HUNTED

THE UNOFFICIAL AND UNAUTHORISED GUIDE TO SUPERNATURAL

HUNTED

THE UNOFFICIAL AND UNAUTHORISED GUIDE TO SUPERNATURAL

SAM FORD AND ANTONY FOGG

First published in the UK in 2012 by
Telos Publishing Ltd
17 Pendre Avenue, Prestatyn, Denbighshire LL19 9SH
www.telos.co.uk

Telos Publishing Ltd values feedback. Please e-mail us with any comments you may
have about this book to: feedback@telos.co.uk

ISBN: 978-1-84583-039-7 (paperback)

Internal design, typesetting and layout by Arnold T Blumberg
www.atbpublishing.com

British Library Cataloguing in Publication Data.
A catalogue record for this book is available from the British Library.

CONTENTS

INTRODUCTION

Some conversations can change your life. Little did we know that a friendly discussion at a convention about our favourite TV show would lead to three years of hard work and this book. But it did and even when we were deep into the writing and research, when finishing the manuscript seemed as likely as Dean Winchester giving up porn sites, we still found time to have a giggle and some fun.

You might guess we're both big fans of *Supernatural*, and it helped that Eric Kripke's vision about a dysfunctional family and their screwed up emotions generated one of the most exciting and leading-edge productions we'd ever seen on TV. It manages to be scary *and* funny, has great character development and features some excellent chemistry between the two gorgeous lead actors. It has provocative stories that are told with skill and the support of an exceptional crew in every single department. It just works on each and every level of production.

For a long time, we read the excellent *Supernatural*-related material on the web and in the books but we decided that nothing quite scratched our inner geeks enough in quite the right place so we set about relieving the itch ourselves. The result is the unofficial guide you are holding and we hope in some small way it satisfies your inner geek too.

Of course, your inner geek may well spot some inconsistencies in our little book. While we've done everything we can short of phoning Eric Kripke to check, we would like to put things right where we can, so please feel free to send any comments or feedback to: sam.ford.supernatural@gmail.com.

Thanks for taking the time to read our first foray into books. We hope you enjoy it.

Antony Fogg and Sam Ford
August 2011

How To Use The Episode Guide In This Book

We've made the sections as self-explanatory as we can but if you want to double check what we're on about then here's what we were trying to say ...

Each episode is broken down into a number of headings. Most are optional and tend to get used when we've got something to mention.

The exception to the rule is the **Squeeze of the Week** section, which has often been included even though the boys weren't getting any squeezes for weeks on end. It's been included in this way to illustrate just how mad this show can be at times – those boys are gorgeous and they just can't seem to get laid! Look, we'll believe anything from vampires to Devil's Traps but the boys not getting laid is one step too far ...

Moving on to the sections:

Episode
The episode number and title – e.g. **3-03 Bad Day At Black Rock**

Transmission dates
First air date for the UK and the US.

Credits
The writer and director can be found here as well as the occasional screenplay writer and anyone else with a finger in the pie at that level.

Recurring Role
Anyone who survives their first episode and makes it back for a second. An elite bunch of characters given *Supernatural*'s track record for blood, gore and bodies.

Guest Stars
Anyone appearing once only as that character.

Synopsis
A short description of what the episode is all about, including spoilers. Given how complicated some of the episodes are, this section was a real challenge to do.

Can You Survive To The Titles?
Supernatural has a very high body count and some of the cast don't get past the opening credits. Here's where you find out who's the first to meet the Reaper in each episode.

Location, Location, Location
Where the boys are visiting in this episode. Of course, it's actually a location in or around Vancouver, BC, Canada in real life but we don't actually care.

Legendary Roots
Real-life facts and folklore about the current monster-of-the-week, with the occasional internal look at the *Supernatural* mythology itself.

Squeeze of the Week
To put it bluntly, do the boys get laid or not? Sometimes we'll give an opinion as to why they've not managed to find anyone but you'll be amazed how often they don't even get a peck on the cheek after rescuing someone.

Sibling Rivalry
This week's brotherly banter and some choice quotes – sometimes it's in fun and sometimes they really mean it.

Body Count
Who gets killed and how they meet their end. Obviously (most of the time anyway) the monster is definitely going to get theirs at the end of the episode so we've stuck to just the grisly deaths of the innocent (and not so innocent) victims.

Toolkit
What you need in the trunk of the car if you're going to dispatch monsters. A surprisingly long list, and improvisations are essential. (Sponge Bob mouse mat anyone?)

Memorable moments
The bits that linger long after the final credits. Where applicable we've included the Top Scare too, but these didn't last much into Season Two, which indicates how the show changed direction towards its own mythology rather than relying on outright frights to keep its audience coming back.

The Car's The Star
Used in episodes where the sexy Impala has contributed something above and beyond being beautiful, sleek and shiny.

Motel Mayhem
Since this isn't a Home and Garden book, we haven't described every single wallpaper or clashing colour scheme – to be honest if you were going to do the motel rooms any kind of justice you'd need a completely separate volume on its own. So we've confined ourselves to the quirks and headache-inducing designs only.

Fashion Observations
Very rare and occasionally sarcastic observations about what the boys are wearing.

Spook Rules
Supernatural's own rules about who and what the current spook/monster/ghost is, how it acts and what special abilities it has, along with how to kill it.

Did You Spot?
As many silly little facts as we could find or observe about each episode.

Going Undercover
All the current disguises and any real-life tie-ins applicable. You'd be amazed how many covers these guys can use in a single episode. How they haven't developed several identity problems we don't know …

Hunter's Lingo
Code words and special hunter's strategies.

Cultural References
Giving the show a solid grounding in our real life culture helps to make it believable. You'll be able to see just how much effort the writers put into each script by the sheer number of cultural references used. You'll also be able to spot some of the homages going on too.

Goofs and Fluffs
The bits that go wrong and still make it to the final cut.

Haven't I Seen You Before?
Mini-biogs of the cast for each episode just in case you needed help with a face you've seen before in a genre show somewhere else. We also identify anyone appearing in other *Supernatural* episodes as well.

Behind The Scenes
Interesting stuff about making the episode.

Musical Interlude
The rock music used in the episode and when you can hear it playing. We'd also like to acknowledge the huge contribution made by Christopher Lennertz and Jay Gruska in composing the wonderful music used throughout. You guys rock.

Analysis
The section where we share our opinion. Please note that we have no professional training in psychology or anything like that but we've done our best to get you into the heads of the characters. We've also explained what we thought was successful and enjoyable, and given any criticism we felt was necessary. For clarity, we've also tried to nail down why a scene or story didn't seem to work. The aim was to give people a different, maybe deeper viewpoint about an episode, and we hope we've achieved that.

Verdict
A quick indication of how we rated the episode out of ten.

SUPERNATURAL GENESIS

Passion is at the heart of *Supernatural* – passion for the stories, for the characters involved, for the quality of the sets, costumes and music and it can be clearly seen in every single episode of the show, even the ones that don't work so well.

That level of passion has to come down from the head of the team to infect and motivate everyone else, so it's perhaps no surprise that *Supernatural* creator Eric Kripke has a deep-rooted love of the stories he's telling. He's often explained that he was fascinated with urban legends and American folklore as a kid, especially the bloody, gory stories with twist endings. And he still believes they offer a sharp insight into American culture.

With that background, it is surprising that when Kripke started his writing career, it was mostly in comedy. He struggled to get anything made and even when he branched out and his *Tarzan* series got picked up, it was cancelled after seven episodes. To work out his frustrations (and therapeutically kill a few people in wonderfully gory ways), he decided to write a horror script. Kripke wasn't interested in getting it made into a movie but a friend showed it to a friend and inside of a year *Boogeyman* became his first produced screenplay.

While *Boogeyman* was being made[1], Kripke started pitching another project. In late 2004, he'd developed an earlier idea for an anthology series into a show about a reporter looking into weird happenings around the US. When his opportunity came, Kripke told Warner Brothers that he wanted to do a series about urban legends. Warner Brothers asked Kripke to make it scary and to come back. When he pitched his reporter idea – which Kripke has admitted was very similar to *Kolchak: The Night Stalker* – Warner Brothers rejected it[2]. But they did ask him if he had anything else.

Kripke had to think on his feet and fast so he told them about another idea he'd had, about two brothers taking Route 66 and stopping off to fight evil along the way. It was an idea he'd only come up with the previous day and had jotted down for use later, but Warner Brothers liked it and wanted more.

Just before Thanksgiving 2004, Kripke handed in his first script to Warner Brothers. In it, Sam and Dean had grown up with an aunt while dad John went off a-hunting, and Dean spent a lot of time trying to convince Sam that demons walk the earth. Warner Brothers rejected this first version, and a second approach was developed between Kripke and soon-to-be-executive-producer Peter Johnson. Warner Brothers

---

1 It was released in 2005. The sequel *Boogeyman 2* was released in 2007 and the movie was mentioned in Season Two's 'Hollywood Babylon' (2-18)

2 A similar series was being made by another studio and was cancelled after one season.

loved this new idea – that had the boys growing up with dad on the road – and Kripke cancelled all his 2004 Christmas plans and locked himself away in his office to get the pilot script written.

However, the green light for the script stayed stubbornly unlit until director David Nutter came onboard – drawn, as he was, by the strong family themes involved.

On the day Nutter signed up to direct the pilot, the studio greenlit the show.

CASTING THE BOYS

The two lead actors were going to be essential to the ongoing success of the show, and it was vital that the right decisions were made in the casting of Sam and Dean Winchester. The recruitment process turned out to be a team effort, fittingly the first of many team efforts that were to make the show so popular …

Kripke knew that finding one suitably talented actor was going to be tough but finding two was even harder. David Nutter had worked with Jensen Ackles on *Dark Angel* and was the first to suggest his name. They brought Jensen in and were immediately impressed by his charisma on and off screen. It seemed they had found their Sam.

For some time, the notion that Ackles would play Sam persisted[3] and in the meantime the hunt continued for the Han Solo to play opposite Ackles' Luke Skywalker. Word of the search reached actor Jared Padalecki but he wasn't going to go for an audition until he had a conversation with *Supernatural* executive producer McG[4], who knew him from when he tested for *Superman*. McG invited Padalecki over for a meal at his house, told him that the show would be more like *The X-Files* than *Buffy*, that there would be the opportunity for real character development and that it was set in reality. Padalecki was convinced and went along for the audition.

Kripke then had a problem – after the audition he thought Padalecki would be the perfect Sam, but they'd already cast Ackles in the part. Once again, the team aspect kicked in. Kripke took tapes of both actors to Warner Brothers to try to figure out who should be Sam. In the ensuing discussions someone (probably Warner Brothers' President, Peter Roth) suggested that Jensen read older and could be Dean. Kripke and Nutter agreed and after that it was just a matter of contacting Ackles' agent and offering him Han Solo instead of Luke Skywalker.

From Jensen Ackles' and Jared Padalecki's point of view, joining the show did not

---

3 There are contradictory accounts of how Ackles came to play Dean. In the *Season One Supernatural Companion* Ackles mentions that Kripke got him to read Dean's part during one of his auditions (without Padalecki present) and they decided he was going to be Dean there and then. Frankly, *how* he got the part is nowhere near as important as the fact that he *did* get it.

4 Joseph McGinty Nichol, nicknamed McG by his mother.

involve a typical audition process, but then this wasn't a typical show. Normally they would have been up against a host of hopeful actors, but when they did the network audition they were the only actors trying out and the executives at the audition told them they had the job before they left. In addition, in any other series, there would have been a number of other regulars, but *Supernatural* centred around just two brothers.

From that moment onwards, the boys' relationship started growing on and off screen. They knew they would be working together all day every day, so they discussed how they were going to tackle the demanding schedule and help each other through the highs and lows. That budding friendship was going to become an important aspect of the show's success.

SORTING EVERYTHING ELSE

From there, the snowball started gaining momentum as each new idea, person or approach got rolled into its mass.

The Impala arrived via a suggestion from one of Kripke's neighbours who was an expert in muscle cars. Since you can fit a dead body in the trunk of a 1967 Chevy Impala it was immediately recruited as the third lead character.

The blue collar feel of the show originated (as so much did) from Eric Kripke, specifically his upbringing in Toledo. And then there's Kripke's love of horror movies like *An American Werewolf in London* and *Evil Dead II* influencing the stories. Other movies like *Poltergeist* were filtered through Kripke's creative process and resulted in decisions about the style and approach. Kripke particularly liked the humour and sense of gritty reality portrayed in *Poltergeist* and both of these seeped into *Supernatural's* development. The trademark heavy metal music (pre-1980 only) is another of Kripke's passions – to the point where he's said in interviews that he'd walk off the show if the music was changed[5].

A pilot episode was made in Los Angeles and approved for series by the studio. While Kripke was having some very specific ideas about the show itself, filming moved to Vancouver, a popular film and television location in British Columbia, Canada. With the move came a new crew and a schedule for each episode that afforded half the time and half the money compared to the pilot episode.

The new crew rose to the challenge admirably and it wasn't long before they were building on the excellent groundwork done on the pilot. Serge Ladouceur, who replaced LA's Aaron Schneider as the director of photography, worked hard to retain the strong sense of reality on the show, keeping light sources justified correctly but not

---

5 *Season One Supernatural Companion.*

over-used, preserving the dark and moody atmosphere.

Kripke's influence continued when Lou Bollo, the stunt co-ordinator, came onboard. Kripke didn't want the *Crouching Tiger, Hidden Dragon* walking-on-tree-tops approach, he wanted the fights to be down-to-earth and brutal. So Bollo selected an Israeli fighting style called Krav Maga.

More key individuals joined the team. Robert Singer was brought in to support Kripke with his experience. The two seemed to complement each other well and Kripke commented that it was Singer who has pushed for the character development while he himself gets more fun out of the gory goings-on.

Following Singer, and on director David Nutter's suggestion, co-exec producer John Shiban arrived to help Kripke build the mythology. With the team fully assembled, the job of writing 22 episodes got underway.

Kripke brought a load of urban legends with him to the writing room for the first few episodes, and for a while that was where the focus lay, but it wasn't long before they realised how good Ackles and Padalecki were and just how deep the story about them could become. The writers started making the boys' relationship more central, but Kripke wanted to avoid being too 'wussy'. Everything started to motor at full speed once they started to understand that it was what the boys didn't say, rather than what they did say, that was important to the story.

Even this early on, as they mapped out the first two seasons of the show, Kripke knew where his story was going. He had the last few episodes mapped out and knew how and when the brothers would end things.

But first they needed to make a successful TV series …

Recurring Cast

JENSEN ACKLES was born on 1 March 1978 in Dallas, Texas to Donna Joan Shaffer and Alan Roger Ackles. He has an older brother Joshua and a younger sister Mackenzie. He attended Dartmouth Elementary School, Apollo Junior High School and LV Berkner High School all in Richardson, Texas and graduated in 1996. Ackles had planned to become a physical therapist but moved to Los Angeles to pursue acting. He had started modelling on and off at the age of four and got his first break in 1996 in *Wishbone* playing Michael Duss. He is married to long term girlfriend and actress Danneel Harris. His acting career includes appearances in *7th Heaven* (Halloween Kid #9 – 1996) and *Sweet Valley High* (Brad – 1996). Between 1998 and 2000 he appeared in 16 episodes of *Days Of Our Lives*. In 2001 he played the role of Eddie G in the Marilyn Monroe fictional biography *Blonde*. *Dark Angel* saw him star as Ben/X5-493 and Alex/X5-495 in 22 episodes mainly in the second season (2001-2002). He also appeared as C J in 12 episodes of *Dawson's Creek* (2002-2003) in the final season. He played Jason Teague in Season Four of *Smallville* (2004-2005), Max Morgan in the series *Still Life* (2005), and Jake Gray in the movie *Devour* (2005). He played Malcolm in seven episodes of *Mr Rhodes* (1996-1997) and appeared in an individual episode of *Cybill* (David – 2007). Also in 2007 he appeared as Priestly in *Ten Inch Hero*[6]. 2009 saw him play Tom Hanniger in the 3D movie *My Bloody Valentine*.

He was also executive producer, first assistant director and appeared in *The Plight of Clownana* (2004).

JARED PADALECKI was born on 19 July 1982 in San Antonio, Texas to parents Sharon L Kammer and Gerald R Padalecki with siblings Jeff and Megan. He attended James Madison High School and started taking acting lessons at the age of 12. He won the National Forensic League national championship in Duo Interpretation in 1998 with partner Chris Cardenas. He was Fox's Claim to Fame Contest 1999 winner and appeared at the Teen Choice Awards, where he met his current manager. He was also a Presidential Scholars Program candidate in 2000, in his senior year. He was going to attend the University of Texas but moved to Los Angeles to pursue acting in 2000. He is married to *Supernatural* co-star Genevieve Cortese. His first roles were Matt Nelson in *A Little Inside* in 1999 and *Silent Witness* (Sam – 2000). In another long running series, *Gilmore Girls*, he played Dean Forester for 63 episodes between 2000 and 2005. Other works include *Close to Home* (2001), an episode of *ER* as Paul Harris (2001) and *A Ring of Endless Lights* (Zachery Gray – 2002). He appeared in *Young*

---

6 Cue dirty giggles …

MacGuyver (Clay MacGuyver – 2003), had an uncredited role in *Cheaper by the Dozen* (2003), and appeared in *Flight of the Phoenix* (John Davis – 2004). 2004 also saw him as Trey Lipton in *New York Minute* followed by a role as Tom in *Cry Wolf* (2005) and another uncredited role in *House of Fears* (2007). More recent credits include the biopic *Christmas Cottage* (2008) playing Thomas Kinkade and the role of Clay Miller in the movie *Friday the 13th* (2009).

THE BLACK 1967 CHEVROLET IMPALA is Dean's car, given to him by his father John Winchester, and damn but it's sexy. It is a fourth generation Chevrolet Impala four door hard top built by the Chevrolet division of General Motors and was named after the southern African antelope. The car was originally introduced in 1958 and has been through various guises up to the current ninth generation. The fourth generation was made from 1965 to 1970. *Supernatural* creator Eric Kripke has said that the Impala was not his first choice of transport for the Winchester brothers. He had wanted an American muscle car like a '65 Mustang. However, his neighbour suggested the '67 Impala as you could fit a body in the trunk, and if you stopped next to one at the lights you would lock your doors.

The interior of the car was specially made for the show with black seats and tan panelling, and the radios in it are non-working props. The studio owns several cars used for different aspects of filming. There are a couple of stunt cars with high performance engines that have 'stomp brakes' that lock the rear end when pressed – this makes the car slide due to its weight – plus a line lock that locks the front brakes to burn the tyres; and there is a 'buck' car – where the shell of the car is on castors and comes apart to allow close up filming inside. It also has removable wing mirrors that are replaceable with cameras for filming.

JIM BEAVER was born on 12 August 1950 in Laramie, Wyoming. He was brought up in Irving attending the High School. He transferred to Fort Worth Christian Academy for his senior year, graduating in 1968. He joined the United States Marine Corps shortly after leaving school and served in Vietnam as a radio operator starting in 1970 before returning to the US in 1971. Upon his return, he worked as a corn-chip dough mixer before attending Oklahoma Christian University, where he became interested in theatre and made his debut in *The Miracle Worker*. He supported himself with numerous jobs including driving a cab, becoming an amusement park stuntman and being a DJ for radio station KCSC before graduating from university in 1975. While at college he wrote several plays and a book on actor John Garfield. He also wrote and performed in numerous plays before starting his television and film career.

His acting work includes playing Leo Sylvestri in *The Young and The Restless*

(1985-2001, five episodes), Detective Earl Gaddis in *Reasonable Doubts* (1991-1993, 13 episodes), and Andy in *Santa Barbara* (1991-1992, five episodes). Other work includes *Sister Act* playing Detective Clarkson in 1992, *Sliver* (Detective Ira – 1993) and as Leland DuParte in *Thunder Alley* (1994-1995, 27 episodes). He has also played Father Timothy Jansen #2 in *Days of Our Lives* (1996-2004, 16 episodes); was in *3rd Rock from the Sun* as Happy Doug (1998-1999, seven episodes); and played Gary in *The Trouble with Normal* (2000-2001, eight episodes).

Further work includes Admiral Daniel Leonard in *Star Trek: Enterprise* (2001) and Sheriff Ritter in *Joy Ride* (2001). He played Whitney Ellsworth in *Deadwood* for 35 episodes from 2004 to 2006 and in *CSI* in 2006 he was Stanley Tanner. More recently he's been in *Criminal Minds* as Sheriff Williams in 2007, *Next* (2007) as Wisdom, Vietnam Joe in *John from Cincinnati* (2007) in eight episodes, 'Uncle' Nick Vukovic in *Day Break* for five episodes in 2007 and in *Harper's Island* as Sheriff Charlie Mills in 2009 for 11 episodes.

JEFFREY DEAN MORGAN was born on 22 April 1966 in Seattle, Washington to parents Richard Dean Morgan and Sandy Thomas. He attended the Ben Franklin Elementary School, Rose Hill Junior High and Lake Washington High School in Kirkland, graduating in 1984, and played basketball throughout high school and university until a knee injury forced him to stop. He was a graphic artist until he helped a friend move to Los Angeles. He was only going to stay for the weekend, but instead, he never left and accidentally fell into acting. His career started in 1995 with a role as a Weapons Officer for one episode of *JAG*. *Sliders* followed in 1996, in which he played Sid. In the same year came *In The Blink of an Eye*, in which he played Jessie. He moved on to *Walker Texas Ranger*, playing Jake Horbart in 2000. He worked on *Angel* as Sam Ryan in 2002, Wally a CIA Technician in *JAG* again for two episodes in 2002, and on *Star Trek: Enterprise* (Xindi-Reptilian – 2003).

His career really started to take off as more roles came in during 2004, when he was Tom Newman in *Six: The Mark Unleashed* and Geoffrey Pine in *Tru Calling*. In 2005 he played Judah Botwin in *Weeds* for two episodes, Joe Zukowski in *The OC* and Detective Cole Davies in *Chasing Ghosts*. He then entered *The Burning Zone* as Dr Edward Marcase for 11 episodes in 2006-2007.

Morgan became a household name when he appeared as Denny Duquette, the heart patient guy, in 23 episodes of *Grey's Anatomy* between 2006 and 2009. During that time he also played William in the movie *PS I Love You* (2007), appeared as Byron in *Days of Wrath* (2008) and as Patrick Sullivan in *The Accidental Husband* (2008). Morgan's career finally went ballistic when he landed the role of another dysfunctional character, Edward Blake, in the 2009 movie *Watchmen*.

SAMANTHA FERRIS was born on 2 November 1968 in North Vancouver, BC. She started working as a television reporter in the mid 1990s for Bellingham, Washington station KVOS TV-12 and Vancouver's BCTV before becoming an actress. Her credits have included *The New Addams Family* (Lacey – 1998), *Stargate SG-1* (Dr Raully – 1999), *First Wave* (Alice – 2000), *Along Came a Spider* (Mrs Hume – 2001) and *Smallville* (Warden Anita Stone – 2004). Further work includes playing Nina Jarvis in *The 4400* (2005-2006, 44 episodes), Lt Alexa Brenner in *The Evidence* (2006, seven episodes) and Pollux in *Battlestar Galactica* (2007).

KATIE CASSIDY was born on 25 November 1986 in Los Angeles, California. Her father is 1970s popstar David Cassidy and her mother is ex-model Sherry Williams. Cassidy grew up in Calabasas, California attending the Calabasas High School, where she started cheerleading and eventually became part of the California Flyers, a competitive team. Her acting roles have included *The Division* (Young CD – 2003), *Listen up* (Rebecca – 2005), *7th Heaven* (Zoe – for four episodes in 2005) and *Sex, Love & Secrets* (Gabrielle – two episodes also in 2005). Other credits include *When A Stranger Calls* (Tiffany – 2006), *The Lost* (Dee Dee – 2006), *Click* (Samantha at 27 – 2006), *Black Christmas* (Kelli Presley – 2006), *You Are Here* (Apple – 2007), *Live!* (Jewel – 2007) and *Walk the Talk* (Jessie – 2007). She has also appeared as Amanda in *Taken* (2008), as Trish Wellington in 2009 series *Harper's Island* and as Ella Simms in *Melrose Place* since 2009.

LAUREN COHAN was born in Philadelphia on 30 November 1982 and lived in Cherry Hill, New Jersey during her childhood before moving to the United Kingdom. Lauren studied Drama and English Literature at University of Winchester/King Alfred's College where she co-founded a touring theatre company. Her first roles came in 2005 starring as Sister Beatrice in *Casanova* and Alessia in *The Quiet Assassin*. She has also played Charlotte in *Van Wilder 2: The Rise of Taj* (2006), appeared in *The Bold and the Beautiful* (2007) and played Leto in *Young Alexander the Great* (2007). Other roles include Emily Fulton in the 2008 movie *Float*, Joanne Clay in *Valentine* (2008), Jackie Amos in *Life* (2009) and in *CSI: NY* as Meredith Muir (2010).

ALONA TAL was born on 20 October 1983 in Herzlia, Israel. She attended Thelma Yellin School of Arts in Tel Aviv and the Lee Strasberg Theatre Institute in New York City. After she served two years in the Israeli army, her acting career kicked off with roles in a children's musical videotape called *Pim Pam Po 2*, a laundry advert and a lead role in the Israeli movie *Lihiyot Kochav* (trans. *Being a Star*). She then landed roles in a soap opera *Zimmerim* (trans. *Guest Rooms*) about a family-run hotel and in a sitcom *Ha-Pijamot* (trans. *The Pyjamas*) about a struggling band. After moving to New York to live with her sister, she appeared in *Cold Case* (Sally – 1998), played Meg Manning in *Veronica Mars* for ten episodes between 2004 and 2006, appeared in *CSI: Crime Scene Investigation* as Tally Jordanin (2005), played Ellie Burke in the 2007 movie *Half Past Dead 2* and Rebecca King in *Cane* (2007). She has also been in *Ghost Whisperer* (Fiona Raine – 2008), *Party Down* (Heather – 2009), *Knight Rider* (Julie Nelson – 2009) and *The Mentalist* (Natalie – 2009).

NICKI AYCOX was born on 26 May 1975, in Hennessey, Oklahoma. She demonstrated an interest in performing even as a child when she learnt piano and sang in beauty pageants. Her acting career started in 1996 when she appeared as Tammy in *Weird Science*, then in 1997 she played Katherine Hanley in *USA High*. Roles as Jennifer in *Boy Meets World*, Alyson in *3rd Rock from the Sun* and Teen Girl in the movie *Double Tap* followed in 1997. She played Brittany in *Significant Others* (1998), Susan in *The Dogwalker* (1999), Chastity in *The X-Files* (1999), Betty Joe in *LA Heat* (1999) and Amy Metcalf in *Cruel Justice* (1999). Other roles saw her as Lily Gallagher in *Providence* in 1999 for seven episodes, and Cecil in *Crime and Punishment in Suburbia* (2000). 2001 saw her feature as Lidia in *Rave Macbeth*, *CSI: Crime Scene Investigation* (Ellie Brass), *Dark Angel* (Syl) and *Opposite Sex* (Joely). She has also been in *Slap Her ... She's French* as Tanner Jennings (2002), *The Twilight Zone* (Ricki – 2002), *Family Law* (Patty Michel – 2002) and appeared as Stella Vessey in *Ed* for six episodes between 2002 and 2004. Further roles include Minxie Hayes in *Jeepers Creepers II* (2003), Tristen Geiger in *Momentum* (2003), Annabelle in *Dead Birds* (2004) and Tammi Campbell in *Las Vegas* (2004). She also played Christina Rush in *Cold Case* (ten episodes between 2004 and 2005), Christine in *LAX* (three episodes 2004-2005) and Pvt Brenda 'Mrs B' Mitchell in *Over There* (ten episodes in 2005). She appeared in *Criminal Minds* (Amber Canardo – 2006), *Defying Gravity* (Grethchen – 2007), *John from Cincinnati* (Jane – 2007) and *Perfect Stranger* (Grace – 2007). In 2008 she had a number of roles including Girl in the short film *Mercenary*, Cheryl Cunningham in *The X-Files: I Want To Believe*, Melissa in *Joy Ride: Dead Ahead*, Nora in *Animal*, Molly Reston in *CSI: Miami* and Kate Westwood in *Law & Order*. More recent roles include Jaimie Allen in *Dark Blue* (2009) and Bridget in *Tom Cool* (2009).

SAMANTHA SMITH was born on 4 November 1969 in Sacramento, California. She has played the former girlfriend in the 1996 movie *Jerry Maguire*, appeared in *Seinfeld* (Hallie – 1996), played Kerry for two episodes in *Nash Bridges* in 1996 and 2000 and Monica in *Caroline in the City* (1998). She also played Nancy Carlson for five episodes in *Two of a Kind* (1998-1999) and Cindy in two episodes of *Family Law*

(1999). She appeared in the comedy *Friends* (Hot Girl – 1999) and as Kate Wilton in *Profiler* (1999-2000, four episodes) and was in *Dark Angel* (as Daphne in 2001). Further work includes *NYPD Blue* (Corrine O'Malley – 2004), *Transformers* (Sarah Lennox – 2007) and *Criminal Minds* (Helen Douglas – 2007).

ADRIANNE PALICKI was born on 6 May 1983 in Toledo, Ohio. After graduating from Whitmer High she moved to New York to enter modelling and talent competitions. Within months she decided to move to Los Angeles to become an actress. Her first couple of roles were in 2003 in *Getting Back with Rachel* and *Rewrite*. Further work includes *CSI: Crime Scene Investigation* (Miranda – 2004), *Smallville* (Kara – 2004) and *The Robinsons: Lost in Space* (Judy Robinson – 2004). She's also appeared as Tyra Collette in *Friday Night Lights* between 2006 and 2009 and as Brianna in *South Beach* (2006). Other credits have included *Robot Chicken* (various characters – 2007-2009) and *Robot Chicken: Star Wars Episode II* (2008), the movie *Women in Trouble* (Holly Rocket – 2009), *CSI: Miami* (Marisa Dixon – 2009). She has also done voice work in *Titam Maximum* (as Clare – 2009).

STERLING K BROWN was born in St Louis, Missouri and attended St Louis Country Day School. He attained a BA in drama from Stanford University and a Master's Degree in Fine Arts from the Tisch School of the Arts at New York University. His main acting roles have included Officer Dade in *Third Watch* for six episodes between 2002 and 2004 and in *ER* as Bob Harris (2004). He has appeared in *NYPD Blue* (Kelvin George – 2004), *JAG* (Sgt Harry Smith – 2004), *Starved* (Adam Williams – 2005), *Alias* (Agent Rance – 2006), *Without A Trace* (Thomas Biggs – 2006) and *Army Wives* (Roland Burton – from 2007).

CHARLES MALIK WHITFIELD was in *Law and Order* (Babatunde's Roommate for three episodes 1992-1998). He has also appeared in *The Guardian* (James Mooney – 2001-2003, 33 episodes), *CSI Miami* (Andre Harding Charles – 2007), *Close To Home* (Benny Boudreaux – 2007), *Private Practice* (Ty – 2009) and *Ghost Whisperer* (Officer Douglas Ramsey – 2009).

CHAD LINDBERG's acting career has included roles in *Mercury Rising* as James (1998), *City of Angels* as Bradford's son (1998), *The X:Files* as Bobby Rich (1998) and Jessie in *The Fast and the Furious* (2001). He has also appeared in *CSI: Crime Scene Investigation* (Brody Jones – 2003), *Cold Case* (Johnny Harkin – 2004), *NYPD Blue* (Eric Keller – 2004) and played *CSI: NY* (Chad Willingham – 2005, five episodes). Other work has included *Buffy the Vampire Slayer* (Dave – 2007) and *Terminator: The*

Sarah Connor Chronicles (Deputy Simmons – 2009).

FREDRIC LEHNE played Eddie Cronin for 19 episodes in *Dallas* (1984-1985), Gordon in *Fortress 2* (1991), INS Agent Janus in *Men In Black* (1997) and a ranger in *Babylon 5* (1995). Further work has included *Firefly* (Ranse Burgess – 2003), *Lost* (Marshal Edward Mars – 2004-2010), *NCIS* (Captain Graves – 2004) and *Without A Trace* (George – 2005). He has also played Charlie Banks in two episodes of *Ghost Whisperer* (2006-2007), David Delaney in *Medium* (2006), Giles Hardewicke in *Bones* (2006), and Jack Vaughan in *Criminal Minds* (2008).

SEASON ONE OVERVIEW

Season One was the biggest workhorse of all the seasons because it had to introduce all the central characters, set up the relationships between them, create the hunters' world and all the internal rules required to work in that world, then kick-start the ongoing story arcs. With such a lot to do, Kripke and his team broke it all down into sizeable chunks and set about weaving the details into the stories while ensuring that the most important ones came out first.

The pilot episode picked out the absolutely essential information and got the ball rolling. Despite Kripke saying in interviews that he was never happy with the (heavily revised) final version of the dialogue for the pilot, it certainly did a good job anyway. We see how dad John Winchester is driven into hunting supernatural beings after his wife Mary is killed in strange circumstances. We meet sons Sam and Dean Winchester, get some idea of what their childhood has been like, and get an insight into Sam's relationship with his father compared with Dean's. We see the monsters they hunt, how they hunt them and the skills required to do the job properly. And we see the cost of the job when Sam loses Jessica.

The similarity of her death to Mary Winchester's starts off the story arc of the yellow-eyed demon – although technically we're actually mid-hunt already since John Winchester has been trying to find this creature for years. But dad's missing and so the brothers have a double search on their hands – to find their dad as well as the yellow-eyed demon.

For most TV series a couple of threads like this would be considered ample and the episodes would be padded out to draw the stories out[7]. *Supernatural* proved to be different. They added in a third story arc of Sam's strange psychic powers, developing this into the wider idea of other children with similar abilities by the middle of the season.

Then they did something else unusual: they started closing down storylines before the end of the season, specifically when the boys found dad (or rather he found them). The show became unpredictable, and there was a very real feeling that it was truly breaking new ground.

The other aspect that broke many of the existing TV rules related to the character development that Dean, Sam and even John underwent in the space of the season. To understand how far they travelled it's important to go back and look at where they started ...

---

7 *Flash Foward* anyone?

Introducing Dean Winchester

Dean is clearly a demon hunter from the start. It's his life, he loves what he does and loves hunting with his father. All of this becomes clear in the first couple of episodes as Dean drags his brother out of his quiet student life and back into the family business[8]. After Sam's girlfriend (Jessica) is murdered, both brothers are now desperate to find dad (John) so they start following the clues he left until they run out and all they can do then is to find monsters to hunt to keep them busy.

As we progress through these early stories, more and more of Dean's personality is revealed. He puts his life at risk fighting monsters to save people like Haley and her family[9]; he doesn't find it easy to talk about his feelings to Sam but has less of an issue talking about them to others[10]; and he's also afraid of flying[11].

By the time we reach 'Skin' (1-06) we're scratching well below the epidermis and discovering how Dean had dreams for his own life but put them aside because his dad needed him. Dean is jealous of Sam's freedom to do what he wants and to lead a normal life. His desire for normality doesn't sit easily with him though. On the surface, he's dissing the normal lifestyle of well manicured lawns[12], and yet he still gets a huge amount of pleasure out of mowing the lawn for his mother quite some time later on[13]. It's an area that will be explored more in the future.

Dean's other personality traits emerge when Sam tells him about the visions and when Dean is close to dying. Sam's visions disturb Dean deeply, but his coping mechanism is to makes jokes and tease Sam about his psychic abilities[14]. It's a mechanism Dean uses often, but especially when in a frightening situation that's outside of his own control. He uses it when he finds out that he's dying too[15] but as soon as he has some control back – where he can save a young girl's life by losing his own – we also start to get a measure of his own sense of self-worth (or lack thereof) in his willingness to die.

As the season enters its final third, Dean's early life with Sam and his relationship with his father are exposed. Dean has always looked after his brother since they were kids and this protectiveness continues even now. Dean's been carrying a lot of guilt

8 See 'Wendigo' (1-02)

9 Again, 'Wendigo' (1-02)

10 Like young Lucas in 'Dead In The Water' (1-03)

11 In 'Phantom Traveler' (1-04)

12 In 'Bugs' (1-08)

13 In 'What Is And What Should Never Be' (2-20)

14 In 'Asylum' (1-10)

15 In 'Faith' (1-12)

around after nearly letting his brother get killed[16]. The change in his dad's attitude towards him after that situation only heightened Dean's reaction and made him listen to his father's orders more closely, since not obeying them could cost someone's life. He is daddy's little soldier and he obeys without question, even when dad is saying that it's safer for everyone if John leaves his boys again[17].

But changes are coming and when John finally hooks up to hunt with his boys, they're more independent. Dean has started to disobey direct orders now[18] and he's seen how Sam's outbursts have changed his dad – by making him share some details about the demon-slaying Colt pistol. Dean is also starting to express his anger about being abandoned by his father, for not being trusted enough to share John's hunt for the yellow-eyed demon. For the first time in his life, Dean is starting to move out from under his father's influence[19].

Overall, it's hard not to like Dean. He's simply trying to do the right things for the right reasons, to help other people and his family. He's accepting of the costs of his lifestyle – to his love life and his longevity – and he loves his dysfunctional family to bits. He's tough, funny, vulnerable and screwed up. How many of us haven't been in any one of those places at some time or another?

Introducing Sam Winchester

Sam, as Dean puts it[20], is like the blonde girl from *The Munsters*. His mother died when he was six months old and the nomadic hunting life is all he's ever known. Both his father and his brother knew their mother and have a solid reason to be looking for her killer. For Sam it's a bit more abstract, given that he can't remember his mother and his bond to her is not so strong. But he doesn't actually want to be a hunter and it makes him odd one out in his family.

There are other reasons he doesn't fit so well too. He's more thoughtful than the others, and a lot less impulsive. He'd rather think something through than go with his gut reaction like the rest of his family and he stands apart because of it.

Even with their differences, it doesn't stop Sam and Dean working together as a lethal team when they're hunting. Sam starts off a little shaky in the pilot – he has been away from hunting for a number of years – but he soon gets back into it, accepting it as his lifestyle[21] and helped along by the need to track down the yellow-eyed demon

---

16 In 'Something Wicked' (1-18)

17 In 'Shadow' (1-16)

18 In 'Dead Man's Blood' (1-20)

19 In 'Salvation' (1-21) and 'Devil's Trap' (1-22)

20 In 'Bugs' (1-08)

21 In 'Skin' (1-06)

after Jessica's death.

It's a difficult period for Sam, still raw after losing the girl he wanted to marry. He's angry that they can't find his dad and that's delaying his revenge for Jessica's murder[22]. We discover more about Sam's pain as the visions he had before her death come to light, and we start to see the guilt that he's carrying. It's this guilt that drives Sam to help the family in their old home in Lawrence, and his need to act on his visions and save lives this time, instead of letting them die needlessly like Jessica did.

Understandably, Sam needs time to work through his grief over Jessica and start to take an interest in girls again, and even when he does, he is worried, because all the women in his life end up dead, and he believes that he's responsible for them dying because he's cursed.

Fact is, he doesn't have too much luck with the men in his life either[23]. Sam's relationship with his father is probably the area of the biggest issues through this season. Sam left his family after a huge bust-up when he wanted to go to college and his father didn't want him to go. Now Sam's looking for his dad and he doesn't even know if John wants to see him or not.

Over the episodes Sam's opinions about his father are challenged as he sees how other people's fathers turned to drink after losing their wife[24] or he learns that John used to swing by Stanford just to check that he was okay[25]. Sam can't stand the way Dean just follows John's orders without question[26] but after the events with the shtriga[27] and knowing how close to death he came because of Dean's mistakes, he starts to understand more about his brother's actions. Yet more change comes when Sam realises that his dad wasn't disappointed with him, he was scared for his son's safety. By the time they finally meet up again, Sam has a far better understanding of his father compared to when we met him. And yet, it doesn't prevent the arguments starting as John continues to treat his sons like children. They eventually achieve some reconciliation as John finally accepts that Sam is just different from him, even though – with Mary's and Jessica's deaths – they actually have more in common than they used to have.

Again, like his brother, it's hard not to like Sam, but for different reasons from Dean. Sam wants to be independent, think for himself, and build his own life. He loves

---

22 In 'Wendigo' (1-02) and 'Faith' (1-12)

23 Behave, not like that!

24 In 'Nightmare' (1-14)

25 In 'Bugs' (1-08)

26 In 'Asylum' (1-10)

27 In 'Something Wicked' (1-18)

his family, he's just different from them. It's not so difficult to see where he's coming from, is it?

INTRODUCING JOHN WINCHESTER

In the first two thirds of the first season, we come to know John mostly through everyone else's opinions and comments. Dean says John writes like Yoda[28]; Sam says he can barely work a toaster[29]; and his old business partner says John loved his wife, doted on his kids, hated to lose and was a stubborn bastard[30].

He's also dragged his boys up on the road with no stable home life. He's often left them alone while he's gone hunting and he's put a huge responsibility on Dean's shoulders – to look after his younger brother in his father's absence. And now he's abandoned them entirely.

No surprise, you're expecting some hard-hearted git to be revealed in 'Shadow'[31] when he finally meets up with his boys. Big surprise, when he's clearly a haunted man, trying to do his best for his family, whom he obviously loves beyond anything else. But he's still ordering his kids around like a drill sergeant and Sam for one isn't taking it anymore unless he gets an explanation about what's going on.

Now it's John's turn to realise he's got to change, and change he does. He starts by giving out more information about the Colt and his search for the yellow-eyed demon. And then he realises how much he needs his boys at his side if he's going to take the demon down in revenge for Mary's and Jessica's deaths[32].

John continues to develop as he finally initiates a reconciliation with Sam – something he hadn't been open enough to do when Sam first left for Stanford – and he begins to realise that leaving Dean the way he did wasn't the best thing he could have done either[33].

By the time he leaves to see Meg, John Winchester has come a long way in a few short episodes. His long-overdue encounter with the yellow-eyed demon is going to show how weary he is of losing good friends and the depth of his obsession with seeing the creature dead. Even John's own life is a fair price if he can take the demon with him, and it doesn't matter if he has to get his own son to kill him.

It's been a brutal life for John since Mary was killed, and he has tried his best to

---

28 In 'Asylum' (1-10)

29 Also in 'Asylum' (1-10)

30 In 'Home' (1-09)

31 Episode 1-16

32 See 'Dead Man's Blood' (1-20)

33 In 'Salvation' (1-21)

protect his remaining family as much as he can. But sometimes you just have to make the best of things and play the cards you've been dealt ...

INTRODUCING THE IMPALA

The final character who deserves an introduction is the ever-present Impala.

After a big start in the pilot (where it gets possessed and is used to try to kill the brothers on a bridge) the Impala had a number of roles through the season. The sleek black beastie is stolen[34], left behind[35], admired[36], hit in the rear by a possessed truck[37] and driven through the front of a house[38].

It takes all the knocks and still manages to complete its most important role effortlessly – being the most stable element in the boys' otherwise chaotic lives. They sleep in it, eat in it and store weapons in it. They also solve cases in it and argue in it – although the most emotionally difficult discussions usually take place while they're sitting on the hood. Its rumbling engine and creaky doors are as much a part of the show as Sam and Dean's bickering, but perhaps the Impala's most significant contribution is by being the one place where the boys can always listen to their favourite rock music.

---

34 In 'Skin' (1-06)

35 In 'The Benders' (1-15)

36 In 'Wendigo' (1-02)

37 In 'Route 666' (1-13)

38 In 'Woman In White' (1-01)

SUPERNATURAL SEASON ONE

SEASON CREDITS

Supervising Producer: Phil Sgriccia
Producer: Peter Johnson
Co-Executive Producer: Richard Hatem
Co-Executive Producer: John Shiban
Co-Executive Producer: Kim Manners
Executive Producer: McG
Executive Producer: Eric Kripke
Executive Producer: Robert Singer
Produced By: Cyrus Yavne
Created By: Eric Kripke
Directed By: David Nutter (1-01, 1-02)
Directed By: Kim Manners (1-03, 1-08, 1-11, 1-16, 1-22)
Directed By: Phil Sgriccia (2-02, 2-12, 2-18)
Directed By: Robert Singer (1-04, 1-21)
Directed By: Peter Ellis (1-05, 1-15)
Associate Producer: Todd Aronauer
Story Editor: Sera Gamble
Story Editor: Raelle Tucker
Director of Photography: Serge Ladouceur, CSA
Production Designer: John Marcynuk
Production Designer: Jerry Wanek
Edited By: Paul Karasick (1-01, 1-02, 1-04, 1-08, 1-12, 1-14, 1-17)
Edited By: Anthony Pinker (1-03, 1-06, 1-10, 1-13, 1-16, 1-19, 1-22)
Edited By: David Ekstrom (1-05, 1-07, 1-09, 1-11, 1-15, 1-18, 1-21)
Music By: Christopher Lennertz
Music By: Jay Gruska
Unit Production Manager: George A Grieve

First Assistant Director: Kevin Parks
First Assistant Director: John MacCarthy
First Assistant Director: Greg Rousseaux
Second Assistant Director: Victor Landrie
Second Assistant Director: Kim Marlatt
Casting By: Robert J. Ulrich, CSA
Casting By: Eric Dawson, CSA
Casting By: Carol Kritzer, CSA
Canadian Casting By: Coreen Mayrs, CSA
Canadian Casting By: Heike Brandstatter, CSA
Stunt Coordinator: Lou Bollo
Set Decorator: George Neuman
Property Master: Chris Cooper
Costume Design: Diane Widas
Key Make-up Artist: Shannon Choppin
Key Hair Stylist: Jeannie Chow
Special Effects Supervisor: Randy Shymkiw
Special Effects Make-up: Joel Echallier
Special Effects Make-up: Toby Lindala
Special Effects Make-up: Flesh & Fantasy Make-Up Effects Inc.
Special Effects Make-up: Schminken Studio Inc

Sound Mixer: Donald Painchaud
Re-Recording Mixers: Dan Highland
Re-Recording Mixers: Gary D Rogers
Supervising Sound Editor: Michael E Lawshé
Music Editorial by: Final Note Productions
Music Supervisor: Alexandra Patsavas
Visual Effects Producer: Scott Ramsey
Visual Effects Supervisor: Ivan Hayden
Cameras Provided by: Clairmont Camera

ADDITIONAL EPISODE CREDITS

1-01
Supervising Producer: Peter Johnson
Executive Producer: David Nutter
Director of Photography: Aaron Schneider

Production Designer: Michael Novotny
Unit Production Manager: Mary Church
First Assistant Director: John G Scotti
Second Assistant Director: Amy Schmidt
Casting By: Patrick J Rush, CSA
Stunt Coordinator: Eddy Donno
Set Decorator: Rich Reams
Property Master: Scott Nifong
Costume Design: Bonnie Mannix
Costume Supervisor: Tom Numbers
Make-up Artist: Nick Pagliaro
Key Hair Stylist: Don Lynch
Special Effects Make-up: Edward French
Mechanical Efx: Paul Lombardi
Sound Mixer: Mack Melson
Visual Effects by: Entity FX, INC

1-02
Post Production Supervisor: Chad E Beck
Production Coordinator: Nancy Carrow

1-03
Script Supervisor: Pattie Robertson
Transport Coordination: Mark Gould

1-04
Gaffer: Chris Cochrane
Key Grip: Harvey Fedor

1-05
Art Director: John Marcynuk
Location Manager: Terry Mackay

1-06
Directed By: Robert Duncan
Location Manager: Russ Hamilton
Construction Coordinator: Chris Thompson

1-07
Directed By: David Jackson
Script Supervisor: Pam Lawrence
Post Production Supervisor: Chad E Beck

1-08
Script Supervisor: Pattie Robertson
Production Coordinator: Nancy Carrow

1-09
Directed By: Ken Girotti
Script Supervisor: Pam Lawrence
Transport Coordination: Mark Gould

1-10
Directed By: Guy Bee
Gaffer: Chris Cochrane
Key Grip: Harvey Fedor

1-11
Location Manager: Terry Mackay
Construction Coordinator: Chris Thompson

1-12
Directed By: Allan Kroeker
Art Director: John Marcynuk
Post Production Supervisor: Chad E Beck

1-13
Directed By: Paul Shapiro
First Assistant Director: Craig Matheson
Location Manager: Russ Hamilton
Construction Coordinator: Chris Thompson
Production Coordinator: Nancy Carrow

1-14
Script Supervisor: Pattie Robertson
Post Production Supervisor: Chad E Beck

1-15
First Assistant Director: Blair Freeman-Marsh
Script Supervisor: Pam Lawrence

1-16
Transport Coordination: Mark Gould
Assistant Editor: Tracy Flannigan

1-17
Directed By: Chris Long
Gaffer: Chris Cochrane
Assistant Editor: Bruce Gorman

1-18
Directed By: Whitney Ransick
Art Director: Dan Hermanson
Location Manager: Terry Mackay
Assistant Editor: Michael Hall

1-19
Location Manager: Russ Hamilton
Key Grip: Harvey Fedor

1-20
Directed By: Tony Wharmby
Edited By: Bruce E Gorman
Production Coordinator: Nancy Carrow

1-21
Transport Coordination: Mark Gould
Post Production Coordinator: Kristin Cronin

1-22
Gaffer: Chris Cochrane
Key Grip: Harvey Fedor

Episode 1-01
Pilot - The Woman in White

Transmission Dates
US first aired: 13 September 2005
UK first aired: 23 January 2006

Credits
Writer: Eric Kripke
Director: David Nutter

Recurring Roles
Jeffrey Dean Morgan (John Winchester), Samantha Smith (Mary Winchester), Adrianne Palicki (Jessica)

Guest Stars
Elizabeth Bond (Amy Hein), Hunter Brochu (Young Dean), R D Call (Sheriff Pierce), Richard Dano (Deputy Swartz), Ross Kohn (Troy Squire), Miriam Korn (Rachel), Kaitlin Claire Machina (Constance's daughter), Robert Peters (Deputy Hein), Steve Railsback (Joseph Welch), Alex A J Rassamni (Constance's son), Sarah Shahi (Constance Welch/Woman in White), Jamil Z Smith (Luis), Derek Webster (Deputy Jaffe), Cletus Young (Motel Clerk)

Uncredited
Baby Sam

Synopsis
Brothers Sam and Dean Winchester embark on a search for their dad, John, who disappeared investigating a series of kidnappings in Jericho, California.

Can You Survive to the Titles?
Mary Winchester takes the honour of being the first person to buy it before the titles.

Location, Location, Location
Twenty-two years ago – Lawrence, Kansas. Present day – Stanford University, Palo Alto (located between San Francisco and San Jose in the heart of Silicon Valley). Present day – Jericho, California.

LEGENDARY ROOTS

In this episode, the harmless phantom hitchhiker, who is picked up but then later disappears, is mixed in with the legend of the Woman in White. There are a number of variations on the Woman in White legend but the version that is used here seems based on the Latin American one, *La Llorona* (The Crying Woman). Again, there are several reasons as to why the woman drowns her children, including having a husband who is forced by his father to marry another woman and a man who will not even marry the Woman in White in the first place. Other 'White Lady' sightings feature in a diverse range of tales, from the Dutch ghosts of wise women and the Germanic elven-like spirits to a whole host of female hauntings from around the world where women have tragically died but remain tied to the mortal plane.

SQUEEZE OF THE WEEK

Sam's girlfriend Jessica appears in a lovely fancy dress outfit. Not sure whether the outfit is a cheerleader or a waitress but doubtless few male viewers care anyway, given how gorgeous she looks. Talking of which, her Smurf T-shirt and sexy shorts sleeping attire will catch everyone's eye (as it does Dean's) when she discovers Sam and Dean fighting in the living room. No surprise that Sam gives her a wholehearted snog in the bar at the party.

The second squeeze in this episode is Ghost Girl Constance Welch, who seems determined to get into Sam's jeans in the driver's seat of the Impala. Can't really blame her, can you?

SIBLING RIVALRY

From the moment they're in the same room together the boys are fighting, starting when Dean breaks into Sam's house. By the time they reach Jericho and are masquerading as US Marshals on the bridge where the latest disappearance occurred, they've regressed into childish tit-for-tat exchanges where Sam stamps on Dean's foot and Dean clips Sam around the back of the head in retaliation.

Back on the bridge later, Sam pushes all of Dean's emotional buttons by taunting him about how their mom isn't coming back – just before the ghost appears and throws herself into the river. After breaking into their dad's motel room, Sam tries to apologise for the incident but Dean insists on 'no chick flick moments', so Sam calls Dean a jerk and Dean calls Sam a bitch.

BODY COUNT

Mary Winchester is the first fatality in the show, burned to death after being stabbed in the stomach and pinned to the bedroom ceiling. Nice.

Troy Squire, an unfaithful Jericho resident, is killed by the Woman in White in his VW on Sylvania Bridge. (It's a bugger getting blood stains out of upholstery, you know.) The cause of death isn't clear because Troy is killed inside the car, out of sight; but based on Constance's actions later when she tries to rip Sam's heart out, we can assume that Troy got his own heart broken in the same bloody way.

Jessica, Sam's girlfriend, is murdered in the same manner as Mary Winchester and it's still horrific even though we've seen it once already.

TOOLKIT

- An unbroken circle of *salt* protects the person inside it because a demon can't cross the boundary, and is used extensively for protection by John Winchester and his sons.
- *Cat's Eye Shells* can be worn on the person to protect against the evil eye – i.e. any kind of nastiness inflicted by merely looking at someone. When your dad starts using them, it indicates that you're dealing with something very serious. The Shells are actually the foot-closure of a Turban Shell sea-snail and measure just under an inch across.
- *Goldwave* is a digital audio editor essential for analyzing electronic voice phenomena (EVP) in telephone messages left by family members.
- A *mobile phone* with speed dial comes in handy when you need to warn your brother of danger – in this case, to tell him that the cops are coming.
- A stolen *pistol* from the police station is very useful for shooting ghosts in the head while they try to murder your brother.
- A *Colt .45* comes in handy for dealing with monsters in the closet when you're nine years old.

MEMORABLE MOMENTS

When Sam yanks Dean into the motel room by the collar and later when Sam tells Dean he smells like a toilet.

Top Scare – when Troy investigates Connie's house and the bird flies out the door at him.

THE CAR'S THE STAR

Our first view of the 1967 Chevy Impala is its rear end, and it's chock full of weapons under the false floor in the trunk. A definite case of 'Does my arsenal look big in this?'

Later on the car is possessed twice – once on the bridge when it nearly runs the boys over and then when Sam is driving and refuses to take Connie home so the car drives him deeper into danger. Just which side is the mechanical beastie on?

The boys get their own back when Sam is attacked by Connie; Dean tries to save him by shooting the ghost, breaking both front windows of the Impala, then Sam drives the car through the front of Connie's house, supposedly damaging one of the headlights.

MOTEL MAYHEM

The boys break into their dad's rented room to find wall-to-wall newspaper and book cuttings. Looks like the set designers got off light for the pilot, because apart from some chintzy lampshades, the underlying décor is hidden by John Winchester's papers and photographs. But the reality – according to the episode's DVD commentary track by Eric Kripke, Peter Johnson and David Nutter – was that this motel room took a lot of time and effort before they got it how they wanted it.

SPOOK RULES

- Ghosts can influence sound and leave hidden messages called electronic voice phenomena (EVP) embedded in digital or analogue recordings.
- When faced with the ghosts of the children you have killed, they have the power to drag you back to hell with them.

DID YOU SPOT?

John Winchester's T-shirt in the opening sequence has USMC on the front – a reference to John's United States Marine Corps background, which is later confirmed in a telephone conversation between Dean and Sam when they discuss the co-ordinates their dad left for them in his journal – an old marine trick.

Sam seems to sleep in a similar T-shirt to the one he goes to the party in, and when Dean breaks into his house in the middle of the night, we never get to see what kind of trousers Sam is wearing. Let's hope he has something on.

The newspaper article about Constance Welch's suicide features quotes from two of her neighbours – Deanna Kripke (perhaps a relation of creator Eric Kripke?) and David Nutter (*Supernatural*'s episode director).

The motel check-in book indicates that some of the crew have stayed at the motel before John, Sam and Dean. Present on the list are the names of production designer Michael Novotny and second assistant director Amy Schmidt.

One of the highway victims is Scott Nifong, who just happens to be the show's property master. Nifong created John Winchester's journal and the look and feel of the trunk of the Impala.

GOING UNDERCOVER

Dean masquerades as a US Marshal, and although Sam never actually shows an ID, he is introduced by Dean as his partner.

Both boys pretend to be Troy Squire's uncles from Modesto in order to talk to Troy's girlfriend, Amy.

Dean gives his name as Ted Nugent when he's arrested, a reference to the guitar-playing rock star who also happens to be a real-life game hunter and a supporter of the National Rifle Association.

John Winchester is currently using a credit card under the name Bert Aframian, and Dean has a credit card for Bert's son Hector. Aframian's name doesn't seem to have any specific relevance, but Hector was a heroic warrior in Greek mythology.

HUNTER'S LINGO

Dean warns Sam about the cops coming by phoning his mobile and saying 'Dude, Five-0. Take off' – a reference to the US cop show *Hawaii Five-0* that first aired in 1968.

CULTURAL REFERENCES

Sam: "Cause we're not exactly the Bradys.'; Luis: 'And I'm not exactly the Huxtables.': Both the Bradys and the Huxtables are fictional families on US TV. The Bradys are the working-class Irish-American Catholics of the soap opera *Days Of Our Lives* while the Huxtables are the upper-middle class African-Americans on *The Cosby Show*.

The Smurfs, featured on Jessica's night-top, came to widespread fame in the 1980s when Hanna-Barbera Productions made a cartoon series about the gnome-like, blue-skinned characters that lived in Smurf Village somewhere in the woods. It was an entertaining enough series but the world really could have done without the cringingly bad Smurf single, made with Father Abraham, that went to Number One in 16 countries worldwide.

Sam: 'So he's working over-time on a Miller Time shift.': The first reference to beer made by the Miller Brewing Company.

Sam: 'He's just deer hunting up at the cabin and he's probably got Jim, Jack, and Jose along with him.': Meaning Jim Beam's bourbon whiskey, Jack Daniel's Tennessee whiskey and Jose Cuervo tequila produced by Tequila Cuervo La Rojeña.

Dean refers to the FBI agents as Agent Mulder and Agent Scully and this *The X-Files* reference is echoed slightly in the next scene with the boys walking past a cinema with a Now Showing board that says 'Be Safe Out There', alluding to *The X-Files'* tag line, The Truth is Out There. 'Be Safe Out There' is also a phrase associated with the 1980s cop show *Hill Street Blues*.

Dean: 'Okay, thank you *Unsolved Mysteries*.': *Unsolved Mysteries* was a documentary-style TV series (airing between 1987 and 2002) that offered viewers the opportunity to contribute to some puzzling police cases. The series covered criminal cases of robberies and homicides as well as more paranormal matters of ghosts and UFO incidents.

Dean: 'We talking like misdemeanour kind of trouble? Or, uh ... "squeal like a pig" kind of trouble?': 'Squeal like a pig' comes from the 1972 movie *Deliverance* and is said just prior to the brutal scene where one of the guys on holiday is forced to strip and go down on all fours before being sodomised.

Sam: 'What were you thinking shooting Casper in the face, you freak?': A name check for Casper, the friendly ghost. Casper has been around since the late 1930s in all forms of media from books, through cartoons and graphic novels, to PC games in 2007. In *The Friendly Ghost*, released in 1945 by Paramount, Casper escapes from the Winchester Mystery House and goes out to make friends.

GOOFS AND FLUFFS

Dean manages to get breakfast (a chocolate bar, crisps and a soft drink) and later goes out to eat at a local diner, but Sam refuses food both at breakfast and later when Dean goes to the diner (and gets arrested instead). Sam must have been one hungry bunny that weekend.

At the petrol station on the way to Jericho, Sam hands Dean a Metallica cassette case, but what actually plays is AC/DC's 'Back in Black'.

As the boys are leaving Jericho, the scenes inside the moving car have a flickering light effect, as if passing under street lights, but long shots show the car on a road without lights.

When the sheriff is interrogating Dean, watch Dean's arms. First they're out of shot, then in again.

After Dean has escaped from the cops and phoned Sam, he turns up at the end of Breckenridge Road, but it's not clear how he got there. And how did he know where to go? It's possible that since Sam dropped the phone when he ran Connie over, that Dean (who was listening) heard Connie asking to be taken home. But unlike when Troy picked up Connie and she asked him to take her to Breckenridge Road, Sam didn't need to be told, because Connie took over the car and drove it there herself. So Dean never heard the address. It's possible he may have remembered her address from the details in the newspaper article, but it's unlikely.

Why did Dean return to Sam's house (to save him again) after he had dropped Sam off and driven away? No reason is given in the aired episode, but in the deleted scenes on the Season One Region One DVD set, it's revealed that Dean's watch stopped while he was driving down the road after dropping Sam off, so he swung the car round and headed back.

After the ghost has been dealt with, Dean drives Sam back to Stanford and the car has only one working headlight. The assumption is that one got damaged when Sam drove the car into the front of Connie's house, but when the car comes to a halt inside the house both headlights are still working. So how did the headlight get broken?

HAVEN'T I SEEN YOU BEFORE?

Hunter Brochu was in *Medium*. R D Call has been in *The X-Files* and *Waterworld*. Richard Dano appeared in *Freddy's Nightmares*. Ross Kohn was in *Autopsy* and

Medium. Miriam Korn has been in *The Tragic Self-Improvement of Ross Lawson.* Robert Peters' credits include *Invasion, Angel* and *Alien Avengers II.* Steve Railsback featured as Duane Barry in *The X-Files* and also appeared in *The Visitor, Alligator II: The Mutation* and *Disturbing Behaviour.* Sarah Shahi played Jenny in *Alias.* Jamil Z Smith played Ronald Greer in *Stargate Universe* and has also been in *Medium.* Derek Webster was in *Night Man, Independence Day* and *Stargate.* Cletus Young's credits include *Wonder Woman, The Hillside Strangler* and *Amazing Stories.*

BEHIND THE SCENES

Jeffrey Dean Morgan believed John Winchester was a good parent, that he always put his kids first and even though John was flawed and the kids are a bit screwed up now, he always acted out of love. [*The Official Supernatural Magazine #2*]

According to the DVD commentary by Eric Kripke, Peter Johnson and Robert Singer, there was a lot of discussion about what would motivate Sam to go hunting. Early versions of the script had John Winchester on the ceiling at Sam's house and Jessica turning out to be evil.

The scenes where Sam agrees to talk outside with Dean, and they discuss their past, were rewritten more times than any others in the episode and Eric Kripke still wasn't happy with the final result.

The pictures of the men already killed on Centennial Highway are actually of two of the prop guys working on the show.

The scene where Troy Squire is startled by the bird coming out of the doorway wasn't in the original script. It was David Nutter's idea.

Eric Kripke had to fight long and hard to keep Dean's 'Agent Mulder, Agent Scully' line on the bridge where Troy's body is found.

The first ever scenes shot for *Supernatural* were in the library when Sam and Dean are searching for information about suicides on Centennial Highway.

In the scenes between Sam and Joseph Welch (Constance's husband), the atmosphere was enhanced by the use of walnut dust blowing around in the background.

Every road in the show is an actual road in Toledo, Eric Kripke's home town.

In an early draft of the script, Constance was going to be a younger girl who had murdered her parents, but David Nutter convinced Eric Kripke to change the story.

In the scene where Dean drops Sam off at home, Sam's scenes were filmed in Los Angeles, while Dean's were filmed on a set. As Dean 'drives' away, the car is actually being pushed by a bunch of grips.

Constance's movements and appearance, as well as the closing scenes where her children drag her back to hell, were influenced by Asian and Japanese horror movies like *The Grudge* and Chris Cunningham's Aphex Twins video 'Windowlickers'.

However, according to director David Nutter in *The Official Supernatural Magazine* #7, it took input from executive producer McG to sort out the ghost's fate.

MUSICAL INTERLUDE

- 'Gasoline' by The Living Daylights – the introduction of Sam and Jessica as they get ready for the party.
- 'What Cha Gonna Do' by Classic – playing as Sam and Jessica are at the Halloween party in the bar.
- 'My Cheatin' Ways' by Kid Gloves Music – Sam and Dean booking a motel room.
- 'Speaking In Tongues' by Eagles Of Death Metal – as Troy drives, speaking to Amy before he sees the Woman in White.
- 'Ramblin' Man' by Allman Brothers Band – while Sam and Dean are at the gas station.
- 'Back In Black' by AC/DC – as Sam and Dean drive away from the gas station.
- 'Highway To Hell' by AC/DC – playing as Dean drives Sam back to Stanford University.

ANALYSIS

'Woman In White' has a wide range of aims to achieve in a short space of time. It has to set up the characters, the story and the sound and tone of the show. The trailer has to hook you so you'll tune in, and the story and characters need to be immediately engaging. Then it has to leave you wanting more. The pilot episode does all this effortlessly.

There is an awful lot of information delivered in this episode, and there's not a scene without another aspect of the boys lives being shown. The most important thing to be set up is the long-term story arc about the search for the demon that killed Mary Winchester 22 years earlier. Husband John embarks on a 'crusade' (as Sam puts it) to exact his revenge and takes his sons with him. It will take two whole seasons before there's any kind of closure for John Winchester, and the foundations laid down at this point need to be solid, so creator Eric Kripke reinforces the storyline by mirroring the opening scenes of Mary's death with almost identical events when Jessica is killed at the end of the episode.

This underlying story arc is wrapped around the investigation of the disappearance of several men on a stretch of hard-top in Jericho. When Dean turns up to ask for his brother's help in finding their father we start to get a feel for the life they had as children – trained to fight with weapons of all kinds, technically adept in analyzing ghostly recordings, knowledgeable about arcane objects, and skilled as conmen. This information is expressed in a number of different ways: some are verbal, with Sam complaining about his upbringing; others are visual, like the weapons in the trunk; and most are through the actions of the boys. We are told how they can afford to live with the conversation about credit cards at the petrol station; Sam's explanation about the pendant given to one of the victim's girlfriends shows their knowledge; and Sam's picking of the lock to the motel room his dad rented indicates shadier skills.

It's an episode with nearly flawless storytelling and structure. Halfway through, Kripke even sets up the ending with a scene in John's motel room, when the boys decide to find the bones of the dead woman and burn them and Sam utters the throwaway line, 'She might have another weakness.' This gives a subconscious cue for the viewer as to Sam's actions at the house at the end of the episode, when the children come to take mommy away.

As well as setting up storylines, this episode introduces Dean and Sam. From the moment the boys appear, their personalities start to build. Sam's scholarly abilities have won him the interview for Law School, and his request for no more shots at the party indicates his attitude to alcohol. Dean's love of the ladies is clear with his Smurf loving flirtatious comment to Jessica (about her night-shirt) while he stares at her chest. Dean's other love, for his precious Impala, is also obvious after Sam drives the car into Connie's house – his threat to kill Sam if he's damaged the car is a slightly hypocritical threat though, given that Dean has just shattered both of the car's front windows by firing a gun through them when rescuing Sam from Connie's deadly grip.

One of the episode's most crucial requirements is that Dean must succeed in convincing his brother to go with him, and it's here that the antagonism between father and youngest son first shows itself. Sam points out that when he said he wanted to go to college, John told him to go and stay gone and that's just what he's doing. Sam's built a good life for himself and it's going to take a lot for him to give that up. Sam doesn't start to give in until Dean says he *could* do it alone but he doesn't *want* to do that. After the rejection from his dad and no contact with his family for almost two years, this is Sam's first indication that they actually care, that at least one family member wants to be with him. The second convincer, while they're by the trunk of the car, is the recording of John saying they are *all* in danger. Sam still cares about his Dad – evidenced by the photo of his parents he keeps on the shelf in his rooms (you're unlikely to keep a photo of someone you hate on display in your home) – and the danger extends not only to Dean but to himself. But even with his loved ones in danger, Sam only commits to a weekend with his brother at first. It takes the devastating event of losing Jessica to convince him to join Dean in his own crusade. He could have stayed for a chance at Law School and a safe life anyway, but it's a measure of his love for Jessica that nothing else matters while her death remains unavenged. Something he learned from his father maybe?

The scene over the car trunk is important for another reason. Just as Dean says he could do it alone but he doesn't want to, he breaks eye contact with Sam and looks decidedly awkward. This is the first indication that Dean struggles to talk about his feelings; a point later underlined when Dean cuts off his brother's apology with his 'No chick flick moments' comment. When Sam baits Dean on the bridge about their mother, we get more evidence of the brothers' different approaches to emotional situations. Sam has accepted the loss of his mother, while Dean still has some seriously unresolved issues that drive him to violence towards Sam.

But most of the time, the rivalry between the brothers is fairly good-natured, and is a frequent feature in the episode. They often regress into foot stamping or cuffs round the head, giving a reassuring and convincing feel that these two are familiar and comfortable with each other, and that there's a history between them.

It's also interesting that the episode deliberately sets up the brothers as equals through the scenes where Dean breaks into Sam's house. In the fight that follows, Dean first pins Sam to the floor, then Sam pulls some fast moves to reverse their positions. Siblings will often establish a specific pecking order early on in life, but maybe their extreme training made it difficult for either Winchester brother to assert dominance. Or more probably, the requirement for them to trust each other with their lives meant that they really didn't want to compete with each other. Now they're in their twenties, there certainly seems to be an even attitude between them.

Equals or not, they are definitely two different personalities. Sam's more cerebral abilities have him booting Dean off the computer while searching for any strange happenings on Centennial Highway. Dean calls him a 'control freak' but that trait doesn't manifest itself in Sam anywhere else in the episode, nor indeed later in the series. Sam goes on to find the information they need, both on the computer and later in their dad's motel room.

Dean's hunter skills are more to the fore in this episode than Sam's, which is understandable given that Sam probably hasn't hunted too many demons while he's been at college. Sam seems a little confused sometimes, but Dean is one sharp and skilful cookie. He's on top when the fight at Sam's house first stops; he's ready to investigate as soon as they spot the cops on the bridge as they arrive in Jericho; he quickly warns Sam (via mobile phone) about the danger when the cops arrive at the motel; and he keeps a perfectly straight face when telling the police that his name is Ted Nugent.

Add to this a strong sense of realism created by a mixture of home-made demon-hunting gadgets, dialogue liberally sprinkled with references to everyday items like Miller beer and cult favourites Mulder and Scully, and an intelligent sense of humour and you get a pilot episode that oozes quality from every frame.

It's no surprise that on the strength of this pilot, *Supernatural* got picked up for a first series.

VERDICT – 9 out of 10

EPISODE 1-02
WENDIGO

TRANSMISSION DATES
US first aired: 20 September 2005
UK first aired: 30 January 2006

CREDITS
Writers: Ron Milbauer and Teri Hughes Burton
Teleplay: Eric Kripke
Director: David Nutter

GUEST STARS
Roy Campsall (Wendigo), Alden Ehrenreich (Ben Collins), Gina Holden (Haley Collins), Tamara Lashley (Paramedic), Cory Monteith (Gary), Callum Keith Rennie (Roy), Wren Robertz (Local person), Donnelly Rhodes (Stevenson Shaw), Graham Wardle (Tommy Collins), Timothy Webber (Ranger Wilkinson), Rhys Williams (Brad)

SYNOPSIS
Looking for John, Sam and Dean travel to the co-ordinates he left in his journal. John's not there but the boys end up helping a family search for their own brother who has gone missing after his camp was attacked by a strange creature in the forest at Blackwater Ridge. Led by Ranger Wilkinson, Sam, Dean and the family are attacked by a Wendigo, which kidnaps Dean and kills the ranger. Sam finds the creature's lair, frees Dean and the lost hitchhiker and they torch the Wendigo using a flare gun.

CAN YOU SURVIVE TO THE TITLES?
Three hikers become the prey of a clever, fast-moving predator. Brad becomes a snack and definitely doesn't make it to the credits.

LOCATION, LOCATION, LOCATION
Flashback: 2 November 1983 (11.27 pm[39]), Lawrence, Kansas.
Present day: Cemetery, Palo Alto; Blackwater Ridge, Lost Creek, Colorado.

---

39 The exact time of Mary Winchester's death is given in the comic series *Supernatural: Origins.*

LEGENDARY ROOTS

The legend of the Wendigo originates with various Native American tribes in Canada and the US but especially the Algonquian people around the Minnesota region. Possibly a cautionary tale to protect tribes in times of hardship, a Wendigo originates as a human being, who in times of famine, resorts to eating human flesh to survive. This imbues the human with magical powers – great strength and speed – and immortality. There are a number of variations of the legend, but most agree that a Wendigo has glowing eyes, vicious claws instead of fingernails, and long fangs. Taller than the average human, they appear gaunt and wasted and have a voracious hunger for human flesh.

SQUEEZE OF THE WEEK

Dean raises his eyebrow cheekily when Haley Collins says she doesn't know how to thank him, but she turns down this silent offer of sex and settles for giving him a delicate peck on the cheek. Is she mad?!

SIBLING RIVALRY

In the bar at Lost Creek, when Sam uncovers historical evidence of hikers going missing, Dean punches his brother on the arm just to emphasise that he'd told Sam that there was something strange going on.

Dean takes the mickey out of Sam for using big words when he calls the monster they're investigating 'corporeal'.

Dean offers to let Sam drive the car for the first time in his life. It's only done to try and cheer Sam up and indicates how much Dean is worried about his brother since Jessica's death.

BODY COUNT

The hikers Brett and Gary are murdered by the Wendigo. Brett is killed near his tent while Gary is gutted alive back at the mine, in the 'larder' where he's being 'stored'. Lovely!

Roy, the back country guide, has his neck snapped and his body strung up in a tree. Shouldn't have been such a sceptic about the Wendigo then, should he?

TOOLKIT

- *Lighter fuel and a beer bottle* to make Molotov cocktails to burn the monsters that are hunting you.
- *M & Ms* chocolate-coated peanuts to leave as a trail behind you when you've been attacked and dragged off by the hairy monster.

- *Flare guns*, conveniently located in mine shafts when you're otherwise weaponless.

MEMORABLE MOMENTS

Dean looks gorgeous again when he's covered in dirt, after the Wendigo has dragged him through the forest and tied him up. (Let's not even go there!) After Sam's tumble down the mine shaft, he challenges Dean strongly for the cutest dirty-face-look but Dean just pips him at the post.

Top Scare – in Sam's nightmare when Jessica's hand thrusts up through the soil of her grave to grab Sam's wrist. An homage to the ending of Brian de Palma's 1976 movie *Carrie*.

THE CAR'S THE STAR

Haley tells Dean she likes his car. Hell, she may as well have been telling Dean he was gorgeous cause the effect is exactly the same. Love me, love my car!

SPOOK RULES

- A Wendigo has never been reported as far west as Colorado. They tend to stick around Minnesota or northern Michigan.
- A Wendigo will steal your GPS, satellite phone and food in order to put you at a disadvantage in the forest. (Either that or they're kleptomaniacs.)
- They know how to last long winters without food and hibernate for years at a time.
- They will take adults to use as food but will leave children behind. The adults are kept alive somewhere dark and safe until they're needed, to keep them 'fresh'.
- They are near perfect hunters – smart, strong, and incredibly fast.
- They're usually hundreds of years old and were once human until they became cannibals.
- They have a constant hunger for human flesh.
- A Wendigo can't cross over an Anasazi symbol of protection.
- The best way to kill a Wendigo is by burning it. Bullets and knives just make it angrier.

DID YOU SPOT?

The book Tom is reading in his tent is Joseph Campbell's *The Hero With A Thousand Faces*, which studies stories about heroes and attempts to identify the patterns in ancient myths.

According to her gravestone, Jessica was born on 24 January 1984 and died on 2 November 2005. Dean was born on 24 January 1979. The January date is Eric Kripke's wife's birthday and the 2 November is the same date Mary Winchester was killed in 1983.

Tom is not due back from his trip until 'the twenty-fourth', that date again.

Dean is wearing the amulet that will be given to him by Sam in the flashback sequences of 'A Very Supernatural Christmas' (3-08).

Sam wears a suit and a tie when he visits Jessica's grave in his nightmare. It's one of the few times he's not wearing one as a disguise.

Dean doesn't do shorts apparently, but he will eventually wear some, luckily – even if does take until Season Four.

The boys go hiking in completely unsuitable clothes – ordinary boots and jeans. Survival in the back country can sometimes depend on something as seemingly insignificant as what you are wearing. Denim is well known for holding onto water and drying out very slowly, which makes it very heavy and energy-sapping to wear on hikes. Fortunately, they get everything sorted out before dark and the weather stays fine.

GOING UNDERCOVER

When they first arrive in Blackwater, Sam tells the Lost Creek ranger that he and Dean are environmental study majors from UC Boulder. This is the University of Colorado and really should have been CU Boulder because that's what they call themselves.

The boys introduce themselves to Haley as park rangers. The ID card Dean holds up has a different name on it, which could possibly be Samuel Cole but it's not clear (even on freeze frame!) They come clean later in the episode, and Dean tells Haley who they really are once they've started hiking to Blackwater Ridge.

CULTURAL REFERENCES

Dean: 'Tell me, uh … Bambi or Yogi ever hunt you back?': Bambi was featured in Walt Disney's third animated movie in 1942. Yogi bear arrived on the scene in 1958 courtesy of Hanna-Barbera Productions. Both indicate what Dean must have been watching on TV when he was growing up.

Ben Collins: 'Like the Donner party?': The Donner family were pioneers in the mid-1800s, emigrating down the California Trail in a wagon train. The train hit snowstorms around Sierra Nevada and they were forced to stop and set up camp. They were low on supplies, and it was several months before a series of rescue parties reached the scene. Unfortunately, food ran out and the remaining pioneers resorted to eating their dead to survive.

Dean: 'Anasazi symbols. It's for protection.': The Anasazi existed around 2,000 years ago and were a prehistoric Native American culture from the south-west United

States who were known for their pottery, basket-making and dwelling construction styles. Their mention in the episode is a bit sudden but makes more sense after viewing the deleted scene (#28 on the DVD) where Ben Collins finds an Anasazi symbol painted onto a rocky outcrop, implying that the tribe have been living in the area.

Sam: 'It's better than breadcrumbs.': A reference to the tale of Hansel and Gretel, where the children leave a trail of breadcrumbs through the forest after their father tries to abandon them because he can no longer feed them.

GOOFS AND FLUFFS

The Wendigo moves with lightning speed in the forest but in the mine shafts it conveniently slows to a more human speed, making it an easier target for Dean's flare gun.

As the Wendigo burns, the front shots seem to show that the creature has hair, whereas the shots from the rear seem to show a bald monster – but maybe it's just a trick of the lighting.

HAVEN'T I SEEN YOU BEFORE?

Roy Campsall has also been in *Alien Trespass*. Gina Holden played Dale Arden in *Flash Gordon*, Coreen Fennel in *Blood Ties* and Carrie in *AVP: Requiem*. Tamara Lashley's credits include *The Dead Zone*, *Jeremiah* and *Battlestar Galactica*. Cory Monteith played Charlie Tanner in *Kyle XY* and has appeared in *Final Destination 3* and *White Noise 2: The Light*. Callum Keith Rennie played Leoben Conoy in *Battlestar Galactica* and has also featured in *The X-Files: I Want To Believe* and *Blade: Trinity*. Wren Robertz appeared in *Dark Angel*, *Stargate SG-1* and *Dead Like Me*. Donnelly Rhodes played Dr Cottle in *Battlestar Galactica* and has also been in *Millennium* and *The Outer Limits*. Graham Wardle has been in *Anna's Storm* and *The Outer Limits*. Timothy Webber's credits include *Friday the 13th: The Series*, *The X-Files* and *Millennium*. Rhys Williams was in *Highlander: The Series*, *Kyle XY* and *Fallen*.

Roy Campsall also appears in 'Asylum' (1-10).

BEHIND THE SCENES

The original footage of the Wendigo getting torched was done with a stunt man and lots of flame gel. But the sequence was a bit too short given the tension and build up, and in post-production the production team decided they wanted to draw out the moment. So visual effects supervisor Ivan Hayden had a wire frame mannequin made, wrapped it in steel wool and ignited it. They then combined those images into the original footage to extend the sequence.

MUSICAL INTERLUDE[40]

- 'Hot Blooded' by Foreigner – Sam and Dean driving after visiting Jessica's grave
- 'Down South Jukin' by Lynyrd Skynyrd – Sam and Dean in the bar
- 'Fly By Night' by Rush – Sam and Dean driving at the end of the episode

ANALYSIS

Eric Kripke learned an important lesson with this episode: Less Is More. He realised that the Wendigo didn't work when it was fully in front of the camera and assigned a lot of that footage to the cutting room floor because he didn't like it.

As a result of Kripke acting upon his own honest opinion and making the cuts, he actually delivers an excellent episode that sets the spine tingling from the opening scare-the-pants-off-the-hikers scene to the give-the-monster-what-for climax in the mine tunnels. By restricting our view of the Wendigo, Kripke heightens both the tension and the believability of the episode, avoiding the disappointment that a fully revealing shot would have generated[41]. Here Kripke enhances the episode's edgy atmosphere with the Wendigo completely *off* the screen, especially in the sickening moment when the monster comes to eat Gary and all we hear are the flesh-tearing, bone-crunching chewing noises in the background. Ew!

As well as providing all the scares, the monster-of-the-week also allows Kripke to reflect back on aspects of the Winchesters' relationship. Haley's determination to find her missing family member parallels Dean's and Sam's search for their dad and results in a more coherent story by creating connections between all the characters. It also gives a more natural feel to the episode's key scene in the forest where Dean decides he's had enough of Sam's 'powder-keg' temper and wants to discuss what's happening in Sam's screwed up head. Sam's anger about Jessica's death and his need to find his dad and the killer are burning him up. Dean then seemingly contradicts his own personality – after all, he doesn't do 'chick flick' moments remember – but he still handles the emotional content of this conversation with Sam competently and comfortably. Both of them are trying to find some direction. Their dad's lack of contact is causing Sam problems because it's delaying his revenge, and causing Dean problems because dad's always been there in the past. Dean explains that he'll use the journal and just carry on as before while trying to find his dad at the same time. By the end of this short scene, both Sam's and Dean's motivations have been clarified.

---

40 At the website http://www.supernaturalwiki.com/index.php?title=Music_%28Season_One%29#Wendigo they mention that the Dave Matthews Band's 'Out of My Hands' is playing when Sam visits Jessica's grave. However, we've been unable to match the episode music with this track.

41 A mistake made in *Alien3*, where total exposure and sub-standard special effects rendered the creature almost laughable.

We see Sam has a good understanding of his own feelings, even if he does need a little guidance from his brother, and Dean has shown that he can do the chick flick moments if he's worried enough.

Sam undergoes more character development with his rediscovered hunter skills coming back to the fore, making him equally as sharp as Dean, but the surprise event occurs towards the end of the episode when they both demonstrate their confidence in each other's abilities by splitting up – Dean going to attract the Wendigo away from Sam, who is trying to get Haley and her family out of the mine. This mutual trust (briefly touched upon in the pilot when Dean says he can't find dad alone and Sam tells him he can) indicates a relationship that has matured over a long period of time to a point where each brother not only knows that the other can look after himself but they also know intuitively what they both need to do. ('Are you thinking what I'm thinking?' says Dean as he breaks off to distract the monster. 'Yeah,' says Sam.) It's these moments of inspired writing enhanced by exceptional acting that lift *Supernatural* above the rest of the genre serials.

VERDICT – 8 out of 10

Episode 1-03
Dead in the Water

Transmission Dates
US first aired: 27 September 2005
UK first aired: 6 February 2006

Credits
Writers: Raelle Tucker and Sera Gamble
Director: Kim Manners

Guest Stars
Amy Acker (Andrea Barr), Amber Borycki (Sophie Carlton), Bruce Dawson (Bill Carlton), Troy Clare (Unknown), D Harlan Cutshall (Unknown), Keira Kabatow (Waitress), Daniel Hugh Kelly (Sheriff Jake Devins), Nico McEown (Lucas Barr), Aaron Rota (Unknown), Bethoe Shirkoff (Unknown)

Synopsis
Sam and Dean investigate a series of disappearances at a lake in Wisconsin. The only survivor is a traumatised young boy, Lucas, who watched his father die in the lake. As more murders occur, the brothers try to uncover the connection between the deaths. Lucas's drawings lead them to a young boy murdered decades before, and it turns out that the current victims were all either involved in the boy's murder or related to the murderers. The killing ends when Lucas's grandfather – Sheriff Devins, the last of the murderers still alive – is claimed by the boy's spirit.

Can You Survive to the Titles?
Sophie Carlton goes for a swim in Lake Manitoc and gets dragged under the water by people/creatures unknown. Hadn't she heard it was dangerous to go swimming alone?

Location, Location, Location
Lake Manitoc, Wisconsin

Legendary Roots
Vengeful spirits are an integral part of folklore in every culture in the world. Some spirits like to create harm for the hell of it; some are looking for souls to replace their own so they can go free; others perpetuate their lifetime of evil long after death, like

the Woman in White; and then there are some whose lives were cut short and ended in an unnatural way – killed in accidents or war or, in this case, murdered. The spirit's need to exact revenge is what binds it to the mortal plain so that it can't pass beyond and continue its journey to its destination, whatever form that may take: heaven, hell, the Pure Lands (Japanese mythology) or the Elysium Fields (Greek mythology) and so on.

SQUEEZE OF THE WEEK

Just another peck on the cheek for Dean as Andrea Barr finally gives in to his roguish charms after Dean saves her son Lucas from drowning. Just what does he need to do to get laid?

SIBLING RIVALRY

There's true anger showing at the start of this episode as Sam (still going through the mourning process for Jessica) challenges Dean about the delay in finding their dad (and of course Jessica's killer). Dean lays into Sam about his attitude, because Dean wants to find his Dad as well, probably more so because Dean has been with his Dad for the last two years while Sam was off at college, so feels the loss more keenly.

The heat of the argument doesn't last long and their banter returns in a number of places: as Sam taunts Dean over his awful chat up lines and his concern about the boy, Lucas, when the Sheriff throws them out of town.

BODY COUNT

The Carlton family really don't do well in this episode. First, daughter Sophie dies in the lake, then son Will is drowned in his own kitchen sink while preparing the fish for tea, then dad Bill's little boat is forcibly capsized and he doesn't re-surface.

The Barr family fare slightly better with non-fatal attacks on both daughter Andrea and her son Lucas. Andrea's dad, Sheriff Jake Devins, eventually throws himself into the lake to save Lucas's life – which only works because Jake and Bill Carlton murdered poor Peter all those years ago and Peter's soul is demanding revenge.

TOOLKIT

- *Salt* starts to show its versatility. In 'Woman in White' it's used to form a protective circle. Now, we discover that to deal with troublesome spirits you need to locate the bones, salt them, then burn them. Good job it's cheap.
- *The ability to swim* means that you can rescue people when vengeful spirits are trying to pull them into the depths of the lake – and in Sam's and Dean's cases, you get to look cute in a wet T-shirt too. Bonus!

MEMORABLE MOMENTS

Dean gets a verbal slap-down from Andrea Barr when she criticises his sense of direction when he's trying to find his way to a good chat-up line.

Sam's battle to free Andrea from the spirit trying to drown her in the bath is wonderfully tense. You can't help but wonder if Dean would have preferred to wrestle the naked woman from the bath though.

Top Scare – Will Carlton's murder in the kitchen sink. Suddenly, it's not just people in/on the lake who are at risk, it's anyone where there's water; and the mundane-ness of the setting makes it even scarier.

MOTEL MAYHEM

The boys are staying in the Lynnwood Inn at the start of this episode. The Lynnwood is a real inn located in north Vancouver (check their website out).

In Lake Manitoc, Wisconsin, they stay at the Lakefront Motel, guided there by Andrea Barr. Coincidentally, there is also a real-life Lakefront Hotel at Lake Manitowoc, Wisconsin.

SPOOK RULES

- Drowned spirits can travel through the water they were murdered in and enter people's homes through their tap water.
- To stop a vengeful spirit you need to find the remains of the body, salt them, then burn them. If you can't find the body, you're in deep trouble – the spirit will only stop once its revenge is complete.

GOING UNDERCOVER

The boys introduce themselves to Will Carlton as Agent Ford (Dean) and Agent Hamill (Sam) from the US Wildlife Service, but their cover is blown later in the episode. The Sheriff's suspicions are first aroused when Sam and Dean don't know about the lake being drained. After contacting the Wildlife Service, who obviously say they've never heard of Ford and Hamill, the Sheriff kicks them out of town.

CULTURAL REFERENCES

The underwater camera shot of Sophie Carlton as she swims in the lake could be a nod to the 1975 movie *Jaws*.

Loch Ness (UK) and Lake Champlain (US) are both locations that have had numerous reports of strange creatures swimming in their waters. Nessie was first sighted in 565AD by a monk called St Columba; and Champ was first seen in 1833 by Sheriff Nathan H Mooney.

Andrea: 'Tell your friend the whole Jerry Maguire thing's not going to work on me.': A reference to *Jerry Maguire* (1996) starring Tom Cruise, where Cruise's character Jerry tries to win the girl by making friends with her son first.

There's a very obvious reference to *Star Wars*. The boys' undercover names are Agent Ford and Agent Hamill, clearly references to Harrison Ford (Han Solo) and Mark Hamill (Luke Skywalker).

GOOFS AND FLUFFS

When Will Carlton first puts his hand into the sink water to get the plug out, you can see the plug chain leading over to the draining board already. He then pulls out the plug and puts it on the draining board, and the chain ends up where it was in the previous shot.

Peter Sweeney is apparently stepping up his killing spree because the lake is going to be drained in the near future. However, Peter can escape the lake and attack people in their kitchen sink, so why is the draining of the lake a problem?

HAVEN'T I SEEN YOU BEFORE?

Amy Acker played Dr Claire Saunders in *Dollhouse* and Winifred 'Fred' Burkle in *Angel* and has also appeared in *Ghost Whisperer*. Amber Borycki's credits include *A Town Called Eureka*, *Kyle XY* and *Blood Ties*. Bruce Dawson played Dr Lawrence Gordon in *Flash Gordon* and was also in *White Noise* and *Hollow Man II*. D Harlan Cutshall's credits include *First Wave*, *The X-Files* and *The Outer Limits*. Keira Kabatow has also been in *Smallville*. Daniel Hugh Kelly was in *Star Trek: Insurrection*, *Cujo* and *The Outer Limits*. Nico McEown featured in *Night at the Museum*, *The Twilight Zone* and *Stargate: Atlantis*. Aaron Rota was in *A Town Called Eureka*. Bethoe Shirkoff has been in *Dark Angel*, *Millennium* and *Roswell: The Aliens Attack*.

BEHIND THE SCENES

Composer Christopher Lennertz likes the idea of a non-human evil that can travel through pipes so he really enjoyed doing the music for 'Dead in the Water'. He used lots of low rumbling sounds and reversed low whisperings of 'evil' and 'kill' to make it creepy. [*The Official Supernatural Magazine #7*]

Jensen Ackles found it challenging to film the scenes in the lake where he's holding Lucas in his arms. There were two divers pulling them under the water and the first time they went for the shot, Ackles kicked free of the divers and had to catch a minute before trying again. [*The Official Supernatural Magazine #1*]

There's a rumour that Padalecki broke his hand during the filming of this episode, as a result of a bar fight that he and Ackles had accidentally got involved with in

Vancouver. This is unconfirmed, but in an interview with TVGuide.com, Ackles mentioned a bit of brawl they got drawn into and when several guys ganged up on Jared, Jensen ran back in and pulled him out by his shirt. Of course, the shirt got ripped and of course it was Jared's favourite shirt but after that, the boys were pretty close.

The lake location used in this episode was the beautiful area around Buntzen lake, near Vancouver. Apparently, this area is quite difficult to film in because you need permission from a particular branch of the government, BC Hydro[42].

MUSICAL INTERLUDE

- 'What A Way To Go' by Black Toast – when Sam and Dean are in the diner
- 'Round And Round' by Ratt – as Sam and Dean are driving to the lake
- 'Too Daze Gone' by Billy Squier – when Sam and Dean are driving and are 'not going to have to hug'
- 'Movin' On' by Bad Company – Sam and Dean driving at end of episode

ANALYSIS

We start to see how brave this series is going to be in terms of creativity. It's clearly not going to be some huge cookie press machine churning out the same shape of episode each week. No, it's going to change its pace, change its influences, and commit to some serious character development.

This episode sees the consequences of a boyhood bullying session that went too far and ended with a young boy, Peter Sweeney, being drowned. Peter has been taking his revenge over the years, killing individuals related to his murderers when opportunity has arisen. This then is the first vengeful spirit story, and it's a premise that will be used for a whole range of episodes in the future (especially in series three). To the production crew's credit, their plundering of myth and folklore will make all their vengeful spirit stories refreshingly diverse, so the approach will not feel over-used.

This is also the first time the danger is not aimed directly at the boys but at people they want to help, and we find that despite being on the scene, the brothers are not superhuman and can't save everyone. It's a slower paced, multi-layered story that holds the viewer's interest. The only flaw is the non-scary appearance of the murderous spirit in the lake, which looks remarkably like an ordinary boy painted blue.

'Dead In The Water' is crammed full of character development, as the strong family theme continues. Following the search for a missing relative in 'Wendigo', 'Dead in the Water' looks at the effects of trauma and grief on those who survive after

---

42 According to location manager Russ Hamilton in *The Official Supernatural Magazine* #4

the loss of a loved one. Sam still seems emotionally closed off after Jessica's death and the focus falls on Dean. His relationship with Lucas reveals how Dean felt after he lost his mother – scared, unable to express his feelings verbally but solid in the knowledge that she would want him to be brave – something he'd never shared with Sam. Dean swings between his open emotions with Lucas and his inability to discuss them with his own brother, where he always shuts down the conversation by retreating behind his wise-cracks. Dean doesn't so much have a problem discussing his emotions, he just struggles to discuss them with his family, especially Sam. It's possibly because Dean's always had to look after Sam as they grew up with their dad missing so often on hunting trips, so he's always had to be the strong one, constantly responsible and in control.

And one other important aspect of Dean's personality that we see for the first time is his changing attitude to children – something that will be touched on and expanded in later shows. It seems Dean is getting rather broody ...

VERDICT – 7 out of 10

EPISODE 1-04
PHANTOM TRAVELER

TRANSMISSION DATES
US first aired: 4 October 2005
UK first aired: 13 February 2006

CREDITS
Writers: Richard Hatem
Director: Robert Singer

GUEST STARS
Benjamin Ayres (Homeland Security), Geoff Gustafson (Lou), Fred Henderson (Unknown), Paul Jarrett (George Phelps), Brian Markinson (Jerry Panowski), Kelly-Ruth Mercier (Woman Passenger), Jaime Ray Newman (Amanda Walker), Dana Pemberton (Guard), Daryl Shuttleworth (Chuck Lambert), Ingrid Tesch (Bonnie Phelps), Kett Turton (Max Jaffey), Amanda Wood (Flight Attendant)

UNCREDITED
Jeffrey Dean Morgan (John Winchester, voice only)

SYNOPSIS
Called in by Jerry Panowski (a previous client of John's) after a plane crash, Sam and Dean discover a hidden demonic message on the cockpit flight recorder saying 'No survivors'. However seven people walked away from the crash. Then the pilot from the first crash is killed – coincidentally 40 minutes into a second flight, the same amount of time as the original journey – and it becomes obvious that the seven survivors are being murdered. Tracking down one of the surviving flight attendants, Amanda, they learn that she is about to fly again. The boys check in on the same plane, despite Dean's fears of flying. Forty minutes into the flight they spot the demon and exorcise it, with Amanda's help. After the plane lands safely, the boys discover that their father has recorded a new voicemail message on his own phone – their first indication that he may still be alive.

CAN YOU SURVIVE TO THE TITLES?
Under the influence of the demon that is possessing him, George Phelps opens a door mid-flight and takes a high-flying dive from an aircraft without a parachute. The

resulting plane crash kills over a hundred passengers leaving only seven survivors – the highest body count before the titles in any episode this season. Not to mention leaving George a two-dimensional smear on the landscape somewhere.

LOCATION, LOCATION, LOCATION

Nazareth, Pennsylvania – the site of the second plane crash; Indianapolis – where Amanda Walker is taking her first flight after the first plane crash.

LEGENDARY ROOTS

There is no actual phantom in this episode; rather we have a demon possessing people and creating chaos. The closest existing mythology to this is in Japan, where they have a complex history of spirits and demons that affect all aspects of living, from health to the afterlife. Japanese demons can do both good and bad deeds and some say their actions depend on the treatment they receive. The demons have supernatural powers and the ability to influence natural phenomena like earthquakes, floods and epidemics, as well as causing man-made disasters like plane crashes. However, you can't vanquish Japanese demons with the *Rituale Romanum* like Sam did. According to the Asianart.com website, the demons must be exorcised with ceremonies known as the 'Oni-Yari' or 'Tsuina'. The ritual requires people to throw roasted soy beans in the four compass directions while calling out, 'Enter, good fortune, demons depart!' The fear of pain causes the demons to run away. Doesn't quite have the same dramatic impact as the Latin rites, does it?

SQUEEZE OF THE WEEK

A lean episode for Dean – all he gets is a sexy 'Hi!' from a passing girl as he leaves the photocopy store. Poor thing!

SIBLING RIVALRY

The surprise is that when Sam finds out that Dean is afraid of flying he *doesn't* spend any time poking fun at his brother[43]. Maybe the seriousness of the situation (the expected plane crash would kill a lot of people) or the time constraints (the plane is leaving imminently) distracted Sam away from giving Dean a good ribbing, but they do have time for couple of fun exchanges at other points – including the moment when they exit the Mort's For Style shop dressed in white shirts and black suits. Dean thinks he looks like one of the Blues Brothers, while Sam thinks Dean's more like a seventh grader at his first dance.

---

43 Although he will poke a little bit of fun at Dean about it in 'Everybody Loves A Clown' (2-02)

BODY COUNT

Approximately one hundred people die in the plane crash in the episode opener. After that, the only unfortunates are Chuck Lambert and his co-pilot when Chuck crashes the little twin-engine plane on a flight that's ironically supposed to give him his confidence back after the first crash.

TOOLKIT

- An *electro-magnetic frequency (EMF)* meter made out of a Walkman, very useful for detecting supernatural presences.
- A copy of the *Rituale Romanum,* the exorcism service that sends those demon critters straight back to hell. Read in Latin for optimum banishment power.

MEMORABLE MOMENTS

There are three surprises in 'Phantom Traveler': Dean's fear of flying; the demon revealing to a stunned Sam that he knows about Jessica's death; and John Winchester's voice message on his mobile phone. The **Analysis** section discusses these in a bit more detail.

SPOOK RULES

- Demons take the form of black smoke when possessing someone.
- Demonic possession leaves behind a residue of sulphur.
- It takes two rounds of Latin ritual to send the demon back to hell – the first to release it from the body it is possessing, which makes it more powerful because it is not limited by the mortal body, and the second to send it back to hell for good (a rule that seems to be forgotten in later episodes).

DID YOU SPOT?

The recurring theme of the number 24 – from Eric Kripke's wife's birthday on 24 January – it's here again in the flight number of the first crashed plane (2485) and the saved flight number (424).

The boys have their emotional moment at the end of episode while they're sitting on the trunk of the Impala. This is unusual because in future episodes, most of the emotional scenes will take place on the hood of the car[44].

According to TV.com, the telephone number quoted by John Winchester in his voicemail was originally aired as a real number that played a message from Dean if

---

44 Like when Dean tells Sam about the night of the fire in 'Home' (1-09) and when they both realise that their dad sold his soul to save Dean's life in 'Children Shouldn't Play With Dead Things' (2-04)

you called it.[45]

Both brothers may look irresistibly cute in their slightly-too-small Blues Brothers suits but Sam turns back the clock further with his 1970s flying collars in Jerry's office. What a cool dude! At least Dean has the sense to keep his collars tucked in or they'd both look daft.

GOING UNDERCOVER

The boys gain access to the remains of the plane by using Homeland Security badges – created in the Copy Jack shop. The cover gets busted when the real Homeland Security team turns up.

Dean tries to convince Amanda Walker that her daughter has been injured in a car crash and tells her that he is Dr James Hetfield from St Francis Memorial Hospital. Unfortunately, this cover also gets busted since Amanda has spoken to her daughter only a few minutes before. James Hetfield is the blond-haired, blue-eyed guitarist and lead vocalist in rock band Metallica.

Sam uses the guise of United Britannia Customer Services to phone around the survivors to find out who will be flying again in the near future. He has a lovely telephone manner too.

CULTURAL REFERENCES

Dean: 'Liar. Cause I was up at three, and you were watching the George Foreman infomercial.': George Foreman is a former heavyweight boxing champion who became the oldest man to win the world heavyweight title and puts his victory down to a healthy diet. Foreman now sells healthy food-grilling machines.

The Poltergeist (1982) movie gets its first of many mentions from one of the workers at Jerry Panowski's firm: '*Poltergeist*? Man, I loved that movie!' The words were added after filming was complete.

Dean: 'Yeah, but this goes way beyond floating over a bed or barfing pea soup.': The first of several references throughout the season to *The Exorcist* movie (1973) and the actions of the young possessed girl Regan (Linda Blair).

The NTSB have the plane wreckage in a secure hanger – The NTSB are The National Transportation Safety Board, an independent US Federal agency that investigates every civil aviation accident in the United States and any significant accidents involving other modes of transportation.

Dean: 'Man, I look like one of the Blues Brothers.': The Blues Brothers Band started on *Saturday Night Live* and wore their trademark black suit, white shirt, black

45 Details at http://www.tv.com/supernatural/phantom-traveler/episode/465117/trivia.html#notes

tie, hat and sunglasses. Their music is a mixture of the electric Chicago Blues sound, and the Memphis Stax Records R&B sound, and they made two movies *The Blues Brothers* (1980) and *Blues Brothers 2000* (1998).

Jerry calls one of his staff Einstein, after the prominent scientist.

Dean: 'All right, this is gonna sound nuts, but we just don't have time for the whole "The truth is out there" speech right now.': Another reference to *The X-Files* sneaking in.

The *Rituale Romanum* is a Roman Catholic exorcism that was first published in the reign of Paul V. The full service is significantly longer than the words that Sam uses in 'Phantom Traveler' but it does involve the use of holy water sprinkled on the possessed person.

GOOFS AND FLUFFS

None of the planes in this episode is real; they are very good special effects. However, in the opening sequence, when you see the plane from the side, you get a clear view of the exits. There are regulations that control the number of exits required to evacuate passengers fast enough, and if this were a real plane, it would be essential to have more exits – in this case probably over the wing.

If Jerry's workplace requires him to wear a security badge around his neck then chances are that the boys will have been badged up in a similar way when they arrived at the building, but neither are wearing badges in any of the office scenes. (Perhaps security were too busy laughing at Sam's collars!)

The twin-engine plane has the registration number C-GBBP when it is on the ground. In flight, it is shown as C-GUTV.

Why does the demon possess the co-pilot on the final plane? Pilots are usually very calm and competent people and not prone to emotional chinks in their armour that demons can wiggle through. Even when the pilot is interviewed at the end of the episode, he doesn't explain why the demon picked him. Maybe he picked the wrong day to give up glue-sniffing?

The scene of the car driving down a stretch of road at the end of this episode (set in Pennsylvania) is on the same stretch of road used at the end of 'The Woman in White' (set in Jericho, California).

HAVEN'T I SEEN YOU BEFORE?

Benjamin Ayres' credits include *Fantastic 4: Rise of the Silver Surfer*, *Smallville* and *Battlestar Galactica*. Geoff Gustafson featured in *The Odyssey*. Fred Henderson was in *Millennium*, *The Outer Limits* and *Final Destination 2*. Paul Jarrett's credits include *The X-Files*, *The Outer Limits* and *Millennium*. Brian Markinson played Dr

Sam Carr in *Dark Angel* and has also been in *Millennium* and *The X-Files*. Kelly-Ruth Mercier featured in *Smallville*. Jaime Ray Newman appeared in *A Town Called Eureka*, *Stargate: Atlantis* and *Heroes*. Dana Pemberton featured in *Dead Like Me*, *Tru Calling* and *Jeremiah*. Daryl Shuttleworth was in *Watchmen*, *Lost Boys: The Tribe* and *Stargate SG-1*. Ingrid Tesch appeared in *Poltergeist: The Legacy*, *Painkiller Jane* and *Blood Ties*. Kett Turton was in *Blade: Trinity*, *Kingdom Hospital* and *Millennium*. Amanda Wood's credits include *The Dead Zone*, *Dead Like Me* and *The Immortal*.

Behind the Scenes

Director Robert Singer was originally bought on board to lend the benefit of his experience rather than direct but he got a phone call while he was in Chicago to say that another director had dropped out and could he go to Vancouver and stand in. After seeing the episode everyone wanted to know how many more he was going to direct. [*The Official Supernatural Magazine #2*]

According to the DVD episode commentary by Jensen Ackles and Jared Padalecki, Padalecki was eating a doughnut while Sam was pulling Dean's knife from under the pillow. He had to do several takes and got through about 15 doughnuts but the scene was never used.

Shooting of the airport scenes took place at Vancouver International Airport and in a private hangar.

The crew had problems filming outside the Copy Jack shop because of the noise from construction happening next door and the big trucks trundling past.

Filming outside the psychiatric hospital, there was a woman and her dog who kept moving so she could be in the background of the shot.

In between filming, Padalecki and Ackles stood in the Mort's For Style shop window and pretended to be mannequins.

After scraping the 'sulphur residue' off the wreckage, Padalecki cut his thumb wide open wiping the knife clean. From then on, the crew didn't allow him to touch sharp things.

The scenes where the co-pilot is sprinkled with holy water was filmed about two months after the rest of the show.

Musical Interlude

* 'Paranoid' by Black Sabbath – when Sam and Dean are looking like the Blues Brothers before entering the air-hanger with the plane wreckage.
* 'Working Man' by Rush – as Sam and Dean track down Amanda Walker.
* 'Load Rage' by Nichion Sounds Library – when Sam and Dean are driving away

at the end of the episode (Note: This song is listed at several sources, but Nichion Sounds Library might not be a band but a website library of music. Nichion is Japan's largest music publishing company).
- Dean is probably humming Metallica's 'Some Kind of Monster' to calm himself down onboard the plane. Sam does ask him if he's humming Metallica.

ANALYSIS

'Phantom Traveler' is a straightforward story of a single demon causing death and mayhem in the modern world. We discover that demons aren't perfect. Even when they're unhindered they don't always get everyone they were after and they have to go round clearing up the stragglers. Enter Sam and Dean to give the nasty demon a bad day ...

There are some nice touches of humour and some great eye-bulging acting from Jensen Ackles in this story, but there's not a lot of tension and there are certainly no real scary moments of the kind done so well previously. On the surface, it seems to be a less than perfect episode, but the strength of 'Phantom Traveler' lies a little deeper.

Kripke and his writing team are starting to seriously layer the stories now. For starters, 'Phantom Traveler' achieves its own spin on 2000's *Final Destination* movie in less than half the time of the film. From the fated plane crash, through the survivors being bumped off, to the climactic resolution, it's all there.

And we're also introduced to the first black-eyed demon – a type of creature that will turn out to be rather important in the future.

Then we're given the first indication of Sam's visions starting. They're just showing as sleepless nights so far and are reasonably explained as Sam worrying about the hunting and Jessica's death, but the foundations being established will provide a solid base for the next and upcoming episodes.

In terms of story arcs, we get a hint that Jessica's death had a hidden purpose when the demon tells Sam: 'She must have died screaming! Even now, she's burning!' With this and the voice message on John Winchester's phone, it's difficult not to get your curiosity piqued. This voice message is the second clue from John (the first being the co-ordinates in the journal), and this one at least confirms that he is alive. The message also deepens the mystery around John's disappearance, because he clearly knows Dean's phone number but hasn't called him. Why?

On top of all this, there's even some character development going on. Dean's fear of flying makes him seem a lot more vulnerable than we'd so far believed after all his invincible kick-monster-ass attitude. And Sam gets to take the lead in defeating the demon, showing that his hunter skills are back up to speed and he's just as capable as his brother.

So 'Phantom Traveler' has no in-your-face scares? So what?

VERDICT – 7 out of 10

Episode 1-05
Bloody Mary

Transmission Dates
US first aired: 11 October 2005
UK first aired: 20 February 2006

Credits
Writers: Terri Hughes Burton, Ron Milbauer
Director: Peter Ellis
Story: Eric Kripke

Guest Stars
James Ashcroft (Coroner), Genevieve Buechner (Lily Shoemaker), Jovanna Huguet (Bloody Mary/Mary Worthington), Jessica King (Unknown), Kristie Marsden (Donna Shoemaker), Duncan Minett (Steven Shoemaker), Adrianne Palicki (Jessica Moore), Marnette Patterson (Charlie), Chelan Simmons (Jill), William Taylor (Detective Jackson Riley), Michael Teigen (Teacher), Victoria Tennant (Unknown)

Synopsis
A vengeful spirit is taking lives every time someone utters the words 'Bloody Mary' three times in the mirror. Her victims all have guilty secrets that resulted in someone getting hurt. Sam and Dean discover who Mary was and how she killed herself in front of a mirror. Given that the girl was cremated, the boys realise that her spirit must be residing in the mirror. Sam volunteers to summon Mary from the mirror she's trapped in, since he has a guilty secret about Jessica's death. When he summons her, we discover why he was guilty about letting Jessica die – he'd seen visions of her death days before it happened but didn't warn her. Dean breaks the mirror then uses another to turn Mary's powers back on herself and kill her.

Can You Survive to the Titles?
Steve Shoemaker bleeds to death – though his eyes – on his own bathroom floor. Made such a mess of the tiles.

Location, Location, Location
Toledo, Ohio; Fort Wayne, Indiana

LEGENDARY ROOTS

This is the second vengeful spirit to appear – the first being murdered boy Peter in 'Dead In The Water' (1-03) – but this time the it isn't an unknown child but the very popular figure of Bloody Mary. Across America, she's the subject of many young girls' late night slumber parties, where they sit in the dark trying to scare each other by summoning her frightening spirit, who appears in a mirror and often attacks the caller. There are many variations of both Mary's original story and the ritual that summons her. Mary herself is always a tragic figure – whether she was tortured and burned at the stake as a witch, a mutilated bride, or a modern girl killed in a car crash. It's no surprise she has anger management issues and often causes harm when called.

She's known by many different names – including Mary Worth, Mary Whales, Hell Mary, Mary Lou and Mary Worthington – and although the ritual to call her takes many forms there are some marked similarities between them: they all involve a dark room, a mirror and a repeated chant to call the spirit, who then arrives, usually to inflict harm.

That harm can be anything from scratching your eyes out or biting your face, to knife attacks and murder. Other variations are driving a person mad, pulling you into the mirror with her or turning your bathwater to blood.

Call her at your own risk.

Also worth a mention here is the use of mirrors in rituals. The mirror has a long and versatile history in folklore. In early Celtic times, the reflective surface of water was utilised for scrying, and lakes and ponds were considered portals to other lands, usually the Underworld. The man-made mirror has been around in one form or another since we started polishing metals and has had a number of properties including reflecting your soul, trapping the spirits of the newly dead and bringing bad luck if broken.

Even today in *feng shui* it is considered negative to have a mirror (or any glossy surface) reflecting your head and upper body while you sleep – either because it will startle your spirit as it leaves your body during sleep and give you nightmares, or because it will reflect the negative chi energy, that is discharged as you sleep, back into you.

SQUEEZE OF THE WEEK

Dean's acting a bit strange as he lasts the entire episode without so much as a leer at the pretty women around him. Who is he, and what have they done with the real Dean?

SIBLING RIVALRY

The boys are way too busy discussing Sam's nightmares to worry too much about banter, and there's only one light hearted comment from Dean where insists he's an awesome brother for letting Sam catch up on his kip.

BODY COUNT

After Steve Shoemaker's death, only Jill manages to get herself killed by not taking the Bloody Mary legend seriously enough and repeating 'Bloody Mary' in a mirror. That'll teach her to scoff. Teach her to run people over too.

TOOLKIT

- A *hand held camcorder with night vision* is a must for detecting traces of evil spirits but works best when used in conjunction with a *black light* (UV lamp) to help show up words written in blood.
- A *crowbar* is one of the most efficient ways of breaking mirrors that have spirits in them, and is also useful when breaking into shops.

MEMORABLE MOMENTS

The brother's scenes are really starting to gel in this episode, and the two of them supply an intense moment in the car when Dean is trying to stop Sam calling Mary's spirit and challenges him that it's all about Jessica's death.

The second memorable moment is when Sam's reflection reveals the secret – and we find out that Sam could have saved Jessica's life if he'd acted on his dreams.

FASHION OBSERVATIONS

Dean doesn't seem to be wearing his amulet – not something that happens very often.

SPOOK RULES

- Spirits don't see shades of grey.
- If a person has a secret linked to someone who has died, that's good enough to justify murder. It doesn't matter whether that person had any part in the actual death or not, only that they believe they did.
- To kill Bloody Mary you need to summon her back to the mirror that reflected her death and break the mirror. When this doesn't work and the spirit crawls out of the mirror, frantically grab any handy mirror nearby and let her see her own reflection. Her own power will then self destructively reflect back on her as she realises she's murdered several other people. (But since that's not a secret, the logic doesn't quite work, does it? Must be one of those shades of grey).

DID YOU SPOT?

There are a lot of visual similarities between Bloody Mary and Samara in *The Ring*, from the grubby dress and the way Mary's dark hair falls over her face to the way Mary crawls out of the mirror (similar to Samara crawling out of *The Ring*'s television).

GOING UNDERCOVER

In order to view Steven Shoemaker's body, the boys masquerade as medical students from Columbus doing a paper.

To learn more about Shoemaker's death, they tell his daughter they were her father's colleagues – a cover that gets busted a short time later by Charlie when she says that Shoemaker worked alone.

When they visit the detective who worked on Mary's murder case, they tell him they are reporters.

Dean tells the police he's the boss's son when they break into the antique shop in Fort Wayne. Since Mr Yamashiro owns the shop, the police are suspicious of Dean, who insists he was adopted.

CULTURAL REFERENCES

Dean: 'Do I look like Paris Hilton?': Paris Hilton is a socialite and heir-apparent to the vast Hilton hotel and real estate dynasty. She also appeared in *House of Wax* (2005) along with Jared Padalecki.

Dean does a search of the NCIC – a computerised index of criminal justice information, run by the FBI for use by Federal, state and local law enforcement and other criminal justice agencies.

GOOFS AND FLUFFS

At the Shoemakers' house, there is a woman drinking coffee by the door when Sam and Dean arrive. As they walk into the next room, the woman starts to walk off, but in the next shot, she's suddenly back in her original position by the door.

HAVEN'T I SEEN YOU BEFORE?

James Ashcroft's credits include *Battlestar Galactica*, *Dead Like Me* and *Black Sheep*. Genevieve Buechner featured in *The 4400*, *Jeremiah* and *The Final Cut*. Jovanna Huguet was in *Smallville* and *Blade: The Series*. Kristie Marsden appeared in *The 4400*, *Masters of Horror* and *Beyond Belief: Fact or Fiction*. Marnette Patterson's credits include *Starship Troopers 3: Marauder*, *A Nightmare on Elm Street 5: The Dream Child* and she played Christy Jenkins in *Charmed*. Chelan Simmons played Hillary in *Kyle XY* and also featured in *Final Destination 3* and *Carrie*. William Taylor was in *Twilight*

Zone: The Movie and *Scary Movie 3*. Michael Teigen's credits include *Jeremiah*, *Dark Angel* and *Reaper*. Victoria Tennant appeared in *Tru Calling*.

BEHIND THE SCENES

The mirrors caused several issues in this episode. For Director of Photography Serge Ladouceur the main problem was keeping the lights, cameras and crew out of the reflections [*The Official Supernatural Magazine #5*]; for set decorator George Neuman the issue was actually buying enough mirrors in the first place. Not only did he need to buy several of each style but they also had to be quite large. He blew half his budget on the mirrors alone and they all ended up broken by the end of the episode. [*Season One Supernatural Companion*]

George's Taverna in Steveston is seen behind Jessica as Sam and Dean drive away from Toledo. The Taverna is actually located on Moncton St in Richmond, BC, Canada. This stretch of road will be seen again in 'Mystery Spot' (3-11).

MUSICAL INTERLUDE

- 'Sugar, We're Going Down' by Fall Out Boy – during Jill's encounter with Bloody Mary.
- 'Rock Of Ages' by Def Leppard – when Sam and Dean are driving, talking about the mirror and Mary.
- 'Laugh, I Nearly Died' by The Rolling Stones – at the end of the episode

ANALYSIS

From the opening scenes, it's clear that the moody visuals and tense atmosphere, lacking from 'Phantom Traveler', are back with 'Bloody Mary'. Mirrors (like clowns) are traditionally scary, and director Peter Ellis certainly spooks it up in all of the mirror sequences: when Lily Shoemaker's dad is followed through the house and into the bathroom; when Charlie is terrorised by Mary in her school; and especially in the climax when Sam summons Mary to a shop full of mirrors.

One of the main reasons the tension is so successful is the soundtrack by Christopher Lennertz. Music should enhance the emotional content of the scenes and add depth to the story. If you're sitting there thinking 'Oooh, this sounds nice' or 'Hmm, don't like that music' then you aren't engrossed in the story and the music hasn't done its job. The music throughout Season One is so singularly unintrusive that it's superb.

In the character development department, if 'Phantom Traveler' gave a gentle hint of Sam's nightmares, then 'Bloody Mary' is the full-blooded smack in the face. This episode seems to be full disclosure about why Sam isn't sleeping well – for the viewers at least. In a neat turn around of personalities, poor Dean can't get his brother to spit out the problem to him. It seems both brothers have difficulty telling the other about their issues, in this case possibly driven by Sam's fear of what Dean would think of him once Dean knew the facts about what he did.

Sam is obviously guilt-ridden about not warning Jessica, but he can't know for sure that a warning would have changed events. And it's not like Sam knew the dreams were premonitions anyway; this was probably the first time he'd had them. Which indicates that Sam is actually very hard on himself but more forgiving with other people – he didn't blame Dean for taking him away from Jessica for the weekend, did he? – and the situation goes some way to explain Sam's withdrawn nature in the earlier episodes.

The other thing that Sam gives away about himself is his attitude to his brother: 'You're my brother and I'd die for you.' It's said quietly, understated, and the conversation quickly moves on, but the meaning behind those words is immense.

And Kripke et al have been layering again, if extremely subtly this time. The biggest mystery at the end of this episode is the fact that as well as Sam's eyes bleeding when Mary comes out of the mirror, Dean's eyes bleed as well – implying that Dean also has a secret where someone got hurt. But what is it? Although it's not mentioned anywhere in the episode, Eric Kripke has confirmed in various interviews that there is something in Dean's past, that it has always been there, and that it will be revealed.

It's just going to take a long time to find it out.

VERDICT – 7 out of 10

EPISODE 1-06
SKIN

TRANSMISSION DATES
US first aired: 18 October 2005
UK first aired: 27 February 2006

CREDITS
Writer: John Shiban
Director: Robert Duncan McNeill

GUEST STARS
Anita Brown (Lindsay), Amy Grabow (Rebecca Warren), Marrett Green (Anchorman), Shiraine Haas (Person with iPod on arm when police take suspect away), Aleks Holtz (Zachary Warren), Peter Shinkoda (Alex)

UNCREDITED
Nick Allen (SWAT Teamer) (Assistant stunt coordinator on the episode), Ron Blecker (SWAT Captain)

SYNOPSIS
Sam is contacted by fellow Stanford student Rebecca who tells him that her brother (and Sam's friend) Zach is accused of murdering his girlfriend, but Zach would have needed to be in two places at the same time to manage it. A second girl is killed only blocks away, and Sam and Dean deduce a shapeshifter is responsible. But then the shapeshifter captures the boys and goes off to attack Rebecca. Now pay attention, it's getting complicated … The boys escape and call the police, who stop shapeshifter Dean before he can kill Rebecca. After the cops have gone, Dean goes to reassure her it wasn't really him who attacked her, while Sam goes back to the shapeshifter's lair – where he finds the real Rebecca tied up. Sam races to Rebecca's house, where the creature has knocked Dean unconscious. Sam takes the creature on after realising that it's changed into Dean again, and the fight is evenly matched until real Dean manages to shoots the shapeshifter before it strangles Sam[46].

---

[46] It's much, much easier to follow in the episode, honest.

CAN YOU SURVIVE TO THE TITLES?

This is the first time that no-one dies on screen before the titles. The pre-title sequence does feature a bloody female victim (Rebecca) tied to a chair but she survives the ordeal. Pre-episode, Emily was killed by the shapeshifter disguised as Emily's boyfriend Zach.

LOCATION, LOCATION, LOCATION

A gas station, 400 miles from St Louis on the way to Bisbee, Arizona; St Louis, Missouri

LEGENDARY ROOTS

The most well-known shapeshifters are werewolves, and there will be more detail about them later[47], but for now it's sufficient to say that werewolves belong to a group of empowered humans who can transform themselves into a wide range of animals.

In Native American Indian lore there are the Bearwalker (who transform into bears, duh!) and the Yenaldooshi (coyotes); from South America come stories of the Nahuales who can turn into almost any animal from snakes to jaguars to eagles; and in Europe there is the Slavic forest spirit, a Leszy, that can turn not only into animals but also into plants.

It's rarer to find creatures who can transform themselves into humans. Mermaids can take human form to come on land; selkies are seals who shed their skin to become beautiful men or women, and power can be gained over them if you can separate them from their seal skin; and in Japanese lore, the Tengu were shapeshifters often associated with ninja magic and could take the form of human or bird or a hybrid of the two.

Rarer still are those who can turn themselves into specific copies of individuals, and Japanese lore has more of these creatures. The kitsune are werefoxes who cause mischief by masquerading as other people[48]; some of the tanuki shapeshifters are powerful enough to copy a particular human being or even an inanimate object; and vampire cats shapeshift to a human form, get close to their victim, suck all their blood, then take on their victim's form to get close to other family members.

Human shapeshifters who only change into other humans seem to have kept themselves very well hidden and don't appear to feature in ancient lore.

---

47 In 'Heart' (2-17)

48 For more details see 'Nightshifter' (2-12)

Squeeze of the Week

A complicated squeeze this time. The real Dean maintains his poor form for a second week and doesn't get anything more than a handshake from Rebecca; meanwhile the shapeshifter in his Dean-suit gets to cosy up to the lovely Rebecca on the sofa in front of a romantic log fire. He evens gets close enough to whisper obscenities into her ear before attacking her.

Sibling Rivalry

The rivalry takes a dark turn in 'Skin'. If the shapeshifter can be believed, real Dean is rather bitter because he had dreams of his own but had to stay home with Dad while Sam left for college and got his own life. But that's not all – Dean is deeply concerned about everybody leaving him. Sam went then the pattern was reinforced with Dad leaving, especially given the suddenness of it and the lack of explanation involved.

Body Count

Emily has already bought it before the episode starts and only Lindsay is murdered by the shapeshifter. Rebecca gets beaten and cut and later abducted but makes it to the end of the episode reasonably intact, physically at least.

Toolkit

- It's a good idea to keep a stock of *silver bullets* to hand if you're a hunter. They have the right properties for a number of nasties, including shapeshifters.
- A hefty dose of *suspicion* helps too, especially if your own brother is acting strangely when a shapeshifter is in town.

Memorable Moments

The fight scene between Sam and shapeshifter Dean is excellent. It's much more brutal than the first fight between the brothers (in the pilot episode) and creates a wonderful disquiet in the viewer – intellectually your brain knows that Sam is beating seven shades out of the shapeshifter, but your eyes are seeing Dean get hurt. An emotionally challenging sequence to watch.

It goes without saying that Dean getting his shirt off stands out as one of the finest moments in 'Skin', but this show does its best to deliver things with a twist – they could have stopped with the shirt but no, they had to continue with his skin, ears and teeth. Ew!

Top Scare – The shapeshifter surprises Dean and Sam in a sewer by sneaking up behind them, then getting caught in the torchlight when it's within inches of Dean's back.

THE CAR'S THE STAR

For the second time, the Impala is used by the 'bad guys'. It's a little simpler here than the possessed car scenario in 'The Woman In White' (1-01) – the shapeshifter merely uses it as a mean of driving to Rebecca's in order to attack her and possibly borrow some tools from the trunk. The boys soon track it down but Dean is upset. He can't stand the thought of anyone else driving his baby.

SPOOK RULES

- Security cameras can pick up strange flares in the eyes of demonic beings because a photograph can capture a glimpse of their soul.
- When a shapeshifter changes from one person to another, they leave the skin of the old disguise behind in a 'puke-inducing pile.'
- Once a shapeshifter takes your form, he can start uploading your memories into his own head.
- You can kill a shapeshifter by firing a silver bullet through its heart. Fire twice to be doubly sure if required.
- After a shapeshifter is dead, he retains the last disguise he assumed.

DID YOU SPOT?

On Sam's phone he has an e-mail from Jerry Wanek, 'Subject: Where are you?!' Jerry Wanek was production designer on *Supernatural* for the best part of Seasons One and Two.

A lovely touch by the set designers in Rebecca's parents' house – a plaque on the kitchen table reads 'When In Doubt, Add More Wine'.

If you're a shapeshifter running around in a Dean-suit then you need to be thorough and be sure to include the details to convince people. In Dean's case, this means you need to wear plain clothes (no patterned stuff), several layers (T-shirt, shirt, denim/leather jacket), his little horned amulet and his silver ring. At the end of this episode Dean is seen to take his amulet back from the shapeshifter's body. You don't see him remove his silver ring but he must have, since he's wearing it outside Rebecca's folk's house as they say goodbye.

GOING UNDERCOVER

Sam introduces Dean to Rebecca as a cop, which Dean promptly upgrades to detective. Once more their cover gets blown, this time after Rebecca talks to Zach's lawyers who check Dean out (and who wouldn't want to check Dean out?).

For the first time, Sam can't use a cover at all, because some people already know him.

CULTURAL REFERENCES

The Drive Safe America sign seen at the start of the episode refers to a company launched in 1974 that wanted to 'provide traffic safety instruction nationwide by keeping classes interesting and interactive.'

Rebecca: 'What do you think this is, Hooters?': Hooters is an international restaurant company that describes itself as 'delightfully tacky, yet unrefined'. It is famed for the tight T-shirts and 'assets' of the female waitresses.

Dean: 'Like the Vulcan mind meld?': The Vulcan mind meld comes from the TV series *Star Trek* and was used by Science Officer Spock, who would make physical contact with a person and create a psychic link through which both subjects could share thoughts and memories.

There's a possible nod to the movie *Alien* (1979) in the scene were the shapeshifter comes up behind Dean and Sam in the sewer. This echoes events in *Alien* where Captain Dallas is hunting the alien in the spaceship's air-conditioning ducts and turns his torch down a duct to find the alien almost on top of him.

The scenes where the shapeshifter is removing his Dean-suit echoes Robbie Williams' 'Rock DJ' video where the singer removes his clothes then carries on with skin, layers of muscle and his face. The scene may also be a nod to *An American Werewolf in London*, one of Eric Kripke's favourite movies.

GOOFS AND FLUFFS

The opening sequence of the SWAT team entering Rebecca's house doesn't match the same sequence later in the episode. When shapeshifter Dean is caught at the start, the cop says: 'Freeze! Don't move! Drop the knife!' Later the cop says, 'Freeze! Drop the knife! Drop the knife! Drop the knife!'

Rebecca's e-mail is dated 5 December 2005, but according to 'The Benders' (1-15) this episode took place around 7 March 2006. No wonder Rebecca was surprised to see Sam: he was three months late!

Rebecca first says that Zach arrived home at 22.30 hours but when they're watching the security tape of his return it's only 22.04 hours.

When Sam discovers that Dean is also tied up in the sewer with him, the scene shows Sam with part of a sheet of canvas over his left shoulder. Part way through the conversation the canvas has disappeared, too quickly for it to have fallen off his shoulder naturally.

When shapeshifter Dean has Sam tied up hand and foot in Rebecca's pool room, Sam kicks the shapeshifter and cuts the rope around his hands then stands up to continue the fight. Suddenly, his legs are free even though you don't see him cut the ropes.

Despite having an excellent storyline, 'Skin' had some highly convenient plot points. First, it was very fortunate that Rebecca stole the security footage of Zach arriving at his home for the brothers to watch.

Secondly, at the end of the episode, Sam says that Dean is being blamed for Emily's murder because they found the murder weapon in his lair along with Zach's clothes covered in Emily's blood. The cops are also starting to believe that the surveillance tape had been tampered with. Now, we know that they haven't hidden the shapeshifter's body because Dean says he would have liked to have gone the funeral, indicating that people know he's dead. Which means there was a dead Dean body in Rebecca's house. So who shot him? Rebecca doesn't seem to be in the frame from that one, so how was it explained to the police? And what about Lindsay's husband, Alex? They don't mention that he was cleared too, so do we assume he's going to prison for a crime he didn't commit? Poor chap!

HAVEN'T I SEEN YOU BEFORE?

Anita Brown featured in *Jake 2.0*, *The Dead Zone* and *Dark Angel*. Amy Grabow was in *Charmed*. Marrett Green's credits include *Final Destination 1 & 2*, *X-Men 2* and *Bionic Woman*. Shiraine Haas has been in *Stargate SG-1* and *Smallville*. Aleks Holtz appeared in *Stargate: Atlantis* and *Smallville*. Peter Shinkoda featured in *Dark Angel*, *Andromeda* and *I, Robot*. Director Robert Duncan McNeill played Lt Paris on *Star Trek: Voyager*.

BEHIND THE SCENES

According to a posting on TV.com, Eric Kripke admitted in an interview in *TV Guide* that he got so many requests from the viewers to see Dean and Sam with 'less on', that he included the scene in 'Skin' where Dean removes his shirt, and also added a similar scene in 'Hell House' (1-17) for Sam to get shirtless too.

Stunt doubles were used in only two places during the Sam/shapeshifter Dean fight in the games room – when Sam is thrown into the bookshelves and when he lands on the bookcase. Ackles and Padalecki did the rest of the fight themselves and it looks all the more convincing for all their hard work.

MUSICAL INTERLUDE

- 'In-A-Gadda-Da-Vida' by Iron Butterfly – plays over the scenes of shapeshifter Dean in Rebecca's house as the SWAT team enter the building to rescue her.
- 'Poison Whiskey' by Lynyrd Skynyrd – when Sam is reading e-mails in the car at the gas station.
- 'Hey Man, Nice Shot' by Filter – when Shapeshifter Dean is shedding his skin.
- 'All Right Now' by Free – at the end of episode.

ANALYSIS

In one of the best episodes of Season One, the *Supernatural* team becomes more than the sum of its parts. Everything works: from the most gruesome effects to date when the shapeshifter sheds his skin, to the now completely relaxed interaction between Sam and Dean as the actors settle once and for all into the skins of their own characters.

It's an episode that feels fully 'crafted', with a story that doesn't waste a moment. This is the first time one of boys has been seen in jeopardy in the opening sequence and the timing is spot on – it wouldn't have worked as well if it had been shown earlier in the season while we were still getting to know Sam and Dean. It may be a well known mechanism – to start with the dangerous situation and then go back to fill in how it came about – but it is deployed here with skill, with a suitably shocking situation involving Dean that means you need to find out how it all happened. And from there on in the story doesn't stop for breath: Sam's friend is in trouble, the crime scene is covered in blood, a second victim is tortured, her husband is attacked, the creature is discovered in the sewers, Dean is captured, Sam is knocked unconscious, Rebecca is abused, the police are after Dean for Rebecca's attack, Sam's knocked unconscious again (he's so not having a good day), then Sam and 'Dean' fight until the creature is shot. Blooming heck, pass the oxygen someone!

Hats off to John Shiban *et al* for a very slick story indeed, especially when you notice that you never actually see the shapeshifter monster 'himself', he always appears as someone else, whether Zach, Alex, Dean or Rebecca.

'Skin' is even more impressive when you realise that it still fits in the now expected character development. Firstly, there's the shapeshifter's revelation about how Dean feels about his brother (see the **Sibling Rivalry** section for more details). We discover that for Dean, despite having accepted who and what he is, the lifestyle choice has not been without its costs. He had his own dreams but selflessly sacrificed them in order to support his dad. But he can't help but wonder about the road not taken and now that sacrifice seems wasted because his dad has deserted him, leaving him with Sam's 'sorry ass'. Of course, the one person the shapeshifter doesn't mention is the boys' mother – she was the first to 'leave' Dean and you can't help but wonder if he's ever got over that.

The second character change is Sam's, and to understand it we have to go back to before Jessica's death, in 'The Woman In White', and the scene on the bridge where Dean tells Sam that sooner or later he's going to have to face up to being a hunter. Sam denies that he's like them and refuses to take that life choice.

By the end of 'Skin', Sam has realised something within himself. Jessica may be gone but he's helped his friends and made a difference to their lives. Zach would be in jail if Sam hadn't been who he was. Now Sam implies that he's finally willing to accept his role. He can see that he never really fitted in at Stanford and he's coming to terms with the hunting lifestyle. While Dean wishes that his brother could just be 'Joe College' he's still glad that Sam's a freak like him.

It's an exchange that also has the additional affirmation from Dean that he'll back Sam all the way, probably in response to Sam's confirmation in the last episode ('Bloody Mary') that he'd die for his brother. These scenes are hugely important and they're played so quietly and effortlessly that you're not consciously aware that they're influencing and informing your understanding of the boys' relationship and characters.

Subtlety, atmosphere, tension, action and story. TV with depth. Now that makes such a refreshing change.

VERDICT – 9 out of 10

EPISODE 1-07
HOOKMAN

TRANSMISSION DATES
US first aired: 25 October 2005
UK first aired: 6 March 2006

CREDITS
Writer: John Shiban
Director: David Jackson

GUEST STARS
Dan Butler (Reverend Sorenson), Chelah Horsdal (Librarian), Alfred E Humphreys (Sheriff), Jane McGregor (Lori Sorenson), Christie Laing (Taylor), Sean Millington (Unknown), Benjamin Rogers (Murph Humphreyville), Brian T Skala (Rich), Mike Waterman (Red Head)

SYNOPSIS
Lori Sorenson witnesses a murder by an invisible assailant and Sam and Dean suspect ghostly happenings. Discovering that a local preacher, Jacob Carns, murdered 13 prostitutes in 1862, the brothers decide that Carns is haunting the Sorenson family and killing people on Lori's behalf. This theory is proved when Lori discovers her father's affair with a married woman and her disapproval of his actions causes the Hookman to attack him. The spirit continues to terrorise Lori – who has also realised that it is killing people she doesn't like and now hates herself for harming her friends and family, turning the spirit's intentions against herself. But even after Dean salts and burns Carns' bones, the spirit continues. The boys finally realise that some of the silver from his hook was melted down and made into other objects. They stop the attack by burning Lori's cross pendant – made from the silver in the hook – and put the spirit to rest.

CAN YOU SURVIVE TO THE TITLES?
Lori's boyfriend Rich, looking for a little sexy fun with his girl in a secluded spot under a bridge, gets a little more than he bargained for when the Hookman cuts him open and strings him up from his ankles above his own car. This dating game is downright dangerous you know.

LOCATION, LOCATION, LOCATION
Ankeny, Iowa: Theta Sorority, Eastern Iowa University; St Barnabas Church; Old North Cemetery

LEGENDARY ROOTS
Three classic urban legends are woven into this episode.

Firstly, 'The Hook' tells of two young lovers parked in a quiet side-road starting to make out. A radio broadcast – about an escaped convict who has a hook instead of a right hand – alarms the girl and she insists her boyfriend drives her home. Angry at being denied some fun he starts the car and floors the accelerator, pulling away rapidly. Arriving back at the girl's house, she gets out and shuts the car door before screaming hysterically at the sight of a bloody hook stuck in the door handle.

Secondly, 'The Boyfriend's Death' starts with a similar couple making out in a car under a tree in a remote spot. When it comes time to leave, the car won't start and the boyfriend tells the girl to lock the doors while he goes for help. Some time later he still hasn't returned and the girl hears some scratching sounds on the roof. The girl is so frightened she huddles in the car until dawn. Some people passing by come to her aid and as she gets out of the car, her boyfriend is hanging from the tree above the car, his shoes scratching the roof.

Finally, 'Aren't You Glad You Didn't Turn On The Light?' is a variation of 'The Roommate's Death' legend. Two dorm-mates in college have a test for science the following day. One decides to stay in and study while the other goes to a party with the boy she's fancied for months. Arriving back at two in the morning after a great time at the party, the girl creeps around the room in the dark trying not to her disturb her friend. In the morning, party-girl awakes to find her dorm-mate murdered and the words 'Aren't you glad you didn't turn on the light?' written in blood on the wall.

SQUEEZE OF THE WEEK
It's Dean's third week with nothing more than a leer at the female students at the university party. He doesn't improve his chances when he decides to go and find the Hookman's grave when he could just stay and party.

Sam on the other hand gets both the squeeze and the snog from 'super hot' Lori Sorenson on the bench outside her house. It's rather ironic that Sam gets the first snog of the series given how Dean has been trying so hard for just that and more.

SIBLING RIVALRY
In the coffee shop after Sam has been trying to find where their dad is by checking traffic violations etc, Dean teases Sam about his girly coffee order of a half-caf, double

vanilla latte to which Sam's retort is, 'Bite me'.

Later, at the party, Dean pokes fun at Sam for going to libraries, studying, getting straight As and being a geek, rather than doing all the paaarties!

BODY COUNT

Rich gets gutted in the opening sequence and Taylor, Lori's room-mate, gets cut up in her bed while she sleeps. Lori's father almost loses his life after he interrupts Lori's and Sam's little tryst outside the church, but Sam gives the Hookman both barrels of rock salt and saves the preacher's life.

TOOLKIT

- The usefulness of salt against spirits was identified in 'The Woman in White' (1-01) when John Winchester used it in his motel room to protect himself. Here again, in *rock salt* form, it is used as a general spirit deterrent, but with a long distance delivery system – a *shotgun*[49].
- Salt is also used with *lighter fuel* when burning the bones of vengeful spirits. We heard about this method of spirit eradication in 'Dead In The Water' (1-03) but this is the first time they actually dig the body up and torch it.
- It helps to have a *shovel* handy for that occasional grave digging job. Good for the biceps too.
- A *coil of rope* is one of those things with a thousand and one uses, but they don't get the chance this time 'cause the cops catch them first.

MEMORABLE MOMENTS

It's wonderfully funny when Dean makes Sam brush the male student's naked back with purple paint while they're in the student digs. Then Dean tells Sam that he's missed a bit at the base of the back so Sam has to carry on painting while pulling a face at Dean.

Top Scare – when Hookman materialises right behind the Reverend and reaches over to impale the Rev on his hook.

SPOOK RULES

- Spirits leave behind the smell of ozone in the room after they have materialised there.
- You need to salt and burn the ghost's physical remains in order to stop it haunting this plane. This includes any prosthetics the ghost might have had, like a blooming

---

49 This is where the shotgun with salt ammunition tradition starts – they'll still be using it in Season Three and beyond.

great silver hook, because in this case the hook was also the source of the ghost's power along with the bones.

- Spirits can latch onto your repressed emotions without you even realising it.

DID YOU SPOT?

This is the second time the brothers have had to spend hours searching through paperwork to find the information they need. This time it's probably because the records are so old (dating back to 1851) and just haven't been scanned yet[50].

GOING UNDERCOVER

The boys tell the students at Eastern Iowa University that they are their fraternity brothers from Ohio but tell Lori only that they recently transferred to the University.

Dean tells the Sheriff that Sam was a 'dumb-ass pledge'.

CULTURAL REFERENCES

Lori asks Taylor if she looks okay for her date but decides she looks a bit too 'Martha Stewart': Stewart is a modern day Mrs Beaton with her own TV show. She specialises in tips about cooking, home and decorating, gardening, and runs Cutest Cupcake competitions on her website. She also dresses very conservatively.

Sam: 'One freaked out witness who didn't see anything? Doesn't mean it's the Invisible Man.': H G Wells wrote *The Invisible Man* novella in 1897 and the story was adapted into a Universal movie in 1933 with Claude Rains taking the lead role of the invisible scientist Griffin.

Dean calls Sam 'Dr Venkman' in the library when Sam discovers the details about Jacob Carns' murderous rampage. Peter Venkman PhD was the scientist played by Bill Murray in the movie *Ghostbusters* (1984).

Dean saves Sam's butt and convinces the sheriff that a fine is sufficient punishment, then adds, 'Dude, I am Matlock.': Benjamin L Matlock was a defence attorney working in Atlanta, Georgia in the TV series *Matlock* that ran from 1986 to 1995.

Dean: 'Dude, sorority girls! Think we'll see a naked pillow fight?': A reference to the pillow fight in the movie *Animal House* (1978) although, technically, those sorority girls were only topless, not completely naked.

GOOFS AND FLUFFS

Sam starts painting Purple Student's back with the paint brush in his right hand but it

---

50 The first time was in 'Bloody Mary' (1-05) but that time, the computers weren't working so they had to resort to hard copy

switches to his left momentarily before going back to his right hand.

Sam points the shotgun up into the air as the cop comes out of the trees towards them, then a split second later he's got it back down pointing at the trees.

When Lori goes to bed she doesn't have a reading lamp clipped to her headboard. When she wakes up there's a nice little grey one on the right hand side. Perhaps it was a present from the Hookman?

Loose ends and logic problems: Dean picks some kind of ticket up from under the car wiper but it doesn't seem to have any relevance to the plot, except maybe as a general reality detail to show that no matter where you leave your car someone will stuff advertising leaflets or parking tickets under your wiper.

Jacob Carns was supposedly buried in an unmarked grave at a cemetery but there is a convenient headstone marking the grave after all. Just as well, else Dean would never have found it. The fact that they buried a murderer on hallowed ground is also unusual – with Catholic churches if you'd committed an 'irredeemable sin' you had to be buried outside sacred ground.

On a similar note, it is unusual that the Hookman manages to enter the church and attack Sam and Lori since it's established in 'Route 666' (1-13) that spirits/demons can't enter churches.

And how the hell does Lori (or indeed the next door neighbours) sleep through the Hookman carving 'Aren't you glad you didn't turn on the light?' into the wall in three inch high letters? What does he do, put his hook in stealth mode?

Sam and Dean enter Lori's room through the closet window. Dean falls on top of Sam as they climb in but the cop doesn't hear them stumbling around at all. And it is rather a dangerous thing to do – entering the crime scene that early – given that the miracles of modern forensics could identify any hairs or fingerprints etc they leave behind. They've entered crime scenes before[51] but that was a long time after the crime was committed and forensics had probably finished.

HAVEN'T I SEEN YOU BEFORE?

Dan Butler's credits include *Quantum Leap*, *Star Trek: Voyager* and *The X-Files*. Chelah Horsdal appeared in *Stargate SG-1*, *X-Men: The Last Stand* and *Hollow Man II*. Alfred E Humphreys featured in *Painkiller Jane*, *Tru Calling*, *X-Men 2* and *Final Destination 2*. Jane McGregor was in *Poltergeist: The Legacy* and *The 4400*. Christie Laing's credits include *Smallville*, *The 4400* and *Kyle XY*. Sean Millington appeared in *The Outer Limits*, *Blade: The Series* and *Stargate: Atlantis*. Benjamin Rogers was in *The Twilight Zone* and *Masters of Horror*. Brian T Skala featured in *Heroes*.

---

51 In 'Bloody Mary' (1-05) and 'Skin' (1-06)

Christie Laing also appears in 'Crossroad Blues' (2-08)

BEHIND THE SCENES

In the deleted scenes it becomes obvious how Lori found out about her father having an affair – she found a condom in his pocket when she was putting his trousers in the wash.

This episode was originally supposed to air after 'Wendigo' (1-02) but even though it had good performances, it wasn't considered tense or scary enough. So some re-shoots were done along with some re-editing to improve it. In the end dropping it back in the airing schedule had no detrimental impact on the overall mythology of the show. If anything it was better, because it fitted with Sam's personality more to wait longer for romance after Jessica's death. [*Season One Supernatural Companion*]

MUSICAL INTERLUDE

- 'Higher Mathematics' by Split Habit (often referred to as 'Merry Go Round') – when Lori is getting ready for a date at the start of the episode.
- 'Bang Your Head (Metal Health)' by Quiet Riot – Sam and Dean driving to the fraternity house.
- 'Noise' by Low Five – when Sam and Dean are speaking to Murph.
- 'At Rest' by APM – Sermon music.
- 'Royal Bethlehem' by APM – when Sam and Dean are researching in the Library.
- 'U Do 2 Me' by Paul Richards – at the college party.
- 'Peace Of Mind' by Boston – at the end of the episode.

ANALYSIS

'Hookman' is one of those solid episodes with John Shiban's writing once again coming in tight and pacy[52]. There are lots of things happening with a mixture of three separate urban legends to carry you through the episode and a little extra love interest thrown in too – but somehow the overall result just isn't as good as the earlier[53] 'Skin' (1-06). This may be due to the re-shooting and re-editing that took place when the director proved to be a little less experienced with filming scares than had been hoped. It also could have been because there didn't seem to be a lot of chemistry going on between Lori and Sam or perhaps because there was less character development than usual.

---

52 Although chronologically, this episode was actually written before 'Skin' (1-06) so maybe that should be: Shiban's first script is tight and pacy

53 Technically, later …

Whatever the reason, the end result is certainly enjoyable but it isn't exceptional.

The character development wasn't entirely left out though. Sam looks like he's slowly coming out of his grief for Jessica and starting to show an interest in other girls, even if he's not quite out of the woods yet. He also confesses to Lori that he feels like everyone he cares about ends up dead. An aspect that will get more focus later in the series.

For Dean, the scene at the end of the episode when he waits in the car while Sam says goodbye to Lori is full of emotion. Despite there being only one line of dialogue between them (Dean says they could stay but Sam shakes his head), you can still see both Dean's concern for his brother and the internal conflict on Sam's face – Sam's probably feeling guilty 'cause the attraction to Lori betrays his memory of Jessica and what they had together. Just as well Dean's right there for him.

VERDICT – 7 out of 10

EPISODE 1-08
BUGS

TRANSMISSION DATES
US first aired: 8 November 2005
UK first aired: 13 March 2006

CREDITS
Writer: Rachel Nave & Bill Coakley
Director: Kim Manners

GUEST STARS
Andrew Airlie (Larry Pike), Jim Byrnes (Anthropology Professor Reardon), Michael Daingerfield (Dustin Burwash), Anne Marie Deluise (Joanie Pike), Carrie Genzel (Lynda Bloome), Jimmy Herman (Jo White Tree), Tyler Johnston (Matt White), Mi-Jung Lee (Newscaster), Ryan Robbins (Travis Wheeler)

SYNOPSIS
A construction worker dies suddenly on the Oasis Plains housing estate owned by Larry Pike. The doctors are blaming Creutzfeldt-Jakob Disease but the victim's brain seems to have been eaten from the inside out. Sam and Dean discover a curse on the construction site that releases the power of Nature to kill any trespassers on the land during the six days after the Spring Equinox. The brothers cannot stop the curse so need to get the site evacuated before it's too late. Everyone leaves except the Pikes and they are still at the house – with Sam and Dean trying to convince them to leave – when the attack by Nature begins in the form of a swarm of angry bees. The family and the brothers manage to seal themselves in the house until dawn, using improvised mini-flame throwers to keep off the few bees that get in. It's then seven days after the Equinox and the curse stops.

CAN YOU SURVIVE TO THE TITLES?
Construction worker Dustin Burwash takes on 4,000 beetles in a hole in the ground and loses.

LOCATION, LOCATION, LOCATION
Oasis Plains, Oklahoma, near Atoka Valley; Department of Anthropology at a local university; Sapulpa, Oklahoma

Legendary Roots

Curses are magical workings designed to have a detrimental effect on the target, bringing sickness, harm or even death. Curses can be found in all traditions of magic around the world and date back as far as ancient Greece and Rome, where it was a common practice to write the curse on a sheet of lead, fold it and place it in a gateway to the underworld such as a cave or tomb. Many other methods for casting curses exist – many require objects belonging to the victim such as hair or nail clippings and others require figures of clay or cloth.

Methods of curse breaking are as varied as curse creation and include ceremonially destroying the magically charged objects or performing banishing rituals. One of the side effects of breaking a curse is that the bad intent usually recoils on the person who cast the curse, showing that what goes around, comes around.

Squeeze of the Week

This episode is even worse than 'Phantom Traveler' (1-04) – nobody gets any kind of squeeze at all. Bummer!

Sibling Rivalry

While they're investigating Dustin's death, someone has to go into the hole in the soil to check it out. Dean wants to flip a coin to see who goes but Sam's a little apprehensive about what might be down there. So Dean immediately teases him about being a chicken. A lovely light-hearted exchange.

Body Count

Larry's surveyor was stung to death by bees a year before this episode takes place. Then Dustin gets munched in the opening sequence, and realtor Lynda Bloome is unfortunate enough to die when she's bitten to death by some spiders in the shower.

Toolkit

- An *aerosol can of bug spray* and a *lighter* makes a handy mini flame-thrower. Dean would have been better off with an industrial strength flame-thrower as per Kurt Russell in *The Thing* (1982) but needs must eh?

Memorable Moments

It raises a smile when Larry, and then Lynda, mistake the boys for being a house-hunting couple and keep giving them the line about how they accept people of any sexual orientation. Dean's excellent reaction the second time it happens is to pat Sam on the butt and go off to talk to someone else with an affectionate, 'Okay honey?'.

And of course, Dean pops his head round the bathroom door wearing only a towel wrapped round his hair after his steam shower. Ooooh!

MOTEL MAYHEM

No motel this week. The boys break into a brand new house on the new estate for a spot of squatting. May as well choose somewhere with top-of-the-range facilities.

FASHION OBSERVATIONS

Dean doesn't seem to take his amulet off – even when he's in the steam shower.

SPOOK RULES

- You don't break curses, you get out of their way.
- Curses can control Nature and send beetles, bees, cockroaches and spiders on killing sprees.

DID YOU SPOT?

Sam gets to drive the Impala for a change, though mostly just around the housing estate.

In the final showdown at the end of the episode, several scenes in the house – when the insects are attacking, coming down the chimney and bursting into the downstairs room – seem to be inspired by Hitchcock's *The Birds* (1963).

The concept of building a luxury housing estate on tainted land was made famous by Steven Spielberg's movie *Poltergeist* (1982) where the houses stood over a burial ground but only the headstones had been relocated, leaving the bodies under the foundations.

GOING UNDERCOVER

The boys tell Travis Weaver that they are Dustin Burwash's nephews so they can find out where the accident happened.

Later, they both pretend to be home hunters looking for a house for their father who is getting on a bit.

After finding the Indian bones in the forest, they go to get them identified at the local university, and tell the college professor that they are students in his Anthro 101 class.

Dean tries to use the same student cover when they visit Shaman Joe White Tree from the Euchee tribe to discover the story behind the curse, but Joe sees through Dean's lies straight away and will only talk to Sam after that.

Dean masquerades as Travis Weaver to try to get Larry Pike to leave his house. Unfortunately, Larry knows Travis too well and blows the cover.

CULTURAL REFERENCES

Dean: 'Mad cow. Wasn't that on Oprah?': Broadcast in 141 countries, *The Oprah Winfrey Show* encourages people to 'Live Your Best Life Today'. The show has been on air since 1984 and is produced by Harpo Studios, who are owned by Oprah herself.

Sam: 'You mean, like Willard?'; Dean: 'Yeah, but bugs instead of rats.': *Willard* (2003) is about Willard Stiles, a social misfit caring for his ill but verbally abusive mother in an old mansion, that is also home to a host of rats. Willard discovers he has a connection to the rats and they become his only friends. Constantly humiliated in front of his co-workers, Willard is eventually fired by his cruel and uncaring boss, but when one of his rats is killed at work, Willard sets out for revenge. Directed by Glen Morgan (*The X-Files*, *Millennium*, *Space: Above And Beyond*) and starring Crispin Glover.

When Sam starts talking about how people and animals can have psychic connections, Dean comments, 'Yeah, that whole Timmy-Lassie thing.': *Lassie* is a popular children's show about Timmy and his collie-dog Lassie who went round having adventures and solving mysteries together. (Well, actually Lassie did all the work, Timmy just translated the barking.) Lassie first appeared in a short story by Eric Knight in 1938, with the first movie, *Lassie Come Home*, being released in 1943 starring Elizabeth Taylor, Roddy McDowell and Lassie. A ninth generation, direct line descendent of the original Lassie is still promoting the show.

Dean: 'Yeah, you were kind of like the blonde chick in *The Munsters*.': The blonde chick in the Munster family was Marilyn, daughter of Frankenstein's monster-like Herman and vampiric Lily. Marilyn was the only human-looking offspring in a family of, well, freaks. The black and white show began in 1964 – the same year as *The Addams Family* – and ran until 1966. The show was revived in 1988 as *The Munsters Today* and ran until 1991, and there have been several spin-off films. Several actresses played Marilyn over the course of the show and in the spin-off films: Beverley Owen (1964), Pat Priest (1964-1966), Debbie Watson (1966), Jo McDonnell (1981), Hilary Van Dyke (1988-1991), Christine Taylor (1995) and Elaine Hendrix (1996).

University Lecturer: 'Well … you know, there's a Euchee tribe in Sapulpa.': In 1836 the Euchee tribe moved to Oklahoma where fewer than 500 now reside in the north west part of the Creek Nation. In Euchee mythology, they recognise the power of the Sun as the source of life and mystery so it's actually quite logical for the story to be tied into the equinox.

Sam: 'A gas company employee, Dustin Burwash, supposedly died from Creutzfeldt-Jakob.': Now pay attention, there's some big words coming up: 'Creutzfeldt-Jakob disease (CJD) is a rare and fatal neurodegenerative disease of unknown cause. Patients are usually aged between 50 and 75 and typical clinical features include a rapidly progressive dementia, associated myoclonus and a characteristic electroencephalographic pattern. Neuropathological examination reveals cortical spongiform change, hence the term "spongiform encephalopathy".[54] Got that? Good!

GOOFS AND FLUFFS

The episode is set from 20 to 26 March 2006. Sam comments that the equinox took place on 20 March, which is correct, but as the bees swarm on the estate on 26 March you can see a full moon in the background. The full moon in March 2006 was on 14 March, so by 26 March the moon would have been very small and nearer to a new moon than a full moon.

As Travis runs to rescue Dustin you can see the cameraman's shadow below the opening of the hole.

Immediately after Sam has been down the hole where Dustin died and is showing Dean the beetles in the car, they pass a pick up truck, seen on the left out of the back window. As the conversation continues, they pass the same pick up truck again within seconds of seeing it the first time.

Sam calls Matt's mobile when he's trying to get the family to evacuate the house but it's not clear how Sam got Matt's mobile number since you never see Sam asking for it (not even in the deleted scenes).

The ending of the episode has got its timings all wrong. When Sam and Dean arrive to get Larry and his family out of the house, Sam says it's 12 am (midnight). The bee swarm appears minutes later and they all dash into the house. Their defensive actions downstairs then up into the loft seem to happen in real time (there's no obvious time gap indicated) and yet the sun is rising less than 15 minutes later to save them from the swarms. They're in Oklahoma not the Land of the Midnight Sun!

HAVEN'T I SEEN YOU BEFORE?

Andrew Airlie plays Mr Oliver in *Reaper*, Brian Moore in *The 4400* and can also be seen in *Final Destination 2*. Jim Byrnes was in *Andromeda*, *Jake 2.0* and played Joe Dawson in *Highlander: The Series*. Michael Daingerfield featured in *Earth: Final Conflict*, *Masters of Horror* and *The 4400*. Anne Marie Deluise's credits include *Total Recall 2070*, *Earth: Final Conflict* and *Andromeda*. Carrie Genzel played Vestra in *Flash Gordon* and has been in *Kyle XY* and *Watchmen*. Jimmy Herman appeared in *Jeremiah*, *The Outer Limits* and *The X-Files*. Tyler Johnston's credits include *Decoys 2: Alien Seduction*, *Blood Ties* and *Smallville*. Mi-Jung Lee was in *X-Men 2*, *X-Men: The Last Stand*, *Snakes On A Plane* and *Watchmen*. Ryan Robbins played Charlie Connor in

54 From http://www.cjd.ed.ac.uk/intro.htm

Battlestar Galactica, Ladon Radim in *Stargate: Atlantis* and was also in *AVP: Requiem*.

BEHIND THE SCENES

This episode generated one of Jensen Ackles' favourite anecdotes about being trapped in a small attic with a large number of bees. The beekeeper had told them that as long as they remained calm, the bees wouldn't sting. But the scene called for Dean to wave his arms in the air so of course they did get stung. [*The Official Supernatural Magazine #3*]

And at least they weren't alone. Despite the crew being suited and gloved up against the bees, Director Kim Manners still walked in without protective clothing saying that if the actors were doing it, then he was going to be dressed the same. [*Season One Supernatural Companion*]

Not that people didn't try to minimise the problems. Costume designer Diane Widas found out what colours they shouldn't use around the bees and the costumes all had sleeves and leg openings sealed so nothing could fly up them. So Ackles and Padalecki could have had it worse. [*The Official Supernatural Magazine #9*]

Other people were having close encounters with bugs too. The six-foot three guy who was covered in 25,000 beetles was scared to death, while the naked woman, lying on the floor with hundreds of baby tarantulas on her head apparently never even whimpered. [*Season One Supernatural Companion*]

MUSICAL INTERLUDE

- 'Rock Of Ages' by Def Leppard – when Sam and Dean are in front of the bar at the start of the episode.
- 'I Got More Bills Than I Got Pay' by Black Toast Music – when Sam and Dean are talking to Larry Park at the BBQ.
- 'Poke In Tha Butt' by Extreme Music – when Matt talks to Sam at BBQ.
- 'Medusa' by MasterSource – when Sam and Dean arrive on the university campus with the bones.
- 'No One Like You' by the Scorpions – at the end of the episode.

ANALYSIS

Oh dear. This is quite simply the worst episode of Season One. The problems lie with the main bugs storyline rather than the underlying family story arc, and there are two main areas of disappointment.

First, it's just not scary. Partly that's because we're a little desensitised these days after numerous movies from *Indiana Jones and the Temple of Doom* to *Arachnophobia* getting in on the creepy-crawly act, but the main reason they fail here is because they are obviously CGI spiders and bees. Fair dues, the bee scene was filmed with real critters, but they just couldn't be seen on the finished film and it's such a shame. Instead, we just get unconvincing bees and an attack of the giggles when the spiders appear in the shower.

Secondly, and worse, the story doesn't hang together convincingly – especially with the miraculous sunrise taking place just past midnight saving the household from a painful death and leaving the viewer trying to figure out how the hell it happened so fast.

However, 'Bugs' is redeemed partially by its underlying arc. The main story of Matt's problems with his father blasts open Sam's own family issues. Sam is finally starting to see the wider picture. Until now he's been single-mindedly driven to find Jessica's killer with help from his dad. Now, he's not sure his dad will even want to see him. As Dean picks up the responsibility of representing John Winchester's point of view, Sam starts to realise that there are two sides to the situation. In the scene outside the university, Sam emotionally transforms from being angry at his father for throwing him out to understanding more about how his father was concerned for his safety. It suddenly dawns on him that he might have misinterpreted his father's actions.

VERDICT – 5 out of 10

EPISODE 1-09
HOME

TRANSMISSION DATES
US first aired: 15 November 2005
UK first aired: 20 March 2006

CREDITS
Writer: Eric Kripke
Director: Ken Girotti

RECURRING ROLES
Jeffrey Dean Morgan (John Winchester), Samantha Smith (Mary Winchester)

GUEST STARS
Loretta Devine (Missouri Mosely), Haili Page Phillipe (Sari Cooper), Jerry Rector (Joe the Repairman), Kristin Richardson (Jenny Cooper), Jamie Schwanebeck (Richie Cooper), Don Thompson (Mike Guenther)

SYNOPSIS
Sam dreams about a woman shouting for help through the upstairs window of their old house in Lawrence. To convince Dean that this is the next job, Sam has to admit that his dreams sometimes come true. In their home town, they join forces with psychic Missouri Moseley, an old friend of their dad's, and together they banish one of the poltergeists haunting their old home. But it takes the spirit of Mary Winchester to save her boys from another malevolent spirit.

CAN YOU SURVIVE TO THE TITLES?
For the second time[55], no-one gets killed before the titles, although Jenny's young daughter, Sari, gets scared witless by a flaming ghost coming out of her bedroom closet in the same room where Mary Winchester died in 1983.

LOCATION, LOCATION, LOCATION
The Winchester family ex-residence, house number 1481, Lawrence, Kansas.

---

55 The first time being 'Skin' (1-06)

LEGENDARY ROOTS

Derived from the German words *polter*, meaning to make a noise by knocking or moving things around, and the word *geist* meaning ghost, poltergeists are the most undesirable type of ghost to encounter. They are usually invisible and are almost invariably associated with a young adolescent, male or female, although more often it is attracted to a girl. Poltergeists need to extract energy from living persons, and young people tend to have it in abundance. The poltergeists then use this energy to telekinetically displace objects, often violently, for the purpose of destruction. Nasty buggers.

SQUEEZE OF THE WEEK

Everyone is way too emotional to even think about it this time.

SIBLING RIVALRY

After Sam's nightmare, he's rather preoccupied with drawing the tree outside his old home. Dean is looking for their next job but realises Sam's not listening. To prove his point he suggests they go investigate the Sacramento case where a man shot himself in the head three times. But none of it is blowing up Sam's skirt at all.

BODY COUNT

For the first time, no-one dies at all in the entire episode, but Joe the repairman does get his hand and forearm chewed off by a possessed waste disposal unit and the chopped up remains can be seen sliding out of the waste pipe under the sink – gross!

TOOLKIT

- Some *powerful herbs* will banish those annoying poltergeists – try angelica root, van van oil, and a sprinkle of crossroad dirt.
- A *small axe* and that ever useful *shotgun loaded with salt* are good to have when you've got to rescue your brother from being beaten up by a spirit who's locked all the doors.
- And a *friendly local psychic* is always handy for those ghostly goings-on.

MEMORABLE MOMENTS

Mary Winchester's appearance to save her sons is laden with feeling and John Winchester's secret arrival at Missouri Moseley's house – along with his refusal to talk to his sons until he knows the truth – is just dripping with intrigue.

SPOOK RULES

- Scratching noises and flickering lights are both signs of a malevolent spirit.
- When extreme evil walks through a house, it leaves a wound. Sometimes those wounds get infected by paranormal energies.
- Putting a special concoction of herbs in the north, south, east and west corners of a house, on each floor, will purify it.
- A good spirit can cancel out a poltergeist's energy. When this happens the good spirit is destroyed in the process.

DID YOU SPOT?

There are two references to situations in 'The Woman in White' (1-01). When Sam is saving Sari and her brother from the poltergeist he tells her, 'Take your brother outside and don't look back' – which is what John Winchester told Dean to do during the original fire. What's interesting about Sam saying this is that he'd admitted earlier that he hadn't known that Dean had carried him out of the house that night. If he couldn't remember that, how did he know what his dad told Dean? Unless it was embedded in his subconscious of course …

The second Pilot reference is to things in the closet. Sari's situation echoes Sam's early life, but when Sam told his father there was something in the closet, his dad just gave him a Colt .45.

GOING UNDERCOVER

The boys pretend to be policemen with John Winchester's old business partner when trying to find out more about John's behaviour before and after the house fire.

After that they both jettison any type of cover and be themselves. Sam was himself in 'Skin' (1-06) as well but Dean used a detective cover in that episode, so this is the first time they're both themselves.

CULTURAL REFERENCES

When Sam first reveals that his dreams come true: Dean: 'First you tell me that you've got the Shining?': The Shining was both a novel by Stephen King (1977) and a movie by Stanley Kubrick (1980). In the movie, an evil presence causes the complete mental breakdown of caretaker Jack Torrence (Jack Nicholson). His breakdown turns violent and only his son Danny can save his mother and himself using his psychic gift called the Shining. The Shining also gets a visual reference when Dean is breaking down the front door with an axe and peers into the house through the missing panels.

When Jenny is in bed after the house has been purified, the bed starts to shake and bounce around. This is a tip of the hat to a scene from The Exorcist (1973) when young

Regan is possessed by the devil and develops the ability to move things telekinetically, including making the bed shake.

Poltergeist and *Star Wars* get referenced again as the boys wait outside the house after it has been purified. Dean asks Sam why they are still there. Sam: 'I don't know. I just … I still have a bad feeling.'; Dean: 'Why? Missouri did her whole Zelda Rubinstein thing, the house should be clean.': Zelda Rubinstein played Tangina Barrons, the psychic in Spielberg's movie *Poltergeist* (1982), called in to help rescue little Carol Anne from the evil spirits holding her on the other side. And 'The house is clean' is one of the more famous quotes from the movie.

Eric Kripke has always said that Sam and Dean are like Luke Skywalker and Han Solo so it's not really a surprise to hear Sam echoing Luke's 'I have a bad feeling about this' from *Star Wars*.

GOOFS AND FLUFFS

During the conversation on the garage forecourt, Sam starts by looking over his right shoulder at Dean. Then, as the shot switches between Sam and Dean, Sam starts looking at Dean over his left shoulder despite the fact that Dean hasn't actually moved. At the end of the conversation, Sam is looking over his right shoulder at his brother again.

When Jenny's son Ritchie has disappeared and she's looking for him, the child lock on the fridge is open after we have seen it being closed by the poltergeist when Ritchie was lured inside. What's really funny is watching Jenny fumbling and pretending to open it when she goes to free Ritchie.

When Joe the repairman is fixing the waste disposal, the tap on the sink is pointing to the left. As he puts his hand back into the sink the second time the tap is in the middle, and when you see him with his arm down the sink in the next shot the tap is pointing to the left again.

As the lamp cord tightens around Sam's neck, Dean comes to rescue him, but as Dean strains against the cord, it's actually hanging quite loosely.

HAVEN'T I SEEN YOU BEFORE?

Loretta Devine appeared in *Urban Legends*, *Urban Legends: Final Cut* and *Grey's Anatomy*. Haili Page Phillipe's credits include *The 4400*, *Battlestar Galactica* and *Jeremiah*. Jerry Rector was in *Star Trek: The Next Generation*, *Sliders* and *The Twilight Zone*. Kristin Richardson has featured in *Lost*, *Angel* and *Charmed*. Jamie Schwanebeck was in *Smallville*. Don Thompson played Specialist 3rd Class Anthony Figurski in *Battlestar Galactica* and Uncle Pat McCallum in *Blade: The Series* and was also in *Taken*.

BEHIND THE SCENES

Some fire walkers were needed for 'Home'[56] because these were very dangerous stunts to do. Once alight, if the stunt person should panic and draw a frantic breath, they get a lung full of fire. Which is obviously not very healthy. So there is always a signal agreed where the stunt person can drop to the ground and be put out if needed. [*Season One Supernatural Companion*]

In *The Official Supernatural Magazine* #3, we discover that there's a very good reason why the boys' home is in Lawrence – because it's close to Stull Cemetery. The grave yard is reputedly one of the Gates to Hell and Eric Kripke chose this place because some of the show's mythology is connected to the cemetery. Oooh, intriguing...[57]

MUSICAL INTERLUDE

All music was written specifically for this episode.

ANALYSIS

What a rollercoaster of a story! Everyone – including the viewer – gets an emotional kick-back from 'Home' and right there in the middle is Dean.

He's got plenty to cope with this time as Sam starts the day insisting that they've got to go home. It's going to take some substantial reason for Dean to do that, since he's sworn never to go back there, so Sam drops the bombshell that his dreams have been coming true[58]. Add in the speculation that it could be the demon that killed their mom back at their old home and Dean's reeling. His vulnerability becomes obvious when he secretly leaves a message on their dad's answer phone, seeking support while he tries to deal with resurfacing traumatic memories of the fire and his mother's death. Dean's not really one to get his psychological responses out in the open (all that touchy feely stuff!) so he's bottled his issues and probably never grieved for his mother properly. No wonder he doesn't want to go back – he's been suppressing so many painful memories for two decades that they're probably threatening to overwhelm him. But go back he does; he fulfils his promise of not letting anyone else die in the house, and saves not only the current owner Jenny but also his own brother from the vindictive poltergeists.

Sam meanwhile has less emotional ties to the old house given that he can't remember much about living there and the night his mother died. He spends most of the time trying to avoid talking about his newly-declared psychic skills, then discovers that he can sense spirits that even Missouri can't pick up. It's only at the end that he

---

56 After the char-grilled Wendigo in 1-02

57 But you'll have to wait till the end of Season Five to find out what happens there.

58 Something he avoided telling Dean at the end of 'Bloody Mary' (1-05)

reveals his concerns about it all when he asks Missouri, 'What's happening to me?' Whatever is going on, he's determined to use it to help people. He failed Jessica by not acting on his dreams and now he has a chance to atone for that error by saving others.

For the first time since the Pilot, we meet the entire Winchester family in 'Home'. Mary Winchester's sudden appearance is touching and cryptic. It's the first time she's seen the boys as grown men and she seems to approve of them totally, destroying her own spirit to save their lives. But not before saying she's sorry to Sam. He asks her 'What for?' but the question remains unanswered. As does the question about why John Winchester won't talk to his children. He's in town and staying at Missouri's house but won't contact the boys.

And that brief glimpse of John Winchester is where the episode tantalises and frustrates. John's allusion to finding the truth compounds the situation and the viewer is left both confused and curious. Sam's comment that it feels like something is starting is reinforced with John's appearance, leaving a deep, uneasy sense that you're teetering on the edge and about to tip over into unknown territory ...

VERDICT – 9 out of 10

EPISODE 1-10
ASYLUM

TRANSMISSION DATES
US first aired: 22 November 2005
UK first aired: 27 March 2006

CREDITS
Writer: Richard Hatem
Director: Guy Bee

GUEST STARS
Norman Armour (Dr Sanford Ellicott), Nancy Bell (Female Patient/Spirit), Peter Benson (Lt Walter Kelly), Leif Bridgman (Patient/Spirit), Roy Campsall (Unknown), Nicholas D'Agosto (Gavin), Richard Dieth (Unknown), John Gray (Teen), Nicole LaPlaca (Patient/Spirit), Brooke Nevin (Kat), Tom Pickett (Lt Danny Gunderson), James Purcell (Dr James Ellicott), Karly Warkentin (Kelly's Wife)

SYNOPSIS
After receiving the co-ordinates of the Roosevelt Asylum in a text message from their dad, the boys investigate a multiple haunting in Illinois. Uncovering the history of the Roosevelt Asylum and discovering the unethical actions of the Chief of Staff, one Sanford Ellicott MD, the brothers try to find the doctor's body in order to burn it. But the doctor lures Sam to the boiler room and after a dose of his special anger treatment Sam goes gunning for Dean, managing to pin him down and shoot him with rock salt. Sam tries again with a handgun but Dean manages to disarm his brother and goes hunting for the evil doctor. Attacked by the doc, Dean just manages to salt and burn the bones before Ellicott can kill him.

CAN YOU SURVIVE TO THE TITLES?
After being in the boiler room at the Roosevelt Asylum, cop Walter Kelly goes home and shoots his wife and then puts the gun in his own mouth and blows his brains out.

LOCATION, LOCATION, LOCATION
Roosevelt Asylum (est 1872), Rockford, Illinois; The Old Terminal Pub, Rockford, Illinois

LEGENDARY ROOTS

There are many reports of haunted asylums but the Danvers State Hospital is one of the best known and inspired the *House on Haunted Hill* films (1959 and 1999). The hospital, affectionately known as the Castle on Haunted Hill, was built in 1874 and opened 1878 near to the site where the Salem witch trials took place, which saw 19 so-called witches killed in the 17th Century.

The hospital was designed for a maximum of 600 people but saw the number of patients rise to over 2,400 at its peak. In order to keep the patients in check, experimental treatments including hydrotherapy and electric shock therapy were conducted, and the hospital is also rumoured to be the birthplace of the lobotomy.

Danvers closed its doors in 1992 and was put on full lockdown in 2004 after a fire was started on the site. Following its closure the state guarded the area, so there is little to report in terms of actual spirit activity, but this has just increased interest in the place and its reputation as a haunted site. Over 120 people were arrested for trespass there between 2000 and 2006. The site has now been renovated into a condominium complex.

SQUEEZE OF THE WEEK

Nope, nothing again. Maybe the boys have gone celibate.

SIBLING RIVALRY

As in 'Skin' (1-06), the rivalry takes on a more serious note again. There's still the occasional light jibe (as in the discussion of who's the hottest psychic, see **Cultural References** section) but mostly we get to see more of the very real differences of opinion between the boys around how they relate to their father: Dean always following orders and Sam always questioning why they should do so. The anger increases exponentially after Sam gets the Dr Ellicott treatment and shoots Dean with the rock salt, but not before revealing how he thinks Dean is pathetically desperate for their dad's approval and how only Sam has a mind of his own. Pretty heavy stuff.

BODY COUNT

No-one else dies after Walter murders his wife and shoots himself in the pre-title sequence.

TOOLKIT

- The homemade *electromagnetic frequency (EMF) meter* proves its usefulness again[59].

---

59 Having first appeared in 'Phantom Traveler' (1-04).

- If you're trying to detect ghostly orbs then get yourself an *infrared camera*.
- The trusty *shotgun with rock salt rounds* is out of the trunk of the car once more. As is the *carton of salt* and *tin of lighter fuel* for burning dem bones, dem bones, dem dry bones.
- Carrying an *unloaded handgun* can also be useful – especially when your angry brother is trying to shoot you. Lucky huh?

MEMORABLE MOMENTS

While trying to dig for more information about events at the asylum, Sam gets an appointment with Dr Ellicott, who asks him what he's been doing. Sam's wonderfully awkward as he tries to explain that he's been on a road trip with his brother and that they did some interesting things and met some interesting people while travelling. Just as well he didn't mention that they killed some interesting things too.

SPOOK RULES

- Local rumour has it that a night in the Roosevelt Asylum, with all the ghosts of the patients, will drive you insane.
- Ghosts are attracted to the whole ESP thing that Sam has going on.
- Spirits can be limited to manifest only at certain hours of the day, and the freaks tend to come out at night.
- Ghosts can not only manipulate mobile phones but can also sound just like your brother in trouble, especially when they want to lure you to the boiler room.
- Ghosts have the power to seal the doors and windows of a building to keep the victims inside.
- You need to salt and burn the ghost's physical remains in order to stop it haunting this plane. However, not all ghosts 'die' in the same way. 'Hookman' (1-07) burned away to nothing while Dr Sanford Ellicott's ghost leaves behind solid, if friable, remains.

DID YOU SPOT?

The *Men's Health* magazine that Sam reads in the waiting room at Dr Ellicott's practice had as its cover model one Sean William Scott, an actor who played a lifeguard in the TV series *Sweet Valley High* – an episode of which featured one Jensen Ackles as Brad. It was the July/August 2005 issue, with the headline 'Your Best Body Ever'. The copy Sam reads was probably the subscription version, since the news-stand version had Williams in a side-on pose rather than the front view seen in this episode and more headlines on the cover.

Going Undercover

Dean pretends to be Nigel Tufnel from the *Chicago Tribune* when he's questioning Lt Gunderson. Tufnel is the lead guitarist of the fictional band Spinal Tap.

Sam makes the appointment with psychiatrist James Ellicott under his own name but it's a fair bet that the address he uses is fake.

Cultural References

Both cop Walter Kelly and Sam get nose bleeds as a result of Dr Ellicott's 'treatment'. These were also a spooky feature of *The X-Files*. The first episode to feature Scully having a nosebleed was 'Leonard Betts' where she and Mulder were hunting a creature that fed off cancer. Scully corners the creature who says, 'I'm sorry, but you've got something I need'. Later in the episode she wakes up with a nosebleed – one of the signs of the cancer.

When looking for clues to John Winchester's whereabouts in his journal: Dean: 'I love the guy, but I swear, he writes like frigging Yoda.': Yoda – a diminutive *Star Wars* character who talks topsy-turvy and is awesome with a light-sabre. If you don't know who he is you either need to get out more or stay in and watch the films!

Dean: 'Let me know if you see any dead people, Haley Joel.': Referencing Haley Joel Osment's character, Cole Sear, in the film *The Sixth Sense* (1999). He was able to see and talk to spirits that were still Earthbound.

Dean: 'Hey, Sam, who do you think is a hotter psychic – Patricia Arquette, Jennifer Love Hewitt, or you?': Both women star in successful TV series playing psychics. Jennifer Love Hewitt is Melinda Gorden in the *Ghost Whisperer* while Patricia Arquette is Allison DuBois in *Medium*. And Sam is definitely the hottest of the three.

When Sam insists he has strange vibes not ESP, Dean: 'Yeah, whatever. Don't ask, don't tell.': The Don't Ask, Don't Tell policy was brought in by President Bill Clinton in 1993, and effectively allowed gay, lesbian, bisexual and transgender (GLBT) people to serve in the US military provided they did not disclose their sexuality (in which case they would be discharged from service). The policy also prevented the questioning or investigating of servicepeople who were suspected of being GLBT.

Dean: 'All work and no play makes Dr Ellicott a very dull boy.': The first of two more references to *The Shining* (1980) following the previous two from 'Home' (1-09). Here, it's about Jack Nicholson's character, Jack Torrance, writing a single sentence hundreds of times: 'All work and no play makes Jack a dull boy.'

Dean finds out the horrific ordeals the inpatients went through; Dean: 'Kind of like my man Jack in *Cuckoo's Nest*. So...ghosts are possessing people?'; Sam: 'Maybe. Or maybe it's more like, uh, like Amityville or the Smurl haunting.': We're back with Nicholson again. *One Flew Over The Cuckoo's Nest* (1975) was set in a mental institution, where Nicholson's character is given a lobotomy after attacking the head nurse. Nicholson in *The Shining* is influenced by an evil spiritual entity and becomes violent against his family. 'Amityville' refers to events at 112 Ocean Avenue, Amityville, Long Island. The Lutz family moved into a house where the previous owner's son had shot and killed six members of his family just over a year before. The new family were allegedly terrorised by paranormal activity in the house, and the events spawned a horror novel (1977) and several movies starting with *The Amityville Horror* (1979).

The Smurl Hauntings are said to have taken place over a 15 year period from 1974 in West Pittston, Pennsylvania. They are thought to have been caused by four evil spirits, one a demon, reacting to a deeply religious family and getting energy from the couple's daughters reaching puberty. The TV movie *The Haunted* (1991) brought the events to the screen.

Dean: 'Dr Feelgood was working on some sort of, like, extreme rage therapy.': Dr Feelgood is the nickname given to physicians who over-prescribe psychoactive medications.

GOOFS AND FLUFFS

When Dean first looks in John's journal for the article on the asylum, a drawing of the Wendigo is on the opposite page. When he looks it up the second time, there's an extra page between the Wendigo drawing and the asylum piece.

When Sam shoots Dean with the rock salt, Dean ends up with smears of white dust on his face, but during his conversation with Sam, the white smears alternate between two different patterns with the change of shot. Then, when Dean has knocked Sam out, the smears and dust on his clothes disappear altogether.

HAVEN'T I SEEN YOU BEFORE?

Norman Armour's acting credits include *Millennium*, *Dark Angel* and *Kingdom Hospital*. Nancy Bell has also appeared in *Medium*, *Numb3rs* and *Star Trek: Voyager*. Peter Benson featured in *Smallville*, *The 4400* and *Masters of Horror*. Leif Bridgman was in *Canes*. Nicholas D'Agosto played West Rosen in *Heroes* and was in *Drive Thru* and *Inside*. Richard Dieth was in *Scooby Doo 2: Monsters Unleashed*. John Gray was in *Kyle XY*. Nicole LaPlaca has been in *The Dead Zone*. Brooke Nevin played Nikki Hudson in *The 4400* and also appeared in *Animorphs* and *Charmed*. Tom Pickett was in *Sliders*, *Mysterious Ways* and *Blood Ties*. James Purcell featured in *RoboCop: Prime Directives*, *Friday the 13th: The Series* and *Blade: The Series*.

Roy Campsall also appears in 'Wendigo' (1-02).

BEHIND THE SCENES

After Kripke's gleefulness about hands minced in the garbage disposal[60], we discover he's not the only one who enjoys his work – so does visual effects supervisor Ivan Hayden. Hayden recounts how his team gathered round the computer giggling when they were working on the effects to shoot a little old lady in the head. They enjoyed the twisted opportunity to turn her head into ectoplasmic jelly. [*Season One Supernatural Companion*]

MUSICAL INTERLUDE

- 'Hey You' by Bachman-Turner Overdrive – when Dean and Sam are questioning Lt Danny Gunderson in the bar.

ANALYSIS

'Asylum' is a satisfyingly spooky tale with some nice touches of humour and lots of tense moments, especially in Dr Ellicott's secret room with the shower curtains obscuring the view and an evil ghost lurking, ready to pounce on his next victim.

We may be into traditional horror fare with haunted buildings and kids daring each other to stay overnight but it gets a fresh overhaul for this episode with several unwritten rules being broken. Apart from making the girl the stronger personality, we also discover that our heroes are vulnerable – Sam succumbs to the evil doctor's powers and is overwhelmed by a severe dose of anger therapy. Now, the hero is usually too strong to be affected by such things – he is the hero after all, and where would the world be with that sort of thing happening all over the place, eh?

Secondly, when Sam is aiming the gun at Dean, he actually goes ahead and pulls the trigger – twice, the second time thinking he has real bullets. Hang on a minute, shouldn't the bond of brotherly love be too great for Sam go through with it? It usually does, but apparently not in *Supernatural*. Oh no, Sam goes for both barrels *and* several bullets to the face. As a result of all this, there's a more realistic feel to the story and a sense that you're seeing something new. These are some of the earliest hints that this series is not going to play safe, especially with the boys' relationship, and these foundations eventually build to some wonderfully shocking episodes at the end of the second and third series.

From a character development point of view, 'Asylum' delivers a meaty portion. Sam is in denial about his powers and won't be drawn into conversation about them. Meanwhile, Dean is dealing with the revelation about Sam's ESP in the only way he knows how – by making jokes about it and teasing Sam. Getting Dean to discuss

---

60 In 'Home' (1-09).

anything emotional is proving difficult, despite Sam twice asking direct questions: once early on about discussing their dad's absence at the asylum; and again at the end of the episode, after Sam's angry outbursts, where Dean shuts the conversation down by simply responding that he's not in a sharing mood and would rather get some sleep.

Sam's angry outburst balances out events in 'Skin' (1-06) where it was (shapeshifter) Dean's chance to share some of his darker thoughts about Sam. Dean not only envies his brother's chance to live a normal life but he's also angry that he didn't get a chance to follow his own dreams. Sam, on the other hand, is getting fed-up of taking Dean's orders all the time and thinks his brother is pathetic for always following their dad without question[61]. What's interesting is how accepting both brothers are of the other's attitude – there's very little resentment going on about the other's opinion afterwards, and that makes for a fascinating ongoing relationship.

Add to all this the (first) end of episode cliff-hanger where Sam answers the phone to find their dad on the other end and you've suddenly got a legion of fans baying for the next episode.

VERDICT – 8 out of 10

---

61 Something he'll actually take back after events in 'Something Wicked' (1-18).

EPISODE 1-11
SCARECROW

TRANSMISSION DATES
US first aired: 10 January 2006
UK first aired: 3 April 2006

CREDITS
Writer: John Shiban
Director: Kim Manners
Story by: Patrick Sean Smith

RECURRING ROLE
Nicki Aycox (Meg), Jeffrey Dean Morgan (John Winchester)

GUEST STARS
Tom Butler (Harley Jorgeson), Mike Carpenter (Scarecrow), William B Davis (Professor Humphris), Lara Gilchrist (Holly), Leah Graham (Pauly), P Lynn Johnson (Stacey Jorgeson), Angela Moore (Clerk), Tim O'Halloran (Scotty), Brent Stait (Scotty), David Orth (Sheriff), Brendan Penny (Steve), Tania Saulnier (Emily Jorgeson), Christian Schrapff (Vince)

Note: two actors are listed for Scotty in all the sources checked and both actors are listed in the credits of the episode itself. Go figure.

SYNOPSIS
John Winchester contacts the boys and orders them to investigate a series of disappearances in Indiana. Disagreeing on whether or not to follow that order, Dean goes to Indiana while Sam heads for California to find their father. Dean uncovers a town worshipping Pagan gods, where an innocent couple are sacrificed every year in return for protection. Sam meanwhile meets (the more-than-she-seems) Meg before rushing back to Indiana to save Dean's skin – because Dean's got himself tied to a tree as a sacrifice to the Pagan god and is having trouble thinking up a plan of escape. They finally torch the tree that is the source of the god's power and decide that they should stick together for a while. Meanwhile, Meg is slashing the neck of an unfortunate trucker and using his blood to contact her 'Father'.

CAN YOU SURVIVE TO THE TITLES?

Holly and Vince Parker – an innocent couple on a road trip – become sacrificial victims in a spooky apple orchard when their car breaks down. Holly is unlucky enough to fall over Vince's skinned body while trying to run away from the scythe-wielding, god-possessed scarecrow. Wrecked her shoes.

LOCATION, LOCATION, LOCATION

Starting in Missouri, the day after events in 'Asylum' (1-10); Burkitsville, Indiana; and a bus station somewhere in Indiana where Sam bumps into Meg again.

LEGENDARY ROOTS

The Vanir come from Norse Mythology – they are a group of gods who were at war with the Aesir. The Aesir were concerned with war and power, while the Vanir were gods of earth and fertility, with peace and nature at their core rather than the dominating traits of the Aesirs.

Peace was reached and an exchange of gods occurred – the Vanir sent Njord the sea god, his twin children Freyr and Freyja, and Kvasir, believed to be second to none in wisdom. In return the Aesir sent Honir and Mimir. All was well for a while, and Honir and Mimir were welcomed by the Vanir. But eventually the Vanir thought they had got the worse end of the deal: while Mimir was wise, Honir was extremely indecisive, especially when Mimir was not around. So the Vanir came to the conclusion that Mimir was not only the voice for Honir but also the brains. In anger, the Vanir cut off the head of Mimir and sent it back to the Aesir, causing a rift between the two sides again.

The Vanir are associated with fertility, so it's no surprise they were worshipped by farmers who would pray for a good harvest.

SQUEEZE OF THE WEEK

Gorgeous blonde Meg enters Sam's life and is clearly interested in him. But Sam puts Dean's safety above any desires he might have to travel with Meg, which turns out to be a sound decision. It seems Meg wants his body in more ways than one …

SIBLING RIVALRY

The good-natured banter has been missing recently and the trend continues in 'Scarecrow'. Sam refuses to follow his dad's orders; he just wants to help John get the demon who killed Jess. Dean wants to save lives by following the orders. Their differences in opinion shine through the anger as Sam can't understand why Dean has such blind faith in their father and Dean thinks Sam is a selfish bastard for not thinking of anyone else.

By the end of the episode, after Dean has apologised for disagreeing with his brother and Sam has rescued Dean and Emily from the scarecrow, Sam decides that his brother is stuck with him because, with the rest of the family gone, Dean is all Sam has left and they're going to see it thorough together. The banter returns briefly as Dean asks Sam to hold him and Sam tells Dean to kiss his ass.

BODY COUNT
It's not a good time to be a couple, with the youngsters getting skinned by the scarecrow in the opening sequence; then the surprise stab in the back for Uncle Harley, followed by Aunt Stacy getting dragged away to be dealt with later, in the climax.

TOOLKIT
- A *stolen car* (plus the *abilities to steal it* successfully) are essential when your brother is in trouble and is going to be sacrificed to a Pagan god after sundown.
- The trusty homemade *EMF meter* tips Dean off to the presence of spooky happenings at the orchard.
- You need to have that *lighter fuel* and a *lighter* handy for burning sacred trees if you're going to destroy the occasional Pagan god, you know.

MEMORABLE MOMENTS
John Winchester finally talks to his boys, but the wounds are still very deep. John wants Sam and Dean to stop looking for him but Sam won't listen and demands to know what's going on. When John tries to explain that even talking together is not safe, Sam remains defiant, angry because his dad is still trying to order him around. A very emotionally charged scene.

SPOOK RULES
- If you want to sacrifice humans to a fertility god in return for protection for the coming year, then line up the victims in the second week in April.
- The victims should be a man and woman and should be fattened up like a Christmas turkey before they are killed.
- A Pagan god can possess an effigy like a scarecrow to claim victims' lives.
- A good place for a fertility god to live is in an apple orchard.
- You need to know which god you're dealing with before you can figure out how to kill it – so it's not like one size machete fits all! In this case, the god is a Vanir and the source of its energy is a sacred tree – an old tree that the locals treat with a lot of respect. Torch the tree and bingo.

DID YOU SPOT?

This is the first episode to have an episode title in the opening credits.

The names in Dean's phone are Bren, Carmelita, Christian, Curtis, Dad, Donny, Robin and Sam.

The names in Sam's phone are Rebecca Warren, Jerry, John Marcynuk, Dean and Mary Ann Liu. Rebecca is Sam's student friend we met in 'Skin' (1-06) and Jerry is probably Jerry Wanek the production designer who was previously seen in Sam's phone in 'Skin' too. John Marcynuk is also a *Supernatural* production designer and Mary Ann Liu is a graphic designer.

GOING UNDERCOVER

It had to happen sooner or later – Dean bumps into someone with a similar taste in music who just happens to know that John Bonham is the drummer for Led Zeppelin.

CULTURAL REFERENCES

Vince: 'Check it out. If I only had a brain ...': This references *The Wizard of Oz* (1939) film, featuring a scarecrow that goes with Dorothy to the Emerald City to find the Wizard of Oz.

Dean: 'Yahtzee. Can you imagine putting together a pattern like this?': Yahtzee is a dice-based game in which players roll five dice and score points through various combinations – Yahtzee is where all dice faces display the same value.

Dean: 'Dude, you fugly.': Fugly – a description of someone who takes ugly to a new level.

Emily: 'Well, you know, it's the boonies, but I love it.': If you're living in the boonies, you're out in the sticks, the middle of nowhere. (Very handy for a god-possessed scarecrow!)

When Sam asks Meg if she's on vacation, Meg: 'Yeah, right. It's all sipping Cristal poolside for me.': Cristal is a brand of exceptional Champagne produced by Louis Roederer.

Professor Humphris tells Dean that Pagan worship isn't common in Indiana, Dean: 'Well, what if it was imported? You know, like the Pilgrims brought their religion over. Wasn't a lot of this area settled by immigrants?': Eric Kripke has cited Neil Gaiman's *American Gods* (2001) as one of the influences on *Supernatural* . In that novel, the immigrants into America brought with them all their gods from their homelands.

Stacy: 'The town needs to be safe. The good of the many outweighs the good of the one.': Possibly a reference to *Star Trek II – The Wrath of Khan*, in which Spock sacrifices himself knowing full well he will die in order to save the ship and crew. Spock enters the *Enterprise* engineering section, exposing himself to high levels of radiation to restore power to the ship and thus allow it to escape an explosion. His last conversation with Captain Kirk includes the phrase: 'The needs of the many outweigh the needs of the few'.

Dean: 'Let's just shag ass before Leatherface catches up.': Leatherface is the star of the movie *The Texas Chain Saw Massacre* (1974) and its sequels. He kills his victims in various ways, including by chainsaw and sledgehammer, then wears their skin as a mask.

GOOFS AND FLUFFS

Dean visits the Professor to look into the Pagan god legends and as he's walking towards the door on his way out, there's a camera on screen in the top left of the shot.

The scene where Sam answers the phone when it wakes him up in bed has been re-shot since it first appeared at the end of 'Asylum' (1-10). The sheets on Dean's bed have changed colour, the boys are in different positions in bed and Sam says 'Dad' as a statement this time rather than a question.

HAVEN'T I SEEN YOU BEFORE?

Tom Butler's credits include *Poltergeist: The Legacy*, *Stargate SG-1* and *The Outer Limits*. Mike Carpenter has appeared in *Blood Ties* and *Watchmen*. William B Davis featured in *Masters of Science Fiction* and *Dark Storm* and played the shady 'cigarette smoking man' C G B Spender in *The X-Files*. Lara Gilchrist played Paulla Schaffer in *Battlestar Galactica* and has also appeared in *Bionic Woman* and *Blood Ties*. P Lynn Johnson played Lisa Starr in *Blade: The Series* and also featured in *The X-Files* and *The Outer Limits*. Angela Moore has also been in *Smallville*, *I, Robot* and *The Outer Limits*. Tim O'Halloran was in *The X-Files*, *The Outer Limits* and *Andromeda*. David Orth featured in *White Noise 2: The Light* and *Friday the 13th: The Series* and played Ned Malone in *The Lost World*. Brendan Penny's credits include *Stargate: Atlantis*, *Blade: The Series* and *Kyle XY*. Tania Saulnier was in *Slither*, *Smallville* and *Poltergeist: The Legacy*. Christopher Schrapff also appeared in *Knights of Bloodsteel*, *Blade: The Series* and *Revolution*. Brent Stait appeared in *Blade: The Series* and *The X-Files* and played Rev Bem in *Andromeda*.

Leah Graham also appeared in 'Hollywood Babylon' (2-18).

BEHIND THE SCENES

The scarecrow costume undoubtedly added to the success of this episode. Costume designer Diane Widas had to make allowances in the outfit to hide the harness that actor Mike Carpenter had to wear. She also had to make it safe for him to wear when he was hanging around on his wooden stand. [*Season One Supernatural Companion*]

Musical Interlude

- 'Bad Company' by Bad Company – playing at the end of the episode.
- 'Lodi' by Credence Clearwater Revival – at the bus station where Sam meets Meg again.
- 'Puppet' by Colepitz – playing on Meg's iPod.

Analysis

Two things make this one of the better episodes of Season One – the orchard location and the scarecrow. Ignoring the fact that the 'apple' orchard is actually full of hazelnut trees and the freshly harvested apples at the base of the trees shouldn't be there in April, this little forest is almost as inherently spooky as the asylum in the previous episode. Excellently lit and atmospherically draped with creeping mist, the trees and pathways form the perfect place for a bit of chase and slash with a lumbering scarecrow. Armed with a scythe and a grotesque leather face-mask, this character is one you wouldn't want to meet on a crowded street at high noon let alone in a dark, deserted orchard after sundown.

A couple of things hold the episode back though. There's a vague sense of *déjà vu*, because 'Scarecrow' shares some high level similarities with 'Hookman' (1-07) in terms of weapon of choice and (lack of) personality in the bad guy. And then there's Dean's inability to function without Sam, which contradicts previous episodes (like 'Woman in White' (1-01) and 'Wendigo' (1-02)) where the boys were clearly fully capable of looking after themselves individually.

This is, however, the first time the monster storyline doesn't directly illuminate the boys' relationship – that responsibility is picked up by the arc-related phone call from their father, which flushes out the difference of opinion, demonstrates how desperately Sam needs to find the demon that killed Jessica and shows how deep their childhood training has embedded into Dean's psyche, where he'll let his brother leave in order to follow John's orders.

The boys' arguments are getting more heated and it's more obvious than ever that the centre of the conflict is their father – where he is, why he won't tell them what's happening, what he's doing, and how he brought them up. But despite the increasing intensity of the rows, it is surprisingly Dean who is the first to apologise for the harsh words. It's a brief, heartfelt exchange that echoes the softer side of Dean's opinions about Sam having his own life. The shapeshifter ('Skin' (1-06)) revealed Dean's jealousy for Sam's lifestyle, but here Dean's admiration for Sam's personality comes out. It may be an unexpected outburst of emotion (indeed, it leaves Sam speechless) but perhaps it is understandable – Dean needs to follow the direct order but he also wants to find his father. By supporting Sam's search, Dean gets to do both.

And finally, this episode reveals two new recurring characters. The wickedly lovely Meg arrives with some unknown but clearly dangerous intentions and at last we meet the gorgeous John Winchester. There's a dark gravitas and serious undertone to the way Jeffrey Dean Morgan plays John that's utterly believable. Haunted by the past, obsessed with his war on evil and driven by his need to protect his children, John might just know more about the future than he can handle. And his mysterious mission tips this series from already watchable to positively addictive.

VERDICT – 8 out of 10

Episode 1-12
Faith

Transmission Dates
US first aired: 17 January 2006
UK first aired: 10 April 2006

Credits
Writers: Sera Gamble and Raelle Tucker
Director: Allan Kroeker

Guest Stars
Gillian Barber (Mrs Rourke), Julie Benz (Layla Rourke), Erica Carroll (Nurse), Aaron Craven (David Wright), Jim Codrington (Doctor), Alex Diakun (The Reaper), Rikki Gagne (Holly Morton), Nicholas Harrison (Unknown), John Hainsworth (Unknown), Woody Jeffreys (Marshall Hall), Rebecca Jenkins (Sue Ann Le Grange), Kenya Jo Kennedy (Unknown), Colin Lawrence (Jason), Tiffany Lyndall-Knight (Doctor), Kevin McNulty (Roy Le Grange), Scott Miller (Cop), Shawn Reis (Burly Cop #2), Pat Waldron (Elderly Lady), Conrad Whitaker (Burly Cop #1), Cainan Wiebe (Boy)

Synopsis
Dean is electrocuted while rescuing two children, damaging his heart. The doctors give him a few months to live, but Sam finds a faith healer, Roy LeGrange, who manages to heal him. Dean is convinced there's something sinister going on, because he saw what he thinks is a reaper at the moment he was healed. Meanwhile, Sam discovers that when Roy heals, someone else dies, and there's also a black magic cross on his stage. Sam breaks into Roy's house to discover how he's controlling the reaper, but it turns out that Roy's wife Sue-Ann is actually manipulating the reaper to heal 'good' people by taking 'bad' people's lives. Sue-Ann locks Sam in the house and sends the reaper after Dean, but Sam escapes, arriving just in time to smash the cross controlling the reaper, freeing it to take Sue-Ann's life.

Can You Survive to the Titles?
For the first time it's a monster that doesn't survive the opening sequence. Rawhead is electrocuted with a huge hundred thousand volt whammy. Only problem is, Dean is electrocuted too and does himself some serious damage. Ooops.

LOCATION, LOCATION, LOCATION

Nebraska, The Church of Roy LeGrange, faith healer

LEGENDARY ROOTS

Reaper lore seems to be related to the Greek god Chronos. Associated with time, and hence aging and death, Chronos is often depicted carrying the (now iconic) scythe.

Reapers are said to come for you at your time of death to take your soul away into the afterlife – in a benign way rather than a vengeful, murderous manner. In some tellings, the reaper is said to harvest souls with the scythe; in others he touches the person about to die to pop their souls out so as not to feel any pain at the time of death.

The story of Rawhead originates from Ireland as the bogeyman (also known as bloody-bones). He lives near water and, in newer versions, under sinks. The bogeyman rewards good children but punishes naughty children by drowning them or turning them into objects that their parents won't want so that they throw them away.

SQUEEZE OF THE WEEK

Layla Rourke is a potential but never-quite-happens squeeze for Dean. Feelings seem to have run pretty deep even so – given that Dean volunteers his life to the reaper in order to save Layla. And all she did in return was stroked her hand down his jaw-line. Poor Dean.

SIBLING RIVALRY

When Dean is being cured, he knows it feels wrong then he sees something on the stage. Afterwards, there's sharp exchange as Sam explains that he hadn't seen anything (and he's been seeing a lot recently), while Dean tells the psychic wonder that he will just have to trust Dean's instincts cause they're usually right.

Aside from this, the rivalry just surfaces in Dean's irritability every time Sam tries to look after him because he's not well.

BODY COUNT

The wrinkle-faced reaper goes out and about a couple of times looking for fresh souls to replenish the dying ones. The first victim is an athlete, Marshall Hall, whose life heals Dean's heart problems; the second is a female jogger who is in the middle of her run in the park when old wrinkle-face sucks her life-force dry. Always knew this fitness lark was bad for you.

The final victim is the wicked Sue-Ann, who gets her comeuppance at the hands of the reaper she has controlled for so long.

TOOLKIT

- A couple of *tasers*, amped up to a hundred thousand volts, will take care of any menacing Rawhead lurking in the cellar, but don't use them if you happen to be standing in the same puddle as the monster or you might come out extra crispy as well.
- A good *set of lungs* so you can shout 'Fire!' at the top of your voice when you want to stop another murder.

MEMORABLE MOMENTS

When Dean is resting in hospital after receiving the news that he only has a couple of months to live, he's cracking jokes about daytime TV and threatening to come back and haunt Sam's ass if Sam doesn't take care of the car. Excellent black humour that's not often seen in American shows.

The closing scene where Dean talks to Layla about faith and life is extremely touching. Group hug everyone!

SPOOK RULES

- There are lots of reapers, not just *the* Grim Reaper, collector of souls and angel of death.
- Reapers prefer a white shirt and black suit (like the Blues Brothers) rather than the whole black robe thing.
- As with other supernatural beings, lights tend to flicker when a reaper is in the vicinity.
- You have to use black magic to bind a reaper, and trying to control one is like putting a leash on a great white shark.
- The black magic involves bones, human blood and building a black altar. You'll also need a Coptic cross to put the blood in.
- To identify your next victim, draw a cross in blood on a photo of them.
- A reaper kills by drawing your life-force out through your head (not the sort of laying on of hands you want really).
- To stop a reaper you have to break the spell binding it by destroying the altar and breaking the cross with the blood in it.

DID YOU SPOT?

The first half of this episode is like Season Three in a nutshell. Dean is about to die. Sam is trying to save him. Dean is chasing girls.

Layla Rourke was played by Julie Benz, more familiar to genre fans as Darla in *Buffy the Vampire Slayer* and *Angel*.

GOING UNDERCOVER
Sam uses a credit card in the name of Mr Burkovitz to pay for Dean's medical care.

CULTURAL REFERENCES
Dean: 'That fabric softener teddy bear – oh, I'm gonna hunt that little bitch down.': In reference to a rather too cute and cuddly teddy bear used to market Snuggle fabric conditioner.

HAVEN'T I SEEN YOU BEFORE?
Gillian Barber's credits include *Fear Itself*, *Stargate SG-1* and *The X-Files*. Julie Benz played Darla in *Buffy The Vampire Slayer* and *Angel*, Kathleen Topolsky in *Roswell High* and Rita Bennett in *Dexter*. Aaron Craven starred in *The Day the Earth Stood Still*, *Beyond Belief: Fact or Fiction* and *Tru Calling*. Jim Codrington's credits include *Resident Evil: Apocalypse*, *Earth: Final Conflict* and *Blade: The Series*. Alex Diakun was in *Sanctuary*, *The X Files: I Want to Believe* and *Andromeda*. Rikki Gagne was in *Lost Boys: The Tribe*, *The 4400* and *Masters of Horror*. Nicholas Harrison appeared in *Dark Storm*. John Hainsworth appeared in *Final Destination*, *Smallville* and *Battlestar Galactica: Razor*. Woody Jeffreys' credits include *Blood Ties*, *Blade: The Series* and *Stargate: Atlantis*. Rebecca Jenkins was in *Kingdom Hospital*, *The Twilight Zone* and *The Outer Limits*. Kenya Jo Kennedy was in *The Dead Zone*. Colin Lawrence played Lt Hamish 'Skulls' McCall in *Battlestar Galactica* and was also in *Watchmen* and *The X-Files*. Tiffany Lyndall-Knight played The Hybrid in *Battlestar Galactica* and was also in *Blade: The Series* and *Stargate SG-1*. Kevin McNulty was in *Millennium*, *Stargate SG-1* and *Poltergeist: The Legacy*. Scott Miller featured in *The 4400*, *Stargate: Atlantis* and *Painkiller Jane*. Conrad Whitaker was also in *Painkiller Jane*. Cainan Wiebe's credits include *The 4400*, *Dead Like Me* and *Sanctuary*.

Shawn Reis also appears in 'The Benders' (1-15).

Erica Carroll also appears in 'Something Wicked' (1-18).

BEHIND THE SCENES
Due to the religious content, writer Sera Gamble didn't think they would get this episode past everybody without it being censored. She kept expecting someone to say No, but they just let it through. [*Season One Supernatural Companion*]

You don't see athlete Marshall Hall's death in the aired episode but in the deleted scenes on the Region 1 DVD there's Marshall being chased by the reaper and finally getting caught by the swimming pool, observed by one of the staff. The scene really adds only background information, and the episode doesn't suffer for it being cut.

MUSICAL INTERLUDE

- 'Don't Fear the Reaper' by Blue Öyster Cult – playing when LeGrange is healing an old man and the female jogger dies.

ANALYSIS

We've had three stonkingly good episodes; we've made some real progress towards solving the John Winchester mystery (Where is he? What's he found? And why won't he tell his kids what's going on?), then we get a story that loses all the forward momentum that's been building up. Consequently, 'Faith' has a strange lack of relevance compared to 'Asylum' (1-10) and 'Scarecrow' (1-11); it's also nowhere near as scary and lacks the atmospheric locations that visually lifted both of those previous episodes. It all feels a little out of sync and the episode would probably have worked better if it had been shown between 'Bugs' (1-08) and 'Home' (1-09), before John's story-arc kicked in with a vengeance.

Out of sync it might be, but 'Faith' certainly runs deep. Both (creator) Eric Kripke and (director) Robert Singer have cited this episode as one of their favourites. Kripke has said in interviews that this was the first episode where he realised what the show could do. That it could take on metaphysical and moral questions – about God and about the value of a life – and openly examine them.

Kripke and his writers are clever enough to use the story to examine those issues from several different points of view. Dean hasn't got any faith because he's seen what evil does to good people. Layla has faith in God whether the miracles are happening or not. And Sue-Ann believes that she is doing good by killing people she believes are 'bad' and saving the righteous.

We also get a couple more insights into the brothers' personalities. Dean has difficulty in accepting that Layla will die as a result of his actions to stop the reaper – so much difficulty that he doesn't run away when the reaper comes for him when Layla is going to get cured, selflessly deciding to give his life for hers. Sam meanwhile illustrates his devotion to his brother in searching for a cure and shows a greater moral clarity in realising that playing God is wrong, regardless of the consequences.

Kripke *et al* develop a taste for morally awkward issues with this episode, and they'll be going on to write more, most noticeably in 'Bloodlust' (2-03) …

VERDICT – 7 out of 10

EPISODE 1-13
ROUTE 666

TRANSMISSION DATES
US first aired: 31 January 2006
UK first aired: 17 April 2006

CREDITS
Writer: Eugenie Ross-Leming and Brad Buckner
Director: Paul Shapiro

GUEST STARS
Mike Busswood (Unknown), Megalyn Echikunwoke (Cassie Robinson), Gary Hetherington (Mayor Harold Todd), Dee Jay Jackson (Cyrus Dorian), Kathleen Noone (Audrey Robinson), Ron Robinson (Unknown), Alvin Sanders (Jimmy Anderson)

SYNOPSIS
Dean gets a call from an old flame, Cassie, whose father has just been killed in a car accident. There are signs that the car was run off the road, but there were no other tyre tracks at the scene. The mayor is murdered and a pattern starts to emerge – all the victims were connected to a wealthy local family. When Cassie is attacked, Sam and Dean uncover a secret kept by five people for 30 years, about how local lad Cyrus Dorian was killed after Cyrus attacked Cassie's father. Cyrus' body and car were dumped in the swamp, so the boys dredge both up and burn the body, but the truck is also supernaturally possessed. Dean uses the Impala to lure the truck onto hallowed ground in order to stop it.

CAN YOU SURVIVE TO THE TITLES?
Cassie's father is on the receiving end of a bout of road rage and gets run off the road by a mysterious monster truck.

LOCATION, LOCATION, LOCATION
Cape Girardeau, Missouri; Decatur Road, two miles off the highway, where there's a bloody big truck that wants to kill Dean.

LEGENDARY ROOTS
The Phantom Vehicle is a ghostly apparition, such as a car, motorbike or lorry, that

usually forms some part of an urban legend or occurrence at the site of a fatal accident. The vehicle often appears and suddenly disappears in front of witnesses or drives where a normal vehicle would have crashed. Although the phenomenon has never been verified scientifically there are many examples:

A car driving erratically that outran a police car by turning into a field – that on closer inspection was bordered by an unbroken fence.

A motorist in Britain crashed his car trying to avoid a lorry that appeared out of nowhere heading straight towards him and suddenly disappeared.

A Renault Sedan rolled up an embankment and crashed into a fence in Cape Town, South Africa, even though the engine was off and the handbrake on.

In the mid 1930s a bus bearing the number 7 repeatedly appeared on a curved road at the St Mark's Road and Cambridge Gardens junction in Ladbroke Grove, London. The red bus caused a fatal accident when a driver hit a wall trying to avoid it, as described by an eye witness. The road was eventually straightened and no further reportings of the bus have occurred.

SQUEEZE OF THE WEEK
At last, Dean gets the girl! Cassie is clearly pleased to see Dean and it's not long before an argument results in a little sexy making up in bed.

SIBLING RIVALRY
Most of the rivalry is very good-natured as Sam teases Dean about his relationship with Cassie and his inability to express his emotions. The only angry words are at the start when Dean tells Sam about Cassie's problems and Sam realises that Dean has broken family rule number one and told Cassie about the hunting. Sam's annoyed that he spent 18 months telling Jessica lies about his family while Dean tells Cassie everything after just a couple of dates. Dean at least has the good grace to look a little guilty for doing it.

BODY COUNT
Cassie's father, Martin Robinson, is run off the road by the four-wheeled menace. Newspaper editor Jimmy Anderson suffers a similar fate too but poor old Mayor Harold Todd gets every bone crushed and all his internal organs turned to pudding. That's gotta hurt.

TOOLKIT
- Standard demon-hunter issue this time – make sure you've got *lighter fuel, salt* and a bloody *big flashlight* in your handbag if you're out to banish a few evil ghosts.

MEMORABLE MOMENTS
The car chase sequence is lots of fun but the head-to-head climax is breathless[62].

THE CAR'S THE STAR
Having been in the background for several weeks – and looking particularly handsome in a misty shot in 'Scarecrow' (1-11) – the car is back taking Dean on a hair-raising chase down the back roads and even taking a hit in the arsenal when it's rammed by that nasty infected-with-Cyrus's-spirit truck.

SPOOK RULES
- Spirits can go dormant for long periods of time but can be woken up by remodelling or destroying the house they lived in – they are particularly likely to wake if the demolition is instigated by the cop who covered up the spirit's murder.
- Vengeful spirits can infect and become part of inanimate objects like trucks and ships.
- Burning the body doesn't always stop the spirit, you have to burn the object they've infected too.
- Some spirits are destroyed when they cross onto hallowed ground – 'Hookman' (1-07) (also a ghost) actually managed to get inside a church, but Cyrus's truck is destroyed when it crosses the boundary.
- Hallowed ground stays that way whether the church is still there or not.

DID YOU SPOT?
There's a great special effect when the truck is driving head on at Dean – when the truck crosses onto hallowed ground, the ornate church gates flare up momentarily before the truck breaks up.

GOING UNDERCOVER
While they are investigating the deaths, Dean tells Jimmy Anderson's friends that he and Sam are insurance investigators working for All National Mutual.

CULTURAL REFERENCES
Dean: 'You heard of the *Flying Dutchman*?': According to legend, the *Flying Dutchman* is a ghost ship that is doomed to forever set sail captained by a man who swore he would complete his voyage, battling against rough seas, even if it took him until doomsday. There have been many reported sightings of the ghost ship through the

---

62 As is the one between Dean and Cassie, we suspect.

19th and 20th Centuries, and seeing it is said to bring impending doom.

Sam: 'Demolition or remodelling can awaken spirits, make them restless. Like that theatre in Illinois.': This is possibly a reference to the Lincoln Theatre. It was built in 1916 on the site of the Arcade Hotel, which burnt down the previous year claiming two lives, although many of the hotel guests were unaccounted for afterwards. The theatre has many spirits haunting it – the most famous is supposed to be a stagehand nicknamed 'Red' who died when he slipped from a catwalk above the stage and caught his arm on the way down, ripping it from his body. He died in a bloody pool on the stage. The story is thought to be an exaggeration of the death of a one-armed stagehand called Red, who died in his sleep at the theatre. Red lost his arm years before, during World War I. There have also been many reports of strange noises, whispers and sightings of ghostly apparitions on the theatre's balconies, usually of a woman.

GOOFS AND FLUFFS

A couple of minutes into the episode, when the truck is chasing the first car, it's supposed to be on a dark road in the middle of nowhere, but in the background you can see a light next to the road, like a street lamp or spotlight for the filming.

How did Cassie know Dean's new mobile number? It changed six months before events in 'Phantom Traveler' (1-04), because Dean asked Jerry Panowski where he got the new number. It turned out Jerry had phoned John Winchester and got it off the answer phone. Would Cassie have had John's number?

Sam hands Cassie a cup of tea after her frightening experience when the truck terrorises the house. She takes one sip from it and seconds later the cup is suddenly three quarters empty.

Meanwhile, Audrey Robinson, Cassie's mum, manages a nice bit of ventriloquism when she's telling everyone about Cyrus's murder – she carries on talking even though she's drinking her tea.

How did Dean and Sam locate the submerged truck and get it tied up for towing in the cold and the snow without getting wet?

When Sam is giving Dean instructions about how to get to the church grounds, he tells his brother to drive exactly 0.7 miles. The odometer reading is 70098.2 when Sam gives this instruction and it reads 70100.9 when Dean finally crosses onto hallowed ground. Only two miles out then guys.

HAVEN'T I SEEN YOU BEFORE?

Mike Busswood's credits include *The New Addams Family* and *Jake 2.0*. Megalyn Echikunwoke played Isabelle Tyler in *The 4400* and also featured in *Buffy The Vampire*

Slayer. Gary Hetherington appeared in *The X-Files, The Dead Zone* and *Masters of Horror*. Dee Jay Jackson was in *Smallville, Dark Angel* and *Slither*. Kathleen Noone was in *Quantum Leap* and *Sabrina: The Teenage Witch*. Alvin Sanders has been in *Smallville, The Dead Zone* and *The X-Files*.

Ron Robinson also appears in 'Jus in Belo' (3-12).

BEHIND THE SCENES

Director of photography Serge Ladouceur said in *The Official Supernatural Magazine* #5 that the truck and car chase involved lighting about a mile and half of country road at night without any street lights to help out. It was probably the biggest lighting job they did for the show.

According to the *Season One Supernatural Companion* there was a freak snowstorm. Ackles and Padalecki don't see snow very often (because they're from Texas) and were out tobogganing and having snowball fights with the crew. The snow also turned the scenes where the truck was being towed out of the pond into a mud-bath, making it a really tough shoot. After work, at four o-clock in the morning, the crew finished the night off by having a mud-fight.

Also in the *Season One Companion*, editor Anthony Pinker commented that the only note the network sent down about this episode was that the girl couldn't go on top in the sex scene. The violence was okay, but, Dean had to be on top. It's a credit to the writing team that this was interpreted to mean that, in that case, the girl could go under, next to, in front of, or behind during the sex scene and, by jove, she did.

MUSICAL INTERLUDE

- 'Walk Away' – The James Gang – plays when Dean receives the call from Cassie and Sam is lecturing Dean about telling Cassie their secret.
- 'She Brings Me Love' – Bad Company – during the love-making scene between Dean and Cassie.
- 'Can't Find My Way Home' – Blind Faith – Dean's final kiss goodbye with Cassie and to the end of the episode.

ANALYSIS

An episode of romance and monster trucks that's light on scares but does illuminate a chapter of Dean's life that he's been trying to forget[63].

The rampant revenge-seeking ghost is interesting enough, but the episode just doesn't ignite in the same way others have before it. It's all pretty straightforward, and

---

63 According to *John Winchester's Journal* (2009) by Alex Irvine, this took place around April 2005.

you have to hang in until the end for any kind of adrenalin rush – which comes when Dean and the Impala take on the haunted truck in a great chase sequence and head-to-head climax.

On the flipside, we get some wonderful touches and insights for the characters. Sam's role is to fill in the gaps of Dean's past – because Dean sure as hell isn't the sort to go round sharing it willy-nilly with everyone, especially when it's so painful for him. Sam's gentle teasing of his brother generates some humorous moments and it's nice to see Sam smiling so much – even if it is at his brother's expense. Without Sam's gentle prodding we would never have discovered that Dean was actually in love with Cassie, that she had dumped him and that the two of them had unfinished business to clear up.

For Dean, we start to see the cost of the lifestyle he's pursuing. Romance is difficult when you're moving around so much; but, even worse than that, you've got to find a girl that won't think you're barking mad when you tell her what your job is all about.

Sam's disbelief that Dean finally stayed with a girl longer than one night implies that this could have been the first time Dean was serious about any woman. Cassie's comment that she'd found the guy who might be in her future indicates a possibility that their relationship could have settled down into something more permanent. Add in the shapeshifter's words from 'Skin' (1-06) about Dean having his own (undisclosed) ambitions for his life and we start to see the grounding for a domestic side of Dean that will come to fore again early in Season Two.

This is subtle stuff. These small, almost subliminal hints build quietly until they emerge fully formed – and when they do, it's not some huge, puzzling curve ball of story development but a logical, smooth extension of what you already know. And that, plainly and simply, is excellent story-telling.

VERDICT – 7 out of 10

EPISODE 1-14
NIGHTMARE

TRANSMISSION DATES
US first aired: 2 February 2006
UK first aired: 24 April 2006

CREDITS
Writer: Sera Gamble & Raelle Tucker
Director: Phil Sgriccia.

GUEST STARS
Dalias Blake (Policeman), Beth Broderick (Alice Miller), Brendan Fletcher (Max Miller), Fred Keating (Kenneth Phillips), Cameron McDonald (Jim Miller), Susinn McFarlen (Neighbour), Avery Raskin (Roger Miller)

SYNOPSIS
Sam has a nightmare about a stranger being murdered in his car in Michigan and it turns out to be a true event. Posing as priests, the boys talk to the remaining Miller family members – the dead man's wife Alice, brother Roger and son Max – but there doesn't seem to be anything supernatural happening. Then Sam has a waking vision of Roger being decapitated in his own apartment and the boys are unable to stop it happening. Sam's third vision is of Max murdering his step-mom – furious that she didn't stop the abuse his father and uncle subjected him to while he was growing up. This time Sam and Dean manage to save Alice, but Max commits suicide.

CAN YOU SURVIVE TO THE TITLES?
Jim Miller is trapped in his garage, unable to turn his car engine off. He dies of carbon monoxide poisoning.

LOCATION, LOCATION, LOCATION
Saginaw, Michigan; Roger Miller's pad at 450 West Grove, Apartment 1120, Saginaw

LEGENDARY ROOTS
Psychokinesis is the ability to control objects with the mind, whether this be moving them (telekinesis), altering/distorting them, or the ability to affect an outcome like a random number generator. Details vary – someone with psychokinetic abilities may

123

not have any telekinetic abilities at all and vice versa.

Famous examples of people with supposed psychokinetic and/or telekinetic abilities are:

Uri Geller – able to bend spoons, describe hidden drawings and make watches stop or run faster using his psychokinetic abilities.

Nina Kulagina – examples of her ability were filmed where she was able to separate the whites and yolks of broken eggs in water and remove a marked matchstick from a pile of matches while they were under a glass dome.

Eusapia Palladino – amongst many of her talents she was reportedly able to levitate and elongate herself, produce the hands and faces of spirits in wet clay and play musical instruments without touching them.

SQUEEZE OF THE WEEK
The boys may look obscenely attractive in their priest outfits but it's really no surprise that they don't pull any females this time around when they're dressed like that.

SIBLING RIVALRY
There's not much rivalry going on since Dean spends most of his time trying not to freak out about Sam's powers but he does try to make light of it all at the end when Sam reveals that he moved the big cabinet without touching it. Sam's a bit stunned that he actually moved the thing, but Dean is cheekily more interested in getting Sam to bend a spoon for him.

BODY COUNT
Jim Miller gets his early on, followed closely by Jim's brother Roger, who has a messy accident with a window frame while he has his head stuck out of the window. Luckily, the head lands safely in the window box after separation or it could have brained some poor passerby below.

Alice Miller gets a carving knife through the eyeball (and clean out the back of her head) while the biggest shock comes when Dean takes a bullet between the eyes. Thankfully, these last two are only seen by Sam in his vision and are eventually avoided, at the cost of Max turning the gun on himself.

TOOLKIT
- An *infra-red thermal scanner* can be used in a building to locate cold spots that usually indicate ghostly presences. The scanner uses laser beams to measure the temperature of surface materials without the need for physical contact. Bet the boys would show up as hot stuff if you used it on them.

- A *handgun* is probably not the best weapon to use when your target can use telekinesis to take it away from you, but if it makes you feel safe, why not?
- A *handkerchief* is always useful if you've run up the fire escape to find a severed head on the window ledge and you want to wipe your prints of the hand rail.
- And a *brother who has eerily true nightmares* will always give you a head-start on spooky cases.

MEMORABLE MOMENTS

Dean getting shot through the head in Sam's vision was sneaky, devious, shocking and absolutely marvellous! Poor ole Dean's really been through it in the last few episodes – shot with rock salt in 'Asylum' (1-10); electrocuted and left dying slowly of heart problems in 'Faith' (1-12); and now a bullet between the eyes! Beware the even-numbered episodes Dean, they're out to get you!

SPOOK RULES

- Rather than Max's powers, most of the spook rules relate to hauntings instead. Apparently the classic signs of a spirit presence in a house are: weird leaks, electrical shorts, odd settling noises at night, cold spots and a sulphur aroma. (The latter was first mentioned in 'Phantom Traveler' (1-04).)
- Location can also influence your chance of a haunting, and proximity to graveyards, battlefields, sites of atrocities or tribal lands puts you higher up the probability ladder.
- Vengeful spirits can latch onto families and follow them around for years.

DID YOU SPOT?

Dean's knack for finding free food kicks in again as he raids the sausages at Jim Miller's wake. The last time he did this was at the home buyer's party on the estate in 'Bugs' (1-08).

GOING UNDERCOVER

Sam and Dean turn up to Jim Miller's wake dressed in dog-collars and claiming to be junior priests from St Augustine's – Father Simmons and Father Frehley. Paul Daniel 'Ace' Frehley was co-founder and lead guitarist of the rock band Kiss; Gene Simmons was also co-founder of the band and the driving force behind their merchandising deals.

CULTURAL REFERENCES

Sam: 'MacReady. Detective MacReady, badge number 15A. And I've got a signal 480 in progress.': Detective MacReady or McCreedy – MacReady is the character played by Kurt Russell in John Carpenter's *The Thing* (1982), where an alien is discovered frozen in the ice at the Antarctic and, when defrosted, shapeshifts into dogs or humans to try to escape, killing those it impersonates. McCreedy (with the different spelling) is a character from the 1988 movie *Hobgoblins*, in which the hobgoblins allow your fantasies to come true but kill you in the process.

A signal 480 is a 'Hit and Run – Felony'.

Dean: 'So, he's psychic? He's a spoon-bender?' And Dean (holding up a spoon to Sam): 'Bend this.': These are both references to Uri Geller; see the **Legendary Roots** section above.

Goofs and Fluffs

When Sam and Dean first arrive at the Millers' house and are talking with their backs to the camera, watch out for the guy in the hat walking to and fro in the background. He looks like a cop and he's certainly giving the pavement a good guarding!

In the Millers' house, Sam and Dean are dressed as priests and Alice Miller hands Sam a drink in a straight-sided green cup. In the next shot, Sam is holding a white, curvy cup with flowers on. The green cup appears in Dean's hands later.

When Sam's vision about Max starts, Sam and Dean turn away from Max's old neighbour, and each has an arm around the other. In the next shot, now from the front, the arms have dropped down again.

Both in Sam's vision of Max killing his mother and in the later scene when Sam and Dean interrupt the murder as it's beginning, Alice Miller is chopping celery. When she puts the knife down, there is still some celery on the blade, but as soon as Max starts to use his powers to move it, the blade is suddenly completely clean.

Haven't I Seen You Before?

Dalias Blake played Lt Wood in *AVP: Requiem* and has also been in *Bionic Woman* and *Smallville*. Beth Broderick played Diane Jansen in *Lost*, Zelda Spellman in *Sabrina: The Teenage Witch* and was also in *Bionic Woman*. Brendan Fletcher was in *The Crow: Stairway To Heaven*, *Freddy vs. Jason* and *Jake 2.0*. Fred Keating featured in *The X-Files*, *Millennium* and *Poltergeist: The Legacy*. Cameron McDonald has been in *Dark Angel*, *The Dead Zone* and *Dead Like Me*. Avery Raskin's credits include *Taken*, *Jake 2.0* and *Beyond Belief: Fact or Fiction*.

Behind the Scenes

The crew like to get a local feel on their episodes so they used music by Bob Seger, who's from Detroit, Michigan [the state where this episode is set]; then Director Phil

Sgriccia got his sister to send over Michigan merchandise like caps and mugs. [*Season One Supernatural Companion*]

MUSICAL INTERLUDE

- '2+2=?' – Bob Seger – at the very start of the episode as Jim drives into his garage.
- ' Lucifer' – Bob Seger – as Sam and Dean drive to Michigan to investigate Jim Miller's death.

ANALYSIS

You certainly get value for money with *Supernatural* – not only is there a 'monster of the week' and an ongoing storyline about John Winchester's disappearance but now they're throwing in a second story arc that's going to reverberate into all the upcoming seasons.

Building on the groundwork in 'Bloody Mary'[64] where Sam first reveals his visions about Jessica's death, then 'Home'[65] where he sees their old home being haunted, we now discover that there are other families who have suffered the same tragedy as the Winchesters and other sons who have special abilities that manifested at the same time. In this single episode, Sam's supposedly curious little ability has been put into context. There's a much bigger game plan afoot. We've no idea how far-reaching the implications are and it's all looking much more sinister than it did before. But don't expect any quick resolution; it's going to be some time before anything else is discovered on this front, so be patient.

In terms of character development, there's more going on. For Sam, the more frequent visions – especially the waking ones – are increasing the fear he first expressed on the steps of their old home in Lawrence, when he was talking to the psychic Missouri[66]. He also takes another step towards reconciliation with his dad when he realises his life could have been a whole lot different if John had supped a bit more tequila and hunted a bit less. This reinforces the first small steps taken in 'Bugs'[67], when he discovered that his dad did actually care about him.

For Dean, we can see his growing concern over Sam's abilities, which is both expressed ('I'm worried about you') and unexpressed (when Sam asks if his powers freak Dean out and Dean pauses before answering, trying to control his reaction,

---

64 (1-05).

65 (1-09).

66 In 'Home' (1-09).

67 (1-08).

belying his subsequent verbal reassurance).

And between the two of them we once again see the difference in their approaches to hunting. Dean wants to go in with both guns blazing to sort Max out while Sam insists they talk it through first. These traits, particularly Sam's, are being established in Season One ready to be changed and manipulated in subsequent seasons to very good effect. Those future episodes wouldn't have worked so well if episodes like this hadn't done such a good job.

VERDICT – 8 out of 10

EPISODE 1-15
THE BENDERS

TRANSMISSION DATES
US first aired: 14 February 2006
UK first aired: 1 May 2006

CREDITS
Writer: John Shiban
Director: Peter Ellis

GUEST STARS
Jon Cuthbert (Alvin Jenkins), Ryan Drescher (Evan McKay), Alexia Fast (Missy Bender), John Dennis Johnston (Abraham Bender), Ken Kirzinger (Jared Bender), Sadie Lawrence (Mrs McKay), Shawn Reis (Lee Bender), Jessica Steen (Deputy Kathleen Hudak), Sandra Steier (Barfly)

SYNOPSIS
Sam goes missing and Dean searches for him, assisted by Deputy Kathleen Hudak – whose own brother disappeared several years ago. Sam has been captured by the Bender family and they want to hunt him for fun. Dean and Kathleen finally track Sam down but get caught by the Benders too. After Pa Bender tortures Dean with a red-hot poker, Sam finally escapes and frees Kathleen, and they eventually overpower the Benders.

CAN YOU SURVIVE TO THE TITLES?
Alvin Jenkins disappears from the parking lot but doesn't actually die before the titles, so no deaths this time.

LOCATION, LOCATION, LOCATION
Hibbing, Minnesota; Kugel's Keg Bar.

LEGENDARY ROOTS
The 'Bloody' Benders were a family of serial killers whose murders were known to have occurred from 1872 to 1873. There were four members of the family (John, Kate, John Jr and Marli Bender) who built and set up home between Thayer and Galesburg in Neosho County. The place was also an inn and general store.

The main attraction was 'Professor Miss Kate Bender' as spiritualist and medium, who gave public séances and readings in the nearby towns. This also attracted travellers to stay at the inn. Any wealthy looking guest was given the seat of honour – in front of the canvas wall that divided the main room. While Kate distracted the guest either John or John Jr would sneak up behind the divide and deliver a killer blow to the guest with a sledge hammer. The body was then dragged behind the curtain, stripped and dumped in the cellar until it could be buried.

Reportedly, with so many travellers going missing – including one Dr William York – the townsfolk decided to search the farms between Big Hill Creek and Drum Creek. Many farms volunteered to be searched – the Benders meanwhile remained silent. Their neighbour reported that the inn appeared abandoned and the animals starving. A search party was formed, including Dr York's brother, Colonel York. They arrived to find the inn empty, a terrible stench and a trapdoor in the floor nailed shut. Upon opening the trapdoor they found no bodies but plenty of clotted blood, which was the cause of the stench. They searched the grounds and ten bodies were found including those of Dr York, a woman and a child (apparently buried alive), as well as numerous dismembered and unidentifiable body parts. No-one knows how many people were murdered by the Benders – the family vanished and were never tracked down, so they remained unaccountable for their actions.

SQUEEZE OF THE WEEK
There's a rather pretty Deputy who seems intent on getting the handcuffs on Dean (can you blame her?) but she keeps it all platonic in the end.

SIBLING RIVALRY
They're both taking pops at each other about the same thing at different times. When Dean arrives to rescue his brother, he tells Sam he must be getting rusty if he let mere people jump him. Then at the end of the episode, Sam gets his own back by teasing Dean for getting sidelined by a 13-year-old girl.

BODY COUNT
Alvin Jenkins may have survived the titles but he runs out of luck when Lee and Jared Bender decide to hunt him in the forest. Alvin finally gets impaled on a couple of spears and gets his photo taken with his murderers.

Pa Bender also dies after the final showdown. Boasting about having fun killing people has some rather fatal consequences.

TOOLKIT

- No specialist equipment is required for dealing with humans but *a high pain tolerance* is useful when someone is pressing a red-hot iron into your shoulder and *the ability to kick-ass in a fight* with bear-sized guys is essential.

MEMORABLE MOMENTS

The most gruesome scene is when you see Pa Bender sawing up what is presumably Alvin Jenkins' body in the kitchen sink. Pa has to put some real elbow grease into the sawing motion. You don't actually see any spurting blood or dismembered limbs so the effect is something of an illusion created by good acting and excellent sound effects.

Dean gets the brunt of the violence again (and it's not an even-numbered episode either!) when Pa Bender gets the red-hot iron out of the fire. You just know it's going to be unpleasant, because this show doesn't take any easy options – people are going to get injured. So Dean cops the burning brand right in the shoulder and barely avoids getting his eye poked out.

Top Scare – when Sam is in the car park and he looks under the car, coming face to face with a ginger cat instead of a spooky monster.

SPOOK RULES

- Although this one's strictly a human problem, we still learn that Spring Heeled Jacks and Phantom Gassers will take people anywhere, anytime.

DID YOU SPOT?

The boys are in uniform again at the start of the episode. Gorgeous.

This is the first episode where the boys walk instead of drive away at the end.

The police details for Sam and Dean are as follows:

Sam Winchester:
Record ID: DF-23094
Name Samuel Winchester
Born: May 2, 1983
Place of Birth: Lawrence, Kansas
Physical Description
6'4' Height, 180-190 lbs Brown Hair, Brown Eyes
No distinctive markings or tattoos
Relevant links: Dean Winchester (deceased) – brother of subject

131

Dean Winchester:
Record ID: DF-23094
Name: Dean Winchester
Born: January 24, 1979
Died: March 7, 2006
Place of Birth: Lawrence, Kansas
Place of Death: St Louis, Missouri
Physical Description
6'4' Height 175 lbs Brown Hair, Green Eyes
Relevant links: Sam Winchester – brother of subject
No distinctive markings or tattoos
Subject was prime suspect in multiple homicide investigations in St
Louis area prior to his death.

Unfortunately, it's rather obvious that Sam is taller than Dean, so the police details are a little wide of the mark there. Also it's unlikely that both records would have the same identifier number (DF-23094), so that's a bit of a goof. However, it's only the individual record numbers that are wrong. When the Deputy searches for Sam Winchester, she is offered a list of two – Sam (DF-23094) and Dean (DF-28398) – and it's only when she opens the files that Dean's number changes to Sam's. So half a goof then.

GOING UNDERCOVER
Sam and Dean pretend to be the State Police in order to get an interview with the boy who last saw Alvin Jenkins in the car park; then Dean masquerades as Officer Greg Washington in order to secure Deputy Kathleen's help in finding Sam.

CULTURAL REFERENCES
Evan MacKay: 'Godzilla vs Mothra.': Godzilla is a Japanese fictional monster that was first seen on the big screen in 1954 and has since spawned many movies, comics and cartoons. 1964 saw the introduction of Mothra (a giant moth) in *Mosura tai Gojira* (*Godzilla vs Mothra*).

Kathleen: 'These traffic cams take an image every three seconds, as part of the AMBER Alert programme.': AMBER stands for America's Missing: Broadcasting Emergency Response. This programme is a US voluntary partnership between law-enforcement agencies, broadcasters, transportation agencies and the wireless industry to activate an urgent bulletin in the most serious child-abduction cases.

Sam asks Jenkins what he's waiting for, Jenkins: 'Ned Beatty time, man.': Ned Beatty starred in the 1972 film *Deliverance*. This is the second reference to the character, who is brutally raped in the movie. He was first mentioned in 'The Woman in White' (1-01) when Dean was arrested by the sheriff in Jericho.

Dean: 'If I tell you, will you promise not to make me into an ashtray?': Ed Gein was a famous killer who would use body parts for domestic items – skulls as soup bowls, shin bones as table legs and skin covering lampshades. Gein was said to be major influence for the characters of Norman Bates in *Psycho* (1960), Leatherface in *The Texas Chain Saw Massacre* (1974) and Buffalo Bill in *Silence of the Lambs* (1991).

When Kathleen discovers that Dean's police badge was stolen, she also receives a picture of Dean and shows it to him. Dean: 'I lost some weight. And I got that Michael Jackson skin disease …': pop legend Michael Jackson suffered from vitiligo – a disease that causes the loss of pigment in the skin.

GOOFS AND FLUFFS

Apart from the goofs on the boys' police records listed above (in the **Did You Spot?** section), there are a couple of other problems in this episode:

In the car park at the bar, Sam places John's journal on the trunk of the third car when he stops to investigate the noise he's heard. When he straightens up, he's been looking under the second car, but you don't see him moving over to it.

When Dean is handcuffed to the police car and is trying to pick the lock before the Bender brothers arrive, he's picking the lock of the cuff around his own wrist. When the Benders get to the car, the cuffs are missing entirely, which means he must have picked not only the lock of the cuff round his own wrist but also that of the one attached to the car handle – and still got away from the car in around three seconds flat. Well done lad!

The scene where Dean is tied to the chair seems to consist of several takes cut together – watch Lee Bender's hands on his Pa's shoulders while Pa is talking about hunting humans, as they keep moving from shot to shot. The blood under Dean's nose after he's been thumped in the face also comes and goes. It's unlikely Jared Bender would be wiping Dean's nose for him while he's holding him in that head lock.

HAVEN'T I SEEN YOU BEFORE?

Jon Cuthbert was in *Night Visions*, *The Crow: Stairway To Heaven* and *The X-Files*. Ryan Drescher featured in *Jeremiah*, *Dark Angel* and *Andromeda*. Alexia Fast's credits include *Masters of Horror* and *The 4400*. John Dennis Johnston was in *Close Encounters of the Third Kind*, *Millennium* and *Highlander: The Series*. Ken Kirzinger was in *The Day the Earth Stood Still*, *Stargate SG-1* and *Freddy vs Jason*. Sadie Lawrence was in *The Butterfly Effect*, *Taken* and *Dark Angel*. Shawn Reis's acting credits include *The Chronicles of Riddick*, *The 4400* and *Kyle XY*. Jessica Steen featured in *Stargate SG-1*,

133

Mutant X and *The Outer Limits.* Sandra Steier has been in *Dead Like Me, Millennium* and *Halloween Camp 2: Scream If You Wanna Die Faster.*

Shawn Reis also appears in 'Faith' (1-12).

BEHIND THE SCENES

In the *Season One Supernatural Companion* Eric Kripke confesses that he thought the little girl in this episode – Missy Bender played by Alexia Fast – was the scariest character they had in Season One. He wasn't the only one that thought so. Co-executive producer John Shiban also felt it and Jensen Ackles admitted in the *Companion* that she freaked him out so much that it made acting scared around her easy.

MUSICAL INTERLUDE

- 'Rocky Mountain Way' – Barnstorm and Joe Walsh – when Sam and Dean are in the bar discussing whether it's their type of case or not.
- 'Sweet and Low Down' – Composer – on the record player when Dean is trying to locate the keys/fighting with Pa Bender.

ANALYSIS

A tense episode that misleads the viewer into thinking that another evil monster is on the loose, then reveals the perpetrators are just plain old humans – crazy humans, yes, but humans nonetheless. It's an intelligent move that grounds the series into a more realistic universe; it's quietly saying that bad things happen (especially around Sam and Dean) but they're not always supernatural in origin.

The story traces its own origins back to a mixture of sources: there are elements of the movies *The Texas Chain Saw Massacre* (1974) and *Deliverance* (1972); and influences from the short story, 'The Most Dangerous Game' by Richard Connell (1924), where a big game hunter starts hunting human prey (a theme that has even turned up in James Bond movies too); but the biggest influence is the real-life exploits of the 'Bloody' Bender family who trapped/killed people at their isolated inn in Kansas in the 1870s. As usual, the story elements get the *Supernatural* spin applied to them, and the result is something very dark and disturbing, for both Sam and Dean.

Sam finds himself confined by the Bender family in preparation for the time they'll hunt him down; Dean is the only person who can find him, but he needs Deputy Kathleen's help and she just thinks Dean's a felon and wants to arrest him. It's not often that the boys are separated[68] and it has an uneasy feel to it, especially given Sam's predicament.

---

68 The only other extended break was in 'Scarecrow' (1-11).

That unease is fed continually as we see more of the Bender family. All the cast playing the family members give convincing performances and this helps to give the episode a seriously menacing edge, but Alexia Fast's portrayal of Missy takes it to a much more intense level. Without such a strong performance from her, the episode would have become something almost comical, but to see an innocent child behaving in such a ruthless manner is truly unnerving in its own right.

Then there's an interesting moral conundrum thrown in at the end, as the show builds on its ability to cast light on human issues that began with 'Faith' (1-12). It's Deputy Kathleen's choice this time as she faces Pa Bender's lack of repentance for killing her brother; but did she do the right thing or did she abuse the power of her position? Again (as in 'Faith') the show doesn't preach any answers, it merely presents the problem. Interpretation is left to the individual viewer.

Unlike in many other episodes, there's little character development going on, with a mere revisit of Dean's need to look out for his younger brother being echoed in Deputy Kathleen's own situation. But despite the reduced sense of depth, the episode still delivers a gruesome story and stands out as one of the grimmest of the season.

VERDICT – 7.5 out of 10

EPISODE 1-16
SHADOW

TRANSMISSION DATES
US first aired: 28 February 2006
UK first aired: 8 May 2006

CREDITS
Writer: Eric Kripke
Director: Kim Manners

RECURRING ROLES
Jeffrey Dean Morgan (John Winchester), Nicki Aycox (Meg Masters)

GUEST STARS
Lorena Gale (Mrs Dunwiddy), Nimet Kanji (Pedestrian), Melanie Papalia (Meredith McDonnell)

SYNOPSIS
Sam and Dean arrive in Chicago to investigate the murder of a young girl, Meredeth, who was ripped to shreds in her locked apartment. The brothers discover that Meg, whom Sam met hitch-hiking in Indiana, has summoned some Daevas and is killing people from the boys' home town, Lawrence. But the boys are just the bait to lure their father out of hiding, and when he finally meets up with his sons, the Daevas attack them all until Sam stops them using a flare and they escape.

CAN YOU SURVIVE TO THE TITLES?
Poor Meredeth is followed to her apartment, has her heart removed while it's still beating, then gets dismembered – these shadow Daevas are really nice creatures.

LOCATION, LOCATION, LOCATION
Chicago, Illinois; a disused warehouse on 1435 West Erie.

LEGENDARY ROOTS
A Daeva is a demon of darkness that originates in Persian mythology (Zoroastrianism). The Daevas chose to follow Angra Mainya, who is thought to be the first personification of the Devil. Zoroastrians believed in duality, so for every good god or spirit there had

to be the evil equivalent. These were the demons that caused plagues and disease, who would fight every other form of religion.

There are seven main archdemons of the Daevas:

Aesma Daeva – the demon of revenge, wrath, lust, anger, war, conflict and violence, opponent of Sraosa (obedience).

Aka Manah – the personification of sensual desire and the eternal opponent on Vohu Manah (wisdom).

Indra – personifies apostasy, the rejection of religion. Opponent of Asha Vahishta (best truth).

Nanghaithya – demon of discontentment, who is the opponent Armaiti (holy devotion).

Saurva – the leader of the Daevas; eternal opponent of Khshathra Vairya (desirable dominion).

Tawrich – personification of hunger, the opponent of Haurvatat (perfection).

Zarich – personifies aging; the eternal opponent of Ameretat (immortality).

SQUEEZE OF THE WEEK
Sam gets some unwanted attention from Meg while both he and Dean are tied to a post in the abandoned warehouse. As Dean puts it: Sam and Meg should have got a room.

SIBLING RIVALRY
There's a lot of bitching about focusing on the job at hand rather than the pretty girls that are around. Sam wants Dean to do a little more thinking with his upstairs brain instead of getting the barmaid's phone number, and later Dean teases Sam about thinking too much with his upstairs brain when Meg turns up unexpectedly.

But the best exchange is when Sam is staking out Meg's apartment and Dean phones to tell him about the Daevas, then insists that Sam should go give Meg a personal strip-o-gram.

BODY COUNT
No-one else dies after Meredeth in the opening sequence, but the Daevas start the job of shredding the Winchester family flesh until everyone is cut and bleeding. They're stopped by Sam, first when he overturns the black altar that controls them and later when he lights the flare.

Technically, the 'real' Meg Masters suffers a fatal injury in the fall from the warehouse window after the altar is destroyed, but that's not revealed until 'Salvation' (1-21) and she's not quite dead yet; the demon possessing her is keeping her going.

This possession stuff really makes the dying process complicated, you know.

TOOLKIT

- *Alarm company uniforms* are handy for looking sexy in and for bluffing your way into a murdered girl's apartment. Be sure you have the trusty *EMF meter* in your uniform pocket too.
- *Masking tape* lets you draw patterns in the blood spatters on the carpet.
- *Holy water, a shotgun, exorcism rituals from half a dozen religions* and *a range of non-disclosed weapons* are required when you're not sure exactly what you'll be fighting.
- And *a small, sharp knife* hidden up your sleeve is essential for those tied up moments while your younger brother is busy snogging the bad girl.

MEMORABLE MOMENTS

When John Winchester and his sons are finally reunited there are tears in everyone's eyes. It's sooo emotional! Group hug everyone!

The best humorous moment is when Sam is watching Meg at her apartment and she's standing in her window wearing just her bra. A passing woman sees Sam peeping and she leans in the car window to call him a pervert.

Top Scare: Just when you thought the Daevas had gone and everyone is playing happy families after being reunited, the creatures attack John Winchester, throwing him across the room before trying to rip his heart out.

SPOOK RULES

- Daevas can enter and exit rooms even if the windows are locked and the doors bolted and chained.
- They take the heart out of the victim, then tear the rest of the body to pieces, leaving convenient spatters of blood on the carpet to trap unwary brothers.
- The sigil for the Daeva is from the Zoroastrian religion and dates back to about two thousand years before Christ.
- The name translates to 'demon of darkness', and they're savage and animalistic with nasty attitudes – a bit like a demonic pit bull.
- Daevas have to be summoned and have a tendency to bite the hand that feeds them – and the arms, and the torso etc.
- A black altar is used to summon them. A pendant with the Daeva sigil will also control them, but you have to know your stuff to do it successfully. This is possibly why Daevas haven't been seen for a couple of millennia.
- Daevas are shadow demons, therefore lighting a flare in the same room as one will temporarily disable it.

DID YOU SPOT?

John Winchester's stubbly chin, briefly glimpsed in 'Home' (1-09) then finally seen in full view in 'Scarecrow' (1-11) has transformed into a fully-bearded chin by this episode. Perhaps he's been growing the beard as part of a disguise to keep the demons from finding him.

GOING UNDERCOVER

The boys pose as employees of PF Alarm Systems, using their own first names, to gain access to Meredeth's apartment.

CULTURAL REFERENCES

Meg: 'I came, I saw, I conquered.': From *Veni, Vidi, Vici* – the famous sentence spoken by Julius Caesar in 47 BC.

Meg: 'Oh, and I met what's-his-name, something Michael Murray, at a bar.': Referring to Chad Michael Murray who starred with Jared Padalecki in the *House of Wax* (2005) remake.

Dean: 'You trapped us. Good for you. It's Miller time.': The second reference to beer made by the Miller Brewing Company. Sam was the first one to use the phrase in 'The Woman in White' (1-01).

HAVEN'T I SEEN YOU BEFORE?

Lorena Gale played Elosha in *Battlestar Galactica* and has also featured in *The Exorcism of Emily Rose*, *The Day the Earth Stood Still* and *The X Files: I Want to Believe*. Nimet Kanji was Dr Rajani Mohadevan in *Blood Ties* and was in *The 4400* and *Stargate: Atlantis*. Melanie Papalia plays Amanda Worth in *Painkiller Jane* and has also been in *Smallville* and *Blade: The Series*.

BEHIND THE SCENES

This episode involved some very tricky lighting situations. According to director of photography Serge Ladouceur, director Kim Manners had visualised a 'film noir' look to the episode and there was a lot of hard light used to achieve this. One of the knock on effects of hard light is that everything has to be very accurate from the action blocking to the actors on their marks. Soft light tends to be much more forgiving during filming. [*The Official Supernatural Magazine #5*]

As well as having to hit the mark accurately, actress Nicki Aycox already had a demanding scene to shoot as it was – when Meg had the boys tied to separate poles in the warehouse. The boys were stuck in one place so Aycox had to slide back and forth across the floor, get on top of Jared then it was over and back to Jensen again, crouching down low all the time. [*Season One Supernatural Companion*] You know, there's gonna be a lot of people out there who would have been happy to help out.

Musical Interlude
- 'You Got Your Hooks In Me' – Little Charlie and the Nightcats – playing on Meredeth's headphones at the start before she's attacked.
- 'Pictures of Me' – The Vue – in the bar when Dean is chatting up the bartender then talking to Sam about the case.
- 'The New World' – X – when Sam is chatting to Meg in the bar.

Analysis
By now, we understand that Kripke *et al* are going to tell their story at their own pace, and we viewers will just have to slaver in anticipation until the writers are ready to throw us the next morsel. After the bombshell about the other families sharing the same tragedy as the Winchesters (mom on the ceiling and those spooky powers) we finally return to the John Winchester storyline and the beginning of the explanations as to why John had to disappear so suddenly.

It starts, like many other episodes, with a supernatural murder, but the reappearance of Meg spins it in a whole new direction. Sam and Dean are not yet aware of Meg's neck-slashing, blood-gushing tendencies, but it's not long before they've figured out whose side she's on. And that's when the twists begin – Meg is playing a completely different game to the boys. John Winchester is obviously getting too close to the demons, but they can't pin him down[69], so they use the boys as bait to catch him.

The boys seem to have won when Meg takes a swan dive out of the window and John meets up with them back at the motel but, in a nice twist, Meg sends the Daevas to attack again. Meg almost succeeds in killing them all, but even as they escape, her silent presence hints that everything may still be going according to the demon's plans.

Suddenly, the boys are on a much larger game-board where the opposition is obviously prepared to murder innocent people to manipulate the players. Nothing will be the same again in Season One; everything will now need to be assessed in the new context to ensure it's not some new demon plan being put into action.

Interleaved with all the demonic shenanigans are some poignant scenes for Sam, Dean and John. It's an emotional moment when Sam and Dean discover John in their motel room. Face to face at last, it's Dean who is first to rush over and hug his dad. Unsurprisingly, given their history, Sam hangs back, still unsure whether his dad

69 And who wouldn't want to pin John Winchester down?

140

wants to see him or not. Sam's opinion of his dad has changed through the months, after finding out how John used to swing by Stanford to check he was okay[70]; and realising how different their life could have been if John had turned to alcohol more than he did after Mary's death[71]. But while Sam has changed, he still doesn't know how his dad feels. The answer and their touching reconciliation come with few words but are heavy with emotion – John: 'It's good to see you again. It's been a long time'; Sam: 'Too long.'

However, despite finally being reunited, it appears the Winchesters have actually got to learn to be apart again. Sam makes it clear to Dean in this episode that once the demon is dead then he wants to go back to school. In a rare vulnerable moment, Dean expresses his hope that they could all be together as a family, hunting again, but Sam insists that Dean will have to let him go his own way.

By the end of the episode the tables have turned. Dean can see the danger that he and Sam put their father in and wants John to leave without them. Sam, driven by his need to avenge Jessica's death, desperately wants to help his father find the demon, but this time it's Sam who needs to let go. It's a painful parting in the end, made all too brief by their need to escape before the Daevas recover from the flare and give chase. But that briefness leaves the air laced with expectations for the future.

VERDICT – 9 out of 10

---

70 'Bugs' (1-08).

71 'Nightmare' (1-14).

EPISODE 1-17
HELL HOUSE

TRANSMISSION DATES
US first aired: 30 March 2006
UK first aired: 15 May 2006

CREDITS
Writer: Trey Callaway
Director: Chris Long

GUEST STARS
Krista Bell (Dana), A J Buckley (Ed Zeddmore), Agam Darshi (Jill), Jase-Anthony Griffith (Sheriff), Jay Nicolas Hackleman (First Teenage Boy), Nicholas Harrison (Mordechai Murdoch), Britt Irvin (First Teenage Girl), Colby Johannson (James), Kyle Labine (Second Teenage Boy), Gerry Mackay (Mr. Goodwin), Shane Meier (Craig Thursten), Natasha Peck (Second Teenage Girl), Travis Wester (Harry Spengler)

SYNOPSIS
Sam finds stories of a haunted house on an amateur ghost-hunting website called Hell Hound's Lair. At first, it seems to be a teenage hoax but then a girl is murdered in the cellar by an axe-wielding ghost called Mordechai Murdock. The story of Mordechai turns out to be made up, but the ghost has become real because of the large number of people believing in his existence. Sam and Dean try to manipulate that belief through the two inept ghost-hunters who run the website, but the attempt fails and they have to burn the house down instead.

CAN YOU SURVIVE TO THE TITLES?
A mysterious girl is seen hanging by the neck from the rafters in Mordechai's cellar, but no body is found when the police investigate. The girl later turns out to be very much alive, so everyone survives to the titles this time.

LOCATION, LOCATION, LOCATION
Richardson, Texas; Collin County Public Library, Texas.

LEGENDARY ROOTS
Tulpa is a discipline, concept and teaching tool originating from Bonpo, Vajrayana

142

and Tibetan Buddhists, which has been rendered into English as 'Thoughtform', an object or being created through the collective visualisation and willpower of a group of monks.

The concept of a tulpa was first brought to the West in 1929[72] by Alexandra David-Néel. She journeyed through Tibet studying mystical techniques and decided to try and create one. She claimed to have created a tulpa in the form of a little plump monk, which eventually took a life of its own appearing when she had not willed it. When the tulpa started to take on a more menacing form, David-Néel eventually had to destroy it by reabsorbing it into her mind.

SQUEEZE OF THE WEEK
Another lean period for the boys. Dean doesn't even get to flirt with anyone.

SIBLING RIVALRY
The sibling rivalry steps up a notch as the boys start playing pranks on each other.

Dean sticks a plastic spoon in Sam's mouth while he's asleep.

Sam turns everything on in the car – radio, wipers, the works – so that when Dean turns the key in the ignition it all goes off together.

Dean puts itching powder in Sam's underwear.

Sam uses superglue and Dean gets his hand stuck to his beer bottle.

They call a truce after that, but the pranks will appear again in 'Tall Tales' (2-15).

BODY COUNT
Young Jill is Mordechai's first victim. She gets hung from the rafters in the Hell House after taking a dare to go in and retrieve one of the jars from the cellar.

TOOLKIT
- Standard ghostbusting equipment is required: *rock salt rounds* in the *shotgun*; a *lighter* and *lighter fuel*.
- A *.45 handgun loaded with wrought iron bullets* can be used to kill a ghost if you can get people to believe it'll work, but that can be unreliable so have a backup plan laid out.
- No salt is required when the ghost is a tulpa as it does not have a body to burn. Instead, use an *aerosol can* with the lighter to make a flame thrower[73]. This will

---

72 David-Néel's *Mystiques et Magiciens du Thibet* was published in France in 1929. The first English edition followed in 1931.

73 As previously used in 'Bugs' (1-08).

distract the ghost from throttling your younger brother and you can then use it to set fire to the house so there's nothing left for the ghost to haunt.

MEMORABLE MOMENTS
Sam coming out of the bathroom wearing nothing but a towel round his waist. Sweet.

SPOOK RULES
- Ghosts are usually pretty strict and follow the same pattern over and over.
- If you meditate hard enough on something, with enough people, you can bring that something to life – as per the incident in Tibet in 1915 when 20 monks brought a golem into existence.
- With 10,000 web surfers believing that a ghost exists and seeing a Tibetan spirit sigil at the same time, it is possible to think a ghost into reality.
- Change what people believe about the ghost and you change the actual ghost.
- Tibetan spirit sigils concentrate meditative thoughts like a magnifying glass.
- Tulpas can't be killed by traditional methods because they aren't traditional ghosts. To stop a tulpa you need to make people believe that something specific can kill that ghost – like a .45 pistol loaded with wrought iron bullets.
- If you can't make people believe in the ghostly weakness, then burn the house down so there's nowhere for the ghost to haunt, and be prepared to come back if the tulpa changes again.

GOING UNDERCOVER
When interviewing Craig Thursten, who started the Mordechai rumours, Sam and Dean pretend to be reporters with the *Dallas Morning News*, a real-life newspaper whose website is www.dallasnews.com.

CULTURAL REFERENCES
Ghostbusters (1984) gets a couple of references. First there are the characters Ed Zeddmore and Harry Spengler: Dr Egon Spengler and Winston Zeddmore were characters in both the 1984 film and the 1989 sequel. Then there's Dean's 'Who you gonna call?' – one of the most famous lines from all the *Ghostbusters* movies.

Ed: 'Remember – WWBD. What would Buffy do?': This is a play on WWJD (What would Jesus do?), but referring to *Buffy the Vampire Slayer*.

Ed: 'Would John Edward go?': John Edward – famous US psychic medium who communicates with the dead, delivering messages to loved ones. TV programmes featuring Edward are *Crossing Over with John Edward* (1999-2004) and *John Edward Cross Country* (2006-).

Ed: 'The power of Christ compels you!': Another reference to the *Rituale Romanum* exorcism rites[74] and *The Exorcist* (1973)[75]. In *The Exorcist* the line is spoken by the characters Father Merrin and Father Damien Karras.

Harry: 'Sweet Lord of the Rings – run!': Referring to the J R R Tolkien series of books consisting of *The Lord of the Rings: The Fellowship of the Ring* (1954), *The Two Towers* (1954) and *The Return of the King* (1955), later adapted by Peter Jackson into a trilogy of films, (2001), (2002) and (2003) respectively.

Dean: 'You afraid you're gonna get a little Nair in your shampoo again, eh?': Nair is a hair removal product made by Church and Dwight UK Ltd and gives you hair control in the face, legs and, most importantly, bikini line areas of the body.

Dean: 'Ugh, I hate rats.': Probably a tip of the hat to the movie *Indiana Jones and the Temple of Doom* (1989) in which Indy's dad, played by Sean Connery, also hates rats.

Craig: 'I write for my school's lit magazine.'; Dean: 'Oh, good for you, Morrison.': A possible reference to Toni Morrison, who in 1993 became the first Afro-American and the first American woman in 55 years to win the Nobel Prize for Literature.

Dean: 'Yeah, so much for curb appeal.': Curb appeal is all about making the front exterior and gardens of a property attractive to entice buyers to look round the house. Something the Hell House in this episode so doesn't have.

Dean: 'Looks like Old Man Murdoch was a bit of a tagger during his time.': A tagger is a graffiti artist.

GOOFS AND FLUFFS

It's stretching believability a little when Sam and Dean send the cops guarding the Hell House off on a wild goose chase twice and even though the cops aren't too far away from the house they don't seem to hear the shotgun blasts or come back to investigate.

The fisherman sculpture on the wall in the restaurant is holding the fish with its head on the left in the close-up but when you see it with Sam and Dean sitting in front of it, the fish's head is on the right.

And there's a couple of goofs in the final face-off against Mordechai inside the house: first, when Sam and Dean leave Ed and Harry, the camera pans right, and the left shoulder and back of one of the crew are visible on the right hand side; then, shortly afterwards, when Harry takes the camera off Ed, it's clearly the body double who gets thrown to the floor by Mordechai.

---

74 First referenced in 'Phantom Traveler' (1-04).

75 Also referenced in both 'Phantom Traveler' (1-04) and 'Home' (1-09).

HAVEN'T I SEEN YOU BEFORE?

Krista Bell is a stunt woman who has performed stunts in *Fantastic Four*, *X-Men: The Last Stand* and *Night at the Museum: Battle of the Smithsonian*. Agam Darshi's credits include *Final Destination 3*, *Stargate: Atlantis* and *Watchmen*. Jase-Anthony Griffith featured in *The 4400*, *Dark Angel* and *The Crow: Stairway to Heaven*. Jay Nicolas Hackleman was in *The Day the Earth Stood Still*, *Smallville* and *The Dead Zone*. Nicholas Harrison has been in *Stargate SG-1*, *Dark Angel* and *The Dead Zone*. Britt Irvin was in *Beyond Belief: Fact or Fiction*, *The Outer Limits* and *Taken*. Colby Johannson appeared in *Reaper*, *Battlestar Galactica* and *Freddy vs Jason*. Kyle Labine's credits include *Halloween: Resurrection*, *The Twilight Zone* and *Freddy vs Jason*. Gerry Mackay was in *Painkiller Jane* and *The Dead Zone*. Shane Meier has been in *The 4400*, *Tru Calling* and *Stargate: Atlantis*.

BEHIND THE SCENES

Good television music is seldom noticed, and *Supernatural* has two great composers in Christopher Lennertz and Jay Gruska. For example, did you notice that the show has a musical humour motif (a guitar line) that has been used since the Pilot[76]? The same motif that was used with the Pilot's bridge scene – where Sam stamps on Dean's foot and Dean clips Sam round the head – is also used in 'Hell House'. Try watching the show with your eyes closed occasionally[77] …

MUSICAL INTERLUDE

- 'Fire of Unknown Origin' – Blue Öyster Cult – when Dean and Sam are driving at the start.
- 'Slow Death' – Extreme Music – talking to Craig in the record shop, first time.
- 'Anthem' – Extreme Music – talking to Craig in the record shop, second time.
- 'Point of No Return' – Rex Horbart and The Misery Boys – in the diner when Sam and Dean are talking about the tulpa theory and drinking coffee.
- 'Fast Train Down' – The Waco Brothers – in the diner the second time when Sam and Dean are talking about the tulpa theory.
- 'Burnin' for You' – Blue Öyster Cult – as they drive away at the end of the episode.

ANALYSIS

There's a good mixture of humour and horror going on in 'Hell House' with a

---

76 'Woman In White' (1-01).

77 No, not easy to do when the boys are on screen, but you can do it if you really try, honest.

plenty scary ghost, some amateur ghostbusters and the boys regressing back to their childhood to play pranks on each other. The scenes at the haunted house are very atmospheric, with some delightfully taut moments that probably seem all the more scary because they're surrounded by the contrasting funnier scenes. The action is sharp and swift and the story twists along, provoking some deeper thoughts between the laughs.

But the most notable contrast of the episode is the difference between the ghostbusters and Sam and Dean, and it indicates how credible the Winchesters' universe has become. If you ignore the fact that Ed and Harry are complete dorks, when the two parties first meet what you have is Ed and Harry representing the real-life methods of paranormal detection coming face-to-face with two experienced but fictional demon-hunters. How many viewers took one look at Ed and Harry and thought, 'These guys have no idea about what's really going on. Leave it to Sam and Dean cause they know what they're doing'? If the *Supernatural* universe was any less convincing, the geeks would have had a very different impact.

To produce that level of conviction in the viewer requires writing that is structured, detailed, realistic and well thought-out, not to mention support from the costume department, music score and actors etc to deliver an all-round believable experience. Because if even one of those aspects fails to hit a high enough standard the viewer will cease to accept any of it. With the exception of 'Bugs' (1-08), *Supernatural* has been consistently believable up to now, and now they're reaping the rewards and building on that ground work.

As in 'The Benders' (1-15), there's little character development happening, although Sam's and Dean's escapades certainly show what they must have been like as kids, which reinforces the sense of history these two have together. Instead, we have something more profound: the concept that people's beliefs can create something real. Corporate businesses have long been aware that 'perception is reality' for their customers, and the concept was also explored in Mark Chadbourn's *Age of Misrule* fantasy trilogy (1999-2001). Here it is applied with frightening consequences to an urban legend. Sam comments, 'Kind of makes you wonder, of all the things we've hunted, how many existed just because people believed in them?' It does indeed make you wonder, rather a lot actually.

VERDICT – 8 out of 10

EPISODE 1-18
SOMETHING WICKED

TRANSMISSION DATES
US first aired: 6 April 2006
UK first aired: 22 May 2006

CREDITS
Writer: Daniel Knauf
Director: Whitney Ransick

RECURRING ROLE
Jeffrey Dean Morgan (John Winchester)

GUEST STARS
Chandra Berg (Bethany Tarnover), Mary Black (Elderly Patient), Ridge Canipe (Young Dean), Penelope Cardas (Nurse), Erica Carroll (Mother), Ari Cohen (Miles Tarnower), Stacee Copeland (Nurse Betty Friedman), Jeannie Epper (The Shtriga), Alex Ferris (Young Sam), Adrian Hough (Dr. Heidecker), Colby Paul (Michael Sorenson), John Prowse (Tavern Owner), Venus Terzo (Joanna Sorenson)

SYNOPSIS
A set of co-ordinates from John sends the boys after a monster that is sucking the life-force out of children in Fitchburg. For Dean, it's a chance to correct a mistake he made when he and Sam were growing up. The Shtriga almost killed Sam when Dean left him alone in a motel room in Fort Douglas. John returned in time to save Sam, but the Shtriga got away. Now they've found the monster again, so Dean has a chance to do the job properly. This time, he enlists the help of Michael, whose mom owns the motel Sam and Dean are staying in. Using Michael as bait, they finally kill the Shtriga, saving its current victims, including Michael's younger brother.

CAN YOU SURVIVE TO THE TITLES?
Young Bethany doesn't get killed by the Shtriga but she does get her life-force drained – which means she doesn't have long to live because her body will start to wear out.

LOCATION, LOCATION, LOCATION
Flashback: Fort Douglas, Wisconsin; Present Day: Fitchburg, Wisconsin; 2400 Court

148

Motel; A W Stowe Public Library; Dane County Memorial Hospital

LEGENDARY ROOTS

The Shtriga, generally pictured as an old haggard woman, comes from Albanian folklore and is a type of witch that drains the blood out of a person, usually a child, while they are sleeping. After feeding, she would leave by turning into an insect. (The most common beliefs have her turning into a bee, moth or fly.) The only cure for being drained is for the Shtriga to spit into the victim's mouth; those not cured eventually sicken and die.

It is believed that there are a couple of methods of protection against a Shtriga. A cross made of bone placed at the entrance of a church on Easter Sunday will trap any Shtriga inside. She can then be captured and killed as she tries to escape. The other method relates to the fact that once a victim has been drained of blood, the Shtriga goes off into the woods and regurgitates it. A silver coin soaked in the blood and wrapped in a cloth can be used as an amulet offering permanent protection from the Shtriga.

SQUEEZE OF THE WEEK

Despite meeting a gorgeous motel owner, Sam and Dean both behave themselves admirably.

SIBLING RIVALRY

Several fun comments fly back and forth as Dean tries to pull rank on Sam because he's the oldest, and as Sam congratulates Dean for being wise enough not to open fire on the monster in a paediatrics ward.

The sarcasm really shows through when they're talking about the hospital being geographically at the centre of the victims' houses and Dean explains that he saw an old person in one of the rooms. Sam suggests that a call to the coast guard must be in order if Dean was seeing old people at the hospital.

BODY COUNT

Apart from the Shtriga, no-one else dies in the entire episode[78]. There are a number of children in comas at the hospital dying slowly, but no-one actually pops off.

TOOLKIT

- The *EMF meter* is out again and the *black light* gadget (UV lamp[79]) to help find traces of blood and supernatural beasties.

---

78 Which has happened only once before, in 'Home' (1-09).

79 Last seen in 'Bloody Mary' (1-05).

- A *camera with night vision, a pair of headphones* and a *laptop with an image feed from your camera* are essential if you're going to shoot a really nasty witch with *consecrated wrought iron rounds.*

Memorable Moments
Dean finally comes clean about what really happened in Fort Douglas, when he screwed up and put Sam in danger.

Spook Rules
- A Shtriga does not give a reading on an EMF meter.
- The creatures feed off the *spiritus vitae* or life-force/essence of children (because kids have a stronger life-force).
- They are invulnerable to all weapons made by God and man at all times except when they're feeding. Then you can kill them with consecrated wrought iron rounds or buckshot.
- They take on a human disguise when they're not hunting – something like a feeble old woman or a doctor.
- They hit a new town every 15 to 20 years. They feed for months on dozens of children before moving on.
- They have superhuman strength and can move very quickly.
- When you lose your life-force to a Shtriga, your immunity goes to hell and pneumonia sets in.

Going Undercover
In order to gain access to the sick children at the hospital, Sam says he's Dr Gerry Caplan from the Centre for Disease Control, although his ID badge claims he's a bikini inspector.

When they book into the motel, Dean uses his Mastercard in the name of Kris Warren.

Cultural References
Sam: 'Dude, I ran LexisNexis, local police reports, newspapers – I couldn't find a single red flag.': LexisNexis: a popular site that allows subscribers to search archive printed content from newspapers, magazines, legal documents and other printed sources. www.lexis.com is for legal documentation while www.nexis.com is for journalism research.

Sam: 'Hi, I'm Dr Gerry Caplan, Centre for Disease Control.': The Centre for Disease Control and Prevention (CDC) is a federal agency in the US Department of

Health and Human Services that investigates, diagnoses and tries to control or prevent diseases (especially new and unusual ones).

The old woman at the hospital is staying in Room 237: Room 237 in *The Shining* (1980) is where Torrence encounters the ghost of a beautiful and naked young woman who ages in his arms, her skin decaying as she tries to follow him out of the room.

When Sam is researching previous Shtriga locations, the towns in the newspaper clips are Brockway, Ogdenville and North Haverbrook. These towns all appear in *The Simpsons* episode *Marge vs the Monorail* (1993), as ones that have already been sold the dodgy monorail. Ogdenville and North Haverbrook also appear in other episodes of the show.

GOOFS AND FLUFFS

As the boys arrive in Fitchburg, the sign saying 'Population 20,501' manages to spell the town name wrong – it says 'Fitchberg'. A second sign, further right, does get the name right.

When Michael starts pouring a glass of milk for his brother, his hand is on the bottom of the glass, but from the next angle it's moved away.

The blood from the Shtriga's forehead accidentally sprays the camera lens when Dean shoots her.

Watch Joanna's hands as she tells Michael that his brother is okay: they keep shifting from his arms to his head, depending on the camera angle.

Cell-phones are usually banned from use in hospitals, so Dean wouldn't have been allowed to talk to Sam while he was in the hospital room with Asher and his mom.

HAVEN'T I SEEN YOU BEFORE?

Chandra Berg's credits include *Battlestar Galactica: Razor* and *Masters of Horror*. Penelope Cardas was in *Jake 2.0*. Erica Carroll was in *The Outer Limits*, *The 4400* and *Battlestar Galactica*. Ari Cohen played Regan Matthews in *Smallville* and was also in *Relic Hunter* and *Andromeda*. Stacee Copeland featured in *The X Files: I Want to Believe*, *Smallville* and *The X-Files*. Jeannie Epper appeared in *Wonder Woman*, *Charmed* and *Tales from the Crypt*. Alex Ferris has also been in *X-Men: The Last Stand*, *Smallville* and *Masters of Horror*. Adrian Hough credits include *A Town Called Eureka*, *AVP: Requiem* and *X-Men: The Last Stand*. Colby Paul featured in *Star Trek* the 2009 movie, *Ghost Whisperer* and *Night Stalker*. John Prowse was in *The 4400*, *Stargate SG-1* and *Jake 2.0*. Venus Terzo's credits include *Masters of Horror*, *Painkiller Jane* and *The Dead Zone*. Erica Carroll also appears in 'Faith' (1-12).

Ridge Canipe also appears in 'A Very Supernatural Christmas' (3-08).

Mary Black also appears in 'Bedtime Stories' (3-05).

BEHIND THE SCENES
Just in case it wasn't obvious yet, Eric Kripke confirms in the *Season One Supernatural Companion* that he has a deep seated fear of really old ladies, especially ones in wheelchairs with misty cataract eyes.

The 2400 Court Motel is a real motel that is scheduled for redevelopment by the City of Vancouver. You can find out more about it by going to http://vancouverneon. com and clicking 'Hotels'.

MUSICAL INTERLUDE
* 'Rock Bottom' – UFO – when Sam and Dean are driving at the beginning of the episode.
* 'Road to Nowhere' – Ozzy Osbourne – as Sam and Dean drive away at the end of the episode.

ANALYSIS
For the first time we meet a monster that the Winchesters have hunted before, and its appearance brings the flashback technique to *Supernatural*. It also allows for some interesting themes to be revisited.

There's a huge back history of stories waiting to be told with the Winchester family and while we've had hints of this before ('When I told Dad when I was scared of the thing in my closet he gave me a .45.'[80]) this is the first glimpse of Sam's and Dean's upbringing.

And it looks so lonely.

Dad is away for days at a time; they have no mother to look after them; and all the responsibility for Sam falls on Dean's shoulders. It's no wonder that even now Dean feels the need to look after his little brother. And that's the strongest theme in the episode – Dean's situation of protecting Sam is reflected in young Michael's bravery in volunteering to be bait for the Shtriga in the hope that it will make his younger brother better. Michael will do anything for his brother and so will Dean. It all nicely echoes Sam's assertion in 'Shadow' (1-16) that he'll do anything for Dean. Which, in turn, echoes similar exchanges in 'Bloody Mary' (1-05) and 'Skin' (1-06), showing how this theme runs right the way through Season One like the proverbial letters in a stick of rock.

These flashbacks break up the linear pattern we've seen in episodes to date and allow for a more detailed explanation of the boys' history. They show how the past can influence the present and demonstrate what the boys'll do when they get a second

---

80 'Woman in White' (1-01)

chance, a way to rectify an old mistake.

That isn't the only character development going on either. Sam starts to understand his brother more. He couldn't understand why Dean followed orders, and in 'Asylum' (1-10) he'd had a go at him about it. (Okay, it was a bit more serious than that: Sam had tried to kill Dean with a shotgun loaded with rock salt.). Sam also stormed off in 'Scarecrow' (1-11) over it, having previously described Dean as pathetic for doing whatever John told them to do. Back then, Dean took all the comments on the chin (and both shotgun barrels in the chest), unwilling to defend himself because then he would have had to admit to screwing up. Now Dean has no choice, so Sam belatedly gets the full explanation.

For Dean, this is the second time in almost as many episodes that he's opened up to Sam. In 'Shadow' (1-16) Dean expresses his wish that the family could stick together after the demon has been killed, and here he's confessing about a past mistake that almost cost Sam's life. For years, Dean has carried the guilt for the children who lost their lives, because he believes he should have stopped in Fort Douglas; but he's also carried the shame for failing his father and leaving Sam in danger. Dean desperately needs his father's approval, and it was difficult for him to have his father 'look at him differently' after his mistake.

But for all his sudden need to share, it's not long before Dean's back being disparaging. When Sam apologises for giving Dean a hard time about taking orders, Dean's typical 'shoot me now' response has returned.

'Something Wicked' showcases the main themes of *Supernatural* – killing monsters, saving innocent lives, taking responsibility to change things, and the ties that bind a family together. With more flashback episodes to come, we'll soon be getting a deeper understanding of the Winchesters' lives, and that can only be a good thing.

VERDICT – 8.5 out of 10

EPISODE 1-19
PROVENANCE

TRANSMISSION DATES
US first aired: 13 April 2006
UK first aired: 29 May 2006

CREDITS
Writer: David Ehrman
Director: Phil Sgriccia

GUEST STARS
Linden Banks (Isaiah Merchant), Jay Brazeau (Darryl), Curtis Caravaggio (Mark Telesca), Josh D Clark (Workman), Taylor Cole (Sarah Blake), Jodelle Micah Ferland (Melanie Merchant), Barbara Frosch (Evelyn), Keith Martin Gordey (Daniel Blake), Sarah Mutch (Unknown), Kenton Reid (Waiter), Jody Thompson (Ann Telesca)

SYNOPSIS
A couple are murdered in their own home and the *modus operandi* matches three other murders dating back to 1912. Sam and Dean track the source of the problem to a haunted painting. They are helped in this by Sarah, who works at the auction house handling the sale of the painting. When burning the canvas fails to stop the killings and the painting rejuvenates itself, Sam and Dean investigate the Merchant family featured in the painting, who all had their throats cut. Assuming the father is haunting the picture, Sam and Dean burn his remains, but when they try to remove the painting so they can bury it, Melanie, the young girl of the family, tries to murder Sam and Sarah. Dean saves the day by burning Melanie's remains at the family crypt.

CAN YOU SURVIVE TO THE TITLES?
Mark and Anne Telesca have their throats cut in their own bedroom after bringing home the haunted painting. They should have had better taste in art, shouldn't they!?

LOCATION, LOCATION, LOCATION
New Paltz, New York

LEGENDARY ROOTS
Can an object be haunted? There are a few well known examples of objects that are

supposedly haunted and you can even buy haunted items on the internet these days!

Robert the Doll is probably one of the most famous examples of a haunted object. The doll was given to Robert Eugene 'Gene' Otto in 1896 by a maid who practiced voodoo. Gene named the doll after himself and the doll became his constant companion. Gene could be heard talking to the doll, which the family just thought was like an imaginary friend, until they heard the doll talk back in an entirely different voice.

Strange things began to happen in the house. The family would hear the doll giggle, catch glimpses of it running around the house, and find Gene and Robert in a room with all the furniture overturned, to which Gene would say 'Robert did it'.

Robert was eventually confined to the attic, only to be rediscovered by Gene when he inherited the house, where he was then given his own room. People walking by would feel Robert's glare from the turret room of the house, earning Robert a place in the attic again – after which visitors would claim they could hear giggles and footsteps coming from upstairs. After Gene's death in 1972 a new family moved in. The ten year old daughter found Robert and not long afterwards claimed the doll was alive and tortured her. Robert now resides in the Key West Martello Museum and employees report he is still up to his old tricks, giggling at visitors and moving, even though he is within a glass case.

SQUEEZE OF THE WEEK

Finally, Sam gets a little more female attention[81]. Sarah is a feisty number and takes ghost hunting in her stride. Sam finally gets a decent snog right at the end of the episode, but he has to work his way up to it since he's not as fast a worker as Dean.

Dean puts in some nifty footwork with the ladies too. Early on, he spends an obviously tiring night with Brandy, whom he picked up that same afternoon in a bar. And since Brandy had a friend, it's never quite clear whether Dean hit the jackpot with one or both of them...

SIBLING RIVALRY

There's typical brotherly banter as Dean tries to convince Sam that he needs a little R&R between jobs, indicates the young lady he's already pulled, and offers to arrange a date for Sam as well. Sam is rather disparaging about Dean masquerading as a Reality TV Scout and insists he can get his own dates thank you very much.

---

81 Something he's not had since Jessica died, save for that fumble on the bench with Lori in 'Hookman' (1-07).

BODY COUNT

An increase in the body count after recent weeks with the double murder in the opening sequence and the sweet old lady, Evelyn, getting what Dean refers to as a 'Columbian necktie'[82] while relaxing in her comfy chair in the evening. She should have had better taste in paintings too.

TOOLKIT

- A *lock pick* and the *know-how to disable a building alarm* are both useful when you need to steal a haunted painting from an auction house.
- *Chain cutters* are essential for breaking into the occasional mausoleum.
- The boys are also packing standard ghostie detecting kit and weapons – *the EMF meter; salt; lighter fuel; a lighter;* and *wrought iron* (the purer the better). It seems the lighter has been getting so much use recently that it's gone on the blink. If you want stop your brother and his girl from getting a really close shave then check your equipment regularly. (Dean's equipment certainly gets checked regularly enough!)

MEMORABLE MOMENTS

The discovery of Evelyn's body, as the head tilts backwards off the torso and the neck gapes open is just wonderfully gruesome.

MOTEL MAYHEM

The motels have been pretty low-key through Season One, with only the log cabin containing all the stuffed animals (in 'Nightmare' (1-14)) showing any unusual character so far. But now the boys are in a 1960s psychedelic motel room with Travolta/disco overtones, and according to the label on the Do Not Disturb sign, it's a place called The Boogie Inn.

The highly patterned walls, combined with the black, white and chrome colour scheme, are simply migraine inducing.

SPOOK RULES

- With haunted paintings, it's usually the subject that haunts them.
- A painting can be haunted by more than one subject and if one of those subjects is going around slitting people's throats, the other one can change the painting to give clues about the evil spirit.

---

82 Technically this is the throat being slashed and the tongue pulled out through the open wound, although Evelyn just got her throat cut through.

- You can bury a haunted painting to stop the evil spirit from attacking more victims.
- When a ghost leaves a painting, their image goes missing from the canvas too, and even though they look normal in the painting, their three-dimensional body looks pretty decayed.
- To stop the evil spirit you need to burn some remains from the body. If you can't salt and burn the bones because they've been cremated then burning anything of them you can find (like their hair) will work as well. This rule first appeared in 'Hookman' (1-07) but in that case they had to burn the metal from the spirit's hook.

DID YOU SPOT?

Dean is back munching his way through free mini quiches and quaffing free champagne again. It's a habit of his that we've seen before in 'Bugs' (1-08) and 'Nightmare' (1-14).

In the parking lot outside the auction house near the start of the episode, one of the luxury cars has a number plate 'THE KRIP' – a reference to series creator Eric Kripke.

GOING UNDERCOVER

Sam introduces himself to the auction house owner as Sam Connors, an art dealer, with Dean as his brother. They both work for Connors Limited.

CULTURAL REFERENCES

Sam: 'What, like a Da Vinci Code deal?'; Dean: 'I don't know, I'm still waiting for the movie on that one.': *The Da Vinci Code* – originally a novel by Dan Brown published in 2003 and later turned into a film in 2006 starring Tom Hanks. The film opened after this episode of *Supernatural* first aired.

Dean: 'Daddy dearest isn't here.': *Mommie Dearest* (1981) was a movie of the life of Joan Crawford from a book written by her adoptive daughter Christina Crawford.

Sam: 'Well, I'd say it's more Grant Wood than Grandma Moses.': Grant Wood (1891-1942) was an American painter best known for his works depicting American rural Midwest. His most famous painting is 'American Gothic'. Grandma Moses (1860-1961) was Anna Mary Robertson Moses, an American folk artist who was one of the most important self-taught artists of the 20th Century.

Sam: 'I'm not talking about a broken heart and a tub of Haagen-Dazs.': Like you don't already know, but Haagen-Dazs is an American brand of ice cream established in 1959 that is often used as a comfort food when a relationship has ended (or any damn time of the day, let's face it).

GOOFS AND FLUFFS

When Evelyn is relaxing in her chair, with the painting overlooking her, she puts her glasses down on her book with the lenses furthest away from her and the arms closest to her. In the next shot the lenses are closest to her.

When Dean, Sam and Sarah go into Evelyn's house and see her sitting quietly in her chair, Sarah goes over to the body. When Sam says, 'Sarah, don't!' he's got his mouth closed in the background of the shot.

When talking about the differences in the painting at Evelyn's house, Dean calls Sam 'Jared'.

HAVEN'T I SEEN YOU BEFORE?

Linden Banks' acting credits include *Smallville, Painkiller Jane* and *The X-Files*. Jay Brazeau's credits include *Watchmen, Blood Ties* and *The Outer Limits*. Curtis Caravaggio played a Special Forces Commander in *AVP: Requiem* and has also featured in *Battlestar Galactica* and *Stargate: Atlantis*. Taylor Cole played Rachel Mills in *Heroes* and was also in *Numb3rs*. Jodelle Micah Ferland played Mary Jensen in *Kingdom Hospital* and Sharon/Alessa in *Silent Hill*. Keith Gordey was in *The Dead Zone, The 4400* and *Poltergeist: The Legacy*. Sarah Mutch has been in *Jake 2.0* and *Smallville*. Kenton Reid appeared in *Stargate SG-1, Dead Like Me* and *Beyond Belief: Fact Or Fiction*. Jody Thompson played Devon in *The 4400* and was also in *Blade: The Series* and *Andromeda*.

BEHIND THE SCENES

In *The Official Supernatural Magazine* #3, visual effects co-ordinator Ivan Hayden cited this episode as having one of his favourite effects – the one where Sam swipes the little girl with the poker and she turns into smoke.

For the auction house, according to set decorator George Neuman in the *Season One Supernatural Companion*, the production team used a real two-level furniture store. But just because you've got a ready-made location doesn't mean the work's over. The crew still took the time to fill it with their own antique furniture rather than risk some expensive pieces getting damaged.

MUSICAL INTERLUDE

- 'Night Time' – Steve Carlson – when Dean is getting the girl's number in the bar and talking to Sam over a beer.
- 'Bad Time (To Be In Love)' – Grand Funk Railroad – when Dean is in the car while Sam and Sarah check the painting.
- ' Romantic Pieces, No. 1' – Extreme – at the auction site.

- 'One More Once' – Black Toast Music – when Sam and Sarah are having dinner at the restaurant.

ANALYSIS

For the first time, Sam and Dean talk about having a little R&R and taking a break from the intensity of demon-hunting. Things don't really turn out the way they want though and Sam's R&R is interleaved with solving the mystery of the killings. It's these aspects that add to the overall believability of the show – who hasn't wanted a breather from the day job at some point? This won't be the last time they try to take a break either, and somehow it's always Dean who voices the need for a break first – curious, given he's more keen on the hunting than Sam ...

The object of the hunt this time is another ghost, the staple *Supernatural* adversary[83], and we're treated to yet another interesting variation that plays more like a murder mystery story with a few gory bits, than straight horror.

And while they're collecting the clues to solve the mystery, Dean is also helping his brother through some significant character development. Dean has already established himself as a ladies man, but he's getting concerned that Sam needs to move on. It's now about a year since Sam lost Jessica and he's shown no interest in other women yet – he even backed off when looker Lori gave him a huge sloppy kiss in 'Hookman' (1-07).

When Sam and Sarah are clearly attracted to each other, Dean goes out of his way to get them together – he even goes on his own to do the research into the county death certificates to find Isaiah's body so they can spend more time together.

For Sam, his women problems are complex. First, he doesn't particularly want to get involved with someone when he knows he's just going to leave them behind when he moves on. He seems to form deeper relationships with women than his brother and the constant travelling will hurt Sam each time he has to leave.

Secondly, Jessica's memory is still fairly fresh in his mind, and getting involved with another woman probably feels like a betrayal of that memory. But Dean helps Sam by pointing out that Jessica would want him to have fun, and Sam takes another step through the grieving process by admitting that Dean is right.

But Sam's issues go deeper. The two most significant women in his life – his mother and Jessica – have both died because of demons, and he carries around a huge amount of guilt, particularly for Jessica's death, which he feels he could have prevented because he'd been warned by his dreams. Sam desperately doesn't want anyone else to get hurt, so he stops himself from getting too involved, even when he's attracted to someone.

And even deeper down is Sam's belief that it's his fault that the women in his life

---

83 Eight of the episodes so far have featured our ethereal friends.

die. Not just that it's a side-effect of the job he and Dean do but that it is specifically his fault because he is cursed. He's subconsciously taken on responsibility for their deaths even though it isn't his to shoulder.

Even Sam's actions, in going back and snogging Sarah just before they leave, show that while he might be getting over Jessica's memory and wanting to get closer to other women, he probably still feels cursed – otherwise he wouldn't have waited until it was safe and they were just leaving before making his move with Sarah. It seems he believes his leaving will ultimately protect her, so he can risk expressing his feelings

Even though this depth makes the episode a worthy addition to the series, there's still an underlying sense of impatience building, because it lacks any hints about the other story arcs. It's highly probable that the writing team were aware of this, because the final three episodes of the season are going to be dedicated to John, and it's going to be spectacular …

VERDICT – 8 out of 10

EPISODE 1-20
DEAD MAN'S BLOOD

TRANSMISSION DATES
US first aired: 20 April 2006
UK first aired: 5 June 2006

CREDITS
Writer: Cathryn Humphris & John Shiban
Director: Tony Wharmby

RECURRING ROLE
Jeffrey Dean Morgan (John Winchester)

GUEST STARS
Brenda Campbell (Beth), Christine Chatelain (Genny), Warren Christie (Luthor), Terence Kelly (Daniel Elkins), Anne Openshaw (Kate), Damon Runyan (Ted), Sean Tyson (Trucker), Dominic Zamprogna (Bo)

SYNOPSIS
A group of vampires attack and kill Daniel Elkins, an old vampire hunter, stealing an old Colt revolver from him. Elkins has left a message for John Winchester, and when Sam and Dean retrieve it, John turns up to see what it says. John needs the Colt to kill the demon that murdered Mary, and the Winchesters track the vampire's nest down to an abandoned barn. There, vampire leader Luthor is the new owner of the Colt. When the Winchesters fail to steal the gun back, John uses blood from a dead body to poison and capture Luthor's girlfriend. John offers to trade her for the Colt but Luthor knocks him unconscious. Sam and Dean arrive just in time to save John's life. It demonstrates to John how much he needs his boys with him, so he agrees to let them hunt Mary's killer with him.

CAN YOU SURVIVE TO THE TITLES?
Daniel Elkins is tracked down by the neck nibbling brigade and provides them with an early dinner in his own home. At least he manages to scratch the details of a Post Office box on the floor before croaking.

LOCATION, LOCATION, LOCATION
Manning, Colorado.

LEGENDARY ROOTS

The most famous origins of the vampire lore are from South-East Europe in the 18th Century, when the oral traditions were published for the first time. There are many different regional variations on what a vampire is, but similarities between them do occur within the folklore. It is said that vampires are the spirit of an evil being returning to possess a corpse, witches, suicide victims, victims of unnatural death or birth defects, or those conceived on certain days. It was the Romanian belief that those bitten by a vampire would become a vampire themselves after death.

Ways of protecting yourself against a vampire also differ between cultures and regions, but include garlic, holy water, the crucifix, and rosary beads. Vampires are said to be unable to walk on consecrated grounds, so churches are considered safe. The most popular ways of killing a vampire are a stake through the heart, decapitation and dismemberment.

Perhaps the most famous depiction of the modern-day vampire is from the 1897 novel *Dracula* by Bram Stoker, which draws on various aspects of folklore and has led to numerous novels and movies proliferating the vampire legend.

SQUEEZE OF THE WEEK

Dean offers to take Sam to see Sarah again[84] but they head off to find out what happened to Daniel Elkins instead – so no romance for anyone again this time.

SIBLING RIVALRY

There's no sibling rivalry going on at all this week, it's all Dad Rivalry as Sam tries to rip a strip off John Winchester instead. Despite their truce in 'Shadow' (1-16) the old animosity is still there, and it doesn't take long for it to flare up.

Dean finds himself playing referee as Sam vents his long-held bitterness about being told not to come back if he walks out of the door; and John counters with his own anger about Sam walking out on him and Dean when they needed him. You could almost see the emotional sparks flying!

BODY COUNT

After Daniel supplies the opening sequence snack, the vampires tuck into a man they kidnapped on the nearby highway for a little bit of supper. No-one else gets killed outright (except vampires) although technically the woman who was also kidnapped on the highway must have died at some point, since she was converted to a vampire during the night. (Dying is rarely straightforward on the show!)

---

84 From 'Provenance' (1-19).

TOOLKIT

- *Knives* feature heavily in the episode – mostly because you need to behead a vampire to kill it. Hence, Daniel Elkins has a *dagger with symbols engraved down the blade*, Sam and Dean both have *large machetes*, but John has the biggest blade of all. Boys and the size of their weapons, eh? Some things never change.

- Daniel Elkins has been using *lines of salt* to protect himself from evil – something Sam and Dean also found in John's motel room in 'Woman in White' (1-01).

- A *bottle of dead man's blood* is useful for those moments when you need only to incapacitate a vampire temporarily rather than kill it.

- *Crossbows* are the ideal way to introduce dead man's blood into a vampire's body.

- *Knowledge of what a three letter/six digit code might be* can help you find clues at the Post Office.

- And the soon-to-be-famous *Colt* is introduced in this episode. It was created in 1835 by Samuel Colt on the night when Halley's Comet was overhead and all those men died at the Alamo. It was made for a horse-riding demon-hunter and there were only 13 bullets ever made. Six of those were used before the gun disappeared but it eventually made its way into Daniel Elkins' hands. The gun has a protective star carved into the grip and *non timebo mala* – no evil will I fear – engraved down the barrel.

MEMORABLE MOMENTS

John Winchester finally sees sense and confesses that even though it scares the hell out of him because he could lose his boys, he can't deny that they are stronger working as a family. The hunt is on and they're all in it together at last.

SPOOK RULES

- Most vampire lore is untrue: crosses don't repel them; sunlight only hurts them like a bad sunburn; and a stake through the heart won't kill them.

- The bloodlust part is true – they need fresh human blood to survive.

- They look like ordinary people – although their eyes flash white if the light catches them – so you'll probably not realise they're a vampire until it's too late.

- Vampires have a second set of pointed teeth that descend over the top of their 'human' ones.

- They nest in groups of eight to ten and send small packs out to hunt for food.

- Victims are taken back to the nest, where they are kept alive and bled for food over days or weeks.

- They sleep during the day but that doesn't mean they won't wake up.

- Once a vampire gets your scent it's able to remember it for a lifetime. To block that scent, burn a mixture of saffron, skunk cabbage and trillium, then dust your clothes with the ashes.

- Vampires mate for life.
- Dead man's blood acts like a poison in a vampire's bloodstream but the sickness wears off after a while.
- The only way to kill a vampire is by beheading it.

DID YOU SPOT?
John has shaved off his beard[85] and is back to his sexy stubble[86].

GOING UNDERCOVER
John must have gone undercover when he was talking to the police to get more information about the kidnapped couple, but we're never told what disguise he used. For the first time, the boys don't use any kind of cover at all.

CULTURAL REFERENCES
Trucker in bar: 'I thought they caught the Unabomber.': Theodore Kaczynski, once America's most wanted criminal, was jailed for four terms of life in 1998 for sending 16 bombs during his bombing spree between 1978 to 1995 that left three dead and 23 injured. Kaczynski was dubbed the Unabomber by the press as the FBI used the handle 'UNABOM' ('UNiversity and Airline BOMber'). It wasn't excellent detective work that caught him though – Kaczynski's brother recognised the style of writing and beliefs in his *Industrial Society and Its Future* manifesto published by the *New York Times* and *The Washington Post*.

Dean: 'Sounds more like *That's Incredible* than *Twilight Zone*.': *That's Incredible* (1980-1984) was a US reality TV show where re-enactments of paranormal activity would take place and people would perform stunts, some of which producers deemed dangerous, including juggling with knives and a man catching bullets in his teeth. *The Twilight Zone* (1959-1964, 1985-1989, 2002-2003) was an anthology TV show that combined a mixture of horror, science fiction and thriller for its tales about unusual or extraordinary experiences.

Male voice over scanner: 'Copy that. Possible 207. Better get forensics out here.': 'A 207' is the police code for a kidnapping.

---

85 Last seen in 'Shadow' (1-16).

86 From 'Scarecrow' (1-11).

GOOFS AND FLUFFS

In John Winchester's journal, Daniel Elkins is listed without the 's' on the end of his surname.

When John knocks on the window of the Impala, the window is completely closed, when he gets in the car, the window is half open. When he gets out again, it is almost completely open. But you don't see or hear Dean opening the window at any point.

John says that the Colt was made in 1835, on the night that Halley's Comet was overhead and the men died at the Alamo. Halley's Comet was indeed visible in 1835 but the Battle of the Alamo took place in 1836.

HAVEN'T I SEEN YOU BEFORE?

Brenda Campbell was in *First Wave*, *Tru Calling* and *Snakehead Terror*. Christine Chatelain featured in *The Collector*, *Sanctuary* and *Andromeda*. Warren Christie has been in *Battlestar Galactica*, *Ghost Whisperer* and *Andromeda*. Anne Openshaw's credits include *Stargate: Atlantis*, *Mutant X* and *Earth: Final Conflict*. Sean Tyson was in *Stargate SG-1*, *BattleQueen 2020* and *The 4400*. Dominic Zamprogna played James 'Jammer' Lyman in *Battlestar Galactica* and *The Resistance* and appeared in *Tru Calling* and *Stargate: Atlantis*.

Terence Kelly also appears in 'Time Is On My Side' (3-15)

BEHIND THE SCENES

The Colt turned out to be one of the most important props of Season One. Property master Chris Cooper explained in the *Season One Supernatural Companion* that the first gun was a powder and cap type but his team went on to make a second revolver, the montage of which appeared in the show. Cooper's crew also engraved the numbers into the 13 silver bullets, along with the pentagram on the gun and the Latin words on the barrel.

MUSICAL INTERLUDE

- 'House is Rocking' – Stevie Ray Vaughan – when Daniel Elkins is in the bar at start of the episode.
- 'Searching For the Truth' – Brian Keith Nutter – while Sam and Dean sit in the diner looking for the next job.
- 'Trailer Trash' – 88 Crash – when John explains vampire lore to Sam and Dean.
- 'Strange Face of Love' – Tito And Tarantula – while the victims are tied up in barn and the vampires are partying.

ANALYSIS

The first iconic monsters to appear in the show, vampires get the *Supernatural* makeover to give them a fresh and more realistic feel. By throwing out a lot of the traditional vampire characteristics and killing methods, the programme-makers bring the vampire to a simpler, more frightening position. These are creatures that look human and for the most part act human, and there's no escape from them using sunlight or stakes. You're not going to realise what they are until it's too late, and then their superior strength and senses will swing the advantage in their favour.

Their normalness is emphasised in their attitudes too – they don't want to be hunted, they don't want to bring attention to themselves, they want to be left alone because, as Luthor puts it, they've as much right to live as everyone else. It's an intelligent interpretation of a vampire's world that keeps away from *Buffy*-style comparisons and gives the Winchesters a significant challenge.

Not that they need it, since the challenges within their own family seem to be more than enough to keep them fully occupied. We've been bursting with impatience to discover more about John's story, and 'Dead Man's Blood' starts filling in the gaps. The back-story to the Colt is told and its power demonstrated when John kills Luthor with it to save Sam, but as always with *Supernatural* it's the interaction between the characters that gives a rich depth to the story.

We finally get to meet John Winchester properly and he starts out as the gruff drill sergeant we've been led to believe he is, barking out his orders with no explanation and picking fault with his boys. ('Dean, why don't you touch up your car before you get rust?') But Sam's repeated outbursts make John think again, and he realises that he can't keep treating the boys as if they were still young kids. He decides to explain about the Colt and then goes further and explains his reasons for getting mad at Sam when he left for college. It takes John a while to get around to what he really wants to say – since he doesn't seem to discuss emotional stuff with anyone very often (wonder where Dean gets it from?) – but the conversation results in a long-overdue reconciliation with Sam.

It's Sam's behaviour that causes this change in John. Sam might have started to appreciate his father's point of view but he can't stand being kept in the dark and being expected to follow orders blindly. The eventual face-off between Sam and John results in Sam summing up what he believes the true problem is: that John is angry because he can't control Sam anymore. John later admits that he thinks the problem is that he can't accept that Sam and he are just different. They make their peace once John accepts Sam as he is, and Sam realises that they actually have quite a lot in common after Mary's and Jessica's deaths.

And if you think Dean has been a bit left out with all these exchanges going on between John and Sam, you're very wrong – because in his typical, quiet, Dean-style way he's started his own process of growth that is fundamental to his relationship with John. Dean has always been daddy's little trooper, eager to please him as a youngster and obedient as an adult. He doesn't like to see the two people that matter most in his life at each other's throats regularly, and he adopts the peacekeeper role between Sam and John. Up to this point, he's always sided with John, even as far as letting John leave at the end of 'Shadow' (1-16) because they'd almost caused his death. But in 'Dead Man's Blood', Dean has not only seen how much stronger they are as a team but he's seen the changes in John (brought about by Sam's outbursts). This time he doesn't want John to leave them behind. When Dean changes his allegiance to side with Sam, it's a powerful moment that surprises both Sam and John; and while it takes the further event of Sam and Dean saving John's ass to fully convince John of the need to stick together, the moment signifies a shift inside Dean from unquestioning son to an independent person in his own right. Dean will continue to grow in this new direction in the future.

The Winchesters are no longer the people we met at the start of the series. They're stronger when they're working together; and it's just as well given the coming storm.

VERDICT – 8 out of 10

EPISODE 1-21 SALVATION
EPISODE 1-22 DEVIL'S TRAP

TRANSMISSION DATES

Salvation
US first aired: 27 April 2006
UK first aired: 12 May 2006
Devil's Trap
US first aired: 4 May 2006
UK first aired: 19 May 2006

CREDITS

Salvation
Writer: Sera Gamble & Raelle Tucker
Director: Robert Singer
Devil's Trap
Writer: Eric Kripke
Director: Kim Manners

RECURRING ROLES

Jeffrey Dean Morgan (John Winchester), Nicki Aycox (Meg Masters), Jim Beaver (Bobby Singer)

GUEST STARS

Salvation
Josh Blacker (Caleb), David Lovgren (Charlie Holt), Erin Karpluk (Monica Holt), Rondel Reynoldson (Nurse), Richard Sali (Pastor Jim Murphy), Sebastian Spence (Tom), Serinda Swan (Nurse)
Devil's Trap
Chad Bellamy (Mechanic), Guy Brews (Husband), Monique Ganderton (Wife), Matt Riley (Firefighter), Sebastian Spence (Tom)

SYNOPSIS

The demons want the Colt from John Winchester, and Meg starts killing his friends to convince him to hand it over. After Pastor Jim and Caleb have had their throats slit, John agrees to hand over the gun, alone, in Lincoln, but he takes a fake gun along instead.

The real gun is left with Sam and Dean because, with the help of Sam's visions, the Winchesters have finally predicted which family will be visited by the yellow-eyed demon next. They save the family but don't kill the demon, wasting a precious Colt bullet in the process.

Meanwhile, Meg has discovered that the Colt John gave her is a fake, and John has been captured.

The boys seek help at Bobby's. Meg follows them there but gets trapped, and the boys exorcise her demon. As the real Meg dies, she tells them where their father is. Sam and Dean leave for Jefferson City to rescue him. They set off the fire alarm in the building where he is being held, then pose as firemen to gain access. As they escape, Dean has to use another bullet from the Colt to stop a demon from beating Sam to death.

Escaping to an isolated shack, Dean realises that John is possessed. The yellow-eyed demon pins both boys to the wall. As it starts to cut Dean up from the inside out, Dean begs his father to take control back. John does this momentarily, giving Sam time to shoot John in the leg. To kill the demon, Sam would have to kill his father – which he can't do – so the demon escapes. As Sam drives the injured John and Dean to the hospital, their car is hit by a high speed truck with a demon at the wheel ...

CAN YOU SURVIVE TO THE TITLES?
Pastor Jim Murphy may have had a huge armoury hidden in the vestry but it doesn't save him from getting his throat cut by Meg.

LOCATION, LOCATION, LOCATION
Blue Earth, Minnesota; Manning, Colorado; Lincoln, Nebraska; Salvation, Iowa; Jefferson City, Missouri; Unknown rural locations in South Dakota and Missouri

LEGENDARY ROOTS
A demon in Christian terms is a fallen angel from heaven, the greatest being Lucifer, the name frequently given to Satan. Lucifer ruled over the Earth while he was on it, but because of pride, he and one third of the angels rebelled against God and rose up to attack heaven – only to be cast down.

The study of demonology is wide and varied and many writers have tried to depict and describe the various levels of demons.

Alfonso de Spina classified the following in 1467:
- Fates, who alter destiny
- Poltergeists, who cause mischief
- Incubi and Succubi, who stimulate lust and perversion

169

- Marching Hordes, who bring about war
- Familiars, who assist witches
- Nightmares, who disturb sleep through bad dreams
- Demons formed from human semen
- Disguised demons
- Demons who assail the saintly
- Demons who instigate witchcraft

In Francis Barrett's *The Magus* (1801) there's a different set:

- Mammon: seducers
- Asmodai: vile revenges
- Satan: witches and warlocks
- Pithius: liars and liar spirits
- Belial: fraud and injustice
- Merihem: pestilences and spirits that cause pestilences
- Abaddon: war, evil against good
- Astaroth: inquisitors and accusers

Other notable descriptions on demon hierarchy are in Francesco Maria Guazzo's *Compendium Maleficarum* (1608) and Sebastien Michaelis's *Admirable History* (1613).

Demonic possession occurs where a demon inhabits a human body rendering the human soul helpless to use their own free will. The human will often lose memory and personality traits, faint and have fits. Being unable to control the demon, they will also be unable to expel the demon of their own accord, and an exorcism is required.

SQUEEZE OF THE WEEK

Nothing will distract the Winchesters from killing the yellow-eyed demon now – well, except the cute nurse at the hospital who manages to catch Dean's eye for a moment. No change there then.

SIBLING RIVALRY

They say you take your problems out on those closest to you and Dean certainly gets both barrels from Sam this time. All of Sam's frustrations get vented at Dean when the yellow-eyed demon gets away again and Sam loses his chance to end it all but Dean's not completely sorry. He can see that both Sam and their father are willing to sacrifice their lives in order to finish this demon off. He tells Sam he's selfish and refuses to be the one to bury them both.

Later on, Sam does at least eat a little humble pie after Dean saves his life by shooting the demon that is beating Sam to a bloody pulp. Sam's apology is heartfelt, and despite Dean still taking time to score a point about being right to bring the Colt along, he's reasonably gracious in his reply too.

BODY COUNT

A second friend of John's, Caleb, suffers the same fate as Pastor Jim. Meg slits his throat and lets John hear his death throes over the phone.

Technically (it's getting complicated again), an innocent man dies when Dean shoots him through the head. The demon possessing the man dies at the same time. Meanwhile, the real Meg Masters draws her last few breaths after her demon is exorcised, the fall from the seven-storey building[87] proving fatal at last. She is kind enough to give the boys some useful info before she pops her clogs completely though.

And of course, after the road accident, it's not clear whether any of the Winchesters are alive or dead as the final credits roll.

TOOLKIT

- It wasn't a good time for Pastor Jim to discover that *a large throwing knife* wouldn't be enough to stop a powerful demon.
- He should have tried the *holy water* that John uses instead. And John has *Mandaic amulets* on hand as well as a back up. The Mandaean faith pre-dates Islam and Christianity and is based on pacifism. It began in what is now Iraq before the birth of Christ. The followers' amulets are inscribed with prayers that protect the bearer against evil spirits.
- A *rosary* and the appropriate *ritual* have the ability to bless water, thereby converting it to holy water. So you'd best gen up on both if you're walking into a trap.
- The *Rituale Romanum* exorcism rites get dusted off and brought back out of the closet. They've not been used since 'Phantom Traveler' (1-04). Unlike the *EMF meter* and the *salt*, which have been used almost everywhere.
- And keep the supernatural Colt nearby cause it's the only way to save your brother from certain death at the hands of a demon.

MEMORABLE MOMENTS

A double episode with so many memorable moments that it's difficult to pick out just a few of the best, but here goes:

John's emotional reaction to Pastor Jim's death and John's need to end it all now. Followed by his reinforcement of this desire after Caleb is killed. This latest death hits hard and John's weariness with hunting and losing loved ones and friends is heart-

---

87 In 'Shadow' (1-16).

breakingly obvious.

When Meg finally catches up with Sam and Dean at Bobby's place, she walks into Bobby's with one of the best demon speeches ever. Actress Nicki Aycox delivers an outstanding performance in this finale. She may be a slim lass in a leather jacket walking into a room with three large, strong blokes, but she still succeeds in being dangerously intimidating, driving the words 'underwhelmed' and 'chuckleheads' home to the hilt with a sharp, crisp style. Gorgeous stuff.

And the whole final showdown between Sam, Dean and John (possessed by the yellow-eyed demon) is just awesome from start to finish.

On the lighter side, you can't help but notice that John Winchester is tied to the bed part of the time and the boys are running around in firemen's uniforms too. That'll keep the fetishists quiet for a while.

MOTEL MAYHEM
Dead animal trophies on the wall seem to be popular in the motels used by the Winchesters. John is staying in stuffed head central when he finally shows the boys his research into the yellow-eyed demon – and the boys had similar décor in the Escanaba Motel in Michigan too[88].

SPOOK RULES
- In the days before the yellow-eyed demon turns up at a house, the signs of his coming include cattle deaths, temperature fluctuations and electrical storms.
- Demonic possession leaves traces of sulphur behind, even if the demon is travelling in someone else's body. The rule was established in 'Phantom Traveler' (1-04).
- Demons have different levels of power. Black-eyes are able to walk on hallowed ground but are harmed by holy water. The more powerful yellow-eyed ones are immune to holy water and hallowed ground. However, both can be killed using the Colt and its bullets.
- All yellow- and black-eyed demons have superhuman strength and can pin people to the walls without touching them.
- Demons can be trapped within protective symbols – which also seem to stop their ability to pin people to walls without touching them.
- Demons are sent back to hell using the Latin exorcism rite from the *Rituale Romanum*.

---

88 In 'Nightmare' (1-14).

- Some symbols will stop a demon getting through or inside an object (like the trunk of a car).

DID YOU SPOT?

This is the first episode to feature the words 'The Road So Far' in the recap at the start and 'To Be Continued' at the end.

This is the first time we meet hunter Bobby Singer – named after *Supernatural's* executive producer Robert Singer. Bobby's house not only looks cluttered but do you realise that there are between five and six thousand books stacked up in his rooms?

Completing the hat-trick of firsts, the quaint phrase 'meat-suit' makes its debut, uttered by the yellow-eyed demon in possession of John Winchester. The phrase will pop up several times in the future, most notably at the start of Season Four.

The knife that Pastor Jim throws at Meg in the church has the words 'God's Eye' engraved on it. The God's Eye, which is believed to originate with the Huichol people of North-Western Mexico, is symbolic of the power of seeing and understanding the unknowable. Given that the inscription can be seen only on freeze-frame, you start to get an idea of how much care and attention goes into the fine details on this show.

At some time, John Winchester has stayed in a Sleep Easy Motel, because he has headed notepaper from there that has been modified to the Sleep Uneasy Motel.

There's a copy of Danielle Steele's novel *Secrets* on the shelf in John's motel room with his research books. The old romantic!

Dean is bleeding heavily from his chest as the yellow-eyed demon sets about killing him slowly – this won't be the last time Dean will suffer an injury like this but it'll take another two seasons to get there.

GOING UNDERCOVER

In order to find the family in Salvation who will be visited next by the demon, John goes undercover as a medic; and Sam and Dean pretend to be police officers.

Later, after John has been captured, Dean masquerades as a resident of Sunrise Apartments with a nervous dog. Then both he and Sam enter the apartment building disguised as firemen.

CULTURAL REFERENCES

Meg: 'There's a warehouse in Lincoln on the corner of Wabash and Lake.': Wabash and Lake is an exit in *The Matrix* (1999) where Neo exits the Matrix for the last time before the flying sequence.

Dean: 'Oh we're going for it, baby – head spinning, projectile vomiting, the whole nine yards.': Another reference to *The Exorcist* (1973). Young Regan (Linda Blair) does the head spinning and projectile vomiting as the possessed lead character in the movie.

Bobby's dog is called Rumsfeld – probably after Donald Henry Rumsfeld (born 9 July 1932), who was the thirteenth and twenty-first US Secretary of Defense. Rumsfeld resigned in 2006 after several controversial years overseeing two wars in the wake of the 9/11 terrorist attacks.

Meg: 'Still there, John-boy?': John-boy was a character in *The Waltons*, the US television series that ran from 1972 to 1981 with three TV movie sequels broadcast in 1982 and three more following in the 1990s.

Sam is impressed by one of Bobby's rare books, Bobby: 'Key of Solomon? It's the real deal, all right.': *The Key of Solomon* (Clavicula Salomonis) is divided into two books and contains the conjurations and invocations to summon spirits of the dead or from hell and protect the conjurer (termed 'exorcist') from them and against an attempt of possession. There are also curses to compel reluctant spirits to obey.

The last music track playing before the car crash at the end – Creedence Clearwater Revival, 'Bad Moon Rising' – was also used in *An American Werewolf in London*, one of creator Eric Kripke's favourite movies.

GOOFS AND FLUFFS

John acts like he doesn't know anything about Sam's psychic abilities, but back in 'Home' (1-09), he heard Missouri say, 'That boy – he has such powerful abilities. But why he couldn't sense his own father, I have no idea,' so he should already have some inkling that Sam can do some strange things. It's not like you'd forget something like that about your own son[89].

When Dean saves Sam by shooting the demon in the head with the Colt, the demon's body ends up lying with the legs on top of Sam's legs, but in the next shot the body is suddenly further away from Sam and the legs aren't overlapping anymore.

When possessed John is killing Dean, the blood starts pouring down Dean's chest and from his mouth. In the next shot, the blood on Dean's chin is gone. Aw, nice of dad to wipe it off for him.

HAVEN'T I SEEN YOU BEFORE?

Salvation

Josh Blacker's credits include *Stargate Universe*, *Painkiller Jane* and *Blood Ties*. David Lovgren was in *Smallville*, *The Outer Limits* and *The X-Files*. Erin Karpluk was in *Bionic*

---

89 Given events in the comic series *Supernatural: Rising Son*, it's clear that John is in full possession of the facts but is just a good liar when discussing it with his sons.

Woman, Jeramiah and *Taken*. Rondel Reynoldson's credits include *Taken, Tru Calling* and *Millennium*. Richard Sali featured in *Friday the 13th: The Series, Animorphs* and *Total Recall 2070*. Serinda Swan appeared in *Blood Ties, Reaper* and *Smallville*.

Devil's Trap

Matt Riley was in *Zombie Town*. Sebastian Spence played Lt Noel 'Narcho' Allison in *Battlestar Galactica* and Cade Foster in *First Wave*.

Monique Ganderton also appears in 'Hunted' (2-10) and 'Magnificent Seven' (3-01).

Behind the Scenes

In *The Official Supernatural Magazine #1*, special effects supervisor Randy Shymkiw, said that the climactic crash in the Impala was probably the hardest, most stressful stunt they'd ever done. The Impala ran on a 600 foot track and the truck had to hit it dead centre, after which they released it. Getting the timing right releasing the Impala proved to be the most difficult task.

Jeffrey Dean Morgan was glad he finally got the chance to take on the demons. It really was time to kick-ass after all the apologising that had been going on. He said that he enjoyed playing Cowboys and Indians and since John Winchester was the ultimate cowboy, it was a dream job playing him. [*The Official Supernatural Magazine #2*]

Meanwhile, Nicki Aycox shared some behind the scenes insights in *The Official Supernatural Magazine #7* about filming the exorcism scene. When it was Jim Beaver's turn to get his shots, Aycox and Ackles were doing their parts for him while the camera focused on Beaver's face. But despite Aycox and Ackles laughing through the entire filming, Beaver just kept going like a trooper. Even director Manners asked him how he had managed to keep a straight face.

Eric Kripke revealed in *The Official Supernatural Magazine #4* that he should have followed Kim Manners advice and not killed Meg off. He just made the best decision he could, with the resources he had at the time.

Musical Interlude

Salvation

- 'Carry On My Wayward Son' – Kansas – playing over the episode recap at the start.

Devils Trap

- 'Fight The Good Fight' – Triumph – playing over the episode recap.
- 'Turn To Stone' – Joe Walsh – when Sam and Dean are driving to Bobby's.
- 'Bad Moon Rising' – Credence Clearwater Revival – when Sam, Dean and John are driving to the hospital and get hit by the lorry.

ANALYSIS

It's a resounding end to the series – full of action, brimming with emotion and beset with twisting storylines. There's an excellent chemistry between the three male leads and together they manage to become more than the sum of the parts, each one drawing the best out of the others. Their scenes are compelling and that's due to equal measures of top performances and excellent writing.

The writers have never taken their eye off the ball and the overall structure of the story has never been neglected. That's been reflected in the cohesion running through the series that has been achieved by repeating symbols and situations. The strongest one in the finale comes after Sam has failed to kill the demon and he turns his anger on Dean[90]. Dean reminds Sam that no matter what they do now, Mary and Jessica are gone and they're never coming back. Sam grabs Dean by the front of the shirt and slams him against the wall with the words, 'Don't say that!' It's the mirror of the scene played out on the bridge in the Pilot episode before Jessica's death, but now with the boys in reverse roles. This subconsciously brings the viewer full circle, recalling that what's happening started way back in episode one and we're still seeing the ramifications of those events now. What has happened before hasn't just been a string of unrelated monster-of-the-week adventures, it's been a very definite path leading to this point.

And the character development continues in this final double episode too. The differences between Sam and Dean are highlighted once more, mostly outside Monica's house when they are waiting for the demon to arrive. Dean wishes that he was backing their dad up, while Sam wishes their dad was backing them up. Dean's focus is more on ensuring that their dad is okay while Sam wants to be doubly sure they get the demon while they have the chance. And having John backing them up also implies that he's not walking into a trap in Lincoln either, so Sam's wishes (as well as Dean's) imply he wants their dad safe as well.

Before long, Sam is doing the whole 'If anything happens tonight, then you need to know …' speech to Dean, indicating that he's unsure what the night's outcome will be and he's trying to be realistic about it all. Dean however refuses to believe that anyone will die that night, demonstrating the same attitude we saw when he interrogates Meg and insists that John *can't* be dead. While believing that you are going to succeed in a task is essential to achieving it, with Dean this also seems to be part of his coping mechanism in stressful circumstances – total denial of anything bad happening.

We find out more about Dean's personality as he tries to look after those he loves. He is the rational voice and the most objective point of view. He's the only one who

---

90 See the **Sibling Rivalry** section for details.

doesn't think killing the demon is worth dying for, and he's trying to convince both John and Sam to see things differently, because he doesn't want to lose them. He also won't let Sam take the burden of responsibility for their mother's death, trying to reduce his brother's suffering. And last but not least, Dean is growing – he's finally freeing himself from his father's influence – which is obvious when John insists Dean should have called him and Dean answers him back angrily, citing all the times they had indeed tried to call their father but finding they had a better chance of winning the lottery instead.

John doesn't particularly like Dean's new attitude but he's big enough a man to admit that Dean has a point and their relationship shifts, influenced by John's desertion of Dean and Dean's exposure to, and new understanding of, Sam's opinions.

But, for a change, it's the story arcs that see the most movement of all.

For John, we finally find out why he left and how he's been tracking the demon. We discover how he truly feels about the life he's led and passed on to his boys. He's a quiet, haunted man with a few very close, trusted friends. John feels their loss deeply and automatically shoulders the grief and guilt for causing their deaths (a trait he seems to have shared with Sam particularly).

And for Sam, even though his powers curiously fail him when faced with the yellow-eyed demon, he does at least get some answers – and a whole duffle-bag full of new questions too. The demon tells Sam and Dean that their mother and Jessica were killed because they were in the way of his plans for Sam and all the other children he's 'visited'. But there's no more clarification on what the plans are or how many other children are affected, or whether they've all lost their mothers and inherited strange powers. And why has the demon started visiting children again, 23 years after he came to Sam? Or did John miss any earlier signs of the demon? Has he been visiting children non-stop for two decades?

But of course the two biggest outstanding questions after this series are: have the Winchesters survived the crash?; and what is going to happen to the Impala?

It was a blessed relief that the series got picked up for a second season with all this still left unresolved. That second season will certainly be answering some of those questions but it will also be taking the story to places that no-one could have predicted.

VERDICT – 10 out of 10

SEASON TWO OVERVIEW

Was the exceptional quality of Season One just a fluke? Did the studio suits just happen to be distracted when the *Supernatural* scripts went over their desks? Would they now suddenly start to notice this dark, gruesome, exciting series that was daring to develop its characters and experiment with its narrative? Worse, would they decide to stamp on its vital spark of creativity and force it into safe, stifling, boring stories?

Nope. Nope. Nope. And nope.

Thank God[91] for that.

Which means that Season Two arrives brimming with thrills and humour, emotional depth and moral conundrums[92], a large and varied line-up of ghosts and a dark smattering of demons, demi-gods and dead things. Yay!

It's a season of two halves, featuring one helluva lot of damp eyes and sniffles. The opening episode sets up the first half-season story arc as the boys experience the huge emotional wrench of watching their dad die[93] (pass the tissues someone?). Then the focus of the episodes hovers around Sam and particularly Dean dealing with the grief (or not dealing with it, as the case maybe) as they get used to life without John Winchester's influence.

Along with the burden of his grief, Dean is also trying to rationalise the whispered instructions from his dad just before he died. By mid-season he can't shoulder the burden any longer and finally reveals to Sam[94] that John told him to save his brother and failing that to kill him.

The focus now slides smoothly over to Sam as we get to see his angst about turning evil, and we're given a very real example of what it would be like if he did go darkside in 'Born Under A Bad Sign' (2-14).

The angst continues through the late middle season, as we're taken through a series of quality stand-alone episodes before the intense and tear-jerking (more tissues!) 'What Is And What Should Never Be' (2-20) throws some light on Dean's issues about hunting and the inherent sacrifices involved in the job.

Then the season finale kicks in as we discover exactly what the yellow-eyed demon has been planning for his psychic kids, and a minor bloodbath ensues at the deserted Cold Oak township as the kids fight it out to become the leader of the demonic army[95].

---

91 Please do insert the name of any God you hold dear.

92 That Sera Gamble lass has been at it again ...

93 In 'In My Time Of Dying' (2-01).

94 In 'Hunted' (2-10).

95 In 'All Hell Breaks Loose, Part One' (2-21).

The intensity increases as Sam dies at the hands of Jake and a desolate Dean faces an impossible decision about saving his brother (jeez, where are those tissues again?). Dean does a deal with a crossroads demon to resurrect Sam and it's showdown time as the yellow-eyed head honcho is finally killed and John Winchester's soul freed from hell[96]. So it's cheers all round until Sam realises why he's still alive and everyone (Ellen and Bobby included) realises the magnitude of the coming fight against an army of demons.

DEAN'S GRIEF AND DAD'S LAST REQUEST

So how is Season Two for Dean? Pretty traumatic overall given that his entire remaining family is killed – John at the start and Sam at the end. So grief is a pretty significant emotion for him this season. Then he's trying to cope with the message from his dad and the prospect that he may have to kill his brother at some point, and finally he's questioning why he's hunting at all.

Taking the first of Dean's issues – dealing with his grief for his dad – it's a life changing moment. Ever since the fire at the house that killed his mother, he has faithfully followed his dad's orders[97] and now he's cut adrift and directionless. He tries to fill the gap in his life with someone else he might be able to respect: fellow hunter Gordon. Dean faces a choice when he meets Gordon: become more like Gordon and kill every unnatural creature you find without thinking about it; or stick with Sam and a more humane and thoughtful approach to hunting. Dean eventually chooses to stay with Sam, so he has to try to find another way to deal with the huge sense of loss.

Within that sense of loss is Dean's anger at his dad – demonstrated when he crowbars the Impala – and also his sense of guilt – which underlies his admission to Sam that their dad is dead because of him[98]. When they discover the deal that John made to save Dean, there's nothing Sam can say to relieve Dean's pain at knowing that he lives because of John's selfless death[99].

On top of his grief, Dean is struggling with the possibility of having to kill Sam. When his brother is close to dying from the Croatoan virus, Dean hints about carrying around a weight of responsibility. Then, when Sam proves immune to the bug, he calls Dean out on what he's keeping secret. Dean reluctantly tells him, but seems quietly relieved to have done so. Now he can keep an open eye on his brother in case he

---

96 In 'All Hell Breaks Loose, Part Two' (2-22).

97 Okay, with the exception of leaving his brother alone one night as explained in 'Something Wicked' (1-18).

98 In 'Children Shouldn't Play With Dead Things' (2-04).

99 In 'Crossroad Blues' (2-08).

turns darkside and support him through the upcoming angst and revelation with the yellow-eyed demon.

And there's another emotional aspect that Dean is dealing with, underlying all the grief and responsibility for his brother. His dad is gone and with him went the driving force behind the hunting. Now Dean starts to question why they take all these risks and whether the payback is worth it. Dean's internal dilemma shows through when he suggests lying low for a while. He just wants to take a break and do some sightseeing for a change[100]. You get to see just how deep his questioning goes when he enters the Wish World[101] and gets the life he's always wanted. But even Dean knows the WishWorld is a lie, and he returns to reality a little wiser about how much his brother and saving people's lives really mean to him.

Just how important his brother is to him is illustrated in the final episode when he sacrifices his life (plus one year) to bring his brother back from the dead. He has already shown inclinations towards this kind of deal[102] so it comes as no surprise that he's ready to go through with it given the right motivations. But at least he lives long enough to complete one life-long task: putting a bullet between the eyes of the yellow-eyed demon, with a little help from his dad who is now free of hell too.

So Dean ends the year getting some long-overdue revenge for his mom and for Sam's Jessica. It remains to be seen if he can save himself from a fiery trip down under.

SAM'S POWERS

Sam's past truly starts to catch up with him in this season, but the answers come in little pieces that have to be put together like a jigsaw, and it takes some time for the final piece to fall into place.

In the meantime, Sam has to deal with his dad's death. On top of the expected grief, he also has to try to help Dean. Sam has to be strong for his brother and set aside his own feelings, despite any doubts he may have about what the demon told him. And indeed, through the first half of Season Two Sam is always there, revealing only a few small glimpses of his own grief through the curtain of brotherly concern.

By far the biggest impact of John's death is Sam's apparent conversion to being a career hunter, trying to fulfil every dream his father ever had for him. Dean rightly spots this and confronts Sam about it[103], allowing Sam's guilt over his arguments with his dad – especially during their last conversation – to be dealt with.

It's that situation between Sam and John that makes Sam's journey through the

100 In 'Hollywood Babylon' (2-18).

101 In 'What Is And What Should Never Be' (2-20).

102 In 'Crossroad Blues' (2-08).

grief a little easier than Dean's. Sam has been pushing very hard against his dad's whole regime for years and suddenly all that resistance has gone. That rebellious streak defined aspects of Sam's personality as much as Dean's obedience defined aspects of his, and now they both have to redefine themselves. Dean tries to fill the hole in his life with Gordon, Sam tries to be a good hunter, but both of these are rebound attempts, and further soul-searching is required. Dean can't replace his dad, so he has to fundamentally change his outlook and start to trust his own abilities more. Sam has already changed at a deep level, when Jessica died and he had to return to hunting and discard his ideas of a normal life. Once Dean reveals what John whispered to him[104] and Sam becomes more aware of the yellow-eyed demon's plans for him, it's easy for him just to transform his earlier resistance to his dad's wishes into resisting the demon's intentions for him. Sam then continues relatively unchanged.

That doesn't mean Sam has no difficulties whatsoever. Coping with the evil inside him and his own potential actions drives him to drink at one point[105] and even gives him romantic issues at other times[106]. Then he's in the front seat on an evil joyride with the Meg demon[107] and gets a preview of what his life could become if he chooses that darker path.

By now the brothers are both becoming more isolated from support, but particularly Sam. The police are searching for them[108] – something that escalates when the FBI and Henricksen wade in[109] – and the Roadhouse becomes out of bounds when they learn that their dad had a part in Ellen's husband's death[110]. Then Gordon starts gunning for Sam[111], and the general hunting community becomes dangerous for them both when Possessed Sam kills another hunter[112]. Meanwhile, there's also Dean, who's getting freaked out by Sam's powers, especially when he turns out to be immune to the Croatoan virus[113].

So for the latter half of the season they're off on single hunting trips together and

103 In 'Everybody Loves A Clown' (2-02)

104 In 'Hunted' (2-10)

105 In 'Playthings' (2-11)

106 In 'Heart' (2-17)

107 In 'Born Under A Bad Sign' (2-14)

108 In 'The Usual Suspects' (2-07)

109 In 'Nightshifter' (2-12)

110 In 'No Exit' (2-06)

111 In 'Hunted' (2-10)

112 In 'Born Under A Bad Sign' (2-14)

113 In 'Croatoan' (2-09)

taking down monsters while the psychic kids storyline remains an irregular pulse, beating here and there underneath all the people getting saved and the ongoing family business.

And then, like a slap in face, it's time for Sam to stare down his destiny, when the yellow-eyed demon deposits him in a deserted town with only a handful of psychic kids to battle it out with. To Sam's credit, he doesn't defect to the darkside and punches it out in a brutal fight against Jake to prove his point. And he almost does so successfully, except for a knife in the spinal cord when he turns his back on his downed opponent.

By the time Dean has brought him back from the other side and Sam has realised what has happened, Sam is starting out on a completely new journey that will take him through Season Three and beyond.

BEHIND THE SCENES

In the *Season Two Supernatural Companion*, Eric Kripke indicated that this season was a turning point for the show. When John made the deal to exchange his own life for Dean's he went against the natural order of things – and that was always the one thing the Winchesters had fought to maintain: keep the natural order, nobody gets to play God. But John's decision put his family on a very difficult path.

And it was to be a winding road indeed. It started in the writers' room as they threw out all the previous episode formulae they had been using and wheeled in a brand new batch of episode structures and invented different approaches to demons, both internal and external. This gave birth to episodes like 'Crossroads Blues' (2-08), opening in and linked to the 1930s; the claustrophobic 'Nightshifter' (2-12), set mainly in the bank; and the backward reconstruction of events in 'Born Under A Bad Sign' (2-14); along with the more philosophical look at Sam's internal darkness in 'Heart' (2-17).

Eric Kripke commented in the *Season Two Supernatural Companion* that Dean's character wouldn't let the writers move him in any other direction until he'd sorted out all his grief issues; and also that he felt that they had done Sam a small disservice, because the only time they dealt with his grief was in 'Everybody Loves A Clown' (2-02), which showed his desire to be daddy's little hunter. By the time they realised the omission it was episode eight or so and the focus was due to change as Dean revealed John's whispered legacy. Sam did get a fair share of focus on his emotional condition as he wrestled with his dark-destiny-versus-free-will problem, although Kripke said in the *Season Two Supernatural Companion* that, given another shot at it, he would have had Sam doing less hand-wringing and more evil.

By now, the crew were working together smoothly, the writers had more character history to write to and the actors were more comfortable in their characters' skins. So in the finale the writers confidently killed Sam and burned down the Roadhouse – the inclusion of the bar being an external suggestion from the studio that never quite fit the road trip dynamic of the show. Sam of course they subsequently brought back – because there would be a big missing dynamic without him.

All in all, the dangerous path the Winchesters are on is only partially revealed in Season Two, with Season Three (and beyond) going on to build on events so far. The yellow-eyed demon may finally be dead, but this season establishes one thing without a doubt: that the writers on *Supernatural* will happily conclude major story arcs and then ruthlessly move into even more emotionally challenging territories.

SUPERNATURAL SEASON TWO

SEASON CREDITS

Consulting Producer: Ben Edlund
Supervising Producer: Matt Witten
Supervising Producer: Phil Sgriccia
Co-Executive Producer: Peter Johnson
Executive Producer: John Shiban
Executive Producer: Kim Manner
Executive Producer: McG
Executive Producer: Eric Kripke
Executive Producer: Robert Singer
Produced By: Cyrus Yavne
Created By: Eric Kripke
Directed By: Kim Manners (2-01, 2-04, 2-06, 2-13, 2-17, 2-22)
Directed By: Phil Sgriccia (2-02, 2-12, 2-18)
Directed By: Robert Singer (2-03, 2-09, 2-21)
Directed By: Mike Rohl (2-07, 2-19)
Directed By: Charles Beeson (2-11, 2-16)
Associate Producer: Todd Aronauer
Story Editor: Sera Gamble
Story Editor: Raelle Tucker
Director of Photography: Serge Ladouceur, CSA
Production Designer: John Marcynuk
Production Designer: Jerry Wanek
Edited By: Anthony Pinker (2-02, 2-05, 2-08, 2-11, 2-14, 2-17, 2-20)
Edited By: Tom McQuade (2-03, 2-06, 2-09, 2-12, 2-15, 2-18, 2-21)
Edited By: David Ekstrom (2-01, 2-04, 2-07, 2-10, 2-13, 2-16, 2-19, 2-22)
Music By: Christopher Lennertz
Music By: Jay Gruska
Production Manager: George A Grieve
First Assistant Director: Kevin Parks
First Assistant Director: John MacCarthy
Second Assistant Director: Amanda Bartley
Second Assistant Director: Kim Marlatt
Casting By: Robert J Ulrich, CSA
Casting By: Eric Dawson, CSA
Casting By: Carol Kritzer, CSA

Canadian Casting By: Coreen Mayrs, CSA
Canadian Casting By: Heike Brandstatter, CSA
Original Casting: Patrick J Rush, CSA
Stunt Coordinator: Lou Bollo
Set Decorator: George Neuman
Property Master: Chris Cooper
Costume Design: Diane Widas
Key Make-up Artist: Shannon Choppin
Key Hair Stylist: Jeannie Chow
Special Effects Supervisor: Randy Shymkiw
Special Effects Make-up: Toby Lindala
Special Effects Make-up: The Schminken Collective Group Inc
Sound Mixer: Donald Painchaud
Re-Recording Mixers: Dennis Kirk
Re-Recording Mixers: Bill Jackson
Supervising Sound Editor: Michael E Lawshé
Music Editorial by: Final Note Productions
Music Supervisor: Alexandra Patsavas
Visual Effects by: Ivan Hayden
Visual Effects Producer: Grant Lindsay

ADDITIONAL EPISODE CREDITS

2-01
Post Production Supervisor: Kristin Cronin
Production Coordinator: Yale Hussin

2-02
Script Supervisor: Pam Lawrence
Post Production Coordinator: John Marby

2-03
Script Supervisor: Patti Henderson
Transport Coordinator: Mark Gould

2-04
Gaffer: Chris Cochrane
Key Grip: Harvey Fedor

2-05
Directed By: Tim Iacofano
Art Director: John Marcynuk
Location Manager: Russ Hamilton

2-06
Location Manager: Paul Lougheed
Construction Coordinator: Chris Sneddon

2-07
Script Supervisor: Pam Lawence
Production Coordinator: Yale Hussin

2-08
Direct By: Steve Boyum
Script Supervisor: Patti Henderson
Transport Coordinator: Mark Gould

2-09
Gaffer: Chris Cochrane
Key Grip: Harvey Fedor

2-10
Directed By: Rachel Talalay
Art Director: John Marcynuk
Post Supervisor: Kristin Cronin

2-11
Location Manager: Russ Hamilton
Construction Coordinator: Chris Sneddon

2-12
Location Manager: Paul Lougheed
Production Coordinator: Yale Hussin

2-13
Script Supervisor: Pam Lawence
Post Production Coordinator: John Marby

2-14
Directed By: J Miller Tobin
Construction Coordinator: Chris Sneddon
Script Supervisor: Patti Henderson

2-15
Directed By: Bradford May
Transport Coordinator: Mark Gould
Assistant Editor: Nicole Baer

2-16
Gaffer: Chris Cochrane
Assistant Editor: Michael Hall

2-17
Location Manager: Russ Hamilton
Assistant Editor: Bruce Gorman

2-18
Location Manager: Paul Lougheed
Key Grip: Harvey Fedor

2-19
Art Director: John Marcynuk
Production Coordinator: Yale Hussin

2-20
Directed By: Eric Kripke
Script Supervisor: Pam Lawence
Post Production Supervisor: John Mabry

2-21
Script Supervisor: Patti Henderson
Transport Coordinator: Mark Gould

2-22
Construction Coordinator: Chris Sneddon
Post Production Supervisor: Kristin Cronin

EPISODE 2-01
IN MY TIME OF DYING

TRANSMISSION DATES
US first aired: 28 September 2006
UK first aired: 13 July 2007

CREDITS
Writer: Eric Kripke
Director: Kim Manners

RECURRING ROLES
Jeffrey Dean Morgan (John Winchester), Jim Beaver (Bobby Singer), Fredric Lehne (Janitor-Yellow-eyed demon)

GUEST STARS
Nicola Anderson (Nurse), Pete Antico (Wounded Man), Daniel Bacon (Orderly), Sharon Bell (Perky Woman), Julian D Christopher (Doctor), Randal Edwards (EMT), Carrie Anne Fleming (Blonde Nurse), Sarah Groundwater (EMT), Marcel Mallard (Truck Driver), Lindsey McKeon (Tessa), Marsha Regis (Nurse), Benson Simmonds (EMT), Todd Woffinden (Doctor)

SYNOPSIS
A demon-driven truck has crashed into the Impala, running it off the road. The Winchesters are injured and taken to a nearby hospital. In an out-of-body experience, Dean's spirit is off hunting a reaper around the hospital wards while his body lies in a coma; Sam is trying to save both Dean and the now-wrecked Impala; and John Winchester still seems to be obsessed with killing the yellow-eyed demon. But John summons the demon to make a deal instead – the Colt in return for Dean's life. But the demon wants a sweetener and John agrees to exchange his own life for his son's.

CAN YOU SURVIVE TO THE TITLES?
They're broken and bloodied, but all the Winchesters survive to the titles.

LOCATION, LOCATION, LOCATION
Near to Jefferson City, Missouri.

LEGENDARY ROOTS

A grim reaper is seen as the personification of death, usually described as a tall, pale, black- cloaked figure where only its eyes can be seen, although occasionally it's depicted in a white burial gown or as a skeletal figure with a scythe. The scythe is used by the reaper to gather souls of the recently departed by severing their ties to their physical body and guiding them into the next world.

There are those who believe the reaper can actually cause the death of a person; or can be bribed or tricked out of collecting the soul, allowing a person to live on Earth longer.

SQUEEZE OF THE WEEK

The reaper might be wearing a pretty girl exterior and telling Dean he's cute, but there's too much drama and tears going on for anyone to think of romance.

SIBLING RIVALRY

A complete 180-degree turn on the usual banter between the two brothers, partly because Sam can't actually talk to Dean until he gets the Mystical Talking Board. Even so, they're both starting to realise that they're on the verge of losing each other, and their words reflect their need to stay together for a change, with Sam particularly coming to see that they'd just started to be brothers again.

Meanwhile, there's still some dad rivalry going on, and Sam and John can't keep away from each other's throats. Sam thinks John cares more about killing the demon than trying to save Dean and that he is being selfish. John insists that he's going after the demon for Dean. Then Sam wades in calling his dad selfish and obsessed and John explodes in return with how Sam begged him to be part of the hunt and should have finished the demon off when he'd had the opportunity.

Dean is still trying to referee the two of them, but in his spirit form they can't actually hear him so he's finding it rather frustrating.

BODY COUNT

A woman chokes to death on the floor in a deserted hospital room. (Now that's just plain unlucky. You'd think you'd have a better chance of surviving a choking fit in a hospital wouldn't you?) A young girl dies after they fail to resuscitate her and the reaper is on hand to reach into her head to take her spirit.

But of course the most important death is that of John Winchester. Another technically difficult death to define – did he commit suicide by giving his soul to the yellow-eyed demon, or did the demon kill him? Is he really dead? Discuss …

TOOLKIT

- If you're going to summon a demon, particularly the nasty yellow-eyed type, then you'll need: *chalk* to draw the *summoning sigil*; *acacia* to burn as incense; and *oil of Abramelin* – an aromatic oil made from a blend of different extracts including cinnamon, myrrh, cassia and calamus – which provides, amongst other things, a means of consecrating ritual equipment. And don't forget *a sharp knife* for cutting your palm open so you can bleed into the *bowl* of flashy *firework powder* that sparks impressively when you set a *match* to it. And a couple of *candles* will give the whole scene a more intimate feel even if you are in the boiler room.
- And don't forget to take along the demon-killing *Colt revolver* to the summoning to use as a bargaining chip too.
- Meanwhile, you may feel silly using a *Mystical Talking Board* but at least it will allow you to talk to your brother's spirit while he's having an out-of-body experience.

MEMORABLE MOMENTS

Another episode steeped in memorable moments, and they run pretty much from the opening scene to the final declaration of John's death. But if there's one that stands out the most it's John Winchester's last conversation with Dean, where he apologises for not being there when his son was growing up. It's brimming with heart-rending emotion that gets the old eyes brimming too.

THE CAR'S THE STAR

The poor old Impala is in a bad way, so much so that even Bobby Singer is suggesting scrapping it completely. Thankfully Sam won't let him do that and everyone sighs with relief.

FASHION OBSERVATIONS

Dean doesn't seem to be wearing his amulet again, and it's no surprise really since for most of the episode he's a spirit. But then how is he wearing the hospital clothes?[114]

SPOOK RULES

- Reapers have to reach into your head to remove your spirit.
- They can alter human perception and make themselves appear however they want – this one is much prettier than the last Dean encountered (in 'Faith' (1-12)), which was a wrinkled old sourpuss.

---

114 Dean doesn't wear his amulet in 'Bloody Mary' (1-05) either.

- In their true form reapers appear as haggard old women, grey and insubstantial, and it hurts their feelings if their true form flips you out. (They must spend a lot of time feeling hurt then.)
- If you're a spirit, you can see your own spirit form and those of other spirits. You can also see your own physical body.
- You can't be heard or seen by anyone 'alive' except psychically sensitive younger brothers.
- You can physically connect with objects when extremely angry or desperately trying to communicate with a sibling.
- When you snap back into your physical body, you don't remember your out-of-body experiences.

DID YOU SPOT?

'Bad Moon Rising' by Creedence Clearwater Revival is still playing on the stereo after the crash, just as it was before the crash in 'Devil's Trap' (1-22).

When they are resuscitating Dean, the monitor is showing a date of 12 August 2006.

GOING UNDERCOVER

John's medical insurance card is in the name of Elroy McGillicuddy. Once more, the boys don't go undercover at all[115].

CULTURAL REFERENCES

Over the hospital PA: 'Room 237, code blue. Dr Kripke to room 237, code blue.': Room 237 from the movie *The Shining* (1980) makes an appearance again[116]. 'Dr Kripke' is a reference to series creator Eric Kripke, and a code blue is a term for a medical emergency, meaning a person is in danger of immediately dying.

Dean: 'Give me some ghost whispering or something.': Another reference to the *Ghost Whisperer* television series starring Jennifer Love Hewitt, whose character can see and communicate with the dead, helping them to cross over[117].

Dean: 'I full on Swayze'd that mother.': Referring to actor Patrick Swayze's character in the 1990 movie *Ghost*, who learned how to move physical objects using the power of his anger.

Dean: 'You see me messing with crystals or listening to Yanni? It's actually a

---

115 The last time they didn't use a cover was in 'Dead Man's Blood' (1-20).

116 The room number was last referenced in 'Something Wicked' (1-18).

117 Previously mentioned in 'Asylum' (1-10).

very old idea. Got a lot of different names: bilocation, crisis apparition, fetches …':
Yanni Chryssomallis, born 14 November 1954, is a Greek self-taught keyboardist and
composer of contemporary instrumental music who has had the privilege of playing
in the Taj Mahal, India. Bilocation is the state of being, or the ability to be, in two
places at the same time. A fetch is an apparition of a person who is soon to die.

Dean: 'I think I'll pass on the 72 virgins, thanks.': Refers to a controversial
interpretation of hadith (oral traditions relating to the words and deeds of the Islamic
prophet Muhammad) where people in paradise are given 72 wives along with 80,000
servants as a reward. The reference to the women being virgins is because they are said
to have never been touched by man or jinn.

Tessa: 'Stage three: bargaining.': This is probably referring to Elisabeth Kübler
Ross's Five Stages of Grief model for people facing death. The stages are: Denial,
Anger, Bargaining, Depression and Acceptance. Different people go through different
stages for different lengths of time and with varying intensity. Dean has already passed
through at least the Denial stage by the time Tessa makes the comment above.

GOOFS AND FLUFFS
The yellow-eyed demon said that he couldn't bring Dean back himself but he knew
someone who could. So how come the yellow-eyed demon turned up, possessed Tessa
and saved Dean – where was the other 'entity'?

When the doctors are trying to resuscitate John, the monitor says 'Sensor off
patient, check connection at patient'. No wonder it is flat-lining: it isn't even attached
to him.

HAVEN'T I SEEN YOU BEFORE?
Nicola Anderson has featured in *Andromeda*, *Jeremiah* and *Smallville*. Daniel Bacon
has been in *The Day the Earth Stood Still*, *Fantastic Four* and *Stargate SG-1*. Julian D
Christopher's credits include *X-Men: The Last Stand*, *The Exorcism of Emily Rose* and
Smallville. Randal Edwards featured in *A Town Called Eureka*, *Smallville* and *Kyle XY*.
Carrie Anne Fleming's credits include *The 4400*, *Bloodsuckers* and *Masters of Horror*.
Sarah Groundwater was in *Flash Gordon* the TV series. Marcel Mallard has been in
The Outer Limits, *Blood Ties* and *Stargate SG-1*. Lindsey McKeon's credits include *3rd
Rock From The Sun* and *IQ-145*. Marsha Regis featured in *Watchmen*, *The Exorcism of
Emily Rose* and *White Noise*. Benson Simmonds was also in *Stargate SG-1* and *Total
Recall 2070*.

BEHIND THE SCENES
In *The Official Supernatural Magazine* #1, Director Kim Manners said he had tears in

eyes when filming the emotional scenes with John, Sam and Dean.

Jeffrey Dean Morgan was sad to see John Winchester go but was happy that John got to prove that he was a good father who loved his kids after all. [*The Official Supernatural Magazine #2*]

Morgan exposed a lighter side to those emotional scenes with Ackles in the *Season Two Supernatural Companion*. He explained how there was always a lot of laughter on the set in Vancouver after the dying scenes when the camera had cut. Morgan was even trying to make Ackles laugh on camera by whispering rude things into his ear.

Actor Fredric Lehne offered an insight into the yellow-eyed demon in *The Official Supernatural Magazine #3*. He believes the demon prefers inflicting psychological pain since it doesn't take much skill to just tear someone's head off. He was interested in corrupting Sam because the hunter was rather pure of heart and more of a challenge.

MUSICAL INTERLUDE

- 'Stranglehold' – Ted Nugent – playing over the episode recap at the start.
- 'Bad Moon Rising' – Creedence Clearwater Revival – At the beginning of the episode where Sam, Dean and John are in the car.

ANALYSIS

In many ways, the first episode of a new series sets the benchmark for the rest. People will tune in to see what you've got to offer, and if can hook them on episode one, chances are they'll be in for the whole ride.

'In My Time Of Dying' did something exceptional – it delivered everything you could have asked for in an opening episode. It gave the ongoing fan-base resolution to John Winchester's story-arc; it gave new fans an intense story that didn't require any background knowledge (although admittedly, they weren't going to get all the in-jokes about the reaper being prettier this time); there was spiritual comment on the nature of death; there was conflict, sacrifice and relationship therapy. And there was one almighty mystery that would be tickling the curiosity for weeks – what did John whisper in Dean's ear?

The other mystery touched upon relates to Sam's abilities. That intriguing but brief conversation between the yellow-eyed demon and John – where John admits that he's known the truth about Sammy for a while – quietly promises significant revelations to come.

And what about the Impala? What's going to happen to the poor, twisted wreck of a car that Bobby (how could he?!) tries to consign to the scrap heap? Thankfully, Sam steps in, unable to let go of the car in much the same way he can't let go of Dean. The Impala and Dean are the only two constants in his life. Almost everything else –

monsters, women, friends, people they've saved – is just transitory, leaving few lasting impressions. Even John was mostly absent during Sam's childhood – it was Dean who bought Sam up over the early years – and the Impala was already part of the family on the night Mary died. So Dean and the Impala have both always been there, and it's no surprise that Sam is so desperate to keep them both in his life.

Dean meanwhile is struggling to accept death, and even as a spirit he's trying to rid the world of monsters and save people – although this time the reaper is on legitimate rather than malicious work, escorting naturally departing souls to the afterlife. Which, despite the reaper wanting to take Dean away forever, actually makes it one of the good guys'n'gals, the first time we've seen the monster get away at the end of an episode (with the exception of the odd demon here and there).

Instead of killing the reaper, Dean takes time to listen to her. It was always going to take a sound argument to get Dean to agree to leave Sam and John willingly, and the convincer comes in telling Dean that if he doesn't go with the reaper he'll turn into the kind of angry spirit that he's always hunted. The long, lonely years being trapped as a spirit could turn him mad and violent, causing him to harm innocent people – and that is exactly what Dean doesn't want. The yellow-eyed demon turned up only just in time.

The other person who makes a monumental decision is John – agreeing to give his own soul, and endure an eternity in hell, in return for Dean's life. The obvious reason for him to do this is because he loves his son, but could there be any other influencing factors? John's last words to Dean indicate the level of regret and guilt he has for taking away Dean's childhood and making him grow up too fast. Is there a debt there that he feels needs to be repaid? A need to give Dean an adult life, since he took away his early years? Dean was always there for him; is it time for John finally to be there when Dean is in extreme need of him?

And then there's the fact that John knows what the yellow-eyed demon has planned for Sam and the other children. John was concerned about Sam's sudden ability to have visions[118] and of course he's concerned about Sam's future, especially with the yellow-eyed demon involved. So how can John protect Sam? There's always been a lot of conflict between the two of them, so for John to stay close to Sam would not be easy. But Dean? Dean could definitely stay close and protect Sam, it's just that Dean's in a coma and doesn't look like he's going to wake up.

If John could save Dean's life, it's a win-win situation for the two brothers. But is John's own life too high a price? He's already given several indications about how he feels about that. In 'Salvation' (1-21) he told Sam and Dean that he wanted to stop

---

118 'Salvation' (1-21).

losing the people he loves; that he just wanted it to be over. Then in 'Devil's Trap' (1-22) he ordered Sam to kill him with the Colt while the demon was still possessing him. So he's clearly not putting his life over and above everything else.

Conversely, John did try to complete the deal with only the Colt on offer (showing that he wasn't completely self-destructive), but given his previous behaviour, is it a surprise that he decided that his own life was an acceptable price under the circumstances?

The ramifications of John's actions will reverberate through many more episodes in Season Two and further, showing just how important he was to everyone. He's gonna be missed by a lot of people.

VERDICT – 10 out of 10

Episode 2-02
Everybody Loves a Clown

Transmission Dates
US first aired: 5 October 2006
UK first aired: 20 July 2007

Credits
Writer: John Shiban
Director: Philip Sgriccia

Recurring Roles
Samantha Ferris (Ellen Harvelle), Alona Tal (Jo Harvelle), Chad Lindberg (Ash)

Guest Stars
Julius Chapple (Nora's Dad), Lexie Huber (Nora's Mum), Ken Kramer (Mr Cooper), Alexis Llewellyn (Little Girl), Quinn Lord (Evan), Nicole Muñoz (Nora), Colin Naples (Midget Clown), Peter New (Morgue Orderly), Dean Redmond (Little Girl's Dad), David Stuart (Evan's Dad), Kirsten Williamson (Little Girl's Mum), Alec Willows (Amazing Papazian/Clown/Rakshasa)

Synopsis
Sam and Dean find a four month old message on John's mobile and it leads them to the Roadhouse Saloon and Ellen and Jo Harvelle. A folder behind the bar about some nearby killings sends the boys to the carnival on the trail of a murderous clown who happens to be a powerful Rakshasa, a supernatural being who feeds on human flesh. Meanwhile, Roadhouse regular Ash turns out to have the technology to help the brothers locate the yellow-eyed demon.

Can You Survive to the Titles?
The parents of a little girl are ripped to shreds in their own bedroom after their daughter invites a cute little clown into their home in the middle of the night.

Location, Location, Location
Medford, Wisconsin

LEGENDARY ROOTS

A Rakshasa is from Hindu mythology. There are two kinds of Rakshasa: the first is a semi-divine, benevolent being; the second is a cannibalistic demon or goblin, enemies of the gods. The Rakshasa is said to feed on human flesh and, being an excellent mind reader, it will seek out a person's weaknesses and exploit them in order to gain their trust. They are shapeshifters, magicians and illusionists and often appear as other humans or animals such as dogs or large birds. They are said to haunt cemeteries, disturb sacrifices, harass priests and possess humans. In their original form they are described as being yellow, green or blue monsters with fangs and poisonous fingernails. Their eyes are vertical slits and they have large bellies.

SQUEEZE OF THE WEEK

Jo Harvelle is desperately trying to be Dean's squeeze, but the poor boy is just not himself at the moment. He's too busy trying to process the grief after his father's death, and it's a well-known real-life fact that grief can suppress the libido.

SIBLING RIVALRY

Oh, where to start? The boys are at each other's throats and the friendly banter makes only a brief appearance when Dean teases Sam about his fear of clowns and Sam teases Dean back about his fear of flying. Apparently, planes do crash and clowns do indeed kill.

Apart from that it's all pretty serious stuff. A week after they've cremated their father, Sam's getting frustrated that Dean is bottling his feelings so much, and tries to get him to talk about whether he's angry or wants revenge. But Dean says he's just annoyed because they have no way to find the yellow-eyed demon and no way to kill it, because the Colt has gone. So Dean is doing the only thing he can, he's working on the car.

Then later, after saving the family from the clown's attack, Dean turns the tables on Sam because he's noticed Sam's sudden obedience to what dad would have wanted him to do. Dean reminds Sam how he spent most of his life slugging it out with John and even picked a fight with him the last time he ever saw him. When he tells Sam it's too late to make it right, he adds that he's saying this because he needs Sam to be honest with himself about how he's dealing with their dad's death. It's an amazingly deep chick flick moment for Dean, but he's probably just trying to distract Sam from needling him about his own issues.

BODY COUNT

There are only double murders going on this time. A second set of parents get shredded in bed when little Evan lets the nasty clown in after dark.

TOOLKIT

- Break out the standard hunting kit – you'll need the *rock salt loaded shotgun* and the *EMF meter* as usual but add *two sets of binoculars* and a *brass knife* to kill the monster.
- If a brass knife is not to hand (because the Rakshasa happens to be throwing it at your head) then a *pointed length of brass piping* will suffice.

MEMORABLE MOMENTS

One of the most powerful scenes in the entire second season has no dialogue at all – it's when Dean vents his anger and grief by taking a crowbar to the Impala's body work. Shocking and totally heart-rending.

Top Spooky Moment: When Evan leads the clown upstairs and his dad wakes up to see the clown holding Evan's hand at the side of the bed. Surreal *and* spooky – urgh!

THE CAR'S THE STAR

It's in a bad way still after the accident and in a worse state after Dean has finished with the crowbar on its bodywork. But like an old friend it takes the pounding because it will ultimately help Dean through the healing process.

SPOOK RULES

- Rakshasas are ancient Hindu creatures that appear in human form and feed on adult human flesh.
- They have to feed a few times every 20 or 30 years, possibly because they have a slow metabolism.
- They don't munch on children – maybe because there's not enough meat on the bones.
- They can make themselves invisible but can't enter a home without first being invited. They dress as clowns to manipulate children into inviting them in.
- Rakshasas live in squalor and sleep on a bed of dead insects.
- Rock salt has no negative effect on them but a Rakshasa can be killed by a dagger made of pure brass.

DID YOU SPOT?

Ash is named after Bruce Campbell's character from the *Evil Dead* films.

The word fugly – this time applied to the yellow-eyed demon – makes another appearance[119].

GOING UNDERCOVER
The boys try to pretend that they've worked for a carnival before but carnival owner Cooper sees straight through them. They get the jobs as a result of Sam's honest explanation about not wanting to go to college.

HUNTER'S LINGO
When the police are investigating the latest murder at the carnival, Dean refers to them as Five-0. This is a reference to the US cop show *Hawaii Five-0* that first aired in 1968[120].

CULTURAL REFERENCES
Ash: 'I'm on it like Divine on dog dookie.': A movie reference to the character Divine in *Pink Flamingos* (1972), where the infamous transvestite eats dog faeces.

Dean: 'You cry when you see Ronald McDonald.': Doesn't need much explanation – burger restaurant McDonald's famous mascot is a huge scary clown. Was that really a good choice of mascot?

Dean: 'You've gotta be kidding me, this guy's no genius. He's a Lynyrd Skynyrd roadie.': Lynyrd Skynyrd is a Southern US band formed in 1964. The height of their career came in the 1970s – until vocalist and primary songwriter Ronnie Van Zant died in a plane crash in October 1977 along with Steve Gaines (guitarist and songwriter), Cassie Gaines (backup singer) and assistant road manager Dean Kilpatrick. The remaining members reformed in 1987 and are still touring.

Mr Cooper: 'Doing what? Ride jockies? Butcher? A&S men?': All these are circus jobs: a ride jockey is a ride operator; a butcher is someone who walks around the carnival, selling food and drink; and an A&S man is the guess the age and weight operator.

Ash: 'MIT. Before I got bounced for ... fighting.': Massachusetts Institute of Technology (MIT) located in Cambridge, Massachusetts first opened in 1965 as a private research university devoted to the advancement of knowledge and education of students in areas that contribute to or prosper in an environment of science and technology.

---

119 It's not been used since Dean described the Vanir as fugly in 'Scarecrow' (1-11).

120 Last used in 'The Woman in White' (1-01).

GOOFS AND FLUFFS

When Sam and Dean are walking down the road, after abandoning the mini-van in some trees, they're arguing about how to deal with John's death. Watch the mobile phone in Sam's right hand – it comes and goes depending on whether it's a distance shot or a closer view.

In the Funhouse, after the Rakshasa has been stabbed, Dean removes the knife from under his arm that is pinning him to the wall. Then he reaches up to switch the steam off. Then you see him remove the knife from under his arm again.

Just as Sam and Dean are leaving the Roadhouse at the end, Dean takes one last swig from the beer bottle, holding it at the bottom, but as he puts it down, he's holding it at the top.

According to this episode, Ellen and the Roadhouse were never mentioned by John Winchester. However, in *John Winchester's Journal* by Alex Irvine (William Morrow, 2009) the entry on 16 April 1986 mentions the Roadhouse, Ellen and Bill Harvelle and little Jo, who was four years old at the time.

HAVEN'T I SEEN YOU BEFORE?

Julius Chapple's credits include *The 4400* and *Underworld: Evolution*. Lexie Huber has featured in *White Noise: The Light* and *Dead Like Me*. Alexis Llewellyn's credits include *The Chronicles of Riddick*, *Tru Calling* and *The Twilight Zone*. Quinn Lord was in *Blade: The Series*, *White Noise: The Light* and *Smallville*. Nicole Muñoz featured in *Fantastic Four*, *Stargate: Atlantis* and *Jeremiah*. Peter New has been in *Dark Angel* and *Scooby Doo 2: Monsters Unleashed*. Dean Redmond was in *Dark Angel*. David Stuart was also in *The X-Files*, *Touched by an Angel* and *Jake 2.0*. Alec Willows has been in *The Twilight Zone*, *Highlander: The Series* and *Millennium*. Kirsten Williamson's acting credits include *Stargate: Continuum*, *X-Men: Evolution* and *Taken*.

BEHIND THE SCENES

Director Phil Sgriccia played up to Sam's clown phobia during the filming of this episode. In the *Season Two Supernatural Companion* he explained how they included lots of little ad libs to make Sam uneasy around the circus. The clown chair wasn't in the script but Sgriccia had a word with Jensen and ensured it was Sam who had to sit in it.

This episode has the dedication 'In Memory of our Friend, Peter Ellis'. Director of episodes 'Bloody Mary' (1-05) and 'The Benders' (1-15), Ellis died on 24 April 2006, according to *Variety*. He was 58 years old.

MUSICAL INTERLUDE

- 'Time Has Come Today' – The Chambers Brothers – playing over the episode recap at the start.
- 'Shambala' – Three Dog Night – as Dean is fixing the car and talking to Sam.
- 'Do That to Me One More Time' – Captain and Tennille – when Sam and Dean arrive at the Roadhouse.

ANALYSIS

This episode gives a measure of reassurance that being creepy is still on *Supernatural's* agenda for Season Two. Opening your eyes to find your child standing at the bottom of your bed, hand in hand with a clown, has just got to be high on a lot of people's freak-out meter, and it's certainly used to disturbing effect here – although it's not quite as spine-chilling as Pennywise the clown in Stephen King's *It*.

Then, unfortunately, the clown creepiness is totally sacrificed in the second half of the episode in favour of the invisible shenanigans in the Fun House. It's not the invisibility that sabotages the scares – the Daevas[121] weren't directly visible but they still managed to be frightening. The special effects, the music and the sets are all at a high standard in this episode too, so where does the problem lie? It's difficult to nail it down exactly but there is a logic problem with the knives. The Rakshasa has been working for years in a circus as a knife thrower so you'd expect him to pretty handy with them. Yet when he's throwing them at Dean he can't hit the mark. Even when he's pinned Dean's arm to the wall in the Fun House so he can't move out of the way, the next knife doesn't do any damage. This guy should be able to hit a pimple on Dean's forehead from 50 feet with unerring accuracy, but because he can't, he's not a threat to the boys' safety and we subconsciously relax.

What doesn't fail throughout this episode are the scenes of Sam and Dean as they both try to deal with their father's death in their own ways. People react to death in many different emotional ways, but there are patterns to the experiences that are generally grouped into five stages. First up is Shock and Denial. Both Sam and Dean went through the Shock at the end of 'In My Time of Dying' (2-01) as they watched the medical staff try to resuscitate John in the hospital. They will have achieved a certain amount of closure (and had an opportunity to say goodbye) in the burning of John's body at the start of this episode, but a week later, they seem to have skipped Denial (where you often think you see the deceased in the street etc) and landed well and truly in stages two – Guilt and Anger – and four – Depression and Despair, missing out stage three – Bargaining – as well.

---

121 In 'Shadow' (1-16).

Most obviously, because he expresses it more, Sam is feeling the guilt about John's death. In their last moments together, Sam is angry at his father and John is trying to defuse the situation because he doesn't want their last moments to be spent with raised voices. Sam's anger at himself for creating this last encounter spills over into his concern for Dean and helps to fire some of the comments about Dean not saying anything about their father's death.

And then there's Sam's change of heart about hunting. Even back in 'Devil's Trap' (1-22), he was trying to do what his father would want him to do, and now that John is gone, that need has become stronger. Sam wants to atone for his actions by being the son his father wanted him to be, to hunt evil and save innocent lives. If Sam can't find the yellow-eyed demon yet then he'll take any kind of hunt, including creepy clowns.

Dean rightly pulls Sam up on this problem, but that's mostly because (like Sam) it's easier for him to deal with his brother's issues than work through his own. Dean seems to be mostly working his way through the Depression stage – where you've often lost any purpose in life and show little interest in the outside world. This manifests in his single-minded work on the car, in his lack of motivation to go hunting and his loss of libido. He's frustrated that they can't find the demon and couldn't kill it if they did find it, he's concerned for Sam and possibly angry at his dad for whatever was whispered in his ear. All of this emotional fall-out is difficult to contain for long and eventually he loses control of it – expressing it by taking a crowbar to the beloved Impala, something that has always symbolically represented his father to him.

Behaving strangely they may be, but Sam and Dean are still showing familiar traits to remind us that they're not completely off the rails. There's the lovely moment of banter in the car where Dean teases Sam about not liking clowns, countered by Sam reminding Dean about his fear of flying[122]. And of course Sam is tempering Dean's shoot-'em-up attitude once more by insisting that they confirm Cooper is the bad guy before they go stabbing things into him.

No doubt there's going to be more angst in upcoming episodes as the boys continue to deal with John's death, but there could also be some interesting storylines surrounding the newly-introduced Harvelle's Roadhouse. Ellen, Jo and Ash look like they're going to add some back history as well as supply some leads to the yellow-eyed demon, and then there's the whole 'community of hunters' aspect to delve into …

VERDICT – 7.5 out of 10

---

122 Established in 'Phantom Traveler' (1-04)

EPISODE 2-03
BLOODLUST

TRANSMISSION DATES
US first aired: 12 October 2006
UK first aired: 27 July 2007

CREDITS
Writer: Sera Gamble
Director: Robert Singer

RECURRING ROLES
Samantha Ferris (Ellen Harvelle), Sterling K Brown (Gordon Walker)

GUEST STARS
Ralph Alderman (Sheriff), Amber Benson (Lenore), Derek McIver (Orderly), Ty Olsson (Eli)

UNCREDITED
Janene Carleton (Christina Flanigan), Michael Roselli (Conrad)

SYNOPSIS
The Impala is fixed and back on the road, the boys are on a case involving beheadings, and Dean is enjoying being back behind the wheel. But the victims turn out to be vampires and their hunter, Gordon Walker, is still in town. When Sam discovers that the vampires aren't killing humans but drinking cattle blood he wants to let them leave peacefully. Gordon has different ideas, going head to head with the Winchesters but losing the fight with Dean.

CAN YOU SURVIVE TO THE TITLES?
Christina Flanigan thinks she's escaped her pursuer in the forest, only to discover how wrong she was when her head hits the floor while her body stays upright.

LOCATION, LOCATION, LOCATION
Red Lodge, Montana

LEGENDARY ROOTS

When you're an obsessed hunter with a desperate need to cleanse the world of the vampire taint, you have to know how to stop a fanged fiend – and Hollywood has actually given us most of the best methods already:

- A stake through the heart is probably the most well known way to dispatch those pesky vampire creatures and is demonstrated in many movies and series from *Dracula* (1931) to *The Lost Boys* (1987) and *Buffy the Vampire Slayer* (1997-2003).
- Beheading or a snapping of the neck also tends to finish off a vampire nicely – a popular method in *Blade* (1998).
- Burning a vampire works in the short term, but if the ashes are scattered as in *The Vampire Chronicles* by Anne Rice, then they can be brought back to life by the vampire clan with an appropriate spilling of blood.
- Or you could try shooting a vampire with a silver bullet, especially if it's a liquid silver bullet as used in *Underworld* (2003).
- Daylight or sunlight can kill a vampire according to the movie *30 Days of Night* (2007), but use with caution since in the *Twilight* novels by Stephenie Meyer it only makes their skin glisten.
- And the final two options are holy water and garlic, again according to *The Lost Boys* movie.

SQUEEZE OF THE WEEK

Sam talks to Ellen, but she's more like a mother-figure than anything else. And since all the other girls the boys meet are vampires (or beheaded vampires) it's slim pickings in this episode.

SIBLING RIVALRY

As Dean drives his shiny Impala along the road in the early scenes, he marvels about how sweet she sounds and Sam asks him if he wants to get a room.

Then when Sam asks him why he's so happy and finds out it's partly because they've got a case, he teases his brother about how some dead cows can cheer him up so much.

The teasing continues in the mortuary as they argue playfully about who will open the box with the head in it. Dean calls Sam a wuss because he won't open the box and Sam's after a bucket so he can puke in it. It's nice to see some good-humoured teasing back amidst the heavy exchanges and punches being thrown.

BODY COUNT

There's vampire blood getting sprayed everywhere but no innocent humans get bumped off this time.

TOOLKIT

- A *large scythe* is handy for chopping heads off in one strike.
- A *pair of latex gloves* and *a strong stomach* are handy when you're examining the severed head of a victim.
- *Sharp knives* are a must for torturing vampires and be sure to have *Dead Man's Blood* available too[123], as it's known to be poisonous to vampires.

MEMORABLE MOMENTS

It's great to see the Impala back on the road again; the scenes in the hospital as Sam examines Christina's severed head are pretty grisly; Conrad getting his head sawn off is gruesome; but Dean going one-on-one in a fight with Gordon has physical drama and brutality, as well as creating the long-term consequences of going up against a fellow hunter.

THE CAR'S THE STAR

The Impala is gleaming in all its glory as Dean drives it to Montana; the dents in the trunk have been fixed and AC/DC is blasting once more. Everyone is glad it's back

MOTEL MAYHEM

There are some lovely cactus accessories in the Adobe Court motel room, including a cute little cactus for holding your car keys.

SPOOK RULES

- All the *Supernatural* vampire rules are consistent with the boys' previous encounter – the neck nibbling critters live in nests together, can be killed only by beheading (shooting them is as effective as snapping them with a rubber band) and they're poisoned by Dead Man's Blood.
- What's new here is that these are the first vampires we've met that are trying to live without drinking human blood. They're drinking cattle blood so they will fall off the hunters' radar. This is an attempt to survive, since they have been hunted almost to extinction.
- There's also a mention that Satanists mark their victims with a reversed pentacle on the forehead.

---

123 The blood was first used in 'Dead Man's Blood' (1-20).

DID YOU SPOT?

J Manners is the name shown on the intern's ID badge. This is nod to Kim Manners, who directed 14 *Supernatural* episodes in the first three seasons[124].

Dean reveals how he got into hunting to Gordon. Apparently he shot an 'ugly sucker' through the heart with a silver-tipped crossbow bolt when he was 16 years old. Dean and his Dad then take the body into the forest and burn it while Sammy waits in the car.

It's perhaps no surprise that Dean doesn't recount the story of his actual first kill to Gordon. According to the *Rising Son* series of comic stories, in 1990 when Dean was 11 years old, John took him hunting for deer for the first time. Not long after that trip a hunter called Anderson, who had discovered Sam's 'demon destiny', came after the Winchesters in an attempt to take seven year old Sammy away from John. Dean shot Anderson in the head when he tried to kill John.

GOING UNDERCOVER

The brothers pretend to be reporters for the *World Weekly News*, or was it the *Weekly World News*? Ah well, Dean is new, so it's no surprise he can't get the name right ...

CULTURAL REFERENCES

Weekly World News is a supermarket tabloid paper founded in 1979 dealing with bizarre and unusual stories. The paper's slogan is: 'Nothing but the truth: The Weekly World News!' The *WWN* ceased paper publication in 2007 and now exists as an online newspaper.

Dean: 'Put the lotion in the basket.': Quoting Buffalo Bill from the book (1988) and film (1991) *The Silence of the Lambs*. Buffalo Bill wanted his captives to moisturise their skin so that when he killed them the skin would be in peak condition as he made a woman-suit out of it. Urgh!

Dean: 'See if those wackos stuffed anything down her throat. You know, kinda like moth in *Silence of the Lambs*.': A reference to the Death's Head moth that is placed in the victim's throat in *Silence of the Lambs*.

The Bartender tells Dean about the folks who leased the Barker farm. They've been to the bar, drinking, Bartender: 'I've had to 86 them once or twice.': The term '86' is slang for eliminating or removing someone. And it's a bit tenuous, but the Barker name could possibly be a reference to the excellent horror writer Clive Barker.

Ellen: 'And Hannibal Lecter is a good psychiatrist.': Another *Silence of the Lambs* plug, this time for the clever but insane Hannibal Lecter played by the awesome and

---

124 Manners died in January 2009 from lung cancer after directing a total of seventeen episodes of *Supernatural*.

206

talented Anthony Hopkins in that film.

Dean: 'Sleep all day. Party all night. Never grow old. Never die.': Add 'It's fun to be a vampire' and you have the tagline for the movie *The Lost Boys* (1987).

Gordon: 'Whoa. Easy there, Chachi.': Chachi was a character (played by Scott Baio) from the hit TV series *Happy Days* (1974-1984).

Gordon: 'Another one bites the dust.': Despite being the title of a hit song by Queen in 1980, this phrase probably dates back to the days of the Wild West when gunfights were common and a dead gunslinger was the first one to 'bite the dust' as he took the bullet.

Gordon: 'But hey, I hear there's a Chupacabra two states over.': A Chupacabra (the word translates into 'goat sucker') is a mythical creature that sucks the blood of animals. There have been sighting in various regions of Puerto Rico, Brazil, Chile, Mexico and the United States, with the first dating back to the 1950s and the height of its notoriety occurring in the 1990s. The Chupacabra sucks dry any animal it attacks, leaving two (sometimes three) neck puncture wounds but no other signs of injury.

GOOFS AND FLUFFS

The blood splatter department seem to be struggling in this episode: when Dean beheads a vampire with a saw he gets blood sprayed on his face, but the spray pattern changes when he turns to look at Sam and Gordon; then Lenore has Sam's blood dripped onto her face in the farmhouse, but when Sam unties her moments later his blood has disappeared from her face.

When Gordon first grabs Sam's arm to drip that blood on Lenore, Sam approaches Gordon with his arms by his sides. But when the shot cuts to Gordon grabbing Sam, his arms have suddenly moved from his side and are now bent at the elbow in a surrender-style position.

When Dean falls onto the small table while he's fighting Gordon he's left with part of the table sticking up near his feet. But in the very next scene, all the debris from Dean's feet has now disappeared. Nice of Gordon to let Dean clear up before hitting him again.

HAVEN'T I SEEN YOU BEFORE?

Ralph Alderman has been in *Millennium*, *The Outer Limits* and *Taken*. Amber Benson starred as Tara in *Buffy the Vampire Slayer*. Janene Carleton is mainly a stunt woman who has been in *X-Men: The Last Stand*, *Watchmen* and *Blood Ties*. Derek McIver also featured in *Blood Ties*. Ty Olsson played Captain Aaron Kelly in *Battlestar Galactica* and has also been in *AVP: Requiem*, *The Day the Earth Stood Still* and *The Chronicles of Riddick*. Michael Roselli is another stunt performer who has been in *X-Men: The Last*

Stand, I, Robot and *Catwoman.*

BEHIND THE SCENES

Actor Sterling K Brown described Gordon as an intense bloke who truly believes he's doing the right thing but struggles to see the situation from anyone else's point of view. [*The Official Supernatural Magazine* #2]

Brown also said his character connected so well with Dean because they both enjoyed kicking ass and felt a responsibility for their siblings. Gordon's sister may not be with him but he's taken it upon himself to help people and even the score after her death.

MUSICAL INTERLUDE

- 'Wheel in the Sky' – Journey – playing over the episode recap.
- 'Back In Black' – AC/DC – while Dean and Sam are driving in the gorgeously restored Impala at the start of the episode.
- 'Time and Time Again' – Long John Hunter – when Sam and Dean arrive at the bar to ask the barman about newcomers in town.
- 'Golden Rule' – Lil' Ed and The Blues Imperials – as Gordon buys Dean and Sam a drink at the bar.
- 'Funny Car Graveyard' – Lee Rocker – playing at the roadhouse when Sam is talking to Ellen on the phone.

ANALYSIS

The Impala is back, so at least on one front Dean has a piece of his life back again. It's a pity the rest of it is such a mess. Now all we need is a new laptop for Sam and the two of them will be as complete as they can be at this stage after losing their father.

The fallout from John's death once more interleaves with the monster story, but compared with the previous episode[125], this tale of vampires abstaining from human blood is more tightly merged with the underlying arc. Both the actions of the vampires and the sadistic Gordon put the boys in the middle of another moral dilemma, the likes of which we've not seen since 'Faith' (1-12)[126]. This time the question is about what is evil and what should be killed, and it's less ambiguous here than it was in 'Faith'[127]. In 'Bloodlust' there's a very definite set of sides. Gordon is for killing everything unnatural; Sam is for killing only evil; and Dean sits at the crossroads with a choice of

---

125 'Everybody Loves A Clown' (2-02).

126 Another story where writer Sera Gamble was involved.

127 And to an extent less ambiguous than in 'The Benders' (1-15), where the Deputy murders the man who killed her brother and gets away with it.

paths to follow – what he does now has the potential to make him into a hunter just like Gordon in few years time or he can take Sam's path instead.

It's a hard decision for Dean, because his father has taught him to hate monsters – not vampires specifically, since we discovered in 'Dead Man's Blood' (1-20) that John hadn't told his sons that vampires existed, but he still hates all kinds of unnatural creatures, and it's very deeply ingrained. Not even Sam's insistence on killing only 'evil' creatures changes Dean's mind about beheading the vampires, although he doesn't seem to dismiss the idea completely. Once the boys arrive where Gordon is torturing Lenore, Dean starts to make his decision. He seems repulsed by Gordon's actions and concerned about Lenore's suffering – an interesting reaction given that Dean was trying to beat information out of a similarly captive Meg only three episodes earlier in 'Devil's Trap' (1-22). When Sam makes his move against Gordon, Dean has got his gun pointed at Gordon only because he's threatening Sam. But Lenore's refusal of Sam's blood is the final convincer for Dean – he makes his choice and sides with his brother. It seems Gordon is wrong: there are shades of grey after all.

It's just another emotional dilemma that Dean probably feels he could do without. He's already got a huge John-shaped hole in his life and he's finding that trying to fill it with another person is much easier than trying to heal the ragged edges of his loss. It's more comforting to have that gap simply plugged by someone else than to start the tough task of rebuilding his life into a new configuration. Given that Sam can spot what his brother is trying to do, it's reasonable to assume that he is feeling the same way, the only difference being that his phone call to Ellen has tipped him off to the unsuitability of Gordon as a father figure. Desperate to get his brother to see it too, Sam uses their father's memory to get his point to hit home – which it does, but it gets Dean hitting back too (something he clearly feels guilty about later when he offers Sam to chance to punch him back).

This conflict between Sam and Dean makes for a tense episode, and the moral issues between Gordon and Lenore increase the intensity to make it a compelling story. But it's also the delivery of the story that's impressive. The lead performances are excellent and the strong contributions from Sterling K Brown and *Buffy* favourite Amber Benson are both grounding and generate an easy believability – even when cattle-hugging vamps seem slightly absurd when encountered on paper alone. Gordon torturing Lenore, Sam's defiance and the ensuing brutal fight between Dean and Gordon are amongst the best scenes of the season – violent, emotional and convincing.

All of these aspects make 'Bloodlust' one of those special episodes that linger in the memory for a long time after viewing.

VERDICT – 9 out of 10

EPISODE 2-04
CHILDREN SHOULDN'T PLAY
WITH DEAD THINGS

TRANSMISSION DATES
US first aired: 19 October 2006
UK first aired: 3 August 2007

CREDITS
Writer: Raelle Tucker
Director: Kim Manners

GUEST STARS
Tamara Feldman (Angela Mason), Serge Houde (Dr Mason), Christopher Jacot (Neil Levine), Jared Keeso (Matt Harrison), Leela Savasta (Lindsey Franco)

SYNOPSIS
A young woman, Angela, is killed in a car crash but, after she's buried, her grave is surrounded by a perfect circle of unholy ground and her boyfriend has his throat cut in his own home. Sam and Dean discover that Angela has been brought back to life as a zombie by her best friend Neil. She's taken her revenge on her unfaithful boyfriend, and next she's going to go after Lindsey, the girl she caught in bed with him. When the boys foil the zombie's plans for Lindsey, Angela turns on Neil before going after Sam and Dean – who finally stop her by staking her in her own deathbed.

CAN YOU SURVIVE TO THE TITLES?
Poor Angela – heartbroken after being betrayed by her boyfriend – gets killed in a car crash, but for once it is a pure accident with no supernatural influences of any kind.

LOCATION, LOCATION, LOCATION
No location is given at the start of this episode but according to Angela's temporary grave marker, she's buried in Greenville Cemetery, so the episode probably takes place in Greenville, Illinois.

LEGENDARY ROOTS
A zombie is a dead body that has been brought back to life by a supernatural force.

210

The idea originated from the Afro-Caribbean belief system of voodoo where a powerful wizard or a bokor would control people as labourers. The soul would have been removed by magic, or the body been brought back to life after the soul had been removed by the regular rites of death. The god of death Ghede was able to reanimate the corpse and the resulting zombie would have no will of their own, remaining under the control of their creator. The soul of the victim – their 'zombi astral' – is kept in a bottle and either wrapped in part of victim's clothes and buried or sold on for luck or healing.

SQUEEZE OF THE WEEK

No squeezes for the boys, but Neil has raised his love from the dead and gets more post-mortem squeezes from her than he ever got when she was alive. She must be a bit clammy to the touch though …

SIBLING RIVALRY

The differences between the boys' opinions become apparent when they visit Mary Winchester's grave. Sam has to explain to Dean that he's there because of the memory of their mother and because it feels like the right thing to do, but Dean thinks he's just being irrational and stomps off. But before long the teasing is back as they argue about the gruesome stuff again[128]. Sam doesn't want to dig up a newly rotting body and Dean's wondering if he's just afraid to get dirty.

BODY COUNT

After her death on the road, Angela is wreaking revenge all over the place. She slits boyfriend Matt's throat while he's watching telly on the sofa. Then, after failing to finish off her own flat-mate Lindsey – with a pair of scissors and some cutting comments – she takes out Neil by twisting his head off with a deft bit of wrist action. But the saddest, most innocent victim of the entire proceedings is Matt's goldfish, which dies when Angela gets too close to him in Matt's home. Aw, shame!

TOOLKIT

- A *clip of silver bullets* will help to deter a rampaging zombie, but the best way to stop one is with a *metal (possibly silver) stake*.

MEMORABLE MOMENTS

It's the emotional fallout happening with the boys that produces some of the best moments. Sam leaving his dad's dogtags on Mary's grave is touching and his face-off

---

128 Like they did in the morgue in 'Bloodlust' (2-03)

with Dean – after Dean loses his rag about bringing the dead back – shows the depth of the brothers' relationship. Dean's closing confession of guilt about being alive at the cost of John's soul simply melts your heart.

SPOOK RULES

- Creating a zombie will leave a perfect circle of dead plants around the grave, but the perfect circle of deadness is also a sign of demonic presence or the presence of a powerful spirit.
- Zombies can be created using ancient Greek divination rituals. These rituals can also be used to communicate with the dead.
- What comes back to life is a vicious, violent version of the original person. They're so nasty they rot the ground around them and have deadly effects on nearby house plants and goldfish. Because of this, expect revenge to be extracted for any number of perceived slights and hurts including committing adultery; being found in bed with the zombie's boyfriend; and trying to leave without saying goodbye properly.
- There are over a 100 different legends about how to kill a zombie. To name just a few:
  - You can set them on fire;
  - You can feed their hearts to wild dogs;
  - You can nail the undead back into their grave beds.
- Silver bullets are said to kill them but actually will only make them pause.
- You can't just waste them with a head shot because this isn't a Romero flick.
- A zombie can run pretty fast – well, fast enough to get away from Dean and later catch and tackle Sam to the floor in a graveyard anyway.
- Zombies will use any weapon available to kill a person, such as a kitchen knife or a pair of scissors, or just use their bare hands to twist your head off.
- If you're going to pretend that you're going to do a ritual over a zombie's grave then mention some authentic herbal ingredients to convince the zombie that you know what you're talking about. Candles are a must for any ritual; black root was ritually used by American Indians as a cleanser due to its ability to induce vomiting (it's also a laxative so make sure it's a short ritual!); and scar weed just sounds good since it seems to be totally made up.

DID YOU SPOT?

The details on John Winchester's dog-tags are:
Winchester
John

306-00-3894
Type – AB
Non Religious

GOING UNDERCOVER

The boys pretend to be friends of Angela's when they go to visit her father, Dr Mason.

Dean says that he is Angela's cousin, Alan Stanwyck, when he meets Angela's flat-mate Lindsey after he's broken into her home. Alan Stanwyck (Tim Matheson) is a character in the movie *Fletch* (1985) who asks Fletch (Chevy Chase) to kill him because he's suffering from bone cancer, and if he's murdered by Fletch, Alan's family will get the insurance money.

When they visit Neil, the boys pretend to be grief counsellors employed by the college. It's not like Dean to be into the hugging, so it was probably Sam's idea.

CULTURAL REFERENCES

Neil: 'We've got booze, we've got chocolate, and, wait for it ... tortured emo rock.': Emo is a style of rock music that tends to have confessional and emotional (shortened to emo) lyrics that are often thought provoking.

Dean: 'Haven't you seen *Pet Sematary*?': Referring to a horror novel (1983) and film (1989) by Stephen King concerning the reanimation of the dead when buried in the eponymous graveyard. The lead characters reanimate their cat and later their son with disastrous results.

Sam: 'You've been watching way too many Romero flicks.': George A Romero, director of some of the most famous zombie movies including the *Night of the Living Dead* (1968), *Dawn of the Dead* (1978) and *Day of the Dead* (1985).

Dean: 'It's got unrequited Duckie love written all over it.': Duckie (Jon Cryer) is a character from *Pretty in Pink* (1986) who pines for his best friend Andie (Molly Ringwald).

Angela: 'Hi honey, I'm home!': This is the title of an American comedy that ran from July 1991-July 1992 comprising 13 episodes about a 1950s fictional sitcom family relocated to real life suburbia 1990.

Dean: 'Nah, I think she went out to rent *Beaches*.': *Beaches* (1988) is a movie starring Bette Midler, about friendships you'll never forget.

GOOFS AND FLUFFS

Angela has been buried for only three days before the Winchesters arrive, and Neil must have dug her up and put the earth back sometime during those three days too, so how come the perfect circle of deadness Dean examines doesn't show any recently disturbed earth? It's all hard packed soil.

As Dean approaches the dead tree by Angela's grave you can see he's wearing a silver chain under his shirt, with his amulet on top. While he's inside the perfect circle, the chain is over the top of his shirt along with the amulet. Seconds later the chain disappears, never to be seen again.

HAVEN'T I SEEN YOU BEFORE?
Tamara Feldman has also been in *Jake 2.0* and *Smallville*. Serge Houde's credits include *Omen IV: The Awakening*, *John Doe* and *The Day The Earth Stood Still*. Christopher Jacot was in *A Town Called Eureka*, *Relic Hunter* and *Smallville*. Jared Keeso was in *White Noise 2: The Light*, *Smallville* and *The 4400*. Leela Savasta played Tracey Anne in *Battlestar Galactica* and Captain Alicia Vega in *Stargate: Atlantis*.

BEHIND THE SCENES
Visual effects co-ordinator Ivan Hayden, in *The Official Supernatural Magazine #3*, cited this episode as having another two of his favourite effects: where the plant dies when the zombie passes close by; and when the scissors get pulled out of zombie girl's chest. He's satisfied with their work no one remarks about how good they look.

According to the *Season Two Official Supernatural Companion*, Jared Padalecki split his trousers while the boys were digging Angela's grave up. Executive producer Kim Manners kept the cameras running while Jared ran round the graveyard with his undies hanging out. Oh to have been a slug on a gravestone that day.

Sam's comment at the end of this episode about the zombie girl breaking his wrist was written into the script very quickly to cover real life events. Eric Kripke commented in *The Official Supernatural Magazine #3* that Padalecki got a hairline fracture during the between-seasons hiatus but didn't get it looked at. Padalecki then landed on his hand fighting the vampires in the motel room in 'Bloodlust' (2-03), which aggravated the situation and he ended up in a cast.

But this wasn't the only breakage going on around that time. In the *Season Two Official Supernatural Companion*, key makeup artist Shannon Coppin talked about how one of props staff and one of the office workers also broke their wrist. By which time, the accidents were getting blamed on a ghost.

MUSICAL INTERLUDE
- 'Sad Girl' – Supergrass – when Neil's trying to cheer-up Angela with beer, chocolate and music.

ANALYSIS

When the boys stumble across a case of necromancy, it opens the way for the exploration of one of *Supernatural*'s major themes and a story of anger and revenge, conflict and guilt.

It starts with an illustration of the differences between Sam and Dean. Sam is looking for some kind of closure by visiting his mother's grave and delivering John's dog tags to her resting place. It's a symbolic gesture, since her body isn't buried there, but the implication from Sam is that at least his parents can be together again after long, dark years of separation, and Sam can start to move on. Dean, on the other hand, can't see the point of visiting Mary's grave, probably because thinking about her death brings up all sorts of unresolved feelings. His answer is to keep moving so he doesn't have time to consider how he is feeling. He just stays in his comfort zone, doing what he's always done – hunting. But his emotional turmoil is getting harder for him to control, especially when their current case reflects so much of his own situation.

Dean has been questioning what he's capable of since 'Devil's Trap' (1-22)[129] and now he meets Neil, who has resurrected Angela, the love of Neil's life and someone he is willing to do anything for. Problem is, she's going round killing the people who betrayed her in life. The anger she carried in her last moment alive is desperate for expression after her death. And there's a parallel but different anger in Dean. Angela's continued existence after her death is clearly unnatural from his point of view (judging by the way Dean shouts at Angela's grieving father about her staying dead). But that same belief is eating him up inside, turning inward on itself and creating a huge sense of self-loathing. Dean himself should be dead, he's unnatural by his own standards and, worse, he suspects that he's in this condition because his father sacrificed his own life to save him. So he's full of guilt as well, because he feels it's his fault that Sam lost his father too. It's no surprise the poor guy is tail-spinning out of control.

This episode isn't just a demonstration of how the boys are changing though. It also includes some nice touches to remind us that actually these guys are the same people we've known all along, paradoxically keeping them consistent while they're rapidly evolving.

When Dean walks into the motel and Sam is watching a porn movie, it produces one of those 'awkward' situations similar to the time when Meg first met Dean and ripped a strip of him for treating his brother like 'luggage'[130].

Then when Sam thinks that there isn't a hunt to investigate but Dean is adamant

---

129 When he realised just what he is willing to do for his brother and father – including killing Meg and the demon-possessed bloke.

130 In 'Shadow' (1-16).

that there is, he reminds Sam that he does know how to do his job, regardless of his brother's opinion. It's the second time Dean has had to point this out to Sam, the first being in 'Faith' (1-12) when he insisted that he'd been hunting long enough to trust his feelings.

And finally there's Sam's determination to reach his brother and help him, regardless of whether Dean wants to take another swing at him or not. Sam took the punch in 'Bloodlust' (2-03) without any kickback and he'll do it again if that's what it takes.

All these references, along with the development of the characters and the sheer fun of chasing, shooting and staking zombies, build the episode into a complex entity that just keeps you coming back for more.

VERDICT – 8 out of 10

EPISODE 2-05
SIMON SAID

TRANSMISSION DATES
US first aired: 26 October 2006
UK first aired: 10 August 2007

CREDITS
Writer: Ben Edlund
Director: Tim Iacofano

RECURRING ROLES
Samantha Ferris (Ellen Harvelle), Chad Lindberg (Ash), Alona Tal (Jo Harvelle)

GUEST STARS
John Dadey (Police Sergeant), Eric Keenleyside (Dennis), Richard Lett (Hearest), Blu Mankuma (Dr Jennings), Ian Rozylo (Attendant), Gabriel Tigerman (Andrew Gallagher), Elias Toufexis (Richard Webber/Anson Weems), Ivan Vance (Security Guard), Rachel Wainwright (Pretty Woman), Chiara Zanni (Tracy)

SYNOPSIS
Sam's visions lead the brothers to Andy Gallagher, another of the chosen children with a special ability. Andy can manipulate people just by telling them what to do, and he seems to be behind the murder of Dr Jennings. But when a woman sets herself on fire at a petrol station, Andy is with Sam and Dean and couldn't have committed the crime. The three investigate to discover that Andy's evil twin, Webber, has come to find his brother and is killing all the people who were involved with separating them at birth. When Webber threatens to make Andy's ex-girlfriend throw herself off the top of a local dam, Andy is forced to kill his sibling.

CAN YOU SURVIVE TO THE TITLES?
Dr Jennings walks into a store to buy a gun, loads a 12-gauge pump-action with live rounds, and shoots the gun salesman in the chest before putting the second cartridge through his own skull, splattering blood all over the ceiling. But it's never that easy on this show. Of course the Doc and the salesman aren't really dead, it's just one of Sam's visions.

LOCATION, LOCATION, LOCATION
Driving in Nebraska; Harvelle's Roadhouse; Guthrie, Oklahoma.

LEGENDARY ROOTS
The evil twin is a popular idea in many television series, where usually the twin is denoted by some physical difference in appearance. Popular differences are the goatee or other facial hair configurations or scarring of some kind to make it easy for the viewer to distinguish between the two characters being played by the same actor or twin.

Star Trek used this concept in 'Mirror Mirror' (1967), in which the landing party are beamed aboard another ISS Enterprise and evil Spock sports a goatee in the mirror universe. The Buffy the Vampire Slayer episodes 'The Wish' (1998) and 'Doppelgangland' (1999) also featured evil counterparts brought over from alternate universes where some of the main characters were vampires.

South Park's 'Spookyfish' (1998) episode also featured an evil Cartman who came out of a portal to the evil world in the Ancient Indian Burial Ground Pet Shop.

SQUEEZE OF THE WEEK
No squeezing going on at all.

SIBLING RIVALRY
Sam starts to wonder about his future with psychic abilities in the first of many concerned exchanges between the boys over the rest of the season. Dean tries to convince Sam that he's not a murderer because he only kills things that were asking for it, but it doesn't work particularly well, and Sam still looks worried.

BODY COUNT
Sam saves the Doc from using the gun, so the Doc squidges himself under the front wheels of a bus instead. Then Holly soaks herself with petrol and uses the cigarette lighter to set herself on fire. Who said smoking doesn't kill?

TOOLKIT
- *Ash's laptop* and some (probably illegal) research reveals the location of the Blue Ridge bus company and the identity of the baby whose mother died in a house fire.
- *A handgun* and *a sniper rifle* help when there's an evil twin with mind control powers knocking around.
- *Sam's spooky visions* are very helpful when you're trying to track down other

people just like you.

MEMORABLE MOMENTS

Only a couple of stand-out moments this time.

When Sam tells Ellen about his powers, with a disapproving Dean looking on, it seems to be a moment of bonding and trust for their relationship, but future revelations will soon make it a rocky relationship, especially when the info about Ellen's husband leaks out.

And Dean singing REO Speedwagon in the car is a charming comedy moment.

THE CAR'S THE STAR

Andy must have a strong ability to manipulate minds if he got Dean to hand over the keys to the Impala willingly. The only other person to drive the Impala with permission is Sam, although it has been taken by force before[131].

SPOOK RULES

- The psychic kids have a range of different abilities: Sam has visions, Max could move physical objects and Andy can impose his will on people.
- With practice, Andy's abilities could develop into manipulating people without needing to use words – the same way his brother's have evolved.
- Sam's visions don't always occur before an event happens, sometimes they occur at exactly the same time as the event.
- The psychic kids can't be traced simply by locating people born on the same day as Sam, and who have lost their mom in a house fire on their six-month birthday.

DID YOU SPOT?

This is the first episode where Sam has a cast on his right arm after Padalecki injured himself filming 'Bloodlust' (2-03)[132].

GOING UNDERCOVER

Tracy mistakes Sam and Dean for debt collectors, but they introduce themselves as lawyers representing Great Aunt Leta who left Andy a sizable estate.

---

131 The shapeshifter stole and drove the Impala in 'Skin' (1-06); and the woman in white spookily took control of the car to try and kill the boys in (1-01).

132 See the **Behind the Scenes** section of 'Children Shouldn't Play With Dead Things' (2-04) for full details.

CULTURAL REFERENCES

Dean: 'He full-on Obi-Wan-ed me!': Obi-Wan Kenobi featured in the *Star Wars* series and used Jedi mind control on others for his own advantage, as first seen in *A New Hope* (1977).

Andy: 'These are not the droids you're looking for.': Another *Star Wars: A New Hope* reference. This time a quote by Obi-Wan Kenobi to help him get past the stormtroopers and into Mos Eisley spaceport.

Dean: 'It's not exactly a serial killer's lair, though. There's no clown paintings on the wall ...': Referencing serial killer John Wayne Gacy Jr (1942-1994) who killed at least 32 men in Chicago between 1972 and 1978, by means of rope or board pressed against their throats as he raped them. Twenty-seven of the bodies were discovered buried in the crawl space under his home. He was known for collecting and painting clown artwork and was a children's clown entertainer.

Sam: 'Hegel, Kant, Wittgenstein, it's pretty heavy reading, Dean.': Referencing the philosophers Georg Wilhelm Friedrich Hegel (1770-1831), Immanuel Kant (1724-1804) and Ludwig Josef Johann Wittgenstein (1889-1951).

Sam: 'Dean, you had O J convicted before he got out of his white Bronco': The trial of the century in which O J Simpson, the American football player turned movie star, was acquitted of the murder of his estranged wife Nicole Brown Simpson and Ronald Goldman, outside her home in 1994.

The licence plate on Andy's van – RU-OBI-1 – references Obi-Wan Kenobi and *Star Wars* again.

Sam: ''Cause there's a PBR in it for ya.': PBR is Pabst Blue Ribbon, a American brand of beer brewed by the Pabst Brewing Company, founded in 1844.

Sam: 'There's a work address from his last W-2, about a year ago.': A W-2 is a US tax form.

Andy: 'Does anyone have a Vicodin?': Vicodin is a type of medicine used to relieve moderate to severe pain.

Dean: 'Got his picture coming off from the DMV right now.': That'll be the Department of Motor Vehicles.

Dean: 'That was mind control! I mean, it's like, that's like being roofied, man.': Being roofied is to have your drink spiked with a date-rape drug like Rohypnol or Ketamine.

Webber: 'We can, we can push them, we can make them do whatever we want!': This is a reference to the Stephen King novel *Firestarter* (1980), in which Andrew McGee uses his 'mind domination' ability, which he calls the Push, to force people to do his will.

GOOFS AND FLUFFS
If Webber could manipulate people without having to say anything to them, why did he waste time contacting both Dr Jennings and Holly Beckett by phone?

HAVEN'T I SEEN YOU BEFORE?
John Dadey has been in *Painkiller Jane* and *The 4400*. Eric Keenleyside featured in *Poltergeist: The Legacy*, *Kingdom Hospital* and *Highlander*. Richard Lett has been in *Dark Angel*. Blu Mankuma was in *Blood Ties* and *Andromeda*. Ian Rozylo featured in *Battlestar Galactica*. Gabriel Tigerman has been in *Journeyman*. Elias Toufexis's credits include *Smallville*, *Stargate: Atlantis* and *Painkiller Jane*. Ivan Vance was in *Harsh Realm*. Chiara Zanni has featured in *X-Men 2* and *Smallville*.

BEHIND THE SCENES
Supernatural does a good job of pushing the envelope, but one of their stunts went too far and had to be toned down – the part where Doc Jennings gets hit by the bus. Editor Anthony Pinker said in the *Season Two Supernatural Companion* that there was a far bloodier version of the stunt involving a tennis shoe flying through the air but Kripke thought it was a little too much.

Staying with this episode's stunts, there's also a one where Holly sets herself on fire. When stunt artists get kitted up for sequences like this, they wear fireproof underwear that has been soaked in an ice-cold fire gel. So by the time they're ready to be set on fire they're freezing and shaking. Being lit up comes almost as a relief.

MUSICAL INTERLUDE
- 'Women's Wear ' – Daniel May – as Doc is shooting Dennis then himself.
- 'Tired of Crying' – Lil Ed and the Blues Imperials – at the Roadhouse when Sam and Dean are looking for Ash.
- 'Can't Fight This Feeling' – REO Speedwagon – when Jo is offering to help Dean at the Roadhouse, and sung by Dean straight afterwards (badly, which is surprising given that Ackles sings backing vocals with his friend's band).
- 'Stonehenge' – Spinal Tap – when Sam and Dean spy on Andy.
- 'Fell on Black Days' – Soundgarden – when Sam and Dean are at the Roadhouse talking to Ellen about the abilities and the demon.
- 'Uncle John' – Eric Lindell – when Sam asks Ash to do a search for house fires coinciding with a baby turning six months old.

ANALYSIS
Every TV series has to do an 'evil twin' storyline sooner or later and this is *Supernatural*'s

take on the idea. To the programme-makers' credit, they've made sufficient changes to freshen it up a little – the evil twin isn't one of the main characters, isn't an identical twin and stays hidden for most of the episode, making his discovery more of twist. And thankfully, Webber doesn't turn up sporting a nice little goatee beard either (*á la Star Trek*'s Spock).

Webber and Andy also take us back to the psychic kids story that hasn't been touched upon in detail since Sam discovered Max in 'Nightmare' (1-14). Here we get the back-story of another family affected by the yellow-eyed demon's meddling but there aren't any huge nuggets of new information on offer overall. Sam and Dean discover that they can't track the kids by looking for anyone who suffered a similar house fire on their six-month birthday, and that makes it impossible to know how many other similar kids are out there.

Even as this increases the sense of unease, there's more concern over the demon's reasons for influencing all these kids. Sam is starting to see a pattern: how anyone could commit murder in the right circumstances. It's the start of some serious soul-searching for Sam. Like Dean in 'Bloodlust' (2-03), Sam is facing a choice, and we can see the two ways he can go in Andy and Webber, who symbolically represent the good and evil aspects of the psychic powers. These are important events for Sam, his decisions and doubts will be explored in more depth in upcoming episodes in Season Two, but this will run eventually into Season Four as well.

Back in the present, we see a definite break away from the grieving brothers storyline in 'Simon Said', making it significantly less intense than any other Season Two episode so far. While it remains eminently watchable and entertaining – and it even has Dean being unusually reticent about going in with both guns blazing for a change – this is one of the weaker episodes in terms of scares and depth. It's more like a stepping stone episode setting up the increased focus on the psychic kids story arc without actually adding much to it itself.

VERDICT – 6 out of 10

EPISODE 2-06
NO EXIT

TRANSMISSION DATES
US first aired: 2 November 2006
UK first aired: 17 August 2007

CREDITS
Writer: Matt Witten
Director: Kim Manners

RECURRING ROLES
Samantha Ferris (Ellen Harvelle), Alona Tal (Jo Harvelle)

GUEST STARS
Stephen Aberle (H H Holmes), Andrea Brooks (Katie Burns), Lisa Marie Caruk (Theresa Ellis), Brent Chapman (Ed), Christ Eastman (Dad)

SYNOPSIS
In a renovated apartment block, young blonde girls are going missing and Jo Harvelle has spotted a pattern. Sam and Dean investigate and are joined by Jo, who has defied her mother's wishes about getting into hunting. Another girl goes missing, and when they search behind the walls, Jo herself is taken. The building turns out to be the site where H H Holmes – America's first known serial killer – was executed, and he's still there. The boys rescue the trapped women from the sewers beneath the building and trap the spirit inside a circle of salt before sealing the entrance with a couple of tons of concrete.

CAN YOU SURVIVE TO THE TITLES?
When the black ectoplasm starts dripping in your apartment, you just know something's going to happen. Katie Burns gets the evil eye and is never seen again (unless you count the brief glimpse of her decaying corpse in the sewer).

LOCATION, LOCATION, LOCATION
Next door to the old site of the Moyamensing Prison, Philadelphia.

LEGENDARY ROOTS

Dr H H Holmes, born Herman Webster Mudgett (1860-1896), is America's first known serial killer. He started off with life insurance scams using corpses he stole from the university laboratories where he was studying. He disfigured them and claimed they had been accidentally killed, then he would claim the insurance money.

His first known kill was in Englewood, Illinois, where he murdered the wife of a drugstore owner who had recently passed away. Dr E S Holton's store was sold to Holmes on the condition that the wife could live above the store after the death of the husband.

Holmes purchased the lot across from the drugstore, where he constructed his 'murder castle'. It was built over three years by numerous builders that he hired and fired regularly so only he knew the actual design. The castle was a three storey, block long building containing over 100 rooms in a maze like construction, many without windows. There were doors that would open to nothing but a brick wall, stairs that went nowhere, doors that could be opened from only one side, soundproof rooms and even gas chambers, acid vats and dissecting tables. Holmes would torture his victims and eventually kill them, disposing of the bodies in a furnace or selling the organs and skeletons to medical schools. It is not known how many people Holmes murdered but estimates range from 20 up to 200. Holmes was eventually tried and hung at the Philadelphia County Prison. His body was buried encased in concrete at his request so no-one could dig it up and dissect it.

SQUEEZE OF THE WEEK

Dean gives Jo a couple of slaps to the rump and a bit of a hug when they are masquerading as a couple looking for an apartment, but he keeps his hands well off after that and even sleeps on the sofa. That is, until they're in the tight space between the walls and he admits that he 'should've cleaned the pipes' before she rubbed her body up against him to squeeze past. Obviously, he's not thinking of her as a little sister all the time then.

SIBLING RIVALRY

Sam is having a rest and most of the verbal fencing this time happens between Dean and Jo as he tries to convince her not to go into hunting, no matter how mentally twisted she thinks she is right now.

But there's only one thing that needs unravelling and that's Dean's boxers, as Jo points out to him when she turns up at the haunted apartment building and Dean tries to lecture her about lying to her mom.

BODY COUNT

Apart from Katie decaying in the sewer, no-one else suffers anything more than a spot of solitary confinement and a quick lascivious fondle from an evil spirit. Jo and Theresa are rescued before Holmes can do anything dastardly to them.

TOOLKIT

- Hunting the spirits of serial killers requires a wider range of equipment than usual so as well as the standard big bag of *salt* and several *EMF meters*, you'll need:
- A *screwdriver* to remove gratings from the wall.
- A *bowie knife* to show off with when someone else is twirling a 'little pig-sticker' of a knife (that happens to be *made of pure iron*).
- *Sledgehammers* to smash through walls.
- A *metal detector and a shovel* for locating metal drain covers to access the sewers.
- A *shotgun loaded with rock salt* and *a flashlight* for entering the sewer tunnels.
- A *handy iron bar* for prising open the doors of small metal compartments where young girls have been trapped.
- A *cement truck, with a full load of cement,* to fill the access tunnel to the trapped evil spirit.
- And how nice to see Sam with a *laptop* once more. Bet he's been feeling naked without it.

MEMORABLE MOMENTS

Unusually, the best scenes are not between Sam and Dean but their interactions with Jo and Ellen instead.

The exchange between Dean and Jo – where he tries to convince her that she has better options than hunting to pursue – is sharply written; and the scenes of Dean arguing with Jo about telling her mother where she's gone are excellently executed.

Ellen's silent wrath in the car as Dean drives everyone back to Harvelle's is formidable.

SPOOK RULES

- You have to be one majorly pissed off spirit to be able to manifest ectoplasm.
- Ectoplasm created by an evil spirit looks like black goo and can ooze from light fittings or drip out of mid-air (without an obvious source).
- Spirits like to hide in the walls and have creepy, grimy, unkempt appearances – probably because a squeaky clean ghost just ain't scary.
- Haunted buildings are often a location where someone has died in a bloody

manner; or they could have a cursed object with resident spirit stored within the structure somewhere.

GOING UNDERCOVER
In order to gain access to the apartment where the first girl used to live, Dean and Jo pretend to be a couple looking for a place to rent, accompanied by their buddy Sam.

CULTURAL REFERENCES
Dean teases Sam about a girl who's been kidnapped by an evil cult. When Sam asks who the girl is, Dean says it's Katie Holmes: Referring to actress Katie Holmes dating Scientologist Tom Cruise. It was feared she may have been brainwashed into following the religion.

Dean: 'I think I know what we're dealing with here. It's the Stay Puft Marshmallow Man.': The Stay Puft Marshmallow Man is the mascot for the Stay Puft Corporation in the 1984 movie *Ghostbusters*[133].

Jo: 'I'm here to rescue you.': Quoting the 1977 movie *Star Wars Episode IV: A New Hope*.

GOOFS AND FLUFFS
When the boys are opening the drain cover, there's a camera shot looking up from inside the shaft and Dean hands the gun to Sam butt first, with Dean holding the barrel. As the camera shot flips to topside, Dean finishes handing the gun to Sam but is now holding the butt of the gun himself.

When Sam and Dean and Jo are discussing Holmes, one of the photographs on the table is actually of Elizabeth Stride, generally believed to be a victim of Jack the Ripper.

Jo says that Moyamensing Prison was 'built in 1835, torn down in 1963' but it seems to be generally reported to have been closed in 1964 and torn down in 1968.

Holmes did indeed use chloroform on his victims but wasn't very fussy about the type of person he preyed upon. He also used gas chambers and blow torches to kill his victims.

According to this episode, Sam and Dean are unaware of their father's involvement in Bill Harvelle's death, however the details of how Bill died – and mention of Ellen, the Roadhouse and Jo – can be found in *John Winchester's Journal* by Alex Irvine (William Morrow, 2009) under the entry on 16 April 1986. Strange the boys never read that bit …

---

133 Mentioned before in 'Hookman' (1-07), 'Hell House' (1-17) and 'Roadkill' (2-16).

HAVEN'T I SEEN YOU BEFORE?

Stephen Aberle featured in *Dark Angel*. Lisa Marie Caruk's credits include *Final Destination, Dead Like Me* and *The Dead Zone*. Brent Chapman has been in *Freddy vs Jason, Masters of Horror* and *The X-Files*. Christ Eastman was also in *The Entrance*.

BEHIND THE SCENES

This episode started one of the most famous on-set pranking tales of the series so far. Telling the story in *The Official Supernatural Magazine* #3, Jensen Ackles explained that he and Padalecki were crawling through sewer tunnels and getting soaking wet. The camera operator was laughing at them and the boys decided he deserved a dunking. So, after the shot was done, they walked over to the camera operator and pushed him into the water. When Kim Manners objected, the boys picked him up and he got a soaking too.

Manners unsurprisingly wanted revenge, so about a week later, the boys were shooting some scenes for 'No Exit' where they had to climb down into a 15 foot pipe with a ladder in it. The pipe was a set and didn't go anywhere, and as soon as both boys were down inside the tube, Manners had two five-gallon buckets of water tipped over them. Touché.

Samantha Ferris describes Ellen's relationship with John Winchester in *The Official Supernatural Magazine* #3, revealing how she thinks Ellen adored John but struggled after her husband's death because she felt John had been responsible for it. When the boys come back to the Roadhouse, she's torn again because she doesn't want the Winchester boys to be responsible for her daughter's death either.

MUSICAL INTERLUDE

- 'Surrender' – Cheap Trick – when Sam and Dean are driving at the start of episode.
- 'Cold As Ice' – Foreigner – as Sam, Dean, Jo and Ellen travel back to the Roadhouse.
- 'Mama' – Godsmack – unconfirmed, but it's supposed to be Dean's ringtone.
- 'Paranoid' – Black Sabbath – suggested in the TV Without Pity.com website review.

ANALYSIS

This one's almost up to *Supernatural*'s usual high standard of stand-alone episodes. It's got an interesting spook in the form of America's first known serial killer and a good old scare moment when the disgusting eye appears in the light switch when the first girl is taken. The team don't quite achieve the eerie atmosphere that *The X-Files* created in their

227

similar episode 'Squeeze' (1-02) but that may be due in part to the inclusion of more humour in 'No Exit', especially in the relationship between Dean and Jo.

That growing relationship is one of the most interesting aspects of the episode. Jo Harvelle comes into the spotlight, and despite Dean being less emotionally troubled than the last time he encountered her, he's still not showing any real romantic interested (despite quips about 'cleaning the pipes'). Actually, they settle into more of a bickering brother-sister alignment, and he tries to protect her from the dangers of hunting in the same way he tried to protect Sam when he was young. Dean's such a mother hen underneath all that bravado.

Jo may be an amateur but she acquits herself reasonably well. At least she shows she has some courage by being bait to trap the serial killer, even if she doesn't actually rescue anyone because she needs rescuing herself. Not that the boys have a perfect record of not being caught by the bad guy either[134], it's just that one brother is usually available to free the other when this happens.

For Jo, the arguments with her mother and her obvious need to stretch her wings for herself are a new development, since she didn't express any such wishes to escape in the boys' first visit to the Roadhouse (she was too busy flirting with Dean at the time). It's clear Jo is trying to find her own path in life after being surrounded by this crowd of hunters since she was young, but her role in future episodes is unclear – as she swings from wanting the boys' help when they arrive, to insisting that they leave her alone after she finds out about John Winchester's role in her father's death.

Talking of which, John Winchester's involvement in Bill Harvelle's death does account for why he never told the boys about Ellen and Jo, but aside from that making the boys feel unwelcome at the Roadhouse, it's not very clear what difference it is going to make.

Apart from the snippet about John, there's very little in the way of story arcs for the boys – Dean reminisces briefly about his fondest memory of his father, but it's surprisingly dry-eyed, with no hint of the emotional turmoil evident at the end of 'Children Shouldn't Play With Dead Things' (2-04). And the psychic powers aren't mentioned at all.

So while 'No Exit' is not one of the most memorable episodes in Season Two – especially in terms of progressing major story arcs – there's nothing inherently wrong with it either. It delivers a satisfying adventure, some sharp dialogue, a scare and a smile or two. Just sit back and enjoy.

VERDICT – 7 out of 10

---

134 Sam and Dean get captured in 'Skin' (1-06); Dean gets tied to a tree in 'Scarecrow' (1-11); and Sam gets caught in 'The Benders' (1-15) and 'Bloodlust' (2-03).

EPISODE 2-07
THE USUAL SUSPECTS

TRANSMISSION DATES
US first aired: 9 November 2006
UK first aired: 24 August 2007

CREDITS
Writer: Cathryn Humphris
Director: Mike Rohl

GUEST STARS
Linda Blair (Det Diana Ballard), Keegan Connor Tracy (Caren Giles), Diana Dutra (Policewoman), Jason Gedrick (Det Peter Sheridan), Shannon Powell (Claire Becker), Andrew Stahl (Geoff Krause)

SYNOPSIS
Sam and Dean are in police custody, Dean having been caught standing over Caren Giles' recently murdered corpse. Sam escapes and follows up their only clue: the word 'danaschulps' found written in the location where the body was discovered. This leads him, along with Detective Diana Ballard, to discover the body of a young girl, Claire, on Ashland Street. Claire's ghost has been appearing to people just before they are murdered, and now she visits Ballard. The murderer turns out to be Ballard's partner, Detective Pete Sheridan, who gets shot when trying to kill Dean and blame all the killings on him.

CAN YOU SURVIVE TO THE TITLES?
Everyone survives to the titles. The teaser this time shows Dean's predicament as Detective Sheridan tells him that he's up on a murder charge for killing several women in St Louis.[135]

LOCATION, LOCATION, LOCATION
Baltimore, Maryland (various locations including Oak Avenue (Giles' office address) and 45 Upper Alder Heights, Parkway (Giles' home address)); The City Centre Motor Hotel; The Aardvark Motel.

---

135 This is where the shapeshifter Dean did all the dastardly deeds until real Dean finally shot him in 'Skin' (1-06).

LEGENDARY ROOTS

If you are visited by a death omen, then chances are that you are going to die in the near future. The form of death omens varies around the world from culture to culture, country to country; it can be a dream, a creature appearing, or something happening to an object. Common bird omens are a bird flying in through an open window, flying down the chimney, tapping on a window or hovering above a house, or an owl seen during the day. Other animal omens are a cat leaving a house and not re-entering it, and a dog howling during the night for no apparent reason. In Mexico, the Caribbean, or the American Southwest, if the Black Witch moth flies into a house (and, according to some, visits all four corners) someone in the house will die soon. Omens that relate to physical objects are a picture falling off a wall, a mirror breaking while still hanging or a clock stopping or failing to chime. An Irish example of a death omen is the banshee coming to announce the death of a person, which according to tradition cries for only five major Irish families: the O'Neills, the O'Briens, the O'Connors, the O'Gradys and the Kavanaghs.

SQUEEZE OF THE WEEK

Dean spends most of his time handcuffed to a table, while Sam's hacking corpses out of the walls – no time for any kind of squeeze[136].

SIBLING RIVALRY

Not much rivalry going on either since the boys spend most of their time separated. But at the start, when they're discussing the newspaper article about a lawyer who has had his throat slit and nothing showed up on the CCTV, Dean decides that he's Mulder and Sam is definitely Scully, because Sam's a red-haired woman.

BODY COUNT

Heroin addict Claire Becker, lawyer Anthony Giles and his wife Caren Giles are all murdered prior to the episode's start and revealed in flashback. Only Detective Sheridan is shot during the episode – by his partner Detective Ballard to stop him killing Dean.

TOOLKIT

- The standard spook kit is on hand – *EMF meter, salt* and *matches* for burning dem bones.
- *A pocket knife* helps to cut the ropes binding the corpse and a *sledgehammer's*

---

136 Although the proximity of Dean and handcuffs is going to keep a few people happy, no doubt.

just the business for breaking down walls. Sam actually switches to using *his elbow* to get through the wall when he's finished with the hammer – he must have reinforced joints and a high pain threshold.

MEMORABLE MOMENTS
The best humour comes when Dean squares up to the camera to confess to his crimes; the best scary sequence is when the ghost appears to Caren just before she is killed.

THE CAR'S THE STAR
Or not in this case. The poor Impala has been impounded by the cops and stored over on Robertson for the entire episode, all alone. Aw!

SPOOK RULES
- Communicating across the veil isn't easy and sometimes the spirits get things jumbled. At times only word fragments make it across, other times the letters get mixed up.
- Spirits who are death omens appear to the next victim not long before the victim is due to die.
- Death omen spirits can transfer some of the physical trauma they themselves experienced – such as bruising to the wrists – to the person they are trying to warn.
- Vengeful spirits are often created by violent deaths and come back for a nasty reason – like deadly revenge on the people that hurt them. However, sometimes they just want justice and lead people to their corpses in order to expose the person who killed them. Most vengeful spirits do not want you anywhere near their remains, especially if you're armed with salt and a match.
- Salting and burning the bones isn't the only way to stop them – if justice is served the spirit will stop haunting people and places.

DID YOU SPOT?
Caren's house number is 421 – Eric Kripke's wife's birthday is 24/1.

The first victim is one Anthony Giles – a veiled reference to the character Rupert Giles played by Anthony Stewart Head in *Buffy the Vampire Slayer*, perhaps?

GOING UNDERCOVER
The boys are pretending to be insurance representatives again[137].

---

137 Something they haven't done since 'Route 666' (1-13).

HUNTER'S LINGO

Not so much lingo as good practice: the boys have back up plans in place in case things go wrong and they get separated. When Sam escapes from the police station, he finds the first motel in the Yellow Pages and gets a room under the name of Jim Rockford so Dean can find him later.

CULTURAL REFERENCES

Dean: 'No, I'm Mulder. You're a red-headed woman.': Referencing the FBI agents Dana Scully and Fox Mulder in *The X-Files* (1993-2002)[138].

Dean: '*Time-Life: Mysteries of the Unknown*. Look it up.': A 33-volume series of books published by Time-Life (1987-1991), each book concerning a different topic such as mysterious creatures, UFOs, hauntings and spirit summonings.

Dean: 'I'm not joking, Ponch.': Officer Francis Llewellyn 'Ponch' Poncherello (Erik Estrada) was one of the main characters in the TV show *CHiPs* (1977-1983) about two California Highway Patrol motorcycle officers.

Dean: 'Go to the first motel listed in the Yellow Pages. Look for Jim Rockford.': From *The Rockford Files* TV series (1974-1980) starring James Garner as private investigator Jim Rockford.

Dean: 'You remember redrum.'; and Dean: 'All work and no play makes Jack a dull boy.': Two more references to the novel *The Shining* (1977) by Stephen King. 'Redrum' was the reversed communication for 'murder' from little Danny Torrance, and 'All work and no play makes Jack a dull boy' was repeated lots of times by Jack Nicholson's character, Jack Torrance.[139]

Sam: 'Nice lady.'; Dean: 'Yeah, for a cop. Did she look familiar to you?' and Dean: 'For some reason I could really go for some pea soup.': Both referencing guest star Linda Blair's character Regan in the 1973 movie *The Exorcist*, who projectile vomits something that looks like pea soup. The first quote is a direct reference to the actress rather than the movie.

Dean: 'Hey, thanks for the law review, Matlock.'; and Sam: 'Sure thing, Matlock.': Benjamin L Matlock was a defence attorney working in Atlanta, Georgia in the TV series *Matlock* that ran from 1986 to 1995.[140]

Dean: 'You know, Casper the bloodthirsty ghost?': A name-check for Casper the Friendly Ghost. Casper has been around since the late 1930s in all forms of media from books, through cartoons and graphic novels to PC games in 2007. In *The Friendly*

---

138 Last referenced in 'The Woman in White' (1-01).

139 'All work and no play makes Jack a dull boy' was also referenced in 'Asylum' (1-10).

140 The series was also mentioned in 'Hookman' (1-07).

Ghost, released in 1945 by Paramount, Casper escapes from the Winchester Mystery House and goes out to make friends.[141]

Sam: 'Well, then they should have a lo-jack, you've just gotta get it turned on.': Lo-jack is a hidden transmitter device within a vehicle that helps the police track and recover it.

GOOFS AND FLUFFS

When Sam and Ballard are about to leave, you can see Sam pull the sleeve of his jacket up one arm. The very next shot has him without the jacket on at all, it's just in his hands.

The 'Ashland Sup(pliers)' sign is painted on the window so when the sun shines through it, the letters will cast a shadow with light all around them. However, the shadow that Sam and Ballard actually see is of light shining through letters surrounded by dark.

If they salted and burned Claire's remains in the basement, how did she manage to appear and distract Sheridan afterwards?

HAVEN'T I SEEN YOU BEFORE?

Linda Blair played Regan in *The Exorcist* and *Exorcist II: The Heretic* and hosted the TV series *The Scariest Places on Earth*. Keegan Connor played Jeanne in *Battlestar Galactica*, Diane Hughes in *Jake 2.0* and Kat in *Final Destination 2*. Diana Dutra has performed stunts in *Fantastic Four* and *I, Robot*. Jason Gedrick featured in *Ghost Whisperer* and *The Outer Limits*. Shannon Powell has been in *Dark Angel*, *Stargate SG-1* and *Blade: Trinity*. Andrew Stahl's credits include *Fantastic 4: Rise of the Silver Surfer*, *SeaQuest DSV* and *Stephen King's The Mist*.

BEHIND THE SCENES

Toby Lindala, head of the *Supernatural* make-up effects department, was pleased with how the ghost's bleeding neck effects turned out in this episode. They developed some special manifold systems so that, as the ghost starts to talk, the blood starts oozing out driven by air from under the sheet of blood. They could control it from trickling out, all the way up to a burbling flow. [*The Official Supernatural Magazine* #9]

MUSICAL INTERLUDE

All music was written specifically for this episode.

---

141 Casper was first name-checked in 'The Woman in White' (1-01).

ANALYSIS

The *Supernatural* writing team goes out of its way to make sure that their entire show is as realistic as possible, and that's not easy when you're dealing with some pretty unbelievable antagonists (murderous midget clown anyone?). Most of the time their efforts are successful[142] and it's episodes like 'The Usual Suspects' that help to cement the boys' adventures into the real world by creating believable situations for them to deal with.

Up to this point, the boys have had a pretty slack attitude about leaving forensic evidence behind them when they visit crime scenes. They've hardly ever bothered about wiping fingerprints down after searching a room[143] and they'll have left fibres and hairs littered across almost every State in the US (don't they watch CSI?). Now their lack of caution has landed them in a pickle (as it damn well should have), because once the cops start looking, they discover that Dean has something of a history when it comes to violent deaths. Back in 'Skin' (1-06), Sam had to get the police to put an APB out on shapeshifter Dean, which led ultimately to the real Dean being wanted for murder in St Louis. The shapeshifter was killed but now real Dean has been arrested for murder in Baltimore and things are looking seriously difficult for the boys.

Not that it seems to bother them at all, since they appear to have it all under control. That's mostly due to who they are and how well they've been trained, and we get to see them performing under pressure from the cops for a change instead of pressure from supernatural beasties bent on killing them.

At first glance, there's not a lot of character development going on in this episode, but it's just hidden a little bit deeper under the surface. For Sam, we get to see his con artist abilities clearer than ever before, especially when he's trying to be compassionate to Caren while giving Dean a withering 'Will you stop upsetting the witness' look. Then there's Sam's handcuff-picking skills and his athletic ability, the latter indicated by his daring escape from the cops out of a window several storeys up with no fire escape within immediate reach.

For Dean, we see more of his cocky laugh-in-the-face-of-danger attitude demonstrated perfectly in his 'sunsets and frisky women' confession, and there's also an indication of how strongly he feels about saving people when he tells Diana where to find Sam. Diana could easily have just hauled Sam's (rather delectable) ass into the station, but Dean was prepared to take the risk because he thought Sam could help save her life. So their own safety clearly comes second to that of the victim's.

---

142 Unless your title happens to be 'Bugs' (1-08).

143 With the exception of 'Nightmare' (1-14), where they wiped down the hand rail on the fire escape after they found Max's uncle decapitated.

For an episode with no fights, chases or major action it's surprisingly engaging. Performances are excellent throughout, especially Linda Blair's, and the structure of the first half of the episode, with its flashback of alternative events, is a fresh way of telling the tale and building the story ready for the linear second half.

A stronger stand-alone story than the last one, it leaves you wondering what's going to happen when the cops catch up with the boys again[144] ...

VERDICT – 8 out of 10

---

[144] In five episodes' time in fact, when events in 'Nightshifter' (2-12) make matters even worse.

EPISODE 2-08
CROSSROAD BLUES

TRANSMISSION DATES
US first aired: 16 November 2006
UK first aired: 31 August 2007

CREDITS
Writer: Sera Gamble
Director: Steve Boyum

GUEST STARS
La Monde Byrd (Robert Johnson), Leah Cairns (Julie Hudson), Marcus Champagne (Unknown), Richard Cohee (Unknown), Deni DeLory (Syliva Pearlman), Vincent Gale (Evan Hudson), John Lafayette (George Darrow), James Lafazanos (Hotel Manager), Christie Laing (Johnson's Demon), Yvonne Myers (Sadie), Aleks Paunovic (Tony Disalvo), Jeannette Sousa (Crossroads Demon), Catherine Thomas (Maid), Lilian Umrugungii (Unknown)

SYNOPSIS
When a successful architect commits suicide after reporting that he's seen a black dog prowling the area, Sam and Dean investigate. They discover that ten years earlier the deceased made a deal with a crossroads demon for wealth and success in return for his soul. The debt came due and the architect died. Problem is, after being summoned for the first deal, the demon hung around making similar pacts with three other people. Dr Sylvia Pearlman's debt is overdue, and she pays the price before the boys can find her; while artist George Darrow is at home, resigned to his fate and waiting patiently to pay his due. But Sam and Dean manage to free another victim – Evan Hudson, who made a deal to save his dying wife's life. As Dean tricks the crossroads demon into a trap, the demon tempts him with deals that could free John Winchester from hell. Dean barely resists the opportunity to help his father, and instead forces the demon to release Evan Hudson from his commitment.

CAN YOU SURVIVE TO THE TITLES?
Blues player Robert Johnson is terrorised by shadowy dogs that only he can see. He tries to escape but the hell hounds soon catch up with him and he dies lying on the floor in convulsions – maybe from fear, maybe from their invisible fatal attentions.

LOCATION, LOCATION, LOCATION

Greenwood, Mississippi, 1938; Rosedale, Mississippi, 1930. It's not clearly stated where the episode takes place, but the implication is that Lloyd's Bar was the site of Robert Johnson's last performance back in '38.

LEGENDARY ROOTS

According to legend, Robert Leroy Johnson (1911-1938) became an accomplished musician after making a deal with the devil. He was told to take his guitar to a crossroads near the Dockery Plantation where at midnight he met the Devil in the form of a large black man. The Devil tuned his guitar, played a few songs on it and once he'd handed it back, Johnson was an outstanding blues player. However, in exchange for this talent he sold his soul.

Johnson recorded only 29 songs in two recording sessions in November 1936 and June 1937. His life was cut short at the age of 27 when he was poisoned by the husband of a woman he had been seeing – or maybe it was the Devil calling in his soul. He was inducted into the Rock and Roll Hall of Fame in 1986 and his music has influenced many subsequent artists, including Eric Clapton, Led Zeppelin and Jimi Hendrix.

SQUEEZE OF THE WEEK

Dean gets a huge snog and some serious demon tonsil tennis when he seals the deal to save Evan Hudson's life. He may have implied he didn't enjoy it, but the crossroads demon was so decidedly hot it's no surprise he didn't fight her off.

SIBLING RIVALRY

When Sam discovers there's a warrant out on Dean in St Louis, Dean starts teasing Sam because no one has posted anything about Sam even being an accessory or anything. Dean thinks Sam is just jealous of his brother's notoriety.

BODY COUNT

Only one fatality after the credits: Dr Sylvia Pearlman gets shredded on a motel floor by some nasty invisible canines when they come to collect her payment – after her deal to become chief surgeon at a local hospital.

TOOLKIT

- There aren't any effective weapons that you can use against a hellhound directly, but protecting yourself in *a circle of goofer dust* seems to be the best option when they're after you. Goofer dust is an African-American hoodoo mixture with a range of recipes available. The base ingredients are graveyard dirt, powdered sulphur and salt, with additional options including powdered snakeskin, red pepper, black pepper, powdered bones, powdered insects and powdered herbs. Its more common use is to jinx people you don't like, rather than as a protection against supernatural beasties.

- Be sure to pack *a shovel* for digging in the middle of a crossroads and hope for a quiet junction or you'll be dodging traffic as you dig.
- Take *some chalk or similar writing material* with you to draw *a Devil's Trap symbol* on the ground or on the underside of a wooden structure.
- And don't forget a copy of the *Rituale Romanum* exorcism text to use on the demon once you've trapped it.

MEMORABLE MOMENTS

Dr Sylvia's last moments are all the more scary for not being able to see the hellhounds.

And Dean's conversation with the crossroads demon is edgy for two reasons – because Evan is really close to becoming a doggy play-chew and because Dean himself is seriously considering making the deal to free his dad.

SPOOK RULES

- There's big, nasty, spectral black dog lore all over the world. Some say they're animal spirits, others that they're death omens.
- When you summon a crossroads demon, you need yarrow flowers, graveyard dirt, bones from a black cat, a photograph of yourself and a small rusty tin to put the items in when you bury them at the centre of a crossroads.
- You seal your deal by snogging the demon you make it with, tongues optional.
- After you've summoned the demon, there's nothing says it has to leave until it's ready. It can hang around afterwards and make more deals with anybody willing to pay the price.
- When it's payback time on your deal, ferocious black dogs that only you can see and hear will be sent to retrieve your soul. They will hound you for some time while you try to run and hide, but once the hallucinations start – where people's faces start distorting, turning grey with their eyes rolling up in their head – you know you're on the final approach for your trip to hell. Brace yourself!
- Demons can't escape from the Devil's Trap symbol and they'd rather release someone from a deal than be exorcised back to hell.

DID YOU SPOT?

The Devil's Trap symbol is taken from the book *The Key of Solomon* (Clavicula Salomonis) and was last used to hold Meg in 'Devil's Trap' (1-22).

There's a Beware of Dog sign on the front gate of Evan's house. Is that the subtle *Supernatural* humour kicking in again?

GOING UNDERCOVER

The boys are masquerading as reporters working for (real life) magazine *Architectural Digest* when they are trying to get more information about Sean Boyden's suicide from his business partner.

When they are investigating the reports about incidents involving anything big, black or dog-like, they pretend to be animal control workers.

CULTURAL REFERENCES

Dean: 'Nobody put a gun to their head and forced 'em to play *Let's Make A Deal*.': *Let's Make A Deal* first aired in 1963, and a new version launched in October 2009 on CBS. In the show, contestants are asked to trade what they have brought in for a mystery prize.

Dean: 'Though this house probably ain't up next on *MTV Cribs*, is it?': Starting in 2000, *MTV Cribs* allowed viewers the chance to see inside the homes of celebrities.

Dean: 'Maybe this place is full of babes in Princess Leia bikinis.': Referencing the skimpy bikini Princess Leia is forced to wear when enslaved by Jabba the Hutt in *Star Wars: Return of the Jedi* (1983).

Lloyd's Bar is another reference to *The Shining*, in which Jack Torrance states 'God, I'd give anything for a drink. I'd give my god-damned soul for just a glass of beer!' Bartender Lloyd magically appears with a fully stocked bar. Dean is also involved with selling his soul at Lloyd's Bar[145].

Dean: 'Dude, I am like Dillinger or something.': John Herbert Dillinger (1903-1934) was an infamous gangster and bank robber during the Great Depression, who was nicknamed Jack Rabbit due to his ability to jump bank counters and orchestrate many narrow getaways from the police.

Dean: 'That's serious spell work. I mean, that's Deep South hoodoo stuff.': Hoodoo is from South American spiritualistic traditions, including folk magic, fortune telling, remedies and necromancy, but is not a religion. The followers are predominantly Christian. Remedies and spells are usually concerned with objects with powers that are supernatural or spiritual, and if they are to be focused on an individual they need something owned by that person like a nail or hair.

Dean: 'What'd you ask for anyway, Evan? Huh? Never need Viagra?': Viagra is a

---

145 Other mentions of *The Shining* are in the episodes 'Home' (1-09), 'Asylum' (1-10), 'In My Time Of Dying' (2-01), and 'The Usual Suspects' (2-07). And this won't be the last time it's referenced ...

pill taken to aid a man's bedroom performance. Something that Dean probably never needs.

GOOFS AND FLUFFS

There's only one goof but it involves a spoiler so it can be read only in the footnotes to protect those who don't want to know yet[146].

HAVEN'T I SEEN YOU BEFORE?

La Monde Byrd has been in *CSI: Crime Scene Investigation*. Leah Cairns played Lt Margaret 'Racetrack' Edmonson in *Battlestar Galactica* and Emily Hollander in *Kyle XY*. Richard Cohee was in *Jake 2.0*. Deni DeLory features in *The 4400, The Outer Limits* and *Prom Night IV: Deliver Us from Evil*. Vincent Gale played Chief Peter Laird in *Battlestar Galactica* and has also been in *A Town Called Eureka* and *The Dead Zone*. John Lafayette has been in *Fright Night Part 2* and *Watchers II*. James Lafazanos played Wraith in *Stargate: Atlantis* and has also appeared in *Battlestar Galactica*. Christie Laing has appeared in *Dead Like Me, The 4400* and *Kyle XY*. Yvonne Myers featured in *The Outer Limits, Andromeda* and *Stargate SG-1*. Aleks Paunovic was in *Bionic Woman, Battlestar Galactica* and *Wishmaster 4: The Prophecy Fulfilled*. Jeanette Sousa's credits include *Mutant X, Urban Legends: Final Cut* and *Total Recall: 2070*.

Christie Laing also appears in 'Hookman' (1-07).

BEHIND THE SCENES

The picture of the black dog at the start of the episode is by John Bauer and depicts the Norse god Tyr putting his hand in the mouth of Fenris the wolf in order for the gods to bind it and protect Asgard. Tyr lost his hand as a result (but probably didn't get his leg humped at least).

Director Steve Boyum said in *The Official Supernatural Magazine* #5 that this episode would have been easier if they'd have used a real dog so Jared could have had something to react to other than an empty room. While the boys deal with that stuff well, by the middle of a long afternoon Jared couldn't tell where the dog was anymore and Boyum was admitting that it wasn't in the room.

MUSICAL INTERLUDE

• 'Crossroad Blues' – Robert Johnson – as Robert is making his deal with the

---

146 Spoiler: It's established in a future episode ('Time Is On My Side' (3-15)) that Lilith controls all the contracts made by crossroads demons. So how could this crossroads demon let Evan out of his deal without consulting the owner of the contract?

demon.
- 'Downhearted Blues' – Son House – while Sam and Dean are at George Darrow's apartment.
- 'Key to the Highway' – Big Bill Broonzy – when Sam and Dean are in the car talking about their dad's legacy.
- 'Chaos Surrounds You' – Brian Tichy – Dean turns up this music to end the conversation about whether or not he's considered making a deal with a demon.
- 'Hair of the Dog' – Nazareth – playing during the Coming Soon montage.

ANALYSIS

The introduction of the crossroads demon to the *Supernatural* mythology is a surprisingly low-key affair given the significant role they'll have in the future, and 'Crossroad Blues' does the very thing it should do: it gives you a very clear understanding of what dealing demons do. It's all very straightforward – put the right set of objects in a tin, bury them at a nice set of crossroads to summon the demon, ask for what you want, seal the deal with some tonsil tennis, then get dragged to hell shredded and screaming ten years later (or however many years you can barter the demon into giving you). We're starting to see the different varieties of the demons now, as well as indications of how a demon might advance itself in hell, along with our first descriptions of the landscape down under. It's all very fascinating and it's all very important stuff to remember.

But this being *Supernatural*, the programme-makers don't stop there. Around this introduction to the dealing demons, there are a couple of morals slipped in about being careful what you wish for (talent won't always bring you fame and fortune) and taking responsibility for your own actions when the debt becomes due. We're also treated to a diverse range of responses from different people when payback day arrives: some run, some stand and face it.

And underneath all that, giving the episode a cohesive feel, there's another layer about the brothers that reveals more aspects of their inner psychology.

Finally the boys catch up with what the audience already knows and discover what John did to save Dean. Dean's struggling with a huge sense of guilt (for still being here, for being the reason Sam's dad's gone, and now for the suffering that John will almost certainly be experiencing in hell), and he's taking his anger out on Evan who's symbolically done the same thing as John in saving someone he loves.

Sam in the meantime is trying to help these people, possibly because he's got first-hand experience of how demons can manipulate people to their own ends and partly because he has a knack for empathising with others. There's no major character development for him in 'Crossroad Blues' (the focus is mainly on Dean) but he is clearly still concerned about his brother's mental state, especially after his 'tail-spinning' comment on the zombie hunt[147] and now with this situation of Dean being tempted to make a deal to free John's soul.

At the end, leaving Sam's question to Dean about the deal unanswered is another nice touch of ambiguity (although you're pretty sure that Dean has given freeing his Dad some damn serious thought). It also seeds a little piece of groundwork ready for some of the upcoming events. This kind of open-ended close to an episode is something of a mini trademark for writers Raelle Tucker and Sera Gamble, whose scripts tend to take exceptionally deep peeks into the boys' emotional states. There was a similar ending to Gamble's 'Children Shouldn't Play With Dead Things' (2-04), where the suspicion first arose that John did something to save Dean's life. And we'll have a similar emotionally-charged situation in Tucker's 'What Is And What Should Never Be' (2-20).

This may not be the most riveting of episodes – they almost pull it off with the invisible dogs, but in the end Evan's and Sam's danger is significantly less intriguing than Dean's encounter with the demon – but that aside, this is a vital chapter in the overall story.

VERDICT – 7 out of 10

EPISODE 2-09
CROATOAN

TRANSMISSION DATES
US first aired: 7 December 2006
UK first aired: 7 September 2007

CREDITS
Writer: John Shiban
Director: Robert Singer

GUEST STARS
Sonja Bennett (Pamela Clayton), Chilton Crane (Beverly Tanner), Nolan Funk (Jake Tanner), Bobby Hosea (Mark Vargo), Kate Jennings Grant (Dr Amanda Lee), Diego Klattenhoff (Duane Tanner), Simon Longmore (Man at Barricade), Laurie Murdoch (Mr Tanner)

SYNOPSIS
Sam's visions lead the boys to a small town that's on the edge of self destruction as a demon virus rages through the populace. Holed up in the medical centre with the only 'clean' people in town – Dr Lee, nurse Pamela, ex-marine Mark and Duane Tanner, whose family were the first to be infected – Sam and Dean try to figure out how to escape past the road block and crowds of infected folk in the streets. When Sam is singled out by Pamela and purposely infected, he decides to shoot himself rather than let the infection take him over. Dean won't leave Sam, so he sends the others (with some home-made explosives) to try to escape. But the townsfolk have mysteriously disappeared and Sam doesn't succumb to the virus after all. Duane and Mark leave town, but the former kills the latter in order to report back to his demonic master with news of Sam's immunity.

CAN YOU SURVIVE TO THE TITLES?
As with several of Sam's previous visions, we see a killing in the opener that doesn't come to pass in the main story. It's Duane Tanner who is fortuitous enough to survive, despite apparently being killed in cold-blood by Dean before the credits.

LOCATION, LOCATION, LOCATION
River Grove, Oregon.

LEGENDARY ROOTS

Croatoan is the name carved into a fencepost on Roanoke Island by a member of 'the Lost Colony'. The island is near the coast of North Carolina, US and is the site of Sir Walter Raleigh's first attempt to colonise America. It was first touted as an ideal settlement location in 1584 by the explorers Philip Amadas and Arthur Barlowe. Upon their return, Queen Elizabeth granted Raleigh patent over all the land he could occupy and named the land Virginia. In 1585, 100 men were sent to Roanoke but arrived too late in the season to produce crops. After their supplies ran out and they had murdered the Chief of a neighbouring Indian tribe, they returned to England. A week later a supply ship arrived and, finding the area abandoned, the leader ordered 15 men to stay behind and hold the fort.

1587 saw 117 men, women and children try to form a permanent settlement on the island, and they soon learnt that the 15 men left behind had been murdered. A few colonists went back to England for supplies but were unable to return to the island until 1590 due to a war with the Spanish. Upon returning they found the settlement abandoned and the word *Croatoan* carved on a fencepost along with the word *Cro* on a nearby tree. Instructions had been left that in case of danger someone was to carve the name of their destination with a Maltese cross above it. Croatoan was the name of an island where a friendly tribe lived. Due to bad weather, the search for the settlement had to be abandoned, and subsequent expeditions have never been able to establish the fate of 'the Lost Colony'[148].

SQUEEZE OF THE WEEK

Not even the pretty Pamela in her nurse's outfit can light up any interest in the boys – even when she throws Sam to the floor and rips his shirt open. (She really wasted an opportunity there.)

SIBLING RIVALRY

Between Sam and Dean, it's an episode that swings from outright hostility to complete support for each other.

When Sam doesn't shoot young, infected Jake Tanner, Dean is annoyed at him for leaving them one more monster to worry about and rips a strip off him for being compassionate about an 'it'. Then the conflict escalates into a physical exchange when Sam tries to persuade Dean not to kill Duane and Dean pushes Sam out of the way. Dean's insisting it's a tough job, and Sam is trying to convince him to wait and think

---

148 John Winchester's theory about Croatoan was that it was a demon's name – like Deva or Reesha – responsible for plagues.

about it, but Dean's not interested. Sam's started to notice that Dean's not been himself recently but he doesn't yet understand why.

Then, when Sam gets infected and the others are leaving, Dean's attitude changes and he can't leave his brother to die alone. Sam loses all sense of fight when he can see Dean struggling emotionally and offers to help him carrying some of the weight. Powerful stuff.

BODY COUNT

Nurse Pamela is shot by Dean after infecting Sam – and Dean seems to be on a roll. He's already killed Ma and Pa Tanner, then goes after eldest son Duane, but stops before following through. Which isn't good for ex-marine Mark Vargo, because later Duane slashes Mark's throat as they leave town together, just so he can use the blood to talk to his demon boss.

TOOLKIT

- Dean's *handgun* gets a lot of use this time around. Let's hope he's got another clip handy in the car.
- Sam uses *a GPS device on his phone* to find River Grove. He's always had paper maps in the past so maybe they thought it was time to upgrade.
- If you're being rushed by an infected madwoman with a knife, anything handily nearby – like a *fire extinguisher* – will do to stop her, especially when applied to the head with force.
- A *hunting knife* is useful when you're surrounded by blood-hungry, demon-virus-infected monsters (although a sub-machine gun would be preferable really).
- *Knowledge of how to make explosives*, starting with potassium chloride, will help in a tight situation.

MEMORABLE MOMENTS

The most infuriating cliffhanger since that car crash at the end of Season One. How could the writers do that?!

THE CAR'S THE STAR

The Impala is one lucky old motor – despite getting shot at by several angry, infected townsfolk at the road block it sustains no injuries to its rear end at all. Probably a good thing, given the contents of the trunk. A stray spark in the arsenal could have had very explosive results.

SPOOK RULES

- A demonic virus leaves a residue of sulphur in the bloodstream but still increases the lymphocyte percentage like a normal virus.
- Demonic viruses make infected people extremely violent with a desperate desire to infect others.
- The virus is spread by blood-to-blood contact and takes three hours to incubate. The sulphur doesn't appear in the blood until after those three hours are up.
- After you kill someone who is infected with a demonic virus, you don't see any black smoke coming out of the body as they expire.

DID YOU SPOT?

Another 'Awkward' situation turns up when Duane Tanner asks where his parents are. Given that Dean has ventilated both Duane's parents with a couple of bullets that morning, it's probably just as well that no-one actually tells the poor boy what happened to them[149].

This is the second time this season that Dean has willingly handed over the keys to the Impala to someone other than his brother[150].

GOING UNDERCOVER

The boys are masquerading as US Marshals Billy Gibbons and Frank Beard. We're back with the rock music theme again since Gibbons and Beard are members of the band ZZ Top. Dean eventually comes clean and tells Dr Lee that they're not really Marshals after all, but up until then the cover had been sound.

CULTURAL REFERENCES

Dean: 'See if one of us can bang Lindsay Lohan.': Lindsay Lohan (born 2 July 1986) is an actress, model and pop music singer known for being a wild child, and is well known on the celebrity party scene.

Sam: 'That wasn't school, Dean. That was *Schoolhouse Rock!*': *Schoolhouse Rock* was an educational cartoon series that ran from 1973 to 2000. Subjects such as science, history and multiplication tables were made the subject of songs.

Dean: 'I feel like Chuck Heston in *The Omega Man*.': *The Omega Man* (1971), which was loosely based on the 1954 *I Am Legend* novel by Richard Matheson, stars

---

149 Previous 'Awkward' situations occurred when Dean walked into the motel and Sam was watching a porn movie in 'Children Shouldn't Play With Dead Things' (2-04) and when Meg first met Dean and ripped a strip off him for treating his brother like 'luggage' in 'Shadow' (1-16).

150 The last time was when Andy Gallagher 'Obi-wan'd' Dean into giving him the Impala.

Charlton Heston as one of the last few uninfected people on Earth after a virus causes most of humanity to turn into violent, nocturnal, light-sensitive albino mutants.

Dean: 'You've got a neighbour named Mr Rogers?': *Mister Rogers' Neighborhood* was a children's television series that ran from 1968 to 2001 (with a short break between 1976 and 1979) with host Fred Rogers creating the famous phrase 'Won't you be my neighbour?'

Dean: 'That was kind of creepy, right? A little too Stepford?': *The Stepford Wives* is a satirical horror novel (1972) by Ira Levin, and spawned the 1975 movie of the same name and a 2004 remake, in which the women of the town of Stepford are replaced by the perfect wives (robots).

Dr Lee: 'It's about 40 miles down to Sidewinder.': Another reference to *The Shining* – the Overlook Hotel is 40 miles away from the town of Sidewinder.

Dean: 'For what? For him to Hulk out and infect somebody else?': *The Hulk* is a comic book series that spawned a TV and movie series about a mild mannered scientist with large green anger issues.

Jake Tanner: 'Yeah, he went on a fishing trip up by Roslyn Lake.': Roslyn lake is a real-life manmade lake that is part of the Bull Run Hydroelectric Project built by Portland General Electric in Oregon's Sandy River basin. The lake was completed in 1911 and the end of the Little Sandy River diverted by wooden flumes to the lake. 1913 saw a small fraction of the Big Sandy River also diverted into the lake. The lake was finally drained after May 2008 when the dam in Little Sandy River was removed.

Dean: 'If it is a possession there could be more … it could be like a friggin' Shriner convention.': A Shriner is a member of the Ancient Arabic Order of the Nobles of the Mystic Shrine (AAONMS), which was established in 1870 as a group within the Freemasons.

Dean: 'Yeah, good point. *Night of the Living Dead* didn't exactly end pretty.': *Night of the Living Dead* is a 1968 George A Romero movie in which the sole survivor of a zombie attack is mistakenly shot and burned with the rest of the zombies.

Dean: 'Wish we had a deck of cards, or a foosball table or something.': Foosball is a table top game where model footballers are positioned on one of eight rotating arms that players must move to get the ball into the opponent's goal at each end of the table.

Haven't I Seen You Before?

Sonja Bennett featured in *Battlestar Galactica*, *A Town Called Eureka* and *Blade: The Series*. Chilton Crane played Susan Farrell in *The 4400* and has also been in *Poltergeist: The Legacy* and *The X-Files*. Nolan Funk was in *Hollow Man II*, *X-Men 2* and *Taken*. Bobby Hosea's credits include *Heroes*, *Independence Day* and *Xena: Warrior Princess*. Kate Jennings Grant has been in *Blackout*. Diego Klattenhoff was in *Fallen*, *Stargate*

SG-1 and *Smallville*. Simon Longmore featured in *Dead Like Me, Dark Angel* and *Stargate: Atlantis*. Laurie Murdoch has been in *The Outer Limits, The X-Files* and *The Sentinel*.

BEHIND THE SCENES

Director Robert Singer cites this episode as one of his favourites. In *The Official Supernatural Magazine* #2 he comments that the script was much more about the psychology and the characters than it was about the scares and fright moments and he found that interesting. It also meant that Singer balanced out Kripke's love of blood and gore so that as a team they made better episodes.

MUSICAL INTERLUDE

All music was written specifically for this episode.

ANALYSIS

The cover story is not the focus of this episode, and it's just as well given that it's a well-worn road of post apocalyptic, infected zombies and body-snatcher style invasions. No, the narrative concentrates squarely on the brothers as Sam strives to calm Dean's anger down and Dean reaches breaking point.

Sam receives another piece of his puzzle when he discovers he's immune to the virus, but it's still not making any sense – especially since he didn't know Duane was a demon. Combining this piece of information with Webber's comments in 'Simon Said' (2-05)[151], we can see that the yellow-eyed demon is visiting other chosen ones and urging them to do things. With Duane's 'call' to his demon boss implying that the infection was just to test Sam, it's becoming more probable that the yellow-eyed demon is also sending Sam the visions and manipulating him (since one of the visions was the reason the boys went to River Grove in the first place). But although we know more than Sam does, we've still no clear idea what the overall game plan is.

What Sam does know is that, like Dean in 'In My Time of Dying' (2-01), he doesn't want to become one of the things he hunts. With the infection supposedly raging through his bloodstream and his time as a human limited, he'd rather put a bullet in his own head while he can. At this point, Dean does an about-face after shouting and bitching at his brother all episode and decides to stick with him, despite it meaning his own death – leaving Sam even more confused by Dean's behaviour[152].

As for Dean himself, he's starting to crumble and lose control, a situation that has

---

151 And a third mention in the next episode 'Hunted' (2-10).

152 See the **Did You Spot** ... section in 'Hunted' (2-10).

been building up gradually since John's death. Dean is like a pressure cooker about to blow its top as he tries to deal with his kaleidoscope of emotions – the pain, hurt and anger after losing John; then the discovery that John sold his soul in return for his life; and now, increasingly it seems, the burden of carrying around John's final words. He doesn't know how to handle it all, so his response is to run away. When they both believe Sam is going to die, Dean says he's going to quit hunting. This Dean is a far cry from the wise-cracking, gun-toting, saving-people, hunting-things Dean we saw deep in Wendigo country[153], and it gives a very obvious indication of how far he's come since then. But it's interesting that Dean doesn't say he's going to stop hunting because he would have lost everyone he loves to the job (Sam, dad, and mom) but hints that a large part of it is related to what John said to him.

The event that finally tips him over the edge is Sam's immunity to the virus. Dean's already more or less admitted that Sam's abilities freak him out[154], but this immunity aspect creates too much internal pressure for him and he finally has to let it all out. Well, he almost lets it out but, someone decided that (as the show was going into its winter hiatus on the network) it would make a great cliffhanger to have Dean stopping just before spilling the beans. So we won't find out what John whispered in his ear until the next episode. Bugger.

In the meantime, we'll have to content ourselves with observing that this episode, along with the next, 'Hunted' (2-10), marks a distinct change in story arc for the boys. Grieving for dad is done with; what comes from now on will directly relate to the bittersweet events of the season finale.

VERDICT – 9 out of 10

---

153 At Blackwater Ridge in 'Wendigo' (1-02).

154 In 'Nightmare' (1-14).

EPISODE 2-10
HUNTED

TRANSMISSION DATES
US first aired: 11 January 2007
UK first aired: 14 September 2007

CREDITS
Writer: Raelle Tucker
Director: Rachel Talalay

RECURRING ROLES
Sterling K Brown (Gordon Walker), Samantha Ferris (Ellen Harvelle), Chad Lindberg (Ash)

GUEST STARS
Jason Benson (Cop), Richard De Klerk (Scott Carey), Monique Genderton (Biker Chick), Katharine Isabelle (Ava Wilson), Levi James (Brady), Tom McBeath (Scott's Father), Bill Mondy (Dr George Waxler)

SYNOPSIS
Ava Wilson dreams of Sam's death before it happens and sets out to find him and warn him. Dean finally tells Sam what John whispered to him – save Sam, and if you can't save him, kill him. Dean wants to lie low, but Sam leaves him behind and goes searching for answers for himself. Ava finds Sam, Dean finds Sam, then Gordon tries to shoot Sam. Dean stops Gordon but gets captured, and Gordon uses him to lure Sam into a trap. Sam sends Ava home, rescues Dean and stitches Gordon up with the police. When Ava doesn't answer her phone, the boys visit her home to find that her fiancé has been murdered by a demon and she has disappeared. How's that for a lot going on?

CAN YOU SURVIVE TO THE TITLES?
Scott Carey is stabbed to death in a parking lot on his way back from visiting his shrink. That's what you get for frying your neighbour's cat from the inside with your special powers!

LOCATION, LOCATION, LOCATION
Harvelle's Roadhouse; Lafayette, Indiana; Peoria, Illinois.

LEGENDARY ROOTS
The hunters' community and the people who support them with information and weapons haven't had too much focus over the first season and (almost) a half, but their role is essential to the hunters' success. So in recognition of the unsung heroes we've met so far (and in some cases, watched die), let's see who they are:

- Caleb is mentioned in 'Asylum' (1-10) when Dean and Sam have been contacting other hunters to try to track down John; and in 'Shadow' (1-16) when Caleb gives Dean information about the Daeva. Caleb's first and last actual appearance is in 'Salvation' (1-21) when he is killed by a possessed Meg who slashes his throat while John Winchester is listening on the phone.

- Pastor Jim Murphy is first mentioned in 'Something Wicked' (1-18) during the flashback when John asks Dean if he knows what to do if John's not back within a certain time frame, and Dean replies 'Call Pastor Jim'. Dean also mentions that he and Sam were dropped off with the Pastor. Like Caleb, Pastor Jim's first and last actual appearance is in 'Salvation' (1-21), killed by a possessed Meg who slashes his throat after he runs into his weapon store in the church. At least John didn't have to listen to him die too.

- Missouri Mosely is a psychic who appears in 'Home' (1-09). Sam and Dean question her about John's whereabouts and the fire that killed their mother. She manages to bad-mouth Dean by telling him not to even think about putting his feet on the table. Missouri Mosely appears on the first page of John Winchester's Journal[155] and also features in the *Supernatural: Origins* graphic novel.

- Daniel Elkins is the only other hunter we've met apart from Gordon. He dies at the hands of vampires in 'Dead Man's Blood' (1-20) after they follow him from a bar to his home. The last time we see him is when he is struggling to load the Colt before being attacked. He managed to keep the Colt hidden from John Winchester for a number of years.

Other hunters who have been mentioned but haven't yet appeared:
- Jefferson – 'Asylum' (1-10)
- Joshua – 'Faith' (1-12)
- William (Bill) Anthony Harvelle – 'No Exit' (2-06) and 'Born Under A Bad Sign' (2-14)

---

155 Both in the TV series and in the released book by Alex Irvine.

SQUEEZE OF THE WEEK

Dean may think that Sam is a sly dog for having a girl in his motel room when he finally catches up with him, but Sam keeps it all platonic, treating Ava more like a little sister than a love interest. He must be on bromide tablets or something.

SIBLING RIVALRY

Harsh words again between the brothers after Dean finally comes clean. Sam's angry that Dean didn't tell him earlier, Dean wants to lay low, but Sam just sees that as a way that Dean can ensure he doesn't turn into a killer.

By the end of the episode, they've worked through some of the issues and are back to friendly banter again. Sam explains that he going to keep on hunting and face whatever comes at him so Dean'll just have to hang around if he wants to help. Dean predictably lightens the mood, provoking the now well known Bitch/Jerk exchange[156].

BODY COUNT

It's a normal day at the office for the boys, with Scott skewered on Gordon's knife in the opener, and Ava's fiancé ending up sliced 'n' diced by demon claws in the closing scenes.

TOOLKIT

- Surprisingly little equipment is used in 'Hunted', the main piece being a *handgun* to point at the guy who has not only bound and gagged your brother but has also tried to blow you up – twice.
- And then there are a couple of *flashlights* needed to search houses with murder victims in the bedroom.
- Everything else required to solve the mystery of Scott's death and beat Gordon is a soft skill:
  - *Skill One* – car stealing – Sam's not done that since 'Scarecrow' (1-11).
  - *Skill Two* – walking along thin window ledges on the outside of buildings to gain access to confidential patient records. Helps if you don't mind heights too.
  - *Skill Three* – be clever enough to know that a hunter would leave more than one trip-wire when he tries to blow you up.
  - *Skill Four* – influencing abilities to convince Ash to search for others like you when he'd rather be chasing skirt (see DVD deleted scenes).
  - *Skill Five* – kicking ass.

---

156 The last time the bitch/jerk exchange was used was in 'The Woman in White' (1-01), although Sam did call Dean a jerk for putting itching powder in his undies in 'Hell House' (1-17), in response to which Dean just chuckled wickedly.

MEMORABLE MOMENTS

Naturally the moment when Dean reveals John's words was always going to be particularly memorable – we've been gagging to find out for ten damn episodes, so of course we're going to be hanging on every word Dean says. It's a powerfully emotional scene delivered by two actors who know their characters inside out and have the skills to make everyone else believe too.

And the cartoon-style smoking boot moments add a nice touch of humour to a very serious episode[157].

Top Scare: When Gordon starts taking pot-shots at Sam – you just don't see it coming at all.

MOTEL MAYHEM

The Blue Rose motel has a cheery, if slightly corny, matching-motif effect going on with little blue roses turning up everywhere and a fully co-ordinated colour scheme to go with them. And catch that psychedelic swirly wallpaper!

SPOOK RULES

- Duplicate abilities can occur in the psychic kids. Ava has the same ability as Sam – she can also see people's deaths before they happen.

DID YOU SPOT?

Now that we know what John said, it's clearer why Dean wanted to stay with Sam when he was expecting to die in 'Croatoan' (2-09). He couldn't let Sam turn evil alone and join the bad guys, so he had to be there to kill him if he turned – at the cost of his own life if necessary. He takes his promises very seriously does Dean.

The words have changed a little across episodes in the scenes where Dean finally tells Sam what John said before he died. In 'Croatoan' (2-09) it's: Dean: 'Right before Dad died, he told me something. He told me something about you.'; Sam: 'What? Dean, what did he tell you?' By the time we get to 'Hunted' (2-10) its: Dean: 'Before Dad died he, he told me something – something about you.'; Sam: 'What? Dean, what did he tell you?' Yup, that's very, very picky, isn't it?

GOING UNDERCOVER

It's only Ava who goes undercover for a change. She pretends to be a new patient for Dr Waxler in order to distract him while Sam creeps along the window sill and gains

---

157 A mechanism also successfully used in the movie *Shrek* when the ogre is looking around the castle trying to locate Princess Fiona and spots the boots of a knight that arrived before him but got scorched by the dragon.

access to the his records about Scott Carey. For the third time, neither of the boys uses a cover[158].

Hunter's Lingo

Sam and Dean probably have a whole set of agreed code phrases that they use to warn each other of trouble, but the only one they use here is 'funky town', which means that someone has a gun on the speaker.

Cultural References

Sam: 'Am I supposed to go Darkside or something?': The Darkside is portrayed as the evil half of the force from the *Star Wars* universe created by George Lucas.

Sam: 'I just watch a lot of T J Hooker.': *T J Hooker* was a television series that ran from 1982 to 1986 about police officer Sgt T J Hooker played by William Shatner[159].

Gordon: 'Besides Mr Tinkles the cat, no.': Mr Tinkles is a cat voiced by Sean Hughes from the movie *Cats and Dogs* (2001).

Dean: 'Yeah, I talked to Ellen. Just got here myself. It's a real funky town.': 'Funky Town' was a 1980 disco hit for the band Lipps Inc.

Sam: 'These are .223 caliber, subsonic rounds.': Subsonic rounds are a type of ammunition that travels below the speed of sound.

Goofs and Fluffs

The Blue Rose hotel stationery that Sam is seen holding in Ava's vision gives the address where Gordon is holding Dean, but the numbers for the address in the vision don't match the ones Sam writes down when Dean tells him where to find him.

After Sam triggers the second explosion trying to rescue Dean, Gordon see Sam's smoking shoe on the floor. In the fight that follows, just before Sam knocks Gordon unconscious, Sam can be seen wearing both shoes. Maybe Sam was clever enough to bring a spare shoe …

Sam frees Dean's left hand from the rope around the chair and Dean frees his own right hand, but there's clearly no knot in the right-hand rope, so he couldn't have been secured very well. A good hunter like Gordon wouldn't have been so sloppy.

Sam has bruises and a cut under his eye after the fight with Gordon, but in the car afterwards, his injuries have all cleared up, only to return when he and Dean search Ava's house and find her missing.

---

158 The other two times were 'Dead Man's Blood' (1-20) and 'In My Time of Dying' (2-01).

159 Yes, he played Captain Kirk, but you already knew that, didn't you …?

HAVEN'T I SEEN YOU BEFORE?

Jason Benson featured in *Bloody Mary*, *The 4400* and *Reaper*. Richard De Klerk's TV credits include *Andromeda*, *Stargate SG-1* and *Alienated*. Monique Genderton has been in *Blood Ties* and *The 4400*. Katharine Isabelle was in *Sanctuary*, *Knight Moves* and *The Outer Limits*. Levi James' acting credits include *The Wisher*, *Black Rain* and *The 4400*. Tom McBeath was Colonel Harry Maybourne in *Stargate SG-1* and has also been in *The Outer Limits* and *The X-Files*. Bill Mondy featured as Deputy Roscoe in *The Dead Zone* and Det Brian Boone in *Blade The Series* and was also in *The Day the Earth Stood Still*.

BEHIND THE SCENES

Actor Sterling K Brown wasn't too hacked off about Gordon being caught by the police. He felt that as long as he had only been arrested and hadn't taken a bullet to the head then there was an opportunity for him to come back.[*The Official Supernatural Magazine #2*]

Story editor Raelle Tucker said that Ava's name was inspired by her best High School friend. Tucker wanted to write a strong female rather than one that screamed and waited to be rescued. She always saw Ava as the sister that Sam had never had. [*Season Two Supernatural Companion*]

MUSICAL INTERLUDE

- 'White Rabbit' – Jefferson Airplane – during Scott's counselling session and over the death scene at the beginning of the episode.
- 'Lonesome Stranger' – Carey Bell – when Ellen and Sam are at the Roadhouse.
- 'Supermassive Black Hole' – Muse – when Ash gives Sam the names of the other psychics.

ANALYSIS

One of the best episodes in Season Two, 'Hunted' delivers everything – the big reveal about what John whispered in Dean's ear; the brothers in conflict; more about the psychic kids; a worthy adversary; shock moments; clever twists; and even snippets of humour with the smoking boot every time Sam gets blown up.

It's amazing that the writers managed to fit so much into one episode really. There are three major threads on the go and they all intertwine seamlessly. First off there's the surprise introduction of Ava, who turns out to be the person having the vision instead of the usual suspect Sam. With her girl-next-door personality, she's trying to do the right thing and save Sam's life. It's hard for her to accept that she's just one of many, since she's barely begun to accept her own abilities, but the recording of Scott

Carey's interview with his doctor, along with Sam's explanation, is too overwhelming for her. Her disappearance at the end of the episode is going to be left a mystery until the season finale but will dovetail very neatly into the overall story arc.

Ava is the second of the psychic kids not to have lost their mother in a fire[160]. Combine this with Ash's search finding only four people who match Sam's circumstances, and the puzzle of the psychic kids only deepens, because they can't be tracked, can't be counted, can't be investigated for connections or anything – and that's really rather unsettling.

The second thread centres around Gordon – another surprise appearance and a great shock moment when he starts taking shots at Sam in the motel. His presence adds a genuine level of tension to events for a couple of reasons. Gordon is a very good hunter and has a seriously black and white attitude, which means he's got all the required skills to achieve his goal of killing Sam and there's no way you're going to talk him out of it. He's decided Sam's going to be the bad guy and he won't stop until he's finished, because he's doing this for all the 'right' reasons. It's not a personal grudge, it's business; Sam is potentially going to join the demons and cause the deaths of thousands of humans; why not stop him now before anyone loses their life? Wouldn't you kill a young Hitler if you knew what he was destined to do? But the flaw in Gordon's argument is that Sam hasn't done anything evil yet and there's still a chance that he won't. Gordon insists that if John Winchester had known about Sam then he would have killed him himself, but truth is John did know and still gave Sam the opportunity to prove himself one way or the other. John just put a safeguard in place in the shape of Dean.

Suddenly we also get an insight into why John never really introduced his boys to the hunter community, apart from Pastor Jim, Caleb and Bobby. There was the risk that the hunters would do exactly what Gordon has done and work out what John already knew about Sam, then come gunning for him[161]. Now the boys find themselves targets of both the police and the hunters. Talk about getting caught in the crossfire!

They're not as concerned about that as they should be though. With Dean finally coughing up the goods on John's last words, Sam's hell-bent on finding out what's going on. It's Gordon who shares the biggest piece of info with Dean when he says Sam is one of the soldiers needed to fight in the coming war: humans with psychic abilities fighting on the side of the demons. It may be Sam's destiny to become one of those soldiers, but Dean insists that he doesn't believe in destiny. He made a promise

---

160 Webber in 'Simon Said' (2-05) was the first one.

161 Further details can be read in the comic book series *Supernatural: Rising Son* on the early problems the Winchesters had with other hunters.

to try to save Sam and he still thinks the best way is to lie low and stay out of the hunting game for a while. Sam can see that the yellow-eyed demon is manipulating all the psychic kids and there's no point hiding. Whatever is coming, he's meeting it head on, and he'd rather do it with Dean by his side.

And the rest of us want to be there too.

VERDICT – 10 out of 10

EPISODE 2-11
PLAYTHINGS

TRANSMISSION DATES
US first aired: 18 January 2007
UK first aired: 21 September 2007

CREDITS
Writer: Matt Witten
Director: Charles Beeson

GUEST STARS
Jonathan Bruce (Larry Williams), Rob Bruner (Robert Carlton), Conchita Campbell (Maggie Thompson), Matreya Fedor (Tyler Thompson), Brenda McDonald (Rose Thompson), John R Taylor (Sherwin), Annie Wersching (Susan Thompson), Talia Williams (Young Rose Thompson)

SYNOPSIS
Sam and Dean give up searching for Ava[162] and go to investigate two mysterious deaths at a hotel in Connecticut. The owner of the hotel, Susan, lives there with her daughter Tyler and grandmother Rose. Susan is selling the property, but people related to the sale are dying. The culprit turns out to be the spirit of grandma Rose's twin sister, Maggie, who died in the swimming pool at the house. Maggie has been appearing at the house since grandma Rose became ill and could no longer keep her away. Maggie is lonely and doesn't want the family to leave. When Maggie tries to kill Tyler so she'll stay with her as a companion, Sam rescues Tyler, and grandma Rose saves the day by offering to stay with Maggie if she'll leave Susan and Tyler alone.

CAN YOU SURVIVE TO THE TITLES?
One of the removal men, Larry Williams, falls (or more likely is pushed) down the stairs, getting his head turned through 180 degrees in the process. Oooh, bet that hurt.

LOCATION, LOCATION, LOCATION
Peoria, Illinois; Pierpont Inn, Cornwall Connecticut.

---

162 Ava disappeared at the end of the last episode, 'Hunted' (2-10). Do try to keep up!

LEGENDARY ROOTS

A protection spell can be cast to provide protection for a person or object against a range of events or situations. There are fire preventative spells, or ones to defend against an unwanted admirer. There are spells for repelling other spells that are meant to harm a person. You can stop people touching certain objects or entering your house; protect your dreams; or break a curse. You can invoke the protective power of the moon or ask the leaves from the trees to keep you safe. Protective spells can also be used to help remove any bad luck or evil spirits that are surrounding a person.

SQUEEZE OF THE WEEK

Sam gets a very gentle, deeply grateful hug from Susan at the end of the episode after he has saved both her and Tyler's lives. Dean thinks he should take advantage of the attraction but Sam thinks Susan already has enough on her plate with moving house and the death of her mother, Rose. Sam's such a thoughtful guy.

SIBLING RIVALRY

An exceptional episode for Winchester wit, and there are way too many examples to mention here, but watch out for:

Dean being officially uncomfortable about Sam's healthy attitude to finding Ava and not wanting to let other people die either.

Another person thinking the brothers are gay[163] as the boys check in to the hotel and get offered a king-sized bed. Sam just thinks it happens because Dean is kind of butch and overcompensating.

Dean setting Sam up with something embarrassing again[164] when he tells Susan about Sam's doll collection at home.

Sam getting drunk and calling his brother bossy and short.

And Dean giving his brother a backhanded compliment about saving the girl and the mother.

Dean's best moment is when he probably judges his brother by his own standards and asks Sam to check out Grandma and see if she's whacked anybody in the past. And no surfing the porn, he meant a different kind of whacking.

BODY COUNT

After Larry gets a good look over his shoulder, the lawyer handling the house sale is found hanging by the neck in one of the bedrooms, then Maggie goes after Susan by

---

163 They've been mistaken for homosexuals in two previous episodes: 'Bugs' (1-08) and 'Something Wicked' (1-18).

164 Dean previously set Sam up painting a male student's body purple in 'Hookman' (1-07).

trying to run her over with the car[165] but Sam saves her just in time. Susan's grandma is the final victim when she offers to stay in spirit form with her ghostly sister so long as Maggie leaves Susan and Tyler unharmed.

TOOLKIT
- They didn't need to go into the trunk of the car for any hardware this time. Everything was either in the hotel or it was a soft skill they already had.
- The hotel mini bar is perfect when you're feeling down and need to numb your emotional pain with whiskey and Jäger; but beware if you're not a regular drinker, the hangover will have you with your head down the toilet next morning.
- Good hunters always have the following too – *excellent observational skills* to spot hoodoo symbols dotted around the house and grounds; *knowledge of those hoodoo symbols; good timing and the ability to sprint* and grab someone from the path of a car that is trying to kill the hotel owner; *the ability to make up stories* about your brother's embarrassing hobbies on the spot; and *the ability to swim* even fully clothed – which the boys should do more often because that wet shirt moment is always worth it[166].

MEMORABLE MOMENTS
Seeing Sam drunk for the first time is something of a shock since he's never drunk excessively in all the time we've known him. (He was even *refusing* alcohol in 'The Woman In White' (1-01).)

Watching the dagger-looks from Sam to Dean, when Dean is explaining Sam's love of dressing up his doll collection at home, is priceless!

And those twitching dead bodies are just sooo wonderfully gruesome.

SPOOK RULES
- A quincunx symbol, also known as a five-spot, is used in hoodoo spell work. When used in conjunction with bloodweed it forms a powerful charm to ward off enemies. The symbol is used as an artificial crossroads and means to seal a 'trick' or work in a space. The symbol can also be used to create sacred space.
- Bloodweed root and its expressed juice causes vomiting and is a strong laxative.
- Hoodoo is hands-on magic – you need to mix herbs, chant and build an altar. If you've suffered paralysis after a stroke you'll probably be unable to work hoodoo.

---

165 The last car that drove itself was the dear Impala in 'The Woman in White' (1-01), and Sam and Dean were the intended victims.

166 It's been simply too long since the last wet shirt event in 'Dead In The Water' (1-03).

- The quincunx symbol is used near doorways and within a building to protect it.
- Spirits of little girls can be seen by other little girls.
- Spirits have no problem connecting with real-world objects, for example items to strangle people with and children's swings and roundabouts. They even know how to drive a car when they need to run someone over.
- Spirits of little girls can get lonely and feel rejected but can be bribed into leaving your grand-daughter alone if you offer to cross over and stay with them yourself.

DID YOU SPOT?

The brothers leave the hotel twice, once when they are kicked out by Susan and once at the end. The same footage seems to have been used for both scenes.

At the end of the episode, as Sam reminds Dean of his promise to kill him if he needs to, the car is parked at the front of the house, but when they leave, the reused shot has them pulling away from the back of the house and through the archway.

GOING UNDERCOVER

The boys pretend to be antique hunters and Dean's credit card is in the name of Mr Mahogoff. The name Mahogoff is usually used with the Christian name Jack and is a joke name (like Miss Norma Stits and Mr Hugh Garse).

CULTURAL REFERENCES

Dean: 'It's a greasy pork sandwich served up in a dirty ashtray.': 'How 'bout a nice greasy pork sandwich served in a dirty ashtray?' is a quote from the 1985 movie *Weird Science*, said by Bill Paxton's character Chet.

Dean: 'We might even run into Fred and Daphne while we're inside.': Fred Jones and Daphne Blake are two characters from the animated TV and film series *Scooby Doo*, which started in 1969.

Dean: 'Time for bed. Come on, Sasquatch.': Sasquatch is another name for Big Foot, the legendary human ape-like creature. The word comes from the Halkomelem word sésquac meaning wild man. Reports of the creature are mainly from the Pacific Northwest region of the USA.

Dean: 'How you feeling, Sammy? I guess mixing whisky and Jäger wasn't such a gangbuster idea, was it?': Jäger(meister) is a German 70% proof drink made from herb and spices that, imbibed after a meal, is supposed to help the digestion.

Dean: 'Think you could have hooked up some MILF action there, bud.': The acronym MILF was made famous by the 1999 film *American Pie* and stands for 'Mom I'd Like To Fuck'. One thing you can say for Dean – he's not ageist. So long as she's got a pulse …

There are several references to *The Shining* again. Sam and Dean stay in room 237 – the room where Jack Nicholson's character encounters the ghost of a beautiful and naked young woman who ages in his arms. The cinematography is similar to that in *The Shining* and so is the scene in the bar.

GOOFS AND FLUFFS

When Sam is barfing in the toilet and Dean enters the room, we see Sam in the mirror on the left. Dean moves across the room to stand on the left-hand side of the bathroom door and talks to Sam. But when Sam is in shot, Dean's leg has swapped to the right hand side of the door. Dean's position then flips back and forth depending on who's talking. This isn't actually a goof, however. If you look closely you can see that the shots of Sam are the reflected image (from the start of the scene) used throughout the conversation – you can tell because Sam's cast seems to have changed arms as well.

HAVEN'T I SEEN YOU BEFORE?

Jonathan Bruce was in *Millennium* and *Reaper*. Rob Bruner has been in *Dark Angel*, *The Outer Limits* and *The Dead Zone*. Conchita Campbell played Maia Rutledge in *The 4400*. Matreya Fedor was in *Slither* and *A Town Called Eureka*. Brenda McDonald has been in *Reaper*, *Blood Ties* and *Hellraiser: Hellseeker*. John R Taylor's credits include *Watchmen*, *Final Destination 2* and *The Outer Limits*. Annie Wersching has been in *Star Trek: Enterprise*, *Angel* and *Charmed*.

BEHIND THE SCENES

Director Charles Beeson didn't like the dolls in this episode either. In *The Official Supernatural Magazine* #6 he admits that it's the eyes, eyelashes, weird hair and porcelain faces that makes him find them really creepy. He's not the only one.

This is the last episode in which Padalecki wears the cast on his arm.

MUSICAL INTERLUDE

• 'Voodoo Spell' – Michael Burks – when Sam is speaking to Ellen and checking the database on PC.

ANALYSIS

The *Supernatural* writing team are clearly fans of *The Shining* – not only has it been referenced in six previous episodes to date[167] but 'Playthings' runs like a mini homage

---

167 'Home' (1-09); 'Asylum' (1-10); 'In My Time of Dying' (2-01); 'The Usual Suspects' (2-07); 'Crossroad Blues' (2-08); and 'Croatoan' (2-09) in case you were wondering.

without the snow. The similarities are in the details as well as the themes of the main story – although Sam and Dean don't suffer quite as badly with the spirits haunting their hotel as Jack Torrance does with his. The obvious similarity is the setting of a rambling old hotel. *Supernatural*'s Pierpont is nowhere near as big as The Overlook but it has that familiar feel of grandeur and history and secrets nonetheless. It has a bar like The Overlook as well, with a lit back panel for the bottles and a conversation between one of the main characters and a gaunt-faced bartender. The sense of the familiar is further reinforced by the use of tracking cinematography. 'Playthings' can't do the long tracking shots that *The Shining* did, following little Danny around the corridors of The Overlook, but it still manages a shorter representation of the technique as the boys move around Pierpont. The final touch is the room number the boys are allocated on arrival – 237. It doesn't look like there is any naked woman in the bath for the Winchesters though – if there were, Sam would surely have spotted her when he was in there throwing up.

Aside from this, it is a satisfying episode that's stylish, atmospheric and well-paced. There's a good mix of murder; bodies that are still twitching grotesquely shortly after death; creepy dolls; and strange old women living in the attic. The tension builds gradually as Maggie's intentions become clearer, and the finale is suitably tense as the boys fight to save Tyler's life.

But it's in some aspects not a typical episode. It's the first to be resolved by someone other than the boys and the second with an ambiguous ending. 'Croatoan' (2-09) also left unresolved questions for Sam and Dean (why was Sam immune? where did the virus come from?) and in 'Playthings' they don't know why Maggie has stopped her haunting. Both episodes gave the audience more facts than the boys, so at least they get some sense of closure, even though there are still some unanswered questions (like what will happen to the girls when the hotel is demolished?).

There's one question answered that we didn't really know we should be asking – how is Sam coping with the 'Save Sam or kill him' situation?

Ironically, bottle-it-up Dean turns out to be more expressive than we gave him credit for compared with let's-talk Sam, because the first time we have any idea how troubled Sam is about the situation is when he actually tries to hide from his problems in the bottom of a whiskey bottle. Sam's drunkenness indicates two things: the size of the problem, which must be huge; and how ill-equipped he is to cope with the issues, since his drinking implies he has a need to run away from the problem by numbing his senses rather than deal with it.

Dean has spotted this change from a touchy-feely, self-help attitude to a quiet internalisation of problems too and even comments on it, wondering why there hasn't been more 'angst and droopy music and staring out the rainy windows' since Ava

263

disappeared.

So what's Sam not coping with? Well, it seems he's going to turn evil in the future and that's his destiny but he believes that the more people he can save, the more he can alter that destiny. When Sam fails to save Ava and the lawyer, his highly critical about his own lack of ability perhaps indicates that he sees his failure as confirmation of his dark destination. Events then give Sam two chances to redeem himself by saving Susan and Tyler, allowing him to feel like he has some kind of control over his own destiny and that the becoming evil aspect is not a foregone conclusion.

Sam is so concerned about becoming the kind of creature he and Dean hunt that he is prepared to give his own life in order to protect other people from what he might do if he turned darkside. Sam clearly doesn't know if he'll be able to kill himself before turning, so he begs Dean to follow through on his promise to John and kill him if necessary.

For Dean, this goes some way towards Sam forgiving him for what he might need to do in the future. While Dean will do anything to avoid doing the deed, he can at least get some solace from the knowledge that Sam wants him to do it.

All of this interaction is in plain view, but in the shadows, in the attic, lurks the true unsung heroine of this episode. Grandma Rose is one helluva woman. Not only has she been single-handedly protecting her family for decades from the fractious spirit of her twin sister but she also resolves the problem with Maggie and saves her own family in a much understated moment of self-sacrifice. Echoing Sam's own sense of selflessness (he would rather lose his life than murder innocent people) Rose gives her own life in order to save her daughter and grand-daughter from Maggie's destructive loneliness – and no-one except the viewer is aware that she's done it. Perhaps surprisingly for someone who doesn't say a single word throughout, Rose is the central character in 'Playthings'. Her actions underpin all of the events and create coherence effortlessly.

With this much depth going on, there's not much room for out and out excitement and action. Indeed these only really turn up at the end – which weakens the episode compared with some of the previous ones – but you can't have everything all the time, can you?

VERDICT – 8 out of 10

EPISODE 2-12
NIGHTSHIFTER

TRANSMISSION DATES
US first aired: 25 January 2007
UK first aired: 28 September 2007

CREDITS
Writer: Ben Edlund
Director: Philip Sgriccia

RECURRING ROLE
Charles Malik Whitfield (Victor Henricksen)

GUEST STARS
Emy Aneke (Sampson), Georgia Craig (Sherri), Chris Gauthier (Ronald Resnick), Holly Houghman (Frannie), Alison Matthews (Reporter), Stehpen E Miller (Bank Security Guard), Roman Podhora (Lieutenant Robards), Kurt Max Runte (Sergeant Tucker), Sanjay Talwar (Mr Devereaux), Brad Turner (Unknown)

SYNOPSIS
When previously law-abiding people start committing crimes and then killing themselves, Sam and Dean investigate. Talking to Ronald, a friend of one of the 'criminals', they discover he has theories of a Mandroid impersonating people to steal money. It sounds like a shapeshifter is working the area, but Sam tells Ronald he's got it totally wrong. Locating the next likely target, Sam and Dean enter the bank looking for the shapeshifter, but Ronald arrives, fully armed, and holds everyone in the bank hostage. While the police set up for a siege outside, Sam and Dean start trying to uncover the shapeshifter inside. The SWAT team storm the building, and Sam and Dean only just manage to kill the shapeshifter before escaping dressed as SWAT team members.

CAN YOU SURVIVE TO THE TITLES?
No-one dies in the opener – it's just setting the siege scene outside the bank, where Dean is caught on camera freeing one of the sick hostages.

LOCATION, LOCATION, LOCATION
City Bank of Milwaukee – Financial Services and Investments, Milwaukee, Wisconsin.

265

LEGENDARY ROOTS

Following on from the shapeshifter **Legendary Roots** in 'Home' (1-09), we take a more detailed look at two fascinating examples from the huge amount of lore available.

A kitsune is a fox in Japanese folklore that has the ability to transform into a human, usually a young girl, beautiful woman or elderly man. They are seen as great tricksters. They are said to have up to nine tails depending on wisdom and age, and the ability to transform starts only at age 100. They are said to fear dogs, so even in human form they will revert to a fox and dash away when confronted by one. They are said to be able to fly, turn invisible and even have the ability to breathe fire or create lightning. In some regions, lore tells of the kitsune being able to bend space and time or being able to drive a human mad.

The aswang comes from Filipino folklore and is often described as a combination of a vampire and a witch with the ability to transform into a black dog or boar. In human form it is quiet and shy, but the give-away is its bloodshot eyes. The creature hunts human victims at night and preys on children, unborn foetuses and the dead. You can detect an aswang by using a bottle filled with special oil from a coconut, mixed with certain blessed plant stems. When an aswang is nearby, the liquid inside the bottle will boil. Ways to repel an aswang include throwing salt – which is said to burn their skin – or possessing a red pouch of ginger to ward them off.

SQUEEZE OF THE WEEK

It's Dean's week, as Frannie in the jewellery store requests a private 'interview' with him and bank worker Sherri takes an understandable shine to him. Sam doesn't get a sniff of any action at all.

SIBLING RIVALRY

Dean admires Sam's skills at telling Ronald that the Mandroid doesn't exist. He thinks it's very creepy that Sam's so good at playing the Fed.

BODY COUNT

The shapeshifter has already notched up two murders by the time we join the action. He's disguised as the bank manager to start with, but it's unclear whether he's killed the real bank manager or not. He soon slips his skin and slits the throat of one of the male hostages, stuffing his body in the false ceiling.

Meanwhile, Ronald may be clever enough to work out that a shapeshifter took his friend's identity but he's not got the common sense to keep away from the windows in the middle of a bank heist – as a result, he takes a bullet to the heart.

The body of a third victim, Sherri, is found seemingly dead with another throat wound, but this turns out to be the shapeshifter's clever disguise and the real Sherri makes it to the end of the episode after all.

The fate of the security guard with the dicky ticker is unknown.

TOOLKIT

- A *silver dagger* should be carried at all times, even when going undercover in a bank. If someone should take it off you then a *silver letter opener* is a good replacement.
- A *handgun* will keep your hostages in check, but recycle weapons where possible by picking up the dead guy's *rifle* when the SWAT team have just shot him in the back.
- *Flashlights* are essential in corridors when the power has been cut.
- And *a coat stand* will allow you reach the ceiling tiles. Just watch your head for falling bodies hidden in the false ceiling.

MEMORABLE MOMENTS

When Sam stands to tell Ronald the truth about his Mandroid theory and trashes all of his ideas, you can't help but feel sorry for Ronald. After all, he was right on the button, with the exception of the Mandroid's name. At least he finds out the truth before he gets shot.

The finale of 'Nightshifter' is one long, nail-biting event as the boys try to find the shapeshifter in the confines of the bank while the SWAT team sweeps through the corridors intent on killing both Winchesters.

MOTEL MAYHEM

Another themed motel appears this week, with a separating screen made up of Schultz beer paraphernalia and polka stuff.

SPOOK RULES

All the standard shapeshifter rules – established in 'Skin' (1-06) – apply:
- Security cameras will pick up strange flares in the eyes of a shapeshifter.
- When a shapeshifter changes from one person to another, he leaves the skin of the old disguise behind in a 'puke-inducing pile'.
- You can kill a shapeshifter using a silver blade/silver bullets through his heart.
- After a shapeshifter is dead, he retains the last disguise he assumed.

Two additional pieces of information have come to light:
- Different shapeshifters change form at different speeds – this shifter is faster than

267

the one in St Louis.

• Shifters can take the form of a dead body, complete with slit throat.

DID YOU SPOT?

This is the second time slo-mo has been used for a dramatic scene. Last time was the rescue of Tyler in the swimming pool in 'Playthings' (2-11); this time it's when Ronald gets the bullets through his chest.

GOING UNDERCOVER

The boys are FBI agents again, gathering information about the jewellery store robbery. When they interview Ronald, Sam is Agent Johnson (see next section), although the signature on his badge seems to say his name is Han Solo. Solo is a *Star Wars* character played by Harrison Ford in *A New Hope* (1977), *Empire Strikes Back* (1980) and *Return of the Jedi* (1983).

Dean's badge is harder to read. It possibly says 'Jack Ryan'. Harrison Ford stars as Jack Ryan in Tom Clancy's *Patriot Games* (1992) and *Clear and Present Danger* (1994).

Then it's a quick change into Securiserve Guard Service overalls (which show off their trim bodies to perfection) and off to the bank to check the surveillance cameras.

CULTURAL REFERENCES

Dean: 'I don't think he likes you, Agent Johnson.': Agent Johnson played by Daniel Bernhardt is from the movie *The Matrix Reloaded* (2003), the second film in the *Matrix* franchise created by the Wachowski brothers.

Ronald: 'Like the Terminator, but the kind that can change itself, make itself look like other people.': Referring to the T-1000 Terminator in *Terminator 2: Judgement Day* (1991), in which the T-1000 has the ability to change into different forms and people.

Ronald: 'You ain't FBI ... Who are you working for, huh? The Men in Black?': This refers to the *Men in Black* (1997) movie about a government agency protecting the Earth from the scum of the universe, starring Tommy Lee Jones and Will Smith as agents K and J.

Hendrickson: 'He's the Bonnie to your Clyde.': Bonnie Parker (1910-1934) and Clyde Barrow (1909-1934) were notorious outlaws, robbers, and criminals who, with their gang, travelled the central United States during the Great Depression.

The Fortean Times held up by Ronald is an actual issue of the magazine – number 209 from May 2006. The cover story is an article on the Cybermen, who first appeared in the *Doctor Who* story 'The Tenth Planet' (1966) and have featured in numerous other episodes up to the present day.

Ronald: 'See, so not just a robot, more of a, uh, a Mandroid.': A Mandroid is a fictional suit of power armour that appears in the Marvel Comics universe. It first featured in *Avengers* #94 (Dec 1971), created by Roy Thomas and Neal Adams. The suit was made from a titanium alloy that provided the user with protection against physical and energy attacks. It also had a life support system and internal air supply. The weapons in the suit included electrostatic beams, lasers, magnetic force punch-blasters, neuro-stunners and tractor beams.

Dean: 'God, it's like playing the shell game.': The shell game is the well-known wager game where someone places a pea under one of three shells and the player has to guess where it has ended up once the shells have been moved around.

Henricksen says that he can't figure out what kind of whacko John Winchester was, Henricksen: 'White supremacist, Timmy McVeigh, to-may-to, to-mah-to.': Timothy James McVeigh (1968-2001) was convicted and executed for the bombing of the Alfred P Murrah Building in Oklahoma City on 19 April 1995, which killed 168 people – the largest terrorist attack prior to the 11 September attack on the World Trade Centre in 2001. The bombing was on the second anniversary of the Waco Siege.

GOOFS AND FLUFFS
When the boys show Ronald their FBI badges, they remove them from their jackets with their left hands and hold them up to the door. But in the next shot, when you see them from behind, Dean is holding his badge in place with his right hand.

HAVEN'T I SEEN YOU BEFORE?
Emy Aneke's credits include *X-Men: The Last Stand*, *Andromeda* and *Smallville*. Georgina Craig was in *The 4400*, *Stargate SG-1* and *Tru Calling*. Chris Gauthier played Vincent in *A Town Called Eureka* and has also been in *The Butterfly Effect 2* and *Watchmen*. Alison Matthews featured in *Battlestar Galactica*, *Final Destination 2* and *Dark Angel*. Stephen E Miller was in *The X-Files: I Want To Believe* and played Assistant Director Andy McClaren in *Millennium*. Roman Podhora's credits include *Poltergeist: The Legacy*, *Total Recall 2070* and *Painkiller Jane*. Kurt Max Runte was in *The Day the Earth Stood Still*, *AVP: Requiem* and *Kyle XY*. Sanjay Talwar was in *Dawn Of The Dead*, *Lexx* and *Relic Hunter*. Brad Turner was in *White Noise 2: The Light*, *Smallville* and *Blood Ties*.

BEHIND THE SCENES
Actor Charles Malik Whitfield filled in some of Henricksen's backstory in *The Official Supernatural Magazine* #5. Whitfield sees Henricksen as being very isolated, knowing that the isolation would make Henricksen stand up and just get on with things. The

actor quite identified with Henricksen too – both with his personality and his deep obsession to finish the job despite any lingering doubts.

While Whitfield sorted out Henricksen's internal motivations, visual effects coordinator Ivan Hayden was sorting out the external views of the Bank. The interior was filmed in a real bank in downtown Vancouver, but the external shots of roads closed off, SWAT teams and helicopters everywhere needed to show how the boys really didn't have any way to escape. They didn't have the budget to hire a few helicopters so the 12 second shot was done totally in CG. [*Season Two Supernatural Companion*]

MUSICAL INTERLUDE

• 'Renegade' – Styx – when Sam and Dean are driving at the end of the episode.
• 'Rock You Like A Hurricane' – the Scorpions – listed on the Supernatural Planet website only.

ANALYSIS

This episode may have a similar structure to the previous one[168], with its relentless build-up to a final showdown, but the previous emotional introspectives are abandoned in favour of all-out action with bank heists, police snipers, shapeshifting murderers and clever escapes.

It's an enjoyable romp chasing the shifter, never knowing who it is, tripping over oozing pools of skin, teeth and toenails. Any other show would deliver the shapeshifter storyline alone, but *Supernatural* writers like layers, so we have several additional complications. The boys are trapped inside a bank, people are being picked off by snipers and the SWAT team are moving in so close you can almost feel their breath on your neck. Add in the ruthless Agent Henricksen and you're on the edge of your seat by the time you hit the halfway mark.

Then it's topped off with two clever twists: the shifter pretending to be a dead body is an intelligent change of behaviour for the creature; and the eventual escape of the boys as SWAT team members delivers a massive shot of relief.

You don't have time to notice that most of the regular story arcs haven't made an appearance. There's no angst about Sam turning evil. No dad issues for Dean. And not a psychic kid in sight. Instead, that vague theme of the police getting the brothers on their files returns fully fleshed and looking for blood. Not only are the boys wanted by the Feds in relation to several murders in St Louis but for the first time we find that someone has been specifically allocated to their case, watching their every move. He's a hard bastard too, driven by the righteous belief that taking the boys out will be the

---

168 'Playthings' (2-11).

best thing to do if humanity wants to sleep well at night. Of course, the opposite is actually true – which just adds to the friction for the viewer.

In terms of the boys' personalities, there's not much new development. It's more a confirmation of their different approaches that we see – first when Sam wants to protect Ronald by not telling him the truth and Dean wants to come clean and 'fess up everything; then later, when Dean is about to kill Sherri because they think she's the shapeshifter despite her fainting, and it's Sam who thinks it through and works it all out.

But as in the previous episode, the most important role is delegated to a secondary character who doesn't survive to the end; in this case, Ronald. At a symbolic level, Ronald represents both Sam and Dean – he has the same 'crazy' beliefs and uses the same kinds of weapons. When Ronald is shot we understand suddenly how the outside world views those 'crazy' beliefs, and we graphically see what will happen to Sam and Dean if they put a single foot wrong – especially now that the Feds are on their tails. It's a very real and deadly threat and is bound to put Sam and Dean under increasing pressure in future episodes. Can't wait.

VERDICT – 9 out of 10

EPISODE 2-13
HOUSES OF THE HOLY

TRANSMISSION DATES
US first aired: 1 February 2007
UK first aired: 5 October 2007

CREDITS
Writer: Sera Gamble
Director: Kim Manners

GUEST STARS
Denis Arndt (Father Reynolds), Heather Doerksen (Gloria Sytnik), Brent Fidler (TV Evangelist), Dan Mellor (Frank Potts), David Monahan (Father Thomas Gregory), Sean Rogerson (Man), Wesley Salter (Zach Smitt), Zara Taylor (Woman)

SYNOPSIS
Angels are appearing to drunks and hookers and giving them instructions to murder people. When Sam and Dean investigate the victims, they learn that each one has either already committed a crime or was about to commit one. Linking the victims is a church, where the boys are told about the recent death of one of the priests, Father Gregory. During a visit to Gregory's grave, Sam sees the angel and later is given a sign to identify the 'evil' man he must kill. Dean follows the man and Sam holds a ritual to summon Father Gregory. While Gregory's spirit is put to rest, Dean stops the evil man attacking a woman and chases his car as he tries to escape. The attacker is killed in a freak accident when a truck sheds its load of steel pipes and one of them smashes through his windscreen and through his chest.

CAN YOU SURVIVE TO THE TITLES?
Another episode with no deaths before the titles. Instead, Gloria's evening of TV is disturbed by the appearance of a bright white light surrounding an angel who wants to whisper deadly sweet nothings in her ear.

LOCATION, LOCATION, LOCATION
Providence, Rhode Island.

LEGENDARY ROOTS

An angel is a messenger from God. The word is thought to come from the Greek 'angelos', which means messenger. The Bible contains many references to angels that carry out the work of God as an intermediary between Him and humans, acting as agent, attendant or messenger (son of God, messenger of God, messenger of the Lord and the holy ones). Angels do not have a physical body. They appear as spirits but are stronger and more intelligent than humans.

In Christian religion there are nine ranks of angels:

- Seraphim – 'the burning ones' who radiate pure light, are closest to God and constantly sing His praise.
- Cherubim – guards of the gates of Eden; originally depicted as the bearers of God's throne.
- Thrones – carry out decisions made by God.
- Dominions – regulate the duties of other angels and make sure the wishes of God are carried out.
- Virtues – bring the blessings of God to Earth and are associated with creating miracles.
- Powers – stop fallen angels taking over the world and keep the universe balanced.
- Principalities – guardian angels of cities and nations, they try to stop evil angels invading them.
- Archangels – carry God's most important messages to humans and command angel armies against angels of darkness.
- Angels – the closest rank to humans, acting as intermediaries between humans and God.

SQUEEZE OF THE WEEK

Forget it, not a sniff.

SIBLING RIVALRY

There's a vibrating 'Magic Fingers'[169] bed in the motel room and all Dean needs is quarters to run it. Sam feels rather uncomfortable watching his brother vibrate on the bed and refuses to bring him quarters for it. He thinks it's too much like the lab rat that starved because it was obsessed with the pleasure button rather than the food button.

---

169 See **Cultural References** for details on the 'Magic Fingers' vibrating beds.

BODY COUNT

Gloria's victim is killed off-screen between the opener and the start of the episode proper, starting the trend for stabbings through the heart.

Victim Frank answers the door and is stabbed immediately after Zach introduces himself. Not a man for long conversations or preamble that Zach.

TOOLKIT

- A *police scanner* will allow you to keep up to date on all the local murders, especially those incited by angels.
- For that friendly church séance you'll be needing several *small white candles*, one *large black candle, matches*, a *handful of herbs* that will flare when burned and *an altar mat* – which can be a SpongeBob placemat laid face down if you really can't find anything else. Use the séance ritual from *your dad's journal* when you're ready.
- Being *good at guessing someone else's password* is a priceless talent.

MEMORABLE MOMENTS

The car chase and the piercing conclusion are pretty much the only moments worth mentioning. Oh and Dean on the 'Magic Fingers' bed of course – he seems to have found his idea of heaven in lying on the gyrating bed while he listens to his favourite music. Some people are just easily pleased.

THE CAR'S THE STAR

The Impala gets to race through the streets on the tail of the bad guy again[170]. As always, it looks sleek and sexy in the midnight neon glow.

MOTEL MAYHEM

Made up to look like some semi up-market knocking shop, the motel has the boys surrounded by naked women silhouettes on screens and posters. But it's the vibrating bed that's a real winner …

SPOOK RULES

- The presence of an angel will shake the whole house and cause the lights to flicker[171]. There's a blinding white light around them and they send out a feeling of spiritual ecstasy.

---

170 Something it hasn't done since 'Route 666' (1-13).

171 Funny, demons make the lights flicker too.

- Angels aren't the Hallmark card version people think they are – none of that sweet, fluffy white-winged stuff. Nope, they're fierce, vigilant fighters of demons.
- Wormwood is a plant associated with the dead, specifically ones that are not at rest.
- You can't summon an angel using a séance ritual.

DID YOU SPOT?

This is the first time that there's no Then/Now sequence at the start of the episode.

GOING UNDERCOVER

Sam dons an orderly's uniform and infiltrates a government facility to talk to Gloria about why she stabbed a man through the heart. The boys then pretend to be church-goers when they visit Our Lady of the Angels.

CULTURAL REFERENCES

Gloria: 'You mean, am I stark-raving cuckoo for Coco Puffs?': I'm cuckoo for Coco Puffs! is a tagline for the Coco Puffs breakfast cereal

Dean: 'But she seriously believes that she was … "touched by an angel"'; and Dean: 'Yup, Roma Downey made him do it.': *Touched By An Angel* (1994-2003) was a series about three angels sent to tell depressed and troubled people that God still loves and thinks about them. Roma Downey played an angel named Monica.

Dean: 'Since when are you all Mr 700 Club?': 700 Club is a US CBN Christian life programme featuring a mixture of news, commentaries and interviews and amazing stories of healing, deliverance and financial blessing.

Dean: 'You just got to wait for some divine bat signal.': The bat signal was used by the Gotham City police to summon help from the one and only Batman.

When Dean says he needs to get some bits and pieces for the séance ritual, Sam: 'Sounds great. I hope Whoopi's available.': Whoopi Goldberg starred as the psychic medium Oda Mae Brown in the 1990 movie *Ghost.*

Dean: 'We'll just put it SpongeBob-side down.': SpongeBob SquarePants is a Nickelodeon cartoon character. He's a yellow pant-wearing sponge that lives in a pineapple under the sea.

Dean: 'Hey. Man, you gotta try this. I mean there really is magic in the Magic Fingers.': Magic Fingers beds were invented in 1958 by John Houghtaling. Apparently, they're like sleeping on a purring cat.

Woman's voice on the police radio: 'We've got a minor TA, involving a motorcycle.': A TA is a traffic accident.

Father Reynolds: 'Well, I like to think of them as more loving than wrathful; but yes, a lot of Scripture paints angels as God's warriors. "An angel of the Lord appeared to them, the glory of the Lord shone down upon them, and they were terrified." Luke. 2:9.': This is indeed Luke 2:9.

Dean: 'Okay, Ecstasy Boy, maybe we'll get you some glowsticks and a nice Dr Seuss hat, huh?': Ecstasy is a drug associated with the clubbing crowd, and Dr Seuss is the pen name for Theodor Seuss Geisel (1904-1991) whose works includes *The Cat In The Hat*.

Sam: 'So they're not really the Hallmark card version that everybody thinks?': Hallmark is a greetings card company known to make sweet, romantic cards.

Dean: 'This is a, a demon or a spirit, you know, they find people a few fries short of a Happy Meal': Happy Meals are preset menu items you can buy at McDonald's fast food outlets – you know, the company with Sam's favourite big, scary clown as its mascot.

GOOFS AND FLUFFS
Dean's phone shows that he's listening to Led Zeppelin's 'Kashmir', but the track you can hear is 'Down On Love' by Jamie Dunlap.

HAVEN'T I SEEN YOU BEFORE?
Denis Arndt was in *Anacondas: The Hunt for the Blood Orchid*, *SeaQuest DSV* and *Lois & Clark: The New Adventures of Superman*. Heather Doerksen featured in *Battlestar Galactica*, *Stargate: Atlantis* and *Smallville*. Brent Fidler has been in *Highlander: The Series*, *Nostradamus* and *The Immortal*. David Monahan was in *Crossing Jordan* and *Angel*. Sean Rogerson features in *Harper's Island*, *Underworld Evolution* and *Stargate: Atlantis*. Wesley Salter's credits include *Alienated*, *Battlestar Galactica* and *Blade: The Series*. Zara Taylor has been in *Dante's Cove*, *Hollow Man II* and *Masters of Horror*.

BEHIND THE SCENES
Episode writer Sera Gamble explained in *The Official Supernatural Magazine* #3 that Ben Edlund had originally pitched the priest idea for this episode, but both she and Kripke had dismissed it. After a few days working on the script they finally decided that Edlund's idea worked after all and used it.

The real life church location used in this episode was St Andrew's Church in Vancouver.

MUSICAL INTERLUDE
*   'Down On Love' – Jamie Dunlap – when Dean is enjoying the 'Magic Fingers' bed.

EPISODE 2-13 HOUSES OF THE HOLY

- 'There's A Good Time a Comin' – Doug Stebleton – when the evil guy attacks his date.
- 'Knockin' On Heaven's Door' – Bob Dylan – as the boys discuss faith at the end of the episode.

ANALYSIS

While there's nothing wrong with the execution of 'Houses of the Holy', the episode still feels hollow. Identifying the reasons for this is tricky, because so much of the episode is actually quite good – the pace keeps moving, the car chase is fun and the acting is as full of emotion as ever. The religious aspects are handled with sensitivity and the music, locations and sets are top notch.

So, what's wrong?

First, there's not very much mystery surrounding the 'monster' that's inciting all these people to murder. It's established early on that the problem is either an angel or a spirit, so we're robbed of a chance to work out what's going on for ourselves. When we do eventually get to the final disclosure it's more inevitable than surprising and leaves a rather flat feeling.

Secondly, there's very little new supernatural lore involved. We already know about dealing with spirits – salt and burn, baby! – and Father Gregory may be deluded but he doesn't have the depth of history that someone like H H Holmes bought with him[172] (nor the filthy fingernails, thankfully). And there's very little about the angels. They get only a passing mention – enough to establish that they are fierce fighters of demons[173] – and there's nothing more juicy than that on offer.

Thirdly, the character development is a bit weak. It's already been established[174] that Sam has more religious tendencies and a greater need to believe than Dean, and this episode does little more than flesh those points out and continue to emphasise Sam's angst about turning evil.

The only new developments are that Sam prays daily; and that Dean's reason for not believing in angels is rooted in his childhood – when his mother would tuck him up in bed at night and tell him that the angels were watching over the family. Given subsequent burning-on-the-ceiling events, it's not difficult to understand Dean's point of view, that he needs proof that the angels exist before he'll contemplate believing[175].

---

172 As America's first serial killer in 'No Exit' (2-06).

173 Something that will become very significant in Season Four.

174 From 'Faith' (1-12).

175 Viewed through eyes that have seen Season Four episodes, Dean spouting his disbelief in angels is actually quite amusing.

The strongest aspect of the character development is in the change of opinions the boys undergo between the start and end of the episode. Their experiences result in a reversal such that Sam goes from having a bright-eyed belief in angels – and by extension in God – to a desolate conclusion that there's no greater power to lend him strength in his coming trials. For Dean, the fate of the evil guy he was chasing in the car implies that one way or another a greater power was going to take the guy's life, and it wasn't going to stop until it succeeded.

Overall, though, this is one of the weakest episodes in the season, despite having a strong and stylish delivery.

VERDICT – 5 out of 10

EPISODE 2-14
BORN UNDER A BAD SIGN

TRANSMISSION DATES
US first aired: 8 February 2007
UK first aired: 12 October 2007

CREDITS
Writer: Cathryn Humphris
Director: J Miller Tobin

RECURRING ROLES
Jim Beaver (Bobby Singer), Alona Tal (Jo Harvelle)

GUEST STARS
Philip Granger (Manager), Richard Kahan (Clerk), Vince Murdocco (Steve Wandel)

SYNOPSIS
Sam disappears for seven days, and when Dean finally catches up with him, he's covered in blood and has no memory of what's happened. Retracing Sam's steps, the boys watch some CCTV footage that shows him murdering hunter Steve Wandel. Sam begs Dean to kill him before he hurts anyone else. When Dean refuses, Sam knocks him unconscious and goes off to terrorise Jo Harvelle in Duluth. Dean turns up in time to stop Sam injuring Jo and proves that he is actually possessed by a demon. Sam is chased to Bobby's, where the demon – who used to be inside Meg – is finally exorcised and he is freed from its influence.

CAN YOU SURVIVE TO THE TITLES?
No deaths in the opener this time, just a worried Dean frantically trying to find his brother.

LOCATION, LOCATION, LOCATION
Twin Lakes, Wisconsin; Duluth, Minnesota; Bobby's place, South Dakota.

LEGENDARY ROOTS
Demonic possession is where a demon takes control over the body of a human. The person who has been possessed has no control over themselves and the entity usually

has to be forced to leave via an exorcism. A possessed person can go through a number of changes that affect their physical appearance or manifest as a mental state such as loss of memory or the sudden ability to speak or read another language. This can also include a change in the tone of voice, and sometimes even the facial structure can appear different. Some possessed people are said to show superhuman strength or unexplainable injuries.

There are a couple of famous examples of possession. Robbie Doe's situation would eventually lead to the 1973 movie *The Exorcist*. Doe, aged 13, was subject to an exorcism in 1949. The boy started reporting scratching noises coming from inside the walls of the family home in January of that year. Later, noises like someone was walking up and down the hallway were reported and objects would appear to move on their own. The boy's bed would shake on its own, with blankets being pulled off the bed along with the boy himself if he was holding onto them. The boy's personality changed – he became angry, agitated and unsettled.

Thinking he had a poltergeist tormenting him, his parents called Rev Luther Schultze, a Lutheran minister. After witnessing the nightmares and thrashing in bed he recommended that Robbie was sent to the Mental Hygiene Clinic of the University of Maryland. There, nothing abnormal was found, but scratches started appearing on the boy. Rev Schultze decided the case was more a job for the Catholics.

Father Albert Hughes of St James Catholic Church in Mt Rainier decided this was a possession after an interview with the boy, who replied in a diabolical voice and shouted obscenities and blasphemies. Cardinal O'Boyle authorised an exorcism after reviewing the case. It was performed at the Georgetown hospital by Father Hughes. The boy spat, screamed obscenities and continued to blaspheme, broke loose from his restraints and slashed the Father with a metal spring from the bed, requiring him to have 100 stitches.

On 9 March, Father Bishop SJ, Father Bowdern SJ and Jesuit scholastic Fr Walter Halloran interviewed the boy and noticed zigzag scratches on his chest. On 16 March, Cardinal Ritter granted another exorcism. As the Rites of Exorcism were performed, the boy began to make growling noises and howls, then the words 'hell' and 'devil' appeared on his chest. The boy was moved to the psychiatric ward of Lexian Brothers Hospital, where the exorcism continued. Much of the time the boy needed to be held down while Bowdern recited prayers from 'The Roman Ritual'. Doe would scream out in pain every time God's name was mentioned and scratches would appear.

On the night of 18 April the boy was forced to wear religious metals and to hold a crucifix. He started asking about the meaning of the Latin prayers. He later claimed that he was St Michael the Archangel. He ordered the demon to leave the boy's body and went into violent contortions and spasms. The boy woke up speaking in his normal voice, saying he had seen visions of St Michael holding a sword.

Anneliese Michel (1952-1976), was a German Catholic woman. It was said she was possessed by six or more demons. The medical diagnosis, when she was 16 years old, was severe psychiatric disturbances. She died aged 24 from malnutrition and mental illness – she was starving herself to 'atone for the wayward youth of the day and the apostate priests of the modern church'. She requested an exorcism, which was performed by two priests a total of 67 times over a ten month period. The priests and her parents were convicted of negligent manslaughter. Two films have been made based on her story: *The Exorcism of Emily Rose* (2005) and *Requiem* (2006).

SQUEEZE OF THE WEEK
Demon-Sam does try to get into Jo Harvelle's knickers, but frankly, she's much more interested in Dean.

SIBLING RIVALRY
Considering how worried Dean is about Sam, he still manages to get in a quip about suddenly discovering that Sam is a Bon Jovi fan.

BODY COUNT
Hunter Steve Wandel is the only victim in the entire episode, and he bleeds to death in Sam's arms[176].

TOOLKIT
- This is the first time having *a huge wad of money* has been important for the boys. First Dean uses cash to loosen the tongue of the gas station clerk so they can find out which way Sam went after stealing the booze and menthol cigarettes; then he has to pay the manager at the dodgy motel so that he can get Sam's phone GPS switched on using the manager's computer.
- A *lock-pick* is essential equipment. This time it opens the closet hiding Steve Wandel's hunting equipment.
- A *hand gun* is highly versatile. You can press it into your brother's hand when you're trying to convince him to shoot you. And if he won't do it then you can knock him unconscious with it instead.
- *Holy water* is another essential item in the hunter kit bag – and it's especially good at flushing out demons, 'cause they fizz and burn awfully well when they come

---

176 Let's face it, if you've absolutely got to die then spending your last moments in Sam's arms isn't a bad way to go really. There are plenty of worse options out there.

into contact with it.

- You don't just need any old *mobile phone* in this job – it has to be a waterproof one. Otherwise, your friends won't be able to find you after you've taken a fully-clothed dip in the harbour with a bullet in your shoulder.
- A *bottle of whiskey* should be used for medicinal pain-numbing purposes when a pretty young blonde is removing that bullet from your shoulder with a knife.
- *Small, silver charms* will help protect you from future demonic possessions, so make sure you wear them constantly in the future.

MEMORABLE MOMENTS

The conversation between Sam and Jo in the bar is mesmerising. You're trying to figure out what the hell is going on with Sam – who is starting to act very strangely indeed – but you're also trying to absorb the information Sam's giving you about Jo's father and Dean's feelings for her. There's also an underlying threat of danger through the whole scene, because you don't know what Sam will do next.

And the finale is emotionally difficult to watch too. This is the first time we've seen Sam lay into his brother with his fists; the first time we've seen Bobby hit Sam. Okay, technically it's demon-Sam, but that doesn't ease the discomfort as you watch both Dean and Bobby take sides against Sammy and go at each other with murderous intent. It certainly highlights how emotionally involved you can become with the characters.

SPOOK RULES

- Possessed people have an unpleasant burning reaction to holy water when it comes into contact with their skin – internally or externally.
- Demons are well known for lying but they can also tell the truth – although only when they know it'll mess with your head.
- Demons can still be trapped within a protective symbol, but if the lines of the symbol are broken then the demon can use its powers to start throwing people about again.
- The *Rituale Romanum* exorcism rites don't work if the demon has locked itself into the body using a binding link symbol branded onto the forearm of the victim.
- Demons can also use Latin rituals, even from inside a Devil's Trap, to create earthquake-like effects and cause cracks in ceilings.
- Binding links can be broken if you re-brand the skin over the top of the symbol so that it is no longer a perfect binding link pattern.
- For a demon, hell is a prison made of bone and flesh and blood and fear. Despite being demons they still suffer while in hell and will go to great lengths to claw

their way back out.

- Revenge for a demon does not necessarily involve killing the victim. If they can manipulate their targets into emotional chaos then that is more satisfying than a bullet in the head.

DID YOU SPOT?

After discovering that the FBI are on their tails, the boys are smartening up their act and being more cautious about forensic evidence. This time, Sam wipes his prints from the blood-stained knife after handling it in the car. They've not done this very often at all[177] given the number of crime scenes they've broken into or arrived at before the police, so it's no surprise Henricksen's been able to track them so far.

This is the first (but not last) time we see Sam with black demon eyes[178].

GOING UNDERCOVER

Sam signs in at the motel under the name of Richard Sambora from Bon Jovi. Jared Padalecki also starred in a movie with Jon Bon Jovi called *Cry Wolf* (2005).

CULTURAL REFERENCES

Dean: 'No, Justin [Timberlake] is quite the triple threat.': The triple threat description of Justin Timberlake refers to someone who has three talents – in this case presumably singing, dancing and acting. The phrase originates in American football and means a player who excels at running, passing and kicking.

Justin Timberlake (1981-) started on television singing country songs on *Star Search* but was more famous for starring in *The Mickey Mouse Club* from 1993 to 1994 alongside Britney Spears, Christina Aguileria and J C Chasez. He and Chasez went onto become members of NSYNC, a boyband that was together from 1995 to 2002. After this he went solo, so far producing two successful albums, 'Justified' and 'FutureSex/LoveSound'. His concerts and videos are noted for his dancing skills. He has also ventured into acting, appearing in movies such as *Alpha Dog* and *Black Snake Moan*.

Gas Station Clerk: 'Tell your story walkin', pal. Po-Po will be here in five.': Po-Po – associated with a Police Officer (can be Pissed Off Police Officer), derived from the hip-hop culture.

Dean: 'Either this guy's a Unabomber ...': This is the second reference to a Unabomber[179].

---

177 The last time was when they wiped the prints from the handrail on the fire exit stairs in 'Nightmare' (1-14).

178 And you'll have to wait quite a while to see it again.

179 The first reference appeared in 'Dead Man's Blood' (1-20).

GOOFS AND FLUFFS

At the start of the episode, Dean is talking to Ellen on his mobile. When Sam's call comes in, he puts Ellen on hold and we never see him get back to her to say Sam has turned up. Poor love, she must have been worried sick.

According to Jo, Bill Harvelle died because John Winchester jumped out from cover too soon and the hellspawn thing they were supposed to be trapping turned on Bill and killed him. But in *John Winchester's Journal* by Alex Irvine (William Morrow, 2009) under the entry on 16 April 1986, it says that Bill was killed because John made a mistake and smudged the Devil's Trap symbol, rendering it ineffectual. Jo's story in this episode gives Bill's death as happening at Devil's Gate reservoir, and this matches what *John Winchester's Journal* suggests.

The story given by demon-Sam where he says that John Winchester shot Bill Harvelle matches the *John Winchester's Journal* entry, but not surprisingly the demon misses out the details about Bill being possessed at the time and begging John to kill him.

HAVEN'T I SEEN YOU BEFORE?

Philip Granger's credits include *To Die For, Poltergeist: The Legacy, Total Recall: 2070* and *Dead Like Me*. Richard Kahan played Marco Pacella in *The 4400* and has also been in *Stargate: Atlantis* and *Masters of Horror*. Vince Murdocco starred in *Night Hunter*.

BEHIND THE SCENES

In *The Official Supernatural Magazine* #4, director J Miller Tobin explained that the water scenes weren't easy for Ackles, even though the actor was only partly submerged, the water was still only 30 degrees. However, the actor was wearing a wetsuit and that's enough to get anyone hot under the collar.

Tobin also explained in *The Official Supernatural Magazine* #4 that the Doors' 'The Crystal Ship' got onto the soundtrack because of editor Anthony Pinker. They knew Kripke wasn't a Doors fan but the boss didn't take much convincing in the end because the song fitted the scenes so well.

And finally, writer Cathryn Humphris didn't script the last punch from Dean, when Sam was no longer possessed. The boys added it in themselves so Dean could release all his frustration over his brother's actions. [*Season Two Supernatural Companion*]

MUSICAL INTERLUDE

* 'Ashes to Ashes' – Tarbox Ramblers – when Sam arrives at bar where Jo's working.
* 'The Crystal Ship' – the Doors – when Sam is revealing how Jo's dad died.

- 'Rock and Roll Ain't Noise Pollution' by AC/DC – the ring tone on Dean's phone that Jo uses to track him.
- 'Back On The Road Again' – REO Speedwagon – as the boys drive at the end of the episode.

ANALYSIS

The writers picked the right place to start this episode. If they'd shown everything from the point where Sam departs on his week-long adventures, it would have been far less intriguing. Starting at the point where Sam re-appears and is reconstructing his actions – like some three-dimensional Winchester-shaped jigsaw – maintains an air of mystery and momentum right up to the part where Dean starts splashing the holy water around and outing the nasty Meg-demon. From there on in, it's a straight demon hunt: chase, trap and evict, with suitable brutal difficulties for Dean.

It's a brave episode overall. It introduces a strand of seriously dark drama, and while there is still a monster-of-the-week (in the Meg-demon), this is also the first episode that relies on exploiting the boys' relationship as the main driver of the story. Previously, the monsters have been after other victims[180] or just one of the two brothers, but this time they're both in the crosshairs, even though others get hurt around the edges. Which only goes to show how strong the Winchester mythology is, because it supports the whole episode effortlessly.

Along with the mythology, there's a wealth of personality. For Sam, we experience his guilt at having murdered someone and his fear that he'll kill more people. It's all consistent with what we've seen of him before, but this time it's actually demon-Sam spouting the angst with the purpose of pushing Dean towards a deadly decision.

But where is Dean going to draw the line between saving Sam or killing him? It appears that Dean will tolerate pretty extreme situations before pulling the trigger, and indeed at one point he even declares that he'd rather die than kill his brother – although he does punch Sam in the face at the end of the episode, so there's clearly a certain level of violence against his brother that he is prepared to dish out.

Dean is fortunate in this instance that Sam is actually possessed and therefore hasn't technically gone darkside yet; he's actually an innocent bystander in all the murders. Dean gets to save his brother by exorcising the demon (eventually) but the precedent has been set – if Sam turns, then it looks like Dean is more likely to try to find a way to save Sam than put a silver bullet between his eyes.

And while Sam's demon blood storyline is opening up, others are being resolved.

---

180 Even in 'Shadow' (1-16), Meg wasn't directly after the boys, she was just using them to get to John; and Gordon was after only Sam in 'Hunted' (2-10).

We finally find out what happened to Jo Harvelle after she left the Roadhouse and went hunting on her own. It's no surprise she's working in a bar, but it is a surprise that Sam manages to overpower her so easily. This is one part of the story that doesn't feel right. Given Jo's background, being around hunters and working in a bar, it isn't logical that she'd fall so quickly to Sam, and without a fight too. His behaviour is sufficiently weird in the bar that she should be wary of him as soon as he tries to hold her hand, if not before. Maybe his 'dewy sensitive eyes' put her off her guard, but this isn't the Jo we came to know at the Roadhouse, nor the one you'd expect to find if she'd been hunting on her own for some time.

One trait she does still have is her interest in Dean. She finally gets her hands on his naked flesh when she bandages him up after Sam shoots him; but after Sam's earlier comments about Dean seeing Jo as a little sister, she recognises the truth of the situation and lets her hopes go[181].

From Jo's place, the boys move on and end up having the showdown at Bobby's – who'll be needing to get his foundations checked with the Meg-demon giving the place a serious round of the shakes before beating seven shades out of Dean. The Meg-demon's motive for causing all this trouble is never really explained beyond a logical desire for revenge that it felt for being sent back to hell by the Winchesters. But would yellow-eyes have let Dean shoot Sam? Or was it all part of some greater plan? The boys are certainly more isolated now that Sam needs to avoid the hunters even more, while Dean needs to avoid the police, but was that intentional? Only time will tell …

VERDICT – 8.5 out of 10

---

181 That's just unlucky – in a similar scene in *The Terminator* (1984), when Sarah Connor bandages Kyle's wounds, she gets a whole bed full of thanks.

EPISODE 2-15
TALL TALES

TRANSMISSION DATES
US first aired: 15 February 2007
UK first aired: 19 October 2007

CREDITS
Writer: John Shiban
Director: Bradford May

RECURRING ROLE
Jim Beaver (Bobby Singer)

GUEST STARS
Angela Case (Trickster Girl 2), Elena Esovolova (Starla), Matreya Fedor (Alien),
Neil Grayston (Frat Pledge), Chad Hershler (Research Scientist), Barclay Hope
(Professor Cox), Emma Lahana (Jen), Desiree Loewen (Classy Girl), Richard Speight
Jr (Trickster), David Tom (Curtis), Mashiah Vaughn (Trickster Girl 1), Tara Wilson
(Co-Ed)

UNCREDITED
Twan Holliday (Chainsaw Maniac)

SYNOPSIS
Sam and Dean are investigating a suicide at a supposedly haunted university building,
but after one of the students is abducted by aliens and another man is eaten by an
alligator in the sewer, the boys have to call for support from Bobby. As Bobby listens
to their versions of the campus events, he observes that they are bickering worse than
ever. With each of the victims arguably deserving their fate, Bobby concludes that
the mischief is being caused by a Trickster: a demigod with the ability to manipulate
reality. The three hunters eventually kill the Trickster but have to fight their way
through scantily-clad babes and a chainsaw-wielding maniac before they can finally
stake him. Unfortunately, the boys have staked only a copy of the Trickster, and the
real demigod still lives.

CAN YOU SURVIVE TO THE TITLES?
Professor Cox thinks he's onto a good thing when a beautiful girl goes up to his office with him. But within minutes he's flying out of the window and landing head-first with bone-crunching finality on the front steps.

LOCATION, LOCATION, LOCATION
The only clue to where the boys are this time is on their jackets while they're undercover. Their jacket badges are for an Ohio telecommunications company.

LEGENDARY ROOTS
The trickster is a classic character from folklore and religion who can be a god, goddess, spirit, human or anthropomorphic animal. The trickster will break the rules of the gods or nature trying to trick other people, most often leading to a positive effect. Probably the most popular trickster tales belong to Loki, who features in Norse mythology as a mischievous and malicious shape-shifter who offered assistance but also hindered the Gods. Loki was cast out for helping cause the death of the god Balder by getting the blind god Hod to throw mistletoe at him – mistletoe being the only plant that hadn't sworn to not hurt Balder. Once caught, Loki was bound by one of his son's entrails and left with a serpent's venom dripping on him, which when it hit him caused him to writhe in agony, resulting in earthquakes on Earth.

SQUEEZE OF THE WEEK
Dean gets an offer of a massage (and who knows what else afterwards) from two beautiful ladies dressed only in bras and panties, and he's only just strong enough to refuse it. The ladies are so disappointed they start a tag-team style fight with him, and Dean definitely doesn't come out on top.

SIBLING RIVALRY
The rivalry between the brothers is rife in this episode. Their bickering reaches new heights, they get frustrated with each other and overreact to every little perceived slight. By the end of the episode they can see a little clearer, realising that the Trickster has manipulated them and that they were both innocent of any wrongdoing.

　　Their apologies to each other are typically Winchester-esque, each understanding the other without any words needed, but Bobby brings them back to reality, brusquely commenting that his heart his breaking and can't they just leave now.

BODY COUNT
After Professor Cox dives out of his window on the fourth floor, an alligator chows

down on an animal research scientist, leaving only an arm and a leg behind. As for Pledge Master Curtis, he probably wishes he had died after being probed by that alien again and again and again and again.

TOOLKIT

- Since the boys suspect a haunting after the first death, they're in there with the *EMF meter* straight away[182].
- Two interpersonal skills will help you reach your objective – first, you need to be able to *control your laughter* when interviewing victims and they tell you they've been abducted and forced to slow dance with aliens; and secondly, you need *a strong stomach* so you don't throw up in the morgue when viewing the chewed-on stumps of a dismembered scientist.
- On a more physical level, having *a large wooden stake dipped in blood* and hidden in your clothes (or are you just pleased to see me?) can be very handy in dispatching mischievous demigods.

MEMORABLE MOMENTS

It's impossible to forget the slow-dancing alien scene and the stage full of girls kicking Dean's ass! This is the first – but not last – episode to feature such bizarre situations[183] and is all the more entertaining for having them..

And don't forget the two versions of Dean's Purple Nurple experience with Starla – two wonderfully hilarious different points of view.

THE CAR'S THE STAR

Poor Impala – that nasty Trickster let its tyres down and Dean had to send it for some tender loving repairs for bent rims. There, there.

MOTEL MAYHEM

This is probably the dingiest, drabbest hole the boys have visited so far. Dean should be checking both beds for all manner of creepy crawlies and stains before eating food anywhere near them.

SPOOK RULES

- A trickster is a demi-god and they exist in cultures around the world, most notable as Loki in Scandinavia and Anansi in West Africa.

---

182 It's not been used since 'The Usual Suspects' (2-07).

183 Okay, 'Bugs' (1-08) had some bizarre scenes too, but they weren't supposed to be funny.

- They are immortal, enjoy causing mischief and chaos, can create things out of nowhere, making them vanish just as quickly, and can't be detected using an EMF meter.
- Tricksters are known for picking people with high and mighty attitudes and bringing them down a peg or two, often in humorous situations, sometimes with deadly consequences.
- They can disguise themselves as anything but take human form most often.
- And tricksters have a metabolism like an insect – which gives them a very sweet tooth.

DID YOU SPOT?

The girl waiting for Professor Cox outside his building should have raised suspicions from the first – not only is she not shivering when she's hanging around wearing next to nothing in sub-zero temperatures but when she speaks her breath doesn't condense on the air. You can see Professor Cox's breath misting while he is talking but not the girl's.

The Professor's scene where he's snogging the rapidly decaying gorgeous girl echoes Jack Torrance's illicit tonsil tennis with a similarly afflicted beauty in *The Shining*.

The whole episode echoes *The X-Files*' 'Bad Blood' (5-12).

GOING UNDERCOVER

It's not clear what cover Dean is using with Starla but it's probably something like a pilot since he introduces Sam as Major Tom, his shuttle pilot.

Then it's back to being reporters for a local paper when they go to interview the students at the university.

Followed by Telecoms engineers for the Ohio Connect DSL company (Digital Subscriber Line – high speed internet access over telephone lines), when the boys gain access to Crawford Hall and Professor Cox's rooms. All they do is talk to the friendly janitor, who lets them in wherever they want.

CULTURAL REFERENCES

Dean: 'I don't know, man. I think they're called Purple Nurples.': Two main recipes are available for a Purple Nurple shot. First, mix Malibu, triple sec, Blue Curacao and cranberry juice. Combine all ingredients in a cocktail shaker with ice. Shake and strain into an old-fashioned glass and serve. Alternatively, mix Blue Curacao, vodka, apple schnapps, sweet and sour mix and grenadine syrup then shake with ice.

Dean: 'What? You mean between the angry spirit and uh … the sexed-up ET?':

E.T. The Extra-Terrestrial is a 1982 Steven Spielberg movie about a stranded alien.

Weekly World News was first mentioned in 'Bloodlust' (2-03) and is a supermarket tabloid paper founded in 1979 dealing with bizarre and unusual stories. The now-online newspaper at worldweeklynews.com ran an article an article about *Supernatural*'s 'Tall Tales' episode.

Dean: 'This is my shuttle co-pilot, Major Tom.': Major Tom is an astronaut created by David Bowie and appears in the songs 'Space Oddity', 'Ashes to Ashes' and 'Hallo Spaceboy'.

The chainsaw-wielding cannibal in the climax is probably a character reference to Leatherface, the star of *The Texas Chain Saw Massacre* (1974) and its sequels.

Dean: 'Looks like you lost it, Poindexter.': A Poindexter is a person who acts and dresses like a nerd but does not possess the intellect usually associated with a nerd.

Sam: 'Well, I didn't find any candy bars or sugar. Not even Equal.': Equal is an artificial sweetener or sugar replacement.

GOOFS AND FLUFFS

When Sam and Dean examine the remains of the scientist, the alligator scale is easy to spot. Surely the coroner would also have spotted this and removed it already? And it's not like the Trickster would have put it there for the boys to find, because the demigod doesn't want the boys to find him. Does he?!

When Dean has staked the Trickster, all the Trickster-created illusions start disappearing, including the chainsaw maniac and the sexy girls. It's not quite clear why the bed and props remain on the stage when the Trickster probably created those for Dean too.

In the closing scenes you can see the 'dead body' take a deep breath then hold it just before the real Trickster arrives to tidy up his remaining illusion.

HAVEN'T I SEEN YOU BEFORE?

Angela Case was in *Masters of Horror*. Matreya Fedor's credits include *A Town Called Eureka* and *Slither*. Neil Greyston played Douglas Fargo in *A Town Called Eureka* and has also appeared in *Jeremiah* and *Dead Like Me*. Chad Hershler was in *Smallville*, *Dead Like Me* and *Stargate SG-1*. Barclay Hope featured in *A Town Called Eureka*, *Smallville* and played Colonel Lionel Pendergast in *Stargate SG-1*. Emma Lahana has featured in *Stargate: Atlantis* and *Kyle XY*. David Tom was in *Quantum Leap*. Mashiah Vaughn has been in *House of the Dead*. Tara Wilson was in *The Butterfly Effect* and *Smallville*.

BEHIND THE SCENES

Richard Speight (who played the Trickster) deadpanned in the *Season Three*

Supernatural Companion about how he much enjoyed watching girls in their underwear wrestling. He also notes that the director of that episode was very thorough, covering every angle for those scenes.

MUSICAL INTERLUDE

* 'Walk Away' – The James Gang – when Dean is eating on Sam's bed while Sam is researching.
* 'Next To You' – Junk Food – when Sam is in the bar questioning the two students and Dean is drinking with Starla.
* 'Brenda & Me' – Rhythm Machine – during Dean's version of his talk with Starla.
* 'Lady In Red' – Chris DeBurgh – when Curtis is slow dancing with the alien.
* 'Can't Get Enough of Your Love, Babe' – Barry White – when Dean enters the auditorium where the girls on bed and the Trickster are waiting.

ANALYSIS

Supernatural has always made time for humour[184]. In most of the previous episodes[185], the humour has been secondary to the plot, but here it takes a more prominent role.

The laughs come from two separate sources: the tricks being played on the victims, and the brothers' opinions of each other and themselves. Even while you're laughing at the slow dancing alien, the episode still maintains a very real, threatening undertone, with the gory remains of the scientist bringing us back to the deadly nature of the mysterious perpetrator. Then the humour returns as the boys and Bobby find themselves in danger. It's difficult not to smile when Dean is being beaten up by the scantily clad babes, but you never lose sight of the fact that he's taking a brutal beating.

It's a fine balance of horror and humour that's maintained from the moment a rather nonplussed janitor narrowly avoids being squidged by the flying Professor, to Dean's undignified launch from the stage to land at the Trickster's feet.

And while all the laughs are taking centre stage, there's a wealth of character development woven into the story too. Let's take a little aside to explain something called the Rashomon Effect. This is about the subjectivity of a person's perception on recollection and explains why different observers of a specific event produce significantly different but equally plausible accounts. This comes to the fore as Sam and Dean are retelling the events to Bobby, and explains why their accounts are so different.

---

184 An influence that may well come from Eric Kripke's love of the movie *An American Werewolf in London*, a film that first combined horror with laughs.

185 With the exception of 'Hell House' (1-17).

But what do the variations tell us about the boys?

Let's start with how Sam sees Dean. Throughout all the flashbacks, it's clear that Sam believes Dean lacks sophistication. He thinks Dean drinks too much (Purple Nurples) and has no manners (burps and stuffs his face with free food while talking with his mouth full). He thinks Dean has little respect for women (feisty little wildcat), let alone any good taste, choosing women equally unsophisticated as himself (Starla trying to keep her liquor down). Dean also lacks any ability to empathise with someone else's situation ('Some alien made you his bitch'). Sam sees himself, however, as level headed, good at getting people to talk to him about their investigation, and focused (as evidenced in his account of his interview with Curtis and his girlfriend Jen).

Dean has a very different take on Sam. He sees him as being anything but macho (Sam's voice in the bar) with a tendency to rabbit on about unimportant things (blah, blah) rather than doing the job and having some serious fun along the way. He thinks Sam over-empathises with people and is too touchy feely; and that people don't get as traumatised as he thinks they do (the scene with Curtis's fellow student). Meanwhile, Dean sees himself as having great taste (pulling classy chicks) and being on an important mission saving people ('Please … lives are at stake'); but is dogged by the understandable fact that women find him irresistible ('My God, you are attractive').

What lets this episode down slightly is that this gorgeous perceptional stuff isn't consistent throughout the flashbacks, leaving it feel uneven in places. The scenes where the boys break into the morgue and to an extent when they interview Curtis about his abduction are told in the normal straight style, minus the personal colour – although Curtis's tale of alien slow dancing is funny enough to let the scene work without the extra stuff thrown in.

It's great to see the writers are still experimenting with different story-telling techniques and points of view, and after the darkness of 'Born Under A Bad Sign' (2-14), this episode lightens the mood and helps to create a more balanced season.

VERDICT – 8 out of 10

Episode 2-16
Roadkill

Transmission Dates
US first aired: 20 February 2007
UK first aired: 26 October 2007

Credits
Writer: Raelle Tucker
Director: Charles Beeson

Guest Stars
Dan Gauthier (David McNamara), Tricia Helfer (Molly McNamara), Maria Marlow (David's Wife), Winston Rekert (Jonah Greeley)

Synopsis
Molly McNamara runs over a guy on a lonely stretch of highway and wakes up in her crashed car to discover that her husband, David, has disappeared from the passenger seat. She flags down a passing car, that just happens to be the Impala, and pleads for help from Sam and Dean. The guy Molly hit is apparently Jonah Greely, who was actually killed in a car accident 15 years earlier and whose ghost returns each year to exact revenge for his death. While the boys search for Greely's grave to salt and burn dem bones, Molly is captured by Greely and tortured. Finding the grave, the boys save Molly from further suffering by burning Greely's remains. They then take Molly to her husband. But only David survived the crash back in 1992 and both Molly and Greely had been haunting the highway each year since then. Finally aware of the truth, Molly's spirit leaves as the first rays of dawn strike.

Can You Survive to the Titles?
No deaths, just car accidents and spooks before the titles.

Location, Location, Location
An isolated section of Highway 41 somewhere between the Upper Peninsula of Michigan and Miami, Florida. Only 2000 miles of blacktop to choose from then …

Legendary Roots
There are ghosts of people that do not realise they have passed from the physical world.

They have become stuck in limbo and are unable to move onto the next plane of existence. The cause of this is not known but many mediums and ghost hunters reckon these ghosts are born from a traumatic death such as murder or a devastating accident and that assistance is needed for them to be able to move onto the next plane. Veteran ghost hunter Dr Hans Holzer explains that these ghosts are 'Stay Behinds': 'A ghost is a human being who has passed out of the physical body, usually in a traumatic state, and is not aware usually of his true condition. We are all spirits encased in a physical body. At the time of passing, our spirit body continues into the next dimension. A ghost, on the other hand, due to trauma, is stuck in our physical world and needs to be released to go on.'

SQUEEZE OF THE WEEK

Molly McNamara is gorgeous, but Dean is cool and distant towards her throughout. Of course, once you know she's a ghost, it's obvious why he wasn't hitting on her like there's no tomorrow. He does draw the line somewhere then.

SIBLING RIVALRY

Sam's dishing out lots of those 'Do you have to be so insensitive?' stares at Dean as his brother asks Molly if her pursuer looked like he'd lost a fight with a lawnmower, tells her bluntly that they're hunting ghosts, and that if she goes in to see her husband (now she's a ghost) she'll freak hubby out for life.

However, there's one occasion when Sam gets to use the 'Just like you' look instead – when Molly explains that the only time her husband really argued with her was when they were stuck in the car. Sam understood exactly what she meant.

BODY COUNT

This is only the fourth episode where no one gets killed at all[186]. Okay, you could argue that technically Molly finally 'passed away', but she's already dead and doesn't count.

TOOLKIT

- Standard hunter's kit bag only – a *shovel* for exhuming bodies, *lighter fuel*, a *match* and a *rock salt-loaded shotgun*.
- You don't need the *EMF meter* to find the spook when he's running at you with his guts hanging out, bent on blood. That situation kind of speaks for itself.

---

186 The others being 'Home' (1-09), 'Something Wicked' (1-18), and 'No Exit' (2-06).

MEMORABLE MOMENTS
The twist at the end is the only eyebrow-lifting moment in an otherwise unremarkable episode.

Sam's over-empathising with Molly (reminding you of Dean's version of events in 'Tall Tales' (2-15)) is memorable for all the wrong reasons.

As is Sam's awful line of quiz-show-host dialogue: 'Every year, Greeley finds someone to punish for what happened to him. Tonight, that person is you.'

THE CAR'S THE STAR
The Impala's comes under ghostly Greely influence when he stalls its engine so the boys can't leave with Molly. This is the second episode in a row that the Impala has been interfered with[187]. The bad guys just can't keep their hands off it! Can you blame them?

SPOOK RULES
- Most of the spook rules have already been established but there are a couple of new ones.
- The existing rules are:
    - Spooks will come back to a time and place that has some personal significance to them.
    - A spirit is often driven by the desire for revenge and they are bound to the real world by either their own remains or unfinished business.
    - Love or hate can trap a spirit in an eternal loop, repeating the same tragedies.
    - Vengeful spirits weren't necessarily evil people in life; their pain forces them to lash out after death.
    - And salt is a symbol of purity that repels impure and unnatural things – like vengeful spirits.
- And the new information:
    - Some spirits see only what they want to see.
    - A spirit never returns after its remains are burned.
    - Sam and Dean don't know where the spirits go after the remains have been burned.
    - The dead may hold onto life so hard after death because they're scared of the unknown.

---

187 'Tall Tales' (2-15) being the previous episode.

GOING UNDERCOVER

The boys go undercover only when they're talking to Molly's husband. It's not clear what the cover is, but it involves suits, so FBI or insurance people is a fair bet.

CULTURAL REFERENCES

Dean: 'Follow the creepy brick road.': The yellow brick road featured in the 1939 film *The Wizard of Oz*. Dorothy and her friends follow it in order to reach the Wizard.

Dean: 'Sammy's always getting a little J Love Hewitt when it comes to this.': Jennifer Love Hewitt stars as Melinda Gordon in *The Ghost Whisperer*, in which her character can talk to ghosts[188].

Dean: 'Well all right, Haley Joel.': Haley Joel Osment starred in the 1999 movie *The Sixth Sense*, in which his character could see dead people[189].

Molly: 'So this is really what you guys do. You're like Ghostbusters.': Another reference to the 1984 comedy film *Ghostbusters* about a group of ghost catchers, starring Dan Aykroyd, Bill Murray and Sigourney Weaver[190].

GOOFS AND FLUFFS

How did old lady Greely manage to get the sideboard back in place over the opening of the secret door if she was on the inside of the hidden room?

At the start of the scene where Greely scratches Molly, she has only a small section of her midriff exposed. Part way through the scene, she swaps to having a large band of flesh in view, despite not being able to move the position of her arms over her head.

Sam digs Jonah's bones up extremely quickly given that he has only a couple of minutes to do it while Dean is being roughed up inside the hut.

Director Charles Beeson said in his interview in *The Official Supernatural Magazine #6*: 'I made sure [Molly] didn't open any doors that she shouldn't have.' However, if you check on the DVD version of the episode, between six and seven minutes in, Molly can be seen opening and closing the car door herself.

HAVEN'T I SEEN YOU BEFORE?

Dan Gauthier's acting credits include *Star Trek: The Next Generation*, *Sliders* and *Charmed*. Tricia Helfer played Number Six in *Battlestar Galactica* and featured in *Jeremiah*. Maria Marlow has been in *Tru Calling* and *Smallville*. Winston Rekert featured in *Battlestar Galactica*, *Stargate SG-1* and *PSI Factor: Chronicles of the Paranormal*.

---

188 A third reference to *The Ghost Whisperer* – the previous ones are in 'Asylum' (1-10) and 'In My Time Of Dying' (2-01).

189 Previously mentioned in 'Asylum' (1-10).

190 Previously mentioned in 'Hookman' (1-07), 'Hell House' (1-17) and 'No Exit' (2-06).

BEHIND THE SCENES

Snow and rain fell during the filming of this episode but it didn't mean the cast and crew had less fun making it. Interviewed for the *Season Two Supernatural Companion*, stunt coordinator Lou Bollo remembers Ackles and on-set costumer Bren Moore playing in the snow. Jensen had been playing Bren up all day then as they finished Bren dropped snow down Jensen's collar, so Jensen threw her into the snow, rubbing her face in it.

MUSICAL INTERLUDE

- 'House Of the Rising Sun' – The Animals – plays several times during the episode – when David and Molly drive at start of episode, again when Sam, Dean and Molly encounter Greeley on the road and finally on the jukebox in Greeley's house.

ANALYSIS

This then is *Supernatural*'s take on *The Sixth Sense*, with the movie even getting a mention in Dean's comment about Haley Joel. The writers on the show are at least intelligent enough to realise that most of their audience are going to have seen the movie, so they were very careful not to give anything away too early.

Like *The Sixth Sense*, 'Roadkill' relies on making the audience feel that they know what is going on. To create this illusion, 'Roadkill' leads you through a series of highly familiar mechanisms before slapping you in the face with the twist.

It opens with normal people being terrorised by a vindictive ghost. This is the most powerful of the mechanisms, because *Supernatural* has used it numerous times[191] throughout Seasons One and Two. We know the score: uncover why the ghost is so hacked off and bent on revenge, find the body, salt and burn the bones, save the innocent victims.

On top of this, all the tools used by the boys during this kind of hunt are kept the same as in the past – shovel, lighter fuel, matches and salt-loaded shotgun. And not only have we heard the cultural references before but the boys are behaving consistently with our expectations. Dean is professionally focused on the hunt and Sam is empathising with the victim. We're cocooned in familiar surroundings, so it's no surprise that we think we know what's going to happen.

Once we're lulled into that false sense of security we're far more vulnerable to the final surprise – a realisation that we experience at the same time as Molly. It's revealed gently without using shock tactics, and the new information forces you to go back and

---

191 From 'Dead in the Water' (1-03) and 'Bloody Mary' (1-05) through 'Scarecrow' (1-11) and 'Route 666' (1-13) to 'No Exit' (2-06) and 'Playthings' (2-11).

mentally review everything that you've seen (which the episode obligingly gives you along with a visual review and some extra bits slipped in).

As a structure, it certainly works, and Tricia Helfer acts her socks off as the distraught Molly. Considering it's the first time that the boys haven't taken the lead roles, she needed to give a strong performance and she doesn't disappoint.

But no-one could act the episode out of its biggest problem – it's a victim of its own necessities. In order to lull us into making assumptions, it *has* to cosset us in familiar territory. In doing so it loses the exciting, original edge we have come to know and love, making it a somewhat boring experience for the first two thirds of the tale. *Supernatural* has always thrown something new and mysterious, at us but this time we get that experience only if we can hang in there long enough for the pay-off.

Not one of the best episodes in Season Two then. Shame.

VERDICT – 6 out of 10

EPISODE 2-17
HEART

TRANSMISSION DATES
US first aired: 22 March 2007
UK first aired: 2 November 2007

CREDITS
Writer: Sera Gamble
Director: Kim Manners

GUEST STARS
Caroline Carter (Friend), Patrick Currie (Kurt Mueller), Brad Dryborough (Glen), Rob Hayter (Cop), Lindsay Maxwell (Hooker), David Quinlan (Nate Mulligan), Teryl Rothery (Coroner), Emmanuelle Vaugier (Madison Owens), Yasmine Vox (Stripper)

SYNOPSIS
While investigating a series of suspected werewolf attacks in San Francisco, Sam and Dean interview Madison Owens, whose boss is the latest victim. Madison is being stalked by her strange ex-boyfriend Kurt. When the boys investigate his apartment, they discover a cop who's been mauled to death in the alley below. With Sam guarding Madison, Dean goes to find her ex, but the werewolf has already killed Kurt at his apartment, and when Dean arrives, it knocks him unconscious. So now Dean knows that Madison is the werewolf. The boys set out to cure her by finding and killing the werewolf who infected her. Dean does this later that night, and Madison doesn't turn. After spending the daytime in bed with Sam, Madison turns again that night and escapes. Phoning the boys in the morning, she begs Sam to save her by putting a bullet through her heart. He obliges with difficulty.

CAN YOU SURVIVE TO THE TITLES?
Lawyer Nate Mulligan gets more than a little cut up after Madison rejects his advances in the bar then comes back in her werewolf form to shred his hopes further.

LOCATION, LOCATION, LOCATION
San Francisco, California, in and around Hunter's Point.

LEGENDARY ROOTS

A werewolf or lycan is a shape-shifter that turns from a human to a wolf-like character. According to folklore, the most common way to become a werewolf is by being bitten or scratched by another lycan. Other cultures say that you can also become a werewolf through practicing Satanism, taking part in cannibalism or being born as the seventh son of a seventh son. Then there's drinking water from the footprint of a wolf, or stripping and wearing clothing made from the skin of a wolf. Eating the meat of a wolf or that of a wolf prey can also bring on the shapeshifting ability.

The rise of a full moon is said to be linked to the change from human to wolf although this seems to be attributed more to the entertainment industry's take on the lore – a 'real' werewolf can transform at will.

That a silver bullet can kill a werewolf also seems to be based more within modern fiction than real lore – which has it that mistletoe, mountain ash and rye will ward off werewolves, so hiding in a field of rye or climbing into an ash tree would save you from attack. The removal of the wolf skin was said to cure a human, along with striking the werewolf on the head with a knife, although many believe that there isn't a cure once you have become a werewolf.

SQUEEZE OF THE WEEK

Well it's about time Sam saw some more action. He's not been interested in a girl since Sarah in 'Provenance' (1-19), and then he only got a kiss. No surprise that Madison is well up for getting into Sam's boxers as well; she knows a good thing when she sees it. (Sam said she was smart.)

SIBLING RIVALRY

Dean is looking forward to going werewolf hunting and Sam teases him about being a werewolf geek. They've not seen one since they were children so Sam pokes more fun at Dean by saying they can go to Disneyland after they kill it.

After that we slip into pleasantly familiar sniping scenarios where Sam says he knows the type of person who starts hitting on anyone in a five-mile radius after a few scotches and Dean pulls age-rank again[192] so he can stay with the hot chick. Happy days.

BODY COUNT

After Nate's office problems, a passing copper has an unfortunate and very bloody run-in with the werewolf behind the rubbish bins; and the apparently abusive and possessive Kurt loses his last encounter with Madison as she dishes out a very rough form of justice.

---

192 Last used in 'Something Wicked' (1-18).

TOOLKIT

- You need expensive tools to deal with a werewolf because they need to be made out of pure silver, but at least you need only *a small silver knife* and a *handgun loaded with solid silver bullets.*

MEMORABLE MOMENTS

Madison's realisation of what she has become is very well done as she scans the bedroom walls full of scratches. And the final scenes, as the boys decide how to handle Madison's request, are brimming with emotion.

SPOOK RULES

- Werewolves remove the heart from their victims, possibly for eating but there's no confirmed reason for the action.
- They murder in the week leading up to the full moon.
- You become a werewolf if you are bitten by one and survive.
- The infected human will have no knowledge of what they become or what they do in werewolf form.
- The human personality can exert some influence on the werewolf's actions – if you fancy a particular human, you won't necessarily kill them while you are in werewolf form.
- Werewolves turn in the middle of the night rather than at moonrise and possibly have to be asleep to do so. They also change at different times – Madison is only just turning when Dean is chasing the fully changed werewolf around Hunter's Point.
- John Winchester's theory was that you could cure someone by killing the werewolf that bit them, but this proves to be incorrect – it's impossible to reverse it.
- Werewolves can be killed only by a silver bullet to the heart.

DID YOU SPOT?

This is the second episode that doesn't feature a Then/Now sequence at the start[193].

The silver knife is the same style and shape as the one that Ronald throws away in the bin in 'Nightshifter' (2-12).

GOING UNDERCOVER

They're detectives this time – Landis and Dante. Joe Dante and John Landis were the directors of two werewolf horror movies, *The Howling* (1981) and *An American*

---

193 The first one being 'Houses of the Holy' (2-13).

Werewolf In London (1981) respectively.

CULTURAL REFERENCES

Dean: 'Like a really hot Incredible Hulk?': A second reference to the Hulk[194] – originally a comic character and later a TV and movie series about a mild mannered scientist who, when angry, turns into a large, green, muscular man.

Dean: 'I'd say Kurt's looking more and more like our Cujo.': *Cujo* is a horror novel (1981) by Stephen King and a movie (1983) directed by Lewis Teague about a rabid St Bernard dog called Cujo.

Sam: 'Wait, so, so Kendall married Ethan's father just to get back at him?': Kendall and Ethan are both characters in the long running soap opera *All My Children*, which started in 1970 and centres around Erica Kane and her long line of husbands.

Dean: 'What are you, the Dog Whisperer now?': *The Dog Whisperer* is a TV show starting in 2004 where Cesar Millan helps people to rehabilitate their dog's behaviour by becoming a pack-leader.

Sam: 'Maybe there's some human hearts behind the Haagen-Dazs or something.': Another reference to Haagen-Dazs ice cream[195].

GOOFS AND FLUFFS

When Sam and the doctor discuss what killed the victim in the morgue, the corpse blinks half way through the conversation.

HAVEN'T I SEEN YOU BEFORE?

Caroline Carter has featured in *Blade: The Series* and *Masters of Horror*. Patrick Currie was in *Stargate SG-1*, *Blood Ties* and *Battlestar Galactica*. Brad Dryborough played Lt Louis Hoshi in *Battlestar Galactica* and also been in Smallville and *Stargate SG-1*. Rob Hayter's credits include *Smallville*, *Stargate SG-1* and *Blood Ties*. Lindsay Maxwell featured in *The Butterfly Effect 2*, *Lost Boys: The Tribe* and *Blood Ties*. David Quinlan has been in *A Town Called Eureka*, *Jeremiah* and *Stargate: Atlantis*. Teryl Rothery was in *White Noise 2: The Light*, *Dead Like Me* and played Dr Janet Fraiser in *Stargate SG-1*. Emmanuelle Vaugier played Dr Helen Bryce in *Smallville* and was in *SAW II* and *IV* and *House of the Dead 2*.

---

194 The first reference was in 'Croatoan' (2-09).

195 This is also a second link to Season One's 'Provenance' (1-19) (to go with **Squeeze of the Week** comments) since that's the only other episode to refer to Haagen Dazs so far.

BEHIND THE SCENES
Actress Emanuelle Vaugier had no issues playing a werewolf, as she explained in *The Official Supernatural Magazine* #6, she finds them dark but very romantic and strangely sexy. Okaaaaay.

Vaugier also commented in *The Official Supernatural Magazine* #6 on getting sexy with Padalecki. They were both nervous – especially with so many people watching – but Jared was a real gentleman and it all went smoothly.

MUSICAL INTERLUDE
- 'Transformer' – Robert Kennedy – when Madison chats with her friends in the bar.
- 'Smoking Gun' – Kip Winger – during Dean's visit to the strip club.
- 'Down On The Street' – The Stooges – when Dean is being attacked by Madison at Kurt's apartment.
- 'Look At You' – Screaming Trees – while Madison and Sam are in bed together
- 'Silent Lucidity' – Queensryche – at the end of the episode where Sam kills Madison.

ANALYSIS
It's always interesting to see what *Supernatural* will do with the iconic monsters. With two successful vampire episodes under their belt, it's time to turn furry and take on the werewolves. Without having the budget of movies like *An American Werewolf in London* for prosthetics or for *Underworld*-style CGI sequences, *Supernatural* was always going to be the poor relation, so it bravely opts for the minimal approach and brings in a heavy dose of moral issues instead.

It's not too bad a decision in the end, but the episode has a number of flaws that are only balanced by the quality of the performances – not only from Ackles and Padalecki but from Vaugier as well.

In the flaws department, there's no mystery about who the other four-legged fangster is, given that there's only two options – Kurt is too obvious (and dead too, before long) so that just leaves the God-squad neighbour Glen.

Then there's the huge, barely-accounted-for plot hole that Madison doesn't turn on the night that Dean breaks the bloodline by shooting Glen while he's fanged up. The boys are left as confused as the viewers, with only Dean's half-hearted 'Perhaps she only turns if she's asleep' to explain things away. We've not had such poor plotting since 'Bugs' (1-08).

And finally, the episode also suffers from being less scary than your average episode of *Scooby-Doo and Scrappy-Doo*. Even the wolf-cam point of view barely raises an eyebrow and certainly doesn't raise the pulse. The days of 'Asylum' (1-10) and 'Scarecrow' (1-11) seem to have faded into the dim and distant past.

And yet, at an emotional level, the episode has much to recommend it. The boys once again have to wrestle with the moral implications of being hunters[196]. Poor Madison just has evil inside her. She's not intentionally harming anyone, she didn't go looking for the situation and she'd stop if she could. At a symbolic level, she just the same as Sam. (Okay, with one exception, Sam's not going out every lunar cycle to eat people's hearts.) But Madison has the same choice Sam will have – live with it and kill people or kill yourself – so it's no surprise he can identify with her problem.

This is also the first time Sam has allowed himself to become properly involved with anyone since Jessica. The poor boy's words to Sarah in 'Provenance' (1-19) about being cursed are coming back to haunt him as another female in his life exits in fatal circumstances.

It makes the final scenes, with Madison begging Sam to put the bullet in her chest, all the more emotional. Dean doesn't want to see his brother hurting like this when he's just started to get over Jessica, and Dean's tears at the end are probably more for Sam than they are for Madison – and maybe just a little for himself, since he knows he might have to do exactly the same thing to Sam in the near future. For Sam, he finally understands how Dean feels about putting a bullet in his 'evil' brother. He knows why Madison can't live with herself and he sure as hell appreciates that if you've got to go then better to get it done by someone who cares about you than a total stranger.

With great acting all round[197] and an excellent choice of music, these closing scenes lift this episode above the mediocre and leave a melancholic after-image long after the credits have finished.

VERDICT – 7 out of 10

---

196 Similar moral issues have occurred in 'Faith' (1-12) and 'Bloodlust' (2-03), both stories also written by Sera Gamble funnily enough.

197 Let's face it though – the boys have had plenty of practice turning on the waterworks in the early episodes after John Winchester's death so you'd expect them to be good at it by now.

EPISODE 2-18
HOLLYWOOD BABYLON

TRANSMISSION DATES
US first aired: 19 April 2007
UK first aired: 9 November 2007

CREDITS
Writer: Ben Edlund
Director: Philip Sgriccia

GUEST STARS
Morgan Brayton (Maggie), R Nelson Brown (Frank Jaffe/Gerard St James), Regan Burns (McG), Gary Cole (Brad Redding), Torrance Coombs (James Boone/'Mitch'), Graeme Duffy (Dave), Andrew Francis (Rick Craig/'Brody'), Leah Graham (Unknown), Patricia Nudd (Elise Drummond), Julie Patzwald (Tour Guide), Alycia Purrott ('Kendra'), Ben Ratner (Walter Dixon), Gerry Rousseau (Billy Beard), Michael B Silver (Martin Flagg), Don Stark (Jay Wiley), Elizabeth Whitmere (Tara Benchley/'Wendy')

SYNOPSIS
Rumours of a haunted movie set are rife after a stage hand is found dead during the filming of *Hell Hazers II – The Reckoning*. Sam and Dean establish that this first death is a publicity stunt engineered by the movie producers themselves, but when one of the studio execs is hung from the rafters for real, the boys start picking up EMF readings and an actual haunting begins. The next victim is producer Jay Wiley, who is minced in the blades of the set's industrial-sized fan, and Sam realises that the victims are being killed by the ghosts of people who have died on Stage 9 in the past. Walter, the disgruntled writer of the original movie script (which was heavily 'reworked' into the final draft), is summoning the ghosts using a talisman, to get revenge on the people who savaged his work. When Walter breaks the talisman, the spooks take their bloody revenge out on him.

CAN YOU SURVIVE TO THE TITLES?
Frank Jaffe seemingly bleeds all over the forest set from his perch in the rafters but it's all a hoax. So technically no-one gets it before the titles.

LOCATION, LOCATION, LOCATION
Los Angeles, California.

LEGENDARY ROOTS
The word necromancy is derived from the Greek meaning dead prophet. Necromancy is a summoning ritual for speaking with the spirits of divination commonly used for future predictions or spiritual protection but has been associated with demon summoning and black magic. The ritual is usually performed in a forest, a desert or at a crossroads, when planets are aligned and the necromancer and assistant stand within a concentric circle that is on consecrated or blessed ground. Then the dead can be raised.

One famous example of a necromancer is the Witch of Endor who, at the request of King Saul in the Bible (Book 1, Samuel 28), was said to have summoned the spirit of the prophet Samuel, but really conjured a demon impersonating him to predict the King's downfall.

SQUEEZE OF THE WEEK
Dean discovers that being a PA has its perks and finally gets his leg over, off camera, with Tara Benchley. It's been 20 episodes since Dean had a tiring night with Brandy[198] and saving his strength for that long may well have helped put that satisfied smile on Tara's face.

SIBLING RIVALRY
Most of the rivalry this week consists of Sam getting frustrated with Dean. As Dean gets more and more into his role as a PA, Sam finds it harder to get him to concentrate on solving the haunting problem. In the end, Sam does all the solving and Dean does all the macho running around with the shotgun.

BODY COUNT
Studio exec Brad Redding gets to hang out on set after a titillating encounter with a voluptuous naked ghost; then two-faced producer Jay Wiley is on the receiving end of some cutting remarks when he has a close encounter with a wind machine. Script writer Martin Flagg almost gets shredded the same way, but he has one helluva PA to save his skin before it's too late.

TOOLKIT
• A *headset and radio* are essential if you're going to blend in on set with the other

---

198 In 'Provenance' (1-19).

PAs, and it helps if you have the skills to get on with them so they'll play you recordings of spook EVP and lend you the dailies.

- And keep the standard spook eradication kit handy – the *EMF meter*, the *shovels*, the *salt-loaded shotgun*, the *salt bag* and the *lighter fuel* and *matches* for burning dem bones.
- A *mobile phone camera* will help you see the ghosts chasing you so you can blast them with that shotgun.

MEMORABLE MOMENTS
Dean steals all the memorable moments this time around: from stuffing his face (again[199]) with free food and slurping down a sliver of steak as Sam looks on disgusted; to the wonderful shotgun-toting, trailer-rocking hero moments. Priceless!

THE CAR'S THE STAR
Another episode where the car is not seen at all[200].

MOTEL MAYHEM
Looks like the boys have commandeered a rather nice, presumably unused, trailer for their base of operations on this hunt. Definitely more plush than their usual dive of a motel.

SPOOK RULES
- Ghosts can manipulate sound, leaving messages called EVP (Electronic Voice Phenomena) on tapes and digital recordings[201].
- They can also be seen on visual recordings – made either with a movie camera or on a mobile phone.
- Hollywood ghosts tend to murder people in the same manner as their own death – for example, if they hung themselves then their victims will die with a noose round their neck too.
- An Enochian summoning ritual and a talisman are required to bring spirits back from the dead and force them into murdering for you. If the talisman gets broken, the spirits are no longer under anyone's control and will most likely take out their revenge on the summoner (which usually involves murdering them in painful ways).

---

199 As he was in Bugs (1-08), 'Nightmare' (1-14), 'Provenance' (1-19) and 'Tall Tales' (2-15).

200 Last time that happened was in 'The Usual Suspects' (2-07)..

201 Last encountered in 'The Woman in White' (1-01).

DID YOU SPOT?

This is the third episode that doesn't feature a Then/Now sequence at the start[202].

There are number of in-jokes, including references to:

- Ivan Hayden (visual effects supervisor) and his team – the real special effects guys on *Supernatural*.
- The TV series *Gilmore Girls* and the chance to see one of its stars – Jared Padalecki played Dean Forester in *Gilmore Girls*.
- The weather being 'practically Canadian' – poking fun at the weather in and around Vancouver, where *Supernatural* is filmed.
- The TV series *Lois & Clark* – which also had a producer and director called Robert Singer.
- The director McG – McG is actually *Supernatural*'s executive producer and directed *Charlie's Angels* and *Charlie's Angels: Full Throttle* as referenced in this episode.
- The number of the beast, used in numerous horror movies, which appears here on the clapperboard as Roll 6 Scene 6 Take 6.

The studio suit, Brad, asks to make the show a bit brighter and doesn't understand how the ghosts can hear the Latin incantation. These are based on situations Kripke has been involved in with *Supernatural*'s own execs, as mentioned in the commentary track for 'What Is And What Should Never Be' (2-20).

Boogeyman is apparently a terrible script – in real life it was written by Eric Kripke and released in 2005 with a 2007 sequel.

Tara is taking photographs of the cast and crew to kill time – something that Jensen Ackles has said he does on set himself[203].

Tara's comment about having problems acting to a tennis ball matches similar comments made by Ackles himself[204].

The set and story of *Hell Hazers II* are remarkably similar to the set and story for *The Evil Dead*.

R Nelson Brown also played Walt in the movie *Devour*, alongside Ackles.

The back-stabbing personality of Jay the producer fits the stereotypical personality we've all come to expect of Hollywood, and there's a similar dig at the writers when Marty says he had to cut about 90% of Walter's script to make it readable.

One of the few production roles that doesn't get ridiculed here is that of the

202 The first two being 'Houses of the Holy' (2-13) and 'Heart' (2-17).

203 See interviews at: http://www.teenidols4you.com/bio/Actors/490/jensen_ackles.html

204 Mentioned by Ackles at an LA convention: http://www.bebo.com/Profile.jsp?MemberId=4153980617 and http://www.celebritywonder.com/html/jensenackles.html

production assistant. Sam defines them as 'like slaves' in the early part of the show but Dean seems to have a thoroughly good time running round as a PA, and both writer Marty and starlet Tara are extremely grateful for his services by the end of the show.

There are several references to *Supernatural* itself:

- Tara thinks that using salt to scare a ghost off is silly and unrealistic and so are shotguns – funny, seems to work for Sam and Dean most of the time.
- When the boys are walking across the lot, a rack of Sam and Dean clothes are wheeled past them and Sam turns and gives them a quizzical stare.
- In the *Hell Hazers II* trailer, images are used from previous *Supernatural* episodes, including 'Hookman' (1-07); 'Scarecrow' (1-11); 'Route 666' (1-13); 'Bloodlust' (2-03); 'Children Shouldn't Play With Dead Things' (2-04); and 'The Usual Suspects' (2-07).
- In Martin Flagg's office the posters for *Hell Hazers II* and *Monster Truck* have images from 'Scarecrow' (1-11) and 'Route 666' (1-13).
- On the set of *Hell Hazers II* there are more references – the water tower is from 'Crossroad Blues' (2-08) and the cabin is from 'Roadkill' (2-16).
- In the credits for *Hell Hazers II* you can see 'Casting Robert Ulrich', 'Production Designer Jerry Wanek' and 'Director of Photography Serge Ladouceur'. All three work on *Supernatural* in the roles indicated.

GOING UNDERCOVER
The boys are undercover as production assistants on the movie set – well, Dean is anyway; Sam doesn't seem to be doing a lot of PA'ing at all.

CULTURAL REFERENCES
Sam: 'Well, Matt Damon just picked up a broom and started sweeping.': Matt Damon starred as Will Hunting, a janitor, in the 1997 movie *Good Will Hunting*.

Dean: 'What, you mean like *Poltergeist*?': Another mention for *Poltergeist*, the 1982 movie in which ghosts haunt a house, moving objects and kidnapping a little girl[205]. This time it's in relation to the deaths of three actors involved in the film.

Dean: 'You know this is where they filmed *Creepshow*?': *Creepshow* (1982), a movie directed by George Romero, was an anthology of five short stories called 'Father's Day', 'The Lonesome Death of Jordy Verrill', 'Something to Tide You Over', 'The Crate' and 'They're Creeping Up on You!'.

Dean: 'It's like *Three Men and a Baby* all over again.': The 1987 film *Three Men And A Baby* was rumoured to feature a ghost of a nine-year-old boy and the gun he

205 The movie was previously referenced in 'Phantom Traveler' (1-04), 'Bugs' (1-08) and 'Home' (1-09).

committed suicide with. This was later revealed as a hoax.

Dean: 'Hey, we gotta go check out Johnny Ramone's grave when we're done here.': Johnny Ramone (John William Cummings) was the guitarist and founding member of the punk band the Ramones. He died on 15 September 2004 from cancer.

The sketches shown to Tara are a lot like the ones from the *Ghost Rider* movie. *Ghost Rider* (2007) starred Nicolas Cage as Johnny Blaze and was based on the Marvel comic series about a stunt rider who sells his soul in order to save his father from cancer. To get out of the contract he agrees with the Devil to become a Ghost Rider to rid the world of evil souls and drag them back to hell.

The tour guide mentions that *Lois & Clark* was filmed at these studios. *Lois & Clark: The New Adventures of Superman* ran for four seasons from 1993 to 1997, starring Dean Cain as Superman and Teri Hatcher as Lois Lane.

Dean: 'Whoa, whoa, Tara Benchley? From *FeardotCom* and *Ghost Ship?*': *FeardotCom* (2002) was a movie starring Stephen Dorff (as Detective Mike Reilly), in which four people are discovered dead 48 hours after logging onto the feardotcom.com website. *Ghost Ship* (2002) starred Gabriel Byrne and is about a passenger ship, missing since 1962, discovered by a salvage team who try to tow it back to land.

Dean: 'You were Desert Soldier Number Four in *Metalstorm: The Destruction of Jared-Syn*?'and Dean: 'I mean, your turn as a tractor crash victim in *Critters 3* ...': *Metalstorm: The Destruction of Jared-Syn* (1983) was a movie about avenging the death of a family member. Richard Moll starred as Hurok. *Critters 3* (1991) saw Leonardo DiCaprio as Josh leading a group of residents of an LA apartment block against some ugly, furry, violent alien invaders.

Gerard: 'These days, it's all about new media, building buzz. They say I'm the new LonelyGirl.': LonelyGirl15 was an internet video blog that ran from June 2006 to August 2008 concerning a teenage girl called Bree and what she and her family were doing. It was originally thought to be real but its fictitious status was revealed in September 2006.

Gerard: 'I'm playing Willy in a dinner theatre production of *Salesman* at Costa Mesa, all next month.': *Death of a Salesman* is a play written in 1949 by Arthur Miller and may be the play Gerard is referring to here.

Dean: 'Hey, I wanted to ask you ... what was it like working with Richard Moll?': Richard Moll is a real actor best known for his role as Nostradamus 'Bull' Shannon in *Night Court* from 1984 to 1992. He has also been in *Happy Days, Scary Movie 2, The A-Team* and *Metalstorm: The Destruction of Jared-Syn*.

The boys read Walter's script, which is called *Lord of the Dead*: *Lord of the Dead* (2000) was written and directed by Greg Parker. Its plot summary/tag line is 'Who knew the Lord of the Dead had a son who wanted no part of the family business?'

Sounds familiar!

Dean: 'Come out to the coast! We'll get together, have a few laughs!': This is a quote spoken by Bruce Willis's character John McClane from the movie *Die Hard* (1988), referring to the invitation from his wife that he recalls while squeezed inside an air vent.

Martin Flagg and Walter are references to characters in *The Dark Tower* series of books by Stephen King.

Goofs and Fluffs
Dean lights the matchbook to burn Elise Drummond's bones but in the shot where he drops the matches into the grave, they've already gone out before they land on the fuel-soaked body.

If the Latin incantation that Tara reads out was the real thing, why didn't a ghost get summoned every time they did a take?

And if Walter was such an expert in summoning ghosts that he produced a script that reads like a how-to manual of conjuration, then why didn't he know that breaking the talisman would free the ghosts so they could take their revenge?

Haven't I Seen You Before?
Morgan Brayton's credits include *Scooby Doo 2: Monsters Unleashed* and *Smallville*. R Nelson Brown featured in *Taken*, *Millennium* and *The X-Files*. Regan Burns was in *3rd Rock From The Sun*. Gary Cole has been in *American Gothic*, *The Ring Two*, *Crusade* and *The Outer Limits*. Torrance Coombs was in *Battlestar Galactica*. Graeme Duffy played Brady Wingate in *The 4400* and has also been in *Smallville* and *Bionic Woman*. Andrew Francis featured in *Final Destination 3*, *Jeremiah* and *Blood Ties*. Leah Graham was in *Tru Calling*, *Masters of Horror* and *Painkiller Jane*. Patricia Nudd was in *Stargate: Atlantis* and *The 4400*. Julie Patzwald featured in *The Outer Limits*, *Disturbing Behaviour* and *Dead Like Me*. Alycia Purrott was in *Power Rangers S.P.D.* and *Black Christmas*. Ben Ratner appeared in *Kingdom Hospital*, *The Outer Limits* and *Smallville*. Gerry Rousseau was in *The Outer Limits*, *The Dead Zone* and *The 4400*. Michael B Silver featured in *Jason Goes to Hell: The Final Friday*, *The X-Files* and *Heroes*. Don Stark's credits include *Timecop*, *Star Trek: Deep Space Nine* and *Stargate SG-1*.

Leah Graham also appeared in 'Scarecrow' (1-11).

Behind the Scenes
This episode was filmed at Lionsgate Studios because, according to director Phil Sgriccia in *The Official Supernatural Magazine* #3, they were the only soundstages that looked big enough to be Hollywood.

Sgriccia went on to say that many of the people in the background shots when Sam and Dean are on their little train tour are actual crew members, dressed in Western gear and walking horses.

Toby Lindala, head of the *Supernatural* make-up effects department, put some gruesome finishing touches into the death-by-large-fan scene. He explained in *The Official Supernatural Magazine* #9 how they did some extra denture work with actor Don Stark so that they could enlarge the giant wound then knock out and break a few teeth.

MUSICAL INTERLUDE

- 'I've Got The World On A String' – Frank Sinatra – when Sam and Dean are visiting 'Frank'.
- 'Green Peppers' – Herb Alpert – played at the end of the episode.

ANALYSIS

This particular episode seems to polarise the audience into 'love it' or 'hate it' camps (with a smaller 'just drool over it' contingent), and sometimes which of the camps you fall into can just depend on what mood you're in when you watch it.

It's an episode to love if you enjoy spotting all the horror-geek references and *Supernatural* in-jokes. And there's a lot to spot given that the team have been hilariously ruthless with sending up a range of stereotypical personalities in the film industry, like studio execs, producers and writers. They've also sent up their own show's mythology, and the *Supernatural* geek can spend many a happy re-run spotting water towers, clips of blood-soaked knives, poster stills, actors' habits and real crew members.

The script is irreverent to almost everyone – with the exception of PAs – and has Dean fitting in on what is possibly the first 'normal' job he's ever had (although needless to say he still ends up shooting spooks in the head with rock salt before the day's end).

It's tightly plotted, skilfully acted (actually it's appropriately badly acted in the scenes where they're shooting the *Hell Hazers II* movie, with a higher standard for the rest of the time), and has more fun scenes than you can shake a frustrated necromancer at.

So that's a 'Yay!' from the geek camp.

However, it's an episode to hate if you're not a horror geek or were looking for some of *Supernatural*'s trademark character development, which, like the boys, seems to have taken something of a holiday. Most of the references are going to go flying past you unrecognised, and what's left is a somewhat bland trip to a movie set. The ghost yarn on its own isn't strong enough to carry the episode, and it's something of a

Supernatural formula now anyway. There's no new info about Sam's impending plunge to the darkside and the boys are merely being true to existing character traits rather than exploring new ones. (Dean's still gorging on the free food and chasing the skirts, Sam's still spotting the clues and doing the intellectual mileage for the two of them.)[206]

That can only mean one big 'Boo!' from the non-geek camp.

And finally, for a percentage of the audience, this is an episode to drool over – for it has the wonderfully gratuitous shot of Dean's crotch. When Dean has settled into his new PA role, we're treated to a full-bloodied, full-framed shot of the lower half of Dean's body, where his new tool belt is wrapped snugly around his trim waist. Hands up who noticed that the tool belt was there. Hmm, thought not.

So that's just got to be a 'Phwoar!' from the drool camp, don't you think?

Love it, hate it or drool over it, this episode hangs together, it's executed with verve and it delivers laughs. But make the most of the humour. With the inevitable darkness growing as we move towards the series finale, this episode and the next provide the only laughs to be had until Season Three.

VERDICT – 8 out of 10

---

206 Which is following a pattern that started two episodes ago in 'Roadkill' (2-16).

Episode 2-19
Folsom Prison Blues

Transmission Dates
US first aired: 26 April 2007
UK first aired: 16 November 2007

Credits
Writer: John Shiban
Director: Mike Rohl

Recurring Role
Charles Malik Whitfield (Victor Henricksen)

Guest Stars
Alistair Abell (Guard), Kurt Evans (Special Agent Reidy), Andee Frizzell (Dolores Glockner), Jeff Kober (Randall), Clif Kosterman (Tiny), Byron Lucas (Worker), James Michalopolous (Hombre), Steven Cree Molison (Lucas), Chris Nowland (Foreman), Robert Parent (Cop), Garwin Sanford (Deacon Kaylor), Bridget Ann White (Mara Daniels)

Uncredited
Silvio Pollio (Metal Worker Joe) according to IMDB

Synopsis
Deacon, an old Marine buddy of John Winchester's, asks the boys to help out with a vengeful spirit who is killing guards and inmates at Green River County Detention Centre. Getting themselves arrested, Sam and Dean gain entry to the Detention Centre, but Special Agent Victor Henricksen soon arrives on a mission to get the boys on trial for the bank heist in Milwaukee[207] and the murders in St Louis[208]. With Henricksen getting closer to extraditing them, Sam and Dean – who believe the ghost to be serial killer Mark Moody – salt and burn Moody's blood, but it doesn't stop the killings. With the help of their lawyer and an inmate, they discover that the ghost used to be a prison nurse. Escaping with help from prison guard Deacon, they manage to burn the

---

207 See 'Nightshifter' (2-12).

208 See 'Skin' (1-06).

nurse's remains in time to stop her murdering Deacon in the prison bathroom.

CAN YOU SURVIVE TO THE TITLES?

A prison guard is trapped in a suddenly closing door in the solitary confinement wing of Green River County Detention Centre. A mysterious figure is seen approaching him just before he has a heart attack and dies. Given the flickering lights and sudden drop in temperature just before the death, you just know ghostly goings-on were involved.

LOCATION, LOCATION, LOCATION

Museum of Anthropology, Arkansas; Green River County Detention Center.

LEGENDARY ROOTS

There are numerous reports of prison hauntings, and here are but a couple of examples:

Alcatraz (the Rock), on an island in San Francisco, USA, was home to the most notorious prisoners from 1934 to 1963, although it had been used as a prison since 1859 after being taken over by the US military. Reported strange occurrences on the island include the death of a prisoner in hole 14D (one of the isolation cells where prisoners had only a low watt light bulb and a mattress and received only bread and water with the occasional meal). An inmate confined to the cell continually screamed of seeing a creature with glowing eyes, and in the morning the man was found dead with hand marks around his neck. The autopsy showed that he could not have strangled himself. The headcount taken next day reported one too many inmates, and there were reports of guards seeing the dead man in the line up before he suddenly vanished.

A night guard also reported strange clanging noises coming from behind a door to a corridor where inmates Coy, Cretzer and Hubbard had been killed during a botched escape attempt. When the door was opened the noises stopped, but once closed the clanging began again.

There has also been crying heard within the walls by a tour guide and visitors, and banjo playing heard from the shower room, which is reportedly where Al Capone practiced after fearing attempts on his life if he went to the recreational yard.

The Eastern State Penitentiary (ESP) in Pennsylvania, like a number of other disused prisons, now provides ghost tours, and a number of TV programmes like *Most Haunted* and *Ghost Hunters* have been recorded there in search of paranormal activity. Activity at ESP has included a locksmith feeling he was being watched while working. When he turned around to look, there was no one there, so he continued working but got the same feeling of being watched. On turning round again, he saw a black figure leap across the block. Visitors and guides alike have also reported laughter resonating out of cells within Cell Block 12, but no source can be found. A black human-like figure has been seen in the older blocks.

SQUEEZE OF THE WEEK

No squeezes for the boys, but Dean's lawyer probably would have liked to squeeze him if there hadn't be a glass partition between them.

SIBLING RIVALRY

The boys are almost constantly bitching at each other this time, with Sam pulling so many scowls at his brother it's a surprise his face doesn't stick that way. So look out for Sam's face when:

- They enter the prison and Dean promises not to trade Sam for smokes.
- Sam wants Dean to be a little more than 'pretty sure' he's found the ghost • given the circumstances of their incarceration.
- Dean wants a little more than Sam being 'pretty sure' that Dean needs to start a fight with large inmate Tiny.
- Sam wonders about how easily his brother fits in with the prison crowd.

Finally, Dean's modesty shines through again when the lawyer sends the boys the info they need in an envelope and describes himself as 'velvety smooth'.

BODY COUNT

There were three more murders in-between the guard in the opening sequence and Sam and Dean arriving on-site. Then Lucas is killed while in solitary after fighting with Dean, and Tiny gets his in the infirmary, also after fighting with Dean. The nurse then tries a little chest massage on Dean (who can blame her) but gets a face full of spirit-deterring salt for her troubles.

TOOLKIT

- The ability to win at cards is essential if you're to earn enough cigarettes to buy the information you need in a prison.
- And a sub-set of the standard spook stopping stuff – *shovels, salt, lighter fuel* and *matches* for burning dem bones.

MEMORABLE MOMENTS

Dean's encounter with Henricksen is simply dripping with Winchester wit and smarm, right into the face of adversity. And the finale is just a good old fashioned edge-of-the-seat affair.

One moment to try to forget is Dean's awful line of dialogue when he hears that the lawyer will tell Henricksen where they've gone: 'Oh, that's friggin' super.'

Spook Rules

- Spirits can be trapped indefinitely in rooms that are entirely lined with iron.
- Just before they appear, evil spirits can cause clocks to stop, lights to flicker and a temperature drop or cold spot resulting in being able to see your breath mist in front of you.
- Evil spirits will often focus on a reason to justify their murdering tendencies – like only killing people who have broken the law.
- If there's enough blood left behind, it's enough to bind a spirit to the mortal plane. However, just because the blood/remains are left behind it doesn't guarantee that the location will be haunted by the owner – like Mark Moody.

Did You Spot?

Dean isn't wearing his amulet or ring in the scenes where they break into the Arkansas Museum of Anthropology.

When Dean holds up all his cigarettes and asks 'Hey, fellas! Who's ready to deal?' you can see Sam mouthing the words 'Hey, fellas!' with Dean with a big smile on his face.

Going Undercover

No covers involved as the boys are fingerprinted and ID'd as Winchesters from the moment they're arrested.

Cultural References

Dean: '... and get ourselves a couple of teardrop tattoos.': Originally the teardrop meant that the wearer had committed at least one murder. It can mean that the wearer has committed the murder whilst in prison.

Dean: 'Are you from Texas all of a sudden?': Both Jared Padalecki and Jensen Ackles are from Texas, and the State has the highest rate of executions in the US.

Dean: 'I call this one my Blue Steel ... Who looks better? Me or Nick Nolte?': Blue Steel is a modelling pose of Derek Zoolander in the 2001 movie *Zoolander*. The comment about Nick Nolte references his 2002 mug shot for his drink driving arrest.

Lucas: 'You talking to me? You talking to me?'; Dean: 'Okay, another guy who's seen *Taxi Driver* one too many times.': This references a famous line spoken by Robert De Niro playing Travis Bickel in *Taxi Driver* (1976).

Dean: 'I wish I had a baseball, you know, like Steve McQueen.': Steve McQueen stars in *The Great Escape* (1963) as Captain Hilts, who bounces a baseball against the

319 FOLSOM PRISON BLUES

wall during his time in solitary.

Dean: 'You're like Clint Eastwood from *Escape from Alcatraz*.': *Escape from Alcatraz* (1979), based on true events, features Clint Eastwood as Frank Morris, who successfully escaped from the notorious prison on 11 June 1962.

Dean: 'It's a good thing I'm like James Garner from *The Great Escape*.': James Garner plays Flight Lt Hendley aka 'the Scrounger' in *The Great Escape*; he scrounges all the items the prisoners need for their escape.

Randall: 'She did this Charles Bronson thing with a hypodermic.': A reference to the movie *Death Wish* (1974), starring Charles Bronson as a vigilante avenging the death of his wife and daughter.

Henricksen: 'You can hang that up in your cell at Supermax.': Supermax (Super Maximum) is a specific kind of prison or area within a prison that represents the most secure level of custody, designed to house violent prisoners or inmates who might threaten the security of the guards or other prisoners.

Sam: 'We should go to Yemen.': Yemen is also mentioned in the TV series *Friends*, when Chandler claims he has got a job transfer to Yemen to avoid having to break up again with his on-off girlfriend Janice in 'The One With The All The Rugby' (4-15). It does not go completely to plan as Janice won't leave his side until he is actually on the plane to Yemen.

Dean: ''Cause, you know, they're just doughnuts. They're not love.': A possible reference to the *Friends* episode 'The One With the Boobies' (1-13), in which Phoebe's new boyfriend Roger says to Monica, "Mon, uh, easy on the cookies, okay? Remember they're just food; they're not love."

GOOFS AND FLUFFS

There's no explanation as to why the ghost of the nurse changes her kill rate from four people over three months to three people (or attempts) in three days. She could have helped solve the prison overcrowding problem if she'd gone for the a one-a-day rate from the start.

The ghost seems to have been trapped in the old wing of the prison in a windowless, metal-lined room for a number of years. This makes sense, since ghosts can't cope with iron. However, later on, nurse Glockner is seen walking through metal bars, which are most likely also made of iron. This goes against the show's established spook rules.

At the table, when Dean is gathering his cigarettes together, there is one shot from the back that shows his hands and the cigarettes in a different position to the shots immediately before and after it.

When the boys have escaped and reach the car, they swap their prison jackets for more normal ones – presumably so people won't spot the prison garb so easily.

The only problem is, Dean swaps his prison jacket for something that looks almost identical to the one he's just taken off. Great disguise that!

HAVEN'T I SEEN YOU BEFORE?

Alistair Abell's credits include *The New Addams Family*, *Stargate SG-1* and *Tru Calling*. Kurt Evans' acting achievements include *Watchmen*, *Stargate SG-1* and *Jake 2.0*. Andee Frizzell played the Wraith Queen in *Stargate: Atlantis* and has also been in *Andromeda*. Jeff Kober featured in *Buffy the Vampire Slayer*, *Poltergeist: The Legacy* and *The Hills Have Eyes 2*. Clif Kosterman was in *White Noise 2: The Light*. Byron Lucas has been in *Highlander: The Series*, *Taken* and *Painkiller Jane*. James Michalopolous featured in *Jeremiah*, *Smallville* and *Blood Ties*. Steven Cree Molison's credits include *The Dead Zone*, *The Fog* and *Stargate SG-1*. Chris Nowland was in *The 4400*, *Stargate: Atlantis* and *Smallville*. Robert Parent has been in *Jake 2.0* and *Kyle XY*. Garwin Sanford's credits include *Painkiller Jane*, *Stargate SG-1* and *Atlantis* and *Earth: Final Conflict*. Bridget Ann White has been in *Star Trek: Deep Space Nine*.

BEHIND THE SCENES

The whole prison block was purpose-built for the show according to set designer Jerry Wanek quoted in the *Season Two Supernatural Companion*. There was about 90 feet of prison block with some interchangeable parts so different areas could be swapped in and out for filming. Other scenes were shot at real-life location Riverview Hospital in Vancouver. This was the same location as used in 'Asylum' (1-10) and had the benefit of being an inherently spooky place anyway, due to the clinical design and stark building materials used.

MUSICAL INTERLUDE

- 'Green Onions' – Booker T and The MG's – when Sam and Dean are arriving at the Green River Detention Center.
- 'Rooster' – Alice In Chains – played at the end of the episode.

ANALYSIS

For the picky people out there, this episode is going to be rather frustrating, because it's not an accurate depiction of prison life – there's too much freedom for the inmates and they have too much access to things that could be turned into weapons.

But the *Supernatural* writers don't seem to be trying to make this into a seriously accurate prison drama; the realism is taking more of a back seat and their emphasis is a little more on the fun. They've got Dean in prime swagger mode, promising not to trade his brother for cigarettes and declaring himself adorable. Dean may think that humans are crazy[209] but it's not really a surprise he's so fearless about this situation, since he's faced things that are far more powerful and difficult to deal with than any mere human (although the spooks are far less likely to want to sexually abuse him in the way some of the prison inmates would).

As Dean jokes his way through the prison, the plot is revealed in careful stages. There are four major twists – the boys get captured by the police on purpose; the ghost is not Mark Moody; Deacon turns out to be the prison guard; and Henricksen is sent to the wrong cemetery – and each twist transforms the episode into something increasingly different from what you expected when it started. This spices up the now-formulaic ghost hunt approach and breathes new life into it, each turn lifting the story until the three-pronged finale has you perched, expecting Henricksen to be busting Sam's and Dean's asses all over again. The last twist – possibly a homage to *The Silence of the Lambs*, where the FBI also close in on the wrong location – plays out with perfect timing, and we're relieved that our intrepid heroes have got away again (which was kind of expected anyway, but at least it is an exciting confirmation of what we already knew). This kind of tense ending is starting to become a regular feature of Henricksen episodes[210].

What hasn't been a regular feature of this season is effective scares, but here we have a return of some of the jumps that characterised so much of the first season. The self-righteous, murderous nurse is more menacing than anything we've seen for some time, and even the guard rapping his stick on the window bars creates a small surprise to keep us on our toes for a change.

Also returning after a short break is the deeper character development. We see Dean thriving in the prison environment, surrounded by a bunch of violent, dysfunctional social dropouts – yep, it's no wonder he fits in. He's lived with violence all his life and possesses a personal skill-set of hustling and running cons that would be the envy of most of the inmates. So he's bound to identify with them at some level – he's just like them. Perhaps it's no surprise he views them as being innocent victims of a lethal spook and undeserving of that kind of vicious death. What is interesting though is that this is a reversal of his opinions expressed back in 'Crossroad Blues' (2-08) – where he felt that the people who had made the deal with the demon deserved everything they got. So inmates who have committed a crime and are being attacked by a ghost who didn't like wrong-doers seem to be more deserving of his help than people who made a deal with a demon and got attacked when the 'loan' was up. Hmmm.

---

209 Established in 'The Benders' (1-15).

210 The last being in 'Nightshifter' (2-12).

Sam on the other hand has a different background. Yes, he grew up in the same violent and dysfunctional family as Dean, but he is also aware of how an individual can have both a good and an evil side within themselves. For him, what differentiates people is the outcome you achieve with that evil side. Applying violence to save people from harm is a polar opposite of applying violence to murder innocent people. And he doesn't seem to think the inmates of the prison have been saving many people recently. This makes them evil in Sam's eyes and almost deserving of the vicious death Dean is trying to save them from.

Another difference between the two boys is in their sense of loyalty. Dean is unconditionally loyal. It's an important trait to him and it almost seems he'd rather die being loyal than live with himself being disloyal. Sam on the other hand is more pragmatic, in that he'll be loyal, but only if the cost isn't too high.

The boys are going deep undercover as a result of this latest encounter with Henricksen and it'll be some time into Season Three before he'll catch them again. Meanwhile, sit back and prepare to be emotionally manipulated as this season closes ...

VERDICT – 8 out of 10

EPISODE 2-20
WHAT IS AND
WHAT SHOULD NEVER BE

TRANSMISSION DATES
US first aired: 3 May 2007
UK first aired: 23 November 2007

CREDITS
Writer: Raelle Tucker
Director: Eric Kripke

RECURRING ROLES
Adrianne Palicki (Jessica Moore), Samantha Smith (Mary Winchester)

GUEST STARS
Kwesi Ameyaw (Professor Rubin), Michelle Borth (Carmen Porter), Mackenzie Gray (Djinn), Melanie Neige Scrofano (Girl in White/Joy Nicholson)

SYNOPSIS
Dean is captured by a Djinn, knocked unconscious and wakes up with a gorgeous, naked woman next to him in bed. The woman is his girlfriend Carmen, and Dean finds himself in a world where his mother is still alive, the family never became demon hunters and he and Sam were never close. But even as Sam announces his engagement to Jessica, a mysterious girl in a white dress keeps haunting Dean from a distance. Then he finds corpses hanging in his closet. Realising that the Djinn has created this illusion based on his deepest wishes, Dean decides that killing himself within the dream is the only way to wake up. It works, and Sam and Dean kill the Djinn, saving the mysterious girl, Joy, who, like Dean, was also a victim.

CAN YOU SURVIVE TO THE TITLES?
No deaths; the Djinn is too busy putting Dean into his wish-world.

LOCATION, LOCATION, LOCATION
A dirty warehouse belonging to a chemical company in Joliet, Illinois; 53 Barker Avenue, Lawrence, Kansas; the Winchester family residence, Lawrence, Kansas, house

number 1841[211].

LEGENDARY ROOTS

A Djinn is a spirit that is described in Islamic and Arabic lore as an evil and ugly demon that has supernatural powers. It is said to inhabit the earth in the form of a human, an animal or an invisible spirit to exercise influence over mankind.

The Arabic belief was that the Djinn were spirits of the fire that did not take physical form. They could be seen and felt but no-one could touch them.

In Islamic belief, the Djinn has the chance of redemption: those that believe in Islam become good and beautiful spirits, whereas those who choose not to follow Islam become demons. According to the prophet Mohammed there are three levels of Djinn: one that has wings and can fly, another that looks like a snake or a dog, and finally a type that stops for a rest then resumes its journey.

King Solomon is said to have enslaved the Djinn with a magical ring. The tamed Djinn travelled with him and even carried out tasks for him. One such task was to build a temple in Jerusalem surrounded by gardens of paradise.

SQUEEZE OF THE WEEK

Dean finally has a regular girlfriend, Carmen Porter, who knows him very well – especially what beer he likes (El Sol) and his preference for cheeseburgers over fancy restaurant food. Uncharacteristically, Dean refuses Carmen when she offers to see what she can do to 'help him sleep'. Then, then when he finally feels up to it, she has to go to work. Poor Dean, he can't even get laid in his wish-world.

SIBLING RIVALRY

The sibling rivalry takes a trip into the past and starts to reflect the animosity that existed between the boys in the very first episode, only this time it's stronger.

Wish-world Sam can't understand why Dean is acting so chummy and calling him Sammy when they rarely talk these days. Dean thinks they should talk more because they're brothers but Sam has a list of issues against Dean that includes pinching his ATM card, Dean not turning up when he was supposed to and Dean stealing Sam's prom date, Rachel, on prom night. But Sam doesn't want Dean to act differently, he just hasn't got anything to talk about with him. It's quite a bleak moment when he says that.

BODY COUNT

No deaths at all during the episode – for a change. Just a couple of desiccated corpses

---

211 This is not the original, correct house number of 1481 as used in 'Home' (1-09)

hanging around in Dean's closet.

TOOLKIT

- A couple of *silver knives dipped in lamb's blood* are the only tools required this week – and apparently, it doesn't matter whether the knife is a purpose-made hunting knife or one from your mom's cutlery drawer, they'll both do the job.

MEMORABLE MOMENTS

The entire episode from when Dean wakes up in his Wish World is one long memorable emotional rollercoaster of a story.

SPOOK RULES

- Djinns tend to hide in ruins, the bigger, the better.
- A Djinn has only to touch your forehead with its blue-flaming hand to bring you under the influence of its power, but they don't have any other great powers to defend themselves with in a fight.
- They have a god-like power to alter reality however they want, in the past, present or future. But they don't grant you a wish, they just make you believe that they have. While the victim is blissed out in their Wish World, the Djinn drains their blood, which it needs to feed itself.

DID YOU SPOT?

Mary Winchester tells Dean she used to tuck him in bed and say that angels were watching over him. Dean first shared this piece of information in 'Houses of the Holy' (2-13) when explaining why he didn't believe in angels.

Sam's prom date was Rebecca Nave – who was actually the co-writer of 'Bugs' (1-08).

Dean is no longer wearing his amulet, but a silver chain and pendant, maybe a St Christopher.

The movie Dean is watching when he first wakes up in his Wish World is *From Hell It Came* (1957). Later he's flicking through the channels and catches a couple of seconds of the *ThunderCats* cartoon series.

From the news and on the internet, Dean establishes that the following people have died in this 'new' life:

- The passengers on flight 424 who were rescued by the boys in 'Phantom Traveler' (1-04).
- The nine children who were comatose and being fed on by the Shtriga in 'Something Wicked' (1-18).

- The parents mutilated in the double homicide in a quiet residential area in 'Everybody Loves A Clown' (2-02).
- The girl drowned in the pool in 'Playthings' (2-11).

GOING UNDERCOVER

No cover needed for the boys this time – since it's all about Dean's home life – but the Impala is running round in a couple of different guises. To keep the boys safe in the real world, the car has shrugged off its KAZ 2Y5 plates for the more anonymous CNK 80Q3, and in Dean's Wish World it is masquerading as RMD 5H2.

CULTURAL REFERENCES

Dean: 'My god, Barbara Eden was hot, wasn't she? And way hotter than that *Bewitched* chick.': These are references to two TV series: *I Dream of Jeannie* (1965-1970) starred Barbara Eden as a genie, while Elizabeth Montgomery played Samantha the witch in *Bewitched* (1964-1972).

Dean: 'Well, we're not in Kansas anymore.'

And:

Dean: 'Aunty Em? There's no place like home.': These are two references to the 1939 movie *The Wizard of Oz*. The second is a direct quote of what Dorothy says when she wakes up back in Kansas.

The episode is reminiscent of the David Lynch film *Blue Velvet* (1986), which depicts an idyllic suburban town with nice houses surrounded by white picket fences and landscaped gardens, hiding a more sinister underworld.

GOOFS AND FLUFFS

The financial channel that Dean is watching in the late evening shows the time as 10.01 am, so not so late evening after all.

The date on the newspaper running the article about the crash of Flight 424 is 5 December 2005 and the TV says it is the first anniversary of the crash, making it 5 December 2006 at the moment. So that grass that Dean so desperately wants to cut is not likely to need it in the middle of winter. Which is just as well, since the mower Dean uses doesn't have any blades attached, as revealed in a shot from under the mower.

There's a likely looking goof in the scene at the graveside too – where Dean's words and visuals seem to be out of sync. Kripke explains on the commentary track that this scene was done in just one take, shot with two cameras moving up and down on a dolly track. So perhaps not a real goof at all.

HAVEN'T I SEEN YOU BEFORE?

Kwesi Ameyaw's credits include *Dead Like Me*, *The Outer Limits* and *Stargate SG-1*. Michelle Borth has been in *Silent Warnings and Trespassers*. Mackenzie Gray featured in *The Crow: Stairway to Heaven*, *Kyle XY* and *Destination: Infestation*.

BEHIND THE SCENES

Jensen Ackles said in an interview with televison.aol.com that this episode really took him out of his comfort zone. He found it easy to fall into Dean's character in the dark, dismal environments that he's used to but now he had to play him in this colourful, upbeat environment and he found it rather challenging.

This episode marked Eric Kripke's directorial debut, but he didn't write it: that fell to veteran Season One writer Raelle Tucker. Kripke commented in *The Official Supernatural Magazine* #3 that once Tucker knew she was getting the episode she went pale. But the two worked together closely on breaking the story then Kripke stepped back and let Tucker get on with it so it wasn't as hard as she'd expected.

The experience of directing was both fun and stressful for Kripke. He explained in *The Official Supernatural Magazine* #6 how the stress caused him chronic stomach aches and headaches, and that his recent decision to eat healthily had caused a few issues – not least of which was almost passing out on set, something he desperately wanted to avoid doing. Fortunately, he phoned his wife who told him to eat something and he started feeling better after that. Everyone has said in interviews since that they were impressed with the job Kripke did.

Some other interesting snippets of information about this episode come from Kripke's commentary track:

The filming schedule didn't allow time for Mackenzie Gray (who played the Djinn) to be made up each day with all the tattoos required for his part, so the actor graciously agreed to keep the tattoos in place over the couple of days of filming. When he wasn't working, he couldn't get a cab anywhere.

The scenes where Dean returns to his mom's house to steal the silver knife and Sam wakes up and goes downstairs to investigate are almost a rerun of those where Dean and Sam first meet up in the pilot, 'Woman in White' (1-01). Kripke admitted that this was done as a homage to David Nutter, the director of the pilot.

The bright and cheerful weather in the lawn-mowing scene was purely coincidental. Apart from this scene, that needed fine weather, it rained the entire time during shooting.

This episode was shot in two chunks due to the availability of Adrianne Palicki (Jessica). She was considered so important to it that when her current show *Friday Night Lights* refused to release her, *Supernatural* shut down shooting this episode for five days, moving onto 'All Hell Breaks Loose Part One' instead until she was free to film. Even then, she still had to be filmed against a blue screen to be dropped into the episode's finale (where everyone is trying to stop Dean stabbing himself) via the special effects department.

The last scene filmed in this episode was of Dean channel-surfing in front of the TV. It was shot at 3 am after a 15-hour filming session.

MUSICAL INTERLUDE

- 'Saturday Night Special' – Lynyrd Skynyrd – on Dean's radio when he and Sam are talking about the Djinn, and also played when Dean and Wish World Sam arrive at the warehouse.
- 'What A Wonderful World' – Joey Ramone – when Dean is mowing his mom's lawn.

ANALYSIS

At last we get to see Dean naked – emotionally at least. If you hadn't already figured out who Dean really is, beneath all that bravado, then this is like a roadmap to his psyche. From the moment he opens his eyes in the Wish World – with a gorgeous girlfriend beside him – we begin to see what he secretly wants rather than the burden of loss that he carries in his real life.

For starters, his mom is alive, something that clearly affects him deeply and draws a tenderness from him that's been previously buried. You can see how much he's missed her in the scene where she kisses him on the forehead and he leans into the kiss, not wanting it to end.

Another wish he gets is to see Sam happy – settled into studying law and with a gorgeous girl in his life. Dean grew up looking after Sam, something his dad virtually drilled into him. To be able to release that responsibility – as well as the responsibility to 'save him or kill him' that has never sat comfortably with him – would be such a relief for him, so it's no surprise it turns up here.

One wish Dean doesn't get fulfilled, but has the potential to achieve, is his desire to have a family of his own. This was first hinted at as far back as 'Dead In The Water' (1-03), where he saves young Lucas's life in the lake. Here it is more obvious with Carmen, in the Wish World, trying to convince him not to stab himself by offering him a future and a family. It's something he's never discussed openly with anyone else, but it'll become more obvious in one of the Season Three episodes coming up[212].

Other slightly less important desires Dean has been hiding include having a

---

212 'The Kids Are Alright' (3-02).

respectable girlfriend, holding down a regular job at a garage, just being a civilian with no arsenal in the trunk of the Impala, and finally taking a well-earned rest from hunting.

But not everything is perfect in the Wish World. John Winchester, it turns out, died peacefully in his sleep. Sam and Dean are also somewhat estranged since Dean has behaved rather badly toward his brother (including pinching his date on prom night and stealing his credit card) and they don't have anything in common anymore. Then there's also the matter of some people dying whom he had already saved.

Shouldn't Dean's fantasy Wish World include Dad being alive, people being saved and a good relationship with his brother? Not if you view this episode as *Supernatural*'s version of *The Matrix*. Then it makes a little more sense, given that people are suspicious if everything is perfect. An imperfect world contains challenges and a sense of progress to distract the victim, and the Djinn is going to want people to stay distracted and calm in the Wish World while he bleeds them dry in the real world.

And there is another reason for the imperfections, as explained in Kripke's commentary track. There needed to be things that the boys had in the real world that weren't present in the fantasy world, things that the hunting life gave them that they wouldn't have had otherwise, and those things are their relationship and saving people.

It's interesting that in Dean's Wish World he could have rectified his relationship with his brother given time. So that leaves one overriding reason for him not to be able to stay in the Wish World – saving people. And it's emphasised further in Dean's urgency in helping the girl in white back in the real world and Sam's words to him at the end of the episode about how people are still alive because of Dean. Even though it hurts so much, it's still worth saving them.

Rather than respond to this with a nod or an agreement, Dean merely holds an 'Is it?' expression on his face, and maybe that's understandable too. The burden that they are carrying is particularly heavy for Dean. He's been struggling with it for some time. Back in 'Croatoan' (2-09) he was already questioning why the Winchesters always got landed with the responsibility.

It's something that John Winchester also had problems with in 'Salvation' (1-21). John just wanted to stop losing his loved ones and friends. Wanted nice things for his family and his wife back. He wanted it all to be finished.

And even though Dean released some of the load when he told Sam what John Winchester whispered to him back in the hospital, he's still lugging it around with him. No surprise he found it hard to break out of the Wish World then.

The only inconsistency in the entire episode is the scene where Dean wants to mow the lawn. In 'Bugs' (1-08), being faced with a housing estate and a simple life in suburbia Dean just wanted to blow his brains out.

And suddenly the boy wants to mow the lawn?

Still, 'What Is And What Should Never Be' is the single most powerful, emotionally painful episode since the Winchester journey started, and if you happen to well up while you watch it, don't worry because you had company – Kripke reports in his commentary that even the crew 'had something in their eye' during the filming of Dean's conversation at his dad's grave.

VERDICT – 10 out of 10

EPISODE 2-21 AND 2-22
ALL HELL BREAKS LOOSE
(PARTS ONE AND TWO)

TRANSMISSION DATES
Part One
US first aired: 10 May 2007
UK first aired: 30 November 2007
Part Two
US first aired: 17 May 2007
UK first aired: 7 December 2007

CREDITS
Part One
Writer: Sera Gamble
Director: Robert Singer
Part Two
Writer: Eric Kripke
Story By: Eric Kripke and Michael T Moore
Director: Kim Manners

RECURRING ROLES
Part One
Jim Beaver (Bobby Singer), Aldis Hodge (Jake), Katharine Isabelle (Ava Wilson), Fredric Lehne (The Yellow-Eyed Demon), Chad Lindberg (Ash), Samantha Smith (Mary Winchester), Gabriel Tigerman (Andy Gallagher)
Part Two
Jim Beaver (Bobby Singer), Samantha Ferris (Ellen Harvelle), Aldis Hodge (Jake), Fredric Lehne (The Yellow-Eyed Demon), Jeffrey Dean Morgan (John Winchester)

GUEST STARS
Part One
Hannah Dubois (Demon Girl), Jessica Harmon (Lily)
Part Two
Kaare Anderson (Unknown), Ona Grauer (Crossroads Demon)

Synopsis

Sam disappears from a diner, and when Dean investigates, all he finds is a number of dead bodies and a scattering of sulphur. Dean receives a tip off from Ash that Sam might be at the Roadhouse, but when he gets there, the building has been burned down and everyone is dead. Meanwhile, Sam has woken up in a deserted frontier town called Cold Oak. Several other people have been deposited there too, including fellow psychics Andy Gallagher[213] and Ava Wilson[214], along with Lily and soldier Jake. Andy uses his powers to send Dean a vision of where they are being held. That night, the yellow-eyed demon tells Sam in a dream that only one of the psychics – the strongest – is needed to lead his demon army, so it's kill or be killed. Lily is killed while trying to leave; Andy is killed by a demon; Sam realises that Ava is summoning demons and has killed the other two; Jake breaks Ava's neck to stop her calling another demon; then Jake attacks Sam. Dean and Bobby arrive just in time to see Jake stab Sam in the back and run away. Sam dies in Dean's arms.

Dean is devastated and can't bury or burn Sam's body. Instead he summons a crossroads demon and makes a deal: Sam's life in exchange for his own soul in a year's time. With Sam back again, the boys go to Bobby's to try to find out what the yellow-eyed demon is up to. Ellen arrives with information from Ash about the Devil's Gate in South Wyoming. The yellow-eyed demon needs Jake to cross the iron defences around the gate and open it for him. Bobby, Ellen and the Winchesters can't stop the gate being opened but manage to close it quickly afterwards. When the yellow-eyed demon arrives to kill Dean, John Winchester's spirit saves his son and Dean shoots the yellow-eyed demon with the Colt, killing him and finally getting revenge for Mary's and Jessica's deaths. John's spirit fades with a smile for his boys.

Can You Survive to the Titles?

Working in a diner is clearly a dangerous job – especially when one of the Winchester brothers walks in. Sam's little visit for extra onions results in one customer and two employees being murdered by demons, and that's not tomato ketchup spreading out into a large pool on the table from the dude with the cut throat.

Location, Location, Location

Cold Oak, South Dakota; Harvelle's Roadhouse – or at least the smouldering remains of said Roadhouse; Southern Wyoming at the centre of a huge Devil's Trap made of iron railway tracks.

---

213 First encountered in 'Simon Said' (2-05).

214 Last seen in 'Hunted' (2-10).

LEGENDARY ROOTS

Dudleytown is a small village, now lying in ruins, situated in Cornwall, Connecticut and is supposed to be one of the most haunted places in the world. Legend has it that in 1510 a curse of horror and death was put on any descendants of Edmund Dudley, who was beheaded for trying to overthrow King Henry VIII. Generations later the curse was still on the family when in 1747 two Dudley brothers founded a new town after returning from war. The curse claimed its first victim in Abiel Dudley, who went insane, claiming hoofed creatures haunted the town, and later died homeless and alone.

Others seem to get drawn into the misfortune too. The family who bought Abiel's home were murdered in 1764 by Indians. A number of the town's people died of a mysterious plague in 1813. General Heman Swift's wife was struck by lightning on the porch of their house in 1804 and killed instantly, and the General went insane and died soon after. The Brophy family were the last remaining residents of the town as others moved due to poor harvests and because of its location, but tragedy was to strike them too – the wife died of consumption, their two sons went into the woods never to return and the family home was burned to the ground. Shortly afterwards, the father walked into the woods, never to be seen again.

The final death attributed to the town was that of Dr Clark's wife. Dr Clark had a summer house built where they were staying. He was called away to New York, and upon his return 36 hours later, his wife had gone insane and was claiming that a strange creature had attacked her. She later committed suicide.

Since the demise of the town there have been reports of strange, ghostly apparitions and incidents in the area. There have been tales of people being pushed and scratched and the appearance of strange lights. Some of the alleged incidents have now been refuted and actually occurred in other nearby towns.

SQUEEZE OF THE WEEK

Dean gets some demon tongue – but only when he seals his deal for Sam's life in return for his soul in one year's time. That's one very expensive kiss.

SIBLING RIVALRY

It all starts out normally enough, Dean wants extra onions on his burger, Sam going to have to suffer the consequences of those onions in the car. But after this initial exchange as Sam goes to fetch the burgers there's no more rivalry because the yellow-eyed demon's plans come to fruition and it all gets serious.

BODY COUNT

After the cluster of deaths in the opening, there's a larger mass death when the

Roadhouse gets toasted, although the only obvious fatality is Ash in his new crispy coating. The rest of the victims get picked off one at a time – Lily in the forest outside Cold Oak; Andy in the shack with the evil Ava; then, immediately afterwards Ava, helped by Jake to see what's behind her with neck-popping efficiency; then Sam with Jake's knife in his back (okay, technically, it wasn't permanent, but he did die); and finally Jake, peppered with bullets by a ominously vicious Sam.

TOOLKIT

- If you're stuck in the middle of nowhere, up against unknown spooky assailants, then look for *weapons made of iron or silver* and locate some *salt* if you can.
- A *knife* is useful in any kind of fight but be careful you don't get betrayed and stabbed in the back with it.
- A shot of *holy water* is the best way to ensure that someone is who they say they are and not a demon in your friend's meat-suit.
- *The demon-killing handgun* made by Samuel Colt will help you finally take your revenge on nasty ole yellow-eyes.[215] Only one of the original 13 bullets remains, and that's all Dean needs.

MEMORABLE MOMENTS

The shock moment of Sam's death is a surprise worth wading through the rest of the episode for, and John Winchester's brief but significant return is pleasingly sentimental.

SPOOK RULES

Psychic kids –

- Andy could already put thoughts in people's heads and make them do whatever he wanted, but he's been practicing and now he can insert images into anyone's head as well.
- Lily has only to touch people and their hearts stop.
- Jake has extra strength, although he claims he's not like Superman.
- Ava started out just having visions, but can now control demons.
- If you open yourself up to your demonic powers, you hit a real fast learning curve and all sorts of skills manifest themselves.

Acheri demons –

- Usually take the form of a young girl – and are believed to live in mountains and come down into the local villages to spread disease, most often to the

---

215 Introduced in 'Dead Man's Blood' (1-20).

children.
- They can be summoned and controlled by someone who's been practicing their psychic talents for the last five months in remote deserted towns.
- Once the person who summons them is dead, they don't tend to come back to continue killing people.

Miscellaneous demonic directives –
- When you summon a crossroads demon, you need yarrow flowers, graveyard dirt, bones from a black cat, a photograph of yourself and a small rusty tin to put the items in and then bury them at a dead centre of a crossroads[216].
- You seal your deal by snogging the demon who made the deal with you. Remember to agree tongues or not up front so you don't get an unwanted surprise.
- The signs of a demonic presence include cattle deaths and electrical storms[217].
- There seems to be at least one gateway to hell on the surface of the Earth. Opening the doors releases demons into our world. This one was protected by Samuel Colt, who used iron railways lines in the shape of a Devil's Trap – demons can't cross iron lines.

DID YOU SPOT?
Lily says, 'Clearly, the only sane thing to do here is get the hell out of Dodge.' A similar line was used previously in 'Tall Tales' (2-15) by Bobby: 'Let's just get the hell out of Dodge before somebody finds that body' after they've (seemingly) killed the Trickster.

Dean's clearly feeling out of sorts – he's refusing free food from Bobby after Sam's death when he'd usually be in there with both hands and a full mouth[218].

The name on the ID that Dean places in the tin box is Agent Dean Ford of the US Wildlife Service[219].

GOING UNDERCOVER
No need to go undercover this time – all the boys' problems are created because they are who they are – Sam and Dean Winchester.

---

216 Established in 'Crossroad Blues' (2-08).

217 Established in 'Salvation' (1-21) except that episode mentioned temperature fluctuations as an omen too

218 As he was in Bugs (1-08), 'Nightmare' (1-14), 'Provenance' (1-19), 'Tall Tales' (2-15) and 'Hollywood Babylon' (2-18).

219 This was last used in 'Dead In The Water' (1-03).

CULTURAL REFERENCES

Andy: 'I just woke up in freakin' Frontier Land.': Frontier Land is an Old Western section at the Disney theme parks.

The signature on the receipt that Sam gives Andy is D Hasselhoff: David Hasselhoff is the star of the TV series *Knightrider* (1982-1986) and *Baywatch* (1989-2001).

Sam: 'It's a brave new world.': A line from Shakespeare's *The Tempest* (1610-1611) but referring to the novel *Brave New World* (1932) by Aldous Huxley, describing a utopian World State.

Yellow-eyed demon: 'You're it – last man standing. The American Idol.': *American Idol* (2002-) is a US singing talent shows similar to *The X Factor* and *Pop Idol*.

Dean: 'Easy there, Van Damme.': Jean-Claude Van Damme is a former kick-boxing champion who became an actor, most famous for action films such as *Kickboxer* (1989) and *Universal Soldier* (1992).

Jake: 'Once you give in to it, there's all sorts of new Jedi mind tricks you can learn.': Probably the most famous Jedi mind trick is Obi Wan Kenobi's: 'These are not the droids you're looking for ...' from the film *Star Wars* (1977).

GOOFS AND FLUFFS

When the interference starts on the radio, why isn't Dean out of the car and legging it for the diner straight away? It's not like the brothers haven't experienced exactly that kind of interference before when ghosts and demons are afoot.

When Bobby says that Dean doesn't mean it that he's done with hunting, Dean stands up angrily and his chair can be heard falling over in the background, but a couple of seconds later, he walks round the back of the now-standing chair to lean on it.

HAVEN'T I SEEN YOU BEFORE?

Part One:

Jessica Harmon's credits include *Battlestar Galactica: The Face of the Enemy, Hollow Man II* and *Kyle XY*. Aldis Hodge has been in *Bones, Charmed* and *Numb3rs*.

Part Two:

Kaare Anderson has appeared in *Smallville, Dark Angel* and *Poltergeist: The Legacy*. Ona Grauer's credits include *Andromeda, House Of The Dead* and *Sliders*.

BEHIND THE SCENES

Ona Grauer also worked with Eric Kripke on the pilot for the short lived (eight episodes) *Tarzan* series in 2003, which featured genre star Lucy Lawless (Xena from *Xena: Warrior Princess*) and Mitch Pileggi (who played Skinner in *The X-Files* and will turn up in *Supernatural* Season Four).

Director Kim Manners explained in *The Official Supernatural Magazine* #1 that Jeffrey Dean Morgan's footage was all shot against a blue screen in February 2006. The rest of the episode, the background plates and the boys' reactions to their dad, were all shot in April 2006. It was all edited together rather seamlessly really.

From the 'All Hell Breaks Loose: Part One' Commentary:

The location for Cold Oak is actually Bordertown near the Maple Ridge area of British Columbia, run by Virtue Studios. The *Supernatural* team had problems accessing the site due to it being under water with all the rain. There was a brief hiatus in the weather that let all the team get in, but then it didn't look like they'd be able to get out again.

The flashback to the Pilot, when the yellow-eyed demon stood over baby Sam, was re-created for this episode, with an exact replica of the room being built and the blood being dripped in the baby's mouth. This latter shot turned out to be a nightmare to film, because the baby wouldn't stop crying. Creating the effect where Mary Winchester goes up the wall was actually easier than dripping the blood into the baby's mouth!

Eric Kripke's favourite scene in this episode is when Andy gets killed and his blood spatters up the window.

Sera Gamble's favourite scene is the fight between Sam and Jake, especially when Jake dislocates Sam's shoulder but Sam still fights on.

MUSICAL INTERLUDE

Part One

- 'Foreplay-Long Time' – Boston – played during the recap at the start and when Sam goes to get some food.
- 'Wrapped Around Your Finger' – composed by Martyn Laight – when Dean is looking for Sam in the diner.
- 'Opening' – Darker My Love – when Ash calls Dean, telling him to get to The Roadhouse.

Part Two

- 'Carry On Wayward Son' – Kansas – played during the recap at the start of the episode[220].
- 'Don't Look Back' – Boston – at the end of the episode over 'We've got work to do'.

ANALYSIS

This is a typical *Supernatural* finale – the focus isn't on running around breathlessly

---

220 Also used as the recap song at the end of Season One.

trying to solve mysteries and blowing things up, it's about revelation and reactions, all delivered with a fierce intensity.

Part One is really about setting up the final instalment, with a few choice morsels thrown in, while Part Two blows the doors wide open metaphorically as well as literally. It's a little slow getting to the good stuff, but given that there have been hints about the yellow-eyed demon's devious plan since Mary Winchester was murdered, it's no surprise the writers wanted to relish the end game.

And it's a layered end game as you'd expect. First of all, there's the selection process to go through, since it's revealed that only one leader is required. Taking up all of Part One, we watch the candidates drop one by one until it's just the two soldier-types left. With Jake beaten unconscious by Sam we think it's all stitched up as it should be, which is why Jake's belated stabbing of Sam is that much more shocking.

Now ole yellow-eyes has to sort out the gateway to hell in end game layer two. The point wasn't just to create a top notch leader, but to have a human under his control to open those gates and release the hordes (before going on to other equally vile and destructive tasks no doubt). It all holds together as a storyline. Everything we've seen has been pointing this way for two seasons, and not a single event contradicts what's been previously established. Quite an achievement.

Meanwhile, other stories are also coming to a close. The Roadhouse meets its fiery end, with the loss of many hunters' lives including that of young Ash. Ellen survives due to a lucky pretzel run, but no-one else. It won't really be missed, since the boys didn't return after they discovered their dad's involvement in Bill Harvelle's death and all of the contact since then has been over the phone.

Also getting tied up is John Winchester's fate. It's a pleasingly symmetrical event, with John being taken to hell in the first episode of Season Two and escaping from hell to help his boys kill the yellow-eyed demon in the last episode. John can rest in peace now that Mary's killer is finally dead, and it's all unashamedly sentimental in his last moments as he says his silent goodbyes to his boys – who both started the season in tears and end it in the same way.

For Sam, these last two episodes finish off the yellow-eyed demon's interest in him, although he'll still have to deal with the knowledge that he has demon blood flowing in his veins at some point in the future. He didn't turn evil during his trials at Cold Oak, so he can stop worrying about that (for the time being at least) and start to get all angsty about Dean's deal with the demon and finding a solution to save his brother's life. It took Dean a few episodes to come to terms with John's sacrifice for him, so let's see how Sam fares in the same position.

If it's mostly closure for Sam, then it's mostly into new territory for Dean. Now we can see what he is prepared to do for his brother – give his own life. He has always been responsible for Sam, and this was reinforced in the flashback scenes in 'Something Wicked' (1-18), where a young Dean was clearly left looking after his younger brother regularly while John was away hunting. Combine this sense of responsibility with Dean's low sense of self-worth (that has been evident but not explained throughout the seasons so far) and you can see why he would indeed make the deal with the demon.

The only contradiction in Dean's actions harks back to 'Children Shouldn't Play With Dead Things' (2-04). There he blatantly believed that what was dead should stay dead, and shouted as much at zombie Angela's grieving father – and yet here he is doing exactly the same thing in resurrecting Sam. Okay, when it's your own brother's life at stake, it's not so difficult to change your mind, but the yellow-eyed demon does remind Dean that (just as Angela's personality changed in 2-04) it might be a slightly altered Sam who has come back, perhaps evident in Sam's ruthless killing of Jake.

It's the intelligence of the storytelling and the consistency of characterisation throughout all the past episodes that leads us logically to this dangerous situation for Dean. If the story's groundwork hadn't been done previously, the deal would have been just another plot mechanism designed to escape a story corner the writers had painted themselves into and not the solid twist it turns out to be. It's going to be interesting to see how Season Three pans out with Dean's rapidly diminishing time left on Earth.

There's one final point worth mentioning that also comes under the heading of preparing your story well in advance. We discover that Mary Winchester already knew who the yellow-eyed demon was when he was standing over six month old Sammy that fateful night. The reason won't be made clear until early into Season Four, but this is another example of initial establishment taking place. It's only a small point now, but it is very significant in its own, mysterious way.

Overall, this is a slower finale than Season One's, but ultimately it delivers more answers. By killing off the yellow-eyed demon now, rather than stringing it out across another season, the writers give everything a sense of forward movement and something new and exciting to look forward to in Season Three. It'll be fun trying to guess where they're going to take us next.

VERDICT – 9 out of 10

SEASON THREE OVERVIEW

Time-boxed into a single year and packed with both familiar legends and Winchester mythology, Season Three eventually grabs the proverbial horns of the question: 'What do we do now that yellow-eyes is dead?'. Then it pins it down and mauls it with gusto. Yes, it takes a while for the writers to decide the best way to tackle the problem, but after that, the teeth come out and the blood starts to flow.

It's a harrowing year for the boys. Not only is Dean's deal hanging over their heads but a determined FBI agent (Henricksen) is still on their asses and a psychotic fellow hunter (Gordon) is exhibiting an unhealthy obsession with Sam[221]. There's a female demon (Ruby) with questionable motivations watching their every move, and a female mercenary (Bela) with very obvious motivations, taking pot-shots at them. And then there's an army of escaped demons getting up to who knows what, who knows where …

THE DEMON WAR

Let's start with a little history. The army of demons escaped at the end of Season Two when the gates to hell were opened. About two hundred demons (and one very grateful John Winchester) clawed their way to freedom on Earth (and beyond for John of course).

Now, as Season Three opens, we start to realise that the demons have dispersed rather than sticking together and they're being rather subdued. It seems that Sam's abdication of the leadership has left them in disarray and they don't know what to do next. The yellow-eyed demon, Azazel, was a tyrant but he kept them together and gave them direction[222]. So in the absence of a leader, individual skirmishes begin amongst small groups of demons like the Seven Deadly Sins[223] or others that have been together for some time[224].

A new leader ascends eventually[225] and the first item on the agenda is to eliminate the competition – Sam Winchester. It's not until the Winchesters are finally locked in a prison cell by Agent Henricksen (thanks to a tip off from Bela)[226] that we get to see our first battalion of demons and start to understand how organised they've become

---

221 You know everyone gets obsessed with Sam sooner or later!

222 See 'Sin City' (3-04).

223 In 'Magnificent Seven' (3-01).

224 Like Casey and Father Gil in 'Sin City' (3-04).

225 First mentioned in 'Malleus Malificarum' (3-09).

226 In 'Jus in Belo' (3-12).

in their search for Sam. We also get to briefly meet their leader – Lilith – who arrives, disturbingly, clad in a sweet little girl meat-suit.

Lilith's and Dean's storylines finally merge in the season finale[227] and we discover more about her twisted nature, just before she discovers she's badly underestimated Sam's powers.

With the exception of 'Jus In Belo' (3-12), the demon war story is rather disappointing overall. Both 'The Magnificent Seven' (3-01) and 'Sin City' (3-04) give the impression of some interesting battles to come, but these don't fully materialise, and by the end of the season you'd be forgiven for forgetting there was any kind of war on at all.

The reasons for this were explained in the *Season Three Supernatural Companion*. In short, the studio instructed the *Supernatural* creators to increase the scope and go for more epic storylines – citing the Season Two finale as a good example. However, the production team still had to work within a tight budget, creating a constant fight between scope and cost.

Then there was the idea knocking around about using the terrorist cell approach, where the demon attacks could happen anywhere, anytime. Eric Kripke admitted, rather candidly, in the *Season Three Supernatural Companion* that real world terrorism and its politics were not his strong point. His inspirations came from the old stories and legends and that's the sort of stuff he liked to write.

All these points contribute to the weaknesses in the demon war storyline as the season progresses. It is only after the terrorist cell approach is abandoned that the excellent 'Jus In Belo' (3-12) gives us a satisfying encounter. Sadly, that is the only one, and it is Lilith alone (more or less) who takes on the Winchesters for the season's finale.

DEAN'S DEAL

In some ways, Season Three is slightly less emotional for Dean. He's hasn't got to cope with being abandoned by his father or worry about his brother going darkside. There's no grief welling up at inconvenient moments or sudden need to save his brother by selling his soul. But that doesn't mean that Dean isn't struggling with the situation. It's just hidden deeper than usual, that's all.

Dean opens the season with a sense of relief[228]. He's successfully resurrected his brother, and no-one else he cares about is under immediate threat. And that's the telling point – Dean has never really cared about himself. There's always been a streak

---

227 In 'No Rest For The Wicked' (3-16).

228 In 'Magnificent Seven' (3-01).

of self loathing in him that's never been far below the surface. In his own view, his life is expendable compared with the lives of those he loves and his sacrifice for Sam is fully justified. Now he can see an end to his responsibilities and it makes him a little more open than before, happy to say things out loud rather than hide them; and a lot more indulgent of his own desires.

The change begins as Dean learns more about hell and what it'll be like when he gets there[229]. That ignites his fears, and it's not long before they escalate when Ruby explains that she can't save him[230]. But worse than that: his fate will be to turn into a demon – the very thing the brothers hunt – and that terrifies him. Coming face to face with his demon self[231] finally gives Dean a reason to live, but they need to find a way to save him that doesn't forfeit Sam's life as well. That proves to be tough.

Dean is a lot more compassionate than Sam by now – a complete turnaround on the situation back in Season One, where Sam was the one to question what they were doing. Meanwhile, Sam has seen through Dean's happy face to the terror underneath[232] and Dean has accepted that if the worst happens he needs to leave Sam capable of looking after himself and the car.

When there's less than three weeks to go, Dean starts to get desperate – so desperate that he's easily fooled by the croccotta's trick[233] when 'John Winchester' phones him and tells him where to find the demon who owns his contract. But Dean isn't totally out of control yet and never gets to the point where he's willing to sacrifice his humanity to beat the deal[234].

When the deadline arrives, Dean demonstrates how deep his dislike of Ruby is, how well he knows his brother, and how dignified he can be in the face of death– he meant it when he said he would go down swinging, and he doesn't stop trying to break the deal until the bitter and bloody end.

It's truly shocking to see him strung up in hell at the very end, desperately calling for his brother. You have to congratulate everyone involved for making this brave decision and not taking the path to an easy, last minute rescue – somehow that would have felt like a cop-out, and we've come to expect more from this series over the years. As it turns out, sending Dean to hell unleashes a host of changes for the show that just keep getting better …

---

229 In 'Sin City' (3-04).

230 In 'Malleus Malificarum' (3-09).

231 In 'Dream A Little Dream Of Me' (3-10).

232 In 'Fresh Blood' (3-07).

233 In 'Long Distance Call' (3-14).

234 In 'Time Is On My Side' (3-15)

SAM'S ATTEMPTS TO SAVE DEAN

Dean may have been at the centre of the deal, but the fall-out from it engulfs many of the people around him – the biggest effect being felt by Sam. As Dean did with his father, so Sam also has to accept that he is – however indirectly – the reason his brother will spend eternity in hell. In his struggle to come to terms with it, Sam does the only constructive thing he can (short of making his own pact): he starts researching how to break the deal.

Throughout the season, Sam tries everything he knows to find a solution to Dean's deal. When the countdown enters the final weeks he's getting more and more frantic until he believes that the only person who can truly help is Ruby.

Ruby has been working her way into the Winchester boys' confidence for several months by now, and has saved both their lives more than once[235], not to mention offering to sacrifice herself so the boys can escape the demon siege[236]. Sam's not naive, he knows she's a demon, knows that demons lie, but his need to help Dean is overpowering, and he eventually gives in to her manipulations.

It's a different Sam that summons Ruby in the final episode – his experiences throughout the season have had their impact. At the start of Season Three, he was always the voice of caution, thinking through their moral obligations, but not now. His thoughtful approach has evaporated and he's making the decision to kill a lot faster and more ruthlessly than before.

But there are other changes as well. Sam is keeping more secrets from Dean and he's less compassionate than he was, harder. At one point he even looks set to turn to drink when he can't find anything to help Dean. It takes Dean's change of attitude – about helping to find a way out of the deal – to give him hope and allow him to carry on sober.

The biggest change follows 'Mystery Spot' (3-11), in which Sam sees Dean die repeatedly and then spends six months on his own searching for the Trickster. The Sam we see after that has no objections to sacrificing a young virgin girl to save other people's lives[237].

By the time Dean lies on the floor, shredded by Hellhounds, Sam is facing a new revelation – his psychic powers have only been dormant and he is, in fact, more powerful than Lilith. But it's too much, too late. Dean has gone.

SAM AND DEAN

All the way through Season Three, the boys are at odds about what to do about Dean's

---

235 In 'Malleus Malificarum' (3-09).

236 In 'Jus In Belo' (3-12).

237 Again in 'Jus In Belo' (3-12).

deal. Previous seasons have given us similar conflicts – like Sam not wanting to hunt once the yellow-eyed demon was dead – but that didn't cause the same kind of problems that this does.

The brothers are locked in a mutually deadly embrace. Dean won't let Sam break the deal because Sam will die if he does. If Sam doesn't break the deal, Dean dies. So while Dean won't help himself, there's increasing tension as Sam goes against Dean's wishes. It takes Dean meeting his demon-self to make him realise that he doesn't actually want to go to hell, but there's not much time left by this point. The fear of going to hell affects them both (Dean's fear for himself, Sam's fear for his brother) as they become more and more desperate and start taking their frustrations out on each other in big arguments whenever they disagree on things.

And they certainly start disagreeing more and more as the season goes on – about whether or not Dean should actively seek a way out of the deal, about how to break the deal with or without Dean's help, about whether to take Ruby's help or not, and over what's more important: Bela and the Colt or Dean's impending one way trip down under.

In previous seasons, the disputes have been fewer and less important and there's always been a sense of support between the two boys. By the end of Season Three, they've grown apart. Mix in the 'Is he 100% Sam?' question beneath it all, and there's a much edgier feel to the whole thing. And that isn't going to get any better for some time to come …

RUBY (FIRST APPEARS IN EPISODE 3-01 THEN INTERMITTENTLY[238])

Ruby certainly knows how to make an entrance – she arrives without warning, saves Sam's life with a remarkable knife that kills demons then disappears just as mysteriously. It takes time over the season to get to know more about Ruby but by the time Dean's walking the dogs down under we're still not exactly sure what she wants and it doesn't seem to matter anyhow 'cause Lillith's sent her a long way away.

What we do know about her is that she's primarily interested in Sam and her relationship with him creates a lot of friction between the brothers. Sam sees her as a dangerous asset – he wants to use her skills and knowledge but is totally aware that demons lie and that what she says shouldn't be totally trusted. Dean doesn't trust her at all and quite happily points the Colt in her face (even though she helped Bobby to fix the gun in the first place) and he would have killed her without Sam's intervention. When she saves his life[239] (as well as Sam's again) he still manages to uncover her lies

---

238 She appeared in 'The Magnificent Seven' (3-01), 'The Kids Are Alright' (3-02), 'Bad Day at Black Rock' (3-03), 'Sin City' (3-04), In 'Malleus Malificarum' (3-09), 'Jus In Belo' (3-12), and 'No Rest For The Wicked' (3-16)

239 In 'Malleus Malificarum' (3-09)

to Sam about her lack of ability to save him from his deal.

But Ruby's a tough character, she hunts her own kind, she's clearly manipulative and she is always in control, so did Dean uncover her lies or did she want him to know? Why then did she volunteer her life to save Sam (and Dean) again?[240]. She seems to be on the Winchester's side but she's still setting the brothers against each other when she reveals the details about Lillith that Sam hadn't told Dean. And later[241] there's important information about Dean's contract and Sam's powers that she's still withholding. So it's hard to tell what Ruby's agenda truly is, beyond keeping Sam alive (and if she has to, then Dean too). But it must be a pretty heavy agenda given that she's prepared to give her life up to protect Sam and in the end she seems to do just that when they take on Lillith in the final showdown.

BELA (FIRST APPEARS IN EPISODE 3-03, THEN INTERMITTENTLY UNTIL 3-15[242])

She lasts only 12 episodes, but no other human causes as much trouble for the boys as Bela. She steals from them, puts bullets holes in them and hands them over to Gordon. When that fails, she sends Agent Henricksen after them, and then it gets worse.

From the start – when she ends up shooting Sam in the shoulder just to get the rabbit's foot[243] – it's absolutely clear just who's side she's on (her own) and just how far she's prepared to go to get what she wants (murder being totally acceptable). But almost everything else about Bela remains a mystery until we discover a small yet significant event in her past when she sees the ghost ship[244], implying that she's killed at least one person in her own family.

It's a secret she's kept for a long time by becoming defensive and avoiding close relationships of any kind. Along the way, Bela has collected a strong set of skills, including being a con-artist and handling guns, but it's her talent as a thief (mixed with the boys' own naivety) that gives her the Colt and two very angry Winchesters on her tail. In the heat of the chase, it's Dean who uncovers Bela's history after reading Rufus Turner's file on her. Even when he throws the details from the file in her face, Bela doesn't tell him the reason why she made the deal[245]. She doesn't seem to need to

240 In 'Jus In Belo' (3-12)

241 In 'No Rest For The Wicked' (3-16)

242 She appeared in 'Red Sky At Morning' (3-06), 'Fresh Blood' (3-07), 'Dream A Little Dream Of Me' (3-10), 'Jus In Belo' (3-12) and 'Time Is On My Side' (3-15).

243 In 'Bad Day at Black Rock' (3-03).

244 In 'Red Sky At Morning' (3-06).

245 Although the viewer sees the truth of the events in the flashbacks in 'Time Is On My Side' (3-15).

justify the killings to anyone else – showing just how little she shares with other people and just how little she requires other people's approval for her actions.

Bela's abusive history explains a lot about her personality and her motivations, including her final attempt to murder the boys in their motel beds – an act that indicates the extent of her own desperation to be free of her deal (something Dean and Sam already understand). She does manage a modicum of redemption at the eleventh hour by disclosing Lilith's name as the demon holding all the contracts, but the information doesn't prove to be particularly useful anyway (since Dean still goes to hell in the end).

As a character, part of Bela's role – like Victor Henricksen's and Gordon Walker's – is to be a human adversary for the boys and provide a little continuity, coherence and variety to go with the more stand-alone monster-of-the-week stories. But unlike Victor and Gordon, Bela never really fits in somehow. It has nothing to do with the quality of actress Lauren Cohan's performance – which is fine except for the irritating posh British accent. Instead, the unease comes from the boys themselves throughout the stories. In the early episodes, Bela *always* gets the better of them, even to the point of putting that bullet in Sam. No monster or human has ever gone up against the boys and won *every* time before. That's not so much of a problem on its own, but someone who's not on the boys' side is, by definition, 'the bad guy/gal' until they swap to the 'good guy/gal' side[246]. So far, all other nasty characters in the show have been consistently treated like a villain in the stories.

But not Bela.

The boys – and Bobby dammit, they all deserve a good slapping – insist on treating her as an ally in a totally random way, which results in a high level of confusion for the viewer. Somehow Bela is both good and bad at the same time. There's nothing wrong with a little ambiguity – Ruby's hidden agenda also creates mistrust, but her actions place her completely on Sam's side so far as we can see, so there's no confusion.

Bela's actions establish her firmly as a villain but somehow these very experienced, sharp-witted, skilled hunters can't see how stupid it is to help anyone who puts a bullet into one of them for no other reason than greed – even if she does look good in a short trench coat, bra and panties. In all other cases except Bela, the boys are consistent in picking their allies, but teaming up with her doesn't really make sense.

With Sam, Dean and Bobby acting so far out of character and the ambiguity of Bela's role, it's no surprise she doesn't gel with the overall storyline. The decision to kill her off was absolutely the right thing to do.

---

246 Like Henricksen in 'Jus In Belo' (3-12).

BOBBY, GORDON AND HENRICKSEN

Not satisfied with including development for all the central characters, the *Supernatural* writers also run with joyful abandon through the lives of the three main supporting characters – Bobby Singer, Gordon Walker and Victor Henricksen.

BOBBY (EIGHT EPISODES IN SEASON THREE[247])

In general, Bobby continues his underlying support of the brothers' hunting activities. He's exorcising demons all night[248], providing information on rabbit's feet and Bela[249], asking for help as he battles his own nightmares[250], and helping them break Dean's deal[251].

Most of it is normal Bobby stuff, but in 'Dream A Little Dream Of Me' (3-10) we finally get to see how he got into hunting. Having to murder your wife because she was possessed by a demon and then later discovering that you could have just exorcised it and let your loved one live is a huge burden to carry through life. And it's clear from Bobby's nightmares how much guilt he carries.

It also becomes clear how Bobby has come to look on the boys as his own sons and the boys look on him as a father figure, especially since John Winchester's death. But Bobby's relationship is much more relaxed, since the tensions and resentment that characterised John's relationship with his boys (particularly Sam) are not present.

The boys haven't had much luck with family at times and somehow it's comforting to know that he's there for the boys when they need him.

GORDON WALKER (EPISODES 3-03 AND 3-07)

Having someone as skilled as Gordon Walker trying to kill you is a frightening prospect, and getting him locked up in jail is not likely to make the problem go away forever.

In this case, it gave Gordon a lot of free time to plan his next actions and he doesn't waste it. First he sends fellow hunter Kubrick[252] after Sam, then he breaks out himself to finish the job properly[253].

---

247 See 'The Magnificent Seven' (3-01), 'Bad Day at Black Rock' (3-03), 'Sin City' (3-04), 'A Very Supernatural Christmas' (3-08), 'Dream a Little Dream of Me' (3-10), 'Mystery Spot' (3-11), 'Time Is On My Side' (3-15) and 'No Rest For The Wicked' (3-16).

248 In 'The Magnificent Seven' (3-01).

249 In 'Bad Day At Bad Rock' (3-03).

250 In 'Dream A Little Dream Of Me' (3-10).

251 In the last two episodes of the season.

252 In 'Bad Day At Black Rock' (3-03).

253 In 'Fresh Blood' (3-07).

But however much Gordon believes he is doing the right thing, fate disagrees with him, and in the end he's turned into his worst nightmare – a vampire. Even then, Gordon is so obsessed that he uses his new powers to go after Sam, which leads to one of the most memorable fight sequences of the season and a spectacular decapitation.

It'll be some time before anyone forgets Gordon Walker.

VICTOR HENRICKSEN (EPISODE 3-12)

He may appear in only three episodes (two in Season Two and one in Season Three) but Henricksen is a formidable adversary for the boys, with the resources of the FBI at his beck and call. Even so, the boys prove themselves clever enough to slip his grip twice. Henricksen seems to have a grudging respect for their skills of escape but he's determined that it won't happen a third time when catches them again in 'Jus in Bello'.

Then Henricksen's world view is turned upside down when he's possessed and starts to understand the boys' perspective. He takes it in his stride, changes course and puts his considerable abilities into getting out of their difficult situation.

It would have been nice to see what Henricksen would have done (long term) with the information that demons really existed – created an X-Files department at the FBI maybe? – but he doesn't get the chance when an encounter with Lilith ends his life.

It's a dangerous business being on a show like *Supernatural* – Henricksen is the third supporting character to die this season (Bela and Ruby being the other victims). Don't get too close to the new starters in Season Four; you never know when they'll be checking out.

BEHIND THE SCENES

In addition to all this story and character work happening in front of the camera, a couple of changes were made behind it too. Eric Kripke explained in *The Official Supernatural Magazine* #2 that the budget limitations the production team were experiencing meant that very little of the show's usual accompaniment of classic rock music could be used in the first three-quarters of the season. If it was a decision between making the episode without the music or not making the episode at all then obviously they dropped the music. But Kripke and his team were astute enough to see the downside of these cuts and how it was damaging an important part of the show – so the team tightened the purse strings and saved up the money to put the classic rock back into episodes nine, ten and eleven[254].

The other change was to do with lighting. This was partly due to the weather

---

254 'Malleus Malificarum' (3-09), 'Dream A Little Dream Of Me' (3-10) and 'Mystery Spot' (3-11).

and partly due to the writers' strike (more on this below). Filming of each season of *Supernatural* starts in the summer, and the amount of natural light available gradually decreases as the crew shoot into winter. For Season Three, however, Vancouver (where the show is filmed) had some unusually sunny days in the summer, and then the shooting stopped, because of the strike, before the dark winter days kicked in. The combined effect of this was that the show seemed less dark, less moody.

The effect was further emphasised by a specific decision to highlight the contrast between the normal world we live in and the dark, supernatural world that lurks underneath. As a result, the diners and motels featured in the episodes looked more true to life, and the basements and haunted houses became more ominous and colourless.

This style is probably most visible in 'Bedtime Stories' (3-05) and 'A Very Supernatural Christmas' (3-08), although the latter's colourful scenes of gingerbread houses and Christmas jumpers actually magnify the horror of having your fingernail ripped out *because* of the realistically cheerful backdrop.

Getting back to the writers' strike[255], this affected the show in more than just the lighting department. A dispute about DVD residuals and writers' compensation for new digital media, it lasted over 14 weeks[256] and cost the show six episodes from its third season.

Naturally, the storylines were affected by the lost episodes, and according to Eric Kripke in *The Official Supernatural Magazine* #7, Dean was originally going to be saved by Sam. But the strike meant Sam didn't have time to learn how to use his powers and since there was no one else powerful enough to stand against Lillith, Dean had to go down under.

There were other casualties too. In *The Official Supernatural Magazine* #5, Jared Padalecki commented that because the story was condensed so much they lost some of the stand-alone episodes – episodes they enjoyed doing because they're usually a lot lighter and a lot of fun.

Despite all this, Kripke reluctantly admitted in *The Official Supernatural Magazine* #6 that the strike wasn't a wholly negative interruption because the actors and writers (including himself) were feeling rather worn out and tired. The break actually allowed everyone to relax and recharge their batteries for a while, which helped.

The other good thing was that the show did come back after the strike – several other shows didn't survive and were cancelled[257]. The writers on *Supernatural* made

---

255 In full, the Writers' Guild of America strike.

256 The strike ran from 5 November 2007 to 12 February 2008.

257 Like *The Bionic Woman*.

such a good job of the remaining episodes that the quality of the show didn't falter. The worst part for the viewers turned out to be waiting so long to find out what would happen to Dean.

SUPERNATURAL SEASON THREE

SEASON CREDITS

Co-Producer: Todd Aronauer
Producer: Sera Gamble
Consulting Producer: Laurence Andries
Consulting Producer: John Shiban
Co-Executive Producer: Peter Johnson
Co-Executive Producer: Ben Edlund
Co-Executive Producer: Phil Sgriccia
Executive Producer: Kim Manner
Executive Producer: McG
Executive Producer: Eric Kripke
Executive Producer: Robert Singer
Produced By: Cyrus Yavne
Created By: Eric Kripke
Directed By: Kim Manners (3-01, 3-07, 3-11, 3-16)
Directed By: Phil Sgriccia (3-02, 3-12, 3-13)
Directed By: Robert Singer (3-03, 3-09, 3-14)
Directed By: Charles Beeson (3-04, 3-15)
Story Editor: Jeremy Carver
Director of Photography: Serge Ladouceur, CSA
Production Designer: John Marcynuk
Production Designer: Jerry Wanek
Edited By: Anthony Pinker (3-01, 3-04, 3-07, 3-10, 3-13, 3-16)
Edited By: Tom McQuade (3-02, 3-05, 3-08, 3-12, 3-15)
Edited By: David Ekstrom (3-03, 3-06, 3-09, 3-11)
Music By: Christopher Lennertz
Music By: Jay Gruska
Production Manager: George A Grieve
First Assistant Director: Kevin Parks
First Assistant Director: John MacCarthy
Second Assistant Director: Amanda Bartley
Second Assistant Director: Adrian Diepold
Casting By: Robert J Ulrich, CSA
Casting By: Eric Dawson, CSA
Casting By: Carol Kritzer, CSA

Canadian Casting By: Coreen Mayrs, CSA
Canadian Casting By: Heike Brandstatter, CSA
Stunt Coordinator: Lou Bollo
Set Decorator: George Neuman
Property Master: Chris Cooper
Costume Design: Diane Widas
Key Make-up Artist: Shannon Choppin
Key Hair Stylist: Jeannie Chow
Special Effects Supervisor: Randy Shymkiw
Special Effects Make-up: The Schminken Collective Group Inc
Sound Mixer: Donald Painchaud
Re-Recording Mixers: Dennis Kirk
Re-Recording Mixers: Bill Jackson
Supervising Sound Editor: Michael E Lawshé
Supervising Sound Editor: Charlie Crutcher
Music Editorial by: Final Note Productions
Music Editorial by: Dino Moriana
Music Supervisor: Alexandra Patsavas
Visual Effects by: Ivan Hayden
Visual Effects Producer: Grant Lindsay

SPECIFIC EPISODE CREDITS

3-01
Post Production Supervisor: Kristin Cronin
Production Coordinator: Yale Kussin

3-02
Script Supervisor: Pam Lawrence
Post Production Coordinator: Jennefer Teegen

3-03
Key Hair Stylist: Kandace Loewen
Transport Coordinator: Mark Gould
'A' Camera Operator: Brad Creasser

3-04
Gaffer: Chris Cochrane
Key Grip: Harvey Fedor

3-05
Directed By: Mike Rohl
Art Director: Don MacAulay
Location Manager: Russ Hamilton

3-06
Directed By: Cliff Bole
Location Manager: Paul Lougheed
Construction Coordinator: Chris Sneddon

3-07
Script Supervisor: Pam Lawrence
'A' Camera Operator: Brad Creasser

3-08
Directed By: J Miller Tobin
Script Supervisor: Patti Henderson
Transport Coordinator: Mark Gould

3-09
Gaffer: Chris Cochrane
Key Grip: Harvey Fedor

3-10
Directed By: Steve Boyum
Art Director: John Marcynuk
Post Supervisor: Kristin Cronin

3-11
Location Manager: Paul Lougheed
Post Production Coordinator: Jennefer Teegen

3-12
Location Manager: Russ Hamilton
Construction Coordinator: Chris Sneddon

3-13
Script Supervisor: Patti Henderson
Production Coordinator: Yale Kussin

3-14
Edited By: Nicole Baer
Construction Coordinator: Chris Sneddon
Post Production Assistant: Shawn Wagoner

3-15
Sound Mixer: Kristian Bailey
Visual Effects by: Mark K Meloche
Assistant Editor: Michael Hall
'A' Camera Operator: Brad Creasser

3-16
Gaffer: Chris Cochrane
Sound Mixer: Kristian Bailey
Assistant Editor: Bruce Gorman

EPISODE 3-01
THE MAGNIFICENT SEVEN

TRANSMISSION DATES
US first aired: 4 October 2007
UK first aired: 27 January 2008

CREDITS
Writer: Eric Kripke
Director: Kim Manners

RECURRING ROLES
Jim Beaver (Bobby Singer), Katie Cassidy (Ruby)

GUEST STARS
Caroline Chikezie (Tamara), Ben Cotton (Pride/Business Man), Josh Daugherty (Envy/Walter Rosen), Monique Ganderton (Redhead), C Ernst Harth (Sloth/Big Guy), Peter Macon (Isaac), Gardiner Millar (Wrath/Bouncer), Michael Rogers (Gluttony/Bar Tender), Tiara Sorensen (Greed/Waitress), Katya Virshilas (Lust/Hot Girl), Allison Warnyca (Shopper)

SYNOPSIS
An army of demons have escaped from hell and seven of them take up residence in Nebraska to cause chaos. Sam and Dean investigate with Bobby's help and meet other hunters Isaac and Tamara. The latter pair follow one of the demons to its favourite bar but discover that it and the others – who represent the Seven Deadly Sins – have taken over the entire place. Isaac is killed when Gluttony forces him to drink drain cleaner liquid but Tamara is rescued by Sam, Dean and Bobby. Dean captures one of the demons in a Devil's Trap in the trunk of the car. The other six come after their comrade, who has already been exorcised back to hell. In the assault, a blonde stranger arrives to save Sam's life with a blade that can kill demons. Bobby sends the remaining Deadly Sins back to hell.

CAN YOU SURVIVE TO THE TITLES?
No deaths happen but there's a small piece of possessing going on for poor Walter Rosen and a large piece of demon army rampaging across the sky.

LOCATION, LOCATION, LOCATION
Oak Park, Illinois, west of Chicago; Around Lincoln, Nebraska.

LEGENDARY ROOTS
In 1589, Peter Binsfeld (c 1545-1598), a German bishop and theologian, defined the Demons of the Seven Deadly Sins:

- Lucifer: Pride (superbia) – a high or inordinate opinion of one's own dignity, importance, merit or superiority.
- Mammon: Greed (avaritia) – excessive or rapacious desire, especially for wealth or possessions.
- Asmodeus: Lust (luxuria) – excessive thoughts and desires of a sexual nature.
- Satan/Amon: Wrath (ira) – the feeling of extreme hatred or anger.
- Beelzebub: Gluttony (gula) – the over-consumption or over-indulgence of anything to the point of waste.
- Leviathan: Envy (invidia) – resentment and unhappiness caused by desire for someone else's possessions, fame, etc.
- Belphegor: Sloth (acedia) – not forming to one's potential, or seen as laziness or indifference.

SQUEEZE OF THE WEEK
Looks like Dean will be adding more notches to his tally stick now that he has only 12 months left to live. He's starting with a sexy little number seen in silhouette by Sam as he waits outside in the car. Dean gets more demon tongue with Deadly Sin demon Lust later on. Ain't no stopping Dean now. Even the demons can't stop snogging the boy …

SIBLING RIVALRY
It opens with a wonderfully light moment for the boys after Sam disturbs Dean during his session with the Doublemint Twins. As a result of seeing a part of Dean he'd never wanted to see, Sam's looking for a knife so he can gouge out his own eyes.

Before long, Sam is getting frustrated with Dean's lack of support in the hunt and trying to get him to focus on the demon attack and the job at hand. Dean is more concerned with how a girl can fight better than his brother, and Sam eventually loses his rag and stops bending over backwards trying to be nice to him – something his brother meets with a pretty relaxed attitude, observing that Sam's efforts didn't last long.

BODY COUNT
A young woman buys some shoes and gets her head smashed in on a car windscreen by an envious shopper (just like the January sales!); and hunter Isaac suffers a grisly

death after being forced to drink drain cleaning fluid by Gluttony. So that's four dead innocent people to the demons (counting the dried out family in the farmhouse). Unfortunately, after Bobby's done exorcising, only two of the seven Deadly Sins' meat-suits survive their demonic possession, which means the good guys clock up five dead innocents. Way to go boys!

TOOLKIT

- They're keeping their standard demon kit close to hand: *holy water, Devil's Trap inscriptions*, a *shotgun* and *pure salt*, along with the *lighter fuel* and *matches* for burning dem bones.
- The *Rituale Romanum* rites also get dusted off again, especially by Bobby who spends half the night exorcising with them[258].
- There's one new item to add to the toolbox too: *palo santo*. It's a holy wood from Peru that is toxic to demons and keeps them pinned down while you exorcise them.
- And one unlikely weapon turns up in the shape of *Bobby's car* – it's very useful in obtaining entry to barricaded bars by driving straight through the doors[259].

MEMORABLE MOMENTS

Dean bleeding on the porch after having his ass whupped by Isaac raises a smile; and Dean making out to 'You Ain't Seen Nothing Yet' raises an eyebrow and smile, and probably something for Dean as well.

THE CAR'S THE STAR

Bobby's wheels get all the action this week – clearly the Impala is having a day off.

SPOOK RULES

- Demons don't always embark on chaos and mayhem immediately after they have been released from hell. It can take up to a week before they get their acts together.
- Demons don't always leave traces of sulphur behind them when they've been up to wrongdoing.
- A Deadly Sin demon needs to make bodily contact with his victim in order to manipulate them.
- Demons can be trapped if they put their meat-suit within the boundary of a Devil's Trap inscription.

---

258 They've only been used in 'Phantom Traveler' (1-04) and 'Hell House' (1-17) up until now.

259 Something the Impala's not done since 'Woman in White' (1-01).

- You can tell when one or more demons are approaching because the lights will flicker and miscellaneous electrical goods will switch on of their own accord even if they have no power connected (although security cameras seem to be immune).
- Demons can be killed outright only by special Colt guns, and now it appears that there's the odd special hunting blade that can do it too, especially when wielded by mysterious attractive blondes stalking Sam.

DID YOU SPOT?

This is the first time we see Bobby without his cap on.

Dean has finally learned that a misbehaving radio is a demon early warning system – pity he'd not realised that when Sam got grabbed in the café in 'All Hell Breaks Loose Part One' (2-21).

Dean clearly has a favourite way to set light to salted bones – this is the second time he's used an entire book of matches to see off the opposition[260].

Walter (Envy) is missing from the mass grave at the end of the episode. We can only assume he got crispy off-screen earlier on.

GOING UNDERCOVER

Bobby goes all smart suit and slick on his trip to interview the Envy girl. The boys must also have gone undercover to obtain access to the security tapes, but who needs to explain that anymore? It's just a given on this show that they'll be cops or FBI or something. And the car is still undercover as CNK 80Q3, the same as at the end of last season.

CULTURAL REFERENCES

Dean: 'You'd think it'd be *Apocalypse Now*. It's been five days and bupkis.': *Apocalypse Now* is a 1979 Vietnam War film from director Francis Ford Coppola. Bupkis means 'nothing' in Yiddish.

Bobby: 'So where's your brother?'; Sam: 'Polling the electorate.': Polling the electorate is from *The Simpsons* – the local cops joke that it's what Mayor Quimby does when he has a motel-room meeting with an attractive young woman.

Dean: 'Hey, I appreciate you giving me a little quality time with the Doublemint Twins.': The Doublemint Twins advertise Wrigley's Doublemint chewing gum. They first appeared in 1956, and a number of different sets of twins have been used sporadically since.

Isaac: 'This ain't *Scooby Doo*.': *Scooby Doo*, which started in 1969, is a long-running

---

cartoon series – about a detective dog and his four friends who hunt down ghosts and the supernatural – that has also spawned films and spin-off series.

Off-screen voice: 'You better call Grissom.': Gilbert 'Gil' Grissom is the Head Investigator from the TV show *CSI: Crime Scene Investigation* that started in the year 2000.

Dean: 'Looking spiffy, Bobby. What were you, a G-man?': G-man is short for Government man, slang for an FBI agent.

Dean: 'What's in the box? Brad Pitt? Seven?': *Se7en* (1995), a movie directed by David Fincher, tells the story of a serial killer who commits murders based on the seven deadly sins.

Envy: 'My name is Legion; for we are many.': The line is a passage from the Bible, Mark 5:9. Jesus has been approached by a man. Jesus says, 'Come out of this man, you evil spirit!'. Then he asks the man, 'What is thy name?' And the man answers, 'My name is Legion; for we are many.'

Envy: 'Which one of you can cast the first stone, huh?': Another reference to the Bible (John 8:7). An adulterous woman has been brought before Jesus. By law she should be stoned. At first Jesus ignores the scribes and the Pharisees when they ask him what they should do with the woman: 'But when they continued asking him, he lifted up himself, and said unto them, He that is without sin among you, let him first cast a stone at her.' (American Standard Version)

Bobby: 'Fat, drunk and stupid is no way to go through life, son.': This is a line from the movie *Animal House* (1978), spoken by Dean Vernon Wormer (John Vernon).

Tamara: 'I don't care if they're the Three Stooges or the Four Tops!': The Three Stooges were a hugely popular film comedy team of the mid-1900s. The original hit trio were Moe Howard (born Harry Horwitz, 1897-1975), his brother Curly (born Jerome Lester Horwitz, 1903-1952), and Larry Fine (born Louis Feinberg, 1902-1975). There were numerous changes of line-up in later years. The Four Tops were a highly successful singing group who signed to the Motown record label in 1964. Their original line-up, Abdul (Duke) Fakir, Lawrence Payton, Levi Stubbs, Renaldo (Obie) Benson, performed together for a record-setting unbroken run of 44 years, from 1953 to 1997. The group still exists today, although only Fakir remains of the original line-up, the other three having died and been replaced.

Pride: 'Here's Johnny!': Probably the most famous quote by Jack Nicholson's character in *The Shining* (1980). Clearly the movie is a favourite of the *Supernatural* writers since this is the eighth time they've alluded to it[261].

261 Other references are in 'Home' (1-09), 'Asylum' (1-10), 'In My Time Of Dying' (2-01), 'The Usual Suspects' (2-07), 'Crossroad Blues' (2-08), 'Croatoan' (2-09), 'Playthings' (2-11) and 'Tall Tales' (2-15).

Dean: 'I'm just gonna ask it again – who was that masked chick?': This quote refers to *The Lone Ranger*, which ran from 1949-1957, the title character of which always wore a mask.

Sam is reading *Doctor Faustus* in the car while Dean has some sexy fun in the motel room. *Doctor Faustus* is a play first published in 1604 regarding a man who sells his soul to the devil for power and knowledge but can only live on earth for 24 years. Originally titled *The Tragical History of Doctor Faustus*, it was written by Christopher Marlowe and first performed 12 years after his death.

Dallas is on the TV in the family home when Sloth casts his influence. The TV show was a long-running soap cantered around J R Ewing and his family's oil business. It ran for 14 seasons from 1978 to 1991, and is to be revived in 2012.

Goofs and Fluffs

It's not clear how they got Walter (Envy) from the trunk of the car and into the house without freeing him from the Devil's Trap. How would you contain him once you'd opened the trunk lid?

It's also rather convenient that Dean could resist Lust's touch – given that other strong-minded characters couldn't resist killing themselves at the touch of one of these demons. Or is it just that Dean is so used to hunting in a lustful state of mind that it was business as usual?

Haven't I Seen You Before?

Caroline Chikezie has appeared in *Æon Flux* and as Lisa in the 'Cyberwoman' episode of *Torchwood*. Ben Cotton played Dr Kavanagh in *Stargate: Atlantis*, *Taken* and *The Day The Earth Stood Still*. Josh Daugherty featured in *Ghost Whisperer* and *Dexter*. Monique Ganderton's acting credits include *Fallen* and *Blood Ties* but she also has done stunts in *Resident Evil: Apocalypse*, *Underworld: Evolution* and *Watchmen*. C Ernst Harth appeared in *Thir13en Ghosts*, *Dead Like Me* and *The 4400*. Peter Macon has been in *Dexter* and *Without A Trace*. Gardiner Millar was in *Millennium* as Mr Otto, *Stargate SG-1* as Yat'Yir and in *Flash Gordon* as Vorak. Michael Rogers has been in *The Collector*, *Painkiller Jane* and *Smallville*. Tiara Sorensen was in *Mutant X*. Katya Virshilas was in *Dante's Cove*, *Smallville* and *Psych*. Allison Warnyca starred in *Smallville*, *Dead Like Me* and *The 4400*.

Behind the Scenes

According to actor Peter Macon (Isaac), quoted in the *Season Three Supernatural Companion*, the drain cleaner fluid he had to drink was made of Gatorade and Jell-o.

In *The Official Supernatural Magazine* #1, director Kim Manners said the biggest challenge was to make what was essentially just a water fight look like it was amazing. The boys were really just splashing the holy water around but they managed to turn it into an exciting western style episode where a brave group of mortals confronted the dark demonic forces.

MUSICAL INTERLUDE

- 'Hells Bells' – AC/DC– recap song.
- 'You Ain't Seen Nothing Yet' – Bachman Turner Overdrive – while Dean is getting squeezed by the Doublemint Twins and Sam is in the car talking to Bobby.
- 'Mean Little Town' – Howling Diablos – in the bar before the demons surround Isaac and Tamara.
- 'I Shall Not Be Moved' – J B Burnett – playing on the radio before Isaac calls to Tamara as the demons attack.

ANALYSIS

Supernatural has created something of a reputation for having a humdinger of a season opener, with the Pilot and Season Two's tragic 'In My Time Of Dying' setting the benchmark. So it's a shame that those high expectations are not met in 'The Magnificent Seven'. While the episode does have its moments – notably the bar scene where Isaac is killed and the final attack at the end – it fails to develop the Deadly Sin demons to any depth, there's a lot of setting up going on, and there aren't any intense emotional situations save for a short exchange between Sam and Dean in the closing scenes.

But this doesn't mean that the episode has nothing going for it at all – there's a huge amount of info being delivered, storylines starting that will endure across seasons, and new characters manoeuvring into position.

For the first time, we have a very definite sense of what the character story arcs are going to be through the upcoming season. Dean is on a mission to make the most of his remaining time, enjoying himself and taking as many demons with him as he possibly can. There will no doubt be times of reflection but he doesn't regret his decision at the moment.

For Sam, we see his need to save his brother from certain death once more[262]. He's already started searching, beginning with *Doctor Faustus*, and isn't likely to stop. It's frustrating the hell out of him, because he's trying to tolerate his brother's excesses, but by the end of the episode he's lost his patience and is telling Dean that he should care more about trying to break the deal.

---

262 A trait that came to the fore previously in 'Faith' (1-12).

And then we see the brand new Dean emerge fully. He's changed since he made the deal, and rather than keeping the terms of the deal secret for the next eight episodes, he's up-front and honest with Sam – welch on the deal and Sam's dead. It's a rare thing for Mr No-Chick-Flick-Moments and indicates just how much he's changed after two seasons of hunting, coping with his dad's death and making one desperate deal. There are other signs of change too – he says he's happier than he's been for some time. Is this 'cause he knows he won't have to shoulder his responsibilities for Sam and saving people for much longer? He's trying to fit in all the things he's never got round to (a threesome with the Doublemint Twins apparently being at the top of the list) and he's not too worried about his cholesterol levels. He's less cautious with the risks he's prepared to take and significantly more willing to step into suicidal situations, especially if it'll save some lives.

Sam's struggling to accept Dean's actions, in the same way Dean struggled with John Winchester's deal. The only way Sam can cope with it is to try to change the position and keep Dean out of those suicidal situations long enough to find a way out of the deal.

Meanwhile, Bobby is taking a stronger role in the boys' lives. He's always been available to support them, steadfast in his loyalty despite Sam killing other hunters[263] while he was possessed, and even now with the hunter community believing the boys responsible for the gates to hell opening. But for the first time he's imposing some control over them (and later Tamara), stopping them blindly rushing into dangerous situations. It'll be interesting to see how long he continues in this approach.

Someone who is clearly here to stay for some time is the mysterious 'masked chick'. Blonde, sexy and (understandably) obsessed with Sam, she's in possession of a powerful knife and not afraid to use it. She adds an air of mystery to proceedings, and her obviously unhappy history with the Deadly Sin demons is intriguing.

So this is an important episode, full of information and new beginnings, even if it's not one of the best openers we've had. It features some of the best dialogue ('Well, I sold my soul. Got a year to live. I ain't sweating the cholesterol.') and some of the worst ('I'm gonna put you down like a dog.'); some character development; some clues about the upcoming war; and an introduction to the first new kid on the block this season. And that ain't a bad achievement after all.

VERDICT – 7.5 out of 10

---

263 In 'Born Under A Bad Sign' (2-14).

EPISODE 3-02
THE KIDS ARE ALRIGHT

TRANSMISSION DATES
US first aired: 11 October 2007
UK first aired: 3 February 2008

CREDITS
Writer: Sera Gamble
Director: Philip Sgriccia

RECURRING ROLE
Katie Cassidy (Blonde Demon (Ruby))

GUEST STARS
Margot Berner (Katie Keel), Megan Bowes (Changling 1), Mitchell Duffield (Changling 2), Daniel Brodsky (Changling 3), Nicholas Elia (Ben Braeden), Stacy Fair (Mrs Ridgeway), Alberto Ghisi (Ryan Humphry), Michelle Grigor (Changling 4/Dakota Ridgeway), Kathleen Munroe (Dana Keel), Cindy Sampson (Lisa Braeden), Todd Thomson (Richard), Susie Wickstead (Mum 1), Desiree Zurowski (Annette Doolittle)

SYNOPSIS
Dean goes in search of an old flame and stumbles across an infestation of changelings. Children are being stolen from the Morning Hill housing estate and replaced with supernatural beings that look the same as the original kids but have a nasty habit of snacking on their mothers at regular intervals. As the mums are slowly driven insane by children they don't think are their own, Sam and Dean find the changeling nest, free all the children and kill the mother changeling.

CAN YOU SURVIVE TO THE TITLES?
You know, as soon as you see the circular saw start up on its own, that dad Richard Keel doesn't have long to go. In a suitably gruesome spray of blood, the poor man is butchered in seconds over his own DIY bench.

LOCATION, LOCATION, LOCATION
Cicero, Indiana; Cicero Pines Motel; Morning Hill gated community.

LEGENDARY ROOTS

The changeling comes from European lore where the offspring of an elf, troll, fairy or other legendary creature is secretly swapped with a human child as the latter is desired and raised by the creature or used as a servant. The changeling could also be an inanimate object that has been bewitched, typically a piece of wood, that would soon appear to grow sick and die. The parents would recognise the changeling by its ugliness or odd behaviour.

According to the lore, unbaptised babies are particularly vulnerable to being taken, along with blonde-haired, blue-eyed infants. A number of methods are used to keep babies safe. These include leaving a pair of scissors open in the room where the child sleeps, placing a steel or iron object above the infant's cradle, using amulets, or turning the infant's clothes inside-out.

A number of methods, dependant on country, are used to trick the changeling into identifying itself and getting the human child returned. It has been said that putting the changeling into a fire will cause it to jump up the chimney. The changeling infant will be more intelligent than the original, and cooking a meal in an eggshell or brewing beer in an acorn will trick it into talking, thus revealing its true nature. The parent's child will be returned if you are excessively cruel to the changeling and beat it or drown it.

SQUEEZE OF THE WEEK

At the start of the episode, Dean is at his least subtle, turning up at old flame Lisa Braeden's house looking for a quickie since they had a weekend together in Lisa's loft eight years previously. By the end of the episode, he has won Lisa over by saving her son's life, but when she offers him exactly what he came looking for, he turns it down without even thinking about it. Go figure.

SIBLING RIVALRY

Not very much rivalry going on, with the boys spending most of their time apart and talking to other people, but there is one small moment of fun when Dean is trying to cheer Sam up about the demon deal by explaining that he's going to squeeze in as many dying wishes as he can and at least he'll have a grin on his face after a day with Gumby girl.

BODY COUNT

No more bodies arrive during the episode but Sam does investigate a further four killings that occurred before they arrived on the scene, where people have fallen from ladders or drowned in their jacuzzis, that kind of thing.

TOOLKIT

- Knowing how to *kick someone in the nads* is a useful skill if you need to get your toys back.
- A *metal bar* is useful for breaking windows when you're trying to save kidnapped children and for breaking locks on cages with children trapped inside.
- A *brick* is a versatile object – you can even use it to smack an attacking real estate representative in the face.
- Keep a *homemade flame thrower* and a *lighter* around for wasting ladies who just happen to be changelings.
- And have the *holy water* handy in your bag in case people in your motel room turn out to be rather more demonic than you'd expected.

MEMORABLE MOMENTS

Keel's close encounter with the saw is pretty gruesome and the blonde girl revealing her true demonic nature is an intriguing turn of events. But the best moment is when Dana Keel drives her daughter into the lake – a quiet, desperate, truly horrific sequence.

SPOOK RULES

- Changelings are not necessarily evil monster babies; they can perfectly mimic the form of older children too.
- Changelings crawl in through windows and kidnap the real child then substitute one of their own.
- They then feed on the mom's synovial fluids – liquid contained in a membrane that cushions the joints – extracting this by biting the back of the victim's neck.
- The changelings act like clingy, totally well-behaved children once in place in a family but react violently to being separated from their victim.
- They can group together to intimidate a mother if she's trying to escape her 'child'.
- It can take several weeks to drain each victim of the fluids before the victim dies.
- Anyone who gets between a changeling and its victim is killed – including dads and babysitters.
- The stolen children are stored underground for the mother changeling to feed on.
- Fire is the only way to kill them. Kill the mother changeling and all the offspring changelings die at the same time.

DID YOU SPOT?

The list of people connected to his mom that Sam looks up:
- Hardecker – possibly killed in a fire on 24 November 2006 in Lawrence Kansas.

- Robert Campbell – maybe died on 19 July 2001 due to a 'heart condition'.
- Mrs Wallace.
- Ed Campbell.

It's not clear who is who in the story, but Mary's uncle[264] and doctor are both dead.

According to the newspaper report, when they found Richard Keel's body, he was lying on top of his circular saw, on his back in a pool of blood. The blade had penetrated into his thoracic cavity, severing several ribs and his spinal cord in the process.

GOING UNDERCOVER

Dean is just his usual sexy self (although he does give Lisa a credit card with 'Siegfried Houdini' on it). Sam goes undercover as an insurance investigator to gain info about the four deaths around the Morning Hill estate; and as police chief Phil Jones to find out what had happened to his mother's friends and family.

CULTURAL REFERENCES

Dean: 'Gumby girl ... Does that make me Pokey?': *Gumby* (1957-) is a stop-motion clay animation show. Gumby is a green clay humanoid figure while Pokey is its clay horse companion.

Blonde Demon: 'Ding dong, the demon's dead.': A play on the line: 'Ding dong, the witch is dead' from the *Wizard of Oz* (1939).

Blonde Demon: 'Doesn't change the fact that you're special, in that Anthony Michael Hall ESP vision kind of way.': This is a reference to *The Dead Zone* (2002-2007), starring Anthony Michael Hall as Johnny Smith, who is able to see the future by touching someone.

Blonde Demon: 'Generation of psychic kids, yellow-eyed demon rounds you up, celebrity death match ensues.': *Celebrity Deathmatch* is a clay animation programme that parodies celebrities fighting to the death in a wrestling ring. Originally shown as part of the MTV line-up, it ran for 75 episodes from 1998 to 2002 and was revived between 2006 and 2007 for 16 more.

Sam: 'Where did you get it? [The demon killing knife]'; Blonde Demon: 'Skymall.': *Skymall* is an inflight shopping magazine that is published quarterly and distributed to approximately 20 million aeroplane seats annually. It is backed up with an internet shopping site.

Dana Keel (Katie's mom) is reading *The Historian* (2005) by Elizabeth Kostova, a book that examines the factual roots of the Dracula legend in the shape of Vlad Teppes

---

264 Her uncle is likely to be one of the Campbells since 'In The Beginning' (4-03) reveals that Mary's maiden name was Campbell.

(the Impaler). The irony being that both book and episode feature supernatural creatures who feed off humans.

GOOFS AND FLUFFS

The radius of the saw (when seen on the bench) isn't big enough to go through Richard Keel's back and come through the front of his chest.

It's strange that the changelings kill peripheral family members (like dads), since they also have synovial fluid and could therefore be walking snack bars for them.

HAVEN'T I SEEN YOU BEFORE?

Margot Berner featured in *A Town Call Eureka*. Daniel Brodsky was in *Reaper*. Mitchell Duffield has also been in *Blood Ties* and *Smallville*. Nicholas Elia was in *White Noise*. Stacy Fair's credits include *The X-Files* and *Tru Calling*. Alberto Ghisi was in *Final Destination 3* and *Stargate: Atlantis*. Michelle Grigor's credits in *Scary Movie 4*. Kathleen Munroe has been in *The Dresden Files* and *Without A Trace*. Cindy Sampson featured in *Lexx*. Todd Thomson was in *Blade: The Series*, *Stargate SG-1* and *Atlantis*. Susie Wickstead was in *Stargate SG-1*. Desiree Zurowski's acting credits include *X-Men: The Last Stand*, *Stargate SG-1* and *Blood Ties*.

Cindy Sampson also appeared in 'Dream A Little Dream Of Me' (3-10).

BEHIND THE SCENES

Director Phil Sgriccia enjoys working with children. In the *Season Three Supernatural Companion* he explained that he'd often break up the kids' work day by bringing his fart machine in and putting it under people's chairs.

Sgriccia went on to say in the same interview that he added an extra, non-scripted moment – where Lisa Baeden kisses Dean – to the episode but didn't tell Jensen Ackles about it. Actress Cindy Sampson was a little flustered about it at first but then agreed that she'd do it after all. (She had to think about it?!)

In *The Official Supernatural Magazine* #1, Katie Cassidy explained how she was pranked in the scene with the ketchup bottle in the diner. Somebody unscrewed the top of the bottle a little so that on the third take, when she squeezed it the ketchup went all over the table, the plate and Katie's jacket. She's still not sure who loosened the top, but she has her suspicions.

MUSICAL INTERLUDE

* '40,000 Miles' – Goodnight City – when Dean shows up at Ben's birthday party[265].

---

265 It's been claimed that Steve Carlson's 'If It Ain't Easy' was used in this episode, but we've been unable to find it.

ANALYSIS

To *Supernatural*'s credit, it's taken the show two seasons to finally do an episode where the boys accidentally happen upon a case without really looking for it. And even this time, their reason for visiting Cicero has a direct relation to Dean's situation so it's not truly a coincidence. Which just goes to show how much thought is put into the writing of each episode, otherwise cases would be falling into the boys' laps virtually every week.

Nevertheless, this is still only an average *Supernatural* episode, with a couple of fine moments hidden in its depths. There aren't any real scares, no build up of tension, and the children come across as weird rather than particularly spooky. Dean's underlying story about his possible parentage of Ben is a small point stretched out too thinly, and overall the episode lacks a sense of weight and importance when compared with previous ones[266].

However, there are some good points to note. The changelings are creepy and disturbing, and their appearances kept to a minimum without overdoing them unnecessarily. And Dana Keel's descent into insanity is a fine piece of both writing and acting.

In *SFX* magazine (#180), Eric Kripke explained that he specifically wanted to look at this difficult topic – of a mother turning against her own children – because of the strength of the mother/child relationship and society's contempt when women don't give their children their utmost devotion. And the subject matter certainly lays down some uncomfortable undertones throughout the episode.

The other interesting developments are around the blonde girl. We may not know her name yet but we do at least know her demonic nature, and in a piece of true *Supernatural* subversion, unlike any demon we've met on the show before, she's here to help. While you're still trying to get your head round that one, she also highlights the fact that all of Mary Winchester's friends and family have been systematically wiped out, and Sam is at the centre of it somehow. There's nothing like a good mystery to pique the curiosity, and for the first time this season you get the feeling that the game is afoot again and you have no idea where it's going.

Sam doesn't seem too keen to tell his brother all about it yet either – which is something of a reversal, since it's usually Dean who clams up (and he was positively effervescing about his demon deal last week). Which just pings the curiosity even more. We also discover that Sam's visions have stopped since the yellow-eyed demon was killed, and that understandably he's still working (again behind his brother's back) to find a way out of Dean's deal. That his new demonic friend offers Sam help in saving

---

266 Although later seasons will build on the seeds planted here.

his brother makes it very possible that Sam will put differences aside and throw his lot in with the demon – so strong is his need to help Dean.

Meanwhile, for Dean, we see his desire to have kids emerge fully now that he has only a few months to live and he's reflecting on what he could have done with his life. We've seen hints of this before in 'Dead In The Water' (1-03) with Lucas, and more noticeably in 'What Is And What Should Never Be' (2-20) where Carmen tried to convince Dean to stay in the Wish World by offering him a family. By the end of 'The Kids Are Alright', Dean can see that, by leading the life he has, he's leaving people alive behind him, children who would not have grown up if he and Sam hadn't been there to help.

So there are some nice touches sprinkled throughout the episode, but just not quite enough of them.

VERDICT – 7.5 out of 10

EPISODE 3-03
BAD DAY AT BLACK ROCK

TRANSMISSION DATES
US first aired: 18 October 2007
UK first aired: 10 February 2008

CREDITS
Writer: Ben Edlund
Director: Robert Singer

RECURRING ROLES
Sterling K Brown (Gordon Walker), Jim Beaver (Bobby Singer), Lauren Cohan (Bela Talbot), Michael Massee (Kubrick)

GUEST STARS
Forbes Angus (Manager), Stephen Dimopoulos (Foster), Hrothgar Mathews (Grossman), Jon Van Ness (Creedy), John F Parker (Elderly Man), Christian Tessier (Wayne)

SYNOPSIS
A lucky rabbit's foot is stolen from a secret lock-up belonging to John Winchester. The boys track the thieves down, but the rabbit's foot luck is already working for Wayne, one of the thieves. In the fight for the foot, it touches Sam and the luck transfers to him. Meanwhile, Wayne's luck turns sour and he's killed in an accident. Sam becomes lucky while he has the foot, but Bela – a thief who procures unique items for a select clientele – takes it from him. Dean goes after Bela, and Sam's bad luck means that two hunters looking to kill him on behalf of fellow hunter Gordon Walker[267] find him and try to beat some answers out of him about the coming war. Dean saves Sam, then they burn the foot, but not before Bela tries to steal it again and shoots Sam in the shoulder.

CAN YOU SURVIVE TO THE TITLES?
Catching up with Gordon Walker in prison, we discover his need to kill Sam has only grown. No deaths before the credits, just Gordon convincing the other hunters, Kubrick and Creedy, to go after Sam for him.

---

267 Last seen being arrested at the end of 'Born Under A Bad Sign' (2-14)

LOCATION, LOCATION, LOCATION

Black Rock, outside Buffalo; Queens, New York.

LEGENDARY ROOTS

Why is it that a rabbit's foot is considered lucky? Well it certainly isn't very lucky for the rabbit that the foot comes from! The superstition is one of the oldest known to man, going as far back as the 600th Century BC, in ancient Totemism, when man believed that spirits inhabited the bodies of animals and that man was descended from animals. Each tribe was believed to come from a different species and would worship the appropriate animal. Rabbits were seen as the bringers of prosperity, the blessing of many children and a good harvest for the year, due to them being prolific breeders.

The lore says that the charm must be made from the left hind foot of a rabbit, and the foot should be removed while the animal is still alive. The rabbit must have been shot, preferably by a cross-eyed shooter and with a silver bullet, or otherwise captured in a cemetery. The phase of the moon is also important; some say the rabbit must be taken during a full moon, others during a new moon. More lore says that it has to be taken on a Friday, a Friday 13th or a rainy Friday.

As superstition goes, for the rabbit's foot to be of any luck it must be given away by the original owner. The receiver of the foot would receive the good luck. Bad luck would come if the original owner kept the foot or the receiver lost it.

SQUEEZE OF THE WEEK

Bela does a first rate job of flirting with the boys at the diner in her little waitress outfit, but even with the rabbit's foot neither of boys gets so much as a sniff at a squeeze.

SIBLING RIVALRY

Dean is most definitely upset about Sam's chat with Ruby and gives his brother a good telling off for even thinking about trusting a demon. In return, Sam justifies his actions by explaining that Ruby might be able to help with Dean's deal. The rest of the time Dean is just making sure that Sam hasn't hurt himself every time he falls over.

BODY COUNT

Thief Wayne's is the only death in the entire episode, and he trips on an empty beer bottle and skewers himself on a long, two-pronged meat fork through the back of the head and out through the mouth. And the gurgling sounds as he dies! Ew! Spectacularly gross!

TOOLKIT

- It's mostly *handguns* for the boys this time, but Bela also has *a Ouija Board* for contacting spirits and John Winchester has put *a tripwire and sawn-off shotgun* to good use protecting his lock-up.
- Other useful items include *security camera* footage to track down the car belonging to a couple of thieves, and *a lucky rabbit's foot* to protect you from getting shot when you break into someone's apartment.

MEMORABLE MOMENTS

The comedy moments in this episode are simply divine – from Sam losing his shoe down the drain when he tries to scrape the gum off the sole, through the numerous trips and falls, to setting fire to the sleeve of his jacket. Laugh out loud slapstick executed with a keen sense of timing from both lead actors.

It's great to see Dean enthusiastically stuffing his face with free food again, while Sam spends most of his 'good luck' time feeling embarrassed and his 'bad luck' time looking dejected, pathetic and cutely vulnerable.

And there's an excellent piece of acting from Sterling K Brown, where Kubrick explains to Gordon that God is guiding him towards Sam Winchester. Gordon's confused look is quickly replaced by an expression that seems to say 'Okay, he's a religious nut, but if he can help kill Sam Winchester, who cares?' Wonderfully done.

SPOOK RULES

- Curse boxes have symbols on the outside. These form part of the binding magic used to contain the powerful magic of the object in the box.
- A lucky rabbit's foot is real hoodoo, Old World magic.
- This foot was given its lucky properties by a Baton Rouge conjuror woman about a century ago, so the magic can last at least 100 years.
- They are created to kill people – when you touch the foot you get very good luck; if you lose ownership of the foot (if someone else touches it, or it is taken from your possession) then your luck turns so bad that you die within one week.
- Sooner or later, everyone loses the rabbit's foot.
- You can stop the foot's magic using a heavyweight cleansing ritual involving burning the foot with a mixture of bone ash and cayenne pepper.

DID YOU SPOT?

The cemetery was a set built in Heritage Park, Burnaby, near Vancouver.

GOING UNDERCOVER

Sam slips effortlessly into con artist mode when the call comes in on John Winchester's mobile about the break in at the lock-up. Within seconds, he is pretending to be Edgar Cayce (1877-1945), a renowned American psychic considered a major influence of the modern New Age movement.

CULTURAL REFERENCES

Kubrick: 'It's true. The Devil's Gate was opened in Wyoming – big. St Helens big.': Located in Washington State, Mount St Helen's is an active volcano that last erupted in 1980.

Dean: 'Until then I say we hit Vegas. Pull a little Rain Man.': *Rain Man* was a 1988 movie in which an autistic man, Raymond (Robert DeNiro) is reunited with his brother, Charlie (Tom Cruise). Charlie uses Raymond's mathematical genius to win in the Vegas casinos.

Creedy: 'It's like watching Jerry Lewis stacking chairs.': Jerry Lewis (1926-) is an American comedian who originally paired up with Dean Martin in the 1950s and '60s and later was an actor, film producer, writer, director and singer.

Dean: 'I'm Batman!': Batman is a DC comics superhero created in 1939. He is the secret identity of millionaire Bruce Wayne, who is trying to protect Gotham City. His adventures have been made into a TV series and a number of major blockbuster movies.

Dean: 'Say goodbye, wascally wabbit.': 'Wascally wabbit' was a phrase often used by Elmer Fudd when referring to Bugs Bunny in a series of Warner Bros cartoons. Elmer was trying to say 'rascally rabbit' but couldn't pronounce his Rs.

Bobby: 'Lugosi? Oh, crap. It's probably Bela.': Bela Lugosi (1882-1956) was an actor who played Dracula in the 1931 movie of the same name.

Kubrick's character could be named after Stanley Kubrick, who directed seemingly the *Supernatural* team's favourite movie, *The Shining*.

GOOFS AND FLUFFS

Gordon said in 'Hunted' (2-10) that he works alone, so when has he had the chance to work with Kubrick so many times?

That army medic must work miracles, because after he tends to Wayne's shoulder, within a *very* short amount of time Wayne's getting up off the floor and putting all his weight on it as he does so.

Why do the boys find Wayne (and Creedy) at their apartment during the period that Wayne is extremely lucky?

Haven't I Seen You Before?

Forbes Angus played a funeral director in *The X-Files* and has been in *Final Destination*, *Millennium* and *Dead Like Me*. Stephen Dimopoulos was in *Poltergeist: The Legacy*, *Stargate: Atlantis* and *Millennium*. Michael Massee has been in *Revelations* as Isaiah Haden, and in *Alias*, *The Crow* and *Se7en*. Hrothgar Mathews features in *Stargate SG-1*, *Seven Days* and *Night Visions*. Jon Van Ness has been in *Louis and Clark: The New Adventures of Superman*. John F Parker was in *The Tomorrow People* and *Poltergeist: The Legacy*. Christian Tessier appeared as Lt Tucker 'Duck' Clellan in *Battlestar Galactica*, Marmaduke 'Megabyte' Damon in *The Tomorrow People* and in *The Day After Tomorrow*.

Behind the Scenes

You might not be able to see it, but in John Winchester's lock-up there lurks a monkey prop from Harvelle's Roadhouse. In the *Season Three Supernatural Companion*, production designer John Marcynuk revealed that the monkey was hidden at the back as a silent pointer that John Winchester might have survived and brought it back from the remains of the burned-out bar.

The *Companion* also revealed another little touch in this episode: there is some sort of rabbit in every scene where good luck happens. The lottery cards have magician's hats with rabbits on them and there is a patch with a rabbit on the Vietnam vet's clothes.

Musical Interlude

- 'Women's Wear' – Daniel May – in the café where Bela overfills Sam's coffee.
- 'Vaya con Dios' – Les Paul & Mary Ford – Sam and Dean go questioning Grossman about Bella.

Analysis

When you take two strong storylines and weave them around each other seamlessly you tend to end up with an excellent final product, and this episode is exactly that. Opening and closing in the same place gives a pleasing sense of symmetry and cohesion to the proceedings, and there's a really nasty death thrown in for good measure when Wayne takes his dive in the kitchen. As soon as you see the beer bottle on the floor you know it's trouble. By the time you see the large fork, you're already wincing in anticipation.

But gore aside, this is really an episode of introductions for new characters and continuations for established characters

Several characters we already know move forward.

We catch up with Gordon Walker – he's bent on revenge against Sam (but not Dean) and roping in other hunters. And that's scary, because Gordon is a skilled hunter, now supported by someone on a religious crusade, both believing strongly that killing Sam is the right thing to do. Sam and Dean already have FBI Agent Henricksen after them, and Gordon and Kubrick are adding to the tension. There are sure to be some showdowns a-coming, and it's all going to be very intriguing.

We also gain a little more insight into John Winchester's character – amazing that a season after he died, his influence on the boys' lives is still being felt, his legacy never far from the surface and breaking through occasionally[268]. The lock-up almost sums up John's life in a single storage space. It's a very masculine room, full of supernatural artefacts, protective devices and weapons to kill the strange beings he encounters; it's all organised neatly with easy access to everything if needed urgently (although it's not obsessively organised; John saves his obsessive side for the yellow-eyed demon); and there's the other, more emotional, side of his life there too – his love for his boys. He's kept mementos of their childhood achievements – Sam's football trophy, Dean's first sawn-off shotgun – like any 'normal' parent would, and it's quietly touching. The only thing missing that you would have expected to see is something to remind him of Mary.

Sticking with the Winchester family, the other people moving forward are the boys.

Sam has come clean about his demonic female friend and she finally gets a name – Ruby. But Sam doesn't tell it all. Since Dean's already mad at him for chatting to demons, he doesn't mention Mary Winchester's family and friends getting wiped out; and given that he's not told Dean about the yellow-eyed demon dripping blood into his mouth when he was six months old either, it's interesting to watch the ongoing role reversal. Sam used to be the open one, but these days it's Dean who won't shut up.

And talking of Dean, he's expressing yet another major difference in opinion – this time over Ruby[269]. He doesn't trust her and doesn't think Sam should either, but she's got her hooks into Sam through his weak point, which is of course Dean, and he's not happy about it. Dean's also clearly worried about Sam and keeps asking if he's okay. He's possibly still suspicious of Sam going darkside, but more likely he's concerned that when Sam came back after dying he wasn't 100% Sam anymore. (Okay, so Dean's still holding this back from Sam, but old habits die hard don't they?)

But the last thing Sam needs is his brother having doubts and turning against him,

---

268 And will do again in Season Four.

269 The boys have disagreed over things a number of times before. including Sam deciding to go after Dad in 'Scarecrow' (1-11); and Sam wanting to find the other psychic kids in 'Hunted' (2-10).

because the new characters introduced in this episode end up either beating him up or shooting him in the shoulder.

Slapping Sammy around is Kubrick. He actually believes that Sam is just a regular hunter type at the start of the episode, but between Gordon's insistence and Kubrick's own apparently divinely influenced 'luck' at finding Sam, he starts to change his mind. It's only Dean's furry-foot-assisted arrival that saves Sam from a bullet between the eyes.

Sam however doesn't avoid the bullet from the other, major new character, Bela Talbot, and shooting Sam shows just how big a ruthless streak she has. We also find out a few other things about her in this episode: she's clearly a thief and gorgeous with it; she's self-centred, greedy, a skilful con-girl, sharp, quick thinking, good at planning, resourceful, likes Siamese cats, doesn't like hunters and believes the world can't be saved. Her own job, and how it intersects with the boys' world, should make for some interesting future clashes.

After a couple of weaker episodes, this strong one restores your faith in the *Supernatural* team and revives that recently flagging urge to know what happens next.

VERDICT – 8.5 out of 10

EPISODE 3-04
SIN CITY

TRANSMISSION DATES
US first aired: 25 October 2007
UK first aired: 17 February 2008

CREDITS
Writer: Robert Singer and Jeremy Carver
Director: Charles Beeson

RECURRING ROLES
Jim Beaver (Bobby Singer), Katie Cassidy (Ruby)

GUEST STARS
Julia Anderson (Woman at Bar), Gregory Bennett (Cop), Sasha Barrese (Casey), Robert Curtis Brown (Father Gil), Gavin Buhr (Max), Todd Curran (John), Don S Davis (Trotter), Dean Paul Gibson (Bartender), Phoebe Greyson (Nun), Matthew Harrison (Regie Mainard), Richard Keats (Andy Johnson), Elisa King (Cheryl), Martin Papazian (Richie)

SYNOPSIS
Omens indicate demons in Ohio but, on arriving, Sam and Dean can't find any evidence of demonic possessions, despite several cases of murder and suicide. Then fellow hunter Richie disappears and Dean tracks down the demon that killed him. It's possessing the body of a hot bartender, so Dean goes back to her place with her for a little exorcism. But Dean gets trapped with the demon in her basement and Sam turns up with the demon's lover. Only Bobby's timely arrival, with the now rejuvenated Colt (thanks to Ruby's help), saves the day.

CAN YOU SURVIVE TO THE TITLES?
Andy ventilates his skull with his own gun on the balcony in the church while Father Gil and one of the nuns watch from below. He claimed that God wasn't with them anymore, and he sure picked the quickest (and messiest) way to find out for real.

LOCATION, LOCATION, LOCATION
Elizabethville, Ohio.

LEGENDARY ROOTS

Lucifer is a translation from 'helel', the Hebrew word for brightness, and in Latin means light-bearer. He is also known by many other names such as Satan, the Devil and Beelzebub.

Lucifer was a guardian cherub, the highest position possible in heaven, and was placed on Earth to rule over it. Lucifer, the fallen angel, is referred to in a passage from the Bible (Isaiah 14:12-14): 'How you have fallen from heaven, O morning star, son of the dawn! You have been cast down to the earth, you who once laid low the nations! You said in your heart, "I will ascend to heaven; I will raise my throne above the stars of God; I will sit enthroned on the mount of assembly, on the utmost heights of the sacred mountain. I will ascend above the tops of the clouds; I will make myself like the Most High."'[270]

Lucifer and his angel army were thrown out of heaven after waging a campaign to rebel against God. Lucifer was eventually bound in chains and thrown into the abyss for a thousand years (Revelation 20:1-3).

SQUEEZE OF THE WEEK

Dean isn't interested in a hooker – with his looks he doesn't need to pay for what he wants – but hits it off with the hot bartender. And all she wants to do is twist his head off like she did with Richie.

SIBLING RIVALRY

Sam realises that his brother is distracted when he doesn't react at all when there's meat within striking distance.

And there's rivalry with Bobby when Dean asks Bobby to get the Colt fixed by that afternoon and Bobby promises that if it doesn't kill demons by then, it'll certainly kill Dean.

BODY COUNT

By the pool table in the bar, Regie puts a bullet right between the eyes of the guy who slept with his wife (and the victim didn't even get the chance to finish his game first!). Then hapless hunter Richie snuffs it when demon Casey shows him how he can see behind him with just a little bit of stretching – nicely gruesome with additional blood for a touch of atmosphere.

---

270 From the New International Version of the Bible.

TOOLKIT

- The *Colt*[271] returns to its former glory with a little TLC from Bobby and some insider know-how from Ruby. It's not clear how many bullets they have but there'd better be a lot of them, given how many demons they've got to kill.
- Dean's been tracking Richie via the *GPS* in Richie's phone[272] but his own phone doesn't get a signal after Casey has trapped them in the basement.
- It's a good job Sam carries a *wad of cash* with him, since he's had to pay off the bartender for information about Dean's whereabouts[273].

MEMORABLE MOMENTS

It shows just how easy it is to get it wrong when Sam breaks into the office at the back of the bar and discovers that Trotter and his henchman aren't demons. Sam's apologies for dowsing them with holy water are just so comical.

MOTEL MAYHEM

The brothers' room has a mirrored ceiling and one of those vibrating beds again but Dean doesn't get time to give it a whirl this time[274]. And the circles/bubbles motif is just psychedelic.

SPOOK RULES

- Some established Demon rules apply:
  - o Holy water is the best way to deter demons but it also gives you a reliable test to see if someone is possessed or not. If they smoulder when they come in contact with it, they're possessed.
  - o If demons are present in a town, they cause dry lightning and barometric pressure drops in the local vicinity.
  - o Demons can be contained in a Devil's Trap symbol so long as the lines are not broken anywhere.
- New demon rules are also emerging:
  - o Demons have a cruel sense of fun, so it's entirely possible that one could possess a host, force them to blow their brains out and then move out and find another host. A bit like stealing a car for a joyride and then torching it.

---

271 Last seen in 'All Hell Breaks Loose: Part Two' (2-22).

272 A technique that Dean also used to find Sam when he went missing in 'Born Under A Bad Sign' (2-14).

273 But then they know they need to carry cash since Dean had to do a similar thing with the motel manager to find Sam in 'Born Under A Bad Sign' (2-14).

274 The last time they had a vibrating bed, Dean barely had time to go hunting, 'Houses Of The Holy' (2-13).

o   Some trapped demons are still capable of using their power (to create a strong wind, cave a basement in etc) even though they are stuck within a Devil's Trap.
o   Demons believe in a higher power: the light bringer, Lucifer.
o   Demons can form relationships and stay together for centuries probably as a monogamous couple.
o   Demons can like humans and decide not to kill them after all.

DID YOU SPOT?

Father Gil has made a little crucifix out of his stirrer sticks in the bar.

The boys are maintaining their score against the demons. At the end of 'The Magnificent Seven' (3-01), it was four dead innocent people to the demons and five dead innocents to Team Winchester. After this episode the demons get one (Richie) and Team Winchester get three (Bobby shoots Ruby's meat-suit and Sam gets Casey and Father Gil). So Team Winchester increase their lead to eight innocents to the demons' five. Hmmm.

GOING UNDERCOVER

The boys are in the insurance investigator suits again as they quiz the Father about Andy's death. Sam has to keep the bluff going during the drive to Casey's house, where Dean is trapped, as the Father asks him about his 'work'; and for someone who is such a skilled con-artist, Sam is looking very uncomfortable lying to a priest. Bet he'd be fine if he knew the Father's actually possessed by a demon.

CULTURAL REFERENCES

After the people were killed in the hobby shop, Sam asks the Father if he knew the man who did it, Father Gil: 'Sure. Tony Perkins. Good man.': Anthony Perkins (1932-1992) starred as Norman Bates in the Alfred Hitchcock horror classic *Psycho* (1960).

Dean's thinking that there's got to be some demons in South Beach, Sam: 'Sorry, Hef. Maybe next time.': Referring to Hugh Hefner, famous for founding the Playboy empire.

Sam: 'All of a sudden, this town turns into Margaritaville?': 'Margaritaville' is a 1977 Jimmy Buffet song about a laid-back lifestyle in a tropical climate.

Casey: 'Sure. You Winchester boys are famous. Not Lohan famous, but, you know …': A reference to Lindsay Lohan, a young actress who is also known for her partying wild child ways.

Casey: 'And humans are such a lovable bunch? Dick Cheney.': Dick Cheney (1941-) served as the 46th Vice President of the United States from 2001 to 2009 in the administration of George W Bush.

Dean: 'Poor jerk. Only thing possessing him was a sixer of Pabst.': Pabst Brewing Company was founded in 1844 in America.

For the record, the ingredients of a Hurricane cocktail are:

- 2 oz light rum
- 2 oz dark rum
- 2 oz passion fruit juice
- 1 oz orange juice
- juice of a half a lime
- 1 tbsp simple syrup
- 1 tbsp grenadine
- orange slice and cherry for garnish

GOOFS AND FLUFFS

When Sam and Dean first arrive in Elizabethville to discover something more than a boarded-up factory town, Sam gets out of the car, then starts putting the second (brown) bag on his shoulder. When the shot cuts to a new angle, the bag is back down at his side and he lifts it up again.

How does Dean track Richie's GPS on his phone if Dean is struggling to get a signal himself in the basement, even when he is standing by the grating?

If Casey has the power to cave in the basement ceiling so she can trap Dean and herself in the basement, why doesn't she crack the floor with the Devil's Trap drawn on it at the same time?

HAVEN'T I SEEN YOU BEFORE?

Julia Anderson has been in *Stargate Universe*, *Tru Calling* and *Stargate: Atlantis*. Gregory Bennett was in *Scary Move 4* and *Stargate SG-1*. Sasha Barrese can be seen in *The Ring* and *Hellraiser: Inferno*. Robert Curtis Brown's credits include *Spider-man 3*, *Red Dragon* and *Medium*. Gavin Buhr has been in *Stargate SG-1* and *Dead Like Me* and as a stunt man in *I, Robot* and *Fantastic Four*. Don S Davis played Major General George Hammond in *Stargate SG-1*, Major Garland Briggs in *Twin Peaks* and appeared in *The X-Files*. Dean Paul Gibson featured in *Millennium*, *Andromeda* and *Blood Ties*. Matthew Harrison's credits include *Night at the Museum: Battle of the Smithsonian*, *Watchmen* and *Thir13en Ghosts*. Richard Keats acted in *The Day the Earth Stood Still*, *Smallville* and *Blood Ties*. Elisa King was in *Blade: The Series*, *Smallville* and *Blood Ties*. Martin Papazian has starred in *Charmed*, *24* and *Dexter*.

BEHIND THE SCENES

According to the *Season Three Supernatural Companion*, this episode was based on the movie *Enemy Mine* (1985), where a human and an alien are stranded on a planet together. But writer Jeremy Carver said that executive producer Bob Singer went straight back and reminded everyone that *Enemy Mine* was based on *Hell in the Pacific* (1968) where, during World War Two, an American and a Japanese soldier were stranded together on an island and have to learn to get along. This episode just uses a demon as the bad guy instead.

MUSICAL INTERLUDE

- 'Run Through The Jungle' – Creedence Clearwater Revival – Sam and Dean meet Richie at the Trotter's bar.
- 'Bad Seed' – Brimstone Howl – Sam and Dean in the bar talking about Richie's disappearance.
- 'Nikki' – Sasquatch – Dean gets hit on by a prostitute then leaves with the hot female bartender.
- 'Did You See It' – Mother Superior – Sam looks for Dean at the bar and pays the male bartender for information.

ANALYSIS

Along with 'The Magnificent Seven' (3-01), this episode gives possibly the best illustration of how *Supernatural* has changed from the seasons before. 3-01 delivered a huge amount of info, as does 'Sin City'. They both suffer a little from having to take the time to explain situations to everyone, but Season Three no longer has simple storylines. As the *Supernatural* universe has grown, so has the level of complexity around the main characters, and with the introduction of Ruby and Bela, it's only going to get more complicated. As a result, the writers are going to have to take time out to explain things. It's no longer a case of saving a life, stopping the hellhounds (or whatever) and having some angst over John's death. Now, we've got Dean's limited timeline, Sam's attempts to save Dean via Ruby, the hunters trying to figure out how to defend themselves and kill demons, details about what the enemy are up to, and concern over whether Sam came back 100% Winchester. Add in the FBI and Kubrick and Gordon and it's a wonder the boys can sleep at night.

But sleep they do, unlike some of the citizens of Elizabethville who are enjoying a lot of nocturnal vice and murdering each other. The new angle on the humans-corrupting-themselves theme that started in 'The Magnificent Seven' (3-01) is explained by Demon Casey and involves simply nudging humans in the right direction – with a little booze and sex humans will walk into Hell with a huge smile on their face.

This is a symbolic situation and ties in with Sam. Humans can tumble into evil ways without realising it. The implication is that Sam teeters on a similar precipice and it might not take much (like some noble desire to save his brother, maybe) to tip him over too. Can he resist or will he – like the people of Elizabethville – stray from the path?

It's hard to tell at this stage, but Sam is definitely changing. He's becoming harder, more accepting of the violence that surrounds his role. There's Ruby warning him that he'll have to do things that go against his nature in order to save Dean, but he's on that road already. With Dean becoming softer and not wanting the female demon to be wasted (because she tried to save him) it's like the two of them have swapped personalities.

Dean's experiences are transforming him too. He says it's liberating to have an end in sight so he doesn't have to worry about the future. He's enquiring about hell and trying to put a brave face on it, but his eyes are a dead giveaway: he's terrified. Like Casey says, Dean hasn't exactly been nice to the demons so they are likely to make the most of seeing him in hell. But Dean's still worried about Sam and openly shares his concern with Bobby, who lies just as unconvincingly as Dean himself does about thinking Sam's okay. It's like they don't want to believe he's changed, because the implications of what they might have to do if he has are too hard to contemplate yet. Is this possibly going to drive a wedge between them this season? Could it be groundwork for something coming up in future episodes? It's not clear.

What is clearer now is the way the war should have turned out if the yellow-eyed demon had survived and Sam had stepped up to the plate. But neither of those things happened, so we're left with a war without a front. Which is really an analogy for the real-life war on terror we've had since 9/11. The bad guys are out there, somewhere, anywhere, and you don't know where they're going to strike next.

And with some of those demons out for Sam's blood, it's hard to trust demon Ruby's intentions. So she does Bobby a good turn and helps him with the Colt and they manage to get it working again. Which is useful under the circumstances – let's hope Bobby can turn out enough bullets to take out the entire set of escapees from hell.

So plenty to mull over in 'Sin City'. There may be a lack of action and some slightly flat demonic dabblings with the town's populace but it remains a significant contributor to the emerging mythology.

VERDICT – 8 out of 10

EPISODE 3-05
BEDTIME STORIES

TRANSMISSION DATES
US first aired: 1 November 2007
UK first aired: 24 February 2008

CREDITS
Writer: Cathryn Humphris
Director: Mike Rohl

GUEST STARS
Mary Black (Grandmother), Chris Cochrane (Edmond), Michael Coleman (Jack Baycon), Christopher Cousins (Dr Garrison), Victoria Duffield (Little Red), Aron Eastwood (Wolfman), Patrick Gilmore (Ken Watson), Ava Rebecca Hughes (Snow White/Young Callie), Peter Jenkins (Attending Doctor), Derek Lowe (EMT), Sandra McCoy (Crossroad Demon), Maxine Miller (Old Woman), Libby Osler (Cinderella), Malcolm Scott (Kyle), Tracy Spiridakos (Callie), Kimberley Warnat (Julie)

SYNOPSIS
Three construction workers are attacked by a savage animal and Sam and Dean come to investigate, expecting to hunt a werewolf. Then a hiking couple are attacked by an old lady in the deep woods and a fairytale theme (the three little pigs and Hansel and Gretel so far) starts to appear. The spirit of a little girl haunting the attack locations leads Sam and Dean to Callie, the comatose daughter of Dr Garrison. Using the fairytale of Snow White, Callie is trying to tell her father that she was poisoned by her stepmother, but she's lashing out and killing people because no-one will listen. While Dean tries to save the latest victim – little red riding hood – Sam tries to convince the doctor about Callie's message. Once her father knows the truth, Callie passes away and stops the killing. Later that night Sam meets with the crossroads demon to discuss Dean's contract. Before killing the demon, he discovers that the contract is owned by another demon – a very powerful one.

CAN YOU SURVIVE TO THE TITLES?
There's gore splashing all over the place as two of the Baycon Brothers get picked off by the nasty, unseen, growling prowling monster at a construction site.

LOCATION, LOCATION, LOCATION
Maple Springs, New York; Cumberland County Central Library.

LEGENDARY ROOTS
The Brothers Grimm were Jacob Ludwig Carl (1785-1863) and Wilhelm Carl (1786-1859), and together they wrote over 200 fairy tales. Their first volume *Kinder und Hausmärchen (Children's and Household Tales)* was published in 1812 and contained 86 folktales. Further editions followed, adding numerous tales, with the final, 7th edition published in 1857, containing the full 200 fairy tales plus ten children's legends.

Their tales are famous throughout the world and have been made into movies, television programmes, plays and pantomimes, as well as simply read to generations of children. Among the many famous stories are those about Little Red Riding Hood, Cinderella, Sleeping Beauty, Rapunzel and Rumpelstiltskin.

SQUEEZE OF THE WEEK
A lean time for both boys – there's nothing happening in the squeeze department at all.

SIBLING RIVALRY
Sam's determination to help Dean out of his deal is causing some serious problems between the two of them. Dean's got to shouting point, so Sam's decided to sneak around behind his back if that's what it takes. The problem is that Sam wants to use the Colt to kill the demon Dean made the deal with, but Dean doesn't know if it's going to work and won't risk Sam's life on a 'maybe'.

It's not long before Sam's trying to send Dean on another guilt trip. This is when they're at the hospital talking to Kyle after the building site attacks, where Sam pointedly admits that he can't imagine anything worse than seeing his brother get killed.

Dean ignores it all and contents himself with bitching back at Sam in his own unique non-PC way and calling Sam gay for knowing so much about Cinderella and her pumpkin.

BODY COUNT
A busier episode than we've had recently. Following the two wolfie chew-toys in the opener, there's a maniacal granny taking a carving knife to her guests and a particularly brutal attack on a different granny outside a supermarket.

Then Sam takes out the crossroads demon that did the deal with Dean. Which takes the Team Winchester kill score to nine (possessed) innocents while the demons remain at five innocents.

Toolkit

- A *notebook and pencil* are very useful if you're going to pose as a police artist, but it helps if you can actually draw to a decent level of competence. Stick men pictures are not going to convince many people.
- A *lock pick* will help to release the poor girl whose stepmother has flipped, started beating her and handcuffed her to the kitchen furniture.
- A pair of *knitting scissors* are essential to play the part of the woodsman in Little Red Riding Hood. Then when you're attacked by the big, bad Wile E Coyote-tattooed bad guy, you might stand a chance.
- The *Colt* gets its second outing this season as we say farewell to the very hot but very evil crossroads demon, courtesy of a bullet between the eyes.

Memorable Moments

A lot of little moments to enjoy in this one. The murders are all convincing, although the granny-beating is the most horrific and the murdering granny verges on the absurd. The opening argument is downright hostile, and the death of Callie quite touching. But nothing beats the shock of the closing scenes as Sam takes out the crossroads demon so callously.

Spook Rules

- If you're in a coma, your spirit can still wander out of your body, possess people and control them – even to the point of making them commit murder. This is especially likely if you are in the coma because your stepmother forced you to drink bleach and no-one knows it was her fault. That kind of thing can really annoy you and make you lash out in anger.
- It helps if you have something to inspire your killing spree, and the original Grimm's Fairy Tales are a suitably gruesome place to start, especially if your own plight matches one of the fairy tales like, say, that of Snow White.
- When you're watching the bloody results of your possessing efforts, you can be seen by anyone in the vicinity.
- Your spirit form can disappear whenever you want it to, and if required you can leave behind a very real object, like a red apple, to give clues to the people helping you.
- You can be dissuaded from your spree if you can get your father to believe the truth about how you came to be in the coma in the first place.
- Once the truth is known you can pass over to the other side in peace.
- The people you have possessed have no memory of their actions after you leave their body.

DID YOU SPOT?

The crossroads demon is played by Jared Padalecki's girlfriend of the time, Sandra McCoy.

The three little piggy construction workers are called the Baycon Brothers. You can just make out their logo on the bottom left hand corner of the 'Once Upon a Time ...' billboard in the opening sequence.

GOING UNDERCOVER

Dean and Sam use the aliases Detective (Robert) Plant and Detective (Jimmy) Page from the County Sheriff's Department to gain access to the hospital and the victims of the supposed werewolf. Robert Plant and Jimmy Page are former members of the English rock band Led Zeppelin, formed in 1968.

CULTURAL REFERENCES

Dean: 'Could like Mischa Barton. *The Sixth Sense*, not *The OC*.': Mischa Barton (1986-) starred in *The Sixth Sense* (1999) as the ghost of a young girl poisoned by her mother and also features in *The OC* (2003-2006).

Kyle: 'There was one more thing he had a – a tattoo on his arm of a cartoon character. It's, uh, it's the guy who's chasing the Roadrunner.'; Dean: 'Wile E Coyote!': Roadrunner and Wile E Coyote are Looney Tunes and Merry Melodies cartoon characters that first appeared 1949. The stories involve Wile E Coyote hatching a variety of plans to catch the Roadrunner but always, always failing.

Sam: 'Oh yeah, yeah, yeah, uh, Munchausen Syndrome by Proxy.': Munchausen Syndrome by Proxy involves the exaggeration or fabrication of illnesses or symptoms by a primary caretaker as an attention-seeking technique.

Crossroads Demon: 'Doth protest too much if you ask me.': The correct quote is 'The lady doth protest too much, methinks' from William Shakespeare's *Hamlet* (1599-1601).

HAVEN'T I SEEN YOU BEFORE?

Mary Black featured in *The Exorcism of Emily Rose*, *The Fog* and *Millennium*. Michael Coleman has been in *A Town Called Eureka*, *Millennium* and *Blood Ties*. Christopher Cousins was in *The Grudge 2*, *Stargate SG-1* and *Joan of Arcadia*. Victoria Duffield's credits include *Painkiller Jane* and *Smallville*. Aron Eastwood was a stunt man in *Underworld: Rise of the Lycans*. Patrick Gilmore played Dale Volker in *Stargate Universe*, *A Town Called Eureka* and *Reaper*. Peter Jenkins was in *Painkiller Jane*. Derek Lowe has appeared in *The X-Files*, *The 4400* and *Andromeda*. Sandra McCoy was in *Nite Tales: The Movie* and *House Of Fears*. Maxine Miller was in *Millennium*, *Reaper* and *The Outer Limits*. Libby Osler has also been in *Stargate: Atlantis*. Malcolm Scott featured in *White Noise 2: The Light*, *The 4400* and *Stargate SG-1*. Tracy Spiridakos was in *The Bionic Woman*. Kimberley Warnat's credits include *The Outer Limits*, *Millennium* and *Stargate: Atlantis*.

Behind the Scenes
Sandra McCoy was very emotional when they shot her scenes with then boyfriend Jared. They didn't rehearse the scene together until they got on the set and everyone thought it was great but McCoy was so nervous that as soon as she was alone with Jared, she started crying and he had to calm her down. [*Season Three Supernatural Companion*]

McCoy also struggled with the weather. She tried to acclimatise between shots rather than putting a jacket back on to keep warm. So she spent the down time shivering with her teeth chattering and had to resort to squeezing her thumbs during the shots to keep her teeth under control.

Musical Interlude
All music was written specifically for this episode.

Analysis
It's starting to become more obvious as the season goes on that the monsters-of-the-week are changing in nature and the show's own mythology is coming more to the fore. So far, there's been only one new monster – the Changelings[275] – with the other episodes tending mostly towards demons with a rabbit's foot thrown in. The shift to demons is understandable given the mass exodus from hell at the end of Season Two, and there have been new characters like Bela to introduce, but somehow the stories in Season Three just haven't been as strong as those in the previous seasons.

This latest episode returns to the monster-of-the-week approach, giving us fairy tale killings by yet another angry spirit, but sadly it continues the trend of weaker stories.

The problem perhaps comes from a couple of places. First is the familiarity of the subject matter. *Supernatural* has done its fair share of vengeful spirits, and while this is a new twist on it – the spirit belongs to a girl who is still alive – it's pretty familiar territory. Also, the fairy tales are well known to pretty much everyone, so rather than discovering fascinating facts about a strange and unusual creature, we're probably already ahead of the writers from the moment they mention Cinderella etc.

---

275 'The Kids Are Alright' (3-02).

Secondly, the scares are missing again. There's no substantial sense of tension in the episode, short of a need to stop the murderer before more people get killed. And the show's trademark dark, moody sets and lighting are nowhere to be seen either[276]. In the scenes where the old lady hacks the walker to death, even though the content of that scene is very horrific, it's just not scary.

Horrific scenes do seem to be becoming more prevalent in Season Three though. Following on from the mother who tried to kill her own child back in 'The Kids Are Alright' (3-02), we now have the aforementioned mad butcher granny getting down and dirty, followed by the brutal battering of an innocent granny in the supermarket car park. This is pretty dark stuff and probably shows up someone's sweet old lady phobia, especially since we'll return to the old granny theme in later episodes[277].

But perhaps the most subtle and horrific situation going on is between Sam and Dean, where each of them is trying to avoid watching the other one die, while looking on helplessly, unable to stop it happening.

Sam is rebelling again and won't listen to Dean telling him what to do – anymore than he'd take his father telling him what to do in the past. There's a definite stubborn streak in him when he's decided to do something (like go to college) and he won't let some else's opinion stop him doing what he thinks is the right thing. He's got a real cold spot for demons now too – not only did they take his father, but now they're trying to take Dean – and he seems to have a certain sense of achievement and enjoyment in killing them, as demonstrated at the end of 'Sin City' (3-04) and again here. He doesn't care about the innocent person being possessed, he no longer sees them or emphasises with him as he used to in the past. All he has is his rage and need to kill them. There's a lot of focus on these changes in Sam and the fact that he may not have returned 100% Winchester after his trip to the other side and back, but where his journey goes from here can only be wondered about. We can also wonder about the interesting new development concerning Dean's contract and how it is being held by another demon. This new information cranks up the intrigue and prods the curiosity pleasantly as Dean's future becomes potentially darker that it was before.

And Dean, we find out, is actually worried about that future. He may be concerned about Sam and his possible slide to the darkside, but we finally get a glimpse beneath his bravado to the terror that lurks below. The reality of his deal has hit home. What he does with the time he has left to him is going to be very interesting to watch.

VERDICT – 8 out of 10

---

276 See the **Season Three Overview** for more on this.

277 'A Very Supernatural Christmas' (3-08).

Episode 3-06
Red Sky at Morning

Transmission Dates
US first aired: 8 November 2007
UK first aired: 2 March 2008

Credits
Writer: Laurence Andries
Director: Cliff Bole

Recurring Role
Lauren Cohan (Bela Talbot)

Guest Stars
Steve Archer (Security Guard), Michael Denis (Waiter), Ellen Geer (Gertrude Case),
Peter Grier (Ghost Sailor), Steve Lawlor (Ghost Captain), Robert Moloney (Peter
Warren), Samantha Simmonds (Sheila Case), Tobias Slezak (Todd Warren)

Synopsis
Sheila Case goes jogging, sees a spooky clipper ship in the harbour then later sees a
spooky sailor in her shower who kills her. The ghost murders another two victims
and Sam and Dean realise that they're dealing with a ghost ship, since all the victims
saw the clipper before they died. All the victims also killed a member of their own
family – accidentally or otherwise. Bela Talbot, in the area sponging off Sheila's aunt,
identifies the clipper and the ghost, and she and the boys go undercover to steal the
ghost's remains so they can salt and burn them. But Bela double-crosses Sam and
Dean and sells the sailor's remains instead. When she sees the clipper herself, Sam
summons both the ghost and the man who killed him, his brother, so the ghost can
get his revenge and release Bela from certain death.

Can You Survive to the Titles?
It's a wonder any of us get in the shower at all these days, given all the murders that
take place while we're blithely soaping ourselves down. In this case, Sheila realises
that she should have gone for the one-person shower instead – it may be a bit more
cramped, but at least there wouldn't be any room for psycho killer ghosts with water
fetishes.

LOCATION, LOCATION, LOCATION

From the licence plate on Peter Warren's car, it's possibly Rhode Island; they're definitely at the Sea Pines Maritime Museum; and according to Gordon in 'Fresh Blood' (3-07) these events take place in Massachusetts.

LEGENDARY ROOTS

One of the most famous ghost ships was the brigantine merchant ship *Mary Celeste*, which was found in mid-ocean bound towards Genoa on 4 December 1872 completely abandoned and unmanned. The ship had set sail the on 7 November 1872 with seven crew, Captain Briggs, his wife and daughter. The ship was discovered by Captain Morehouse in first class condition with sails, mast and hull intact, the cargo (1,700 barrels of commercial alcohol) lashed in place and enough fresh water and food to last six months. The last entry in the ship's log was entered on 25 November stating that they had reached the island of St Mary in the Azores.

No satisfactory explanation has been found for why or how the ship was abandoned or how it had managed to sail to where it was discovered with no crew. Suggestions include mutiny, piracy, underwater earthquake or a large sea creature, but none of these can account for the condition the ship was found in.

A Hand of Glory is the preserved hand of a murderer – either the right or the left depending on sources, although the general consensus is to use the hand that committed the crime. The hand should be cut off while the body is still hanging from the gallows.

Using a strip of burial shroud the hand is wrung dry of all remaining blood, then placed in an earthenware pot in a concoction of salt, long peppers, crushed black pepper, crushed sesame seed, zimat and salt petre, where it is marinated for two weeks. The hand is then placed in the sun to dry, or placed in a hot oven that is fired with vervain and fir. The drying hand is then moulded into a fist shape with enough space to hold a candle. But you can't use any old candle in a Hand of Glory. The only ones that will work are made from the fat of another murderer, with a wick made from his hair.

SQUEEZE OF THE WEEK

Bela is flirting with both of the boys, calling Sam cute (and a drama queen) and suggesting to Dean, after she sees him in his tuxedo, that they should have angry sex. But instead of following through with Dean, she just double-crosses them and then lobs them a wad of money when they save her life.

SIBLING RIVALRY

The anger between the boys is still burning fiercely as Dean figures out what Sam's been up to behind his back with the crossroads demon and the new Colt. Then Dean tries to explain that he understands how Sam feels, but he just gets more vitriol in return for not trying to find a way out of his deal himself.

Between the harsh words, they do take some time to have a little friendlier banter here and there. When discussing Gert and her obvious attraction to Sam, Dean comments that the old girl is crazy then teases his brother when he sticks up for Gert's belief in ghosts.

BODY COUNT

Another young lady discovers how dangerous jogging is at the start of the show[278]. Seeing the ghost ship results in her being attacked in the shower, where she drowns. Businessman Todd Warren dies at home in the bathroom, then next day his brother Peter dies in his car, also of drowning. Bela comes close to being victim number four, but Sam's smart idea to summon the murderer and his brother (who ordered his death back in 1859) allows Bela to live.

TOOLKIT

- Since they're dealing with a spook once more, the *salt-loaded shotgun* is an essential item to have around, but the *salt, lighter* and *lighter fuel* (for salting dem bones baby) are left in the kit bag on account of Bela stealing the ghost's remains.
- Certain soft skills – including *looking damn hot in a tuxedo*, being able to *disable an alarm* and being able to tolerate *being groped by an old lady* for a hour or so – are essential when retrieving the remains of the ghost's body; and a little more distrust in one's allies might mean you hold onto said remains a little longer too.
- Being able to *complete a long Latin summoning ritual in all sorts of weather* – including rain and high winds – will help you save a life here and there.
- *Candles* help with creating the right atmosphere for the ritual (at least until the rain starts) and some *blood in a bowl* and *a lock of hair* will help give the ritual some kick, especially if you've got the hair inside a pentagram drawn on a grave monument.

MEMORABLE MOMENTS

Some great humorous moments in this one – Dean hyperventilating when he thinks the Impala has been stolen; Sam getting groped by the old lady; and Dean being totally helpless in the face of free food whatever the situation[279].

---

278 Another jogger was murdered in 'Faith' (1-12) by the reaper.

279 As he was in Bugs (1-08), 'Nightmare' (1-14), 'Provenance' (1-19), 'Tall Tales' (2-15), 'Hollywood Babylon' (2-18) and 'All Hell Breaks Loose' (2-21/2-22).

Seeing the boys in tuxedos creates something of a drool problem too.

There's a top scare when Todd is leaning over his bath of dirty water and the hand thrusts out to grab his throat.

But by far the most impressive moment is the ghost-on-ghost showdown as the captain and his brother crash into each other in slow motion. Quite simply the single most stunning special effect since the show started.

THE CAR'S THE STAR

The Impala gets towed away after Bela gets her hands on it but it's soon retrieved intact before the weapons are found in the trunk. It probably appreciated the break, since all the boys seem to do while they're in the car at the moment is argue about what Sam's doing to try to save Dean.

And it seems people who insult the Impala are marked for bad things – Pete Warren calls it a crappy car and is dead within five minutes of passing comment.

SPOOK RULES

- Ghosts often choose a reappearance time period that is personally relevant to them. For this spook, he was 37 years old when his brother had him hanged, so he comes back every 37 years to take revenge on similar people.
- The apparitions of old wrecks appear all over the world, and almost all of them are death omens: *The S S Violet*, the *Griffin* and the *Flying Dutchman*. Once you've seen one you just pucker up and kiss your ass goodbye.
- To find a way of stopping the murderous spook on a ghost ship, you need to first identify the ship you are dealing with.
- Ghosts can affect mechanical items – they can stop your car from working so you can't run away from them[280].
- A ghost can fill your lungs with water just by touching your face (or wrestling with you in the shower).
- When an angry ghost is faced with the brother who killed him, they'll destroy each other in a spectacular display of shattered water droplets.

DID YOU SPOT?

This is the second time the boys have squatted in deserted property[281].

Ellen Geer – who plays Gert Case – might be familiar from her previous role as

---

280 The last time this happened was with the Impala in 'Roadkill' (2-16).

281 First time being in 'Bugs' (1-08).

the Elderly Piper in the series *Charmed* (episode 'Forever Charmed' in 2006).

The location for the posh party is the same house used in 'Playthings' (2-11).

GOING UNDERCOVER

The boys are from the Sheriff's Department again, when talking both to Gert and to Peter Warren about the deaths of their relatives.

CULTURAL REFERENCES

Sam: 'It's not your birthday ... Happy Purim?': Purim commemorates the time when the Jewish people living in Persia were saved from extermination by the courage of a young Jewish woman called Esther.

Gert: 'This will get their tongues wagging, hey my Adonis.': Adonis in Greek mythology was a handsome youth loved by both Aphrodite and Persephone, and the name is now often used to describe an attractive young man.

Dean: 'Screw you.'; Bela: 'Very Oscar Wilde.': Oscar Wilde (1854-1900) was a famous writer, renowned for his witticisms, who spent two years in prison for being gay. His famous plays include *The Importance Of Being Ernest*.

Sam: 'Tell me I didn't get groped all night by Mrs Havisham for nothing.': Miss Havisham is an aged spinster who takes an interest in Pip in *Great Expectation* by Charles Dickens.

Peter: 'A smuggling vessel, with the rakish topsail, a barkentine rigging, angel figurehead on the bow.': The *barkentine* is a type of vessel rather than just the rigging. This type of vessel has at least three masts, and features fore-and-aft rigging on all mast except for the foremast – which features square rigging.

Sam: 'No, not really. I mean, both brothers are Duke University grads.': Duke University was established in 1838, and is a private research university located in Durham, North Carolina, United States.

Sam: 'So, they were brothers, very Cain and Abel.': Cain and Abel were the two sons of Adam and Eve in the Bible. Cain, a crop farmer, committed the first murder by killing his brother Abel after God rejected his offerings but accepted the animal sacrifices from Abel.

GOOFS AND FLUFFS

While waiting for Dean to come downstairs in his tux, Bela says Gert and Sam must be halfway to the party by now. If that is the case, how do Bela and Dean manage to arrive in front of Gert and Sam?

When Sheila is in the shower and the spook is in the bathroom with her, she opens the shower door to check what made the noise and she doesn't have any soap in her hair. In the next shot, she's washing the lather out seemingly without putting any in to start with.

It's not clear, but the assumption is that Sheila is in the shower after her jog round the harbour. Gert says that she came home and discovered Sheila's body, which means she was probably out when Sheila came home after running. So when did Sheila have time to tell Gert about the ghost ship?

HAVEN'T I SEEN YOU BEFORE?

Steve Archer has appeared in *Stargate: Atlantis*, *The Exorcism of Emily Rose* and *Stargate SG-1*. Michael Denis was in *Smallville*. Ellen Geer has been in *Star Trek: The Next Generation*, *Medium* and *Charmed*. Peter Grier played in *The Outer Limits*, *Tru Calling* and *Jeremiah*. Steve Lawlor starred in *Battlestar Galactica*, *Painkiller Jane* and *Smallville*. Robert Maloney featured in *The X-Files*, *Millennium* and *The 4400*. Tobias Slezak's credits include *Stargate SG-1*, *Stargate: Atlantis* and *A Town Called Eureka*.

BEHIND THE SCENES

According to visual effects co-ordinator Ivan Hayden in the *Season Three Supernatural Companion*, the impressive ghost annihilation effect was created by a combination of images, where the team popped water balloons and threw water and shot them at a thousand frames per second, used actual 3D water elements inside the computer and also some live action scenes with the actors.

Lauren Cohan also explains in the *Companion* that she had problems with her line, 'He was tried aboard ship in a kangaroo court and hanged. He was 37.' She ended up saying all sorts of different kangaroo versions of the correct line, and of course Padalecki and Ackles kept mimicking her after she fluffed each take.

Cohan also said, in *The Official Supernatural Magazine #2*, that Padalecki was playing around like a big kid with the mousetraps on the set of the Winchester safe-house, throwing them at people until he caught his own finger in one of the traps

MUSICAL INTERLUDE

All music was written specifically for this episode.

ANALYSIS

On the surface, if you don't think about it too hard, this is an entertaining enough episode with a liberal sprinkle of humour, some great James Bond-style outfits and a stunning special effects sequence at the end.

The humour is spread throughout the episode from the moment Dean starts hyperventilating about the car being stolen and his ribbing of Sam about his new girlfriend Gert; through Bela objectifying Dean in his suit, and Dean being unable to resist free food again; to Sam downing his champagne in one when faced with an evening being groped by 'Mrs Havisham'. It helps the episode to bubble along nicely, as what initially looks like being a 'straight salt and burn dem bones' case twists itself around Bela's presence to become far more intriguing.

And this really is Bela's episode, with much of the focus being about the boys' opinion of her versus her own justifications for what she does. We get to see more about how she works when she's not pointing guns at people, how easily she can play a con and how well she can manipulate people.

She clearly uses her brains and utilises the Impala as a distraction to keep the boys out of her way, although she can't resist a bit of boasting about it when they discover it's missing. If she was truly ruthless, she wouldn't have told them where it had gone.

She's not got any problem conning old women out of money for fake séances – although given that she genuinely contacted the spirits who had touched the rabbit's foot[282], maybe they aren't all fake séances after all. But whatever cons she does pull, she justifies to herself by insisting that she provides comfort for her victims so they do get something out of it. She doesn't see herself as a bad person at all, rather she thinks her motives are purer than the boys' obsessive revenge ideals since hers is just a business transaction.

But she's obviously not that pure given that she must have spilled family blood – by accident or intentionally – somewhere in her past. And she's not giving any clues away as to what happened either. Maybe finding out the details will start to explain why she is the kind of person she's become, and it's a tasty bit of intrigue to look forward to in future episode no doubt.

And yet, somehow, Bela isn't quite gelling as a new character. She's stolen artefacts from the boys, and then when she couldn't have those, she took the lotto cards to the tune of $46,000 – which isn't even mentioned when she tosses the boys $10,000 in notes after they save her ass. But most importantly she shot Sam. She's proved herself untrustworthy, and yet the boys decide to team up with her. This is a strange thing for them to do with someone like Bela, especially when there are obvious alternatives available. Sam and Dean could have crashed the party alone, something they even comment on themselves, so it's seems very out of character.

Dean chewing gum when they go to the party is another thing that's out of character; he's never been much of a gum fan before, so why now? Then there are Sam's comments about Bela getting one over on Dean, which also jar considering that their relationship has been remarkably blame-free up to this point – and it's especially

282 In 'Bad Day At Black Rock' (3-03).

unusual since Bela stole the rabbit's foot from Sam's pocket when they first met, so it's not like he's squeaky clean himself in that department..

There are other little niggles too:

Why do the boys need to squat in a derelict house when they have the credit cards available?

The sailor's body was cremated, but wouldn't a burial at sea be more normal? Wouldn't a funeral pyre on a wooden ship be somewhat risky?

Why does the ghost grab Sheila round the neck and struggle in the shower when all he needs to do is touch her head like he does with the other victims? Fair enough, she is the only naked female to get killed, and you can understand why he'd like to get a bit more ... ahem, hands on ... but it feels contrived, to give the opening scene a bit more drama.

Then there's the unusually big special effect moment at the end. *Supernatural's* effects are always good quality but tend to fit the flow of the story and the down-to-earth, blue-collar approach of the show. They're often not even noticeable as effects – like additional cockroaches on festering bodies etc. The ghost-on-ghost effect here is excellent but something of a showpiece and not your typical *Supernatural* example.

And there's also the strange weather in that climax sequence. It's not clear why it had to pour with rain through part of this scene then suddenly clear up. There's a moment in the car when the radio announcer explains that there will be some severe weather coming in with sudden rainfall involved, but although this justifies its appearance, why have it at all?

All of these little anomalies add up and leave you with a very uneasy feeling about the entire episode – that it just doesn't work on some deep level. Only a couple of moments feel truly comfortable: the use of the two feuding sailor brothers who eventually destroy each other (to reflect the possible future for which Sam and Dean are heading); and the boys arguing at the start and end of the story, revealing a little more about themselves in the process.

Sam is continuing to keep secrets from Dean and doesn't 'fess up until he's faced with the fact that Dean has already figured it out. The only thing Sam needs to add after that is that some other demon holds the contract. The reason for Sam's new subterfuge lies in Dean's insistence that he'll do what he can to stop him finding a way out of the deal if that's what it takes[283]. But Sam won't apologise for trying either, even if killing the crossroads demon has caused problems with finding out who holds the contract.

Sam can't understand why Dean won't take any interest in saving himself. He doesn't want Dean to worry about him and he doesn't want an apology for putting him

---

283 In 'The Magnificent Seven' (3-01).

through this either. Sam wants help saving his brother and he's very frustrated because Dean has just accepted the situation and won't help find a way out of the deal.

But Dean has very good reasons for not helping Sam. He's driven by the need to keep his brother safe – since welching on the deal will cost Sam's life – although he is understandably curious about who holds his contract.

We know all this because Dean is a lot more open these days, probably because he hasn't got that much time left so he may as well just get stuff sorted out before it's too late. He understands his brother well enough to know what the missing bullet means and doesn't wait long before challenging Sam to tell him what happened.

Then Dean tries to explain that he understands how his brother feels and touches on what will happen after he's gone, how Sam will get over him and continue hunting. Sam's commitment to hunting has been swinging to and fro since Season One, with him at one point insisting he'd go back to school after the yellow-eyed demon was dead[284] then swapping and trying to be a good hunter for his dad[285] after John's death[286]. It was always possible Sam would quit the hunting game after the yellow-eyed demon was killed[287] but actually he has had to carry on because it's the only way he can save his brother from the crossroads deal. But once Dean is gone – what then?

Until that happens, Sam is going to carry on trying to save his brother and Dean is likely to keep opposing him. The strong family theme is still there but the harmonious days of Seasons One and Two are far behind us now.

VERDICT – 7 out of 10

---

284 In 'Shadow' (1-16).

285 In 'Everybody Loves A Clown' (2-02).

286 In 'In My Time Of Dying' (2-01).

287 In 'All Hell Breaks Loose Part Two' (2-22).

EPISODE 3-07
FRESH BLOOD

TRANSMISSION DATES
US first aired: 15 November 2007
UK first aired: 9 March 2008

CREDITS
Writer: Sera Gamble
Director: Kim Manners

RECURRING ROLES
Lauren Cohan (Bela Talbot), Sterling K Brown (Gordon Walker), Michael Massee (Kubrick)

GUEST STARS
Katie Chapman (Girl), Clare Elliott (Women at Bar), Daniella Evangelista (Hanging Victim 1), Matthew Humphreys (Dixon), Damon Johnson (Lucy's Victim), Jon Kralt (Driver with Flat Tire), Mercedes McNab (Lucy), Natalia Minuta (Hanging Victim 2), Aliyah O'Brien (Beautiful Woman)

SYNOPSIS
Sam and Dean track down a freshly turned vampire girl. After killing her, they go looking for Dixon, the vampire using a local club as his hunting ground. Meanwhile, hunter Gordon pays Bela for revealing the Winchesters' location. In the ensuing gunfight, the boys escape and Gordon is taken by Dixon, who is trying to create a new nest. Dixon turns Gordon, who then decides to use his new powers to go after Sam. Gordon tries to get Kubrick to agree to kill him after he's killed Sam, but Kubrick attacks Gordon with a machete and Gordon has to kill him instead. Luring Sam and Dean to a warehouse by taking a young girl hostage, Gordon separates Sam from Dean and takes Sam on. Dean deals with the hostage, whom Gordon has already turned, then goes to help his brother. Gordon is too strong for Dean but Sam manages to decapitate him with razor wire.

CAN YOU SURVIVE TO THE TITLES?
Bela comes close to getting a bullet between the eyes from Gordon before they come to a mutually beneficial agreement, but everyone survives the encounter. Which is just

as well given the upcoming body count.

LOCATION, LOCATION, LOCATION
In a 'big city' somewhere in the US; Dixon creates his new nest at the 'Trading Co' warehouse.

LEGENDARY ROOTS
There's been a lot of water under the bridge since the hunters appeared on the scene in the shape of Gordon in 'Bloodlust' (2-03). Here's a look at the other hunters we've met since then:

- Steve Wandell is finished off by a possessed Sam in 'Born Under A Bad Sign' (2-14). Seen via a security video, he is punched and kicked to the ground before Sam slits his throat.
- Isaac and Tamara are a married couple who appear in 'The Magnificent Seven' (3-01). Isaac is killed by the Gluttony Demon who forces him to drink drain cleaner out of a jug.
- Richie is first seen in 'Sin City' (3-04) and killed in the same episode by a demon who promises him sex and leads him down to the basement. Casey reveals she's a demon and is attacked with a knife by Richie; Casey grabs him and snaps his neck.
- Kubrick is first seen in 'Bad Day At Black Rock' (3-03) visiting Gordon in prison. He then tracks Sam down, intent on killing him. He is seen again in 'Fresh Blood' (3-07), in which the vampire Gordon kills him by ripping out his heart.
- Creedy appears in 'Bad Day At Black Rock' (3-03) helping Kubrick track down Sam.
- Rufus Turner is a retired hunter who appears in 'Time Is On My Side' (3-15) giving Dean information on Bella after being bribed by a bottle of scotch.

So with Gordon's death in 'Fresh Blood', it seems that the bottom line is that very few hunters make it to retirement age. Guess that just comes with the territory.

SQUEEZE OF THE WEEK
Dean gets his neck nibbled a couple of times during the episode but decapitates the first girl who tries, and the second time it's Gordon!

SIBLING RIVALRY
Dean can't help ribbing Sam about his change of opinion – from not wanting to kill Gordon to finally seeing it as the only option – although the humour hides Dean's

concerns about his brother since he came back.

Meanwhile, Sam's sick and tired of Dean's kamikaze trip since the deal, but in true form Dean wants to be more like a ninja than a kamikaze.

Then Sam finally tells Dean what's been worrying him. Tells him that he's looked up to his big brother since he was a little kid, wanting to be just like Dean. Tells him that he knows Dean very well, can see how terrified he is and could he please drop the front and go back to being his brother instead. Aw!

BODY COUNT

Two humans get theirs in terribly gory ways. Gordon kills them both – the unfortunate guy who is changing the wheel on his car sprays his blood all over the dash and windows; and Kubrick turns out to have more guts than expected and probably gets to see them close up when Gordon shoves his hand into his abdomen.

There are also a number of vampire deaths cranking up the body count. The boys decapitate poor luckless Lucy; Gordon rips off the heads of the two newly turned family members at Dixon's place; then Gordon gets his comeuppance from Sam in a juicy bit of arterial-spurting slice-work in the warehouse. We never see what happens to Dixon, but it's unlikely the boys would have let him live given that he was going round preying on innocent young girls in nightclubs.

Which brings the count to an unhealthy six.

TOOLKIT

- A *machete* is essential hardware when there are vampires to be decapitated. The bigger the better. And don't forget to get *a sharpening stone* to keep the knife in peak condition.
- The *Colt* can deal with a range of supernatural beasties and works particularly well on vampires when you can't reach your machete.
- A *bottle of dead man's blood*[288] is useful to temporarily incapacitate a vampire rather than kill it, and a *syringe* will deliver the liquid into the vampire's bloodstream with unerring efficiency.
- You may not get to use *your handgun* on the vampires but it pays to keep it in good working order and oil it whenever you've got a spare moment between killings.
- A *talking board* is a good way to contact spirits to tell you where a badass hunter is located, and you can then use this information to buy back some good will from the other hunter who threatened to kill you.

---

288 The blood was first used in 'Dead Man's Blood' (1-20) and later in 'Bloodlust' (2-03) and 'Fresh Blood' (3-07).

- And when it comes to fixing the Impala, make sure you've got *a box wrench* and *a socket wrench* minimum, and that you know the difference between the two.

MEMORABLE MOMENTS
Sam telling Dean that he wants him back as a brother is one of the most emotional scenes so far this season. And Gordon losing his head, up close and personal, almost has you cheering on your sofa.

MOTEL MAYHEM
Looks like the boys are getting into the squatting habit[289] – which is probably just as well, given that Gordon and the FBI are after them and they need to stay under the radar.

SPOOK RULES
Standard vampire rules apply:
- They have a second set of pointed teeth that descend over the top of their 'human' ones.
- They nest in groups of eight to ten and send small packs out to hunt for food.
- Sunshine hurts their skin.
- Once a vampire gets your scent it's able to remember it for a lifetime. To block that scent, burn a mixture of saffron, skunk cabbage and trillium, then dust your clothes with the ashes.
- The only way to kill a vampire is by beheading it, and they have been hunted to the point of extinction.

But some extra rules come to light too:
- You can turn a human into a vampire by getting them to ingest vampire blood or getting vampire blood directly into their bloodstream.
- Artificial lights (like headlights) are too bright for vampire eyes.
- A vampire can hear blood pumping from half a block away.
- They can kill either by biting your neck and draining your blood, or by thrusting their fist into your stomach and letting you haemorrhage all over the floor. Ew, messy!
- As a vampire turns, their eyes become bloodshot and they can still be seen as reflections in windows.

In the spiritual world, ghosts can help you locate psychotic hunters who are bent on

---

289 This is the third time they've done it, the first two being in 'Bugs' (1-08) and 'Red Sky At Morning' (3-06).

killing you because they think you're the Antichrist.

Did You Spot?

The structure in the background of Bela's and Gordon's conversation is the same one seen in the opening sequence of 'Hookman' (1-07).

The name Lucy has had a long association with vampires – Lucy Westenra was Mina's best friend in Bram Stoker's novel *Dracula* (1897) and was turned into a vampire by the fanged guy himself.

After the big fight when Gordon and his head are separated, there's a sign on the left behind Dean as he stands up. It says 'Accidents: The Best Previous Record was 183 days. Safety is your responsibility.' 183 days is about five months, and you have to wonder if it's a reference to the number of days remaining before the hell hounds come for Dean.

Going Undercover

The only people who go undercover are Gordon and Kubrick, as FBI agents, to interrogate the vampire victim about whether or not he's seen Sam and Dean; and to confirm that he's not been turned.

Cultural References

This is the only episode not to contain any cultural references besides the Easter Bunny and the Tooth Fairy (and we suspect you already have a good idea who they are).

Goofs and Fluffs

Okay, this isn't really a goof, but it's so unbelievable it should be … .

When Dean breaks cover and run across the alley in front of Gordon and Kubrick, they both get several shots off and neither of them hits him. There's no cover and Gordon and Kubrick are both experienced hunters, yet they didn't even come close. It's unusual for realism to be sacrificed for the sake of a plot convenience in *Supernatural*, and it's disappointing too.

Haven't I Seen You Before?

Katie Chapman starred in *A Town Called Eureka*. Daniella Evangelista was in *The 4400*, *Alienated* and *Blood Ties*. Matthew Humphreys has been in *Numb3rs* and *Medium*. Damon Johnson has featured in *Millennium*, *Stargate: Atlantis* and *Smallville*. Jon Krait has been in *Bionic Woman* but is mainly a stuntman/co-ordinator who has been in *The Day The Earth Stood Still*, *Watchmen* and *Fantastic 4: Rise Of The Silver Surfer*. Mercedes McNab played Harmony in *Buffy the Vampire Slayer* and *Angel*. Natalia Minuta has been in *Smallville*.

BEHIND THE SCENES

Actor Sterling K Brown wasn't convinced at first that Gordon would actually turn an innocent girl into a vampire, after the character's experiences of his own sister being turned, so he talked to Eric Kripke about it. Kripke explained that they had discussed Gordon's motivations a lot but finally agreed that the bloodlust sensation would be so huge that it would override Gordon's previous instincts. [*The Official Supernatural Magazine #2*]

Ever the fan of gore, Kripke thought that Gordon getting garrotted with razor wire was one of the coolest deaths they've done. Yes, it was illogical in that Sam would severely damage his own hands if he pulled hard enough to decapitate Gordon, but no one really cared because everyone wanted to see Gordon's head come off. [*Season Three Supernatural Companion*]

MUSICAL INTERLUDE

- 'Seven Minutes In Heaven' – Dave Feldstein – Sam and Dean follow Dixon from the club.
- 'Crazy Circles' – Bad Company – Dean working on the Impala and teaching Sam about the engine.

ANALYSIS

All the better episodes in the season so far seem to have featured Gordon, Kubrick and Bela. Since Bela's just not settling in easily (especially with that grating English accent[290]) and Kubrick's just a side-kick, the only conclusion left is that it's Gordon's presence that's helping to lift the quality. And with his warped and damaged personality it's no surprise he inspires some of the better storylines.

He's freshly escaped from prison and on the run, but in true obsessive psychotic style, all he wants to do is kill Sam. Even when he's been turned into the one type of monster he's been slaughtering for the last who-knows-how-many years, all he can think of is using his new-found powers to stop Sam. Add in his existing hunter skill set and that makes him one helluvan adversary and one that challenges and pushes Sam into new territory.

What adds extra depth is that Gordon's and Sam's situations reflect each other. Gordon has evil running in his veins just like Sam, and Gordon illustrates one of the paths open to Sam should he choose it – suicide[291]. Sam tries to tell Gordon that he still has some good in him (*Return of the Jedi* anyone?) and we already know that vampires

---

290 Okay, so what if actress Lauren Cohan lived in the UK for a while? That accent still grates.

291 Whereas he illustrated Dean's choice of paths in 'Bloodlust' (2-03).

can survive on cow's blood if they choose that path, but Gordon loathes what he has become so much that the thought of continuing as a vampire is not an option. Death is the only possible destination, and he thinks Sam should have done the decent thing too. But Sam still believes he can do good with his powers by saving people, which ironically is exactly what Gordon believes he is doing in killing Sam. It's all so wonderfully ambiguous and, dammit, intense stuff.

But then the programme-makers add a bit more depth in vampire Dixon's storyline too. His desire for the company of like-minded friends and his loneliness and despair at losing his previous nest are easy to understand, even if you don't agree with his methods for forming a new nest. His situation of 'staring down eternity alone' is a direct reflection of Dean's. It's something that Sam clearly picks up on and throws back at Dean when he goes all kamikaze again and wants to locate and kill Gordon on his own.

All this breathes previously lacking cohesion back into the story and gives this episode long overdue impact.

But perhaps the single most overdue moment is between Sam and Dean, where they finally discuss Dean's state of mind. This seems to mark a substantial change in Dean's attitude to his fate as he realises that his brother can see through his performance. Dean's still terrified of what's going to happen, but he also sees that he needs to leave Sam in as strong a position as possible in order to survive after he's gone. It's not clear yet whether this means that the kamikaze moments are over or that we'll have more auto shop lessons to come, but it does seem to have cleared the air between the two so maybe they can both move on from the anger.

For Sam, we're also seeing very obvious personality developments. His readiness to accept that they'll have to kill Gordon to stop him makes him a very different Sam from the one that was trying to save vampire Lenore's life because she wasn't evil. Even Dean remarks on Sam's change of attitude, reminding us of the 'maybe he's not 100% Sam' issue still lurking in the background – but wouldn't it be far more surprising if Sam was still willing to try to talk Gordon out of it after all the attacks he's made so far? So this is actually a logical development rather than a suspicious one.

And as for Bela, we discover something new here too – she's not afraid of dying. She stared down the barrel of Gordon's gun and coolly called his bluff. The girl's got balls as well as a grating accent. So what's the story there then? Guess we'll just have to wait to find out.

VERDICT – 8.5 out of 10

Episode 3-08
A Very Supernatural Christmas

Transmission Dates
US first aired: 13 December 2007
UK first aired: 16 March 2008

Credits
Writer: Jeremy Carver
Director: J Miller Tobin

Recurring Role
Ridge Canipe (Young Dean)

Guest Stars
Victoria Bidewell (Molly Johnson), Alex Bruhanski (Slimy Santa), Jennifer Copping (Cindy Caldwell), Dryden Dion (Ronnie), Colin Ford (Young Sam), Merrilyn Gann (Madge Carrigan), Spencer Garrett (Edward Carrigan), Brandy Heidrick (Cheery Elf), Emily Holmes (Melinda Walsh), Connor Levins (Jimmy Caldwell), Zak Ludwig (Eddie Carson), Don MacKay (Grandpa Carson), Douglas Newell (Mr Siler)

Synopsis
The boys look into a strange disappearance (from a house with locked doors and windows) just before Christmas. When they find that this is the second mysterious disappearance, they visit a local Santa's grotto looking for an anti-Claus monster. Instead they find only a sad, lonely drunk in a red suit. Another kidnapping leads them to wreath-maker Madge Carrigan and her husband. Their use of expensive meadowsweet herbs upstairs and a range of power tools (and human remains) in the basement give away their Pagan god status. The Carrigans capture Sam and Dean, preparing them to be the final sacrifices for the year, but the boys escape and stop their killing spree using branches from the Christmas tree.

Can You Survive to the Titles?
Poor ole Grandpa is in the middle of putting the presents under the tree (dressed as Santa) when he's dragged up the chimney, crunched into shape so he fits through the gap and never seen again, leaving behind a bloody, fur-topped boot.

LOCATION, LOCATION, LOCATION
One Year Ago: Seattle, Washington. Present Day: Ypsilanti, Michigan. Flashback – Christmas Eve, 1991: Broken bow, Nebraska.

LEGENDARY ROOTS
There wasn't an actual person called St Nicholas, according to religious historians and folklore experts. St Nicholas is said to be based on a Teutonic god called Hold Nickar, or Poseidon to the Greeks, who was a powerful god of the sea and would gallop through the sky during the winter solstice giving blessings and benefits to all that worshipped him. When the Catholic church created St Nicholas they demonised the Pagan deities. Hold Nickar was associated with the Devil, known as Old Nick and temples that were previously used to worship him or Poseidon were converted to churches or shrines in St Nicholas's honour.

The Anti-Claus is said to be based on a variety of gods with a number of them mentioned in the episode:

- Krampus is said to look like the Devil with a long red tongue, long tail and a goat-like face. He brings a bundle of leafless twigs used for birching and has chains or a basket that carries away misbehaving children and throws them into hell.
- The legend of Black Peter began in Holland in the 15th Century. He was originally depicted as a Spanish pirate due to the political situation at the time and his appearance has evolved throughout the course of history. He is said to accompany St Nicholas and dole out coal and sometimes knock on the heads of misbehaving children.
- Belsnickel's appearance is that of a man clothed entirely in fur. Again he is said to deliver coal or switches to badly behaved children, but would leave gifts for the good kids.

SQUEEZE OF THE WEEK
It's rather sad, but the boys don't get a Christmas hug from anyone.

SIBLING RIVALRY
The rivalry spans the past and the present as the boys show that they started exchanging banter a long time ago. Back in 1991, Sam is told that they moved around a lot because nobody like Sam's face; by the present day Sam is returning caustic comments about how Mr Gung-Ho Christmas is about to put a bullet in Santa.

BODY COUNT
After Grandpa's bone-crunching experience one year ago, Mike Walsh is abducted

off-screen between the opener and the boys arriving to talk to his wife Melinda. Then there's Al Caldwell, who's taken from his bed, after his wife is knocked unconscious, and dragged downstairs in a leather bag, only to be wickedly twisted into an appropriate shape to go up the chimney, while his son looks on.

TOOLKIT

- A *thermos flask of coffee* is an essential item for those cold nights on stake-out, but try not to finish it all too early on.
- *Observational skills* are crucial for a hunter, along with a secret passion for Christmas wreaths made of meadowsweet. This herb is a rare and powerful one in Pagan lore and was used to lure gods to human sacrifices.
- A *large knife* will allow you to whittle down some *evergreen stakes* to a suitably sharp point, and you can place a *large swing bin* next to you as you work for the wood slivers (except they're likely to fly off all over the place so the bin won't be much use until afterwards).
- A *lock pick* will gain you entry to even a Pagan god's suburban domicile.
- A *flashlight* will help you investigate a cellar full of bloody remains and half eaten bones.
- Being able to *think fast in a tight situation* (even when you're in pain 'cause someone's yanked your fingernail out) is a life-saving skill – pulling out the drawer of a dresser to block a door from opening is good lateral thinking and having the strength to move a large dresser in front of another door also helps.

MEMORABLE MOMENTS

There are some lovely heart-rending moments with families coming together, surrounded by moments of gut-wrenching horror as bodies are dismembered. The monster taking one of Santa's biscuits from the plate after bagging a victim is an inspired piece of storytelling, and the reaction of the female elf at Santa's theme park is a well-timed moment of humour.

THE CAR'S THE STAR

The Impala doesn't take a large part in the story, but it's touching to see that it is included in the final scene of a cosy Christmas together with the boys. And it even gets into the spirit of the occasion by sporting a light coat of snow upon the bonnet. Aw.

SPOOK RULES

- In the days before Christmas, a loud thud on the roof is less likely to be Santa and more likely to be an evil Pagan god coming to kidnap someone in the household, but only if you have a meadowsweet wreath over your open fire.

- Pagan gods will always dislodge soot from the chimney on their way down to get you.
- The god's outfit is a grubbier, bloodier and soft leather (or skin!) version of Santa's red and white suit. He also carries a large, soft leather body bag to put the victim in.
- Pagan gods are partial to freshly-baked cookies as well as human flesh.
- If a Pagan god can't get you up the chimney in one piece, he'll break your bones until you do fit.
- In order to fit in to everyday life, a Pagan god will assume the shape and mannerisms of a human (they can get jobs, a mortgage and play bridge on Tuesdays and Fridays – they just have a few strange ideas about fingernails and teeth).
- Pagan gods are sticklers for rituals, and in return for a human sacrifice they'll give you mild weather. The ritual for the human sacrifice involves a dried meadowsweet wreath, blood from the sacrifice, a freshly pulled fingernail and newly removed molar.
- Vervain and mint herbs are used to decorate a Pagan god's house at Christmas.
- A Pagan god's true face is revealed in a torch beam, and once you've confirmed they aren't human, you can go ahead and kill them with an evergreen stake – either a purposely-crafted one or a hastily pulled branch from a Christmas tree.
- The Anti-Claus is also known as Belsnickel, Krampus and Black Peter.
- He shows up around Christmas and punishes the wicked, by hauling their asses up the chimney amongst other things.
- The Anti-Claus walks with a limp and smells of candy.

DID YOU SPOT?

The Special Presentation logo is used only on this episode and was insisted upon by creator Eric Kripke, who remembered it from the Christmas Specials he watched as a kid. It appears here without the usual CBS letters (the original logo said 'A CBS Special Presentation') and dates back to the 1970s.

Also exclusive to this episode is the special *Supernatural* title card with Christmas decoration, snow, Santa's hat and red and blue lettering.

The closing shot of this episode is very similar to that of *The X-Files'* Christmas episode ('How The Ghosts Stole Christmas' (6-08)), looking in through the window watching the two lead characters inside opening presents while the snow starts to fall softly outside. Aw again!

GOING UNDERCOVER

The boys are FBI every inch of the way as they first investigate the disappearance of Mike Walsh and later the brutal kidnapping of Al Caldwell from his bed at home.

CULTURAL REFERENCES

Sam: 'So, I guess we're dealing with Mr and Mrs God.': *Mr and Mrs God in the Creation Kitchen* (2006) is a children's book by Nancy Wood.

Sam: 'Yep. It's uh … it's actually Dick van Dyke.'; Dean: 'Who?'; Sam: '*Mary Poppins*.': *Mary Poppins* is a 1964 live-action-with-animation movie about a nanny and the children she looks after. Dick van Dyke co-starred as a Cockney chimney sweep and bank chairman.

Sam: 'Dean, those weren't exactly Hallmark memories for me, you know.': Hallmark greetings cards are renowned for their sweet, lovey-dovey designs[292].

Dean: 'All right, Grinch.': The Grinch was created in 1957 by Dr Seuss in the children's book *How The Grinch Stole Christmas!*, which has also been turned into a television special (1966) and a live action movie starring Jim Carrey (2000). It features a grumpy hermit hatching a plan to steal Christmas from the Whos of Whoville.

Young Dean: 'Mm. He's James Bond.': James Bond[293] is a character created by Ian Fleming in 1953 for a series of books that have also been made into computer games and films starting with *Dr No* (1963). These follow the adventures of an officer of the British Secret Intelligence Service (or MI6). The latest star of the films is Daniel Craig, who looked particularly nice coming out of the sea in tight swimming trunks.

Dean: 'And all these Martha Stewart wannabes buying these fancy wreaths.': Stewart is a modern day Mrs Beaton with her own TV show. She specialises in tips about cooking, home and decorating and gardening, and runs Cutest Cupcake competitions on her website. She also dresses very conservatively[294].

Sam: 'I mean, since when are you Bing Crosby all of a sudden?': Harry Lillis aka 'Bing Crosby' (1903-1977) was an American singer and actor who starred in the 1954 film *White Christmas* about a song and dance group who try to save the Vermont inn. The song 'White Christmas' sung by Crosby actually first featured in the movie *Holiday Inn* (1942).

Dean: 'So what? Ozzie and Harriett are keeping a Pagan god hidden underneath their plastic-covered couch?': *The Adventures of Ozzie and Harriet* was an American sitcom that ran for 14 seasons (1952-1966), about the ideal American family life.

---

292 Also mentioned in 'Houses of the Holy' (2-13)'

293 Like you don't already know!

294 Last mentioned in 'Hookman' (1-07)'

Mr Carrigan: 'Hardy Boys here make five.': The Hardy Boys are a couple of fictitious teenage amateur detective boys starring in the *Hardy Boys Mystery Stories*. They first appeared in 1927 and were originally conceived by Edward Stratemeyer.

Dean: 'Well, you say it like that, I guess you guys are the Cunninghams.': The Cunninghams were the main family from the long running TV show *Happy Days*, which ran from 1974 for 11 seasons and was set in the 1950s.

GOOFS AND FLUFFS

When we see Al Cauldwell kidnapped from his bed, we hear his wife Cindy scream when she is knocked unconscious, but Al himself doesn't make much noise at all; however when Cindy recounts the story to Sam and Dean she says her husband was 'dragged out of bed, screaming'.

When Madge is cutting Dean's arm with the knife, you can see the blood running but it's obvious that there's no wound on his arm where she should have cut into his flesh.

Dodgy Santa in his caravan is either pretty nifty with his beer, and swaps it from his left hand to his right hand extremely quickly when the boys barge in, or there's a bad bit of editing happening.

HAVEN'T I SEEN YOU BEFORE?

Victoria Bidewell was in *What Lies Beneath* and *AVP: Requiem*. Alex Bruhanski's credits include *Sliders* and *The X-Files*. Ridge Canipe has been in *Angel* and *CSI*. Jennifer Copping featured in *Stargate SG-1*, *The Outer Limits* and *The Invisible Man*. Dryden Dion has also been in *Masters of Horror*. Colin Ford was in *Smallville* and *Close To Home*. Merrilyn Gann featured in *The X-Files*, *Millennium* and *The Outer Limits*. Spencer Gerrett's credits include *Transformers: Revenge of the Fallen*, *The Invisible Man* and *Criminal Minds*. Brandy Heidrick has featured in *The Butterfly Effect*, *The 4400* and *Stargate: Atlantis*. Emily Holmes was in *Battlestar Galactica: The Resistance*, *Taken* and *The Dead Zone*. Connor Levins has also been in *Masters of Horror* and *Smallville*. Zak Ledwig's acting credits include *A Town Called Eureka*, *The Dead Zone* and *Master of Horror*. Don MacKay featured in *The X-Files*, *Millennium* and *Poltergeist: The Legacy*. Douglas Newell was in *The Crow: Stairway to Heaven*, *The Outer Limits* and *The Lone Gunmen*.

Ridge Canipe also appears in 'Something Wicked' (1-18).

BEHIND THE SCENES

Stunt co-ordinator Lou Bollo found this episode memorable, because he thought it was a bit sick in places and it made him want to go home, shower and phone his mother. Bollo particularly liked the bit where the monster bumps his victim down the stairs in the leather bag because they'd taken the time to find a stunt man small enough to fit the bag, rather than going for the less realistic option of something mechanical inside the bag kicking out. [*The Official Supernatural Magazine* #9]

MUSICAL INTERLUDE

- 'Silent Night' – Sam and Dean – Carol singing!
- 'Twelve Days of Christmas' – as Grandpa arrives in the opening sequence.
- 'Silent Night' – when the Pagan god takes Al Cauldwell while his son watches.
- 'Joy to the World' – as Sam and Dean interview Cindy Cauldwell.
- 'Deck The Halls' – in the Christmas shop that sells the wreaths.
- 'Oh Come All Ye Faithful' – as Sam and Dean sneak up on the Carrigans' house for a little breaking and entering.
- 'We Wish You A Merry Christmas' – when the boys wake up in the Carrigans' kitchen.
- And 'Have Yourself A Merry Little Christmas' – Rosemary Clooney – when Sam and Dean exchange presents at the end of the episode.

ANALYSIS

An excellent episode of symmetry and contrast that (almost) stands alone and incorporates all of *Supernatural*'s best features – great storytelling, emotional depth, a touch of series mythology, horror, humour, and interesting monsters from folklore.

The horror is subtle and very twisted. Much of it comes from the contrast between the bright, happy innocence of Christmas and the dark, grisly viciousness of murder. There are unrepentant gods taking what they believe they deserve and distraught wives devastated by the loss of family members. There's the unnerving scene where Sam's fingernail is ripped out with a pair of pliers by someone wearing a novelty Christmas jumper, made so much more disturbing by it being set in a kitchen brimming with Christmas cheer rather than the decaying basement revealed earlier in Sam's flashlight beam. And the whole sequence of having a seven year old boy watch the monster abduct, and probably kill, his father is seriously unhinged. It features a mere three words of dialogue but delivers a terrifying sequence that is contrasted by a moment of humour when the monster takes the biscuit.

The symmetry is a little more subtle to spot and lurks in the storylines that run through the episode. The monster-of-the-week story is about tearing families apart in traumatic circumstances, while the Sam-and-Dean story is about families coming back together and healing past traumas. Lurking in there we have young Dean making the effort to give young Sam his last Christmas as an innocent child before he has to enter the world of real-life monsters; while present-day Sam is making the effort to give Dean one last enjoyable Christmas alive before he has to enter the environs of hell.

These two aspects of contrast and symmetry give the episode an underlying sense of balance, a feeling of completeness that's only re-emerged in these latest two episodes this season compared with the early Season One stories when the monster-of-the-week regularly made a direct connection to the boys' back-story[295].

This time, that back-story features a defining moment in Sam's childhood where he learns the truth about the monsters. It's a powerfully emotional situation, but it never slides too far into cloying sentimentality, because John Winchester never turns up for Christmas Day. That wouldn't fit the dysfunctional family mould these boys grew up with – we're seeing how the bond between the two brothers became so strong, how they've had to rely on each other because Dad wasn't there at crucial times in his children's development (although in John's defence, he was there when they needed protecting from monsters).

With all these good story things going on, there are only a couple of niggles. First, it's clear from 'The Woman In White' (1-01) that one of Sam's most vivid memories is from when he was nine years old when something in the closet scared him and Dad gave him a .45. In the Pilot, Sam is clearly upset about his Dad's actions, but according to this episode, Sam is eight-and-a-half when he finds out that the monsters are real, so why should he be upset to be given the gun six months later? Surely, he'd be grateful to have something to defend himself with?

The second niggle is about how easy it is for the very human Winchester boys to beat the presumably powerful Pagan gods. Okay, Sam doesn't get away unscathed (that must hurt!) but even your average demon gives them more trouble than these two gods.

But hey, these are relatively small problems when compared with the success of the rest of the episode. Its contribution to the show's overall mythology is significant, its humour is almost literally to die for, and it reveals how Dean is preparing for his future while Sam moves from outright denial to an uneasy acceptance that he might not be able to save his brother. And with this show, it's not easy to predict which way Dean is going to go ...

VERDICT – 9.5 out of 10

---

295 Previous episode 'Fresh Blood' (3-07) is the only other story so far in Season Three to show this type of coherence.

EPISODE 3-09
MALLEUS MALEFICARUM

TRANSMISSION DATES
US first aired: 31 January 2008
UK first aired: 23 March 2008

CREDITS
Writer: Ben Edlund
Director: Robert Singer

RECURRING ROLE
Katie Cassidy (Ruby)

GUEST STARS
Kristin Booth (Renee Van Allen), Erin Cahill (Elizabeth Clark), Robinne Fanfair (Janet Dutton), Marisa Ramirez (Tammi Benton/Astaroth), Rebecca Robbins (Amanda), Ken Tremblett (Ron), Jonathan Watton (Paul Dutton)

SYNOPSIS
Sam and Dean get more than they bargained for when they investigate a coven of witches after the mysterious death of a young woman while locked in her own bathroom. After a second murder is attempted by witch Amanda, the boys manage to uncover the members of the coven, but not before some witch-on-witch bitching results in Amanda's death. Then Ruby arrives to warn them that a powerful demon is in town and suggest they leave immediately. When they don't, Dean is attacked with a spell, but Ruby saves his life. Dean goes to support Sam as he confronts the coven members. Both fall victim to the demon, who is masquerading as Tammi, one of the witches; and Ruby has take on her old boss personally to save the boys again.

CAN YOU SURVIVE TO THE TITLES?
Do your gums bleed when you brush them? Poor old Janet Dutton's teeth fall out when she brushes hers, then her gums bleed heavily into the sink. Amanda's spell finally takes Janet's life when the witch uses a knife to complete the magical murder.

LOCATION, LOCATION, LOCATION
There's no indication of which town/city the episode is set in, but Amanda's house

414

EPISODE 3-09 MALLEUS MALEFICARUM

is located at 309 Mayfair Circle and the boys are staying at The Conquistador Motel.

LEGENDARY ROOTS

The *Malleus Maleficarum* is a famous medieval treatise on witches. The name of the book is Latin for 'Hammer of Witches'. It was written in 1486 by Heinrich Kramer and Jacob Sprenger, and the first publication was a year later in Germany. Its main purpose was to challenge the existence of witchcraft, and it allowed courts to decide how to interrogate and convict anyone thought to be a witch.

The book is broken down into three parts. Part One is concerned with the belief that witches exist and can work with the Devil if permitted by God. Part Two deals with the methods used to recruit a witch and the powers they hold, and how to destroy or cure them. Part Three deals with the judicial proceedings, and how to prosecute a witch.

SQUEEZE OF THE WEEK

There are several lovely women in the coven, but they seem to be more interested in lowering their mortgage rates and winning craft competitions than in how tight the boys' butts are – are they mad?

SIBLING RIVALRY

Sam points out how contradictory Dean is being about Ruby. Dean doesn't like Ruby because she's a demon, and humans and demons just need to murder each other. Sam counters with a reminder about how Dean didn't want the Casey demon to be killed.[296]

BODY COUNT

Wicked Amanda gets a taste of her own medicine when a spell causes her wrists to be slit open by an invisible knife (in vertical slashes up her arm too, a sure-fire way of bleeding to death). The boys find her in a large pool of blood in her own home. The irritating witch Renee gets her neck broken by a newly revealed demon – Tammi. Final witch Elizabeth tries to help the boys but has her heart crushed by the demon for her troubles. Adulterous hubby Paul merely gets a maggot-infested reminder that burgers aren't good for you, but he survives the ordeal.

Which is more than can be said for the poor bunny rabbit killed by Amanda for her spell! There hasn't been a murdered animal since zombie Angela inadvertently killed her boyfriend's goldfish[297].

---

296 In 'Sin City' (3-04).

297 In 'Children Shouldn't Play With Dead Things' (2-04).

TOOLKIT

- Breaking into a witch's house is so much easier with a good *lock pick*, and be sure to take your *hand guns* with you in case said witch turns nasty.
- Keep a *lighter* in your pocket for burning hex bags.
- A *friendly demon with a potion* powerful enough to save your life is indispensible when you are attacked by a demon spell. So what if the potion tastes like ass?
- The *Colt* and its demon-killing bullets are essential when taking on the entity that controls a witches' coven.
- And ensure that same friendly demon brings the *demon-killing knife* along too, just in case you screw up and get disarmed.

MEMORABLE MOMENTS

While it's tempting to say that the tooth-losing and maggot-munching moments stand out as the best ones in this episode, it's only because they are the most gruesome. The most important moments, upon which the entirety of Season Four will hinge, are the less prominent ones where Ruby saves Dean's life; takes on the Tammi-demon and saves both Winchesters; then reveals Dean's destiny once his contract is up. Take note of these scenes: it all starts here.

SPOOK RULES

Witches:

- Spell-casting involves an altar, candles, Latin incantations, an item belonging to the victim, animal bones, demonic symbols drawn on a surface, a dagger and the application of bodily fluids – frequently the spell-caster's blood. But the witch has to pledge her soul to a demon for the true power of the spell to flow.
- A hex bag needs to be close to the victim at the time the spell is cast for maximum effect. The bag should contain bird bones, rabbit's teeth, and cloth cut from an item of clothing belonging to the victim. To destroy their power, burn the bag and its contents – this causes the items used by the witch for the spell-casting to burst into flames.
- The item belonging to the victim will influence the injury inflicted – when the item is a toothbrush, the victim will start losing teeth etc.
- The correct kind of spell will also ensure that the victim's loved ones can't reach them to provide help – doors will be forced shut and locked until the victim is beyond saving.
- Radios are sensitive little things. Not only do they go wonky when ghosts[298] and

---

298 Checkout 'Roadkill' (2-16) for details.

demons[299] are around, but they also start changing station on their own when spells are being cast on someone nearby.
- Any self-respecting witches' coven meeting needs a tablecloth with an arcane symbol on it, a set of candles in an elaborate candle holder and a *Book of Shadows*.
- Thrifty witches will grow their own spell ingredients in the garden. Favourite choices are belladonna, wolf's bane and mandrake.
- Black magic will help you go up a few tax brackets, lower your mortgage rate, and win raffles and craft contests, as well as murder your lover's wife.

Demons:
- You know there's a demon in the vicinity when the car's headlights flicker and the engine stalls for no apparent reason.
- When a demon has cast a spell to make you double over in pain and start spitting blood, your only chance of survival is a seemingly human-friendly demon who will force-feed you a potion that tastes disgusting.
- Demons have their own version of an exorcism ritual and can force another demon to leave a meat-suit by chanting the Latin words.
- All demons were human once. Their time in hell causes them to change for the worse.

DID YOU SPOT?

The radio station that Paul Dutton tunes into is 101.1 FM. This is a classic rock station in Vancouver where the series is filmed.

The boys are still not being very careful when they're discovering murdered bodies. They phone the police about Amanda's death before they've wiped fingerprints etc, and it's a big risk delaying their departure from the crime scene considering Agent Henricksen is still out there looking for them.

It's interesting that the Tammi-demon picks up an iron poker as a weapon against Ruby – if the iron is arranged in lines then demons can't cross them[300], so iron clearly isn't the nicest material for them to be near. Still, maybe that's why she wanted to use it against Ruby.

The score in the war against the demons has gone up again. The demons have now killed seven innocents so far this season (they add two out of three of the witches this time: Amanda isn't particularly innocent since she's been murdering people all over the place, but the other two have been merely winning craft competitions and so don't

---

299 See episodes like 'Woman in White' (1-01) or 'All Hell Breaks Loose Part One' (2-21).

300 Established in 'All Hell Breaks Loose, Part Two' (2-22).

really deserve to die). Meanwhile Team Winchester is maintaining a slim lead with ten (adding one for the Tammi-demon's meat-suit).

Going Undercover

The boys spend a short time pretending to be from the CDC[301], the Centre for Disease Control and Prevention, a Federal agency in the Department of Health and Human Services that investigates, diagnoses and tries to control or prevent diseases (especially new and unusual ones).

Then shortly afterwards Sam is masquerading as Detective Bachman and introduces Dean as Detective Turner. So it's back to their music roots: Bachman Turner Overdrive was a 1970s Canadian rock band formed by three Bachman brothers and Fred Turner.

Hunter's Lingo

When leaving Janet's house after examining the bathroom, Sam says to Dean: 'I think we've got everything we need ...' This is the second episode in a row that Sam's used that phrase (he used it when leaving Mrs Walsh's house in 3-08) and it seems to be a code for 'I've found the supernatural evidence so let's split, I need to talk about it'.

Cultural References

Dean: 'So are we looking for some craggy old Blair bitch in the woods?': This is a reference to the 1999 movie *The Blair Witch Project*, which made original use of a handheld camera to capture footage.

Dean: 'It's like *Fatal Attraction* all over again.': The 1987 movie in which Glenn Close's character (Alex Forrest) stalks a family after a brief love affair with Michael Douglas's. In one famous scene, she kills the family's pet rabbit and leaves it boiling on the stove for them to find – creating the term 'bunny boiler' for an obsessively vengeful woman.

Ruby: 'It's called witchcraft shortbus.': Shortbus is used as an insult and refers to the smaller buses that used to take people with learning difficulties to their special schools or classes.

Tammi: 'Nice dick work, Magnum.': Dick work is slang for private detective investigating work. And *Magnum PI* (1980-1988) was a TV show about a private investigator who drove a Ferrari and lived in Hawaii.

Tammi: 'That's what happens to witches who get voted off the island.': A reference to the system of contestant elimination on the CBS reality TV show *Survivor*.

---

301 They haven't used this cover since 'Something Wicked' (1-18).

Tammi: 'What did you think it was? Make believe? Positive thinking? *The Secret?*': *The Secret* (2006, by Rhonda Byrne) is a self-help book and film concerning the law of attraction and positive thinking to hopefully improve people's lives.

Tammi: 'You really telling me you threw your chips in with Abbott and Costello here?': Abbott and Costello were born William (Bud) Abbott (1895-1974) and Louis Francis Cristillo (1906-1959). They formed a famous comedy double act that appeared in radio shows, TV and movies.

Dean: 'I saw *Hellraiser*; I get the gist.': *Hellraiser* is a 1987 horror movie based on a novella by Clive Barker. The main demon characters all wear leather outfits of various descriptions.

Ruby: 'Back when the plague was big.': Plague (the Black Death) was big in Europe between 1348 and 1350. It reduced the population by 30% to 60% (estimates vary) and has returned at various points up to the 19th Century. The London plague in 1665-1666 killed an estimated 100,000 people.

Elizabeth: 'But she was an Episcopalian.': An Episcopalian is a bishop within the Episcopal Church, which considers itself 'Protestant, yet Catholic' and ordains women into the priesthood.

Dean: 'Yeah, a regular Martha Stewart.': A third name check for Martha Stewart[302], whom the boys seem to consider the personification of domesticity.

Dean: 'Burn witch, burn.': This is most likely a reference to the *Night of the Eagle* (1962) movie, which was called *Burn Witch, Burn* when released in America. The film concerns a college professor who discovers that his wife has been practicing magic.

GOOFS AND FLUFFS
Just before Amanda is killed, the breeze blows out three of the four candles in the room. By the time the boys arrive, one of the candles has re-lit itself so there are now two burning.

In the scenes where Sam is pinned to the wall by the Tammi-demon, Sam's fringe changes from scene to scene.

Then later, after the demon has been killed, Ruby's hair gets tucked behind her ear without her touching it – maybe she uses her demonic powers on hairstyling activities.

HAVEN'T I SEEN YOU BEFORE?
Kristin Booth appeared in *ReGenesis* as Daisy Markovic, *Total Recall 2070* and *Salem Witch Trials*. Erin Cahill has been in *Power Rangers Wild Force* and *Without A Trace*. Robinne Fanfair was in *Blood Ties* and *Blade: The Series*. Marisa Ramirez played in *Roswell High*

---

302 Previously name-checked in 'Hookman' (1-07) and 'A Very Supernatural Christmas' (3-08).

and *Without A Trace*. Rebecca Robbins featured in *The Outer Limits, Smallville* and *The Dead Zone*. Ken Tremblett stars in *Watchmen, Dead Like Me* and *The X-Files*. Jonathan Watton's credits include *Mutant X, Masters Of Horrors* and *They Come Back*.

BEHIND THE SCENES

Real life often worms its way into *Supernatural* stories it seems. In the *Season Three Supernatural Companion*, Eric Kripke explained the inspiration for the maggoty hamburger came from when he opened his bin one day to find a maggot-infested possum in there. Unable to forget the maggots later on that day when he was working with Ben Edlund, Kripke had a word with him and they incorporated the wriggly critters into the show.

Composer Christopher Lennertz explained in *The Official Supernatural Magazine* #7 that the climactic moment when the Tammi-demon stops the bullet was deliberately left music-free. It's a frequently used format of theirs, particularly when things get scary or weird – they have a score for the build-up, leave it silent as the event happens, then chip back in afterwards with a musical reaction.

MUSICAL INTERLUDE

- 'Every Rose Has Its Thorn' – Poison – when Paul gets hexed in the car.
- 'I Put A Spell On You' – Screamin' Jay Hawkins – as the radio changes stations by itself while Paul is eating the maggoty burger.

ANALYSIS

In the same way that 'Red Sky At Morning' (3-06) was all about Bella, this one is all about Ruby and her past, but more importantly, it's also about Ruby's relationship with Dean.

We already know from the demonic Seven Deadly Sins that Ruby is a familiar face in hell, and now we find out that she used to be a human witch whose soul belonged to the Tammi-demon. However, Ruby obviously did something to get thrown out of servitude. It's not revealed what it was or even what she did between then and escaping through the Gate[303] (you can't have everything explained in one episode now, can you?) but it's possible that her ability to remember what it was like to be human has something to do with her having been cut loose. And now she's on Earth she seems to want to spend her time saving Sam's and Dean's (tight, sexy) asses from certain death[304]. She's doing a pretty good job of it too – first by saving Dean from the Tammi-demon's spell and then by taking on her old 'boss' in a bit of one-on-one fisticuffs.

---

303 When it was opened in 'All Hell Breaks Loose' Parts One and Two (2-21 and 2-22).

304 And it's easy to understand why she'd want to do that, isn't it?.

With killing the Tammi-demon and saving the boys, Ruby shows where her allegiances lie. She makes an uneasy peace with Dean, comes clean about not being able to save him from hell, slips in a quiet but significant opinion about not believing in the 'Devil', and shares some personal insights into what he can expect when he gets there. Her motivation is, she says, to prepare Sam for life without Dean.

Despite Dean's suspicions that this is not the whole story, Ruby's actions have made a significant change in his attitude towards her – he'll accept her presence without trying to kill her at least. Besides, now he has other things to worry about: not only does he have just a couple of months left before getting dragged down to hell, but Ruby definitely can't save him, and in all probability he's going to be turned into a demon once he gets there. The prospect of becoming something he hunts is troubling for Dean, and something that is going to continue to affect him deeply for some time to come.

On top of all this, Dean is also concerned about Sam. Ever since he came back from the dead, Sam has been losing his sensitive side, and now he's not thinking twice about killing a few human witches. Dean can't understand where the old Sam has gone, so Sam has to spell it out for him – he needs to become Dean if he's to survive after Dean goes to hell. It's not the most convincing explanation of his behaviour – given that he viciously filled Jake with bullets before he even knew that Dean had made the deal – but it is a reasonable concept. Sam does need to toughen up, especially now that there's a load of demons wanting to kill him.

It's a difficult situation for Sam. He abdicates rulership of the demon army, so a new leader is rising, and they want him out of the way – presumably since he's the only one strong enough to be a serious challenge. It's inevitable that the Winchesters and the new demon leader will lock horns at some point in the future, and you just know it's going to get interesting when that happens.

It's just one more event to look forward to as this season starts to gain momentum toward its incredible finale.

VERDICT – 8.5 out of 10

EPISODE 3-10
DREAM A LITTLE DREAM OF ME

TRANSMISSION DATES
US first aired: 7 February 2008
UK first aired: 30 March 2008

CREDITS
Writer: Sera Gamble and Cathryn Humphris
Teleplay: Cathryn Humphris
Director: Steve Boyum

RECURRING ROLES
Lauren Cohan (Bela Talbot), Jim Beaver (Bobby Singer)

GUEST STARS
Martin Christopher (Doctor), Adrian Formosa (Jeremy's Father), G Michael Gray (Jeremy Frost), Tammy Hui (Maid), Elizabeth Marleau (Bobby's Wife), Damon Runyan (Henry Frost), Cindy Sampson (Lisa Braeden), Myriam Sirois (Graduate Student)

SYNOPSIS
Bobby Singer ends up in hospital while he's hunting for the murderer of a doctor who was killed in his sleep. The boys are called in when Bobby falls asleep and can't be woken up. Finding Bobby's hunting notes, they learn that the murdered doctor was running illegal experiments with a special dream root. After digesting the root, a person can walk into and control other people's dreams. Dean phones Bela, who supplies them with the rare root and then hangs around to help out. The boys wake Bobby from his nightmare – where one of the doctor's test subjects, Jeremy Frost, is fooling him into thinking his wife is trying to kill him – but then Jeremy comes after Dean. With help from Sam, the boys defeat Jeremy in Dean's dreams, but not before Dean encounters his own worst enemy – himself.

CAN YOU SURVIVE TO THE TITLES?
No deaths before the titles, but a worrying situation for Bobby, who appears to be sleeping peacefully on the outside but is being chased in his nightmares by a murderous version of his wife.

LOCATION, LOCATION, LOCATION
Pittsburgh.

LEGENDARY ROOTS

A dreamscape is the imaginary landscape that evolves from dreams, the imagination or the inner reaches of the mind.

Dream walking is the ability to enter someone else's dreamscape through a form of telepathy. It is possible to control this ability but usually there needs to be a connection between the dream walker and the person whose dream is being entered. The dream walker starts with meditation while concentrating on the person whose dream they are trying to enter. Once the dream walker is asleep and has achieved a lucid dream, the walker pictures the individual whose dream they want to enter – if they are also in a lucid dream at the same time, it is possible to enter. The dream usually feels real between the two and can be vividly remembered by the person who has had their dream entered.

SQUEEZE OF THE WEEK

An old flame of Dean's, Lisa Braeden[305], is lurking in his subconscious, but with a killer chasing the boys through Dean's dream landscape there's no time to stop for even a cuddle.

But it's the scenes between Sam and Bela that raise the pulse. She's a pretty lass, and the boys haven't exactly had a lot of opportunity to indulge their sexual urges recently, so it's no surprise that they're starting to dream about getting some nookie – but it is a surprise to find Sam rather than Dean engaging in full-on lust. In fact, later on, it's Dean who's dreaming of a steady life of family, picnics and baseball after school.

SIBLING RIVALRY

Sam falls asleep at the keyboard and dreams of steamy sex with Bela. On waking, Dean remarks upon the happy noises Sam was making while he dreamt and asks if he was dreaming of Angelina Jolie or Brad Pitt.

But Sam won't elaborate on who the dream was about, so Dean goes back to his research, grumbling that the doctor had even worse handwriting than Sam's[306].

BODY COUNT

Sam has several close encounters with a baseball bat and takes the brunt of the beatings

---

305 Last seen in 'The Kids Are Alright' (3-02).

306 Dean seems to have a thing about his family's handwriting – he was complaining about John Winchester's writing back in 'Asylum' (1-10)

until he turns the tables and clubs Jeremy Frost to death while the two of them are loose in Dean's dream. No gore at all, but full marks for a most unusual location for the killing.

Toolkit

- Bela dusts off her *Tarot cards* and *Spirit Board* to help the boys for the first time, but she can't find out where Jeremy has gone after all.
- *Drugs* are also used for the first time. The dream root, *silene capensis*, allows you to walk in someone else's dreams and catch any murderers lurking in there.
- On the personal skills side, the ability to *convince a friend that he's trapped in a dream* is invaluable, as is the control required to *manipulate your brother's dream* and *create a weapon* in the shape of your murderer's abusive father.
- And a *high pain threshold* will help you survive a beating with a baseball bat.

Memorable Moments

Sam's beating with a baseball bat is brutally memorable, and Bela stealing the Colt at the end of the episode is an intriguing twist. And of course there's Sam's embarrassment and reluctance to stand up after dreaming of Bela and him in bed together.

But the exchange when Dean meets himself in the motel room stands out the most, with the shocking appearance of the black-eyed Dean and the disturbing message he has to deliver.

Spook Rules

- Victims of a dream walker go to sleep and don't wake up.
- People who can't dream due to Charcot-Wilbrand syndrome may find a cure if they take African dream root. The root (*silene capensis*) has been used by shamen and medicine men for centuries. When brewed as a tea with a sample of the victim's body, it allows the taker to enter the victim's dreams and manipulate events. If you take enough of it you can improve your control until you can turn someone's bad dreams good or their good dreams bad, even to the point of killing them in their dreams. You can also look around in their head and pick out memories and fears to use against them.
- More than one person can walk in the same dream.
- The victim still retains some control over their own dream and they have the ability to force themselves to wake up if necessary. Their best defence is simply not to go to sleep, since they are safe from a dream walker until they drop off.

Did You Spot?

In Bobby's dream, his house can be seen looking like new again. It was last seen in its more beaten-up state in 'The Magnificent Seven' (3-01).

This is the first episode where a drug-enhanced human is the monster.

While they're in Bobby's dream, Dean tells Sam that they shouldn't split up. It seems a strange thing for Dean to say given that they've been splitting up while on a hunt since Season One's 'Wendigo' (1-02), continued doing it through 'Asylum' (1-10) and even hunted separately in Season Two's 'What Is And What Should Never Be' (2-20).

GOING UNDERCOVER

Bobby keeps Dean's number as his emergency contact under the name of Mr Sniderson, and he uses this when he goes to hospital. Then Dean's back in detective mode (Pittsburgh Police Department to be exact) when he goes to question Dr Gregg's lab assistant then on to Jeremy's place.

When he visits Jeremy, we get to see Dean's badge with the following details:

Pittsburgh City Police Department
Name: Detective R Plant
License: 450GH0-23
Issued: 07.12.06
Expiry: 09.01.09
Signed: Robert Plant

CULTURAL REFERENCES

Sam: 'This doctor was testing the stuff on his patients, Tim Leary style …': Dr Timothy Francis Leary (1920-1996) was a psychologist, philosopher, explorer, teacher, optimist, author and revolutionary avatar of the mind.

Dean: 'Well, shall we dim the lights and sync up *Wizard of Oz* and "Dark Side of the Moon?"': Apparently the 1939 film *The Wizard of Oz* and the Pink Floyd 'Dark Side of the Moon' album can be played in parallel, creating the 'Dark Side of the Rainbow' as it is known. It was a favourite trick of college students to do this at parties. There has even been a theatre showing of the two synced up together.

Dean: 'Okay, I don't know what's weirder. The fact that we're in Bobby's head … or that he's dreaming of *Better Homes and Gardens*?': *Better Homes and Gardens* is a US magazine that features articles on a range of topics like cooking, gardening and decorating.

Sam: 'You take enough of it, with enough practice, you can become a regular Freddy Krueger.': Freddy Krueger, played by Robert Englund, is the star of the *Nightmare on Elm Street* (1984) movie, which has enjoyed numerous sequels and two spin-off TV series.

Dean: 'Now, Dr Gregg was testing treatments for a, uh, "Charcot-Wilbrand syndrome"?': Charcot-Wilbrand syndrome is the loss of the ability to dream after a stroke.

Dean: 'Thanks for the news flash, Edison.': Thomas Alva Edison (1847-1931) was an American inventor whose claims to fame include the light bulb, the motion picture camera and the phonograph.

Dean: 'I'm my own worst nightmare, is that it? Huh? Kind of like the *Superman III* junkyard scene?': The scene in question is where Superman fights Clark Kent in the 1983 movie.

GOOFS AND FLUFFS
Plenty of curious points in this one:

Why do the boys call Bela when the most obvious place to try to get the dream root first would be the doctor's office?

How does Sam manage to brew the dream root so quickly in the middle of nowhere, in the Impala, when Dean finally decides to go to sleep?

Jeremy is awake while Bobby is fighting his wife off – we know he is because Dean visits him while Bobby is in hospital. So how does Jeremy control Bobby's dreams for so long?

How does Jeremy know when Dean and Bobby will be asleep? These guys are hunters and often spend most of the night out killing things, so it's no general rule that these guys sleep at night.

And then there are the scratches on Bobby's face in his dream – in the close-ups, it's obvious that they are just painted on and the skin isn't broken at all.

Staying with Bobby, or more specifically Bobby's kitchen in the dream sequence, when did that suddenly arrive? It wasn't there in 'Devil's Trap'[307] but it's sure there now. Most people have a conservatory added, but not our Bobby.

HAVEN'T I SEEN YOU BEFORE?
Martin Christopher played Major Marks in *Stargate SG-1*, *Stargate: Atlantis* and *Stargate: The Ark of Truth* and has also been in *Night At The Museum* and *Painkiller Jane*. G Michael Gray was in *Dark Angel*, *Tru Calling* and *Blood Ties*. Tammy Hui featured in *Battlestar Galactica*, *Grand Star* and *Stargate: Atlantis*. Damon Runyan was in *Smallville*. Cindy Sampson has been in *Lexx* and *Reaper*. Myriam Sirois was in *Babylon 5: The Legend of the Rangers: To Live and Die in Starlight*.

---

307 Episode 1-22.

Cindy Sampson also appeared in 'The Kids Are Alright' (3-02).

BEHIND THE SCENES

In the Scene Specifics section on the DVD, Eric Kripke explained that Jason from the *Friday the 13th* movies was due to appear in this episode, hockey mask and all. The crew were fully prepared with all the props and everything exactly how they wanted it, but three days before filming, there was some confusion over who owned the character and a hasty re-write had to be done.

In the *Season Three Supernatural Companion*, Jared Padalecki talked about trying to make Jim Beaver (Bobby) laugh in one of the scenes. The close up was on Jim's face and Jared was standing at the bottom of the bed, squeezing Jim's toes really hard. Jim soldiered through like a pro and Jared made himself laugh more than he did Jim.

In *The Official Supernatural Magazine #3*, Jim Beaver said that he thinks Bobby feels like a father to the boys, but only since events in 'Devil's Trap'[308]. He doesn't think they were that close before then.

MUSICAL INTERLUDE

- 'Long Train Runnin'' – The Doobie Brothers – while Sam is getting drunk on whiskey in the bar.
- 'Dream A Little Dream Of Me' – The Mamas and The Papas – during Dean's dream about the picnic with Lisa Braeden.

ANALYSIS

Dream walking is one of those mystical activities that seem to have been around since the dawn of time, so while not strictly an urban legend, it's no surprise it makes an appearance in the series. Dreams are a huge topic that stretches from specific dream types that occur throughout history and across cultures, to theories of the collective unconscious. This episode keeps the subject matter tightly focused on killing other people in their own dreams and delivers some suitably surreal, dream-sequence scenery changes (especially when the boys are running through the forest and Dean ends up in a corridor lined with tree wallpaper instead).

But this is really a character-driven episode that exposes the depths of Dean's psyche liked a gutted carcass while dissecting Sam's emotions and exposing Bobby's past.

Let's get Bela out of the way first though – since she only puts in a brief but significant appearance. She really just confirms what we already know and what the

---

308 Yep, also episode 1-22.

boys and Bobby seem totally incapable of understanding – that she's only on her own side and people matter far less to her than money. You just want to slap some sense into the boys and Bobby for being stupid enough to allow her within a ten mile radius of them.

Talking of Bobby, we finally discover how he got into hunting, and it's not so different from how John Winchester started – with a manipulating demon causing the death of his wife (although there's no evidence to say it was the same yellow-eyed demon that attacked both their families). From the conversation in Bobby's dream, it seems that his wife was possessed and Bobby stabbed her to death because she was rabid. It can't be easy for Bobby to know now that he could have saved his wife with a simple exorcism ritual, but it does account for why he tends to be the one who exorcises more than the others[309].

Another aspect of Bobby we see clearly for the first time is the depth of his relationship with Dean. We knew the boys had always referred back to Bobby when they were struggling to solve a mystery[310] or when they were in really serious trouble[311], but now we see that not only does Dean treat Bobby as a father figure but Bobby trusts Dean with his life and is prepared to believe that he's in a dream if Dean says so. And it's nice to see Bobby's big enough to admit he needed Dean's help and to thank him for it – which probably makes Bobby one of the least dysfunctional people on the show.

All this additional info, along with this being the first time he's been sick and the first time we've seen him scared of an assailant, makes Bobby a far more vulnerable, sympathetic character and not just a smart-assed, hard-nosed hunter who always covers his tracks and never misses a thing (like the fact that Sam's powers might have helped him beat Jeremy).

Sam clearly hadn't considered that his powers could have made a difference in his fight with Jeremy. That might be because Sam's still a bit distracted. He's struggling to cope with losing hope about saving Dean. This is only the second time we've seen Sam get drunk[312], and it shows how desperate he's become – he's trying to run away from the situation by numbing his senses with alcohol. Fortunately there are changes afoot and there will be more hope than ever by the end of the episode.

Meanwhile, Sam's lusting over Bela. The humour of these scenes and the follow-up ones works well and lightens an otherwise very serious episode, but nevertheless the

---

309 He exorcised all the demons in one night in 'The Magnificent Seven' (3-01).

310 In 'Tall Tales' (2-15).

311 In 'Devil's Trap' (1-22).

312 The last time Sam was drunk was in 'Playthings' (2-11) when he was trying to come to terms with not being able to save the guy who hung himself at the house, the same as he couldn't save Ava at the end of 'Hunted' (2-10).

sequence feels very out of place. It doesn't fit with Sam's known personality – he doesn't usually lust after women and has been more interested in long-term relationships than one-night stands so far. But people are complex beings, and why shouldn't we discover some new aspect of Sam, even after all this time?

Dean on the other hand stays completely consistent with what we already know, except now we see deeper into his soul than ever before. Hiding in his head are his hopes and his fears, and it's still heart-wrenching to see how he longs for a normal family life. This was explored in more depth in 'What Is And What Should Never Be' (2-20) and was bubbling beneath the surface in 'The Kids Are Alright' (3-02). Here it's obvious that Lisa Braeden and her son have now become the focus of his dreams of a lost life.

Dean's fears are also lurking in his dreamscape. Ruby's revelation in 'Malleus Maleficarum' (3-09) that all demons were once humans and that Dean will turn demon too has terrified him. When he was lying comatose in the hospital during 'In My Time Of Dying' (2-01), the reaper had to frighten Dean into going with her – by telling him that he would become what he hunted if he stayed[313]. And you can see just how deep the terror goes in the exchange between Dean and his demon-self.

But the more interesting exchanges are older and more entrenched, starting with Dean's contradictory feelings about his father. Dean has always been the good little soldier and tried to please his dad but he clearly has a realistic handle on his dad's behaviour (calling him an 'obsessed bastard'). The negative aspects of Dean's relationship with John are hung out like dirty laundry for all to see – how Dean blames John for Mary's death; how John loved Sam more; and how John dumped all his crap on Dean's young shoulders. Dean's not really had the opportunity to get this off his chest to anyone who would understand – with the exception of Cassie[314] maybe, the only girl he's ever been serious about – and he wouldn't find it easy to discuss given his bottle-it nature anyway. So it's no surprise that the only place he can share it is in his dreams with himself.

The other aspect that is harshly exposed is Dean's lack of self-esteem, how he exists like a jigsaw picture of other people's pieces. The leather jacket is his dad's, as are the car and the music. And his *raison d'etre* is to look after Sam. Which bit of Dean is truly and purely his own identity? The answer appears to be nothing; he's made up of bits of everyone else, and with those beliefs about yourself, it's no wonder you've got low self-esteem.

But hate himself or not, Dean takes a huge step after facing these home truths. He

---

313 A common trait in hunters it seems to have given Gordon similar problem in 'Fresh Blood' (3-07).

314 In 'Route 666' (1-13).

doesn't want to go to hell, and now he's prepared to help Sam find a way to save him. But it might just be too little too late.

VERDICT – 8.5 out of 10

EPISODE 3-11
MYSTERY SPOT

TRANSMISSION DATES
US first aired: 14 February 2008
UK first aired: 6 April 2008

CREDITS
Writer: Jeremy Carver and Emily McLaughlin
Teleplay by Jeremy Carver
Director: Kim Manners

RECURRING ROLES
Jim Beaver (Bobby Singer), Richard Speight Jr (Trickster)

GUEST STARS
David Abbott (Judge Myers), Lloyd Berry (Mr Pickett), Rob deLeeuw (Clem), Derek
Green (Ed), Katherine Horsman (Ms Hasselback), Brock Johnson (Sid), Kasey Kieler
(Kel), Andrew McIlroy (P J Karpiak), Dean Moen (Randy), Denalda Williams (Doris)

SYNOPSIS
When investigating a disappearance at a tourist attraction, Sam gets caught in a time
loop where he relives Tuesday over and over again, and each day Dean is killed. After
watching Dean die over one hundred times, Sam finally realises that the Trickster
is manipulating reality. Forcing the Trickster to end the loop, Sam wakes up on
Wednesday, only for Dean to get shot for real. Sam goes on an obsessive bender for
the next six months, killing monsters and trying to locate the Trickster. Then Bobby
finds a blood ritual to force the Trickster to come to them. But Sam figures out that
Bobby is just one of the Trickster's illusions and puts a stake through his back. When
the Trickster appears, he admits he's bored of getting revenge and sends Sam back to
the Wednesday when Dean was alive.

CAN YOU SURVIVE TO THE TITLES?
Dean bleeds all over the floor after taking both barrels to the chest while prowling
around the Mystery Spot tourist attraction. But the boy isn't finished dying yet ...

LOCATION, LOCATION, LOCATION

The Mystery Spot, Broward County, Florida; then, when Sam goes on the rampage, he visits Death Valley, Nevada and Austin, Texas plus others places not mentioned.

LEGENDARY ROOTS

A time loop is usually centred around an individual who relives the same series of events for a set amount of time, usually a few hours or a day. The memory of events for the individual concerned remains intact. Anyone else who has been in contact with the individual for the length of the time loop has no idea what's happening and just carries on as normal, repeating exactly what has happened before.

The person stuck in the time loop usually has to figure out why they are there and fix or amend something during in order to release themselves from the loop and move on with their lives.

SQUEEZE OF THE WEEK

It's more of a body-check of the week as Dexter Hasselback's daughter gets to bump repeatedly into Dean's rather gorgeous shoulder as she wanders up the street with her leaflets about her missing dad. Clearly she just can't help being drawn towards his handsome features, whether she's looking or not.

BODY COUNT

Dean doesn't make it to the titles and he doesn't make it to the first advert break either or the second one. It's morbid fun watching the myriad ways he gets bumped off through this episode, and you should be able to spot him getting: shot in the (firm, muscular) chest, run over, crushed under furniture, choked on a sausage, head injury/ broken neck in the shower, poisoned by a taco, electrocuted by his razor, killed by Sam with an axe, then shot with an arrow by the waitress (not seen on screen). On the one hundredth Tuesday, Dean is savaged by a golden retriever. On the one hundred and first day, Sam unmasks the Trickster and wakes up on Wednesday, when Dean dies for the last time, shot with a hand gun by Cal.

TOOLKIT

- Having your favourite *hand gun* tucked down your trousers when you head off for breakfast is the hunter's way – to be ready for anything, anytime, anywhere – and will probably get you better service at the table.
- The trusty *EMF meter* has been dusted off and brought out of the cupboard[315].

---

315 We haven't seen the boys use this since 'Hollywood Babylon' (2-18).

- A *good torch* will help you search a building after dark but isn't much of a defence against a man with a shotgun and a twitchy finger – especially if you've just put your handgun on the floor.
- The *ability to pick pockets* helps when you're trying to keep the roads safer.
- Threatening a demi-god would be impossible without *a large wooden stake dipped in blood* to hand. Just make sure you've got the actual demi-god cornered rather than one of his illusions of himself this time.

MEMORABLE MOMENTS

Every single damn time Dean pops his clogs – they're all so very, very funny.

And the excruciatingly long moment after Sam has killed the fake-Bobby – or is it the real Bobby?

THE CAR'S THE STAR

The arsenal gets a clear-out once Sam is in charge. There's no mess and all the weapons are neatly stored in their own foam settings. Wonder if he dusted the interior too?

MOTEL MAYHEM

The flamingo-themed motel doesn't raise Sam's spirits at all, and after 100 days with a flamingo mural above the bed, plastic flamingos in the bathroom and flamingo wallpaper, no wonder he's grumpy.

SPOOK RULES

Mystery Spots:
- The lore is pretty nuts about these places – the magnetic fields are so strong that they can bend space-time, balls roll uphill, furniture is (nailed) on the ceiling and holes can open up and transport victims to unknown destinations.

Psychic powers:
- Sam's visions are not overly vivid, and the differences between one of his visions and living through a Tuesday for real are very obvious to him.

Tricksters:
- A Trickster's *modus operandi* is to pick someone who needs to be taken down a peg or two and give them their just deserts – in this case, the vindictive journalist who puts Mystery Spot tourist attractions out of business gets thrown down a wormhole.
- A Trickster is one of the few creatures capable of making reality out of nothing.

- And when a Trickster is controlling your reality, it makes it impossible for you to save your brother. You can rip the local Mystery Spot apart, burn it down or visit it at a different time of day; you can have something different for breakfast or not have breakfast at all; you can even steal car keys from the guy who could knock down your brother as well; but it won't make any difference.

Fake Spook Rules from the Fake Bobby:
- To summon a Trickster you need to be in a location where he used his magic, and it has to be done at a specific time or you'll have to wait another 50 years.
- The Trickster-summoning ritual requires a gallon of fresh human blood, red candles, two undisclosed herbs and spices and chalk to draw the symbol on the floor.

DID YOU SPOT?

The moment when Dean gets run over seems to be a quiet homage to the horror movie *Final Destination* (2000).

George's Taverna in Steveston is seen behind Sam and Dean as they walk away from the breakfast diner (blue and white sign). The taverna is actually located on Moncton St in Richmond, BC, Canada, which means Dean gets run over on the corner of Moncton St and 2nd Ave, next to the drugstore. This stretch of street was also used in 'Bloody Mary' (1-05) when Sam sees Jessica's ghost (in a white dress) on the corner near the taverna as he and Dean drive past in the Impala.

GOING UNDERCOVER

The boys trot out the tried and trusted reporters disguise to interrogate Mr Carpiak, the owner of the Mystery Spot, but no names or publications are given.

CULTURAL REFERENCES

Dean: 'Sounds pretty *X-Files* to me.': *The X-Files* is another supernatural series about unexplained occurrences. Kim Manners directed this episode and the similar *The X-Files* episode 'Monday' (6-14).

Dean: 'Dingo ate my baby crazy.': Refers to an incident that occurred in Australia in 1980, when Azaria Chamberlain, a nine month old baby, disappeared under mysterious circumstances near Uluru (Ayers Rock). The Chamberlain family were camping and the mother, Lindy Chamberlain, claimed to have seen a dingo carrying her baby from their tent. She was convicted of murdering her baby but later acquitted when new evidence suggested that the baby was, in fact, killed by a dingo.

Dean: 'Like *Groundhog Day*?': *Groundhog Day* is a 1993 comedy movie starring

Bill Murray, whose character is forced to relive the same day over and over, until he becomes a better person and wins the heart of Rita (played by Andy McDowell).

Dean: 'Okay Kojak, let's get you outside.': *Kojak* was a detective series about a tough, folliclely-challenged cop played by Telly Savalas, which ran from 1973 to 1978.

Trickster: 'You're like Travis Bickle in a skirt.': Travis Bickle was played by Robert DeNiro in the 1976 Martin Scorsese movie *Taxi Driver*. Bickle is an unstable Vietnam veteran who protects a prostitute.

Trickster: 'Whoever said Dean was the dysfunctional one has never seen you with a sharp object in your hand. Holy *Full Metal Jacket*.': *Full Metal Jacket* is a Stanley Kubrick movie released in 1987 that follows a group of young men training to become soldiers. It portrays the dehumanisation of the group leading them to be psychotic killers in the Vietnam War.

Sam: 'Okay, look, I'm just saying that there are spots in the world where holes open up and swallow people. The Bermuda Triangle, the Oregon Vortex ...': The House of Mystery is a cabin belonging to the Old Grey Eagle Mining Company in Gold Hill, Oregon, and was built in 1904. It was used as assay office and later a tool shed. It is reported to sit on the Oregon Vortex. In the area around the cabin, tennis balls roll upwards, brooms stand on their end and people seem to grow in height depending on where they stand.

The Bermuda Triangle is an area in the Atlantic Ocean near Bermuda, Florida and Puerto Rico, where a number of aircraft and vessels have reportedly disappeared without trace.

GOOFS AND FLUFFS

When Dean first pops his head out from behind the shower curtain, his hair is soaped flat to his head. In the next shot, where he hasn't moved since talking to Sam, it is suddenly soaped into a Mohawk style.

On the second Tuesday, after the blonde has bumped into Dean, a couple start walking from right to left and manage to do it twice – once when Dean is talking then again when Sam is talking.

The rule seems to be that only Sam can make the repeating events change – by stopping Dean going to the diner or pinching Mr Pickett's keys. This theory is upheld when Sam spots the strawberry syrup instead of the maple syrup – how did it change if Sam didn't influence it? But there are a couple other things that change without Sam's influence: on the first Tuesday, a couple come out of the shop (the lady is wearing a red coat) behind Sam and Dean as they walk down the street, but they aren't there on any of the other days we see; and on the second Tuesday, Dean's gargling comes with bubbles (whereas it didn't on the first Tuesday).

HAVEN'T I SEEN YOU BEFORE?

Lloyd Berry's acting credits include *AVP: Requiem*, *Poltergeist: The Legacy* and *Highlander: The Series*. Rob deLeeuw has also been in *Dark Angel* and *Big Wolf on Campus*. Derek Green's credits include *Kyle XY*, *Blood Ties* and *Smallville*. Katherine Horsman appeared in *Blade: The Series*, *Dead Like Me* and *Smallville*. Brock Johnson was in *Andromeda*, *Smallville* and *Painkiller Jane*. Kasey Kieler can be seen in an episode of *Reaper*. Andrew McIlroy was in *Battlestar Galactica*, *Blade: The Series* and *Tru Calling*. Dean Moen featured in *Stargate SG-1* and *Tru Calling*. Richard Speight Jr has been in *Jericho*, *Alias* and *Independence Day*. Denalda Williams was in *Six Feet Under* and *The X-Files*.

BEHIND THE SCENES

The Season Three Supernatural Companion reveals that this was one of the episodes on which the crew pranked Ackles and Padalecki. The boys are Texans, and production designer Jerry Wanek is a fan of the Wisconsin-based Green Bay Packers American football team. There was a big football game on, so Wanek:

- Put Packers memorabilia all over the boys' trailers.
- Got the caterer to cook Wisconsin bratwurst for lunch.
- Got everybody to wear Packers helmets and masks of Packers star Brett Favre, so when the boys came out of one the buildings on set they saw 75 Brett Favres staring at them.

MUSICAL INTERLUDE

- 'Heat Of The Moment' – Asia – on the radio as Sam and Dean wake up each Tuesday at 7:30 am.
- 'Back In Time' – Huey Lewis and The News – when Sam finally wakes up on Wednesday.

ANALYSIS

This is simply the funniest episode since *Supernatural* started, and there's some pretty stiff competition out there – what with slow dancing aliens[316], unlucky rabbit's feet[317] and swarms of bees[318]. What makes the giggles worse is that it's really a serious situation, but from the moment Dean dies under the falling furniture and we see his little legs sticking out from underneath, it's impossible to keep a straight face. By the

---

316 In 'Tall Tales' (2-15).

317 In 'Bad Day At Black Rock' (3-03).

318 The unintentionally funny 'Bugs' (1-08).

time he gets savaged by the golden retriever, you're wiping away the tears in your eyes. Then the first stupendous plot twist arrives with Wednesday and Dean dies 'for real'.

. The episode then transforms into something far darker, as Sam's psyche is exposed and he heads full-tilt into obsession-fuelled rage (something of a family trait that) but strangely without the presence of Ruby – which gives a vague undertone that this is actually still the Trickster's reality he's in.

With Sam hunting alone, things align more to his preferences – the car trunk is more organised[319], with foam packing keeping everything safely in place; Sam's research papers are still pinned to the wall but there's nothing random about their placement, they all line up in perfect order; the top of the toothpaste tube is clean; and Sam straightens his bed after getting up to keep the room tidy. It's obvious that Dean is the slob influence, and it's no wonder that they've bickered about it in the past.

But Sam can't really cope with the emotional fall-out of losing Dean, and his focus on getting his brother back is so narrow that it excludes Bobby and the pleasures of eating, except as a necessity, and he's even numb to pain – as seen when he extracts the bullet and sews up his own wounds. Nothing can stop him in his search for the Trickster.

Then the second excellent twist kicks in, and it takes the loooongest moment for Bobby to start shimmering before disappearing. It's just a shame that what follows in the final exchange between a supposedly impulsive Trickster and the puppy-dog-eyed Sammy undermines the entire episode. That the Trickster would want to get revenge on the Winchesters is understandable, but all the stuff about wanting to teach Sam a lesson is just too flimsy – the Trickster has the world at his beck and call, why should he care about how Sam copes with watching his brother die?

It's possible that the Trickster's involvement is part of some bigger picture, but until that connection is revealed this remains the strongest and weakest of episodes at the same time.

VERDICT – 8 out of 10

---

319 Much like John Winchester's trunk in 'Dead Man's Blood' (1-20).

EPISODE 3-12
JUS IN BELO

TRANSMISSION DATES
US first aired: 21 February 2008
UK first aired: 13 April 2008

CREDITS
Writer: Sera Gamble
Director: Philip Sgriccia

RECURRING ROLES
Lauren Cohan (Bela Talbot), Katie Cassidy (Ruby), Charles Malik Whitfield (Special Agent Victor Henricksen)

GUEST STARS
Val Cole (News Anchor), Peter DeLuise (Steven Groves), Kurt Evans (Special Agent Carl Reidy), Aimee Garcia (Nancy Fitzgerald), Tyler McClendon (Deputy Phil Amici), Rachel Pattee (Lilith), Ron Robinson (Cop), Stoney Westmoreland (Sheriff Melvin Dodd)

SYNOPSIS
While raiding Bela's flat for the Colt, the boys are arrested by Victor Henricksen (acting on a tip-off from Bela). Henricksen calls in the good news to his boss, Steven Groves, who immediately flies out to the small town jail where the boys are incarcerated. But Groves is possessed, and after trying to kill Sam and Dean, the demon flees Groves' dead body to tell the demon hordes where the brothers can be found. Returning ahead of the hordes, the demon possesses Henricksen and kills the Sheriff. Finally Henricksen knows about demons, and he and the boys join forces to defend the jail. Ruby fights her way into the jail to offer her life – along with virgin Nancy's life – in a spell to kill all the demons, but Sam and Dean lure all the demons inside the jail, trap them and exorcise them instead. The new demon leader, Lilith, arrives at the jail after Sam and Dean have left, and kills everyone inside.

CAN YOU SURVIVE TO THE TITLES?
No-one dies in the opening; it's all about the boys being screwed over by Bela yet again (will they ever learn?) then being detained in custody by Agent Henricksen.

LOCATION, LOCATION, LOCATION
Monument County Sheriff's Office, Colorado; The Wagon Trail Motel, room 12, after the siege is over.

LEGENDARY ROOTS
Magical traditions often call for virgins to be involved in proceedings due to their purity, but in the broader sense this need for purity also applies to the instruments and materials used during traditional magical operations – like wax and parchment etc – as they need to be free of the influence of other activities.

Some sources say that in the older magical traditions, clairvoyants and scryers should be virgins to ensure the clarity and accuracy of the visions received.

SQUEEZE OF THE WEEK
No squeezes, but it is a surprise that Dean doesn't make Nancy an offer to upgrade her virginity status for her.

SIBLING RIVALRY
When Sam is cleaning and bandaging Dean's bullet wound in his shoulder and Sam calls him a wuss.

BODY COUNT
FBI Deputy Director Steven Groves' meat-suit is dead as soon as the demon moves out of residence. Then the chopper pilot gets it, along with the four cops working for Sheriff Dodds, the demon cutting their throats. Then a bit of meat-suit hopping takes out FBI Agent Reidy. Dodds himself is killed by Henricksen's meat–suit, but Henricksen survives the possession experience thanks to Sam's inventiveness with a toilet full of water and a rosary. And just when everyone thinks they're safe, Lilith turns up to take out the jailhouse survivors – Deputy Amici, Nancy and Henricksen. A body count into double figures for a change.

Given that Team Winchester don't actually kill any of the possessed townsfolk, that changes the demon war score to: Team Winchester – still on ten (possessed) innocents killed; the Demons – a whopping 18.

TOOLKIT
- *Hand guns* are essential when you're going after a double-dealing thief with no moral fibre and a totally self-centred attitude.
- Knowing the *Rituale Romanum* off by heart is crucial. Learn it once and it'll pay you back time after time after time. And for scaling up your efforts for maximum

effect, why not use a *tape recorder and speaker system* to ensure your work reaches the largest audience possible?

- The blessing to turn ordinary water into *holy water* is another bit of ritual that will pay you back repeatedly if you take the time to learn it. But you'll need a *rosary* too for this one – so pickpocket skills will be needed if you can't get down to the store in time.
- *Flasks* for holding the holy water will make fighting off a horde of demons just so much easier, so always put them in the trunk.
- *Red spray paint* is ideal for drawing those protective *Devil's Traps* but keep a knife handy to scrape off the paint and break the seal should you trap someone on your own side.
- *Protective amulets* will keep newbies safe from possession, but for the regular hunter you're better getting a permanent *tattooed amulet* done on your firm pectoral muscles for round-the-clock protection.
- Hex bags from a friendly demon will keep the big bad demon from finding you too.
- And where would anyone be without *half a ton of salt* to seal windows and doors when the hordes are baying for your bloody carcass.

MEMORABLE MOMENTS

The anticipation is divine when Henricksen walks into the room and the boys strain to look up to see his face..

Both of the demonic possessions are a surprise – the first one really hits home because Dean takes the bullet in the shoulder; the second one works because you're expecting it to be the Sheriff and his death happens so quickly that it takes time to catch up with the plot. Dean's 'But you didn't shoot the Deputy' quip is just a wonderful example of black humour (one of many throughout this episode)[320].

SPOOK RULES

Four standard demon rules are used, plus three new points:

- Demons can be trapped if they put their meat-suit within the edges of a Devil's Trap inscription.
- You can tell when one or more demons are approaching because the lights will flicker.
- They can't cross an unbroken salt line at a door or window.
- Possessed people's eyes turn black and they can be exorcised using the *Rituale*

---

320 A feature this episode shares with 'Faith' (1-12).

Romanum.
- Big, bad, nasty, powerful demons that run the pack have white eyes.
- Certain spells are capable of vaporising demons within a one mile radius, but they require a person of virtue (a virgin) and their heart must be cut out of their chest at the right moment during the casting. The spell won't harm the meat-suits the demons are using.
- The more energy that is expended in a destructive blast, the more powerful the demon that caused it.

DID YOU SPOT?

This is the first episode that features all four main characters.

According to the *Season Three Supernatural Companion*, the petrol station – Gibson's Gas – was named after visual effects supervisor Ivan Hayden's girlfriend; and one of the Wanted posters features a photograph of director Phil Scriggia's daughter.

CULTURAL REFERENCES

Henriksen asks Dean if he knows what decision he is trying to make, Dean: 'Oh I don't know, what – whether Cialis will help you with your little condition?': Cialis is a drug used for erectile dysfunction, similar to Viagra.

Henricksen: 'Think Hannibal Lecter and his half-wit little brother!': Hannibal Lecter is the serial killer from the novels by Thomas Harris. He has appeared in *Red Dragon* (1981), *The Silence of the Lambs* (1988), *Hannibal* (1999) and the prequel *Hannibal Rising* (2006), which have all been adapted into feature films.

Dean: 'How do we Houdini out of this one?': Harry Houdini (1874-1926) was a famous escapologist noted for the Chinese Water Torture Cell escape.

Henriksen: 'I shot the Sheriff.'; Dean: 'But you didn't shoot the Deputy.': A quote from the Bob Marley 1973 record 'I Shot The Sheriff'.

Henricksen: 'Look, I get it, you're Mayberry PD.': Mayberry, North Carolina, was the setting for the fictional sitcom *The Andy Griffith Show* (1960-1968), which followed the misadventures of widowed sheriff Andy Taylor and his deputy Officer Barney Fife. Fife was the kind of cop who sat on a porch all day eating doughnuts, hence Henricksen's comment.

Henricksen: 'I'll get them out of your hair and on their way to Supermax, and you'll be home in enough time to watch the *Farm Report*.': *Farm Report* is a US television show focusing on agriculture and its related business and rural life.

GOOFS AND FLUFFS

When Henricksen phones his boss, he starts to remove his bullet-proof vest by undoing the velcro on his left-hand side. In the next shot, he opens the velcro fastenings on the same side again.

When Dean says, 'You don't poke a bear with a BB gun, it's just gonna make him mad,' for the second half of the sentence his lips aren't moving in the foreground of the shot.

HAVEN'T I SEEN YOU BEFORE?

Vale Cole has been in *AVP: Requiem*, *The 4400*, *Smallville* and *Blade: The Series*. Peter DeLuise features in a number of *Stargate SG-1* episodes, *SeaQuest DSV* as Dagwood and *21 Jump Street* as Officer Doug Penhall. Kurt Evans has also been in *Watchmen*, *Stargate SG-1*, *Taken* and *Battlestar Galactica* as paramedic Howard Kim. Aimee Garcia's acting credits include *Angel* and *7eventy 5ive*. Tyler McClendon's other credits include *Stargate: Atlantis* as Kenny Wraith, *Watchmen* and *A Town Called Eureka*. Rachel Pattee was in *Tin Man*. Ron Robinson has featured in *Star Trek: Voyager*, *The Crow: Stairway To Heaven* and *The Sentinel*. Stoney Westmoreland's credits include *Seven Days* and *Star Trek: Voyager*. Charles Malik Whitfield features in *Law & Order* and *The Guardian*.

Ron Robinson also appears in 'Route 666' (1-13).

BEHIND THE SCENES

Writer Sera Gamble was out of her comfort zone with this episode. She explained in *The Official Supernatural Magazine* #5 that they often have a few episodes that come up with no particular owner. Gamble usually goes for the misfits, witches or student stories but this time got the one that was full of cops. She found it a challenge but was ultimately proud of the episode.

Lauren Cohan (Bela) and Katie Cassidy (Ruby) finally appear in the same episode, but back when they were cast, their roles could so easily have been reversed. Cohan auditioned for Ruby's part but was called back to audition for Bela, while Cassidy auditioned for Bela and (yes, you got it) got called back to audition for Ruby.

MUSICAL INTERLUDE

All music was written specifically for this episode.

ANALYSIS

A very tense, action-filled episode with the definite feel of *Assault on Precinct 13* (1976) about it, with the siege scenario and the prisoners being held in the jail being freed to help with the defence of the station. The *Supernatural* version substitutes demon-possessed townsfolk instead of gang members and throws in Special Agent

Henricksen too. When he's involved, you just know it's going to get claustrophobic for the boys and only the cleverest ideas and local support are going to get them out of trouble[321]. The episode delivers on both of these fronts (claustrophobia and clever ideas) but also mixes in a series of shock attacks, a set of gory deaths, an impressive cloud of electrified demonic smoke and an exploding helicopter.

But as usual, it's how the characters deal with events that gives the episode depth, and it's Henricksen who forms the focal point this time, with some interesting points for Ruby and a couple of quiet but significant changes for the boys.

We finally get to learn more about Henricksen's background, and given that he's FBI it's no surprise he has a string of ex-wives behind him and no-one waiting at home. He's an intelligent bloke and understands the people he's tasked to apprehend. He knows that the threat of a small cell will worry two guys who currently roam the length and breadth of the US; he knows that threatening to split them up so they never see each other again will deeply affect two people who live out of each other's pockets; and he thinks he understands their (in his view 'distorted') family values, so he spends some time bad-mouthing John Winchester to obvious effect.

Along with that intelligence, Henricksen carries an unflappable demeanour, even when everyone around him is panicking. The combination of these two traits probably accounts for the ease with which he slips into the boys' world of monsters. He can't deny being possessed, so he accepts the situation quickly and moves onto more important issues like protecting himself and the boys.

For Sam and Dean, protection against demons is business as usual, but even between them there's a role reversal happening. It's probably the impact of Sam's experiences of watching Dean die[322] and then having to cope without him, but he doesn't object to Ruby's suggestion to kill Nancy as part of the ritual[323]. This time Dean is taking the compassionate route and representing someone else's point of view – something Sam did regularly back in Season One. But the change is mutual: Dean is trying to balance Sam's more extreme decisions while Sam is learning to kill more efficiently without procrastinating so much about the situation (thereby improving his chances for survival after Dean has gone).

The other interesting point is that Sam hadn't told Dean that the demons are out

---

321 They've eluded Henricksen twice before, in 'Nightshifter' (2-12) where they disguised themselves as SWAT Team members to escape; and in 'Folsom Prison Blues' (2-19) where Henricksen was sent to the wrong cemetery after the boys escaped from prison.

322 In 'Mystery Spot' (3-11).

323 Slightly illogical given Sam's attitude with fake-Bobby in 'Mystery Spot' (3-11) about only agreeing to kill an innocent person for their blood because he knew Bobby was not real.

to get them or that there is a new leader rising from the demon ranks. The Tammi-demon told Sam about it before Dean arrived on the scene[324] but Sam clearly forgot to pass this info on – there's no reason to think that he kept it back deliberately, but it does continue to raise the question of trust between the two boys.

It's Ruby who is at the source of creating that mistrust by stirring it between Sam and Dean, but she's becoming a whole bunch of contradictions now, because we find that she's willing to give her life to save Sam's. The big unanswered question is, why? Also, it's not entirely clear whether she would actually have been killed or just sent back to hell after the spell. But she fights her way into the jail, killing her own kind to help the boys, and the implication is that she's on Sam's side all the way. But there's still a nagging doubt that she has a hidden agenda – she's still a demon, after all.

There are more details about the other demons freed from hell too. We get solid confirmation that there's a contract out on the boys' heads, giving the lower demons the motivation to search for them. But it's an organised approach rather than a free-for-all, and they have scouts possessing key people, like Steven Groves, Henricksen's boss, to help find Sam and Dean. The scouts also have communication lines set up to call for back-up when they've found the boys, so they can have a substantial demon force available in just a couple of hours.

And we finally meet the most important demon of Season Three, Lilith, who is all the more fundamentally disturbing because of her choice of little girl meat-suit. Her presence establishes her ruthlessness as well as her differences from the main demon horde – with her white eyes rather than the normal black. She also delivers the final twist in the story by killing everyone in the jail that Sam and Dean have fought to save, something that gives Ruby the moral high ground over the boys' decision not to go with her plan[325].

So this is a packed episode that fleshes out the demonic threat that's been looming since the gates to hell were opened, and it'll be interesting to see how it develops from here – especially with the rest of the season being compacted due to the 2008 writers' strike.

VERDICT – 9 out of 10

---

324 In 'Malleus Mallificarum' (3-09), although the Tammi-demon didn't mention Lilith's name.
325 Well this is a Sera Gamble story, there had to be some moral grey area included somewhere.

Episode 3-13
Ghostfacers

Transmission Dates
US first aired: 24 April 2008
UK first aired: 8 June 2008

Credits
Writer: Ben Edlund
Director: Phil Sgriccia

Recurring Roles
A J Buckley (Ed Zeddmore), Travis Wester (Harry Spengler)

Guest Stars
Austin Basis (Kenny Spruce), John DeSantis (Freeman Daggett), Dave Hospes (Shooting Victim/Travelling Salesman), Brittany Ishibashi (Maggie Zeddmore), Dustin Milligan (Alan J Corbett), Tony Morelli (Train Victim/Staggering Man)

Synopsis
The *Ghostfacers* pilot episode: Harry Spengler and Ed Zeddmore[326] introduce their first case as their team investigates the repeated haunting at Morton House. Sam and Dean arrive to investigate the same haunting and try to get the Ghostfacers out of the house and out of harm's way. But the house is sealed and Corbett (one of the *Ghostfacers* team) and then Sam both disappear. While Dean tries to find out where they are being held, Corbett is murdered by the ghost, Freeman Daggett. Dean finds Sam just in time to save his life, then Corbett's ghost attacks Daggett's ghost and drags it into the afterlife. Sam and Dean view the film footage of events at *Ghostfacers* HQ but leave an electromagnet in the room that erases all evidence of the haunting.

Can You Survive to the Titles?
No deaths, action or excitement in the opener. There's just Harry and Ed introducing *Ghostfacers*.

---

326 Who first appeared in 'Hell House' (1-17).

Location, Location, Location

It may be Wisconsin, but it's hard to tell from Ed's and Harry's car plates; Corbett said he saw the flyers at the outlet mall in Scogan, but an extensive search with varied spellings doesn't turn up anything to indicate where they might be.

Legendary Roots

Ghosts come in many different forms, from a quiet, chilling presence to a mischievous or vindictive poltergeist[327]. Some spend all their time repeating the same set of actions over and over again.

It's believed that a dead person can leave behind some residual energy that is an imprint or recording of an event. This event is often replayed without deviation even if the location where the recording is being played out has undergone changes, such as doors or walls being moved. The situation recorded by the spirit varies from a simple event to something much more traumatic.

Squeeze of the Week

The only people seeing any action are Harry and Maggie, who are caught snogging on camera.

Sibling Rivalry

When Sam realises that they're locked in with a murderous ghost, he has a go at Dean – because despite having two months left before the deal comes due, it looks like they might be dying that night instead and he's not happy about it. Understandable really.

Body Count

Only Corbett loses his life, but it's a gruesome way to go – stabbed through the back of the neck, right the way through to the front and out of his throat. Ew!

Toolkit

- *Bolt cutters* to remove the chains on the fencing around the haunted building.
- To enable you to record the ghostly happenings, *normal cameras* and *night vision cameras* will be needed, along with *audio equipment* to capture EVP (Electronic Voice Phenomena)[328].
- *Flashlights* will help you to see where you're going.
- The trusty *EMF meter* and a *thermometer* will forewarn you about spooky

---

327 See 'Home' (1-09) for more on poltergeists.

328 EVP was first heard in 'The Woman in White' (1-01), then recorded again in 'Hollywood Babylon' (2-18)

appearances.
- *Chairs* can be handy if you find yourself in a house experiencing a supernatural lock-down and you need to try to break the doors down.
- *Salt* is one item you should never leave home without – it's protective in any number of situations but especially useful against ghosts.
- And of course the *salt-loaded shotgun* is another must-have piece of kit.
- The final piece of hardware required if you need to keep the details of the haunting secret is an *electromagnet 'bomb'*, which once set off will erase all the hard drives and tapes in the vicinity.

MEMORABLE MOMENTS
Corbett really is the star of this episode, probably sacrificing his eternal soul to save his friends and the man he loves.

SPOOK RULES
Most of the spook rules have already been established, but there are a couple of modifications to include.

The existing rules are:
- Spooks will come back to a time and place that has some personal significance to them, often at regular intervals, like each year or on every 29 February.
- A spirit is often driven by the desire for revenge, and they are bound to the real world by their own remains, unfinished business or in this case extreme loneliness.
- Love or hate can trap a spirit in an eternal loop, repeating the same tragedies.
- Just before they appear, evil spirits can cause flashlights to go off, cameras to register static and a temperature drop.
- Ghosts have the power to seal the doors and windows of a building to keep the victims inside.

The new rules are:
- Death echoes are ghosts trapped replaying the moment of their death forever. They're about as dangerous as a scary movie.
- Death echoes can be shocked out of their eternal loop, usually by someone connected to the deceased, if they can talk to the part of the spirit that is still human.
- Death echoes will usually haunt the places where they lived or died, but

occasionally they will haunt buildings where their bodies have been stuffed and stored.

- A harmless death echo will register around 10.6 or 10.7 on the EMF meter; a psychotic ghost bent on murdering you will register well over 11.0.
- Some ghosts can make your (not so) little brother disappear in an instant.
- A person doesn't have to be murdered in order to come back and haunt – even a ghost who commits suicide can come back and kill if they're determined enough.
- A good spirit can cancel out an evil spirit's energy. When this happens, the good spirit is destroyed in the process. This is probably what happens when Corbett grabs Daggett.

DID YOU SPOT?

There are a couple of in-jokes loitering in the script. First, Ed mentions the writers' strike in the opening sequence; this refers to the real-life Writers' Guild of America strike in early 2008 that delayed filming of this episode and shortened Season Three from 22 episodes to 16.

Secondly, Harry wonders who those 'assholes from Texas' are and while it's true enough that 'Hell House' (1-17) was indeed set in Texas, it's also a fact that both lead actors are from that State too.

This is the first episode where all the swear words are bleeped out and none of the credits roll until the end.

CULTURAL REFERENCES

When Dean learns that Daggett's problem was loneliness, Dean: 'What, he's never heard of a RealDoll?': RealDoll is supposedly the world's finest sex doll.

Sam: 'Daggett was the Norman Bates stuff-your-mother kind of lonely.': Norman Bates is the main character in the 1960 movie *Psycho*, directed by Alfred Hitchcock. He looks after his mother at their motel, but it is revealed at the end that her preserved corpse is actually in the cellar, and Norman has been portraying her himself throughout the film. There were three sequels produced in later years.

Spruce: 'I am 15/16ths Jew, but 1/16th Cherokee. My grandfather is a mohel, my great-grandfather was a tallismaker, and my great-great-grandfather was a degenerate gambler and had a peyote addiction.': A mohel is a Jewish man skilled in circumcision. A tallismaker is someone who makes a shawl, with a ritually-knotted fringe at each corner, which is worn by Jews at morning prayer. And peyote (lophophora williamsii) is a small cactus known for its psychoactive properties.

Spruce: 'Yo Corbett dude. You're Robocop.': Robocop is a character from the 1987 film of the same name. He is a murdered cop, brought back to life as a cyborg to fight crime in Detroit.

Dean: 'You and Rambo need to get your girlfriends and get out of here.': Rambo is a character originally from a novel by David Morell and later featured in a series of action movies.

Maggie: 'What are these, c-rations?': C-rations were the canned rations that were pre-cooked or prepared and issued to the US military in the 1940s and 1950s, usually for the land forces when fresh items (A-rations) or unprepared food (B-rations) or survival rations (K- and D-rations) were not sufficient.

Ed: 'Hey, Menudo left their dance bag behind.': Menudo was a boy band from Puerto Rico, formed in 1970 but having their main success in the '80s.

Harry: 'Yeah, but Ed and I pretty much call the shots at the Kinko's where we work.': Kinko's was a copy shop before being bought out by FedEx.

GOOFS AND FLUFFS

If Daggett has murdered a whole string of people over the years, why isn't the bomb shelter overflowing with stuffed cadavers enjoying the party? And the house should be overrun with lots of different death echoes replaying too.

When the second death echo turns up, Dean asks if it is the same one the Ghostfacers have seen before – but Dean has watched the footage of the first death echo with everyone else, so he should know it is a different death echo.

Sam's party hat is on his head when Dean breaks the door down but not when Dean comes to untie him.

HAVEN'T I SEEN YOU BEFORE?

Austin Basis featured in *7eventy 5ive* and *American Zombie*. A J Buckley has been in *The X-Files*, *Nightstalker* and *Silent Walking*. John DeSantis played Thorne in *Blade: The Series* and also featured in *The Dresden Files*, *Flash Gordon* and *Dark Angel*. Dave Hospes has mainly featured as a stuntman, including in *AVP: Requiem*, *Watchmen*, *Fantastic Four* and *Fantastic Four: Rise Of The Silver Surfer* and the X-Men movies. Brittany Ishibashi has also been in *Angel*. Dustin Milligan played Marcus in *Final Destination 3*, Trevor Eastman in the *Butterfly Effect 2* and has also been in *Dead Like Me* and *Andromeda*. Tony Morelli's other acting credits include *The X-Files*, *Final Destination 3* and *Stargate SG-1*, and his stunt career includes *The X-Files: I Want To Believe*, *X-Men: The Last Stand* and *Fantastic Four: Rise of the Silver Surfer*. Travis Wester appeared in *Mr Rhodes* as Ethan alongside Jensen Ackles.

BEHIND THE SCENES

According to the *Season Three Supernatural Companion*, director Phil Sgriccia created an extra scene that wasn't in the script – he put the rat on the floor and didn't tell actor Travis Wester that it was there. Wester just played along with it and really freaked out.

The *Companion* also says that the actors were asked to carry their own cameras and lights – the only episode where this has happened. Director of photography Serge Ladouceur expanded on this aspect of the episode in *The Official Supernatural Magazine* #5 explaining how the episode was scripted with imperfections so it would look like it wasn't planned, and feel more like a reality TV show.

Musical Interlude
- 'Ghostfacers Theme' – plays at the end of the opener and repeats as Sam and Dean drive off.
- 'We're An American Band' – Grand Funk Railroad – as Sam and Dean drive past the Ghostfacers as they break into Morton House.
- 'Hocus Pocus' – Focus – when the Ghostfacers set up the eagles' nest.
- 'It's My Party' – Lesley Gore – at Daggett's party and during Corbett's death.

Analysis
When this was originally aired, it was the first episode after the writers' strike, and besides feeling immense relief that the show hadn't been cancelled (as many others were), viewers had also been deprived of their Sam and Dean fix for some time. Events in 'Jus in Belo' (3-12) had left a mini cliff-hanger around what Lilith was going to do next, and after the forced break of the strike, expectations were (perhaps unusually) high.

So when 'Ghostfacers' came along, with its emphasis on amateur morons, with only a small sweetener in the shape of Sam and Dean, it's no surprise that it disappointed. There were so many things that needed exploring in the overall arcs of Lilith and Dean's deal that sitting through the Ghostfacer shenanigans at the time was almost painful.

But time heals all wounds (or at least some) and it's easier to appreciate the episode more when you're watching it back on DVD and the wait between episodes is as small as you want it to be. You can even fast–forward, if you want, to take out the irritating scenes where a gaggle of Ghostfacers go running round the house, shouting loudly with flashlights akimbo.

Now it's easier to see that there are lots of different homages going on, with the hat being tipped to shows like *Ghost Hunters* from the 1970s through the 1980s *Friday the 13th*[329] to the ground breaking 1999 movie *The Blair Witch Project*[330].

---

329 Corbett's death is reminiscent of when Kevin Bacon's character gets the arrowhead through the neck.

330 With similar shaky handheld camerawork.

They aren't particularly serious homages either, with lots of slapstick and bungling going on as the Ghostfacers stagger through the hunt, unwittingly hampering Sam and Dean at every opportunity. It does all get a little tiresome after a while as it descends into pointless immature infighting between the Ghostfacer team, and the situation is only made worse by the tragic (and horrific) death of Corbett. This serious situation sits awkwardly in the middle of the silliness and the overall effect is really rather uncomfortable.

But awkward laughs or not, these are going to be the last we'll get before events turn dark again. Dean has two months before his deal becomes due, and the boys still don't have any clue who owns the contract. And even if they did, they have no way of killing them since Bela stole the Colt. Just what can they try next to save Dean's soul?

VERDICT – 6 out of 10

EPISODE 3-14
LONG DISTANCE CALL

TRANSMISSION DATES
US first aired: 1 May 2008
UK first aired: 15 June 2008

CREDITS
Writer: Jeremy Carver
Director: Robert Singer

RECURRING ROLE
Jeffrey Dean Morgan (John Winchester)

GUEST STARS
Eric Breker (Mike Stubbs), Thomas Michael Dobie (Ed), Dawson Dunbar (Simon Greenfield), David Neale (Mark Greenfield), Anjul Nigam (Stewie Meyers), Tom O'Brien (Clark Adams/Crocotta), Anna Mae Routledge (Museum Tour Guide), John Shaw (Ben Waters), Ingrid Torrance (Margaret Waters), Cherilyn Wilson (Lanie Greenfield)

SYNOPSIS
Frustrated that they can't find Bela, the Colt or anything to break Dean's deal, the boys investigate a suicide that could be a haunting only to discover that nearly a dozen people in the same town have been receiving phone calls from dead loved ones. Then Dean gets a call from John Winchester, who says that the demon that owns Dean's contract is in town and he'll phone with the location shortly. Dean wants to go after the demon but Sam's instincts say to wait until they know what's actually going on. Sam goes to see one of the victims, Lanie, whose dead mother has been asking Lanie to kill herself. Sam realises from its *modus operandi* that they're dealing with a crocotta, but the monster lures him to its lair at the phone company by faking a call from Dean. While Sam heads off there, Dean gets a call from John with the location of the demon and breaks into the house to set up his demon defences (Devil's Traps etc). When the innocent owner of the house – a cop – arrives home, Dean attacks him. However, he soon realises that the owner isn't a demon, and that that wasn't John on the phone. He stops fighting the cop at the same time Sam kills the crocotta.

CAN YOU SURVIVE TO THE TITLES?

Ben Waters finally gives in to the demands of his dead high school sweetheart and goes to her by blowing his brains out in his study.

LOCATION, LOCATION, LOCATION

Milan, Ohio – the birth place of Thomas Edison.

LEGENDARY ROOTS

Gaius Plinius Secundus (Pliny the Elder) first wrote about the crocotta in his *Naturalis Historia* (Natural History) encyclopaedia published in AD 77-79. The crocotta was described as a cross between a dog and a wolf, with extremely strong teeth and instant digestion. Some mythologies say the crocotta was a gluttonous beast that would dig up the remains of the dead and search for prey around farms.

The crocotta's cry sounded like a human in distress, which would lure dogs as prey. They were also said to be able to mimic human voices and could lure farmers into the forest by calling their names. Once far enough into the forest, the crocotta would attack and consume its prey.

Some legends have also described the crocotta's ability to change sex and colouration and suggested that other animals that attempted to hunt them would freeze in their own tracks. The eyes of a slain crocotta were said to be striped gems that if placed under a person's tongue would give them precognitive powers.

SQUEEZE OF THE WEEK

It's an absolutely squeezeless week this time.

SIBLING RIVALRY

There's lots of bickering and differences of opinion going on as well as some great one-liners. Dean telling Sam to pack his panties; Dean explaining that civvies are supposed to be freaked out ghosts; both of them observing that their respective beatings improved their looks; then Sam offering help now that Dean has realised that the only person who can get him out of this mess is himself. But Dean is unimpressed by Sam's flat response to his deep revelation and not even the offer of a poem will salvage the moment.

BODY COUNT

After Ben ventilates his own skull, it's a pretty quiet episode until the crocotta reveals himself as Clark. By then he's got a starter course (technician Stewie Meyers) and main course (Sam) tied up in the bowels of the phone company building. Stewie gets a knife

453

through the heart and his soul is devoured first, which gives Sam time to free himself and get off the menu.

TOOLKIT

- A *cool, sporty rental car* will allow you to check out people on your list at the same time as your brother, thereby getting results faster. However, it can also break your cover if the person you want to talk to is intelligent enough to spot it.
- Keep the *Rituale Romanum* on a piece of paper with you if you don't know it off by heart.
- The blessing to turn ordinary water into *holy water* is another bit of ritual to keep written down and to hand, but you'll need a *rosary* to go with it.
- Holy water can be kept in any type of receptacle – from a toilet basin[331] to a plastic water bottle from the supermarket.
- *Red spray paint* is ideal for drawing those protective *Devil's Traps*, and why not keep it economical by using the same paint you used at the jail in Monument[332].
- The trusty *EMF meter* can check if Edison's spirit phone is working for real or not.
- Keep a knife handy for assaulting innocent (if unsanitary) phone company employees at their car.
- Never be afraid to improvise, and if the only sharp instrument available is *a metal tool holder prong* attached to the wall, then by all means be sure to thrust the back of the monster's head onto it to stop him killing you first[333].

MEMORABLE MOMENTS

There are lots of interesting moments to see: Sam's careful conversation with Lanie to get her to talk about the phone calls; Dean's desperately brief conversations with his father; the boys' arguments about what to do; and Dean's final apology to Sam for giving him a hard time.

MOTEL MAYHEM

This is the kind of motel room that you really don't want to wake up in after a heavy night out on the town. The frantic bubble pattern on the bedspread combined with the metallic star panel and the firework bursts on the wallpaper are guaranteed to give you

---

331 As in 'Jus in Belo' (3-12).

332 Well, it's the same shade of paint as the stuff they used in 'Jus in Belo' (3-12), so it's probably the same can too unless they bought in bulk.

333 Sam's good at improvising – he brained an infected woman with a fire extinguisher in 'Croatoan' (2-09).

a bad headache whether you've got a hangover or not!

THE CAR'S THE STAR

Sadly, in 'Long Distance Call', you see more of Sam's car – the sporty, silver rental car with plates EM701A – than the Impala. Humph.

SPOOK RULES

A crocotta:

- Lives in filth.
- Is a scavenger.
- Mimics loved ones.
- Whispers 'come to me' to its victims to lure them into the dark and swallow their soul.
- Has a sharp set of jagged teeth and can unhinge its jaw when swallowing souls.
- Used to hide in the woods for days or weeks, whispering to people and drawing them out into the night, but they tended to look out for each other.
- Used to eat one or two souls per year but finds it easier now everyone is so connected, yet so alone.
- Eats souls in a similar way to a Shtriga[334].

A crocotta can:

- Use a phone number over a century old to phone his victims.
- Manipulate webcams to show images of people who aren't there.
- Change website weather information so it looks like there's a demon following you.
- Find all your deleted voice-mails, e-mails and phone numbers of family and friends, then use the information to convince you to kill yourself.
- Make disconnected phones and toy phones ring and allow you to have a conversation with your dead loved one on it.

And finally:

- To kill a crocotta, ram a sharp metal instrument into the base of its skull.

DID YOU SPOT?

The last time any computers went crazy and filled the screen with typing was in 'The Usual Suspects' (2-07), when the word was 'danaschulps'.

There's a certain repetitiveness going on for Sam: in both this episode and the

---

334 In 'Something Wicked' (1-18).

last[335] he sits opposite an innocent victim and watches them die after the monster has stabbed them (although this one is stabbed through the heart and the last one (Corbett) through the neck).

BustyAsianBeauties.com was last mentioned in 'Tall Tales' (2-15).

GOING UNDERCOVER
Sam and Dean slip into detective mode when interviewing Ben Waters' widow, although we don't get to hear the names they use. After that they're pretending to be from the phone company's HQ and are using the aliases Mr Raimi and Mr Campbell. This is a reference to the *Evil Dead* movie (1971) and its sequels (1997 and 1992), which were written and directed by Sam Raimi and starred Bruce Campbell.

CULTURAL REFERENCES
Dean: 'Like Oprah.': Oprah Winfrey is a world-famous chat show host, has her own production company and has starred in a number of movies including the 1985 hit *The Color Purple*. At one point she was the world's only black billionaire. This is her second name check[336].

Dean's Voicemail: 'This is Herman Munster. Leave a message.': Herman was the Frankenstein's monster-type character out of *The Munsters* TV show, which ran from 1964 to 1996.

Dean: 'Just watch out for Chris Hansen.': Chris Hansen features on the NBC programme *Dateline*. He is a reporter who tracks down sexual predators who find their victims on the internet.

Dean: 'Then believe it! I mean, if we get this sucker, it's Miller time.': The third reference to beer made by the Miller Brewing Company[337].

GOOFS AND FLUFFS
When Sam is tied up and trying to free his hands, there's blood on his wrist, but when he's fighting the crocotta the blood has disappeared.

HAVEN'T I SEEN YOU BEFORE?
Eric Breker appeared in *Stargate SG-1* as Colonel Reynolds and can also been seen in *The X-Files*, *The 4400*, *Tru Calling* and *X-Men Origins: Wolverine*. Dawson Dunbar has

---

335 In 'Ghostfacers' (3-13).

336 First name check in 'Bugs' (1-08).

337 Sam was the first one to use the phrase in 'The Woman in White' (1-01); Dean used it in 'Shadow' (1-16) when talking to Meg and again here.

been in *Smallville*. David Neale's credits include *The Outer Limits*, *Stargate: Atlantis* and *Millennium*. Anjul Nigam features in *Cloverfield* and *Medium*. Tom O'Brien played Roger Nixon in *Smallville*, *The X-Files* and *Stargate SG-1*. John Shaw played Doug Roth in *Watchmen* and also been in *Smallville* and *Stargate: Atlantis*. Ingrid Torrence's other roles include Lucy in *The 4400*, *Blade: The Series* and *Dead Like Me*.

Behind the Scenes

Graphic designer Lee Anne Elaschuk in the *Season Three Supernatural Companion* gave an insight into how much detail is added to the sets when he revealed that Stewie's 'Employees of the Month' poster had photos of the crew on it. But since Stewie was the sort who would draw moustaches and things on the photos, graphic designer Mary Ann Liu passed it round the office and they all graffitti'd on someone else's face.

Musical Interlude

All music was written specifically for this episode.

Analysis

After the disappointment of the last episode ('Ghostfacers' (3-13)) it's a relief to be catching up with the boys properly and finding out where they're up to with Dean's deal and the Bela/Colt situation[338]. Okay, so not much progress has actually been made, but at least we get a sense of movement as we see how the situation has started to affect the Team Winchester morale.

'Long Distance Call' illustrates both how desperate Dean is to find a solution to his deal[339] and how it is affecting the boys' relationship. Sam and Dean don't often totally disagree, but the lack of progress has Dean understandably frustrated. As a result, he's not only more vulnerable but his sense of perspective is wrecked and he's taking his anger out on Sam – something that's inevitable given there's no-one else around to lay it on.

Sam, meanwhile, is trying to keep a level head and not argue with his brother, since he seems to understand exactly where his brother's emotions are rooted. He also knows Dean's weakness when it comes to family and particularly their father. Dean has been hard-wired from a young age to obey his father, while Sam has questioned things more readily. It's no different here, and it leads the two brothers in different directions.

When Dean finally realises his mistake, we see more evidence of how he's finding

---

338 Bela stole the Colt in 'Dream a Little Dream Of Me' (3-10).

339 The next episode looks into how desperate Sam is about to get.

it easier to be open with his brother – a trait that started back in 'The Magnificent Seven' (3-01) – although of course he still doesn't tell Sam everything[340]. But as with the old Dean, when things get too emotionally heavy between them, he's still there with a joke to cover over the awkwardness. It seems some things will never change.

The seamless mixture of emotional reaction and the monster-of-the-week storyline is what makes episodes like this one stand out. The crocotta hunt stands on its own as a perfectly viable job for the boys, but the crocotta's actions directly highlight the problems that Dean is having and the final showdown indicates that Sam can indeed survive without his brother when necessary. But perhaps cleverest of all, the crocotta's manipulations confirm to Dean his best hope for breaking the deal – killing the demon who owns his contract.

There's going to be a lot of ground to cover in the last two episodes of this truncated season[341], but with this sort of story quality being maintained, you can bet it's going to be an interesting finale.

VERDICT – 9 out of 10

---

340 As will be seen in 'Time Is On My Side' (3-15).

341 Reduced to only 16 episodes because of the writers' strike.

EPISODE 3-15
TIME IS ON MY SIDE

TRANSMISSION DATES
US first aired: 8 May 2008
UK first aired: 22 June 2008

CREDITS
Writer: Sera Gamble
Director: Charles Beeson

RECURRING ROLES
Lauren Cohan (Bela Talbot), Jim Beaver (Bobby Singer)

GUEST STARS
Peter Birkenhead (Victim), Roan Curtis (Schoolgirl (Crossroads) Demon), Billy Drago (Doc Benton), Adrian Holmes (Demon), Terence Kelly (Coroner), Kaleena Kiff (Young Woman), Nathaniel Marten (Jogger), Marilyn Norry (Nurse), Tiera Skovbye (Young Bela), Kavan Smith (Jules), Craig Veroni (Thomas), Steven Williams (Rufus Turner)

SYNOPSIS
Sam convinces Dean to investigate a series of human organ robberies because he has a hunch that an old adversary of their father's – Doc Benton – is having to replace body parts that have failed during his immortal lifetime. Sam turns out to be correct, but before the brothers can hunt Benton down, Bobby phones with a lead on Bela from hunter Rufus Turner. Sam stays to hunt Benton but Dean goes to see Turner, who reveals Bela's past to him. Confronting Bela, Dean realises that she hasn't got the Colt but also notices that she is warding her room against hellhounds. Meanwhile Sam has found Benton's hut in the woods and frees one of his victims. But Benton chloroforms Sam at the motel while he's on the phone to Dean and takes him to his hut. Dean finds Sam just in the nick of time and subdues Benton. They bury him alive since they can't kill an immortal. That night, Bela tries to kill both of the brothers, but Dean has figured out her deal with the demon. Just as her deal deadline arrives, Bela tells Dean that Lilith holds his contract.

CAN YOU SURVIVE TO THE TITLES?
A plastic surgeon, Jules, is abducted outside his health club and isn't seen again until

459

he turns up at a local hospital in a long coat, clutching his stomach and clearly in great pain. A nurse convinces him to show her under his coat, whereupon his intestines hit the floor and Jules keels over dead.

LOCATION, LOCATION, LOCATION
Cristal Spa and Racquet Club, Erie, Pennsylvania; The Erie Motel, 267 West Huron; Boulevard, Erie, Pennsylvania; Rufus's house, Canaan, Vermont; Hotel Canaan, Canaan, Vermont.

LEGENDARY ROOTS
For many years, an urban legend has been told of a traveller who is drugged in a bar (often by a prostitute) and then wakes up later in a bath full of ice with a pain in his lower back and a note attached to his body saying 'Call the emergency services'.. On speaking to the operator, he is told his kidneys have been surgically removed by an organ-harvesting gang to be sold on the black market. Investigation confirms a precision cut in the victim's back that has been professionally stitched.

This story has been retold in virtually the same format with many different locations. For example, one version has it that in New Orleans in 1997, just before Mardi Gras, an organised gang planned to drug visitors to remove their organs for later resale.

Despite the story being told globally, it seems no-one has ever actually come forward and reported such an occurrence officially.

Another rumoured practice is that of stealing babies for body parts. The story usually involves the adoption or kidnapping of children from Latin America to be taken to America for use as an unwilling organ donor.

In some places, foreign visitors have been attacked because it was believed that the reason for their visit was to steal babies. According to the press, American tourist June Weinstock was attacked by a mob on 29 March 1994 after being accused of abducting a Guatemalan boy. She suffered serious head injuries and has been left permanently incapacitated.

SQUEEZE OF THE WEEK
With only three weeks to go, Dean's thinking less about squeezing someone else and more about saving himself.

SIBLING RIVALRY
The boys have a difference of opinion again[342]: Dean wants to go after Bela and the

---

342 The previous one being in the last episode, 'Long Distance Call' (3-14).

Colt while Sam wants to stay and hunt Benton. Dean tries to assert himself by telling Sam that he won't let him go after the Doc but Sam just strops back that Dean can't stop him – and indeed he can't.

BODY COUNT

There's plenty of gore on offer from the opener onwards. After Jules spills his guts in the hospital corridor, a poor jogger is abducted from the park. It's a close call as to which part of his death is the most gruesome – the scalpel cutting his chest open, the crunching as his ribs are broken and his chest cavity opened, or the removal of his still-beating heart. Then a kidnapped girl gets away with her life but loses the skin on her forearm. She does gain a couple of friendly maggots to keep the wound clean though.

Then the Winchesters have been trying to find out the name of the demon who owns Dean's contract and end up exorcising a lower-ranking demon in the process – which leaves behind an already dead, hard-ridden corpse. Making the latest demon war scores: Team Winchester still on nine (possessed) innocents; and the demons increasing by one to 19.

TOOLKIT

- The whole *holy water, Devil's Trap, Rituale Romanum* demon sub-toolkit is needed to interrogate the black-eyed monsters and get them to tell you who holds your contract.
- A *flashlight* and *a map* are essential for a bit of fumbling around in the woods as you search for an evil doctor's pad for dirty deeds.
- A reliable *four wheel drive rental car* will be priceless should you suddenly need to get away from the evil doctor after freeing one of his victims.
- Your trusty *pearl-handled handgun* will save your brother's life, then *a hunting knife* dipped in chloroform will save your own life.
- A *bottle of Johnny Walker (Blue Label)* will loosen the tongue of even the most hardened and cynical hunter.
- Your trusty *handgun* is also useful for threatening someone who has repeatedly screwed you over.
- And two *blow-up sex dolls* are perfect decoys when you have a murderous bitch trying to screw you over permanently this time.

MEMORABLE MOMENTS

Despite all the gruesome moments happening around Doc Benton, it's Bela's tragic storyline that stands out. Not only do the boys finally out-think her, but we now

461

understand more about the events that shaped her personality and see the price of her actions catch up with her.

Spook Rules

- Doctors who became immortal around 1816 continue to use the surgical procedures of their day – like using silk thread to sew up incisions and maggots to eat away infected tissue.
- If you need to kidnap people and operate on them to remove body parts without anaesthetic then a remote location is essential and a nearby stream or river will supply fresh water as well as allowing you to dump the bile, and intestines, and faecal matter relatively safely.
- Immortality can be achieved through pure (if very weird) science – no blood sacrifices and no black magic required.
- Even monsters have moral standards – Doc Benton insists he didn't do anything that wasn't necessary for his own survival. Which means he isn't the bad guy in his own eyes. But there's one jogger at least who will definitely dispute that point of view
- The herb Devil's Shoestring has protective properties against hellhounds that are trying to drag you down under.
- It's possible to try to wriggle out of your demon-deal – for example you could steal a weapon they desperately want. But demons are unlikely to honour the terms of the deal and will change them after you've fulfilled your side of the bargain.
- Lilith apparently holds every deal made by a crossroads demon.

Did You Spot?

The sticker on Sam's car says Lariat Auto Rentals. This is the rental company regularly used by Mulder and Scully in *The X-Files*.

Doc Benton's fate is very similar to that of Dr H H Holmes, the evil spirit in 'No Exit' (2-06). Both bad guys get trapped forever so they can't hurt anyone else.

The date of the Erie Hotel receipt is 6 November 2008 – that makes it 25 years to the month since John Winchester first took Doc Benton down. John's hunt is dated in the *Supernatural: Origins* graphic novel as happening on 24 November. This ties-in with what is written in *John Winchester's Journal* by Alex Irvine.

Going Undercover

The boys are playing incompetent detectives when they visit the coroner's office to investigate the first victim's gut-spilling, liver-extracting killing. Since they've clearly not read the coroner's report, they're in danger of having their cover blown, but the coroner just assumes they're useless and throws them out at the earliest opportunity.

CULTURAL REFERENCES

Sam tells Dean he won't need a new pancreas for at least half a century, Dean: 'Well we can't exactly get those at a Kwik-E-Mart can we?': The Kwik-E-Mart is the convenience store in the long-running cartoon series *The Simpsons*.

Dean: 'Okay, great. My man Dave Caruso will be stoked to hear it.': Dave Caruso stars as Lieutenant Horatio Caine in *CSI: Miami*, running since 2002, about the Miami-Dade, Florida police department's Crime Scene Investigations unit.

Dean: 'Zombie with skills. Dr Quinn, Medicine Zombie.': A reference to the 1993-1999 series *Dr Quinn, Medicine Woman*, starring Jane Seymour as the good Dr Quinn.

Bobby: 'Rufus Turner.'; Dean: 'Is that like a Cleveland Steamer?': A Cleveland Steamer is a sexual act involving faeces.

Dean: 'A little Antiques Roadshow surgery, some organ theft.': *The Antiques Roadshow* is a long running TV series in which members of the public bring in objects so that experts can appraise their value.

Dean: 'Ah, what is this, Sid and Nancy?': Sid Vicious (John Simon Ritchie) was the bassist for '70s punk band the Sex Pistols, and Nancy Spungen was his girlfriend. They were famous for their drug-addicted relationship. Nancy was found murdered in the bathroom of Sid's hotel room. Sid died of a heroin overdose four months later.

Bobby: 'British accent, went by the name Mina Chandler.': Actress Helen Chandler played Mina Harker in the 1931 version of *Dracula*, starring Bela Lugosi.

Bela: 'I'll call the buyer. Speak Farsi?': Farsi is the language spoken in Iran.

Dean: 'Wakey, wakey, eggs and bakey.': This is a line spoken by Jerry Goldsmith (played by Chris Hardwick) in *House of 1000 Corpses* (2003) and by Budd 'Sidewinder' (played by Michael Madsen) in *Kill Bill Vol 2* (2004).

GOOFS AND FLUFFS

When the jogger wakes up on the operating table, his heart-rate monitor watch is now upside down on his wrist.

As Sam is attacked by Doc Benton in the motel, he drops his Blackberry phone in the tussle. Dean is still on the call at the time, but the Blackberry screen shows that there is no call is progress – the home page/desktop screen is displayed, and this is not visible during a call.

HAVEN'T I SEEN YOU BEFORE?

Peter Birkenhead can be seen in *Medium*, *Six Feet Under* and *NCIS: Naval Criminal Investigative Service*. Roan Curtis has appeared in *The Bionic Woman* and *Smallville*.

Billy Drago's CV includes *Charmed*, *The Hills Have Eyes*, *The X-Files* and *Friday the 13th: The Series*. Adrian Holmes has appeared in *White Noise 2: The Light*, *Stargate SG-1*, *Smallville*, *Tru Calling* and *Highlander The Series*. Terence Kelly's acting credits include *Watchmen*, *Kyle XY*, *The Exorcism Of Emily Rose*, *Dead Like Me* and *Millennium*. Kaleen Kiff has also appeared in *Smallville*. *Flash Gordon* is Nathaniel Marten's other television work. Marilyn Norry can be seen in *Battlestar Galactica*, *Reaper*, *Tin Man*, *The Exorcism Of Emily Rose* and *Knight Moves*. Tiera Skovbye was in *Painkiller Jane*. Kavan Smith appears in *Stargate Atlantis* and *SG-1* as Major Evan Lorne, *The 4400* as Jed Garrity, *Mission to Mars* and *Battlestar Galactica*. Craig Veroni's credits include *Stargate Atlantis* as Dr Peter Grodin, *Smallville*, *Blood Ties* and *Battlestar Galactica*. Steven Williams has appeared in *Stargate SG-1* as General Vidrine, *The X-Files* as Mr X and *Jason Goes to Hell: The Final Friday* as Creighton Duke.

Terrence Kelly also appears in 'Dead Man's Blood' (1-20), but as Daniel Elkins.

Behind the Scenes

Actor Billy Drago commented in *The Official Supernatural Magazine* #5 that Benton was a loner and that carving people up the way he did meant he lived out in sticks – so he didn't have many people to talk to unless he was operating on them. But clearly John Winchester had had lengthy conversations with him since John knew what he was up to and why he was doing it.

Like 'Malleus Malificarum' (3-09), this episode required a 'maggot wrangler' on set to look after the maggots used in some of the scenes. The maggots were counted each day to ensure none had escaped, they had their own trailer, and they had their own stunt doubles – grains of rice – for the running-through-the-field scenes to ensure none got dropped.

Kaleena Kiff was usually behind the camera on the *Supernatural* set, rather than in front of it as in this episode – she was director Kim Manners' assistant.

Musical Interlude

All music was written specifically for this episode.

Analysis

Forget the subtle horror of a mother being driven mad by a child who's acting strangely or the quiet fear of not knowing who will be the next possessed person to attack you – 'Time Is On My Side' goes for the full gross-out of gut-spilling, rib-cracking and maggot-infesting, with butchered flesh all over the place. Although you have to concede that the final resting place of Doc Benton is actually a more subtle solution compared with carving the monster up into iddy-biddy little pieces and feeding the bloody chunks to the fishes.

Along with the bloody horror are lots of other interesting snippets, including an immortal monster-of-the-week, a Sam storyline, a Dean storyline and a (surprisingly) concluding Bela storyline.

For the monster-of-the-week, we learn of the second time that John Winchester failed to conclude a hunt successfully[343]. Then again, John did rip Doc Benton's heart out in their first encounter[344] so you can't blame him for thinking he'd sorted the maniac out for good. And this is exactly the point that causes this episode's logic problem: if Doc Benton could survive having his heart cut out, his neck getting broken and being shot several times in the chest (not to mention being stabbed), why does he need replacement organs, since clearly he could carry on living without them?

Apart from this point, the Doc is one nasty character, especially since he insists that he's never done anything that he hasn't needed to do to survive[345], the implication being that he feels he's not really done anything wrong. In his own eyes, he's justified in doing what he's doing.

Which is a similar point of view to Sam's too, because he believes that using Benton's formula to make Dean and himself immortal (with the mere side effect of having to kill innocent people sometime in the future) would be justified, since it would save Dean from having to go to hell. We're starting to see just how desperate Sam is becoming, and as with Dean in the last episode[346], it's affecting his common sense. Fortunately, Dean doesn't want to become what he hunts[347], and hell looks like a better option on balance. These differences of opinion – about immortality and the best way to avoid going to hell – are showing up regularly now, as the deadline draws nearer and the boys both become more tense and worried that they can't stop Dean being dragged off to hell.

Dean's got only three weeks left now, and the plan that started to form in 'Long Distance Call' (3-14) – of finding and killing the demon that owns his contract – has now become his focus. In order to do this he needs the Colt, so he makes the decision to confront Bela as soon as he knows where she is – regardless of what Sam thinks they should be doing.

It's a confrontation that brings some big revelations about Bela's past and,

---

343 The first was that of the Shtriga that attacked Sam as seen in flashback in 'Something Wicked' (1-18).

344 As shown in the *Supernatural: Origins* comic series.

345 That's Sera Gamble's writing influence again.

346 'Long Distance Call' (3-14).

347 As seen before in 'Time Is On My Side' (2-01) and touched on in 'Malleus Maleficarum' (3-09) and 'Dream A Little Dream Of Me' (3-10).

ultimately, a piece of information that Dean desperately needs: the name of the demon who owns his contract, and who turns out to own Bela's contract too.

Doc Benton's immortality may have some logic issues, but Bela's past history and motivations are so perfectly formed that they're positively elegant. Her deal with the demon explains everything from her extravagant lifestyle, where she's clearly enjoying as much life as she possibly can before her time is up, to the reason she's been stealing from the boys (to break her own deal). The abuse by her father when she was a child explains why the deal was made, and maybe she included her mother in it too because she did nothing to stop the abuse?

Bela came through those traumatic experiences not trusting anyone, so money became the motivation in her life. She burned her fingerprints off, changed her name from Abbey to Bela, took her inherited millions and put her parents' car accident behind her. Except now, the debt has come due, and the hellhounds are circling. In one last attempt to save herself, she tells Dean that Lilith holds their contracts in the hope that he'll kill her and she'll be free as well.

It's an appropriate end for Bela, and she's finally done something useful on her way out. The character never really gelled within the show; the boys and Bobby seemed to have had lobotomies whenever she was around since they trusted her every time despite her past history of shooting Sam and repeatedly betraying them; and let's not forget that her English accent was irritating beyond words.

The question now is: what are the boys going to do with the new information about Lilith? And will Dean end up going to hell or will they find a way to save him? The season finale has all the answers …

VERDICT – 8.5 out of 10

EPISODE 3-16
NO REST FOR THE WICKED

TRANSMISSION DATES
US first aired: 15 May 2008
UK first aired: 29 June 2008

CREDITS
Writer: Eric Kripke
Director: Kim Manners

RECURRING ROLES
Katie Cassidy (Ruby), Jim Beaver (Bobby Singer)

GUEST STARS
George Coe (Pat 'Grandpa' Fremont), Anna Galvin (Barbara Fremont), Peter Hanlon (Tom Wepram), Brad Loree (Police Officer), Sierra McCormick (Zoey Fremont/ Lilith), Vince Murdocco (Mailman), Jonathan Potts (Jimmy Fremont)

SYNOPSIS
Dean has 30 hours left before the hounds come sniffing for his soul. Bobby has located Lilith. Sam has summoned Ruby against Dean's wishes – but Dean knew he would do that, so he's ready when the demon turns up. Dean leaves Ruby stuck in a Devil's Trap after taking the demon-killing knife from her in a fight, but not before she's told Sam that the way to save Dean is by using his psychic powers. But Dean won't let Sam do this, because he sees that path as too dangerous for him and he wants their family to stop martyring themselves for each other. Along with Bobby, the boys go to kill Lilith, but on the way there they get stopped by a demon possessed traffic cop. Dean spots the demon because he can now see a demon's real face below the human one, and they eventually arrive at the house where Lilith is 'playing' with the Fremont family. She's possessing their little girl and, having killed the nanny, then Grandpa Fremont and the family pet, she's asleep in bed when the Winchesters (with a very annoyed Ruby) break in to the house. But Lilith jumps bodies to Ruby, and in the final showdown: Sam discovers his powers are stronger than Lilith's; Dean experiences what it's like to be ripped to shreds by hellhounds; and Lilith does a runner before Sam can kill her. The closing shot is of Dean suspended by chains in hell, with meat hooks through his flesh, desperately calling his brother's name.

CAN YOU SURVIVE TO THE TITLES?
No deaths in the opener, just a lot of angst about the upcoming demise of the elder Winchester brother.

LOCATION, LOCATION, LOCATION
Bobby's place (probably), South Dakota; New Harmony, Indiana; and an unknown location in hell.

LEGENDARY ROOTS
It has long been believed that deals with the Devil – or a trickster or demon – can be made in return for long-sought-after things such as power, wisdom, wealth or extended life. The price is high: a soul or a person's first born child. The contract made is either written or agreed orally. The written contract is believed to be signed in blood. The oral contract is made by invoking the demon through conjuring or a ritual and agreeing face to face. Examples of people who have supposedly made deals with the Devil are:

- The Orthodox cleric Theophilus of Adana in the 6th Century, whose deal gave him the position as Archdeacon of Adana but who claimed that his soul was saved by the Virgin Mary.
- Niccolò Paganini, an amazingly talented Italian composer and violinist, who was rumoured to have made a deal with the Devil to become so good – and he played along with the rumours.
- Tommy Johnson, a blues musician unrelated to Robert Johnson, who claimed he sold his soul after going to a crossroads and making a pact with the Devil so he could become an outstanding musician.

SQUEEZE OF THE WEEK
Dean has done all his squeezing and time has run out.

SIBLING RIVALRY
As the deadline approaches, the tension between the boys is getting worse. They are disagreeing about more and more things. Dean thinks Ruby is the Miss Universe of lying skanks but Sam's still hoping she can help; Dean wants an end to the Winchester family members sacrificing themselves for each other and playing into the hands of the demons; Sam wants to ninja in to the house and kill a ten year old girl; and Sam thinks using his powers is the only way to save Dean – which frightens Dean because of John's warning.

But they still find a little time to joke gently with each other when the chick flick moments get too heavy. It's Sam doing the joking this time for a change, as Dean explains his plan to go down swinging if he has to and Sam telling him that his little speech really should have been to a soundtrack of 'Eye of the Tiger'.

BODY COUNT

Lilith may have already killed the nanny by the time we catch up with her on her holiday, but the body has been left on the hall floor to attract the flies and everybody is stepping over it. Then after Grandpa Fremont tries to raise the alarm with his (little did he know, possessed) neighbour, Lilith breaks his neck with a flick of the wrist.

Lilith's other Fremont victim is poor little Freckles. We never find out what kind of pet he was, but judging by the amount of blood on Lilith's dress, he won't be begging at the table for food ever again[348].

Ruby's meat-suit doesn't get up again after Lilith's finished with it either (which is no surprise since Bobby stuck a bullet in her chest when he first met her[349]).

Meanwhile, Team Winchester manages to kill an innocent cop who was unfortunate enough to have been possessed, along with the possessed mailman and the Fremonts' possessed neighbour Mr Rogers.

Which brings the final scores for this season to: demons 21 innocents; Team Winchester 13 (possessed) innocents (not a bad score considering these are the good guys).

But of course, there's another very important and shocking death to mention: the flesh-shredding, blood-gushing, leg-humping hellhound attack on Dean Winchester himself. Bugger!

TOOLKIT

- The *Rituale Romanum* will always exorcise those demons.
- The blessing to turn ordinary water into *holy water* is necessary to turn ordinary sprinklers into something a lot more powerful. Don't forget the *rosary* to go with it.
- *Red spray paint* is ideal for drawing those protective *Devil's Traps*.
- A *demon-killing knife* will deal with possessed traffic cops but you're unlikely to get a chance to use it against a powerful white-eyed demon.
- For finding demons, you'll need *a map, a wooden tripod, a glass ball with two metal strips inscribed with appropriate symbols, a pendulum with an elegant sharp pointer on it*, the *right ritual* and the *right name*. Then there's nothing you can't locate, including the street where you can find the demon that holds your

---

348 Freckles is the third animal to be murdered in three seasons. Zombie Angela killed her boyfriend's goldfish in 'Children Shouldn't Play With Dead Things' (2-04) and witch Amanda butchered a poor little bunny in 'Malleus Malificarum' (3-09).

349 In 'Sin City' (3-04).

contract.

- For summoning demons, you'll need *chalk* to draw the *summoning sigil* and a *bowl* of flashy *firework powder* that sparks impressively when you set a *match* to it. A trio of *candles* will give the whole location a more intimate feel, even if you're completing the ritual in an old barn[350].

- For protection against incoming hellhounds, you'll need *goofer dust*. This is an African-American hoodoo mixture with a range of recipes available[351]. The base ingredients are graveyard dirt and powdered sulphur and salt, with additional optional ingredients including powdered snakeskin, red pepper, black pepper, powdered bones, powdered insects and powdered herbs.

- And finally, *lock picking skills* will get you into the house where the really powerful demon lies ready to kill you and your brother – so *stupidity or blind bravery* are also useful traits.

MEMORABLE MOMENTS

The Winchester duet to Bon Jovi's 'Wanted, Dead or Alive' is a light moment in a very serious situation, and they're in much better tune than they were when they sang 'Silent Night' together[352].

And Dean's final moments can't fail to stand out in the whole season let alone the final episode. The suspense of the 'will he/won't he' situation is finally decided in a tense and exciting climax to an excellent season.

SPOOK RULES

- For demon deals, as you get closer to your deal deadline, you start getting hallucinations. These usually start with people's faces distorting and twisting for a few seconds as you look at them then escalate until you can actually see a demon's face under its meat-suit face. This happens because you're getting closer to hell as your deadline approaches, so you start piercing the veil.

- The more powerful the demon, the less effective weapons such as holy water are in stopping it.

- When it's payback time on your deal, ferocious black dogs that only you (and any

350 When John Winchester summoned the yellow-eyed demon he also used *acacia* to burn as incense and *oil of Abramelin* – an aromatic oil made from a blend of different extracts including cinnamon, myrrh, cassia and calamus – which provides, amongst other things, a means of consecrating ritual equipment. And he also used *a sharp knife* to cut his palm open to bleed into the bowl. Sam seems to have found a less bloody summoning ritual. See 'In My Time Of Dying' (2-01).

351 First encountered in 'Crossroad Blues' (2-08) – see episode write-up for more goofer dust details.

352 In 'A Very Supernatural Christmas' (3-08).

attending demons) can see and hear will be sent to retrieve your soul and shred your flesh.

DID YOU SPOT?

Both Bela's and Dean's final word, before the hellhounds took them, was 'bitch'.

In the scene where Dean takes on Ruby, the shot where Dean falls down after being head-butted is the same footage as when he falls down after being kicked in the head.

There's a familiar note to Dean's speech about how the members of his family tend to sacrifice themselves for each other:

Dean: 'Sammy, all I'm saying is that you're my weak spot. You are. And I'm yours … And those evil sons of bitches know it too … They're using it against us … We stop being martyrs, man.'

Compared to the Trickster in 'Mystery Spot' (3-11), who gave an almost identical speech:

Trickster: 'The way you two keep sacrificing yourselves for each other? Nothing good comes out of it, just blood and pain. Dean's your weakness. The bad guys know it too … Sometimes you just gotta let people go …'

If you hadn't already spotted it, this episode was based on *The Twilight Zone* episode 'It's a Good Life', which starred Bill Mumy, in which the family's surname was also Fremont.

The 1960s comedy *Car 54 Where Are You?* gets a sly reference in the police car that pulls the Winchesters over for a broken tail light.

It's possible that the opening sequence is an homage to the opener of the first *Evil Dead* movie (without the dangerous driving or the singing in the car).

GOING UNDERCOVER

The boys are always ready with a disguise of some sort, whatever the occasion, so when the traffic cop pulls them over because the tail-light is out, the registration documents are already prepared in a Mr Hagar's name (although it wouldn't be a surprise to find the glove compartment full of lots of different registration documents in lots of different names).

CULTURAL REFERENCES

Dean: 'Hell, she probably wants you to become her little Antichrist Superstar.': Either a reference to Marilyn Manson's second album, also called *Antichrist Superstar* and released in 1996, or a play on words about the musical *Jesus Christ Superstar*.

Dean: 'What, are you gonna give her the Carrie stare and Lilith goes poof?': *Carrie* is a 1974 novel by Stephen King, later made into a movie, TV movie and musical, about a girl with a telekinetic ability that she uses to get revenge on those who have teased her at school.

Dean: 'Our slutty little Yoda.': Yoda is the Jedi Master who, amongst other things, trains Luke Skywalker in the ways of the Force in the *Star Wars* movies. Yoda was first mentioned in 'Asylum' (1-10).

Sam: 'A sure-fire way to confirm it's Lilith and a way to get us a *bona fide* demon-killing ginsu.': A ginsu is a brand of knife made famous in the 1970s by the various ways it was advertised, which lead to the modern day infomercial.

Dean: 'Well, this is a terrific plan. I'm excited to be a part of it. Can we go, please?': This is a variation on a quote from the *Ghostbusters* movie. The actual quote in *Ghostbusters* is: 'I love this plan! I'm excited to be a part of it! Let's do it!'

Haven't I Seen You Before?

George Coe has appeared in *The Stepford Wives*, *Star Trek: The Next Generation*, *Smallville*, *Numb3rs* and *Bones*. Sierra McCormick has also appeared in *Criminal Minds*. Jonathan Potts has been in *Reaper*, *Relic Hunter*, *Jason X*, *Earth: Final Conflict* and *The Twilight Zone*. Anna Galvin featured in *Stargate: Atlantis*, *The Andromeda Strain*, *Smallville*, *Blood Ties*, *Stargate SG-1* and *The Sentinel*. Peter Hanlon has been in *Smallville*, *The 4400*, *Dead Like Me*, *Scary Movie*, *Poltergeist: The Legacy*, *Millennium* and *The X-Files*. Brad Loree can be seen in *Smallville*, *Battlestar Galactica*, *X2*, *Stargate SG-1*, *The Outer Limits* and *Timecop*.

Behind the Scenes

The sweet suburban cul-de-sac where Lillith takes her R&R was an actual location that was taken over by the *Supernatural* crew for two whole nights. Location manager Russ Hamilton explained in the *Season Three Supernatural Companion* that the residents from all 16 of the million-dollar homes were put up in a hotel during filming. However, even with access to such a perfect location, sets also had to be used. For the scene where Sam and Dean watch the grandfather die from the house across the street, the actors were actually on a two-storey piece of scaffolding further up the street. And for the shot where the camera is focused on the boys as they talk after seeing grandpa die, they were in the basement of one of the houses.

Also in the *Season Three Supernatural Companion*, Jensen Ackles explained that this episode caused him the most physical pain. The closing scene where he was suspended with the hooks was done using prosthetics and then actually hanging the actor 14 feet in the air. Ackles had most of his weight on the harness around his waist, but it slipped past the belt of his jeans until he had his entire weight supported by the metal buckle on the harness, which was digging into his hip. Ouch!

Stunt co-ordinator Lou Bollo agreed that Ackles had a hard time shooting those final scenes, commenting that the actor had been abused – thrown on the table, then dragged off it, followed by a fun half day running and falling in the woods. [*The Official Supernatural Magazine #9*]

MUSICAL INTERLUDE
- 'Carry On Wayward Son' – Kansas – recap song[353].
- 'Wanted Dead Or Alive' – Bon Jovi – Sam and Dean singing as they drive towards New Harmony to kill Lilith.

ANALYSIS
There's nothing like a ticking clock to ratchet up the tension, especially when the life of one of the main characters hangs in the balance. In most series, that fact that a main character is threatened would actually release the tension, because you'd know that some miraculous solution would be found at the eleventh hour. But *Supernatural* has never been that comfortable to watch and the track record – with John Winchester's death, then Sam's knife in the back – brings you into this finale with a rather nervous disposition, knowing it could go either way.

The journey to finding which way it is going to go is not as exciting as previous finales, but is rather revealing on a few points.

Starting with Ruby, we begin to see how manipulative she has been with the brothers, but especially Sam. She's been withholding info about Lilith owning Dean's contract and she's been hiding details about Sam's powers and what he can do with them for Dean. She cites very reasonable points about why she didn't share – because they'd have run off after Lilith and got killed if they'd known earlier, or because Sam wasn't ready to use his powers again with his fear of being a sideshow freak – but it makes you wonder what else she's manipulating. And she's very protective of Sam's life and only Sam's life. Although she's helped Dean in the past[354], it's mainly been so he could then go and help Sam, or perhaps to make him less disapproving of her so she could get more access to Sam.

For Sam, he's become increasingly desperate to save his brother, to the point where he defies his wishes and summons Ruby anyway. He still believes she can be useful even if she is manipulating him. Once Dean has taken the knife from her, Sam's back to helping his brother kill Lilith whatever the odds are against them. And those odds are high; so high that Sam tries to launch into the 'If we don't make it out of this' speech again. (He did the same when they were waiting for the yellow-eyed demon to

353 Also used as the recap song for finale episodes in Season One and Two.
354 In 'Malleus Malificarum' (3-09).

turn up at the end of Season One[355].) Just like before, Dean slaps him down – except this time Dean's not in outright denial and insisting that no-one is going to die. This whole episode shows how Dean is finally adjusting to the fact that he's probably not going to win against Lilith so he's trying to prepare Sam for the worst and stop him making the same mistake he and John made. Even though nothing is going to stop Dean from trying to take Lilith out and giving it his best shot, he's still trying to protect the people around him – why else would he try to leave Bobby behind?

He's also trying to be sensible about what they're trying to do and raising some solid questions. How do they kill Lilith? Should Sam go anywhere near Lilith since the demon wants his head on a plate? And is it the right intel from Bela? (*Now* he starts to mistrust her, when she's not lying for once! Oooh, you could slap him.) He's only going to get one shot at killing Lilith so he's trying to make it count.

But even after all that, Lilith beats him. In the shocking climax, a very dignified, if terrified, Dean faces the hellhounds and loses, only to find himself painfully suspended in hell, all alone and screaming for his brother.

All of the scenes with the Winchesters and Bobby leading up to this point are riveting and emotionally charged. What weakens this finale are the elements in the Fremont household, which tend to be significantly slower and, in the end, rather irrelevant. The scenes certainly establish Lilith as a twisted bitch with no respect for human life (well, any life if you include poor Freckles), and her little girl meat-suit does come across as a little unnerving, but the effect isn't menacing enough for a demon with such power. Then there's the question of why she's on R&R in the first place. It's not as if she's been leading a full-time assault on mankind in any kind of demon war. In fact, despite the demons having a new leader, they seem to have completely forgotten there's even supposed to be a war.

It's probable that the writers' strike had a hand in making this one of the less intense season finales so far – especially when you consider the unerring quality of the seasons that came before it. The fact remains that there are a lot of fans that are eternally grateful that the show survived the strike full stop, when many series were cancelled in that aftermath.

One thing is sure though. With Dean suffering in hell and Sam's future uncertain, the Winchesters are facing a grim outlook. So put your trust in Kripke and the *Supernatural* team – they clearly love the show too, and they'll certainly be doing their best to deliver a cracking Season Four. We can hardly wait …

VERDICT – 9 out of 10

---

355 In 'Salvation' (1-21).

SUMMATION

It's been one helluva road trip. Three seasons in and the *Supernatural* cast and crew still have the pedal to the metal and they're not going to slow down as they zip past the Season Four boundary.

There's been plenty of action and angst along the way. In between exorcising, dismembering and incinerating demons and monsters, Sam spends Season One grieving for Jessica, the love of his life, while getting back into the hunting groove that he's been trying to leave behind. Fuelled by revenge for Jessica's death, he gets reacquainted with his brother and goes in search of Dad's help to find Jess's killer, discovering his strange psychic abilities along the way.

Dean meanwhile is already firmly in the hunting groove, enthusiastically dispatching monsters all over the place and saving people, yet still hell-bent on finding his father.

Eventually they find their Dad – or rather he finds them – as well as the long-sought-after demon-killing Colt. The yellow-eyed demon then becomes the focus of their hunting skills, but the demon has his children – Meg in particular – hot on the Winchester asses.

The season ends with a violent face-off between the Winchesters and the yellow-eyed demon, with the demon coming out on top and the Winchesters badly injured in a car crash.

What started as an interesting idea about a couple of brothers looking for their dad and taking on a monster-of-the-week turned into something very different, with its themes of revenge and the importance of family. It avoided using formulaic stories, revelled in both the scares and the gore and tangled us all in the issues of the Winchesters' relationships, so much so that we even cared about the damn Impala getting damaged, let alone the main characters.

Not content to sit back, the show delivered an emotional kick to the guts in the Season Two opener with John Winchester's death. Having him sell his soul, and the Colt, in order to save his son, only served to bolster the show's themes of family and what you're prepared to do for them.

It takes time for the two brothers to go through the grieving process after their dad's departure, but once Dean has shared John's last words about saving Sam or killing him, they're forced to face Sam's growing psychic powers and the existence of other people with similar abilities. Then the yellow-eyed demon's long term game plan kicks in and there are psychic kids – including Sam – dying all over the place as the demon army leader emerges in the shape of Jake.

A desperate Dean then does a demon deal to save his dead brother, and with the help of Bobby and Ellen, manages to close the doors to hell again. And there's a truly spiritual moment as John Winchester's ghost, now freed from hell, helps his son finally kill the yellow-eyed demon with the Colt before heading off for realms unknown.

Much of this second season is about loss and how to deal with it, especially for Dean, but there's also a strong theme around the issue 'What is "evil"?'. This becomes crucial for Sam with his demon blood coming to the fore and raises the question of what it would take to push him over the edge to the 'darkside' – apart from a demon riding his meat–suit, that is. To his credit, even when the chips are down, Sam decides not to follow the evil path, but the decision costs him his life. Then we discover how far Dean, now bereft of all his family and full of self loathing, is prepared to go to have his brother back.

But, in Season Three, it's not long before a recently-resurrected Sam discovers what his brother has done, and the race is on to save Dean's life before the deal's deadline arrives. In the meantime, there's a minor army of demons creating chaos across the country that need sorting.

Both of the brothers are now on very specific journeys. Sam is spending all his spare time trying to break the deal with help from new demon pal Ruby. He's hiding it from Dean and he's becoming more and more desperate as the season goes on.

At the same time, Dean is facing up to the consequences of his actions and the fact that in hell he's likely to become exactly the type of demon he currently hunts. At first, he has no desire to break the deal, but eventually – after a little *tête à tête* with his demonic self – he can see the downside of visiting the underworld and starts chipping in with Sam's efforts.

Sam's and Dean's experiences have changed them so much by now that, in personality terms, they've almost swapped places. Sam has become harder and responds to his gut instinct more in order to toughen himself up for a life without Dean; while Dean spends more time thinking about what they're doing, questioning and reviewing his life before it runs out. His own self-loathing and his need to protect Sam from harm create a barrier that he eventually overcomes; but even when they start to find ways to cheat on the deal, Dean discovers that some things are worse than hell.

But in the long run, they both fail in their attempts, and Lilith, the owner of Dean's contract, wins the day. Dean is shredded and dragged to hell, leaving Sam reeling from his loss and the sheer strength of his own psychic powers – which becomes obvious when Lilith is unable to kill him too.

And so we move into Season Four, which is if anything darker and emotionally more difficult than anything that's gone before. We'll see what use Sam makes of his powerful abilities; we'll meet new supernatural beasties and a brand new winged race who are in the middle of a war. We'll see Ruby's influence over Sam grow and the boys embroiled in situations that'll damage their relationship. There will be blood and death and fire. And there will be one helluva humdinger of a season finale.

For a show that has already achieved so much, it's not even pausing for breath as it pushes on to greater heights...

APPENDIX:
SUPERNATURAL MERCHANDISE

All good television series generate a range of spin-off items for the fans, and *Supernatural* is no exception. In this Appendix, we'll take a brief look at the ever-growing range of items available, and throw in some candid opinion when we think it's deserved.

AUTOGRAPHED PHOTOS AND POSTERS
With *Supernatural*-themed conventions on the increase, there are more and more autographed items coming onto the market. Most of these are likely to be limited in availability, so it's always advisable to try to verify the source as reputable before purchasing.

BLANKETS
The most readily available blanket has a cartoon design featuring Dean's quote, 'Dad wants us to pick up where he left off … saving people … hunting things … the family business.' The image features Sam and Dean along with a collage of Hookman, a werewolf and a hotel called Kripke Manor (named after series creator Eric Kripke of course). Can't say that Sam or Dean look like much the characters though.

BOOKS/MAGAZINES/NOVELS/COMICS

Non-Fiction
The Official Supernatural Companion books started being published back in October 2007 and have been released fairly regularly by Titan Books ever since. They all follow the same basic format of interviews and episode guides throughout each volume, and author Nicholas Knight does a good job of giving readers an insight into working on the *Supernatural* set, the problems faced, decisions made and various opinions on the episodes and characters. There's an excellent range of interviewees in these from Eric Kripke through directors, actors, stunt co-ordinators, the special effects team, make-up staff and music composers.

Staying with the interviews and behind the scenes stuff but mixing in news and some occasional bits of fiction is the bi-monthly *Supernatural* magazine from Titan Magazines. It keeps readers up to date with what's going on with the show and supplies some yummy pictures and posters. It's good quality and well worth the cover price.

There's one other official non-fiction book around – *The Supernatural Book of*

Monsters, Demons, Spirits and Ghouls by Alex Irvine. Released by Titan Books in November 2008, this is a thorough examination of the creatures encountered in the first two seasons of the show. Informative and written in an entertaining, Winchester journal style.

Fiction

Moving into fiction but reading almost like a factual book is *John Winchester's Journal*, also by Alex Irvine, released by HarperEntertainment in February 2009. Physically the book could have been made to look much more like the real journal on the show – even the artwork inside is different from that of its on-screen counterpart; for example the Wendigo picture featured so prominently in the episode (1-02) has not been used – and you can't help but think someone missed a trick with it. However, a lot of effort has been put into the written words, and they do indeed sound like the thoughts and ramblings of John Winchester. Well worth reading, and only a couple of mismatches of fact with the TV series. The book is out now from HarperCollins in both hardback and paperback formats.

There is also a series of stand-alone fiction adventures available, published by Titan Books and featuring Sam and Dean. At the time of writing there are eight titles available from some well-known authors in the tie-in novel arena. So if you're in need of a stand-alone adventure with the boys while you're waiting for the next series then you have a choice from:

Released in 2008:
Nevermore by Keith R A DeCandido
Witch's Canyon by Jeff Mariotte
Bone Key by Keith R A DeCandido

Released in 2010:
The Heart of the Dragon by Keith R A DeCandido
The Unholy Cause by Joe Schreiber
War of the Sons by Rebecca Dessertine and David Reed

Released in 2011:
Supernatural: One Year Gone by Rebecca Dessertine
Supernatural: Coyote's Kiss by Christa Faust

If you're looking for more than just a one-off adventure and something that fills in the back mythology, especially around John Winchester and the boys' childhood, then head for the comic shelves.

Best read in release order, the three comics out so far from WildStorm take you chronologically from Mary Winchester's death to the argument between Sam and John that led to Sam leaving for Stanford.

Supernatural: Origins by Peter Johnson and Matthew Dow Smith (released May 2008[356]) tells how John Winchester tries to cope with the strange circumstances of Mary's death. It peels back the layers of his personality and shows why he made the seemingly dysfunctional decisions that led to him to a life on the road with his two sons, hunting demons. It also shows how a very young Dean started to protect his younger brother and look after his dad when he came back from hunting trips. Essential reading.

Supernatural: Rising Son by Peter Johnson, Rebecca Dessertine and Diego Olmos (released May 2009) joins the family when Sam is about 12 years old. We always suspected that John Winchester knew more about Sam's destiny than he was letting on – especially when he whispered the legendary 'Save him or kill him' phrase to Dean just before the demons took his soul at the start of Season Two[357]. In *Rising Son* we see John discovering Sam's future, as a small team of hunters try to kill Sam and stop him fulfilling that destiny; there are also powerful demons running round in sexy meat-suits trying to take Sam away from John in order to groom the boy for his future leadership role. Also essential reading.

Supernatural: Beginning's End by Andrew Dabb, Daniel Loflin and Diego Olmos (released September 2010) throws a light on the reason Sam and John had that big bust up that ended with John telling Sam to leave and not bother coming back. The Winchesters follow a lead about Mary's killer to New York City where John meets up with an old military buddy now running a team of hunters in the city. There's plenty of hunting going on and lots of Winchester arguments too. Another essential tome for mythology lovers.

The comics have also been collected in some graphic novel releases from Titan Books in the UK and DC Comics in America.

And last but not least in the books section is an unofficial tie-in book, *In The Hunt: Unauthorized Essays on Supernatural* edited by Supernatural.tv and published by Benbella Books in March 2009. This is an intriguing collection of essays that cracks open topics like what the show says about the human/demonic potential of us all; why the boys' biggest weakness – each other – is also their biggest strength; and how the boys are the new keepers of the lore.

---

356 UK graphic novel release date.

357 In 'In My Time of Dying' (2-01).

BOOKMARKS
Available with images of Sam, Dean or Sam and Dean. An inexpensive way to enjoy *Supernatural* merchandise.

BUTTONS/BADGES
Another affordable *Supernatural* fix, and these are mostly unofficial. Designs range from the entire Latin exorcism speech through to 'I <heart> purple nurples'.

CALENDARS
A Sam Winchester calendar and a Dean Winchester calendar were available in 2010. So you're stuffed if you have broader tastes and want to see a more general all rounder on your wall.

DVDS
Like you need us to tell you that you can get all the seasons of *Supernatural* on DVD or Blu-ray – either in separate part one and part two format, released earlier on; or as complete season box sets containing some additional extras. What you might not have heard about are some copies of the complete Season Four box set being erroneously issued with the part one and part two DVDs being used – which meant there were no extras on them – but this seemed to be rectified pretty quickly. The early Season One UK DVD box sets were also short of the extras that appeared on the US versions. The Season Two UK DVDs onwards did have the extras included.

GAMES
You can go round hunting things and saving people with the *Supernatural Role Playing Game* by Digger Hayes, Jamie Chambers, Cam Banks and Jimmy McMichael, released by Margaret Weis Productions. This core book, published in August 2009, is supported by *Supernatural RPG: Guide to the Hunted* by Jeff Preston, Kevin Stein, Cam Banks and Rob Donoghue (released May 2010) and the *Supernatural RPG: Road Atlas* by Margaret Weis Productions and Jimmy McMichael (released September 2010).

GLASSES/MUGS
Featuring the boys, the Roadhouse or the Impala, you can get a travel mug, a cappuccino mug or your standard type of mug as required. And there's a disappearing logo mug if you want to be fancy.

There's also a nice frosted shot glass available for those who want something more potent than just putting Sam and Dean to their lips.

HATS

Only one of these seems to be available so far – Sam and Dean and the *Supernatural* name logo on a baseball cap. Wear it with pride.

JEWELLERY

Not surprisingly, you can get hold of Dean's ring and Dean's amulet in a good few places, but the boys are also quite big on bracelets, including Dean's black (apparently elephant hair!) Season One bangle, his skull bracelet and Sam's jelly bracelet. Perhaps they inherited this trait from Mom, since Mary's charm bracelet is also available, although this is sometimes listed as a hunter's charm bracelet. There are lots of different kinds of dog tags available too, and a pentagram necklace and earring set for the occult minded.

KEYRINGS

Various designs exist featuring either the boys or, understandably, the Impala and the 'shotgun … cakehole' quote. Great if you want the boys in your jeans rubbing up and down your leg as you walk.

KOOZIE

A drinks can cover with the famous 'Shotgun … cakehole' quote on it. Perfect for fizzy drink addicts.

LICENCE PLATES/PROPS

If you want a replica of the Impala's KAZ 2Y5 licence plate or a replica of the Impala itself, they're out there, although the latter seems difficult to get. A little easier is the licence plate holder that says 'My other car is a '67 Chevy Impala', and there's a licence plate with a montage of Sam and Dean images mostly from Season Four onwards. Everything here is based on a US licence plate only, including the holder.

PATCHES

Nothing too exciting. You can get Sam's name, Dean's name, Dean with a pentagram or a range of Sam and Dean photos.

PHOTOGRAPHS

The boys are obviously depicted in lots of photos, but it's nice to see Season Four hunk Castiel featuring here too. Still sadly lacking on the Jeffrey Dean Morgan side though – there are very few of him available.

PILLOW CASES

Yes, you can now rest your weary head against Sam or Dean when you go to bed. There's an I <heart> Jensen and an I <heart> Jared pillow case available to give you sweet dreams.

PLATES

Featuring the boys, and pretty hard to get hold of overall, this is a crockery plate for eating your toast off. It features a photo montage of the boys rather than artwork and is probably a collector's item if that kind of thing floats your boat.

POSTERS

Who wouldn't want a lifesize Sam and Dean staring out from your bedroom wall? Of course you can get posters from the show, but there's not a huge amount of choice – just the boys really, and a couple with Jeffrey Dean Morgan as well, but they'll do well enough. Watch out on Amazon too – in the UK they're listed under the Kitchen and Home category, in the US they're under Home and Garden!

STATUES/BUSTS

Oh my god. While people are entirely entitled to go and buy a statue or a bust of whatever they please, why can't the bust at least look like the character it's supposed to be? Pick from not-Dean, not-John Winchester, or not-Lenore (the vampire). Only the scarecrow shows a resemblance, but it still misses the target in the creepy department.

STICKERS

Officially, you're limited to the Impala licence plate – the KAZ 2Y5 one. Unofficially, you can get a large range of bumper stickers from 'I'd rather be watching Supernatural' to 'Salt and Burn'.

TATTOOS

Temporary ones for those with a low pain threshold. You can get Dean's name, Sam's name or the cool pentagram tattoo to protect you from possession as displayed on a couple of hunky chests in 'Jus In Belo' (3-12).

TRADING CARDS AND BINDERS

These were produced by Inkworks and cover several seasons, but it's not clear if any more are coming as Inkworks seems to have ceased trading.

Several standard base packs were produced for each of the first three seasons and included a range of special cards including autograph cards, foil cards and 'Pieceworks' cards, the latter of which had attached to them a piece from an item of clothing worn by one of the cast.

Inkworks also released two special themed boxed packs: 'Connections' and 'A Very Supernatural Christmas'. The former included an extra high quality set of Sam and Dean cards with autographs and Pieceworks cards, and a range of themes within them including 'The Road to Ruin' six card set and 'Fear No Evil' nine card set. Meanwhile the latter boxed pack is linked to the Season Three Christmas favourite[358] and features seven cards and a Pieceworks card.

And when you've bought all your cards, you can get a cool *Supernatural* ring binder to store them in and keep them in mint condition.

T-SHIRTS/HOODIES/ETC
Very popular, with lots of styles available – mostly in black. Have your very own Sam and Dean staring out from your chest, or any number of skulls, ravens, Roadhouse or Impala designs to suit your every mood.

---

358 Episode 3-08.

BIBLIOGRAPHY

[n researching this book we have used countless sources across the internet and in books to confirm our information, and we can't list every single one here. However, these are the websites, books and magazines we found ourselves referring to time and time again:

BOOKS

Season One Supernatural Companion by Nicholas Knight
Season Two Supernatural Companion by Nicholas Knight
Season Three Supernatural Companion by Nicholas Knight
The Official Supernatural Magazine #1 to #9 published by Titan Magazines
Supernatural: John Winchester's Journal by Alex Irvine
The Supernatural Book of Monsters, Demons, Spirits and Ghouls by Alex Irvine
Hero with a Thousand Faces by Joseph Campbell
The Vanishing Hitchhiker: American Urban Legends And Their Meanings by Jan Brunvand
The Encyclopedia of Witchcraft and Demonology by Russell Hope Robbins
SFX magazine

WEBSITES

www.supernaturalwiki.com – hats off to you guys'n'gals, you're awesome.
www.supernatural.tv – great site.
www.tvwithoutpity.com – the *Supernatural* episode recaps are hilarious.
John Keegan's *Supernatural* reviews at www.mediablvd.com magazine.
www.tvguide.com
http://www.itv.com/supernatural/
www.Twiztv.com
www.tv.com
www.wikipedia.org
http://www.angelfire.com/indie/anna_jones1/endor.html
http://www.angelfire.com/realm/shades/demons/bookdevilsanddemons/exorcromcath.htm
dana.thedudes.nu/roadhouse/supernatural/index.html

... and assorted other websites and books on general mythology, all sorts of ghosts, werewolves, vampires, urban legends, crossroads, folklore, *The X-Files*, *The Simpsons*, exorcism, Latin rituals, online Bibles, Japanese spirits, hunting rifles, the Blues Brothers,

Norse gods, the Amityville murders, Smurfs, urban slang, police codes, tulpas, djinn, pink flamingos, demons, Grimm's fairytales, dream walking, necromancy, George Foreman and many, many more. And not forgetting a whole range of horror movies, but especially *The Shining*, *Evil Dead II* and *An American Werewolf in London*.

ACKNOWLEDGEMENTS

So many people help in the production of a final published book that it's impossible to mention them all, but special thanks should go to the following: Mark for his endless patience and lonely nights while the continuous keyboard tapping came from upstairs; all our work colleagues who knew what we were up to – their encouragement made a huge difference; our other friends who encouraged us when the task seemed never-ending; Roger for his early support and humorous additions; the wonderful *Supernatural* fans for their fantastic websites; and to our publishers David J Howe and Stephen James Walker for all their efforts and their equally endless patience in waiting for the book to be delivered.

Other Telos Titles Available

TIME HUNTER

A range of high-quality, original paperback and limited edition hardback novellas featuring the adventures in time of Honoré Lechasseur. Part mystery, part detective story, part dark fantasy, part science fiction ... these books are guaranteed to enthral fans of good fiction everywhere, and are in the spirit of our acclaimed range of *Doctor Who* Novellas.

THE WINNING SIDE by LANCE PARKIN

Emily is dead! Killed by an unknown assailant. Honoré and Emily find themselves caught up in a plot reaching from the future to their past, and with their very existence, not to mention the future of the entire world, at stake, can they unravel the mystery before it is too late?

An adventure in time and space.

£7.99 (+ £2.50 UK p&p) Standard p/b ISBN: 1-903889-35-9

THE TUNNEL AT THE END OF THE LIGHT by STEFAN PETRUCHA

In the heart of post-war London, a bomb is discovered lodged at a disused station between Green Park and Hyde Park Corner. The bomb detonates, and as the dust clears, it becomes apparent that *something* has been awakened. Strange half-human creatures attack the workers at the site, hungrily searching for anything containing sugar ...

Meanwhile, Honoré and Emily are contacted by eccentric poet Randolph Crest, who believes himself to be the target of these subterranean creatures. The ensuing investigation brings Honoré and Emily up against a terrifying force from deep beneath the earth, and one which even with their combined powers, they may have trouble stopping.

An adventure in time and space.

£7.99 (+ £2.50 UK p&p) Standard p/b ISBN: 1-903889-37-5

£25.00 (+ £2.50 UK p&p) Deluxe signed and numbered h/b ISBN: 1-903889-38-3

THE CLOCKWORK WOMAN by CLAIRE BOTT

Honoré and Emily find themselves imprisoned in the 19th Century by a celebrated inventor ... but help comes from an unexpected source – a humanoid automaton created to give pleasure to its owner. As the trio escape to London, they are unprepared for what awaits them, and at every turn it seems impossible to avert what fate may have in store for the Clockwork Woman.

An adventure in time and space.

£7.99 (+ £2.50 UK p&p) Standard p/b ISBN: 1-903889-39-1

£25.00 (+ £2.50 UK p&p) Deluxe signed and numbered h/b ISBN: 1-903889-40-5

KITSUNE by JOHN PAUL CATTON

In the year 2020, Honoré and Emily find themselves thrown into a mystery, as an ice spirit – *Yuki-Onna* – wreaks havoc during the Kyoto Festival, and a haunted funhouse proves to contain more than just paper lanterns and wax dummies. But what does all this have to do with the elegant owner of the Hide and Chic fashion chain ... and the legendary Chinese fox-spirits, the Kitsune?

An adventure in time and space.

£7.99 (+ £2.50 UK p&p) Standard p/b ISBN: 1-903889-41-3

£25.00 (+ £2.50 UK p&p) Deluxe signed and numbered h/b ISBN: 1-903889-42-1

THE SEVERED MAN by GEORGE MANN

What links a clutch of sinister murders in Victorian London, an angel appearing in a Staffordshire village in the 1920s and a small boy running loose around the capital in 1950? When Honoré and Emily encounter a man who appears to have been cut out of time, they think they have the answer. But soon enough they discover that the mystery is only just beginning and that nightmares can turn into reality.
An adventure in time and space.
£7.99 (+ £2.50 UK p&p) Standard p/b ISBN: 1-903889-43-X
£25.00 (+ £2.50 UK p&p) Deluxe signed and numbered h/b ISBN: 1-903889-44-8

ECHOES by IAIN MCLAUGHLIN & CLAIRE BARTLETT

Echoes of the past … echoes of the future. Honoré Lechasseur can see the threads that bind the two together, however when he and Emily Blandish find themselves outside the imposing tower-block headquarters of Dragon Industry, both can sense something is wrong. There are ghosts in the building, and images and echoes of all times pervade the structure. But what is behind this massive contradiction in time, and can Honoré and Emily figure it out before they become trapped themselves … ?
An adventure in time and space.
£7.99 (+ £2.50 UK p&p) Standard p/b ISBN: 1-903889-45-6
£25.00 (+ £2.50 UK p&p) Deluxe signed and numbered h/b ISBN: 1-903889-46-4

PECULIAR LIVES by PHILIP PURSER-HALLARD

Once a celebrated author of 'scientific romances', Erik Clevedon is an old man now. But his fiction conceals a dangerous truth, as Honoré Lechasseur and Emily Blandish discover after a chance encounter with a strangely gifted young pickpocket. Born between the Wars, the superhuman children known as 'the Peculiar' are reaching adulthood – and they believe that humanity is making a poor job of looking after the world they plan to inherit …
An adventure in time and space.
£7.99 (+ £2.50 UK p&p) Standard p/b ISBN: 1-903889-47-2
£25.00 (+ £2.50 UK p&p) Deluxe signed and numbered h/b ISBN: 1-903889-48-0

DEUS LE VOLT by JON DE BURGH MILLER

'Deus Le Volt!'…'God Wills It!' The cry of the first Crusade in 1098, despatched by Pope Urban to free Jerusalem from the Turks. Honoré and Emily are plunged into the middle of the conflict on the trail of what appears to be a time travelling knight. As the siege of Antioch draws to a close, so death haunts the blood-soaked streets … and the Fendahl – a creature that feeds on life itself – is summoned. Honoré and Emily find themselves facing angels and demons in a battle to survive their latest adventure.
An adventure in time and space.
£7.99 (+ £2.50 UK p&p) Standard p/b ISBN: 1-903889-49-9
£25.00 (+ £2.50 UK p&p) Deluxe signed and numbered h/b ISBN: 1-903889-97-9

THE ALBINO'S DANCER by DALE SMITH

'Goodbye, little Emily.'
April 1938, and a shadowy figure attends an impromptu burial in Shoreditch, London. His name is Honoré Lechasseur. After a chance encounter with the mysterious Catherine

Howkins, he's had advance warning that his friend Emily Blandish was going to die. But is forewarned necessarily forearmed? And just how far is he willing to go to save Emily's life?

Because Honoré isn't the only person taking an interest in Emily Blandish – she's come to the attention of the Albino, one of the new breed of gangsters surfacing in post-rationing London. And the only life he cares about is his own.

An adventure in time and space.

£7.99 (+ £2.50 UK p&p) Standard p/b ISBN: 1-84583-100-4

£25.00 (+ £2.50 UK p&p) Deluxe signed and numbered h/b ISBN: 1-84583-101-2

THE SIDEWAYS DOOR by R J CARTER & TROY RISER

Honoré and Emily find themselves in a parallel timestream where their alternate selves think nothing of changing history to improve the quality of life – especially their own. Honoré has been recently haunted by the death of his mother, an event which happened in his childhood, but now there seems to be a way to reverse that event ... but at what cost?

When faced with two of the most dangerous people they have ever encountered, Honoré and Emily must make some decisions with far-reaching consequences.

An adventure in time and space.

£25.00 (+ £2.50 UK p&p) Deluxe signed and numbered h/b ISBN: 1-84583-103-9

CHILD OF TIME by GEORGE MANN

When Honoré and Emily investigate the bones of a child in the ruins of a collapsed house, they are thrown into a thrilling adventure that takes them from London in 1951 to Venice in 1586 and then forward a thousand years, to the terrifying, devasted London of 2586, ruled over by the sinister Sodality. What is the terrible truth about Emily's forgotten past? What demonic power are the Sodality plotting to reawaken? And who is the mysterious Dr Smith?

All is revealed in the stunning conclusion to the acclaimed *Time Hunter* series.

An adventure in time and space.

£9.99 (+ £2.50 UK p&p) Standard p/b ISBN: 978-1-84583-104-2

£25.00 (+ £2.50 UK p&p) Deluxe signed and numbered h/b ISBN: 978-1-84583-105-9

TIME HUNTER FILM

DAEMOS RISING by DAVID J HOWE, DIRECTED BY KEITH BARNFATHER

Daemos Rising is a sequel to both the *Doctor Who* adventure *The Daemons* and to *Downtime*, an earlier drama featuring the Yeti. It is also a prequel of sorts to Telos Publishing's *Time Hunter* series. It stars Miles Richardson as ex-UNIT operative Douglas Cavendish, and Beverley Cressman as Brigadier Lethbridge-Stewart's daughter Kate. Trapped in an isolated cottage, Cavendish thinks he is seeing ghosts. The only person who might understand and help is Kate Lethbridge-Stewart ... but when she arrives, she realises that Cavendish is key in a plot to summon the Daemons back to the Earth. With time running out, Kate discovers that sometimes even the familiar can turn out to be your worst nightmare. Also starring Andrew Wisher, and featuring Ian Richardson as the Narrator.

An adventure in time and space.

£14.00 (+ £3.00 UK p&p) PAL format Region-free DVD

Order direct from Reeltime Pictures, PO Box 23435, London SE26 5WU

HORROR/FANTASY

URBAN GOTHIC: LACUNA AND OTHER TRIPS edited by DAVID J HOWE
Tales of horror from and inspired by the *Urban Gothic* televison series. Contributors:
Graham Masterton, Christopher Fowler, Simon Clark, Steve Lockley & Paul Lewis, Paul
Finch and Debbie Bennett.
£9.99 (+ £2.50 UK p&p) Standard p/b ISBN: 1-903889-00-6

KING OF ALL THE DEAD by STEVE LOCKLEY & PAUL LEWIS
The king of all the dead will have what is his.
£8.00 (+ £2.50 UK p&p) Standard p/b ISBN: 1-903889-61-8

THE HUMAN ABSTRACT by GEORGE MANN
A future tale of private detectives, AIs, Nanobots, love and death.
£7.99 (+ £2.50 UK p&p) Standard p/b ISBN: 1-903889-65-0

BREATHE by CHRISTOPHER FOWLER
The Office meets *Night of the Living Dead*.
£25.00 (+ £2.50 UK p&p) Deluxe signed and numbered h/b ISBN: 1-903889-68-5

HOUDINI'S LAST ILLUSION by STEVE SAVILE
Can the master illusionist Harry Houdini outwit the dead shades of his past?
£7.99 (+ £2.50 UK p&p) Standard p/b ISBN: 1-903889-66-9

ALICE'S JOURNEY BEYOND THE MOON by R J CARTER
A sequel to the classic Lewis Carroll tales.
£6.99 (+ £2.50 UK p&p) Standard p/b ISBN: 1-903889-76-6
£30.00 (+ £2.50 UK p&p) Deluxe signed and numbered h/b ISBN: 1-903889-77-4

APPROACHING OMEGA by ERIC BROWN
A colonisation mission to Earth runs into problems.
£7.99 (+ £2.50 UK p&p) Standard p/b ISBN: 1-903889-98-7
£30.00 (+ £2.50 UK p&p) Deluxe signed and numbered h/b ISBN: 1-903889-99-5

VALLEY OF LIGHTS by STEPHEN GALLAGHER
A cop comes up against a body-hopping murderer.
£9.99 (+ £3.00 UK p&p) Standard p/b ISBN: 1-903889-74-X
£30.00 (+ £3.00 UK p&p) Deluxe signed and numbered h/b ISBN: 1-903889-75-8

PRETTY YOUNG THINGS by DOMINIC MCDONAGH
A nest of lesbian rave bunny vampires is at large in Manchester. When Chelsey's ex-
boyfriend is taken as food, Chelsey has to get out fast.
£7.99 (+ £2.50 UK p&p) Standard p/b ISBN: 1-84583-045-8

A MANHATTAN GHOST STORY by T M WRIGHT
Do you see ghosts? A classic tale of love and the supernatural.
£9.99 (+ £3.00 UK p&p) Standard p/b ISBN: 1-84583-048-2

SHROUDED BY DARKNESS: TALES OF TERROR edited by ALISON L R DAVIES
An anthology of tales guaranteed to bring a chill to the spine. This collection has been published to raise money for DebRA, a national charity working on behalf of people with the genetic skin blistering condition, Epidermolysis Bullosa (EB). Featuring stories by: Debbie Bennett, Poppy Z Brite, Simon Clark, Storm Constantine, Peter Crowther, Alison L R Davies, Paul Finch, Christopher Fowler, Neil Gaiman, Gary Greenwood, David J Howe, Dawn Knox, Tim Lebbon, Charles de Lint, Steven Lockley & Paul Lewis, James Lovegrove, Graham Masterton, Richard Christian Matheson, Justina Robson, Mark Samuels, Darren Shan and Michael Marshall Smith. With a frontispiece by Clive Barker and a foreword by Stephen Jones. Deluxe hardback cover by Simon Marsden.
£12.99 (+ £3.00 UK p&p) Standard p/b ISBN: 1-84583-046-6
£50.00 (+ £3.00 UK p&p) Deluxe signed and numbered h/b ISBN: 978-1-84583-047-2

BLACK TIDE by DEL STONE JR
A college professor and his students find themselves trapped by an encroaching horde of zombies following a waste spillage.
£7.99 (+ £2.50 UK p&p) Standard p/b ISBN: 978-1-84583-049-6

FORCE MAJEURE by DANIEL O'MAHONY
An incredible fantasy novel. Kay finds herself trapped in a strange city in the Andes ... a place where dreams can become reality, and where dragons may reside.
£7.99 (+ £2.50 UK p&p) Standard p/b ISBN: 978-1-84583-050-2

HUMPTY'S BONES by SIMON CLARK
Something nasty is found in a village garden by an amateur archaeologist, something which has lain buried for centuries.
£9.99 (+ £2.50 UK p&p) Standard p/b ISBN: 978-1-84583-051-9

THE DJINN by GRAHAM MASTERTON
Graham Masterton's terrifying 1977 novel is republished by Telos in a brand new edition, complete with an exclusive introduction by the author.
£9.99 (+ £2.50 UK p&p) Standard p/b ISBN: 978-1-84583-052-6

RULES OF DUEL by GRAHAM MASTERTON and WILLIAM S BURROUGHS
A clever and pervasive novel, which turns literature on its head, and makes the reader work to be part of the evolving plot. Complete with original introduction by Burroughs, written before his death in 1997, *Rules of Duel* is a previously unpublished masterpiece from two of the greatest writers of their generations.
£9.99 (+ £2.50 UK p&p) Standard p/b ISBN: 978-1-84583-054-0

ZOMBIES IN NEW YORK AND OTHER BLOODY JOTTINGS by SAM STONE
Thirteen stories of horror and passion, and six mythological and erotic poems from the pen of the new Queen of Vampire fiction.
£12.99 (+ £2.50 UK p&p) Standard p/b ISBN: 978-1-84583-055-7

ART BOOK

ALTERED VISIONS by VINCENT CHONG
Vincent Chong burst onto the horror and fantasy scene several years ago with a sequence of incredible artworks. Since then he has gone on to provide cover artwork for authors such as Stephen King, and has worked with publishers all around the world, as well as providing illustration for record covers and websites. Now some of his incredible artwork is collected in *Altered Visions*.
£30.00 (+ £2.50 UK p&p) Signed Limited Edition Hardback ISBN: 978-1-84583-053-3

TV/FILM GUIDES

DOCTOR WHO

THE HANDBOOK: THE UNOFFICIAL AND UNAUTHORISED GUIDE TO THE PRODUCTION OF DOCTOR WHO by DAVID J HOWE, STEPHEN JAMES WALKER and MARK STAMMERS
Complete guide to the making of *Doctor Who* (1963 – 1996).
£14.99 (+ £5.00 UK p&p) Standard p/b ISBN: 1-903889-59-6
£30.00 (+ £5.00 UK p&p) Deluxe signed and numbered h/b ISBN: 1-903889-96-0

BACK TO THE VORTEX: THE UNOFFICIAL AND UNAUTHORISED GUIDE TO DOCTOR WHO 2005 by J SHAUN LYON
Complete guide to the 2005 series of *Doctor Who* starring Christopher Eccleston as the Doctor
£12.99 (+ £3.00 UK p&p) Standard p/b ISBN: 1-903889-78-2
£30.00 (+ £3.00 UK p&p) Deluxe signed and numbered h/b ISBN: 1-903889-79-0

SECOND FLIGHT: THE UNOFFICIAL AND UNAUTHORISED GUIDE TO DOCTOR WHO 2006 by J SHAUN LYON
Complete guide to the 2006 series of *Doctor Who*, starring David Tennant as the Doctor
£12.99 (+ £3.00 UK p&p) Standard p/b ISBN: 1-84583-008-3
£30.00 (+ £3.00 UK p&p) Deluxe signed and numbered h/b ISBN: 1-84583-009-1

THIRD DIMENSION: THE UNOFFICIAL AND UNAUTHORISED GUIDE TO DOCTOR WHO 2007 by STEPHEN JAMES WALKER
Complete guide to the 2007 series of *Doctor Who*, starring David Tennant as the Doctor
£12.99 (+ £3.00 UK p&p) Standard p/b ISBN: 978-1-84583-016-8
£30.00 (+ £3.00 UK p&p) Deluxe signed and numbered h/b ISBN: 978-1-84583-017-5

MONSTERS WITHIN: THE UNOFFICIAL AND UNAUTHORISED GUIDE TO DOCTOR WHO 2008 by STEPHEN JAMES WALKER
Complete guide to the 2008 series of *Doctor Who*, starring David Tennant as the Doctor.
£12.99 (+ £3.00 UK p&p) Standard p/b ISBN: 978-1-84583-027-4

END OF TEN: THE UNOFFICIAL AND UNAUTHORISED GUIDE TO DOCTOR WHO 2009 by STEPHEN JAMES WALKER
Complete guide to the 2009 specials of *Doctor Who*, starring David Tennant as the Doctor.
£14.99 (+ £3.00 UK p&p) Standard p/b ISBN: 978-1-84583-035-9
£30.00 (+ £3.00 UK p&p) Signed h/b ISBN: 978-1-84583-036-6

WHOGRAPHS: THEMED AUTOGRAPH BOOK
80 page autograph book with an SF theme
£4.50 (+ £2.50 UK p&p) Standard p/b ISBN: 1-84583-110-1

TALKBACK: THE UNOFFICIAL AND UNAUTHORISED DOCTOR WHO INTERVIEW BOOK: VOLUME 1: THE SIXTIES edited by STEPHEN JAMES WALKER
Interviews with cast and behind the scenes crew who worked on *Doctor Who* in the sixties
£12.99 (+ £3.00 UK p&p) Standard p/b ISBN: 1-84583-006-7
£30.00 (+ £3.00 UK p&p) Deluxe signed and numbered h/b ISBN: 1-84583-007-5

TALKBACK: THE UNOFFICIAL AND UNAUTHORISED DOCTOR WHO INTERVIEW BOOK: VOLUME 2: THE SEVENTIES edited by STEPHEN JAMES WALKER
Interviews with cast and behind the scenes crew who worked on *Doctor Who* in the seventies
£12.99 (+ £3.00 UK p&p) Standard p/b ISBN: 1-84583-010-5
£30.00 (+ £3.00 UK p&p) Deluxe signed and numbered h/b ISBN: 1-84583-011-3

TALKBACK: THE UNOFFICIAL AND UNAUTHORISED DOCTOR WHO INTERVIEW BOOK: VOLUME 3: THE EIGHTIES edited by STEPHEN JAMES WALKER
Interviews with cast and behind the scenes crew who worked on *Doctor Who* in the eighties
£12.99 (+ £3.00 UK p&p) Standard p/b ISBN: 978-1-84583-014-4
£30.00 (+ £3.00 UK p&p) Deluxe signed and numbered h/b ISBN: 978-1-84583-015-1
HOWE'S TRANSCENDENTAL TOYBOX: SECOND EDITION by DAVID J HOWE & ARNOLD T BLUMBERG
Complete guide to *Doctor Who* Merchandise 1963–2002.
£25.00 (+ £5.00 UK p&p) Standard p/b ISBN: 1-903889-56-1

HOWE'S TRANSCENDENTAL TOYBOX: UPDATE No 1: 2003 by DAVID J HOWE & ARNOLD T BLUMBERG
Complete guide to *Doctor Who* Merchandise released in 2003.
£7.99 (+ £2.50 UK p&p) Standard p/b ISBN: 1-903889-57-X
HOWE'S TRANSCENDENTAL TOYBOX: UPDATE No 2: 2004-2005 by DAVID J HOWE & ARNOLD T BLUMBERG
Complete guide to *Doctor Who* Merchandise released in 2004 and 2005. Now in full colour.
£12.99 (+ £2.50 UK p&p) Standard p/b ISBN: 1-84583-012-1

THE TARGET BOOK by DAVID J HOWE with TIM NEAL
A fully illustrated, large format, full colour history of the Target *Doctor Who* books.
£19.99 (+ £5.00 UK p&p) Large Format p/b ISBN: 978-1-84583-021-2

WIPED! DOCTOR WHO'S MISSING EPISODES by RICHARD MOLESWORTH
The story behind the BBC's missing episodes of *Doctor Who*.
£15.99 (+ £3.00 UK p&p) Standard p/b ISBN: 978-1-84583-037-3

TIMELINK: THE UNOFFICIAL AND UNAUTHORISED GUIDE TO THE
CONTINUITY OF DOCTOR WHO VOLUME 1 by JON PREDDLE
Discussion and articles about the continuity of *Doctor Who*.
£15.99 (+ £3.00 UK p&p) Standard p/b ISBN: 978-1-84583-004-5

TIMELINK: THE UNOFFICIAL AND UNAUTHORISED GUIDE TO THE
CONTINUITY OF DOCTOR WHO VOLUME 2 by JON PREDDLE
Timeline of the continuity of *Doctor Who*.
£15.99 (+ £3.00 UK p&p) Standard p/b ISBN: 978-1-84583-005-2

TORCHWOOD

INSIDE THE HUB: THE UNOFFICIAL AND UNAUTHORISED GUIDE TO
TORCHWOOD SERIES ONE by STEPHEN JAMES WALKER
Complete guide to the 2006 series of *Torchwood*, starring John Barrowman as Captain
Jack Harkness
£12.99 (+ £3.00 UK p&p) Standard p/b ISBN: 978-1-84583-013-7

SOMETHING IN THE DARKNESS: THE UNOFFICIAL AND UNAUTHORISED
GUIDE TO TORCHWOOD SERIES TWO by STEPHEN JAMES WALKER
Complete guide to the 2008 series of *Torchwood*, starring John Barrowman as Captain
Jack Harkness
£12.99 (+ £3.00 UK p&p) Standard p/b ISBN: 978-1-84583-024-3
£30.00 (+ £3.00 UK p&p) Deluxe signed and numbered h/b ISBN: 978-1-84583-025-0

SURVIVORS

THE END OF THE WORLD?: THE UNOFFICIAL AND UNAUTHORISED GUIDE
TO SURVIVORS by ANDY PRIESTNER & RICH CROSS
Complete guide to Terry Nation's *Survivors*
£12.99 (+ £3.00 UK p&p) Standard p/b ISBN: 1-84583-001-6

24

A DAY IN THE LIFE: THE UNOFFICIAL AND UNAUTHORISED GUIDE TO 24 by
KEITH TOPPING
Complete episode guide to the first season of the popular TV show.
£9.99 (+ £3.00 p&p) Standard p/b ISBN: 1-903889-53-7

TILL DEATH US DO PART

A FAMILY AT WAR: THE UNOFFICIAL AND UNAUTHORISED GUIDE TO TILL
DEATH US DO PART by MARK WARD
Complete guide to the popular TV show. PUBLISHED SEPTEMBER 2008
£12.99 (+ £3.00 p&p) Standard p/b ISBN: 978-1-84583-031-1

SPACE:1999

DESTINATION: MOONBASE ALPHA: THE UNOFFICIAL AND UNAUTHORISED
GUIDE TO SPACE:1999 by ROBERT E WOOD
Complete guide to the popular TV show.
£15.99 (+ £3.00 p&p) Standard p/b ISBN: 978-1-84583-034-2

SAPPHIRE AND STEEL

ASSIGNED: THE UNOFFICIAL AND UNAUTHORISED GUIDE TO SAPPHIRE
AND STEEL by RICHARD CALLAGHAN
Complete guide to the popular TV show.
£12.99 (+ £2.50 p&p) Standard p/b ISBN: 978-1-84583-032-8

THUNDERCATS

HEAR THE ROAR: THE UNOFFICIAL AND UNAUTHORISED GUIDE TO THE
HIT 1980S SERIES THUNDERCATS by DAVID CRICHTON
Complete guide to the popular TV show.
£16.99 (+ £3.00 p&p) Standard p/b ISBN: 978-1-84583-038-0

FILMS

BEAUTIFUL MONSTERS: THE UNOFFICIAL AND UNAUTHORISED GUIDE TO
THE ALIEN AND PREDATOR FILMS by DAVID McINTEE
A guide to the Alien and Predator Films.
£9.99 (+ £3.00 UK p&p) Standard p/b ISBN: 1-903889-94-4

ZOMBIEMANIA: 80 MOVIES TO DIE FOR by DR ARNOLD T BLUMBERG &
ANDREW HERSHBERGER
A guide to 80 classic zombie films, along with an extensive filmography of over 500
additional titles
£17.99 (+ £5.00 UK p&p) Standard p/b ISBN: 1-84583-003-2

SILVER SCREAM: VOLUME 1: 40 CLASSIC HORROR MOVIES by STEVEN
WARREN HILL
A guide to 40 classic horror films from 1920 to 1941.
£12.99 (+ £3.00 UK p&p) Standard p/b ISBN: 978-1-84583-026-7

SILVER SCREAM: VOLUME 2: 40 CLASSIC HORROR MOVIES by STEVEN WARREN HILL
A guide to 40 classic horror films from 1941 to 1951. PUBLISHED 2009.
£14.99 (+ £3.00 UK p&p) Standard p/b ISBN: 978-1-84583-029-8

TABOO BREAKERS: 18 INDEPENDENT FILMS THAT COURTED CONTROVERSY AND CREATED A LEGEND by CALUM WADDELL
A guide to 18 films which pushed boundries and broke taboos.
£12.99 (+ £3.00 UK p&p) Standard p/b ISBN: 978-1-84583-030-4

IT LIVES AGAIN! HORROR MOVIES IN THE NEW MILLENNIUM by AXELLE CAROLYN
A guide to modern horror films. Large format, full colour throughout.
£16.99 (+ £5.00 UK p&p) h/b ISBN: 978-1-84583-020-5

The prices shown are correct at time of going to press. However, the publishers reserve the right to increase prices from those previously advertised without prior notice.

TELOS PUBLISHING
c/o Beech House, Chapel Lane, Moulton, Cheshire, CW9 8PQ, England
Email: orders@telos.co.uk
Web: www.telos.co.uk

To order copies of any Telos books, please visit our website where there are full details of all titles and facilities for worldwide credit card online ordering, as well as occasional special offers, or send a cheque or postal order (UK only) for the appropriate amount (including postage and packing – note that four or more titles are post free in the UK), together with details of the book(s) you require, plus your name and address to the above address. Overseas readers please send two international reply coupons for details of prices and postage rates.